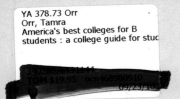
Praise for *America's Best Colleges for B Students*

"This book contains practical information for any student searching for the right college 'fit' instead of simply trying to 'fit in' at the wrong college. From this small college's perspective, the 'solid B' student has the same chance as an A student to be successful in an environment where each is encouraged to develop his/her potential."

— **Sandy Speed**
Dean of Admission and Financial Aid
Schreiner University

"This book offers practical information and advice for students and parents alike. There is a great school out there for you — *America's Best Colleges for B Students* will help you find it!"

— **Mark Campbell**
Vice President for Enrollment Management
McKendree College

"At last, a college resource book for real students and real families. We hear so much about how only overachievers get into good schools that we forget that college isn't just about grades and tests scores; it's about learning, living and moving forward. This is something that all students need, regardless of their high school performance. Tamra Orr has given families the tools to help their young adults find the perfect college for them. An invaluable resource!"

— **Teri Brown**
Author of Day Tripping: Your Guide to Educational Family Adventures

"Tamra Orr's refreshingly candid approach to the college search dispels the fear that B students and their families often face. An easy yet information-packed read!"

— **Bethany Bierman**
Assistant Director, Office of Undergraduate Admissions
Augsburg College

"Many hard-working kids (this book calls them B students) don't think they're college material because they don't have high college boards or the highest grades. In short order, this book dispels that myth! Tamra Orr has gathered helpful insights and suggestions that will, thankfully, elevate the expectations of such students to achieve college success."

— **Patrick J. O'Brien**
Retired high school counselor, former Marquette Northern California admissions representative and current ACT ambassador

"This excellent 'advice' book is a must read for those students and their parents who want to understand and navigate the process and find the right match toward that important degree."

— **Karen P. Condeni**
Vice President and Dean of Enrollment
Ohio Northern University

"This book will be a terrific introduction to the college search process. The format offers helpful suggestions in a non-intimidating approach. For many high school students the college process becomes a seemingly insurmountable task. *America's Best Colleges for B Students* is a terrific introductory tool that outlines the basic steps to begin the college search process."

— **Amanda (Mandy) Warhurst Webster**
Senior Associate Director of Admission
Salve Regina University

"Tamra Orr's book is just what the 'not so perfect' student needs. The advice is to the point and incredibly useful. You don't have to attend a huge Ivy League school to get a superior education. Orr's book should be required reading for individuals of all ages who are thinking of attending college."

— **Sandra Roy**
Educator and author

Praise for *America's Best Colleges for B Students*

"What really makes a great student great? Is greatness limited to a letter grade on paper or a score on the SATs? There is so much more that factors into it like the sincere desire to not only succeed in the classroom, but succeed in life. There are some outstanding institutions of higher learning that understand that reality and offer programs from which B students will benefit the most as well as learning services that help them become better students. By offering an in-depth analysis of the best schools catering to the needs of real world students, this book will go far in helping families identify the best schools that suit individual needs. Education is not 'one size fits all,' and this book helps explain that — and will help anyone in search of higher education find the 'right fit.'"

— **Jennifer A. Fiorentino**
Director, Public Relations & Communications
Dean College

"With humor and insight, Tamra Orr sets the record straight about college admission, offering practical advice and hope to college-bound students. This book makes the important point that the college admission process doesn't need to be fraught with stress and anxiety. Many bright, interesting teens that underperformed in high school will recognize themselves in the pages of this book. Orr guides students in how to explore colleges where they can find themselves and achieve as never before."

— **Joan Casey**
College Planning Consultant
Educational Advocates

"Finally! A guide for motivated late bloomers — solid students who in the right environment will flourish. Tamra Orr has done her homework to provide you with the guidance and tips you need to find the college that's right for you — and help you succeed once you're there. Pack your suitcase for adventure and bring your drive, energy and personal commitment to achieve!"

— **Esther Goodcuff**
Associate Vice President for Enrollment Management
and Student Affairs
Adelphi University

America's Best Colleges for B Students

Third Edition

A College Guide for Students Without Straight A's

TAMRA B. ORR

America's Best Colleges for B Students: A College Guide for Students without Straight A's
3rd Edition
By Tamra B. Orr

Published by SuperCollege, LLC
3286 Oak Court
Belmont, CA 94002
www.supercollege.com

Credits: Cover design TLC Graphics, www.TLCGraphics.com. Design: Monica Thomas.

Trademarks: All brand names, product names and services used in this book are trademarks, registered trademarks or tradenames of their respective holders. SuperCollege is not associated with any college, university, product or vendor.

Disclaimers: The author and publisher have used their best efforts in preparing this book. It is intended to provide helpful and informative material on the subject matter. Some narratives and names have been modified for illustrative purposes. SuperCollege and the author make no representations or warranties with respect to the accuracy or completeness of the contents of the book and specifically disclaim any implied warranties or merchantability or fitness for a particular purpose. There are no warranties which extend beyond the descriptions contained in this paragraph. The accuracy and completeness of the information provided herein and the opinions stated herein are not guaranteed or warranted to produce any particular results. SuperCollege and the author specifically disclaim any responsibility for any liability, loss or risk, personal or otherwise, which is incurred as a consequence, directly or indirectly, of the use and application of any of the contents of this book.

ISBN-13: 978-1-932662-43-6

Manufactured in the United States of America
10 9 8 7 6 5 4 3 2 1
Library of Congress Cataloging-in-Publication Data

Orr, Tamra.
    America's best colleges for B students : a college guide for students without straight A's / By Tamra B. Orr. -- 3rd ed.
        p. cm.
    ISBN 978-1-932662-43-6
    1. College choice--United States--Directories. 2. Universities and colleges--United States--Directories. I. Title.
    LB2350.5.O77 2010
    378.73--dc22
                2010005072

*To my kids who brighten my life, my husband who enriches my life
and my parents who gave me life.*

CONTENTS

FOREWORD

If the prospect of receiving an A- in AP calculus keeps you up at night, this book is not for you. If, on the other hand, you are ecstatic about scoring that B in English, this book is exactly what you need!

One of the greatest myths about a college education is that you need to have straight A's or be the class valedictorian to get into an excellent college. The truth is that there are terrific colleges out there that want you — whether you are a B student or, gasp, even a C student. But don't assume that these colleges are looking for slackers. Quite the opposite: These schools know that good students don't always perform at their true potential in high school. For example:

● Maybe you didn't take high school seriously and only now have come to realize the importance of doing well academically.

● Maybe you managed your time poorly or were overcommitted with a job or activities.

● Maybe you were distracted by events in your life beyond your control.

● Maybe you were just bored with high school.

Whatever the reason, these schools know that your grades and test scores are not always reflective of who you are and how well you will do in college. So, if you are now committed to getting a college education and are willing to put in the time and effort to be a successful student, these colleges want you.

The key is: How do you find these colleges? What do you need to look for to make sure that you will excel? And how do you show the college that you are serious about getting a great education and will be an asset to their student body?

That's where this book will help. Here are just a few of the things that you will learn:

● How to identify colleges that accept students with less than perfect grades and test scores.

● What characteristics to look for in a college to ensure that you succeed academically as well as socially.

● How to best position yourself — both the positives and negatives — in the college application, essay and interview.

● Ways to pay for your education. (Scholarships are not just reserved for the A students. There are literally thousands also available for students based on non-academic skills and talents.)

● Tips for making that sometimes difficult transition from high school to college.

Tamra Orr has written this book just for you. She has been there, done that as a student like you without perfect grades or test scores. She knows there is no shame in being a B student. (In fact, Tamra knows how to present this as a huge positive to a college!) She also knows that just because you may not be in the "Ivy-League-Wannabe" crowd doesn't mean you are not motivated and committed to being successful.

Let her help you find that perfect college! We wish you the best in your journey!

— Gen and Kelly Tanabe
Authors of eleven books on college planning
including *Get into Any College* and
Get Free Cash for College

INTRODUCTION

Once upon a time, long, long ago, almost anyone who wanted to go to college and could find a way to afford it went to college. SAT just meant the past tense of "sit" and GPA was an odd combination of letters that might have been a neat abbreviation for "Grandpa." After World War II, tests and test scores started to gain in importance, but it would be some time before they would become the determining factor behind going to college. Sure, if you had a great SAT score or a really high GPA, it was easier to get scholarships or get the really BIG colleges to give you more than a glance. But I remember applying to colleges without much thought at all about my numbers (I'm dating myself now, as that was back in the late 1970s). I was too busy scoping out the campus, checking the ratio of guys to girls and, oh yeah, seeing what majors were offered. (I must say, however, that 30 years later, I can STILL tell you my SAT scores.)

The picture is quite different today. Getting into college is not only more expensive but also much tougher. Colleges have become so selective that even valedictorians with a 4.0 average and perfect SAT scores are being turned away from some of the Ivy League institutions.

Because of this, many students are ready to throw their hands in the air and say, "Okay, I get it! I don't have good enough numbers, so I obviously can't go to college. I'll just forget it!" If you are among these, realize this: You, yes YOU, are the reason for this book. It is designed to give you two things: help with what it takes to get into many colleges (and an overview of what happens after you do) and leads on which colleges are eagerly awaiting your application.

For starters, get rid of the myths/assumptions you might have about choosing a college. If you believe any of the following, take them from the "The Earth is Round" list (truth) and put them in the "Santa Claus/Tooth Fairy" list (fantasies). Here we go:

- You need a perfect GPA or SAT to get into a good college.

- The best way to pick a college is by reading the rankings in a magazine article/taking your best friend's recommendation/choosing the names you recognize the most.

- Traditional four-year colleges are the only ones employers will accept.

- Only the large colleges are worth attending.

- Your college should have more students than your high school does.

- Small colleges offer inferior classes, faculty and degrees.

  None of the above statements is true.

- A perfect score or transcript is not required at most colleges, as you will see as you read this book.

- The best way to select a college is to *not* accept someone else's opinion as absolute truth and to do your homework (yes, MORE homework) and find out which colleges best suit you and your preferences.

- While four-year colleges are the norm, there are many two-year programs and other options that are just as appealing to future employers.

- Small colleges often offer the conditions and student/teacher ratio that will ensure a high-quality, successful education. In no way are their classes, faculty or degrees inferior to those of the larger universities.

One of the biggest myths of all about college, of course, is that even if you find one that you like and will accept you, you will not be able to afford it. We will dispel that myth as well in Chapter Six.

You, standing right there in the middle of the library or bookstore (or at home scanning the intro because your parents told you, "READ THIS!"), you with the 2.9 or 3.1 GPA or the 1560 new SAT score or 19 composite ACT, *can* go to a college or university. You can find yourself at a wonderful institution where you will make friends, have fun, grow up and yeah, learn a lot of stuff and get a degree. These colleges are not runners-up to the "good" places; they are wonderful schools that are willing to look beyond the numbers to the person standing behind them. They have admissions departments that give your scores some thought, and then put them down and search for the human being on the other side of the digits. And really, isn't that what you would want them to do anyway? You are certainly more than any group of numbers could possibly represent.

This book was written to guide you to lots of helpful information about 100 colleges and universities that want you to be a part of their student population. It will also show you how to:

- Make the best use of the time you still have left in high school

- Make a great impression on the college admissions department through both the essay and interview

- Explain those less-than-stellar numbers and let your strengths shine through

- Survive in college once you get there

Belonging is one of the strongest natural drives inside each and every person. You want to find a college where you are happy, comfortable and accepted. The administrations of these colleges want students who feel like they have found a new home. Let this book be your guide to that relationship.

SECTION ONE

CHOOSING

**HOW TO CHOOSE
THE RIGHT COLLEGE
FOR YOU**

WHERE TO FIND COLLEGES THAT WELCOME B STUDENTS

We Really Do Want You
(Or, Why Colleges Love B Students . . .)

Why would a college want you, the B STUDENT, instead of Ms. Straight A's or Mr. Perfect SAT Score? Easy! Colleges want diversity. They want all kinds of students and that means you too. You are so much more than your GPA or your ACT scores and most colleges realize that. They want you because you are curious, enthusiastic and interesting!

You want the chance to shine, and there are colleges that want to help you do it. Think about it for a moment. There are more than 3,400 four-year, accredited colleges and universities in this country. That's a lot of places to learn! You can be sure that there are many schools for everyone and there certainly are many choices for B students. Your statistics may make the search a little longer and a bit challenging but no less rewarding.

Nothing is as important to your educational success as finding a college where you feel comfortable. A key to success is being flexible and prepared to give the avenues open to you a fair chance. You have to be willing to look a little deeper and explore options, some of which you may not have thought of before. For instance, "Keep an open mind about going out of state," encourages Lynda McGee, college counselor at Downtown Magnets High School in Los Angeles. It is McGee's personal goal to find schools for all students. "Some students fear leaving the area, especially those in sunny California," she explains.

Judi Robinovitz, an educational consultant for more than 25 years, suggests that students be open to exploring colleges they may not already know about. "You have to dispel the notion that just because you have not heard of a college, it's a bad college," she says.

"There are no bad colleges," explains Patrick O'Brien, former admissions officer and consultant-ambassador for the ACT. "Remember, the 'best' school is the one that is best for you, not necessarily the ones that are highlighted in the books," says O'Brien.

But, why would a college be willing to take a chance on a student who doesn't have the kind of scores and grades thought to be required by a majority of colleges? It's simple: They have common sense.

First, a number of universities want a diverse student body roaming around their campuses. To achieve this, they have to broaden their ideas of what kind of student they will accept. Just as colleges accept people from all kinds of financial, ethnic, religious and racial backgrounds, they often will accept those with various levels of academic achievement.

Second, admissions officers often realize that while students may not have the most perfect numbers, they can still add greatly to the student body. They may be tremendous leaders, facilitators, speakers or organizers. They may exhibit strength in a variety of skills that can't be pinpointed with the average test score. For example, while a student may not perform well in math, he or she may excel in the humanities. These students can enrich the campus community in untold ways.

Last, colleges know that some students are genuinely working toward starting over, to changing their priorities and standards. Often this can be seen in school transcripts. Grades are improving with time; a new leaf has been turned over. Colleges recognize that some students really do go through difficult times such as the severe illness or death of a family member. Because of this, they are frequently willing to overlook some weak numbers and support that new dedication by accepting you into their college and giving you another way to continue your trend.

So the college that you assumed was out of reach because of your grades or test scores may actually be entirely possible if you can give them a reason for why you deserve to be there.

Looking Outside the Box

One secret to finding the right college is to look beyond the most popular schools that everyone you know is applying to and then to think outside of the box. Are there other colleges in your area? Before you start shaking your head because these "other" colleges aren't what you had in mind, at least do a little research. Look at their sites online, and check out the profiles at the end of this book. You can't say you don't like a place until you have enough information to know if you like it (otherwise known as innocent until proven guilty!).

Some schools that may be more open to B students include these:

- career-oriented colleges

- community colleges

- all men's colleges

- all women's colleges

- very small colleges

Don't Overlook Community College

For many students, one of the best options remains the local community college. Yeah, you still have to live in your hometown, and most likely, still at home with your family, but you benefit from a good education while saving some big bucks for the future or for transferring to a four-year college. Community colleges are more open to students with B or C averages than some four-year institutions, so they can be a great solution for you.

But hey, you've heard some rumors about community colleges, right? You've heard them called everything from "Only Chance College" to "Harvard on the Highway." Like everything else, community colleges have a few myths surrounding them, and — here's a real surprise — most of them just aren't true. For instance:

- A degree from a community college is not as good as a university degree.

  That just doesn't make any sense. An apple is an apple. A degree is a degree. You did the work and earned the diploma. Is it the same thing as a degree from Harvard? Okay, maybe not, but most of the time it will still get you through the front door and into the job.

- The people who go to community college couldn't get in anywhere else.

  Not true. Students go to community college for a variety of reasons. Maybe it is more convenient and less expensive for some people because it allows them to keep working, giving them a chance to save money while providing a quality education that sometimes may even serve as a stepping stone to a traditional college.

- The faculty at community colleges is inferior to that of four-year institutions.

  The faculties and staff at community colleges and other colleges are quite comparable. They both have their degrees and years of experience to share with you.

- The credits from a community college will not transfer to other colleges.

  This is a myth. Credit hours from community colleges transfer in the same way that credit hours from four-year universities do.

COMMUNITY COLLEGE FACTS

Here are some of the current stats on community colleges, thanks to the helpful people at the American Association of Community Colleges (www. aacc.nche.edu):

Public institutions	979
Private institutions	148
Tribal institutions	30
TOTAL	1,157

11.6 million students currently enrolled

6.6 million for credit and 5 million for non-credit

- 46% of all U.S. undergraduates
- 45% of first-time freshmen
- 58% women; 42% men
- 62% part time; 38% full time
- 47% of African American undergrads
- 56% of Hispanic undergrads
- 48% of Asian/Pacific Islander undergrads
- 57% of Native American undergrads

Average tuition and fees: $2,076, and 37.8% of students receive some kind of financial aid.

More than 490,000 associate degrees

Almost 235,000 two-year certificates

● Since community colleges cost so much less, they can't be any good.

Community colleges are fine institutions. The difference in tuition can be due to many reasons, but it is mainly because community colleges do not have the incredible overhead that residential colleges have.

In 2004, the American Association of Community Colleges conducted a survey to see what the hottest programs at these colleges were. The survey found that the top five fields to study were allied health (46.6 percent), skilled trades/industrial, public services, information technologies and business.

Go, Team, Go!

Remember that choosing a college is not usually an individual choice. Instead, it takes a team of people all working together, including your teachers, advisers, guidance counselors, principals, coaches and family members. You need help with a decision this big, because it is a complex one.

There are so many colleges that accept B students that it is important for you to consider several different elements when you start your search. Ask yourself these questions:

● What kind of student am I now, and what are my career plans for the future?

● What parts of school do I like the best and least now?

● What does the idea of success actually mean to me?

● Where do I see myself in two years? Five years? Ten years?

● What part of the country appeals most to me?

● Do I want a small, intimate college or a bustling, exciting university?

● What percentage of males and females would be ideal for me?

● What is the cost and how much financial aid does each school offer?

● What are the most popular majors and is mine on that list?

● Do I want to be involved in a sorority/fraternity?

● Will I have any scholarships or grants that affect where I can go?

● Do I want a philosophical or religious college?

You may not know the answers to all these questions yet. Many of them will only come after you have taken some tours, read your research and talked to your team. Giving them some thought now, however, will give you a head start.

What to Look for in a College

When you start your college search, you have to find a happy balance between being optimistic and realistic. Look at the GPA and ACT/SAT scores that each college lists and analyze those numbers in relationship to yours. If a college's cut-off on the SAT verbal score is 510 and yours is 520, go ahead and apply — it's a "safety" college. What if your score is 480? Give it a try — it's a "fairly good chance" college. How about a score of 410? Not likely — but you could still apply to this college; just don't hold your breath. Be willing to stretch a little and know that those numbers are not carved in stone but are general guidelines.

The colleges profiled in this book do more than just accept B students. They are dedicated to helping them. They may offer a first-year general studies, remedial or transition class to help get you started. Many offer on-campus writing clinics and tutoring services. When you get in touch with the representatives from these colleges, be prepared to ask them what services they might offer. Can you record lectures? Are there faculty advisers for each student? Are classes offered to help with the transition to college? Even if they don't have any plans in place (which is unlikely) your request might be just enough to implement one.

Let's take an up-close look at each of these options for a moment. It's important for you to think about which of these features is important to you and will help you succeed in college. Take notes so that when you contact a college rep or admissions officer, you can ask if these choices exist at the school:

TUTORING: A variety of types of tutoring are available on virtually every campus. The only question is what format you prefer. You can check into peer tutoring from either a classmate or friend; faculty tutoring from a willing professor; in-depth tutoring from a teacher's assistant or at special on-campus centers and clinics. While some tutors may charge a fee, most services tend to be free. When you speak with a college rep, ask what might be available if you should need extra assistance.

COUNSELING: While tutoring is helpful to understanding a certain assignment or class subject, counseling is a wider scope. A counselor will help you make bigger decisions like what major to choose, what classes to take and in what direction you should go to achieve your goal. An academic counselor will

A COLLEGE WHOSE DOOR IS ALWAYS OPEN

The core philosophy of the community college in America can be captured in the phrase "access and excellence." Community colleges, like all institutions of higher education, struggle to be excellent. But when it comes to "access," there is no struggle at all; community colleges are the access institutions of the 21st century.

The community college has emerged as the institution of the second chance — even the third and fourth chance. Community colleges take great pride in their "open-door philosophy," which means that any student who has graduated from high school or who has reached a certain age will be admitted. This philosophy and practice is remarkably different from those of most four-year colleges and universities. Historically, most four-year colleges and universities require that students meet certain criteria for admission, eliminating those who are under-prepared or unqualified to compete.

Community colleges are willing to give all applicants an opportunity to succeed regardless of their history. That does not mean that an unprepared student will be admitted into a very challenging program such as nursing or engineering technology. Instead, through assessment and advising, students who are not prepared for more challenging work will be guided into developmental education programs where they will receive special tutoring and courses in which they can develop the skills for more advanced work.

The focus of the community college — through its faculty and innovative programs and practices — is to help students succeed, regardless of their level of achievement when they enter.

— TERRY O'BANION, former president of the League for Innovation in the Community College

Chapter 1: Where to Find Colleges That Welcome B Students

not only help you reach academic goals, but he or she also will often help you with emotional and mental stress. To do your best academically, you need to be in good shape mentally. Counselors can recommend resources, give suggestions and tips, connect you with helpful mentors or organizations and much more.

CLASS SIZE AND PROFESSOR/STUDENT RATIO: One of the biggest advantages of small colleges is their small class size. While many universities, even the really large ones, state that their average class size is between 10 and 30, a number of small colleges have fewer students per class. Instead of 22:1 student to professor ratios, they may have 5:1. This can be good because your professors are much more likely to be aware of you; if you are struggling or having a problem, they will be more apt to recognize it and reach out. Small classes mean you can ask more questions and discuss things on a deeper level. It also frequently means that participation will play a role in your overall grade.

There are many positive things about small classes, but some students might say that small classes have a negative side as well. For example, if you miss class, professors know (in a class of several hundred, it is a lot less noticeable, believe me!). If your homework isn't turned in, it will be observed right away as well. Truthfully, these can be good things. Professors who notice you are getting behind can remind you to catch up before you've dug your hole so deep that it takes a miracle to pass the class.

Overall, small classes can make the transition from high school to college easier. You will not feel so much like a minnow floundering in a huge ocean. You will get to know your fellow classmates much easier and quicker if there are a half dozen in your class rather than hundreds. Smaller classes often create more of a sense of cooperation between students rather than competition. Instead of trying to do better than another person, you will only be trying to do better than you have done before — and that is the best kind of competition there is.

It's important to go beyond the statistics when you look at the numbers you find for professor/student ratio. Ask students who attend the school how much they interact with their professors and how much of an effort the professors make to help their students. More important than the ratio of professors to students is how involved the professors will be in your studies.

TEACHING STYLES: Another question to look into when choosing your college is what different teaching styles the school may offer. What emphasis does it have on lab time? Is there a period of internship? How much of class time is comprised of hands-on activities for kinesthetic learners? How much is pre-printed or written in forms that are student-friendly for visual learners? How much can be taped for auditory learners? Are there many field trips? All these options can make learning easier for many students. They are alternatives to the typical lecture/listen teaching format that has dominated your education up until now. Colleges offer new ways to learn and excel.

PASS/FAIL or CREDIT/NO CREDIT CLASSES: Not all colleges offer classes with pass/fail grading systems but a number of them have used it effectively, including the following: Millikin University, University of Iowa, University of Illinois, Ohio State University, Stanford University, Tufts University, University of California (Berkeley), Syracuse University, Pennsylvania State University, Pomona College and Grinnell College.

There are certainly a number of perks to this type of grading system. It often encourages students to explore classes that they might otherwise have ignored. For example, if you are an English major, you may not be brave enough to take an advanced math class because you will be surrounded by students who excel in math and competing with them might be overwhelming. However, if you know that you are only going to have to achieve a passing grade, you might be willing to go for it. With pass/fail, there is often less pressure on you; conversely, you may mistakenly think that you don't have to try at all (then you are just wasting everyone's time!).

In addition to regular classes, some types of learning fit the pass/fail system better than the traditional A, B, C, D and F. This is especially true for laboratory experiments, hands-on activities, thesis work and research.

Is there a downside to this type of grading system? Naturally. Some of these courses can't be counted toward your major. While taking a class that doesn't count toward your major may seem unwise, it can be a smart move. You might discover a new passion, interest or direction for your education. You might also discover that you are better at a subject than you had imagined. Pass/fail classes might even lead you to decide on a supplemental course of study, a double major— or you might even consider changing your major. Think of the pass/fail credit simply as an invitation to go down another new college pathway.

THE EMPHASIS ON FINAL EXAMS: Another option to explore is how much influence final exams have on your overall grades. If you are the type who suffers from test anxiety (more on that later) or just does not test well, you want to look for colleges that offer options to traditional testing. Maybe oral tests are possible. Maybe you can earn most of your grades through homework, class participation or other activities.

SUPPORT NETWORK AND LEVEL OF COMPETITION: Besides the formal support network provided by the school from tutoring and counseling, some colleges offer an informal support network. You will want to find out more about this. Do students tend to help each other or compete against each other? At some schools, students frequently work together on group projects or have study sessions together. At other schools, students work more independently. This is especially important if you learn better in a group environment.

SPECIAL PROGRAMS: Investigate what kind of special programs the colleges may offer. For example, some colleges offer co-op programs in which students are able to spend a semester gaining hands-on work experience with a company while earning credits. Most schools have study-abroad programs that allow some students to study internationally, but they vary in their size and scope. Special programs like these may appeal to you and may be just what you need to get motivated.

POSSIBLE AND POPULAR MAJORS: As you look through colleges listed in this book, take special note of the majors listed with each one. These are the most popular majors associated with the particular school. Why is it important to choose a college that features your major? It is just like going shopping. If you really want a pair of boot-cut jeans, you aren't going to go to a shoe store. You want to go where the clerks know what you are talking about and can lead you directly to many choices that fit your needs, right? It's the same thing with a college. If you want to be in computer tech, a college that specializes in art may not be the best choice. You want the school that is familiar with your major and can offer a strong faculty and curriculum in your choice.

You also want to check with a college rep for a school that interests you and ask if you can have a double major at that college (and not just CAN YOU, but will you get the support and guidance you need if you choose to) or can you create your own major. The more options you have, the better the chance of having a college education tailored to your unique needs and the stronger the possibility of overall success.

What if you are undecided about your major when you start your college search? Relax—you are far from being the only one. Make a list of the most likely areas you'd like to explore and then look to see which colleges offer them. It is a first step and that's where every journey begins.

Where to Find Out More about Colleges

- **College fairs.** Dozens or even hundreds of college representatives will come to your town for college fairs. This is your opportunity to ask questions and get a personal perspective from those associated with these colleges without leaving the city limits. Get a list of upcoming college fairs from your counselor or at www.nacac.com/fairs.html.

- **College representatives at your school.** Be sure to meet representatives from colleges when they come to your school! You may be tempted to spend the time doing something else, but these events are designed to give you an opportunity to learn a lot about various colleges. You may also be meeting people who will eventually review your application, should you decide to submit one to any of the schools involved. If you make a good impression, your chances of admission may improve.

- **College catalogs/view books.** These may vary from a simple, colorful tri-fold pamphlet to a 40-page catalog, complete with DVD and/or CD, business cards with contact names, testimonials from students and dozens of photographs. Read them through carefully because they can answer many of your questions.

- **College websites.** Whether you look online at home, in the library or at school, take the time to look over the websites of some of the colleges you are interested in. They almost always have an FYI/FAQ section that will provide answers to basic questions. You also get a chance to see what the campus looks like, what some students have to say about the place (all glowing, of course!) and much more.

- **College alumni.** For great suggestions and insight into a college, see if you can get in touch with someone who actually attended it. It might be your cousin, your father's co-worker, someone your guidance counselor suggested or a person the college itself refers to you. Make a list of questions for that person ahead of time so you are sure to cover what you most want to know. If the person graduated more than a few years ago, some information might not be as current as you need, but you can still learn some important facts.

My biggest piece of advice is that there IS a school for everyone and you WILL be accepted. Remember, you have power over your own life. Get connected with knowledgeable people, invest in books like this one and in the *Fiske's Guide* and Princeton Review's *361 Best Colleges*. Check out *U.S. News & World Report's* "A+ Schools for B Students."

In your junior year, start making plans. Use the summer before your senior year the best way you can. Look for opportunities that open doors and windows for you—think big. If you can't find something, start your own. My son and his friends started a driveway sealing business and did great. Paint, mow lawns—show initiative. It will be a great topic for the essay you should be working on before summer ends.

- **College visits and tours.** While this topic will be discussed in greater depth later in this book, it is important to say at this point that college visits must be given the value that they deserve. Nothing makes a place come

When school starts again, take the most challenging curriculum you are capable of handling. If your school is small and does not offer the more advanced courses, look elsewhere: go online, take distance learning classes or check out the community college.

— **Shirley Bloomquist**, *MA, College and Educational Counselor*

alive as much as visiting it. You can read about a university in every possible source, but you can't really know it until you visit it. That's when you can personally taste the cafeteria creations, hear the conversations in the student union and see the layout of the dorms in some of the residence halls. Go on a tour with your class, counselor, friends or family. The information you will gather is immeasurable.

- **College online virtual tours.** While going to a college in person is the best option, it is not always possible for a variety of reasons. In that case, be sure to at least go to a college's website and check out its virtual tour. You can get a better idea of whether this is the kind of place that calls to you — or not.

- **Guidance counselors.** These wonderful people can give you a lot of helpful information about individual colleges. They may have printed material, website suggestions, contact names and more. Just ask!

- **The school or local community library.** While this book is a great source for finding out about schools that welcome B and C students, there are tons more books out there that list college options. Check them out and look up the schools in which you are most interested. You'll find out useful information that can help you in your decision making. Spend some time just browsing through these books. You may encounter some colleges that you have not heard of before but that are intriguing possibilities.

- **Current college students.** Are there any students in your neighborhood or community already going to a college that interests you? Ask if you can meet for a snack and a chat and have all those questions you haven't been able to ask anyone else ready. Currently enrolled students are the real "been-there-done-that" experts. They will tell you the real truth about college life, not just what the writers of the college's marketing materials want you to know. If you can't find a college student in your area, go to the college and dialog with the students there. Can't get to the campus? Give the place a call and ask the admissions officer to connect you with some students.

- **Decoding college lingo 101.** When you are reading college literature (and believe me, you will get a TON of it), look for key words that will tell you more about how they evaluate applications. For example, they may say that they do a "comprehensive" review of a student's application. Typically, this means they will look beyond the numbers to things like background, extracurricular activities, essays, interviews, recommendations and more. Check online to see if the colleges you are interested in list information about their admissions process online; it might give you some great insight into how they make their decisions.

- **Right from admissions itself.** Skip the middle men and the media and go straight to the college's admissions office. Call and ask to speak with an admissions officer. Be honest. Explain your situation and ask what your chances of admission are or what you might be able to do to improve those chances. You might get some fantastic insider information (the legal kind!).

Visit Colleges Sooner Rather than Later

Don't wait a moment longer to go and visit schools. Seeing is believing! Reading about a place in a book or online is fine for background information, but it is a visit that will give you the true feel of the college's atmosphere, attitudes and activities. (To find out what college tours are like, check out the website www.campustours.com).

Patrick O'Brien, former admissions officer and consultant-ambassador for the ACT, says, "The more opportunities to visit college campuses as a junior or in the first part of senior year, the better. And don't just go for the standard college tour of the campus and facilities. Check out the dorms and dorm life," he advises. "Insist on visiting a class in a field of interest—it will show you how the college academic system really works."

Try not to visit colleges during summer, however. As O'Brien says, "Never visit a campus when school is not in session; that's like visiting your high school on a weekend—dullsville." Don't depend on Mom, Dad or your guidance counselor to contact the school for a tour either. Do it yourself; it shows that college that you have initiative.

When you go for a campus tour, take part of your college-finding team with you so that you can get their impressions of each place too. Don't spend your time exploring the things you can get from the school's website. Pretend you are an anthropologist from the future and study the place like we study primitive cultures today. Watch the students interact, check out the food sources, find out how the place accepts those from different ethnic, political or religious backgrounds, gays or married couples. Read the posters in the buildings and the bulletin boards in dorms. What announcements do they have? What are some of the upcoming events and activities? Do they have a choir, band or orchestra? How about a drama group? Hang out in the student union and see what goes on there. Is there a lot of diversity on the campus? Go by the bookstore and see what souvenirs you like. Check out the shopping area around the campus. Pick up a campus newspaper to read later.

Remembering all your impressions of the places you have seen will not be easy. After you have seen a couple of campuses, facts and opinions will begin to mesh and soon you will find yourself asking which college had that great library. Do you remember what campus had those huge trees and large green lawns? To prevent this from happening, make up a form to write down your thoughts as you tour a place. You can create a form that reminds you to give schools a score of 1 (horrible) to 10 (perfection itself), and that offers a spot for general comments, thoughts and questions to follow up on later.

On Page 15 is an example of the kind of form you could use. If you don't like it, my feelings aren't hurt. Create your own! Design it the way that fits best for you.

The Sky's the Limit

Once you start looking for colleges, you'll be overwhelmed at how many great choices there are. In fact, your problem may be that you have too many options!

After you have a list of colleges, the next step is to fill out the applications. This is your opportunity to make your case (why you should be accepted) to each college. While most colleges do look at the numbers from your GPA, SAT and ACT scores, they will also look to your character. They will want to know your aspirations, your passions, your level of responsibility and maturity and how you choose to spend your time. Who inspires you? Who influences you? What do you expect of yourself? College admissions officers see countless numbers of applications, many with high numbers, but it is the student that shows integrity, curiosity, originality and independence that will catch their eyes. Unlike grading those little #2 pencil-filled dots on the standardized tests, this kind of information is much harder to measure. The college application will go a long way to help paint that very unique portrait of you as a person.

But before we hit the application, let's take the next chapter to look at some things you can do now to make sure you maximize your time in high school and set yourself up to create the strongest application possible.

DON'T GET CAUGHT UP IN THE FRENZY

Many students get totally caught up in the college admissions frenzy without actually realizing that there are more than 4,000 colleges in the United States that have to stay open, so they are looking for students. In other words, you have a much better chance of getting in than you think.

Some advice for you:

● Remember that it is not what college you get into but what you do while you are there that matters the most.

● Even if you think you cannot get into a college, apply anyway.

● Make sure to apply to colleges other than just your favorite one. Even if you consider them a back-up plan, take the time to make a list and apply.

● Be true to yourself about what you want out of a college experience. If you really do not want one that is academically rigorous, that's totally fine. Just be up front about it.

● If one certain college is your dream but you don't fit the academic requirements, apply anyway. If you stand out in any way at all, you just may make it in after all.

— LAURA JEANNE HAMMOND,
Editor in Chief, *Next Step Magazine*

COLLEGE SCORE SHEET

Name of school: _____

Date visited: _____

Who went with me: _____

Contacts I made at the school: _____

_____

FOOD	1	2	3	4	5	6	7	8	9	10
CAMPUS	1	2	3	4	5	6	7	8	9	10
DORMS	1	2	3	4	5	6	7	8	9	10
GREEK	1	2	3	4	5	6	7	8	9	10
COMMUNITY	1	2	3	4	5	6	7	8	9	10
_____	1	2	3	4	5	6	7	8	9	10
_____	1	2	3	4	5	6	7	8	9	10

TOTAL SCORE: _____

Questions:

How does this place make me feel? _____

Best thing about this place: _____

_____

_____

Worst thing about this place: _____

_____

What is the city like? _____

_____

What special services are offered to help B students? _____

_____

Overall comments: _____

_____

_____

_____

CHAPTER TWO

IT'S NEVER TOO LATE: TAKE THE NECESSARY STEPS TO MAKE A CHANGE FOR THE BETTER RIGHT NOW

Procrastination (pro-kras-ten-a-shun): that annoying habit that tends to follow us throughout our lives, convincing us that we can easily put off until tomorrow what we should be doing today (or yesterday) and not have to pay any consequences. (For an example, see the character of Scarlett O'Hara in the classic *Gone with the Wind*, who coined the phrase, "Fiddle-dee-dee, I'll think about it tomorrow!")

We've all done it. You will start the project/diet/chore/report/whatever tomorrow. Tomorrow, as little red-headed Annie reminded everyone in a relatively annoying song, is always a day away. It's eternally full of promise and potential. Unfortunately, when tomorrow arrives, it's today already, so we just repeat the mantra and everything is bumped one more time.

When it comes to getting ready for college, procrastination can be positively lethal. You already know that multiple forms have to be turned in early, from applications to financial aid requests. It doesn't stop there.

If your grades and test scores are not where you want them to be, there are no overnight miracles, potions or cures you can use. But there are steps you can take to brighten the picture a bit, especially if you are still in your sophomore or junior year.

Here is the list. Read it now (don't wait until tomorrow!) and you will already have a leg up on the competition. Some of these things are fairly simple; others take a lot of self-discipline. Fortunately, that is good practice for your college days ahead.

(1) Improve your grades ASAP.

Don't try to get out of improving your grades just because the school year is already partially over. Unless it's less then two weeks until summer vacation, there is still time to make a difference in that GPA. Here are some great ideas to try—TODAY, not tomorrow or next week. Don't be a Scarlett.

First of all, don't generalize your grades or the challenges of certain subject areas. If you're like most students (or human beings for that matter), you're stronger in some subjects than others. Think about which subjects give you the most trouble. Pinpoint the class or classes. Now narrow it down further. WHAT in that class is tough for you? In English, is it the reading or the writing? Is it the grammar or the composition? If it's science, is the difficulty in the lab or in reading the text? What formula or concept in math is bogging you down? If you can be specific about the problem, it is easier to find steps that will help you change things.

Once you know what issues are giving you the most trouble, do something about it. Here are just a few suggestions:

● Ask your teacher for help before or after class.

● Find a student who can help explain certain concepts.

● Join or create a study group.

● Get a tutor.

● Ask your parents for help.

What else can you do? If you are not already doing so, TAKE NOTES. By taking down what the teacher is saying and putting it in your own words, you are focusing and repeating key information. These notes should be as organized and neat as possible and then they should be read over at least once a day to make sure the material is sinking in. Studies have proven that you can learn far more reading short amounts of material each day rather than cramming lots of details in a few hours.

Go over your past tests, quizzes, worksheets and homework assignments. If you did something wrong on them, make sure you understand what it was. If you don't, then ask. There is nothing wrong with making mistakes if you turn around and use the experience for learning and understanding more.

Lastly, check to see if there is a way to earn some extra credit in the class where you are struggling. If there is, do it. It will help your overall grade and make a better impression on your teacher.

(2) Reorganize your priority list.

At the risk of sounding like your parents (and one day, you will realize how intelligent they really are), one of the most important steps you can take in high school is to make your studies a top priority. Does that mean that you will never see your friends and that you must give up any semblance of a social life? No. Instead, it simply means that when you think about your day, school should be high on the list, somewhere below breathing, eating and drinking, but way above watching *The Three Stooges* marathon on television.

If you have homework and your best friend calls and asks you to come over and hang out, give it some thought. Do your best to look beyond the fun of the moment to the potential reward down the road. It's not easy—but it is the mature thing to do (so be sure and let your parents know you made the responsible decision and earn a few brownie points in the process).

By making school a priority, other things will fall into line. Doing homework and studying for tests means better grades, and better grades mean a higher GPA and most likely a better performance on the SAT or ACT. In turn, both of those will strengthen your chances of getting into more colleges. Amanda (Mandy) Warhurst Webster, senior associate director of admissions at Salve Regina University, says, "Students must realize that the senior year is very important. You have to remain focused on academics and come in with a very strong first semester."

(3) Use your summers wisely.

Counting down the days to summer break is an educational tradition. Imagining how you are going to spend those long, hot, lazy summer days can keep you occupied for hours. Chances are that your plans include sleeping in, being with friends, finding a beach, exploring a career as a couch potato and generally doing as little as possible. Without ruling out those possibilities, why not include a few things that could actually raise your chance of college admission? Here are a few possibilities:

● **Get a job that will teach you important skills.** Colleges value students who work because it demonstrates responsibility and maturity. The skills you gain will also help you move up the ladder so that the next job you have will be better.

● **Read that list of books your English teacher handed out.** Doing this will not only give you a head start on the fall but will also help you prepare for the standardized tests.

● **Volunteer in your community.** Colleges like to see students who are involved and give back to their neighborhood or community. Plus, think of the sense of satisfaction that you'll receive from helping an elementary school child read or by making the life of a senior citizen less lonely.

● **Take a summer school class at your high school or a community college.** You can do this to review material from a class that you didn't do as well in or to get a jump start on your classes for the fall. The biggest question that college admissions officers ask when reviewing your application is this: Will you be able to handle the academic courses at this college? Show that you will by taking a class.

You still have lots of days to be lazy or sleep in, so find a balance.

Please remember that difficulty of admissions does NOT equal quality of education. Just because a school is really difficult to get accepted into does not guarantee that it is the highest quality or best fit for you. Keep an open mind. If you haven't heard of the college, it doesn't mean that it isn't a wonderful place. I am personally biased towards small colleges—they give you individual attention, professors and other administrators know your name and you have the chance to develop the academic self-confidence you need.

— **Judith Mackenzie**, *Mackenzie College Consulting*

19

(4) Start on that college essay NOW.

College essays (as you'll see in Chapter Four) can be extremely helpful in getting admitted to colleges. Don't wait to plan what you will say in an essay until you have to actually write it. Begin to brainstorm ideas and work on the basics you will need to know to write an outstanding essay. Don't put it off! That would be like waiting until the homecoming game to work on your tackling or waiting until the debate tournament to think about what position you are taking on an issue. Start now!

Brush up on basic English skills and start thinking about what ideas you might want to write about. Refer to the sample questions listed in Chapter Four and think about how you would answer each one. Go to the library and check out a book on writing a quality, winning college essay. Read the samples to get a feel for what admissions officers seem to prefer. Think how you would approach the same or similar topic. Line up your reasons, examples and anecdotes now, not later.

(5) Get to know your guidance counselor.

For many students, the guidance counselor is just one of those people in the background of your high school life. You rarely see him or her except on special occasions (or if you are in trouble). You have time to change all that! Schedule a visit with your guidance counselor. Ask for tips on how to improve your chances of getting into college. Ask for help in searching out the best options. A guidance counselor is a person that is there to help you, so make yourself accessible. Ask questions. Follow up on advice.

(6) Shed the fluff and take advanced placement, honors or college prep courses.

A number of colleges do some rearranging of your grades that you might not be aware of. They will look at the classes you took in high school, throw out the "fluff" classes and recalculate the "core" classes. Journalism, shop, drama, home economics—all gone. Only science, math and English might remain. For many students, this is an unpleasant surprise because the grades they got in their elective classes were the ones responsible for driving up their overall GPA. Knowing this, you might want to choose different classes for your junior and senior years. Throw out the easy classes and take advanced placement or college prep courses instead. Some suggestions include these classes: algebra, geometry, foreign language, laboratory science and English. The honest fact is that a B in a core class will benefit you more than an A in any fluff class.

Patrick O'Brien adds, "Junior year for many is like boot camp, or to say it another way, it's more like college while the frosh and sophomore years are more like middle school. It is a breakthrough year with greater opportunities but also greater challenges. More self-direction is expected," he adds. "You should expect it of yourself. Keep all things in balance."

Mark Campbell, vice president for enrollment management at McKendree College, advises high school students, "Don't be tempted to take the soft senior year. Continue to develop your writing!"

Here is a helpful chart for converting your grades over to the point system used for computing GPAs.

A	4.0
A-	3.7
B+	3.3
B	3.0
B-	2.7
C+	2.3
C	2.0
C-	1.7
D+	1.3
D	1.0
D-	0.7
F	0.0

(7) Get passionately involved in your community.

Another factor that can help you get accepted into college is a history of being actively involved in your community in some way. Don't wait until the summer of your senior year to do this. Start looking around now for ways to play a part in your community. Make sure that you are sincere; don't become involved just to impress the admissions departments of colleges. Do it to learn and explore, and to discover more about yourself. Find a place of service that is in an area of great interest to you. Then you will find your passion, and it will mean more to you than just wanting to look good on a piece of paper. And there's another plus—you will be able to write or talk about that passion in your essay or interview.

Some possible areas in which to get involved include volunteering at places such as these:

- schools

- crisis intervention centers

- homeless shelters

- park and recreation centers

- community gardens

- nursing homes

- libraries

- hunger relief centers

- humane society

- theatres

(8) Get a coach, tutor, mentor and/or study buddy.

Just like it is better to study several days before a test rather than several hours (or minutes!) before, why wait to find someone who can help you succeed in so many ways? If you are not doing well in a class, do not hesitate to ask for help. Talk to your teachers. Get a tutor. Find a student who will study with you. Hire a study coach. Learn from a mentor. Do what you need to do now to improve those grades, as well as your own enthusiasm, dedication and passion.

If the term "mentor" is new to you, here is some helpful information. A mentor is a guide and counselor, someone that gives advice and helps you think through decisions. The term "mentor" carries with it the connotation

THE TOP FIVE FACTS ABOUT LEARNING DISABILITIES

When someone has a learning disability, what he or she should be able to do is different from what he or she is able to do. Learning disabilities are invisible, life-long conditions. You can't tell by looking at a person that he or she has one, and learning disabilities can't be cured. One in every ten people has a learning disability.

A learning disability may mean you have difficulty with any of the following:

- spoken language
- written language
- coordination
- self-control
- organizational skills
- attention
- memory

FACT 1: People with LD are smart. People with LD have average to above average intelligence. Some people prefer to think of LD as a "different learning style" or a "learning difference." That's because you CAN learn, but the way in which you learn is different. You have a unique learning style.

FACT 2: There are many types of LD.

Dyslexia is usually thought of as a reading disability although it also means having problems using language in many forms.

Dyscalculia causes people to have problems doing arithmetic and understanding math concepts. Many people have issues with math, but a person with dyscalculia has a much more difficult time solving basic math problems.

Dysgraphia is a writing disorder that causes people to have difficulty forming letters or writing within a certain space.

Dyspraxia is a problem with the body's system of motion. Dyspraxia makes it difficult for a person to control and coordinate his or her movements.

Auditory memory and processing disability describes problems people have in understanding or remembering words or sounds because their brains don't understand language the way typical brains do.

FACT 3: LD is hereditary. No one knows the exact cause of LD but it is believed to be a problem with the central nervous system, meaning it is neurological. LD also tends to run in families. You may discover that one of your guardians or grandparents had trouble at school. LD is not caused by too much sugar, guardians who aren't strict enough or allergies.

FACT 4: LD must be assessed by a psychologist. Diagnosing LD involves a number of things. You and your guardians will be interviewed to find out what kind of problems you have had, how long you have had them and how seriously they have affected you. Your teachers should be interviewed as well.

You will be given several tests. These aren't the same kind of tests you take in school. Instead, the person testing you will ask you questions and get you to complete certain tasks. Once the tests are finished, the examiner looks at how you are doing at school and compares that with how you should be doing given how smart you are (your intelligence). If there is a difference between these that can't be explained by other reasons, then a diagnosis of LD is often made.

FACT 5: There is no cure for LD but lots can be done to help. One of the most important things you can do to help yourself is to understand what your particular LD is. It is also important for you to recognize and work on your strengths. Your guardians and teachers will help you learn about how to cope with your learning problems better by teaching strategies that can minimize their effect.

Source: Reprinted with permission from the Learning Disabilities Association of BC

that the person brings a certain knowledge that comes from wisdom and experience—in other words, a mentor is someone who "knows the ropes"—a friend, coach, tutor, teacher, counselor or even a relative that has been where you are. Research has shown that mentoring relationships can help students to develop work ethics and a sense of responsibility, as well as help raise self-esteem, strengthen communication skills and improve personal relationships. The skills that mentors can teach you will most likely help in high school and certainly in college.

(9) Make sure you aren't working "around" an undiagnosed learning disability.

If you have been continually struggling in school and it has been showing up in your grades and test scores, make sure that you have been tested for learning disabilities. It is possible that you have an undiagnosed issue that has caused you to develop a different learning style. Talk to your guidance counselor or family physician. Many of the colleges today welcome students with various learning disabilities and they have special programs geared especially for them.

Not sure what qualifies as a learning disability? It's a blanket term that covers everything from not being able to sit still in class to not being able to read very well. There are many people who dislike the phrase "learning disability." They believe that instead of calling areas of challenge "disabilities," people should realize that some students simply have found other approaches to gaining knowledge that are perhaps different from most people's ways of learning.

Review the information about learning disabilities from an organization called the Learning Disabilities Association of BC. Know the facts about learning disabilities.

Worried that learning disabilities will interfere with your education? There are many successful people who have made the "LD" list, such as Whoopi Goldberg, Magic Johnson, Nelson Rockefeller, Jay Leno and Charles Schwab. Not too shabby, eh? You wouldn't mind being in such good company, would you?

(10) Take classes at your local junior college.

Start your college career while you are still in high school by taking classes at your local junior or community college. Many of these institutions are open to the idea. Terry O'Banion, former president of the League for Innovation in the Community College, explains the possibilities. "In the last decade or so, many high schools and community colleges have created articulated programs to allow students enrolled in high school to take courses for community college credit," she says. "Called 'dual or concurrent enrollment,' the practice is very widespread and is likely to expand in the next few years.

"The practice emerged because able high school students often exhaust the supply of solid courses by their senior year; there is no reason to wait until they graduate from high school to begin taking college-level courses," adds O'Banion. "Additionally, community colleges and high schools in the same region share common purposes of preparing students for the workforce or for further education, and they can enhance that purpose by creating opportunities for high school students to take courses at the local community college to round out their schedules," she concludes.

Tonia Johnson, associate director of admission at Guilford College, also discourages students from leaving school early in their senior year. Just because you have all the credits you need doesn't mean you need to cut your year short. A better plan is to use this time to do something that will impress admissions officers. "Take courses somewhere, get involved in an internship, but use the time wisely," she says.

Regardless of the stage at which you need to make changes, don't look back at your mistakes: look forward to your possibilities. Making that difference can be enough to get your admissions application placed in the "accepted" pile instead of that other stack. Write out a list of the top ten things you want to change, pin it up and give it the attention it needs. You might be surprised at the results!

GETTING IN

**BEYOND THE BASIC
APPLICATION FORM:
EXPLAINING
WEAKNESSES AND
BUILDING ON
STRENGTHS**

GPAS, SATS AND ACTS, OH MY!

Let's face it. If you're reading this book, it means those wonderful acronyms in the title of this chapter are not among your strong points. For one reason or another, your overall GPA or your test scores are just not that remarkable.

What can you do about that? One possibility is to check out the colleges that do not require standardized test scores as part of their admissions process. "What?" you ask in amazement. There are colleges that don't want those all important numbers? That's right. In fact, there are more than 700 of them and they can all be found at www.fairtest.org.

Why would some colleges choose not to rely on ACT and SAT scores? Here is how Fair Test explains it:

> *"Test scores are biased and unreliable.* Standardized college admissions tests are biased, imprecise and unreliable, and therefore should not be required for any college admissions process or scholarship award. If test scores are optional, students who feel that their strengths are reflected by their SAT or ACT scores can submit them, while those whose abilities are better demonstrated by grades, recommendations, a portfolio or a special project are assured that these will be taken into full account. Sometimes admissions officers use low test scores to automatically reject qualified candidates without even considering their schoolwork. That's simply not fair.

> *"Test scores are nearly useless in college admission.* Research shows that the SAT and ACT do not help colleges and universities make significantly better admissions decisions. The University of Chicago Press book, *The Case Against the SAT*, found that the SAT is 'statistically irrelevant' in college admission. It also proves that the SAT undermines the goal of diversity by reducing the number of qualified minority and lower-income students who are admitted."

If you are applying to a school that requires SAT or ACT scores, Fair Test encourages you to ask some important questions including these:

- How does your school use the SAT and/or ACT?

- Are cut-off scores used? If so, do they apply to general admissions or to particular programs?

- Does your school use any statistical formula which includes SAT/ACT scores to judge applicants' academic records?

- Do you take possible coaching into account when considering ACT or SAT scores?

- How does your college report SAT and ACT scores in handbooks and brochures?

- Does this college report simple averages or a range of scores? Does this include all entering students' scores in these figures, in compliance with the Good Practice Principles of the National Association for College Admission Counseling?

So, if all of this is true, why do most colleges rely so heavily on the results from standardized tests? It's a matter of "measurement." If you think about it, an A at a high school in Chicago may be different than an A at a high school in Los Angeles. In fact, an A at two high schools in the same school district or even with two different physics teachers at the same high school may be different. Because schools have varying ways of awarding grades and varying levels of difficulty, colleges need a uniform way to measure students. The SAT and ACT have become those measures. A great deal of importance is given to the scores achieved on them.

In fact, a good performance on college-entrance tests has become the focus of many a student's "free" time past the hours when the high school doors are closed for the day. In recent years, "test prep" has become more than just an option. It's a booming business! During the last few years, it has grown from $100 million to more than triple that. More and more students are putting out big bucks to prepare themselves to take the SAT.

So while standardized tests may be unreliable and not every college requires them, it doesn't look like they are going away anytime soon. If you are applying to a college that requires test scores, then you have little choice but to "bite the bullet" and take the test.

Meet the New Tests

As you probably know, the SAT and ACT tests have recently been changed. Let's take a look at these "new" exams:

SAT Reasoning Test (www.collegeboard.com)

- The exam has three sections—Critical Reading, Math and Writing—each scored between 200 and 800 points for a total possible score of 2400.

- The Critical Reading section is 70 minutes long with two 25-minute sections and one 20-minute section. It contains reading comprehension, sentence completion and paragraph-length critical reading sections. This section replaces the old verbal section.

- The Math section is 70 minutes long with two 25-minute sections and one 20-minute section. It contains multiple-choice questions and student-produced responses on numbers and operations, algebra, geometry and statistics, probability and data analysis.

- The Writing section contains a 25-minute essay that is first and a 35-minute multiple choice section that has questions on identifying sentence errors, improving sentences and improving paragraphs.

ACT (www.actstudent.org)

- This exam has four multiple-choice tests and an optional Writing test. There is a score for each of the four tests (English, Math, Reading and Science) from 1 (low) to 36 (high), and the composite score is the average of the four test scores between 1 and 36.

- The English section has 75 questions in 45 minutes that test standard written English (punctuation, grammar and usage, sentence structure) and rhetorical skills (strategy, organization, style).

- The Mathematics section has 60 questions in 60 minutes that test pre-algebra (23 percent), elementary algebra (17 percent), intermediate algebra (15 percent), coordinate geometry (15 percent), plane geometry (23 percent) and trigonometry (7 percent).

- The Reading section has 40 questions in 35 minutes that test reading comprehension.

- The Science section has 40 questions in 35 minutes that test the "interpretation, analysis, evaluation, reasoning and problem-solving skills" of natural sciences.

- The optional Writing section has one essay prompt in 30 minutes that tests writing skills.

Tips for Getting a Higher Score

It goes without saying that doing well on the standardized college entrance exams (ACT/SAT) helps you get in the front door of most colleges. There are dozens of books to tell you how to do well on these standardized tests, so I will not attempt to do it here. Instead, here's a quick list of the most basic things you can do to assure that you do the best you can:

- Make a decision that the test is important to you and that you will give it time and effort.

- Get familiar with the test format so that this is not a surprise to you. Know what each test will cover. You can get free sample exams from the creators of the exams by going to www.collegeboard.com for the SAT and www.act.org for the ACT.

- Consider hiring a coach or tutor to help you prepare for the tests. There are intensive test preparation courses available from companies like Princeton Review (www.review.com) and Kaplan (www.kaplan.com), but there are also lower-cost options from community colleges and maybe even your high school.

- Go to the library or bookstore and start looking at all the test prep books. They come in several different formats. A recent trend is exciting novels of all kinds that entertain you while they introduce you to all of the vocabulary words you need to know for the test. Check the stories out at www.amazon.com or use a search engine to find "vocabulary SAT novels." The stories are so captivating that you completely forget that you are learning at the same time. SAT and ACT prep books are easy to find and will de-mystify the process for you.

- Check out websites on the Internet for test help. Just put "SAT test preparation" in the search box. Here are just a few of the many out there:

  www.review.com

  www.kaplan.com

  www.number2.com

  www.act-sat-prep.com

  www.4tests.com

  www.petersons.com

A last bit of advice before you take one of these standardized tests: Do not attempt to cram for them; it will never work. This is not that type of test. Instead go into the test well rested, following a good breakfast. Take the entire three hours and 35 minutes to complete it. Don't rush. If you get done early, just take the time to go back over your work. Don't panic when you see other students turning in their tests when you are far from done. Everyone has a different test pace, and getting done faster is not an indication of how anyone did. Know that you did the best you could and despite the scores, forge ahead. Colleges are waiting for you!

Taking the Credit; Taking the Blame

There will come a time within the application, essay or interview where you will be expected to either explain or discuss your SAT/ACT score and GPA. It's better to offer an explanation than to ignore your scores or GPA and hope that the admissions officers don't notice them. In fact, they will notice them, and without an explanation, they will have no reason to give you the benefit of the doubt.

Remember that admissions officers are human beings. They have made mistakes or struggled in some way in their lives. They will understand and listen, so take the time to explain honestly why you believe your numbers are not as high as you had hoped they would be.

Here is a list of the general do's and don'ts that you need to remember when discussing your less-than-stellar numbers. The key is to be honest at all times.

DO: Explain any circumstances that may have affected your numbers such as these:	DON'T:
frequent moves	whine
test anxiety or health issues	complain
learning disabilities	place blame on others (parents, teachers, etc.)
part-time jobs	adopt a "poor me" attitude
extenuating personal or family issues	be emotional

As you can see, it's important to take responsibility for your performance. Instead of making excuses or blaming others, state the facts and own up to how you did. There are legitimate and understandable reasons for not doing as well as you are capable of doing. Some of these reasons were listed above. But make sure that you do not confuse explanations with excuses. Not having a date to the spring formal is not a good reason.

Also have a balance between providing enough information to make your case but not so much information that your explanation is overwhelming. For example, you might write that having a severely ill parent affected your ability to concentrate on your studies for a semester, but you don't need to also provide the detail of every medical procedure your parent has had.

If your grades are low in a specific subject, explain this. You can describe how you have sought extra help in the subject or how you took a summer school class to make sure you really understood the material, but it's still a weak area. You can also explain that you plan to major in another subject area in which you are stronger when you reach college.

It's important as well to note any progress that you've made. If you have since improved your grades in a subject area or overall, indicate this and explain that you have a renewed commitment to your studies.

Once you have discussed this topic, you can move on to focus on your

Chapter 3: GPAs, SATs and ACTs, Oh My!

HOW WILL MY SAT ESSAY BE GRADED?

Each essay will be scored independently by two high school and college teachers. Neither scorer will know what points the other one gave. Each reader will assign the essay a score ranging from 1 to 6. Essays with a 6 are outstanding, with few to no errors at all. These essays are built on a main point that is supported by stories, examples and reasons. Essays with scores of 6 are organized, focused, coherent, smooth and are indicative of a wide vocabulary. But not every essay is a 6. Let's look at what other scores can mean:

- A score of 5 indicates that the essay is effective, without being stellar. It is effective with only a few grammar/usage/mechanics errors.

- Essays that are scored with a 4 are considered competent, but with some gaps in quality.

- An essay with a score of 3 is adequate but has a number of errors, including grammar/usage/mechanics, vocabulary, focus or development.

- A score of 2 means that the essay is seriously limited with a number of weaknesses.

- An essay that is scored with a 1 is severely flawed.

For more detailed information on how the scoring is done, check out the College Board website at www.collegeboard.com.

strengths instead. Without dwelling on the negative, you have the opportunity to highlight how much you have to offer the college.

Include a Resume to Highlight What You Have Accomplished

Many colleges will let you submit a resume. You may already have one on hand thanks to summer job searches. This can provide a beginning. The resume you used for looking for a summer part-time job might give you some quality information to use, but it probably will need changes before you share it with a college. Why? Two reasons: one, time has most likely passed since you wrote it and there may be new things to add, and two, your intention is different. You aren't trying to impress a potential employer so that he or she will give you a weekly paycheck. This time, the goal is to impress a college admissions officer and get you through the front door of the school.

Resumes are like the *Cliffs Notes* of your academic/educational and community life. They are the condensed version of the great stuff you have accomplished thus far. Resumes can be very effective. Here are some tips:

- Have high-quality paper.

- Choose a font size and style that is easy to read (at least 12 and below 18 and Arial, Times New Roman, Garamond or Franklin Gothic Book).

- Do not handwrite this resume. Even if you have to use the school or library computer, make sure this is neat and looks professional.

- Many word processing programs include a built-in resume wizard, so check and see if you can find one. This template walks you right through where to put what and then puts it in a format that looks great.

Here is what you need to include on your resume:

- full name

- current address

- telephone number (home and cell)

- email address

- all awards or honors you have earned

- all forms of community service

- all part-/full-time jobs

- references

- sports and extracurricular involvement—remember that these can be in school or outside of school!

One of the most important aspects of the resume is to include the pertinent details that truly explain what you have accomplished. For example, if you worked as a volunteer at a local children's day care center, include how many children you worked with and what responsibilities you held. This is the place where you can really shine in ways that your numbers do not reflect.

On Page 35 is an example of a typical type of resume you might want to include in your application. Look it over to see how you can adapt it to your needs.

After you have done all this hard work, don't blow it by not checking your spelling and grammar. The greatest resume will make a rotten impression if it has errors. Have someone else read over it before you finalize it. They may catch a mistake you missed—or remember something wonderful that you forgot to include.

A resume gives the opportunity to share with the college more than your grades and test scores. It gives them a snapshot of your achievements that will really help them understand what you have to offer.

A WORD ABOUT TEST ANXIETY

Feeling worried or pressured about taking a test is normal. Indeed, a slight edginess can often enhance your performance. However, if the worry turns into panic and/or fear and makes it almost impossible to study or take the test, you probably are suffering from test anxiety.

Test anxiety can strike before and/or during a test. It can make you feel physically sick, from a headache or nausea to faintness and hyperventilating. You might have a dry mouth, pounding heart or sweaty hands or be unusually emotional. It is often very difficult to concentrate at all.

How can you combat it? Here are some tips:

1. **Be prepared as much as possible for the test.** The SAT and ACT are cumulative exams that assess years of study in high school. They are not tests for which you can "cram." Get a good study guide and become familiar with what the SAT and ACT test. Try a few of the practice tests. Then relax and just do your best.

2. **Take good care of yourself.** Get enough sleep, eat healthy and get some regular exercise. Don't have any coffee before the test because caffeine increases your level of anxiety.

3. **Learn how to relax.** Sounds simple, but it can be challenging when your body and mind are trying to do just the opposite. Like with other things, practice is the key. Spend time learning how to think about each muscle group in your body. Start with your feet. Tighten them and then let them go. Work your way all the way up to your head. Breathe slowly and deeply.

4. **Replace negative thoughts with positive ones.** Instead of telling yourself, "I am just going to blow this entire test," say, "This may be a difficult test but I will do the best I can on it." Visualize yourself doing well on the test.

5. **When you are taking the test, remember those deep, slow breaths.** Be sure to read the test directions carefully. If you don't know a question, skip it and go back later.

6. **If you find yourself tensing up during the test, put down your pencil, take a few deep breaths, relax your neck and shoulders and then go back to it.** Go to another question or problem and come back to the one that made you anxious. Sometimes answering a few problems that you do know will help you remember the answer to the one that threw you a curve.

7. **When you are done, do something fun.** See a movie, go out to eat, meet with a friend or just take a well-deserved nap.

123 4th St.
Anytown, USA 10000

Phone 555-555-5555
Fax 555-555-5556
Email anystudent@aol.com

CHRIS SMITH

Community Involvement	Volunteered for six months (2007) at The Boys and Girls Club: helped organize and guide 30 children between the ages of 8 and 13 in multiple after-school activities. Learned skills of organization, teamwork, cooperation and discipline.
	Intern at Wheels Unlimited, my grandfather's bicycle repair shop, after school for two years (2005-2007). Learned how to serve customers, run a register and basic mechanics/engineering skills.
Extracurricular Activities	Participated in the Chess Club (2005) and the Debate Club (2006-2007). Director of the Drama Club (2006) and President of the Ski Club (2007).
Employment	June-August 2006 20 hours a week at Marin County Public Library
	June-August 2007 18 hours a week at the Community Theatre
Education	2004-2007 East County High School
	Summer 2006 Theatre Workshop
	Summer 2006 Sign Language 101 at St. Martin's Community College
References	Mr. Bob Smith, Youth Coordinator at the Boys and Girls Club, 555-222-1111
	Mrs. Jean Youngblood, English/Language Arts Teacher, East County High School, 555-982-1120
	Mr. Rod Cooper, High School Debate Coach, 555-888-1210
	Miss Lindsay Francis, Professor of Sign Language, St. Martin's Community College, 555-333-0101
Awards received	Debate Team Regional First Prize, 2006
	First Place, State Library Essay Contest, 2006
	Heart of Gold, Volunteer Ribbon, 2007

CHAPTER FOUR

WINNING IN WRITING: THE ALL-IMPORTANT COLLEGE ESSAY

Not every college requires an essay, but most of them want to see one. If you are applying at one of the colleges that do not require ACT or SAT scores, for example, the college essay is extremely important. Bottom line: The chances are pretty good you will have to write an essay. And, putting aside your fears for a moment, you will come to realize that this is a good thing.

For many admissions officers, your essay is the first chance they get to see the real you. They already know your grades, test scores and what classes you have taken for the last four years, but they don't know YOU. Sure, they are looking at how well you remember those grammar and punctuation rules, as well as what kind of vocabulary you use, but they also want a glimpse of your personality, ambitions, talents, goals and dreams.

College essays have become such an important part of the admissions process that there are many books dedicated to showing you how to write them. Many also give sample essays to read from students who were accepted by colleges. One excellent book is *Accepted! 50 Successful College Admission Essays* by Gen Tanabe and Kelly Tanabe. Check out the many websites on the Net dedicated to the topic.

Be aware there are unscrupulous companies and people willing (for a price) to take the headache out of your hands and write the essay for you. Yes, you can buy your college essay. Is this ethical? What do you think? Not only is this wrong, but it also won't help you get into college. Purchased essays are never able to convey the real you to a college. Don't ask a friend or relative to write it for you either. The admissions officers are good at spotting styles that don't fit with students. Also consider that if you turn in something that reads like Ernest Hemingway, but your GPA in English class has always been a B or less, a red flag will pop up immediately.

But the best reason for writing your own essay is that regardless of your skill, you can write a successful essay that will reflect your personality and your passion for life. It's not as hard as you might imagine! Read on to learn how.

The questions and/or topics you might be given to write about in college essays vary a great deal in subject area. Regardless of the question, the point

TYPICAL ESSAY QUESTIONS

- Describe your most significant personal experience. How has it influenced you?

- Identify and discuss a problem facing your generation.

- What have you read that has had a special significance to you? Explain why.

- Describe a person or experience of particular importance to you.

- Describe the reasons that influenced you in selecting your intended major field of study.

- If you could travel through time and interview a prominent figure in the arts, politics, religion or science, whom would you choose and why?

- Describe your experience in living in a racially, culturally or ethnically diverse environment; what do you expect to need to know to live successfully in the multi-cultural society of the future?

- Make up a question, state it clearly and answer it. Feel free to use your imagination, recognizing that those who read it will not mind being entertained.

- Indicate what you consider your best qualities to be and describe how your college education will be of assistance to you in sharing these qualities and your accomplishments with others.

- Evaluate a significant experience, achievement or risk that you have taken and its impact on you.

- Indicate a person, character in fiction, a historical figure or a creative work (as in art, music, etc.) that has had a significant influence on you and describe that influence.

- Why do you want to spend two to six years of your life at a particular college, graduate school or professional school? How is the degree necessary to the fulfillment of your goals?

- Use this space to let us know something about you that we might not learn from the rest of your application.

- How have you grown and developed over the four years of your high school career?

- What is the biggest risk you have ever taken? Explain why you took it and what you learned afterward.

- Discuss some issue of personal, local or national concern and why it is important to you.

- Write about your favorite book or film and tell why it has influenced you.

- Relate the most humorous experience in your life.

- You have just finished writing your 300-page autobiography. Please submit page 217.

is to say who you are. You will show that in how you respond, what anecdotes you use, what examples you include and so on.

Essay Mistakes to Avoid from the Get Go

Remember that you want your essay to stand out from the others in the pile on that admission officer's desk. You want to make a favorable and memorable impression and you want the reader of the essay to feel as if he or she is getting to know you. To make sure that your essay sounds unique and individual, take care to avoid certain pitfalls; for example, don't respond with the answers that everyone else does. If you are asked to write about a book you have read, don't pick the one that all high school students were required to read. Pick something unusual or different, a book that tells the admissions personnel something about you for choosing it. It does not matter if the admissions officer has ever heard of it. What matters is how you explain why it was an important book to you.

If you are asked to write about an event in your life, go beyond just describing it. Show how it affected your life and how you are different because of it. The trick here is not writing what everyone else does. Along with Dr. Seuss essays, admissions officers weary of reading essays that focus on the "I've seen the light" philosophy. You lost the game, but achieved a goal. Your parents got divorced/took drugs and it taught you a lesson. You had this favorite teacher or coach. It's one thing to write about something that you learned from the experience, but it's over the top to write that you've found the purpose of life through these experiences. It's easy to think that you have to be profound and philosophical when you write this essay, but the truth is that admissions officers see more than enough of this approach.

THIS IS YOUR CHANCE!

Quite often, the college application essay is the perfect opportunity to tackle the subject of your less-than-stellar-quality test scores or GPA. Many times you can tie the question you are asked to write about to the subject of your strengths and weaknesses. If you can directly address the issue in your essay, do so. Look back over the list of the most commonly asked questions. Can you see how you could relate your strengths to the topic? For example, "Use this space to let us know something about you that we might not learn from the rest of your application." You could explain how you have been persistent, dedicated, strong, determined, creative or any other admirable trait through examples. You can show the admissions officers that while your numbers may not be the strongest they have seen, you are a bright, skilled and wonderful student that would be an excellent addition to any college. Think of the essay as your time to shine!

Other things to avoid

Don't try to be cute by adding poetry or illustrations unless they directly relate to your topic or your specific talent, don't use unusually fancy paper and never handwrite the essay. While it is okay to be emotional, do not whine, complain or be sarcastic. Avoid using current films, actors or television shows for your examples, and don't try to sell yourself. Represent the special person you are, but don't sound like an overzealous salesman working on commission. Don't use anyone else's idea even if it is interesting. It won't sound like you and your support will sound hollow.

Be funny, be enthusiastic, be reflective—but make sure it is not something that you and 4,000 other students wrote about. Go beyond the expected and you will get noticed. The college essay is often the deciding factor in whether you are accepted or rejected. You want your words to push you over the top.

Putting Words on Paper

College essays are typically 250 to 500 words. That is about one to two pages of typing, double spaced. According to the Common Application (www.commonapp.org), that limit is a guideline because colleges do not actually count the words. They won't mind if it is a little shorter or longer because quality is far more important than quantity. "College admissions officers are far more concerned that the essay is well written, proofread (not just spell-checked), well thought out, etc. Do not get caught up in the 'micro' (words, spacing, font size, color of ink)," states the website. "They are looking for the 'macro': does the student write well and what can they learn about this person from his/her essay?" Their website has more helpful information on what you will find on many college application forms.

Once you know the question, sit down and brainstorm possible answers. Just let your mind wander around the topic and write it all down without judgment or self-censorship. When you have run out of ideas, start going through what you have. What looks best? Throw out the things you could only write a paragraph about and keep the ideas that you can build into several pages of examples and facts that support a topic sentence. Look for the ones that make you feel emotional; that probably means they impacted your life in some way. Then choose one.

Now, write out an outline, just like you have done for other papers and reports you've done in school. What are the main points you want to cover? What details go under each point? For example, imagine that you have been asked to write about something you have read that was significant to you. Some points you might want to cover include these: Why you chose to read the book, how you felt while reading it, what new perspectives or points of view the author taught you, what questions the material raised in your mind, what you learned from the experience.

Once your outline is done, it is time to write your first draft (and yes, that means there will be second, third and more drafts before you're done). Do not start your essay with any of the following opening sentences:

- My name is Kevin Jones and I . . .

- I was born in Los Angeles, California, and . . .

- My college admissions essay is going to be about . . .

- I am writing this because I really want to go to your college . . .

- This is the story of my life so far . . .

- I am such a great person that you will want to read my story . . .

- My parents, Jean and Jasper Carpenter, first moved . . .

These are boring lead-ins and you will most likely have lost the reader's attention in the very first paragraph. Start with something interesting, eye-catching and unique. Grab the admissions officer's attention by writing something that will make him or her put down that cup of coffee, sit up straight in the chair and want to read what comes next.

Your first draft should be written without worrying about grammar, spelling or punctuation. You want to get your best thoughts down first, without being slowed down by rules. In case you don't remember the basic structure from endless English classes, you need the minimum of a five-paragraph essay. It should look pretty much like this:

INTRODUCTION thesis statement
BODY: Paragraph 2 support for thesis statement
BODY: Paragraph 3 support for thesis statement
BODY: Paragraph 4 support for thesis statement
CONCLUSION summary of main points

When you are done, show the first draft to your friends and family. Ask their opinions. Should you give more detail? Was everything clear? Did it represent your personality? Is this how they would have imagined you answering the question? Listen carefully to their feedback so you can use it in your revisions.

Now write a second draft, pulling in any extra details you remembered and keeping others' comments in mind. This time, fix any spelling, grammar or punctuation errors. Share it with a favorite teacher or your guidance counselor. Get their comments. Go back to the desk. Go through it again, keeping the new feedback in mind. Run spell check (but do not depend on it) and print. You're ready.

What If I'm Not a Writer?

It is entirely possible that you are a whiz at math or a mad scientist, and writing just isn't your forte. If this is true, the college essay may be all that much more intimidating. So let's give your essay some thought before you begin to put words on paper.

Here are some ways to take your brilliant ideas and eventually come up with an essay. Which one sounds best to you?

- Get a tape recorder and tell what you would like to have in your essay. Consider this your first draft. Listen to it and refine it and when

Remember in Chapter 3 how I talked about "taking the credit; taking the blame"? Let's return to this theme for a moment. An essay is one of your best opportunities to explain your grades. If you can do this clearly and honestly without resorting to whining and complaining, then you are doing yourself a huge favor.

Let's take a look at three partial sample essays that explain, in three very different ways, why these students' grades are less than stellar. Can you relate to what they say? How could you write your essay?

Example 1

Reaching and then maintaining high grades has always been a struggle for me. It wasn't that I didn't care about school, because I did. Basically, there were so many issues going on inside my house that I rarely had a moment to give to homework or studying. I have a younger brother named Kevin and he has cerebral palsy. He has to spend most of his time in a wheelchair and since both of my parents work, it is my job to take care of him as soon as I get home from school each afternoon. I don't mind doing it, but it really makes it hard for me to sit down and study for more than a few minutes at a time. Sometimes it also meant that I was up later than I should have been and then I was tired for class the next day.

Has your family experienced something that has made it harder for you to study and maintain good grades? It might be an illness or sickness, moving, divorce, a parent in the military, etc. Think about it for awhile. Maybe to help your family you have had to work two jobs. Perhaps you have had to help out in the family business. What are some reasons that you simply could not study or do as well in school as you had hoped?

Example 2

The only person that I can blame my poor grades on is me. For the first two years of high school, I just did not put the effort and time into my classes that they deserved. I spent most of my time playing sports and spending time with my friends. In my junior year, however, that all changed. One of my best friends died in an automobile accident. It came as quite a shock to me. I guess, like a lot of other teenagers, I thought I was immortal and this accident proved me wrong. Moreover, it made me realize that time really is limited and if I wanted to go to college and pursue music, I had to start taking school a lot more seriously. Since that time, I have been working to make high school my first priority. It has not been easy and I am still struggling in a couple of my classes, but my GPA has steadily gone up.

Does this story sound familiar? Did something happen to you during your high school years that changed your perspective on things? Did you blow off school for a while and then something got your attention focused in a different direction? If you admit that once you didn't do so great but you're better now and why, it can be quite persuasive.

Example 3

My GPA is low for one reason and that is math. My teacher was very supportive and spent a great deal of extra time tutoring me but it never seemed to work. For whatever reason, math just continues to be incredibly difficult for me. As abysmal as I am at numbers, however, I excel with words. I love to read the writings of other authors as well as pen my own. I have kept journals since I was six years old and have written more than 100 short stories. I've won a number of local and regional contests and truly believe that my future will center on the publishing world. In the meantime, however, my math grades will keep pulling down my GPA and I will keep muddling my way through numbers while I am covering my notebooks with words.

Is there an area in which you stand out from the pack and another that is a constant struggle? Talk about it. Explain this challenge and what you have done to address it and even compensate for it. It is okay to honestly state that you are not as strong in one subject as you are in another. Show how you use that experience to fuel your productivity in areas where you do excel.

it centers on what you want to say, either type it as you listen or ask someone else to transcribe it for you.

- Sit down and talk to your parents or a special friend about your response to the essay question or topic. As you speak, have that person make a list or an outline of what points you mention. Once you have a basic roadmap, it can be easier to start writing the essay.

- Find some friends who are writers and ask for their tips, ideas and suggestions. Have one of them tutor you through the process as you write the essay.

- Get some books from the library that have sample essays and see if you can use them as inspiration.

- Ask your English teacher for some guidance in putting your ideas on paper.

- Check to see if the college you are applying to allows for some flexibility in the format of your essay. If so, you might be able to write it as a lab report or some other format that feels more comfortable to you. You might also see if a college will accept a verbal essay rather than a written one.

- Write the essay as best you can and then let someone who writes very well go over it for suggestions, corrections and revisions.

Out of Your Hands

It is done, gone and out of your hands. What happens to your essay now? That depends on the college. At least one person will read your essay. At smaller, more intimate colleges, it will probably be read by more than one person. Quite often the first person to see it is an admissions officer, commonly an alumnus of the college or someone with a strong background in education. If there are multiple readings, your essay passes next to another admissions officer or perhaps a director. At some colleges, it will even be presented to an entire admissions committee.

The college essay is important, so give it the time, attention and effort it deserves. In turn, the colleges will give your essay the time, attention and effort it deserves.

Winning in Admission—With Someone Else's Words

There is another important element of the admissions process that we don't want to overlook—personal reference letters. This time you don't have to sell yourself with your words; other people will do the job for you.

Whom should you ask to write a letter of reference? Common sense says to make it someone who likes you, right? Just don't make it your grandmother, best friend or boyfriend. Sure, they like you—even love you—but you need a letter that will show how a person has evaluated you as a potential student, not something about how you are the best granddaughter, friend or girlfriend in the world. Here are some potential people to ask:

- co-workers, employers or supervisors
- teachers
- coaches
- other school faculty
- your pastor
- karate instructor or sponsor of other activities outside of school
- if you have done volunteer work, ask the organization's leader

It may be tricky to ask someone at school for a letter of recommendation if you haven't done well in his/her class but don't rule it out. Explain to your teacher or counselor what you are trying to accomplish and you may find you have more of an ally than you had originally thought. If you have a reason for not performing to your full potential, let your teacher know. Explaining your circumstances can help your teacher write a more supportive letter that gives a fuller picture of who you are.

How do you go about asking for a letter of reference? Ask in person rather than by email or telephone. This way you can show how much it would mean to you to have this individual's personal recommendation.

Be sure to give the person plenty of time to write a quality letter. Don't walk up to your boss at the end of the shift and say, "Before I go home tonight, could you write a reference letter for me?" Ask weeks ahead if possible. If there are word limits or other restrictions on the letter's format, be sure to tell the person before he or she begins writing.

Some people may not know how to write a personal reference letter, so be ready to tell them what it should include. Provide a resume or summary of some of your achievements to help the different individuals that you ask to write letters, and include a stamped, addressed envelope to the school. The typical letter should be about one to two pages in length and should include these elements:

- The identity of the writer
- The writer's relationship to you (teacher/student; employer/employee, etc.)
- Why the writer has chosen to recommend you as a potential candidate for college
- Examples and illustrations of the strong points that he or she has observed in you
- An overall evaluation of you as a student, community volunteer, all-around person
- A conclusion

Afterwards, always, always, always show your appreciation and gratitude for each person's help. A thank you note is really good manners, but a direct and sincere thank you face to face is great too.

CHAPTER FIVE

WINNING IN WORDS: THE ALSO-IMPORTANT COLLEGE INTERVIEW

You may or may not have won over those admissions officers or committee members with your written words, so now it's time to dazzle them with your verbal wit. The college interview is important as it is another chance to show a school just who you are, why you want to attend their college and why they should count themselves lucky to get you (in a humble fashion, of course). It is also another chance to explain why your numbers are not as high as they could be.

While not all colleges require an interview, if you are given the opportunity, take it. Interviews may be held at the college with an admissions officer, which requires a trip to the school. But sometimes interviews are conducted in your community by local alumni. You should look forward to the opportunity of an interview. In fact, you might find it easier to discuss issues face to face rather than on paper.

Of course, unlike the essay, an interview doesn't afford you the chance to brainstorm, outline, think about, mull over, ponder and weigh the questions. Your responses are going to be on the spot, so preparation is the key to not looking like a befuddled idiot desperately searching for the right answers.

What kinds of questions will you be asked during the interview? They are similar to the kinds of questions that are used as essay topics. But the essay has just one question to answer or one topic to explore. In the interview, however, you typically answer a number of questions and converse with an interviewer or panel for 15 minutes to an hour. Topics to be discussed are often divided into categories like school/classes, teachers, extracurricular activities, community, college and the world in general. Here are some typical examples. As you read these questions, think about how you would answer each one.

- How would you describe your high school?

- How do you fit into your school?

- If you could change one thing about your school, what would it be? Why?

- What has been your favorite/least favorite class in school?

- Who was your favorite/least favorite teacher in school? Why?

- How do you spend your free time and/or summers?

- Do you have a hobby of some kind? Tell me about it.

- Why are you interested in coming to this college?

- Where do you see yourself four years from now?

- What would you like to change about yourself?

- What are the three words that best describe you?

- What accomplishment are you most proud of?

- Why do you think you are a good match for this college?

- What do you think about _____ (current event, literature, art, music or other contemporary subject)?

Who will ask you these questions? It depends on the college. It may be an admissions officer, another student, faculty member, alumnus or panel of interviewers.

Keep in mind that a college interview is usually more like a casual chat over coffee, not a white-light-in-your-face interrogation. If you have a good sense of humor, the interview is the time to show it. If you have a talent, skill or ability that just did not fit on the application form or in your essay, speak now or forever hold your peace. If you can, find out if the interview is considered to be informational (just getting some facts about you and a time for questions and answers) or evaluative (part of the admissions criteria).

Feeling nervous as you go into the interview is understandable. In a way,

DON'T JUST TALK ABOUT YOU

Since the interviewers are real people, they value real conversations. Which would you prefer: listening to a one-hour soliloquy with Socratic references on the merits of academia as perceived through the eyes of an 18-year-old, or participating in an intriguing conversation about current events, life experiences and personal opinions? Needless to say, interviewers prefer the latter as well.

Throughout your interviews, remind yourself that your goal is to achieve two-way conversation. Be careful of any interview where the subject is you and you dominate the interview talking about your accomplishments. Don't worry about trying to mention all your achievements—your interviewer will ask about them. At the same time, however, this is not the only thing the interview is about.

Common sense tells us that most people enjoy talking about themselves, and interviewers are no different. Your interviewers volunteered for this job because they enjoyed their college experience and they like talking to potential students. Interviewers are usually the kind of people who love to give advice to young prospects. Think of this as a time not only for your interviewers to learn about you but also for you to find out as much as you can about them and their experiences.

Reprinted with permission from Get into Any College by Gen and Kelly Tanabe

it is a good thing because it will give you that extra boost of adrenaline you need to keep on your toes and pay attention. A person who isn't at least a little bit nervous may not do as well as one who is!

To make this less of a stressful event, practice what you are going to say ahead of time. Entertain your friends and family with it. Speak in front of the mirror or to an understanding guidance counselor. Prepare an answer for all the possible questions so you are ready, no matter which one the officer may ask.

The bottom line of the interview is simple—it is not the end all, be all of the admissions process. It will not usually make or break your acceptance. The person talking to you is a human being and may well have gone through the exact same thing you are going through right now. This means you will glimpse some compassion, empathy and even a smile during the interview. Relax, take a few deep breaths and let the special person that you are shine out!

According to the people at www.collegeboard.com, there are 13 things to avoid in a college interview. Are you paying attention? Here they are!

Don't:

- Be late

- Memorize speeches—instead sound natural and conversational

- Ask questions covered by the college catalog

- Chew gum

- Wear lots of cologne or perfume

- Swear or use too much slang

- Be arrogant—there's a fine line between being confident and boasting

- Lie—it will come back to haunt you

- Respond with only "yes" or "no" answers

- Tell the school it's your safety or last choice

- Be rude to the receptionist or any other staff you meet

- Bring a parent into the interview

- Refuse an interview

During the interview, more than your words count. While you don't have to come to the interview in a suit and tie or wear a dress, you shouldn't show up in shorts and tank top either. Be professional in your appearance. As you talk to the interviewer, sit up straight and don't fidget. Be sure to make eye contact. Never interrupt, and shake hands at the beginning and the end.

HOW DO I RESPOND TO QUESTIONS LIKE "TELL ME ABOUT YOUR GREATEST FAILURE" OR "WHAT IS YOUR BIGGEST WEAKNESS?"

Contrary to what it may seem, these are not trick questions. They ask you to examine yourself closely and to be honest. Admissions officers often ask questions like these to draw out meaningful experiences in your life that show you have coped with a variety of challenges. To prepare for a question like this, just think a moment about what kind of difficult moments you have had to deal with in your life. Did your parents get divorced? Did you lose a friend? Think about what you have had to struggle with. Did you have trouble with a certain subject? How did you overcome your difficulty? What personality trait gives you the most trouble? What do you do about it? When you answer a question like this, you may just find out some amazing things about yourself that you had not realized yet!

YOUR INTERVIEW HOMEWORK

Remember those college brochures filled with pictures, statistics and text cultivating dust balls under your bed? Dig them out before your interview and do something really radical—read them! It is not necessary to read them cover to cover, but knowing such basic facts as where the school is located, what kind of environment it has, some of the courses it offers and some of the activities you may choose to participate in is a good idea. It does not impress interviewers to discover that students who are applying to their beloved alma mater do not even know what state it is located in or that the college is single sex. (There was an applicant who actually made it to the interview before he learned that the college he was applying to was an all-women school!)

Try to talk to relatives or friends who attend or have attended the college. They can give you insights into the college that are not found in the glossy brochures. The more you know the better.

Doing your homework will allow you to be able to ask intelligent questions. You are making the most important decision of your life so far. It makes sense that you would have a question or two about it. Having prepared questions not only helps create the two-way conversation dynamic, but it also demonstrates that you are serious about attending the college.

Not all questions are good questions, and in particular, avoid asking those obvious ones where the answers are on the first page of the college's brochure. Instead, the best questions to ask your interviewers are those that make them reflect on their own experiences, require them to do a little thinking and elicit an opinion. Making your interviewers think or express their opinions makes the interviews more interesting for them and makes your question seem insightful and probing. Some examples:

● What do you think about the X department?

● How did the small/large class size affect your education?

● How did X college prepare you for your career?

● What was the best opportunity you felt X university provided you?

● What is the best/worst aspect of X university or X city?

● If you had to do it again, what would you do differently?

Think of some more questions like these and write them on a list with the most interesting ones at the top. Take this list into the interviews and refer to them when the conversation begins to stall and when your interviewers ask you if you have any questions.

Reprinted with permission from Get into Any College by Gen and Kelly Tanabe

Your college interview is also a chance for you to ask questions. By doing so, you often show initiative and curiosity—two traits most colleges are looking for in their students. Ask if the officer has any advice for you, ask a question about your potential major or ask about dorm activities and college lifestyle. Find out if there will be a new student orientation program, what activities are available for freshmen, what part-time job opportunities there are in the area or end with a zinger like, "Is there anything you would like to know about me in order to help you make a fair and final decision about my application?"

The interview is a unique opportunity to establish rapport with a person who previously only knew you as numbers and words on paper. Use it wisely and show the interviewer(s) what a fantastic person you really are!

THE MOMENT OF TRUTH

What happens when the admissions officer asks you, "How do you explain the fact that your SAT score or GPA is a little less than wonderful?" First, expect it. That way you can prepare for it. If it doesn't happen, then whew! you are off the hook. If it does, you're ready. Second, be honest. Don't say there was a computer error or you really did better than that. Third, don't place blame. Don't try and put those numbers off on rotten teachers, stupid tests or unfair grading. On the other hand, you can explain with a truthful assessment of factors that have affected your life. Was there a crisis during that time? Did you have to work extra hours that cut into study time? Were you heavily involved with sports or other extracurricular activities? Did you find high school boring or stifling? Without accusing others, tell the interviewer why you believe those numbers do not represent your real potential.

What should you do if the admissions officer does not ask about your numbers? That's a judgment call, and the answer rests with your gut instinct. If the interview has gone really well and you feel like you have established a good rapport with the officer, explaining those numbers without being asked can be seen as admirable. If you have not clicked with the officer, however, and the interview has had some awkward pauses, you might want to just skip this so things don't go downhill.

SECTION THREE
PAYING

**B STUDENTS CAN WIN
SCHOLARSHIPS TOO**

CHAPTER SIX

B STUDENTS CAN WIN SCHOLARSHIPS TOO

"My GPA is not that hot . . . and my SAT scores were lousy because I had a temperature/didn't get enough sleep/forgot to prepare/had an argument with my boyfriend, so I wonder if I can even get into college. But heck, college costs thousands and thousands of dollars and my family cannot afford that. Why even apply? My parents don't have the money and scholarships only go to the straight A students anyway . . ."

Have you had that conversation with yourself? If so, you aren't the first and certainly won't be the last to do so. But be advised: Such thinking is a big mistake.

Without question, college costs a lot, and most families struggle to find enough money to pay for it. But those scholarships you keep hearing about are not just for the eggheads or overachievers who excelled in everything from U.S. history to trigonometry.

So who exactly gets scholarships besides those with high numbers? Let's take a look.

Students who show genuine financial need

And you thought growing up without a Porsche in the driveway was a bad thing? Scholarships were originally set up for these very students. They were put into place to support students' families financially so that college could be possible for many more than just those who can afford it. If your family has a genuine need to help you attend college, many scholarships may be available for you. The key to snatching one of them is simple: be honest about ALL your numbers, including finances; don't try to fudge those income levels. That isn't honest, and you will get caught. Also be prepared to show any extenuating circumstances behind those numbers. Was your mother laid off? Was there a medical emergency? Does your family have three kids in college already? These are important factors to include.

Students with a disability or illness

Not that you would wish for one, but if you happen to have a documented disability or illness, there is assistance for you because of it. A number of organizations support students with some kind of physical challenge. Scholarships are available from such sources as the Alexander Graham Bell Association, American Foundation for the Blind, Hemophilia Resources of America and the National Center for Learning Disabilities.

Students with specific majors

Already know what you want to do with the rest of your life? Countless organizations support young people who are pursuing certain careers. You must show that you are genuinely passionate about whatever field it might be, from digital photography to interior design. You will need to let the scholarship people know how you found out about the field, who mentored or inspired you, how your dedication grew and what skills you learned or developed. Have truthful, profound stories ready to share. Have you started your own business in this career already? Have you supported your fascination through volunteer work? Do you have recommendations from people in a related field? These are the factors that will help a committee select you above all others for that cash. Consider these examples: The American Nursery and Landscape Association has money for those who love flowers, trees and the outdoors. The Arabian Horse Foundation helps those who adore horses. Other organizations have money for those whose focus is cooking, construction, forestry, hospitality, the performing arts and more.

Students who show leadership

Are you known for taking charge and putting things together? Do you already have a few groupies that really like you? Scholarship committees are impressed with young people who have shown some form of leadership. If you have helped others by using your abilities in organization and guidance, or if you have inspired others, then this is the place to let it be known.

What have you done? Show it, don't just tell it. Give concrete examples

---

MYTH:
YOU NEED STRAIGHT A'S TO WIN MONEY FOR COLLEGE

The Truth: While straight A's certainly don't hurt your chances of winning [scholarships and awards for college], you may be tempted to place too much importance on your grades. Many scholarships are based on criteria other than grades and are awarded for specific skills or talents such as linguistic, athletic or artistic ability. Even for scholarships in which grades are considered, GPA is often not the most important factor. What's more important is that you best match the qualities the scholarship committee seeks. Most students who win scholarships do not have the highest GPA. Don't let the lack of a perfect transcript prevent you from applying for scholarships.

— **GEN AND KELLY TANABE,**
Get Free Cash for College

such as letters of recommendation, photographs and projects. Point out the responsibilities you have taken on and what they have taught you. Places like the Financial Service Centers of America, the Coca-Cola Scholars Foundation and Discover Card promote their own businesses by sharing their profits with students like you.

Students with particular religious backgrounds

If you have been wondering if God has been listening to those prayers, this might be your answer. To promote the growth and development of their religion or denomination, many church organizations offer students college scholarships. Okay, time for real honesty here. Do not try to get one of these scholarships or awards if the only times you go to church are to attend weddings, funerals and pray right before a major test. You have to be a true believer and show it through your active involvement with the church. Perhaps you lead a youth group, work in the church nursery, take classes from the pastor or participate in other areas of ministry. It is common to see scholarships from the Methodist, Catholic, Baptist and Presbyterian churches.

Students with superior athletic ability

Love to chase some kind of ball around? If you are the star football, basketball, baseball, tennis, golf or track star, chances are there is a college or organization that wants to give you the money to go to college. As Gen and Kelly Tanabe say in their book on scholarships, "Athletic scholarships are the Holy Grail. At their best, they can cover tuition and fees, room and board and books. That's not bad for doing something that you enjoy." Not sure if your sport is covered? Even the Ice Skating Institute of American Education Foundation and the National Archery Association have money to share. Check it out!

Students with a specific ethnic background

Time to look through your family tree. To celebrate their history and culture, some ethnic organizations are willing to give you money for school. This helps increase the number of minorities on campuses and also encourages students to go into professions they might have ignored or otherwise overlooked. Many groups are represented, including such organizations as the Sons of Norway and the National Italian American Foundation. Look for information regarding your heritage.

Students with hobbies

And your friends tried to say you were wasting your time! Not so. Scholarships are out there for young people who have serious hobbies. Of course, you have to show that you don't just pursue this hobby on rainy weekend afternoons, but that you are involved on a regular basis. You also want to prove dedication to this hobby by showing a consistent effort to improve the skills it takes to be good at what you do. Perhaps your hobby has even led you to awards and honors or to the creation of your own business.

WHERE TO FIND SCHOLARSHIPS

For most students, the hunt for scholarships is a short one. Many start with a scholarship book or head to the Internet. Unfortunately, most students end their search after exhausting these two sources.

Big mistake!

Books and the Internet are only the tip of the iceberg, and neither comes close to listing all the available scholarships. If you do your own detective work and canvass the community, you will uncover additional awards. Keep in mind that local scholarships may have smaller overall awards, but the chances of your winning them are much higher. Here's where to begin:

High school. The first stop in your scholarship hunt should be the high school counseling office. When an organization establishes a new scholarship (awards are created every year), high schools are the first places to get a notice. Over the years, most counseling offices have assembled a long list of scholarships. Don't reinvent the wheel if the counselor has already collected the information. Also remember that some high schools give out a set number of scholarships to their students each year and often less than that apply. In other words, all you would have to do to get the scholarship is fill out the papers!

Prospective colleges. Contact the financial aid office at every school you are interested in attending. Not only do the colleges themselves offer scholarships, but their financial aid offices also maintain lists of outside opportunities.

Civic and community organizations. Every community is home to dozens of civic organizations, such as the Rotary Club, Lions Club, Knights of Columbus, American Legion, Elks Club and VFW. Part of their mission is to support the community by awarding scholarships.

Businesses big and small. Many businesses such as newspapers, shopping malls, supermarkets and retailers offer scholarships to local students. For example, every Wal-Mart and Target store awards scholarships to students in the community. To find these opportunities, contact the manager at these businesses. You can get a list of businesses from the chamber of commerce or in the reference section of the public library.

Parent's employers/union. If your parents work for a large company, have them ask the human resources department about scholarships. If they are limited to the children of employees, there may be little competition for these awards. Also, if your parents are a member of a union, have them ask the union representative about scholarships.

Professional or trade associations. From accounting to zoology, every profession has its own associations, and many of these professional associations use scholarships to encourage students to enter the field. Start by looking at groups related to your future career.

Religious organizations. Your church or temple may offer scholarships to support members. If your local church does not have a scholarship program, check with the national headquarters.

Ethnic and cultural organizations. To promote a certain culture, develop leaders or encourage members to pursue higher education, many ethnic organizations sponsor scholarships.

Discuss how this hobby has affected your life and what skills it has taught you. Be sure to include letters of recommendation from people who have seen what you are capable of. Do you spend hours doing graphic design on your computer? Have you sold some of your original logos to local companies? The Rhythm and Hues Studios might have money for you. Is photography all you can think about? Have you had your own displays at local stores? Do people call you to take pictures at their weddings or parties? Have your shots already popped up in the community newspaper? Talk to the National Press Photographers Foundation. Whatever your hobby, it's worth doing a little research to see if there are organizations with scholarships and awards for students just like you!

Students with parents who have generous employers

Check out your mom and/or dad's places of employment. It is not uncommon for businesses and corporations to include in their employee package some scholarship money for workers' children. Ask your parents to read through their employee handbooks again or just ask some questions. Who knows what hidden benefits your parent will find?

I hope you're convinced by now that just as colleges will happily take students with less-than-stellar grades and test scores, so will they just as happily take students who do not come from the wealthiest families. Financial aid is a huge part of college admissions and one that often means you can get that education you once told yourself was way out of reach. It's time to start an all-new conversation with yourself. Try something along these lines: "Hey, colleges really DO like me, and my family really CAN afford it now. So, what am I waiting for?" There you go.

Where Not to Find Scholarships

Watch out for scams. You already know this but it bears repeating: if it sounds too good to be true, it most likely is. Avoid any scholarship that asks you for payment, promises scholarships that NO ONE else has access to or asks for too much personal information like your Social Security number or bank account information.

Setting Your Priorities

Once you start searching for possible scholarships, you may easily find that there are so many that you are somewhat overwhelmed. Too many scholarships, too little time! It will help if you take time to prioritize them, i.e. decide which ones are the best fit for you. Ask yourself the following questions to help narrow down the list:

- How do you fit the mission or point of the award? Does it sound just like you or do you only match about 3 out of the 10 criteria?

- How much do academics count in each of the scholarships? Most organizations provide this information. If the only mention is a minimum GPA and yours is above that, you are set.

- How many awards are being given out? What are your overall chances of getting one?

- What is the scope of the competition? You will have a better chance of winning a scholarship that is only open to students in your county than one that is nationwide.

- How much is the award? Is it enough to make a difference? Consider the amount given, but don't just apply to the scholarships with the largest prizes because those often have the most competition.

Scholarship Essays

Scholarship essays and college admissions essays are not the same thing. When you are scheduling time to write your scholarship and college admissions essays, remember that the two are very different. While an admissions essay is geared to providing college admissions officers with an overall picture of who you are, the scholarship essay is targeted to the purpose of the scholarship itself. The people reading this are looking for something specific about you. For example, if you are applying for a sports scholarship, include information on the reason you play, what you have learned and how you have improved. If the scholarship is for future teachers, write about your experience with children and teaching or tutoring. Don't just list these things either in some kind of bulleted format. Instead, talk about the why, how or what behind it all.

How did you get involved? What new perspectives have you learned? Why do you want to pursue this further?

Time to recycle. You have been throwing your soda cans and water bottles in recycling containers for years now, so keep up the spirit and see if you can recycle any of your essays. The good news is that, naturally, this saves you time and effort. The bad news is that it isn't quite that simple. Before you decide to use Essay B for scholarship XYZ, make sure it actually fits. Read the question carefully and make sure you are addressing it specifically. You may be able to tweak certain parts of an essay and adapt something written for one college or scholarship to meet the criteria of others.

I hope you've seen from this chapter that scholarships are a possibility for any student, regardless of college-entrance exam scores or GPA. There are awards given for every background, talent or achievement. Many scholarship or award committees don't count grades or test scores as the most important factor. It is well worth taking some time to prioritize the scholarships you apply for. Then write the best application and essay that you can. With that combination, you have a good chance of winning funds for college.

THE COLLEGES

A GUIDE TO THE COLLEGES THAT WELCOME B STUDENTS

A GUIDE TO THE COLLEGES THAT WELCOME B STUDENTS

As a B or C student, you have many options when it comes to finding a college that is right for you. In fact, there are far more colleges that want you than you could ever apply to in a single year. Your challenge will not be finding the right college but narrowing down your list of possibilities. As you will see, not all colleges require certain GPAs or test scores to make it past the velvet rope. Now it's time to meet some of the schools that not only accept B and C students but that also embrace them. These colleges are competitive and offer the highest quality educations, but they also recognize that students like you have much to offer and are committed to ensuring your success.

How These Colleges Were Chosen

All the colleges and universities listed in this directory were chosen for several reasons.

● They each offer very high quality educations. Just because the colleges listed here accept students with less-than-perfect scores doesn't mean that they sacrifice quality. These schools are committed to preparing you for your future.

● B and C students are welcome. These colleges have test scores and GPA averages that fit well with the typical B student's range. In addition, the schools offer programs such as tutoring or mentoring that will help students succeed once they are in college.

● They are competitive. While not as selective as many of the colleges at the top of news magazines' lists, the schools listed here do have standards for admission. Because they generally draw from a smaller geographic area, community colleges are not included.

● They offer diversity. These schools represent all parts of the country and all sizes, from small to large.

ADELPHI UNIVERSITY

1 South Avenue, Garden City, NY 11530
Admissions: 800-ADELPHI · Financial Aid: 516-877-3365
Email: admissions@adelphi.edu ·Website: http://www.adelphi.edu

From the College

"Founded in 1896, Adelphi University was Long Island's first private co-educational institution of higher learning. Since 2007, Adelphi has been cited as a 'Best Buy' by the *Fiske Guide to Colleges*, one of only a handful of private universities to make the list. *The New York Times* wrote in fall 2006, 'By practically every measure, the university is thriving.' As Adelphi grows, our academic programs evolve to reflect the needs and interests of our more than 8,400 students from 37 states and close to 50 countries including an acclaimed Honors College; career-advancing joint degree programs; performing arts programs; and professional programs in social work, nursing, business, psychology, and education. Internationally recognized scholars and artists fill the ranks of Adelphi's more than 900 full- and part-time faculty members.

"Adelphi's main 75-acre campus in historic Garden City has six residence halls and is conveniently located 45 minutes from New York City, and just a few miles from beaches, parks and cultural centers.

"Students may join Adelphi's more than 80 student organizations, including fraternities, sororities and academic honor societies. Access to professional internships in all industries, whether in New York City or on Long Island, abounds. An expanded career center connects students with a range of professional opportunities. Specialized extracurricular and academic programs promote student involvement in civic and community service. Adelphi has NCAA Division I and II intercollegiate athletic teams, including its Division II National Championship women's lacrosse team as well as an array of intramural activities. In fall 2008, Adelphi opened a state-of-the-art performing arts center and center for recreation and sports. The carefully designed building complex serves as a hub for student activities, cultural performances, athletic competitions and academics. Adelphi students have free access to student counseling, financial aid advising, mentoring and other life improvement services. Students wishing to study abroad will find ample opportunities and personalized assistance in selecting programs through Adelphi's study abroad office.

"Through its schools, the College of Arts and Sciences, the Gordon F. Derner Institute of Advanced Psychological Studies, the Honors College, University College, the Ruth S. Ammon School of Education and the Schools of Business, Nursing and Social Work, Adelphi offers more than 100 undergraduate and graduate programs of study at our main Garden City campus and at off-campus centers in Hauppauge, Manhattan, and Hudson Valley."

Campus Setting

Adelphi is a private, four-year, multipurpose university. Founded as a boys' preparatory school, it became a college in 1896 and gained university status in 1963. Its 75-acre campus is located in western Long Island, 20 miles from New York City. In addition to a large, well-stocked library, the campus facilities include: art gallery · bronze-casting foundry · sculpture and ceramics studios · theatre · language labs · observatory. Adelphi University provides on-campus housing with 542 units that can accommodate 1,202 students. Housing options: co-ed dorms · special housing for disabled students. Recreation and sports facilities include: basketball · tennis and volleyball courts · baseball · lacrosse · soccer and softball fields · fitness center · swimming facility.

ADELPHI UNIVERSITY

Adelphi University
Garden City (Pop. 23,000)
Location: Large town
Website: http://www.adelphi.edu

Students
Total enrollment: 8,177
Undergrads: 1,498
Freshmen: 964
Part-time students: 18%
From out-of-state: 10%
Male/Female: 29%/71%
Live on-campus: 23%
In fraternities: 7%
In sororities: 6%
Off-campus employment rating: Good
Caucasian: 53%
African American: 12%
Hispanic: 6%
Asian or Pacific Islander: 6%
Native American: 0%
International: 3%

Academics
Student/faculty ratio: 9:1
Class size 9 or fewer: 10%
Class size 10-29: 68%
Class size 30-49: 20%
Class size 50-99: 2%
Class size 100 or more: -
Returning freshmen: 78%
Six-year graduation rate: 64%

Most Popular Fields of Study
Business, Finance, Sales and Marketing
Protective Services, Criminal Justice and
   Public Administration
Psychology
Visual and Performing Arts
English and Literature
Computer and Information Sciences
Mathematics
Parks, Recreation and Fitness
Health Professions, Medicine and Re-
   lated Sciences

Student Life and Activities

Most students (77 percent) live off campus, which does impact the on-campus social scene. Nevertheless, like any college, students find time to create their own recreational outlets. Adelphi is what you make it, reports the student newspaper. If you want to meet people, there are plenty of opportunities. Popular gathering spots include University Center dining room, Post dining, commuter lounge, fire-side lounge, UC Plaza (when the weather is warm), New York City and Roosevelt Field Mall. Popular campus events include visual and performing arts exhibitions, Disabilities Awareness Week, International Week, Black History Month, Endowed Lectures Series, student theatre and dance performances, concerts and performances by top music groups and comedians, lectures by U.N. Ambassadors, intercollegiate and intramural sports, Spring Fling Spring In/Spike It Festival, Homecoming and Career Day. Adelphi University has 80 official student organizations. Influential groups include Greeks, Circle K, Environmental Action Coalition, Christian Fellowship, African People Organization (APO), athletes, Caliber and La Union Latino. For those interested in sports, there are intramural teams such as: badminton · baseball · basketball · dodge ball · flag football · soccer · volleyball. Adelphi University is a member of the Atlantic Soccer Conference (Division I), New York Collegiate Athletic Conference (Division II).

Academics and Learning Environment

For the B student, the learning environment of a college is just as important as the quality of its academic program. Adelphi University has 295 full-time and 639 part-time faculty members, offering a student-to-faculty ratio of 9:1. The most common course size is 10 to 19 students. Adelphi University offers 89 majors with the most popular being nursing, education and business administration/management and least popular being French, philosophy and Spanish. The school has a general core requirement. Cooperative education is not offered. All first-year students must maintain a 2.0 GPA or higher to avoid academic probation. Other special academic programs that would appeal to a B student: self-designed majors · pass/fail grading option · independent study · double majors · dual degrees · accelerated study · honors program · internships · weekend college · distance learning.

B Student Support and Success

This school has offered a General Studies program since 1985. According to the university, it is designed for "motivated high school seniors who demonstrate the potential for academic success, but who have not met the traditional academic admission requirements. Counselors, faculty members and administrators identify potentially successful candidates on the basis of their applications and letters of recommendation, as well as through personal interviews." The program offers small classes and personal advisement for each student. At the end of the year, students who have met all of the requirements continue as sophomores in the school's other undergraduate programs.

Adelphi University provides a variety of support programs including dedicated guidance for: academic · career · personal · psychological · minority students · veterans · non-traditional students · family planning · religious. Recognizing that some students may need extra preparation, Adelphi University offers remedial and refresher courses in: reading · writing · math · study skills. Other remedial services include Computer lab, English conversation for international students. The average freshman year GPA is 3.0, and 78 percent of freshmen students return for their sophomore year. What do students do after college? While many enter the work force, approximately 41 percent pursue a graduate degree immediately after graduation. Among students who enter the work force, approximately 93 percent enter a field related to their major within six months of graduation. Companies that most frequently hire graduates from Adelphi University include: NYC Public Schools · Enterprise Rent-A-Car · North Shore L.I.J. Health System · AHRC · Bethpage Federal Credit Union · Long Island Public Schools · JP Morgan Chase · KPMG · 1-800-Flowers · XL Capital Assurance · Price Waterhouse Coopers · Schwartz & Co · GEICO · Ernst & Young · Marcum & Kleigman · St. Francis Hospital · BDO Seidman · Marks, Paneth & Shron · Winthrop University Hospital · Weiser.

Support for Students with Learning Disabilities

Students with learning disabilities may take advantage of specific support programs offered by Adelphi University. If necessary, the college will grant additional time to students with learning disabilities to complete their degree. Also, a lightened course load may be granted to LD students. High school foreign language waivers are accepted. According to the school, writing, math and content labs are available for all students through the Learning Center and writing center. Students with learning disabilities will find the following programs at Adelphi University extremely useful: tutors · learning center · testing accommodations · extended time for tests · take-home exam · oral tests · readers · typist/scribe · note-taking services · reading machines · tape recorders · texts on tape · early syllabus · diagnostic testing service · priority registration · waiver of math degree requirement. Individual or small group tutorials are also available in: time management · organizational skills · learning strategies · writing labs · study skills. An advisor/advocate from the Learning Disabilities Program is available to students.

How to Get Admitted

For admissions decisions, non-academic factors considered: interview · extracurricular activities · special talents, interests, abilities · character/personal qualities · volunteer work · work experience · state of residency · alumni relationship. A high school diploma is required, although a GED is also accepted for admissions consideration. SAT or ACT test scores are required of all applicants. SAT Subject Test scores are required from all applicants. *According to the admissions office:* Minimum combined SAT Reasoning score of 900 and minimum 2.5 GPA recommended. *Academic units recommended:* 4 English, 3 Math, 3 Science, 2 Foreign Language.

Insight

"Our admissions process is holistic," says Esther Goodcuff, associate vice president for enrollment management and student affairs. "We carefully read every single piece of documentation in each application. Our General Studies program is not a remedial program but

ADELPHI UNIVERSITY

Highlights

Admissions
Applicants: 6,865
Accepted: 4,551
Acceptance rate: 66.3%
Average GPA: 3.3
ACT range: 20-26
SAT Math range: 500-590
SAT Reading range: 470-580
SAT Writing range: 470-580
Top 10% of class: 23%
Top 25% of class: 51%
Top 50% of class: 87%

Deadlines
Early Action: December 1
Early Decision: No
Regular Action: Rolling admissions
Common Application: Accepted

Financial Aid
In-state tuition: $22,725
Out-of-state tuition: $22,725
Room: $7,230
Board: $2,800
Books: $1,000
Freshmen receiving need-based aid: 66%
Undergrads receiving need-based aid: 59%
Avg. % of need met by financial aid: 52%
Avg. aid package (freshmen): $16,400
Avg. aid package (undergrads): $16,500
Freshmen receiving merit-based aid: 27%
Undergrads receiving merit-based aid: 32%

Prominent Alumni
Thomas J. Donohue, president and CEO of the U.S. Chamber of Commerce; Gary Dell'Abate, producer of the Howard Stern Show; Alice Hoffman, best-selling novelist and author of more than 20 books.

School Spirit
Mascot: Panther
Colors: Brown and gold

one that challenges students, while at the same time supports them. Our faculty does individual tutoring outside of class, and students are given an academic counselor to help with college transition issues." Goodcuff says that Adelphi's admissions department looks at trends in how students have been performing in high school, watching for an upward movement. "Letters of recommendation and the essay also give us a sense of just who you are," she adds. "We look for students who are highly motivated and truly want to do well."

How to Pay for College

To apply for financial aid, students should submit the following: Free Application for Federal Student Aid (FAFSA) · state aid form. Adelphi University participates in the Federal Work Study program. *Need-based aid programs include:* scholarships and grants · general need-based awards · Federal Pell grants · state scholarships and grants · college-based scholarships and grants · private scholarships and grants · United Negro College Fund · Endowed and restricted donor funds. *Non-Need-based aid programs include:* scholarships and grants · state scholarships and grants · creative arts and performance awards · special achievements and activities awards · athletic scholarships.

AGNES SCOTT COLLEGE

141 East College Avenue, Decatur, GA 30030
Admissions: 800-868-8602, extension 6285 · Financial Aid: 800-868-8602
Email: admission@agnesscott.edu · Website: http://www.agnesscott.edu

From the College

"Agnes Scott College educates women to think deeply, live honorably and engage the intellectual and social challenges of their times. Students are drawn to Agnes Scott by its academic reputation, faculty and metropolitan Atlanta location, offering myriad cultural and experiential learning opportunities. A diverse and growing residential community of scholars, this highly selective liberal arts college presents its curriculum with international context. Study abroad is encouraged by offering faculty-led travel tied to classroom study to broaden understanding of cultural values and contrasts. A strong record of student achievement is found in the numbers of Agnes Scott students who earn prestigious scholarships and fellowships including Fulbright grants, Rhodes Scholarships, Thomas R. Pickering Foreign Affairs Fellowships and Benjamin A. Gilman International Scholarships. An array of experiential learning opportunities also encourages students to apply learning to career development."

Campus Setting

Agnes Scott, founded in 1889, is a church-affiliated, liberal arts college for women. Its 100-acre campus is located in Decatur, six miles from downtown Atlanta. Campus buildings are Gothic and Victorian in style. A four-year private women's college, Agnes Scott College has an enrollment of 832 students. The school is also affiliated with the Presbyterian Church. In addition to a large, well-stocked library, the campus facilities include: art gallery · observatory · science center. Agnes Scott College provides on-campus housing with 446 units that can accommodate 752 students. Housing options: women's dorms · single-student apartments. Recreation and sports facilities include: physical activities building · swimming pool and diving facility · basketball and courts · weight room · track and field.

Student Life and Activities

With 87 percent of students living on campus, there are plenty of social activities. Popular on-campus gathering spots include the Alston Student Center and Eddie's Attic. Popular campus events include Writers' Festival, Spring Fling, Black Cat Week, Black Cat Formal, Cultural Events Series, Senior Investiture, Sophomore Family Weekend, Planetarium Shows, Fall Fest and Spring Fest. Agnes Scott College has 85 official student organizations. Some of the most popular are: Collegiate Chorale · Georgia Association of Educators · Inter-Organizational Council · Circle K · Habitat for Humanity · The Collective (LBTQIA) · Student Senate · Pre-Med Association. For those interested in sports, there are intramural teams such as: bowling · cross-country · cycling and triathlon · Hearts · karate · swimming · yoga. Agnes Scott College is a member of the Great South Athletic Conference (Division III).

Academics and Learning Environment

For the B student, the learning environment of a college is just as important as the quality of its academic program. Agnes Scott College has 83 full-time and 34 part-time faculty members, offering a student-to-faculty ratio of 8:1. The most common course size is 10 to 19 students. Agnes Scott College offers 34 majors with the most popular being English, psychology and economics. The school has a general core requirement as well as a religion requirement Cooperative education is not offered. All first-year students must maintain a 1.5 GPA or higher to avoid academic proba-

AGNES SCOTT COLLEGE

Agnes Scott College
Decatur, GA (Pop. 18,000)
Location: Major city
Website: http://www.agnesscott.edu

Students
Total enrollment: 832
Undergrads: 5
Freshmen: 179
Part-time students: 4%
From out-of-state: 47%
Male/Female: 1%/99%
Live on-campus: 87%
Off-campus employment rating: Excellent
Caucasian: 54%
African American: 21%
Hispanic: 3%
Asian or Pacific Islander: 4%
Native American: 0%
International: 4%

Academics
Student/faculty ratio: 8:1
Class size 9 or fewer: 37%
Class size 10-29: 60%
Class size 30-49: 3%
Class size 50-99: 2%
Class size 100 or more: -
Returning freshmen: 82%
Six-year graduation rate: 71%

Most Popular Fields of Study
Biological and Life Sciences
Area, Ethnic and Gender Studies

Admissions
Applicants: 1,593
Accepted: 763
Acceptance rate: 47.9%
placed on wait list: 30
Average GPA: 3.6
ACT range: 22-28
SAT Math range: 500-610
SAT Reading range: 520-680
SAT Writing range: 520-660
Top 10% of class: 34%
Top 25% of class: 68%
Top 50% of class: 93%

tion, and a minimum overall GPA of 2.0 is required to graduate. Other special academic programs that would appeal to a B student: self-designed majors · pass/fail grading option · independent study · double majors · dual degrees · accelerated study · Phi Beta Kappa · internships.

B Student Support and Success

Besides being the setting for the horror flick "Scream 2," Agnes Scott offers smaller classes, often with fewer than a half dozen students. The school offers "talking study halls," centers where students can discuss homework assignments as a group. Every student is given an admission counselor who works from beginning to end on the application process. Agnes Scott features a Center for Writing and Speaking, a peer tutoring organization that helps students with written and oral communication skills.

Agnes Scott College provides a variety of support programs including dedicated guidance for: academic · career · personal · psychological · minority students · non-traditional students · family planning · religious. The average freshman year GPA is 3.0, and 82 percent of freshmen students return for their sophomore year. What do students do after college? While many enter the work force, approximately 31 percent pursue a graduate degree immediately after graduation. Among students who enter the work force, approximately 57 percent enter a field related to their major within six months of graduation. Companies that most frequently hire graduates from Agnes Scott College include: CGI · CIEE Teach Abroad · College Republican National Committee · Coxe Curry & Associates · Dean & Deluca · Georgia Shakespeare Theatre · Georgia Tech Campus Christian Fellowship · International Medical Press · Service Employees International Union · Skyland Trail · Teach for America · The Campaign to Save the Environment · thinkoutside · TESL Teacher · TRX.

Support for Students with Learning Disabilities

Students with learning disabilities may take advantage of specific support programs offered by Agnes Scott College. If necessary, the college will grant additional time to students with learning disabilities to complete their degree. Students with learning disabilities will find the following programs: tutors · testing accommodations · untimed tests · extended time for tests · oral tests · readers · typist/scribe · note-taking services · reading machines · tape recorders · texts on tape · early syllabus · priority registration · waiver of math degree requirement. Individual or small group tutorials are also available in: time management · organizational skills · learning strategies · writing labs · math labs · study skills. An advisor/advocate from the Office of Academic Advising and Student Disability Services is available to students.

How to Get Admitted

For admissions decisions, non-academic factors considered: interview · extracurricular activities · special talents, interests, abilities · character/personal qualities · volunteer work · work experience · geographical location · minority affiliation · alumni relationship. A high school diploma is required, although a GED is also accepted for admissions consideration. SAT or ACT test scores are required for some applicants. SAT Subject Test scores are required for some applicants. *According to the admissions office:* Rank in top fifth of secondary school class recommended. *Academic units recommended:* 4 English, 3 Math, 2 Science, 2 Social Studies, 2 Foreign Language.

How to Pay for College

To apply for financial aid, students should submit the following: Free Application for Federal Student Aid (FAFSA). Agnes Scott College participates in the Federal Work Study program. *Need-based aid programs include:* scholarships and grants · general need-based awards · Federal Pell grants · state scholarships and grants · college-based scholarships and grants · private scholarships and grants. *Non-Need-based aid programs include:* scholarships and grants · general need-based awards · state scholarships and grants · special achievements and activities awards · special characteristics awards · tuition waivers for employees and their dependents.

AGNES SCOTT COLLEGE

Highlights

Deadlines
Early Action: November 15
Early Decision: No
Regular Action: March 1 (priority)
Common Application: Accepted

Financial Aid
In-state tuition: $29,890
Out-of-state tuition: $29,890
Room: $4,925
Board: $4,925
Books: $1,000
Freshmen receiving need-based aid: 75%
Undergrads receiving need-based aid: 69%
Avg. % of need met by financial aid: 94%
Avg. aid package (freshmen): $29,977
Avg. aid package (undergrads): $29,153
Freshmen receiving merit-based aid: 23%
Undergrads receiving merit-based aid: 28%
Avg. student debt upon graduation: $25,577

Prominent Alumni
Katherine Krill, CEO, Ann Taylor Stores Corporation; Jennifer Nettles, Grammy-winning country and folk musician; Jean Toal, Chief Justice, South Carolina Supreme Court.

School Spirit
Mascot: Scotties
Colors: Purple and white

ALBION COLLEGE

611 East Porter Street, Albion, MI 49224
Admissions: 800-858-6770 · Financial Aid: 517-629-0440
Email: admissions@albion.edu · Website: http://www.albion.edu

From the College

"Albion College offers a strong liberal arts curriculum with a purposeful focus on professional preparation in law, medicine, education, economics and management, and the sciences. Consistently ranked among the top ten colleges for vibrant campus activities and opportunities for service and leadership, Albion also enjoys the support of its alumni, ranking 15th among all colleges and universities in annual giving. As a member of the Michigan Intercollegiate Athletics Association (MIAA), the oldest athletic conference in America, and NCAA Division III, a strong tradition of developing scholar-athletes continues as over 33 percent of all full-time students are involved in varsity athletics. A 144-acre preserve with nature trails and an interpretive center is located adjacent to campus along the Kalamazoo River. Recently, the college opened the Held Equestrian Center on 340 acres immediately south of the main campus."

Campus Setting

Albion, founded in 1835, is a church-affiliated, liberal arts college. Its 574-acre campus is located in south central Michigan, 65 miles from Detroit. Campus architecture includes both mid-nineteenth century and modern buildings. A four-year private institution, Albion College has an enrollment of 1,860 students. The school is also affiliated with the Methodist Church. In addition to a large, well-stocked library, the campus facilities include: astronomical observatory · equestrian center · science complex. Albion College provides on-campus housing with 888 units that can accommodate 1,848 students. Housing options: co-ed dorms · women's dorms · fraternity housing · cooperative housing. Recreation and sports facilities include: aquatic center · basketball · racquetball · tennis and volleyball courts · equestrian center · field house with track · football stadium · recreation and wellness center · softball field.

Student Life and Activities

With 91 percent of students living on campus, there are plenty of social activities. One popular hot spot is the Kellogg Center. Popular events include Friday Night Live Series, Day of Woden, Greek Week, Homecoming Week. Albion College has 129 official student organizations. Popular groups on campus are fraternities and sororities. For those interested in sports, there are intramural teams such as: basketball · football · racquetball · soccer · softball · swimming · tennis · ultimate frisbee · volleyball. Albion College is a member of the Michigan Intercollegiate Athletic Association (Division III).

Academics and Learning Environment

For the B student, the learning environment of a college is just as important as the quality of its academic program. Albion College has 138 full-time and 33 part-time faculty members, offering a student-to-faculty ratio of 12:1. The most common course size is 10 to 19 students. Albion College offers 32 majors with the most popular being economics/management, biology and psychology and least popular being physics, theatre and philosophy. The school has a general core requirement. Cooperative education is not offered. All first-year students must maintain a 2.0 GPA or higher to avoid academic probation. Other special academic programs that would appeal to a B student: self-designed majors · pass/fail grading option · independent study · double majors · dual degrees · honors program · Phi Beta Kappa · internships.

B Student Support and Success

Albion wants its new students to transition well into college life and provides a First Year Experience, as others do. It offers Common Reading, followed up by presentations by the author, as well as a program called Student Orientation, Advising and Registration (SOAR). This takes place in May before the freshman year begins and is two days of touring the campus, meeting people, eating in the dining hall, speaking to faculty, planning student schedules and even registering for fall classes. The first three days of the first year center around get-acquainted activities such as skits, singing, lectures, ice cream breaks and comedians.

Albion offers classes smaller than 20 students, and many undergrads speak highly of the casual and friendly attitudes of the faculty.

Albion College provides a variety of support programs including dedicated guidance for: academic · career · personal · psychological · minority students · veterans · non-traditional students · family planning · religious. Recognizing that some students may need extra preparation, Albion College offers remedial and refresher courses in: reading · writing · math · study skills. The average freshman year GPA is 3.2, and 86 percent of freshmen students return for their sophomore year. What do students do after college? While many enter the work force, approximately 37 percent pursue a graduate degree immediately after graduation. Among students who enter the work force, approximately 55 percent enter a field related to their major within six months of graduation. Companies that most frequently hire graduates from Albion College include: Ernst & Young · Epic · PricewaterhouseCoopers.

Support for Students with Learning Disabilities

Students with learning disabilities may take advantage of specific support programs offered by Albion College. If necessary, the college will grant additional time to students with learning disabilities to complete their degree. Also, a lightened course load may be granted to LD students. Students with learning disabilities will find the following programs at Albion College extremely useful: tutors · learning center · testing accommodations · untimed tests · extended time for tests · take-home exam · oral tests · readers · note-taking services · reading machines · tape recorders · texts on tape · videotaped classes · early syllabus · priority registration · waiver of math degree requirement. Individual or small group tutorials are also available in: time management · organizational skills · learning strategies · specific subject areas · writing labs · math labs · study skills. An advisor/advocate from the LD program is available to students.

How to Get Admitted

For admissions decisions, non-academic factors considered: interview · extracurricular activities · special talents, interests, abilities · character/personal qualities · volunteer work · work experience · state of residency · geographical location · alumni relationship. A high school diploma is required, although a GED is also accepted for admissions consideration. SAT or ACT test scores are required of all applicants. SAT Subject Test scores are not required. *According to the admissions office:* Albion takes a holistic approach to applica-

ALBION COLLEGE

Highlights

Albion College
Albion, MI (Pop. 9,000)
Location: Small town
Website: http://www.albion.edu

Students
Total enrollment: 1,860
Undergrads: 864
Freshmen: 492
Part-time students: 1%
From out-of-state: 6%
Male/Female: 46%/54%
Live on-campus: 91%
In fraternities: 41%
In sororities: 39%
Off-campus employment rating: Good
Caucasian: 88%
African American: 3%
Hispanic: 1%
Asian or Pacific Islander: 2%
Native American: 0%
International: 1%

Academics
Student/faculty ratio: 12:1
Class size 9 or fewer: 15%
Class size 10-29: 75%
Class size 30-49: 9%
Class size 50-99: -
Class size 100 or more: 6%
Returning freshmen: 86%
Six-year graduation rate: 73%

Most Popular Fields of Study
Biological and Life Sciences
Business, Finance, Sales and Marketing
Visual and Performing Arts
English and Literature
Philosophy, Religion and Theology
Physical Sciences, Chemistry, Physics and Astronomy
Mathematics
Interdisciplinary Studies
Health Professions, Medicine and Related Sciences
Foreign Languages, Literature and Linguistics

ALBION COLLEGE

Admissions

Applicants: 1,958
Accepted: 1,630
Acceptance rate: 83.2%
Average GPA: 3.6
ACT range: 23-27
SAT Math range: 500-650
SAT Reading range: 560-630
SAT Writing range: 500-630
Top 10% of class: 27%
Top 25% of class: 61%
Top 50% of class: 91%

Deadlines

Early Action: December 1
Early Decision: No
Regular Action: Rolling admissions
Common Application: Accepted

Financial Aid

In-state tuition: $29,488
Out-of-state tuition: $29,488
Room: -
Board: -
Books: $900
Freshmen receiving need-based aid: 65%
Undergrads receiving need-based aid: 61%
Avg. % of need met by financial aid: 88%
Avg. aid package (freshmen): $23,987
Avg. aid package (undergrads): $23,332
Freshmen receiving merit-based aid: 33%
Undergrads receiving merit-based aid: 37%
Avg. student debt upon graduation: $26,053

School Spirit

Mascot: Britons
Colors: Purple and gold
Song: *Fyte Onne*

tion review. We place highest importance on a student's academic record, including the rigor of their curriculum and grade trend. Also important is a student's ability to make a difference on campus through extracurricular involvement and the student's essays. Finally we will consider the teacher/counselor recommendation. Standardized test scores are used mostly for scholarship purposes, but may be used for admission decisions in certain circumstances. *Academic units recommended:* 4 English, 4 Math, 4 Science, 4 Social Studies, 3 Foreign Language.

How to Pay for College

To apply for financial aid, students should submit the following: Free Application for Federal Student Aid (FAFSA). Albion College participates in the Federal Work Study program. *Need-based aid programs include:* scholarships and grants · general need-based awards · Federal Pell grants · state scholarships and grants · college-based scholarships and grants · private scholarships and grants. *Non-Need-based aid programs include:* scholarships and grants · state scholarships and grants · creative arts and performance awards · alumni affiliation scholarships.

ALBRIGHT COLLEGE

P.O. Box 15234, 13th and Bern Streets, Reading, PA 19612-5234
Admissions: 800-252-1856 · Financial Aid: 610-921-7515
Email: admission@alb.edu · Website: http://www.albright.edu

From the College

"Our mission is to inspire and educate the scholar and leader in each student, building on a strong foundation in the liberal arts and sciences and a commitment to the best of human values, fostering a commitment to a lifetime of service and learning."

Campus Setting

Albright, founded in 1856, is a church-affiliated, liberal arts college. Its 110-acre campus is located at the edge of a residential section of Reading, 45 miles from Philadelphia. A four-year private institution, the school is also affiliated with the United Methodist Church. The campus facilities include: art gallery · educational technology center · Holocaust resource center. Albright College provides on-campus housing with 17 units that can accommodate 1,148 students. Housing options: co-ed dorms · single-student apartments · special housing for international students.

Student Life and Activities

With 69 percent of students living on campus, there are plenty of social activities. Albright College has 75 official student organizations. The most popular are: College Activities Council and Commuter Student Association. Albright College is a member of the Commonwealth Conference (Division III), Middle Atlantic States Collegiate Athletic Conference (Division III).

Academics and Learning Environment

For the B student, the learning environment of a college is just as important as the quality of its academic program. Albright College has 118 full-time and 49 part-time faculty members, offering a student-to-faculty ratio of 12:1. The most common course size is 10 to 19 students. Albright College offers 53 majors with the most popular being business administration, sociology and history. The school has a general core requirement. Cooperative education is available. All first-year students must maintain a 1.7 GPA or higher to avoid academic probation. Other special academic programs that would appeal to a B student: self-designed majors · pass/fail grading option · independent study · double majors · dual degrees · accelerated study · honors program · internships.

B Student Support and Success

At Albright, students have the ability to focus on a single field of study, or combine several to create an individualized major. The college offers a Learning Resource Center that is open daily for free individual tutoring or group sessions. A Writing Center gives students the chance to have their papers proofread and edited before they are turned in. The center offers workshops on time management, test taking tips, study skills and success strategies. Students

Highlights

Albright College
Reading, PA (Pop. 85,000)
Location: Large town
Website: http://www.albright.edu

Students
Total enrollment: 2,305
Undergrads: 951
Freshmen: 509
Part-time students: 2%
From out-of-state: 42%
Male/Female: 42%/58%
Live on-campus: 69%
In fraternities: 13%
In sororities: 23%
Off-campus employment rating: Good
Caucasian: 73%
African American: 10%
Hispanic: 5%
Asian or Pacific Islander: 2%
Native American: 0%
International: 6%

Academics
Student/faculty ratio: 12:1
Class size 9 or fewer: 20%
Class size 10-29: 68%
Class size 30-49: 12%
Class size 50-99: -
Class size 100 or more: -
Returning freshmen: 73%
Six-year graduation rate: 64%

Most Popular Fields of Study
Business, Finance, Sales and Marketing
Biological and Life Sciences
Psychology
Visual and Performing Arts
English and Literature
Philosophy, Religion and Theology
Computer and Information Sciences
Mathematics
Interdisciplinary Studies
Physical Sciences, Chemistry, Physics and Astronomy

ALBRIGHT COLLEGE

Admissions
Applicants: 4,561
Accepted: 2,814
Acceptance rate: 61.7%
Average GPA: 3.3
ACT range: 18-20
SAT Math range: 450-560
SAT Reading range: 440-550
SAT Writing range: Not reported
Top 10% of class: 16%
Top 25% of class: 45%
Top 50% of class: 77%

Deadlines
Early Action: No
Early Decision: No
Regular Action: March 1 (priority)
Common Application: Accepted

Financial Aid
In-state tuition: $30,800
Out-of-state tuition: $30,800
Room: $4,870
Board: $3,900
Books: $1,000
Freshmen receiving need-based aid: 76%
Undergrads receiving need-based aid: 68%
Avg. % of need met by financial aid: 72%
Avg. aid package (freshmen): $23,472
Avg. aid package (undergrads): $19,988
Freshmen receiving merit-based aid: 13%
Undergrads receiving merit-based aid: 10%
Avg. student debt upon graduation: $31,720

Prominent Alumni
R. Scott French, '87, fashion designer; Saidah Ekulona, '92, actress, (*Law & Order*, *Sex and the City*); Bob Beal, '65, President and CEO of Cystic Fibrosis Foundation.

School Spirit
Mascot: Lions
Colors: Red and white
Song: *Hail Alma Mata*

with learning disabilities can contact the vice president of student services for individual arrangements. Class sizes average 15 to 20 with general classes slightly larger and advanced classes sometimes having fewer than 10 students.

Albright College provides a variety of support programs including dedicated guidance for: academic · career · personal · psychological · minority students · military · non-traditional students · religious. The average freshman year GPA is 2.8, and 73 percent of freshmen students return for their sophomore year. What do students do after college? While many enter the work force, approximately 26 percent pursue a graduate degree immediately after graduation. Among students who enter the work force, approximately 98 percent enter a field related to their major within six months of graduation. Companies that most frequently hire graduates from Albright College include: Beard Accounting · Herebein · Ernst & Young · Pfizer · Vanguard · SEI · Accenture · Boscov's · Jefferson Hospital.

Support for Students with Learning Disabilities

Students with learning disabilities may take advantage of specific support programs offered by Albright College. If necessary, the college will grant additional time to students with learning disabilities to complete their degree. Also, a lightened course load may be granted to LD students. Students with learning disabilities will find the following programs at Albright College extremely useful: tutors · learning center · testing accommodations · extended time for tests · take-home exam · oral tests · readers · typist/scribe · note-taking services · tape recorders · texts on tape · early syllabus · priority registration. Individual or small group tutorials are also available in: time management · organizational skills · learning strategies · specific subject areas · writing labs · study skills. An advisor/advocate from the Academic Learning Center is available to students. This member also sits on the admissions committee.

How to Get Admitted

For admissions decisions, non-academic factors considered: interview · extracurricular activities · special talents, interests, abilities · character/personal qualities · volunteer work · work experience · state of residency · alumni relationship. A high school diploma is required, although a GED is also accepted for admissions consideration. SAT or ACT test scores are considered, if submitted, but are not required. SAT Subject Test scores are not required. *Academic units recommended:* 4 English, 3 Math, 4 Science, 2 Social Studies, 3 Foreign Language.

How to Pay for College

To apply for financial aid, students should submit the following: Free Application for Federal Student Aid (FAFSA). Albright College participates in the Federal Work Study program. *Need-based aid programs include:* scholarships and grants · general need-based awards · Federal Pell grants · state scholarships and grants · college-based scholarships and grants · private scholarships and grants · Federal ACG/SMART. *Non-Need-based aid programs include:* scholarships and grants · general need-based awards · state scholarships and grants · creative arts and performance awards · special achievements and activities awards · special characteristics awards.

ALCORN STATE UNIVERSITY

1000 ASU Drive #359, Alcorn State, MS 39096
Admissions: 800-222-6790 (in-state) · Financial Aid: 601-877-6190
Email: rbrooks@alcorn.edu · Website: http://www.alcorn.edu

From the College

"Alcorn State University is located on 1,756 acres of scenic land in southwest Mississippi. The campus has a blend of rich, historic buildings and modern, innovative facilities. Alcorn State University has received recognition throughout the United States for its excellence in liberal arts, agricultural research, technology, nursing and fine arts. We also have one of the largest marching bands in the United States and have won numerous athletic championships in men's and women's sports.

"For more than 125 years, Alcorn State has educated leaders in the full range of professions agriculture, the arts, business, human services, education, law, politics, medicine and nursing. An important reason for our graduates' success: At Alcorn, students form close, collaborative relationships with faculty mentors.

"A look at our campuses will show you that we're growing. A $10 million math and science building with $3 million in state-of-the-art equipment is one of the newest additions to Alcorn's 1,700-acre Lorman campus."

Campus Setting

Alcorn State, founded in 1871, is the oldest historically black, land-grant university in the country. Its 1,756-acre campus is 90 miles southwest of Jackson. A four-year public institution, Alcorn State University has with 3,252 students. Although not originally a co-educational college, Alcorn State University has been co-ed since 1903. The school also has a library with 335,252 books. Alcorn State University provides on-campus housing with 8 units that can accommodate 2,411 students. Housing options: women's dorms · men's dorms. Recreation and sports facilities include a sports complex.

Student Life and Activities

With 53 percent of students living on campus, there are plenty of social activities. Popular on-campus gathering spots include the cafeteria and game room; off-campus, students gather at the Trace Theater. Popular campus events include Probate Shows, concerts and Homecoming Week. Alcorn State University has 78 official student organizations. Popular groups on campus are Greek sororities and fraternities. Alcorn State University is a member of the NCAA, Southwestern Athletic Conference (Division I, Football I-AA).

Academics and Learning Environment

For the B student, the learning environment of a college is just as important as the quality of its academic program. Alcorn State University has 176 full-time and 41 part-time faculty members, offering a student-to-faculty ratio of 13:1. The most common course size is 10 to 19 students. Alcorn State University offers 64 majors with the most popular being general studies, nursing and biology and least popular being economics, history and applied science. The school has a general core requirement. Cooperative education is not offered. All first-year students must maintain a 2.0 GPA or higher to avoid academic probation. Other special academic programs that would appeal to a B student: independent study · double majors · accelerated study · honors program · internships · distance learning.

ALCORN STATE UNIVERSITY

Alcorn State University
Alcorn State, MS
Location: Small town
Website: http://www.alcorn.edu

Students
Total enrollment: 3,252
Undergrads: 871
Freshmen: 402
Part-time students: 9%
From out-of-state: 20%
Male/Female: 33%/67%
Live on-campus: 53%
In fraternities: 7%
In sororities: 10%
Caucasian: 5%
African American: 92%
Hispanic: 1%
Asian or Pacific Islander: 0%
International: 1%

Academics
Student/faculty ratio: 13:1
Class size 9 or fewer: 25%
Class size 10-29: 55%
Class size 30-49: 16%
Class size 50-99: 4%
Class size 100 or more: -
Returning freshmen: 59%
Six-year graduation rate: 39%

Most Popular Fields of Study
Biological and Life Sciences
Business, Finance, Sales and Marketing
Agriculture, Aquaculture and Animal Sciences
Social Sciences, History, Economics, Political Science
Protective Services, Criminal Justice and Public Administration
Visual and Performing Arts
Family and Consumer Sciences, Nutrition and Home Economics
Computer and Information Sciences
Communications, Journalism, Advertising and Comm. Technologies
Liberal Arts, Humanities and General Studies

B Student Support and Success

This is primarily an African American college, although about 8 percent of the students are Caucasian or of other ethnic backgrounds. Classes are small, and College for Excellence is offered for all freshmen, returning and transfer students. This program plans, supervises and coordinates all academic experiences of these students. It has an advising and tutoring staff and state of the art computer labs. Professional advisors support students by helping them adjust to college life, teaching them about Alcorn and its policies, exploring career options and solving any problems that come along. Additionally, staff is available to teach good test-taking, studying and time management skills and to monitor progress. Students who need additional help in reading, writing or thinking skills are assisted so that they can quickly reach college-level proficiency.

Alcorn State University provides a variety of support programs including dedicated guidance for: academic · career · psychological. Additional counseling services include: alcohol/substance abuse. Annually, 59 percent of freshmen students return for their sophomore year. What do students do after college? While many enter the work force, approximately 34 percent pursue a graduate degree immediately after graduation. Among students who enter the work force, approximately 84 percent enter a field related to their major within six months of graduation. Companies that most frequently hire graduates from Alcorn State University include: Cargill · Dow Chemical · Eastman Chemical · Entergy Operations · Enterprise Rent-A-Car · Ergon Refining · Exxon · FDIC · John Deere · Monsanto · Mississippi State Tax Commission · Mississippi Valley Gas · Naval Oceanographic Office · Primerica Financial Services · Sanderson Farms · Trustmark · Tyson Foods · USAE Corps of Engineers · U.S. Department of Agriculture · U.S. Department of Energy · Walgreens · Wells Fargo Financial.

Support for Students with Learning Disabilities

Students with learning disabilities may take advantage of specific support programs offered by Alcorn State University.

How to Get Admitted

For admissions decisions, non-academic factors considered: interview · state of residency. A high school diploma is required, although a GED is also accepted for admissions consideration. SAT or ACT test scores are required for some applicants. SAT Subject Test scores are required for some applicants. *According to the admissions office:* Complete the College Prep Curriculum with: a minimum 3.2 GPA; minimum 2.5 GPA, minimum composite ACT score of 16 (combined SAT Reasoning score of 790), or rank in upper 50 percent of class and minimum composite ACT score of 16 (combined SAT Reasoning score of 790); minimum 2.0 GPA and minimum composite ACT score of 18 (combined SAT Reasoning score of 870). *Academic units recommended:* 1 Foreign Language.

How to Pay for College

To apply for financial aid, students should submit the following: Free Application for Federal Student Aid (FAFSA) · institution's own financial aid forms. Alcorn State University participates in the Federal Work Study program. *Need-based aid programs include:*

scholarships and grants · general need-based awards · Federal Pell grants · state scholarships and grants · college-based scholarships and grants · private scholarships and grants. *Non-Need-based aid programs include:* scholarships and grants · state scholarships and grants · athletic scholarships · ROTC scholarships.

ALCORN STATE UNIVERSITY

Highlights

Admissions
Applicants: 3,065
Accepted: 2,619
Acceptance rate: 85.4%
Average GPA: 3.0
ACT range: Not reported
SAT Math range: 360-480
SAT Reading range: 370-440
SAT Writing range: Not reported
Top 50% of class: 75%

Deadlines
Early Action: No
Early Decision: No
Regular Action: Rolling admissions
Common Application: Not accepted

Financial Aid
In-state tuition: $4,498
Out-of-state tuition: $10,692
Room: -
Board: -
Books: $1,392
Freshmen receiving need-based aid: 93%
Undergrads receiving need-based aid: 91%
Avg. % of need met by financial aid: 75%
Avg. aid package (freshmen): $9,798
Avg. aid package (undergrads): $8,670
Freshmen receiving merit-based aid: 17%
Undergrads receiving merit-based aid: 14%
Avg. student debt upon graduation: $18,123

Prominent Alumni
Alyce Griffin Clarks, Mississippi State Representative

School Spirit
Mascot: Braves
Colors: Purple and gold
Song: *Alcorn Ode*

ALFRED UNIVERSITY

1 Saxon Drive, Alfred, NY 14802-1205
Admissions: 800-541-9229 · Financial Aid: 607-871-2159
Email: admissions@alfred.edu · Website: http://www.alfred.edu

From the College

"At Alfred University we value: -A learning environment that promotes open exchange of ideas, critical thinking, global awareness, technological literacy, intellectual honesty and community involvement; -A work environment that promotes open communication, recognition of achievement and the development of personal potential; -Research and scholarship that advance the frontiers of knowledge, contribute to graduate and undergraduate teaching and demonstrate creativity in all fields of endeavor; -Diversity in people and cultures, ideas and scholarship -A campus that is safe, attractive and promotes health and wellness; -A caring community that respects each individual, fosters intellectual curiosity and growth, promotes and models good citizenship and encourages enlightened leadership."

Campus Setting

Pioneer Seventh Day Baptists founded Alfred University as a select school in 1836. Alfred became the first co-educational institution in New York State and the second in the nation. The nonsectarian University is comprised of the College of Business, the College of Liberal Arts and Sciences, the Inamori School of Engineering and the School of Art and Design. About 2,000 full-time undergraduate and 300 graduate students work and live on a 232-acre hillside campus in Alfred, New York. A four-year private institution, Alfred University has an enrollment of 2,416 students. In addition to a large, well-stocked library, the campus facilities include: art galleries · ceramic art museum · carillon · observatory. Alfred University provides on-campus housing with 26 units that can accommodate 1,425 students. Housing options: co-ed dorms · single-student apartments.

Student Life and Activities

With 73 percent of students living on campus, there are plenty of social activities. Popular gathering spots include Powell Campus Center, Brick Lawn, the Bandstand, the Moka Joka and Terra Cotta. Popular campus events include Hot Dog Day, Glam Slam and The Alfies. Alfred University has 83 official student organizations. The most popular are: Chamber singers · Habitat for Humanity · Kanakadea · Spectrum · Pet Pals · Student Activities Board · SAFE · Green Alfred · Alfred Steppas · AU Swing Society · Friday Night Live · Pirate Theater. Alfred University is a member of the Empire Eight (Division III).

Academics and Learning Environment

For the B student, the learning environment of a college is just as important as the quality of its academic program. Alfred University has 158 full-time and 39 part-time faculty members, offering a student-to-faculty ratio of 12:1. The most common course size is 10 to 19 students. Alfred University offers 67 majors with the most popular being business administration and ceramic engineering and least popular being sociology, economics and Spanish. The school has a general core requirement. Cooperative education is available. All first-year students must maintain a 1.7 GPA or higher to avoid academic probation, and a minimum overall GPA of 2.0 is required to graduate. Other special academic programs that would appeal to a B student: self-designed majors · pass/fail grading option · independent study · double majors · dual degrees · honors program · Phi Beta Kappa · internships.

B Student Support and Success

Rumored to have been the inspiration for the 1980s sit-com *Northern Exposure*, this college is quiet and small but active. The school is especially known for its School of Engineering's glass and ceramic programs and is one of the few schools that offers a degree in Ceramic Engineering. Classes are typically less than 10 students at Alfred. The general atmosphere appeals to the back-to-nature student who likes cold, snowy winters.

Alfred University provides a variety of support programs including dedicated guidance for: academic · career · personal · psychological · minority students · family planning. Additional counseling services include: women's, wellness. The average freshman year GPA is 2.6, and 78 percent of freshmen students return for their sophomore year.

Support for Students with Learning Disabilities

Students with learning disabilities may take advantage of specific support programs offered by Alfred University. If necessary, the college will grant additional time to students with learning disabilities to complete their degree. Also, a lightened course load may be granted to LD students. According to the school, progress of students receiving services from Special Academic Services is monitored. Students with learning disabilities will find the following programs at Alfred University extremely useful: tutors · testing accommodations · untimed tests · extended time for tests · oral tests · readers · note-taking services · tape recorders · diagnostic testing service · waiver of math degree requirement. Individual or small group tutorials are also available in: time management · organizational skills · learning strategies · specific subject areas · writing labs · study skills. An advisor/advocate from the Special Academic Services is available to students.

How to Get Admitted

For admissions decisions, non-academic factors considered: interview · extracurricular activities · special talents, interests, abilities · character/personal qualities · volunteer work · work experience · state of residency · minority affiliation. A high school diploma is required, although a GED is also accepted for admissions consideration. SAT or ACT test scores are required of all applicants. SAT Subject Test scores are considered, if submitted, but are not required. *According to the admissions office:* There are no minimum requirements. Admission is determined on an individual basis. *Academic units recommended:* 1 Foreign Language.

Insight

Sue Goetschius, director of communications, says Alfred University has always been an institution "championing the underserved." Alfred was the first co-educational institution in New York State and among the first to enroll students regardless of ethnicity or religion. A large percentage of students today continue to be economically disadvantaged; more than 90 percent receive institutional financial aid, which is one reason why both *U.S. News & World Report* and the *Fiske Guide to Colleges 2010* rate Alfred as being a good value. Another population the university has traditionally served is those whose high school records might not be the strongest, but who the

ALFRED UNIVERSITY

Highlights

Alfred University
Alfred, NY (Pop. 3,000)
Location: Rural
Website: http://www.alfred.edu

Students
Total enrollment: 2,416
Undergrads: 998
Freshmen: 502
Part-time students: 5%
From out-of-state: Not reported
Male/Female: 51%/49%
Live on-campus: 73%
Off-campus employment rating: Poor
Caucasian: 66%
African American: 4%
Hispanic: 2%
Asian or Pacific Islander: 2%
Native American: 0%
International: 2%

Academics
Student/faculty ratio: 12:1
Class size 9 or fewer: 18%
Class size 10-29: 65%
Class size 30-49: 14%
Class size 50-99: 3%
Class size 100 or more: 1%
Returning freshmen: 78%
Six-year graduation rate: 67%

Most Popular Fields of Study
Business, Finance, Sales and Marketing
Biological and Life Sciences

Admissions
Applicants: 2,557
Accepted: 1,945
Acceptance rate: 76.1%
Average GPA: 3.2
ACT range: 21-26
SAT Math range: 510-620
SAT Reading range: 500-605
SAT Writing range: 480-590
Top 10% of class: 19%
Top 25% of class: 54%
Top 50% of class: 88%

ALFRED UNIVERSITY

Deadlines
Early Action: No
Early Decision: December 1
Regular Action: February 1 (priority)
August 1 (final)
Common Application: Accepted

Financial Aid
In-state tuition: $24,366
Out-of-state tuition: $24,366
Room: $5,766
Board: $5,084
Books: $950
Freshmen receiving need-based aid: 74%
Undergrads receiving need-based aid: 74%
Avg. % of need met by financial aid: 85%
Avg. aid package (freshmen): $23,510
Avg. aid package (undergrads): $21,253
Freshmen receiving merit-based aid: 5%
Undergrads receiving merit-based aid: 8%
Avg. student debt upon graduation: $26,962

Prominent Alumni
Joel Moskowitz, CEO of Ceradyne.

School Spirit
Mascot: Saxons

admissions officers believe have the potential to do well. Goetschius explains, "Often, when I speak with our alumni, I hear the recurring theme, 'Alfred took a chance on me.' "

How to Pay for College

To apply for financial aid, students should submit the following: Free Application for Federal Student Aid (FAFSA) · institution's own financial aid forms · state aid form · Non-custodian (Divorced/Separated) Parent's Statement · Business/Farm Supplement. Alfred University participates in the Federal Work Study program. *Need-based aid programs include:* scholarships and grants · general need-based awards · Federal Pell grants · state scholarships and grants · college-based scholarships and grants · private scholarships and grants. *Non-Need-based aid programs include:* scholarships and grants · state scholarships and grants · creative arts and performance awards · leadership scholarships.

ALMA COLLEGE

614 West Superior Street, Alma, MI 48801-1599
Admissions: 800-321-2562 · Financial Aid: 800-321-2562
Email: admissions@alma.edu · Website: http://www.alma.edu

From the College

"Alma College, a four-year liberal arts college in the middle of Michigan's Lower Peninsula, offers a personalized education that engages students in transformative learning experiences. Founded in 1886 and affiliated with the Presbyterian Church (U.S.A.), Alma is committed to a quality undergraduate education and the development of responsible leaders through its Center for Responsible Leadership. Academic excellence and a deep regard for students as individuals are fundamental to its educational residential programs. Its small size enables many opportunities for one-on-one collaboration with faculty. Students also participate in research, community service and study abroad activities."

Campus Setting

Alma College, founded in 1886, highlights personalized education, social responsibility and achievement in a supportive, small-college environment emphasizing active, collaborative learning and close student-faculty interaction. Its 125-acre campus is within walking distance of downtown Alma, 40 miles from Saginaw, in the middle of Michigan's Lower Peninsula. Alma maintains a close relationship with the Presbyterian Church but also offers an environment that welcomes students of all religious backgrounds. A four-year private institution, Alma College has an enrollment of 1,384 students. In addition to a large, well-stocked library, the campus facilities include: planetarium · science center · center for exercise and health science. Alma College provides on-campus housing with 25 units that can accommodate 1,187 students. Housing options: co-ed dorms · women's dorms · sorority housing · fraternity housing. Recreation and sports facilities include: baseball · soccer and softball fields · basketball and volleyball courts · football · track and swimming pool stadium · tennis and recreation center.

Student Life and Activities

With 88 percent of students living on campus, there are plenty of social activities. Popular events include: Homecoming, All Nighter, Songfest and Honors Day. Alma College has 75 official student organizations. The most popular are: Alma Ambassadors · Union Board · Student Congress · Students Offering Service · Alma College Republicans/Democrats · Amnesty International · Big Brothers/Big Sisters · Model UN · Pride. For those interested in sports, there are intramural teams such as: basketball · disc golf · dodgeball · flag football · floor hockey · ice hockey · racquetball · soccer · softball · tennis · ultimate Frisbee · volleyball. Alma College is a member of the Michigan Intercollegiate Athletic Association (Division III).

Academics and Learning Environment

For the B student, the learning environment of a college is just as important as the quality of its academic program. Alma College has 86 full-time and 52 part-time faculty members, offering a student-to-faculty ratio of 13:1. The most common course size is 10 to 19 students. Alma College offers 30 majors with the most popular being business administration, biology and exercises and health science and least popular being economics, computer science and philosophy. The school has a general core requirement. Cooperative education is not offered. All first-year students must maintain a 2.0 GPA or higher to avoid academic probation, and a minimum overall GPA

ALMA COLLEGE

Alma College
Alma (Pop. 10,000)
Location: Small town
Website: http://www.alma.edu

Students
Total enrollment: 1,384
Undergrads: 615
Freshmen: 433
Part-time students: 3%
From out-of-state: 3%
Male/Female: 44%/56%
Live on-campus: 88%
In fraternities: 25%
In sororities: 27%
Off-campus employment rating: Good
Caucasian: 92%
African American: 2%
Hispanic: 2%
Asian or Pacific Islander: 1%
Native American: 1%
International: 0%

Academics
Student/faculty ratio: 13:1
Class size 9 or fewer: 18%
Class size 10-29: 103%
Class size 30-49: 11%
Class size 50-99: 3%
Class size 100 or more: 1%
Returning freshmen: 75%
Six-year graduation rate: 70%

Most Popular Fields of Study
Business, Finance, Sales and Marketing
Biological and Life Sciences
Visual and Performing Arts
English and Literature
Philosophy, Religion and Theology
Computer and Information Sciences
Mathematics
Health Professions, Medicine and Related Sciences
Foreign Languages, Literature and Linguistics

of 2.0 is required to graduate. Other special academic programs that would appeal to a B student: self-designed majors · pass/fail grading option · independent study · double majors · dual degrees · honors program · Phi Beta Kappa · internships.

B Student Support and Success

Alma College's Academic Effectiveness Program is designed for students who are struggling academically. A counselor works with you to figure out the source of the problem and then develop a plan of action. The Center for Student Development also offers "Learning Lunches" each term on the topics of time management methods, note taking, classroom strategies, study skills, test taking strategies, test anxiety, preparing for employment and graduate school and pursuing internship options.

Alma College provides a variety of support programs including dedicated guidance for: academic · career · personal · minority students · non-traditional students · family planning · religious. Recognizing that some students may need extra preparation, Alma College offers remedial and refresher courses in: reading · writing · math · study skills. The average freshman year GPA is 3.0, and 75 percent of freshmen students return for their sophomore year.

Support for Students with Learning Disabilities

Students with learning disabilities may take advantage of specific support programs offered by Alma College. If necessary, the college will grant additional time to students with learning disabilities to complete their degree. Students with learning disabilities will find the following programs at Alma College extremely useful: remedial math · tutors · learning center · testing accommodations · untimed tests · extended time for tests · take-home exam · oral tests · exam on tape or computer · readers · note-taking services · proofreading services · reading machines · tape recorders · early syllabus · priority registration · priority seating · waiver of foreign language degree requirement. Individual or small group tutorials are also available in: time management · organizational skills · learning strategies · specific subject areas · writing labs · math labs · study skills. An advisor/advocate from the Academic and Career Planning is available to students. This member also sits on the admissions committee.

How to Get Admitted

For admissions decisions, non-academic factors considered: interview · extracurricular activities · special talents, interests, abilities · character/personal qualities · volunteer work · work experience · state of residency · alumni relationship. A high school diploma is required, although a GED is also accepted for admissions consideration. SAT or ACT test scores are required of all applicants. SAT Subject Test scores are not required. *According to the admissions office:* Minimum composite ACT score of 22 (combined SAT score of 1030) and rank in top half of secondary school class required; minimum 3.0 GPA recommended. *Academic units recommended:* 2 Foreign Language.

How to Pay for College

To apply for financial aid, students should submit the following: Free Application for Federal Student Aid (FAFSA). Alma College participates in the Federal Work Study program. *Need-based aid programs include:* scholarships and grants · general need-based awards · Federal Pell grants · state scholarships and grants · college-based scholarships and grants · private scholarships and grants. *Non-Need-based aid programs include:* scholarships and grants · state scholarships and grants · creative arts and performance awards · special characteristics awards.

ALMA COLLEGE

Admissions
Applicants: 1,891
Accepted: 1,354
Acceptance rate: 71.6%
Average GPA: 3.5
ACT range: 21-26
SAT Math range: 528-680
SAT Reading range: 518-678
SAT Writing range: Not reported
Top 10% of class: 27%
Top 25% of class: 60%
Top 50% of class: 88%

Deadlines
Early Action: No
Early Decision: No
Regular Action: Rolling admissions
Common Application: Accepted

Financial Aid
In-state tuition: $25,838
Out-of-state tuition: $25,838
Room: $4,196
Board: $4,322
Books: $722
Freshmen receiving need-based aid: 81%
Undergrads receiving need-based aid: 79%
Avg. % of need met by financial aid: 82%
Avg. aid package (freshmen): $20,846
Avg. aid package (undergrads): $19,768
Freshmen receiving merit-based aid: 19%
Undergrads receiving merit-based aid: 20%
Avg. student debt upon graduation: $18,583

Prominent Alumni
Louis G. Ferrand '64, head legal advisor for Secretary General of the Organization of American States (OAS); Karen Magnuson '78, editor and vice president of the Rochester Democrat and Chronicle

School Spirit
Mascot: Scots
Colors: Maroon and cream

ALVERNO COLLEGE

3400 South 43rd Street, P.O. Box 343922, Milwaukee, WI 53234-3922
Admissions: 800-933-3401 · Financial Aid: 800-933-3401
Email: admissions@alverno.edu · Website: http://www.alverno.edu

From the College

"Alverno College, a four-year independent, Catholic, liberal arts college for women, promotes the personal and professional development of its students. The college is known for its ability-based, assessment-as-learning approach to education, and has consulted with three U.S. presidential administrations on accountability and outcomes in higher education. The Alverno environment actively engages students in their education through hands-on practical learning and a highly developed off-campus internship program inherent to the curriculum, and provides students professional support in their educational endeavors including a professional advising office and a fully staffed career education center. Alverno College also employs the Diagnostic Digital Portfolio, a unique Web-based system which helps students process the feedback they receive from faculty, external assessors and peers. Alverno offers more than 35 major program areas of study, including graduate programs in education, nursing and business that are open to women and men."

Campus Setting

Alverno College, founded in 1887, has a 40-acre campus and is located 12 miles from downtown Milwaukee. The school is affiliated with the Roman Catholic Church. Campus facilities include: art gallery · theatre · teaching · learning · and technology center · clinical nursing skills lab · student-centered multimedia production facility · career center · international and intercultural center · communication resource center · math center. Alverno College provides on-campus housing with 184 units that can accommodate 269 students. Recreation and sports facilities include: athletic training room · fields · fitness center · gymnasium · soccer and softball complex.

Student Life and Activities

Most students (90 percent) live off campus, which does impact the on-campus social scene. Nevertheless, like any college, students find time to create their own recreational outlets. Popular events include: Celebrate Cultures Week, Community Day, Homecoming/Spirit Week, Boo Bash, Orientation, Weekly Roundtable Discussion, Alverno Idol, Giving Thanks Week, Love Your Body Week, Alverno Presents Performing Art Series, Rotunda Ball and the Alverno Debate Series. Alverno College has 41 official student organizations. Popular groups include: Alpha, student newspaper, Alverno Student Education Organization, Artourage, Circle K, Hispanic Women of Alverno, Women of Asian Ethnicity, Psych Forum, Students in Free Enterprise, Student Athlete Advisory Council. Alverno College is a member of the Northern Athletics Conference (Division III).

Academics and Learning Environment

For the B student, the learning environment of a college is just as important as the quality of its academic program. Alverno College has 113 full-time and 136 part-time faculty members, offering a student-to-faculty ratio of 13:1. The most common course size is 10 to 19 students. Alverno College offers 53 majors with the most popular being nursing, elementary education and psychology. The school has a general core requirement. Cooperative education is not offered. Other special academic programs that would appeal to a B student: self-designed majors · independent study · double majors · internships · weekend college · certificate programs.

B Student Support and Success

Alverno College offers a number of instructional services to help students achieve their academic goals. Basic courses in math, algebra, reading/writing, ESL and computer skills are offered. Communication and math resource centers are available, as well as peer and instructor tutoring. The college website states that the primary purpose of the Communication Resource Center is to help students with their writing, speaking or reading assignment by conferencing with them and responding to their individual questions and concerns. The center offers help with everything from prewriting skills (brainstorming, mapping, etc.) to revising, proofreading and editing.

Alverno College provides a variety of support programs including dedicated guidance for: academic · career · personal · psychological · religious. Recognizing that some students may need extra preparation, Alverno College offers remedial and refresher courses in: reading · writing · math · study skills. Annually, 73 percent of freshmen students return for their sophomore year. What do students do after college? While many enter the work force, approximately 10 percent pursue a graduate degree immediately after graduation. Among students who enter the work force, approximately 85 percent enter a field related to their major within six months of graduation. Companies that most frequently hire graduates from Alverno College include: Alverno College · Aurora Health Care · Blood Center of Wisconsin · City of Milwaukee · Children's Hospital of WI · Community Memorial Hospital · Froedtert Hospital · Kohl's · Medical College of Wisconsin · M & I Corp.· Milwaukee area schools · Milwaukee Public Schools · Milwaukee County government · Northwestern Mutual · U. S. Government · State of Wisconsin · Wheaton Franciscan Healthcare.

Support for Students with Learning Disabilities

Students with learning disabilities may take advantage of specific support programs offered by Alverno College. If necessary, the college will grant additional time to students with learning disabilities to complete their degree. Also, a lightened course load may be granted to LD students. Students with learning disabilities will find the following programs at Alverno College extremely useful: remedial math · remedial English · remedial reading · tutors · learning center · extended time for tests · take-home exam · note-taking services · reading machines · tape recorders · early syllabus. Individual or small group tutorials are also available in: time management · organizational skills · learning strategies · specific subject areas · writing labs · math labs · study skills.

How to Get Admitted

For admissions decisions, non-academic factors considered: interview · state of residency. A high school diploma is required, although a GED is also accepted for admissions consideration. SAT or ACT test scores are required of all applicants. SAT Subject Test scores are not required. *Academic units recommended:* 2 Foreign Language.

How to Pay for College

To apply for financial aid, students should submit the following: Free Application for Federal Student Aid (FAFSA) · institution's own

Highlights

Alverno College
Milwaukee, WI (Pop. 600,000)
Location: Major city
Website: http://www.alverno.edu

Students
Total enrollment: 2,782
Undergrads: 6
Freshmen: 535
Part-time students: 28%
From out-of-state: 4%
Male/Female: 0%/100%
Live on-campus: 10%
In sororities: 2%
Off-campus employment rating: Good
Caucasian: 64%
African American: 17%
Hispanic: 13%
Asian or Pacific Islander: 5%
Native American: 1%
International: 1%

Academics
Student/faculty ratio: 13:1
Class size 9 or fewer: 12%
Class size 10-29: 81%
Class size 30-49: 7%
Class size 50-99: 3%
Class size 100 or more: 1%
Returning freshmen: 73%
Six-year graduation rate: 39%

Most Popular Fields of Study
Business, Finance, Sales and Marketing
Protective Services, Criminal Justice and
    Public Administration
Psychology
English and Literature
Philosophy, Religion and Theology
Mathematics
Health Professions, Medicine and Related Sciences
Liberal Arts, Humanities and General
    Studies
Communications, Journalism, Advertising
    and Comm. Technologies
Education

ALVERNO COLLEGE

Admissions
Applicants: 560
Accepted: 496
Acceptance rate: 88.6%
Average GPA: 3.0
ACT range: 17-22
SAT Math range: Not reported
SAT Reading range: Not reported
SAT Writing range: Not reported

Deadlines
Early Action: No
Early Decision: No
Regular Action: Rolling admissions
Common Application: Accepted

Financial Aid
In-state tuition: $18,624
Out-of-state tuition: $18,624
Room: -
Board: -
Books: $1,056
Freshmen receiving need-based aid: 79%
Undergrads receiving need-based aid: 79%
Avg. % of need met by financial aid: Not reported
Avg. aid package (freshmen): $15,625
Avg. aid package (undergrads): $13,151
Freshmen receiving merit-based aid: 13%
Undergrads receiving merit-based aid: 9%
Avg. student debt upon graduation: $27,976

Prominent Alumni
Sister Joel Read, President-Emeritus, Alverno College, Education Reformer; Stephanie Arend, Superior Court Judge, State of Washington; Cathy Rick, Chief Nursing Officer, Veteran's Health Administration, Washington DC

School Spirit
Mascot: Inferno
Colors: Red and white and black
Song: *Where All Belong*

financial aid forms. Alverno College participates in the Federal Work Study program. *Need-based aid programs include:* scholarships and grants · general need-based awards · Federal Pell grants · state scholarships and grants · college-based scholarships and grants · private scholarships and grants · Federal Nursing scholarships · transfer scholarships · referral scholarships. *Non-Need-based aid programs include:* scholarships and grants · state scholarships and grants · alumni scholarships · community service scholarships · leadership scholarships · minority scholarships.

ANGELO STATE UNIVERSITY

2601 West Avenue N, San Angelo, TX 76909
Admissions: 800-946-8627 · Financial Aid: 800-933-6299
Email: admissions@angelo.edu · Website: http://www.angelo.edu

From the College

"As a comprehensive institution of higher education, Angelo State University provides a strong academic experience while offering significant financial support to students. As a result, the university's academic quality and low student-faculty ratio (19-1) prepare students for success in their chosen professions or acceptance to graduate and professional school, such as medicine and law. Because of major scholarship and gift aid support which does not have to be repaid like many academic loans, ASU boasts one of the nation's lowest student debt burdens upon graduation.

"Students desiring a more rigorous academic experience can apply to ASU's dynamic Honors Program while those desiring study abroad can participate in a growing International Studies Program that provides a more global experience while keeping costs within reach. ASU has the only Physics Department in Texas ranked in the top 20 among undergraduate programs nationwide and a nationally recognized Biology Department which in 2007 became the first department in the nation to have its biology honor society named the top chapter in the nation a record six times.

"Academically, the university is organized with six colleges: Business; Education; Liberal and Fine Arts; Nursing and Allied Health; Sciences; and Graduate Studies as well as 21 academic departments. Those departments offer 40 undergraduate programs, 23 graduate programs, including a doctorate, and one associate degree as well as nearly 100 majors. As a member of the Texas Tech University System, ASU provides options for a variety of pre-professional and two-plus-two and four-plus-one programs with Texas Tech. ASU draws students from practically every county in Texas (215 of 254) as well as from 37 states and 21 countries. With more than half of its graduates as first generation college students, ASU is attuned to the academic and social needs of a new generation of college students.

"In addition to (its) academic offerings, ASU provides a 268-acre campus that offers an attractive and safe setting for a college education. ASU's campus facilities are valued at over $345 million and include the Math-Computer Science Building, which houses one of the most sophisticated computer systems in the state; the Junell Center/Stephens Arena, one of the top facilities in all of NCAA Division II athletics; and the Houston-Harte University Center; the center of campus student life. Additionally, the university operates 6,000 additional acres in farm and ranch lands that also serve as home for ASU's Management, Instruction and Research Center as well as the Food Safety and Product Development Laboratory.

"Angelo State also manages one of the nation's largest scholarship endowments. Funded by the Robert G. and Nona K. Carr Scholarship Foundation, Carr Scholarships today benefit one in every six ASU students with grants ranging from $2,000 to $6,000. Established in 1978 exclusively to benefit needy and deserving ASU students, the Carr Foundation today holds assets of more than $81 million. For the 2008-09 academic year, more than $3.4 million in Carr Scholarships were awarded to ASU students."

Campus Setting

Angelo State was founded as a junior college in 1928, became a four-year college in 1965 and gained university status four years later. Its 268-acre campus is located in San Angelo, a cattle and sheep ranching region. A four-year public institution, Angelo State University has an enrollment of 6,155 students. In addition to a large, well-stocked

ANGELO STATE UNIVERSITY

Angelo State University
San Angelo, Texas (Pop. 95,000)
Location: Medium city
Website: http://www.angelo.edu

Students
Total enrollment: 6,155
Undergrads: 2,583
Freshmen: 1,467
Part-time students: 15%
From out-of-state: 2%
Male/Female: 46%/54%
Live on-campus: 36%
In fraternities: 3%
In sororities: 4%
Off-campus employment rating: Fair
Caucasian: 65%
African American: 8%
Hispanic: 25%
Asian or Pacific Islander: 1%
Native American: 1%
International: 0%

Academics
Student/faculty ratio: 19:1
Class size 9 or fewer: 6%
Class size 10-29: 49%
Class size 30-49: 34%
Class size 50-99: 10%
Class size 100 or more: 1%
Returning freshmen: 56%
Six-year graduation rate: 33%

Most Popular Fields of Study
Business, Finance, Sales and Marketing
Agriculture, Aquaculture and Animal Sciences
Biological and Life Sciences
Protective Services, Criminal Justice and Public Administration
Psychology
English and Literature
Computer and Information Sciences
Mathematics
Parks, Recreation and Fitness
Interdisciplinary Studies

library, the campus also has a planetarium. Angelo State University provides on-campus housing with 7 units that can accommodate 1,696 students. Housing options: co-ed dorms · women's dorms · men's dorms · single-student apartments · special housing for disabled students. Recreation and sports facilities include: arena · center for human performance · intramural fields · tennis courts · baseball complex · lake facility and lake house.

Student Life and Activities

Most students (64 percent) live off campus, which does impact the on-campus social scene. Nevertheless, like any college, students find time to create their own recreational outlets. As a residential campus, Angelo State University is active year-round with events and opportunities for students to enhance their classroom experience with broad social, cultural and entertainment opportunities. The university social network centers around the Houston Harte University Center. The UC houses the Student Government Association, student organizations, the University Book Store and a branch of the Concho Educators Federal Credit Union branch. The university's Intramural Fields are also popular. Angelo State also sponsors 76 student-led organizations. Popular campus events include Rambunctious Weekend, Homecoming, Ram Jam, CMA Moon Lectures, football, baseball, Midnight Madness and planetarium shows. Tri Beta Biological Honor Society, Block and Bridle, Intramural and Recreation Program, and the Society of Physics Students are popular organizations on campus. For those interested in sports, there are intramural teams such as: basketball · boxing · flag football · gymnastics · handball · indoor soccer · martial arts · racquetball · softball · tennis · ultimate Frisbee · wrestling · volleyball. Angelo State University is a member of the Lone Star Conference (Division II).

Academics and Learning Environment

For the B student, the learning environment of a college is just as important as the quality of its academic program. Angelo State University has 241 full-time and 81 part-time faculty members, offering a student-to-faculty ratio of 19:1. The most common course size is 20 to 29 students. Angelo State University offers 64 majors with the most popular being business, psychology and kinesiology and least popular being French, German and drama. The school has a general core requirement. Cooperative education is not offered. All first-year students must maintain a 2.0 GPA or higher to avoid academic probation. Other special academic programs that would appeal to a B student: independent study · double majors · honors program · internships · distance learning.

B Student Support and Success

Angelo State University provides a variety of support programs including dedicated guidance for: academic · career · personal · psychological · veterans. Annually, 56 percent of freshmen students return for their sophomore year.

Support for Students with Learning Disabilities

Students with learning disabilities may take advantage of specific support programs offered by Angelo State University. Students with learning disabilities will find the following programs extremely useful: remedial math · remedial English · remedial reading · learning center · extended time for tests · oral tests · note-taking services · tape recorders · diagnostic testing service.

How to Get Admitted

For admissions decisions, non-academic factors considered: state of residency. A high school diploma is required, although a GED is also accepted for admissions consideration. SAT or ACT test scores are required of all applicants. SAT Subject Test scores are not required. *According to the admissions office:* Minimum composite ACT score of 30 (combined SAT Reasoning score of 1270), and rank in top three-quarters of secondary school class, or rank in top half of secondary school class required. *Academic units recommended:* 4 English, 4 Math, 3 Science, 4 Social Studies, 3 Foreign Language.

Insight

Preston Lewis, director of communications and marketing, says that while ASU welcomes students graduating in the top 10 percent of their graduating class, the university has as a strategic move paid special attention to recruiting students in the top 11 percent to 25 percent of their graduating class. Special scholarships are targeted to students graduating in this range. More than half of students are first-generation college students. He says, "We are accustomed to welcoming not just students but their families into the college experience."

How to Pay for College

To apply for financial aid, students should submit the following: Free Application for Federal Student Aid (FAFSA) · institution's own financial aid forms. Angelo State University participates in the Federal Work Study program. *Need-based aid programs include:* scholarships and grants · general need-based awards · Federal Pell grants · state scholarships and grants · college-based scholarships and grants · private scholarships and grants · Federal Nursing scholarships. *Non-Need-based aid programs include:* scholarships and grants · state scholarships and grants · athletic scholarships · ROTC scholarships.

ANGELO STATE UNIVERSITY

Highlights

Admissions
Applicants: 3,010
Accepted: 2,934
Acceptance rate: 97.5%
Average GPA: Not reported
ACT range: 17-23
SAT Math range: 430-540
SAT Reading range: 410-520
SAT Writing range: 400-510
Top 10% of class: 14%
Top 25% of class: 28%
Top 50% of class: 73%

Deadlines
Early Action: No
Early Decision: No
Regular Action: August 15 (final)
Common Application: Not accepted

Financial Aid
In-state tuition: $6,136
Out-of-state tuition: $14,447
Room: $3,398
Board: $1,820
Books: $1,000
Freshmen receiving need-based aid: 58%
Undergrads receiving need-based aid: 54%
Avg. % of need met by financial aid: 61%
Avg. aid package (freshmen): $4,359
Avg. aid package (undergrads): $5,206
Freshmen receiving merit-based aid: 7%
Undergrads receiving merit-based aid: 4%
Avg. student debt upon graduation: $11,400

Prominent Alumni
Satcha Pretto, Univision network anchor; Dr. Arnoldo De Leon, nationally recognized historian on Mexican American history; Grant Teaff, executive director, American Football Coaches Association.

Anna Maria College
Paxton, MA (Pop. 4,047)
Location: Rural
Website: http://www.annamaria.edu

Students
Total enrollment: 1,200
Undergrads: 336
Freshmen: 182
Part-time students: 26%
From out-of-state: 22%
Male/Female: 42%/58%
Live on-campus: 68%
Off-campus employment rating: Good
Caucasian: 70%
African American: 3%
Hispanic: 3%
Asian or Pacific Islander: 1%
Native American: 0%
International: 0%

Academics
Student/faculty ratio: 10:1
Class size 9 or fewer: 31%
Class size 10-29: 68%
Class size 30-49: 16%
Class size 50-99: 10%
Class size 100 or more: 1%
Returning freshmen: 59%
Six-year graduation rate: 49%

Most Popular Fields of Study
Business, Finance, Sales and Marketing

Admissions
Applicants: 712
Accepted: 621
Acceptance rate: 87.2%
Average GPA: 2.5
ACT range: 16-18
SAT Math range: 380-470
SAT Reading range: 390-480
SAT Writing range: Not reported
Top 50% of class: 39%

92

ANNA MARIA COLLEGE

50 Sunset Lane, Paxton, MA 01612
Admissions: 800-344-4586
Financial Aid: 800-344-4586, extension 366
Email:admission@annamaria.edu
Website: http://www.annamaria.edu

From the College

"Anna Maria College, a Catholic institution of higher education, recognizes its obligation to serve its immediate community, the Commonwealth of Massachusetts, the nation, and the world through the provision of education, the preservation of learning, and the sponsorship of research. Rooted in the Roman Catholic tradition of higher education, Anna Maria College is maintained and operated in conformity with the values of the Judeo-Christian tradition and in keeping with the ideals of its foundresses, the Sisters of Saint Anne. These ideals, which reflect the development of the total human being, also include increasing access to quality education, educational innovation and respect for practical skills.

"The college offers its undergraduate students a program integrating a liberal arts education and strong career preparation. To its graduate students, the college offers an education fostering high standards of personal development and professional achievement, as well as a mature sense of responsibility."

Campus Setting

Founded in 1946 as a college for women, it began admitting men in 1973. Its 180-acre campus is set on the grounds of a 19th century estate, eight miles from Worcester. A four-year private institution, the school is also affiliated with the Roman Catholic Church. In addition to a medium-size library, the campus facilities include: art gallery · art studio classrooms · dark room. Anna Maria College provides on-campus housing with 207 units that can accommodate 396 students. Housing options: co-ed dorms · special housing for disabled students.

Student Life and Activities

With 68 percent of students living on campus, there are plenty of social activities and gathering spots. Popular activities include men's soccer games, men's and women's basketball games, Spring Weekend, the Variety Show and productions by the Drama and New England Theater Company (in residence at AMC). Anna Maria College has 13 official student organizations. The Ski Club, the Drama Club, the History Club and intramural sports are popular on campus. Anna Maria College is a member of the Commonwealth Coast Conference (Division III).

Academics and Learning Environment

For the B student, the learning environment of a college is just as important as the quality of its academic program. Anna Maria College has 40 full-time and 141 part-time faculty members, offering a student-to-faculty ratio of 10:1. The most common course size is 10 to 19 students. Anna Maria College offers 42 majors with the most popular being criminal justice and least popular being Spanish, English and art therapy. The school has a general core requirement. Cooperative education is not offered. All first-year students must maintain a 2.0 GPA or higher to avoid academic probation. Other special academic programs that would appeal to a B student: self-designed majors · pass/fail grading option · independent study · double majors · dual degrees · accelerated study · internships · certificate programs.

B Student Support and Success

Anna Maria College offers an $8,000 scholarship based upon involvement in the high school community and the community at large. Anna Maria does not require minimum scores on the SAT. In addition, the admissions department states that there are many B and C students who are highly involved in their high school and are welcomed at Anna Maria.

Anna Maria College provides a variety of support programs including dedicated guidance for: academic · career · personal · psychological · religious. Recognizing that some students may need extra preparation, Anna Maria College offers remedial and refresher courses in: reading · writing · math · study skills. The average freshman year GPA is 3.0, and 59 percent of freshmen students return for their sophomore year.

Support for Students with Learning Disabilities

Students with learning disabilities may take advantage of specific support programs offered by Anna Maria College. Students with learning disabilities will find the following programs at Anna Maria College extremely useful: Learning Center · tutoring · study skills workshops.

How to Get Admitted

For admissions decisions, non-academic factors considered: interview · extracurricular activities · special talents, interests, abilities · character/personal qualities · volunteer work · work experience · state of residency · alumni relationship. A high school diploma is required, although a GED is also accepted for admissions consideration. SAT or ACT test scores are required of all applicants. SAT Subject Test scores are not required. *According to the admissions office:* Minimum combined SAT score of 900, rank in top half of secondary school class and minimum 2.5 GPA recommended.

How to Pay for College

To apply for financial aid, students should submit the following: Free Application for Federal Student Aid (FAFSA) · state aid form. Anna Maria College participates in the Federal Work Study program. *Need-based aid programs include:* scholarships and grants · general need-based awards · Federal Pell grants · state scholarships and grants · college-based scholarships and grants · private scholarships and grants · Federal Nursing scholarships · United Negro College Fund. *Non-Need-based aid programs include:* scholarships and grants · general need-based awards · state scholarships and grants · special achievements and activities awards · special characteristics awards.

ANNA MARIA COLLEGE

Highlights

Deadlines
Early Action: No
Early Decision: No
Regular Action: Rolling admissions
Common Application: Accepted

Financial Aid
In-state tuition: $22,360
Out-of-state tuition: $22,360
On-campus room and board: $11,050
Off-campus room and board: $6,700
Supplies: $800
Freshmen receiving need-based aid: 81%
Undergrads receiving need-based aid: 82%
Avg. % of need met by financial aid: 73%
Avg. aid package (freshmen): $16,589
Avg. aid package (undergrads): $16,424
Freshmen receiving merit-based aid: 17%
Undergrads receiving merit-based aid: 15%
Avg. student debt upon graduation: $29,366

School Spirit
Mascot: AMCAT
Colors: Royal blue and white

ARIZONA STATE UNIVERSITY

P.O. Box 870112, Tempe, AZ 85287
Admissions: 480-965-7788 · Financial Aid: 480-965-3355
Email: ugradinq@asu.edu · Website: http://www.asu.edu

From the College

"Arizona State University offers a combination of academic excellence, entrepreneurial energy and broad access as a single, unified institution comprising four distinctive campuses impacting the economic, social, cultural and environmental health of the communities it serves. Its research is inspired by real world application blurring the boundaries that traditionally separate academic disciplines. ASU serves more than 67,000 students in metropolitan Phoenix, Arizona, the nation's fifth largest city. ASU champions intellectual and cultural diversity, and welcomes students from all 50 states and more than 100 nations across the globe."

Campus Setting

Arizona State University is a public, comprehensive university. Founded as a Normal school in 1885, it gained university status in 1958. Its 1,548-acre campus is near downtown Tempe, close to the center of metropolitan Phoenix. A four-year public institution, Arizona State University has an enrollment of 67,082 students. In addition to a large, well-stocked library, the campus facilities include: art, anthropology, geology, history and sports museums · early childhood development lab · herbarium · robotics lab · semiconductor clean room · high-resolution electron microscope facility · solar research facilities · biodesign institute · institute of sustainability · arboretum. Housing options: co-ed dorms · sorority housing · fraternity housing · single-student apartments · married-student apartments. Recreation and sports facilities include: aquatic area · athletic fields · centers.

Student Life and Activities

Most students (86 percent) live off campus, which does impact the on-campus social scene. Nevertheless, like any college, students find time to create their own recreational outlets. Popular gathering spots on- and off-campus include the Memorial Union, Cady Mall, Student Recreation Center and Old Main Lawn. Popular campus events include Homecoming, Family Weekend and World Festival. Arizona State University has 654 official student organizations. There are many religious, minority and international student groups as well as music, theatre, political, service and special-interest groups. For those interested in sports, there are intramural teams such as: badminton · basketball · bowling · dodgeball · flag football · floor hockey · golf · racquetball · sand volleyball · soccer · softball · table tennis · tennis · ultimate Frisbee · wiffle ball · wrestling. Arizona State University is a member of the Member of Pacific-10 Conference (Division I, Football I-A).

Academics and Learning Environment

For the B student, the learning environment of a college is just as important as the quality of its academic program. Arizona State University has 2,520 full-time and 382 part-time faculty members, offering a student-to-faculty ratio of 21:1. The most common course size is 10 to 19 students. Arizona State University offers 297 majors with the most popular being interdisciplinary studies, communication and psychology. The school has a general core requirement. Cooperative education is available. All first-year students must maintain a 1.6 GPA or higher to avoid academic probation, and a minimum overall GPA of 2.0 is required to graduate. Other special academic programs that would appeal to a B student: pass/fail grading option · independent study · double majors · dual degrees · accelerated study · honors program · internships · distance learning certificate programs.

B Student Support and Success

Like other colleges, ASU offers First Year Experience for freshmen. According to the college, this program is designed to "provide a strong foundation for all first-year students and students in transition that will foster their academic and personal success. We will achieve this mission by providing academic support services, opportunities for the exchange of ideas, workshops, generating and supporting research and scholarship, hosting visiting scholars and practitioners, faculty interaction within living and learning communities, administering a website and student involvement opportunities with the university community."

The Learning Resource Center offers tutoring to help students develop study skills and strategies. This nationally certified program offers tutoring in more than 100 courses, either in a group or individual settings. Peer coaching teaches time management, study habits and test-taking skills. The program also includes software training and Academic Skills Workshops.

Arizona State University provides a variety of support programs including dedicated guidance for: academic · career · personal · psychological · minority students · military · veterans · non-traditional students · family planning · religious. Annually, 80 percent of freshmen students return for their sophomore year.

Support for Students with Learning Disabilities

Students with learning disabilities may take advantage of specific support programs offered by Arizona State University. If necessary, the college will grant additional time to students with learning disabilities to complete their degree. Also, a lightened course load may be granted to LD students. Students with learning disabilities will find the following programs at Arizona State University extremely useful: tutors · testing accommodations · extended time for tests · take-home exam · oral tests · readers · note-taking services · reading machines · early syllabus · waiver of math degree requirement. Individual or small group tutorials are also available in: time management · organizational skills · learning strategies · study skills.

How to Get Admitted

For admissions decisions, non-academic factors considered:. A high school diploma is required, although a GED is also accepted for admissions consideration. SAT or ACT test scores are required of all applicants. *According to the admissions office:* Minimum combined SAT Reasoning score of 1040 (composite ACT score of 22), rank in top quarter of secondary school class, or minimum 3.0 GPA recommended of in-state applicants; minimum combined SAT Reasoning score of 1110 (composite ACT score of 24), rank in top quarter of secondary school class, or minimum 3.0 GPA recommended of out-of-state applicants.

How to Pay for College

To apply for financial aid, students should submit the following: Free Application for Federal Student Aid (FAFSA). Arizona State University participates in the Federal Work Study program. *Need-based*

ARIZONA STATE UNIVERSITY

Highlights

Arizona State University
Phoenix (Pop. 1,400,000)
Location: Major city
Website: http://www.asu.edu

Students
Total enrollment: 67,082
Undergrads: 25,799
Freshmen: 9,707
Part-time students: 19%
From out-of-state: 29%
Male/Female: 48%/52%
Live on-campus: 14%
In fraternities: 5%
In sororities: 6%
Off-campus employment rating: Excellent
Caucasian: 65%
African American: 5%
Hispanic: 15%
Asian or Pacific Islander: 6%
Native American: 2%
International: 2%

Academics
Student/faculty ratio: 21:1
Class size 9 or fewer: 9%
Class size 10-29: 57%
Class size 30-49: 20%
Class size 50-99: 9%
Class size 100 or more: 4%
Returning freshmen: 80%
Six-year graduation rate: 56%

Most Popular Fields of Study
Business, Finance, Sales and Marketing
Visual and Performing Arts
Social Sciences, History, Economics, Political Science
Protective Services, Criminal Justice and Public Administration
Family and Consumer Sciences, Nutrition and Home Economics
Computer and Information Sciences
Communications, Journalism, Advertising and Comm. Technologies
Philosophy, Religion and Theology
English and Literature

ARIZONA STATE UNIVERSITY

Admissions

Applicants: 27,089
Accepted: 24,473
Acceptance rate: 90.3%
Average GPA: 3.4
ACT range: 20-26
SAT Math range: 480-610
SAT Reading range: 470-600
SAT Writing range: Not reported
Top 10% of class: 31%
Top 25% of class: 58%
Top 50% of class: 85%

Deadlines

Early Action: No
Early Decision: No
Regular Action: Rolling admissions
Common Application: Not accepted

Financial Aid

In-state tuition: $5,997
Out-of-state tuition: $18,592
Room: $5,610
Board: $3,600
Books: $1,270
Freshmen receiving need-based aid: 40%
Undergrads receiving need-based aid: 41%
Avg. % of need met by financial aid: 60%
Avg. aid package (freshmen): $10,395
Avg. aid package (undergrads): $10,062
Freshmen receiving merit-based aid: 24%
Undergrads receiving merit-based aid: 16%
Avg. student debt upon graduation: $17,732

Prominent Alumni

Phil Mickelson, professional golfer; Kate Spade, designer/owner, Kate Spade LLC; Al Michaels, sports commentator, NBC.

School Spirit

Mascot: Sparky
Colors: Maroon and gold
Song: *Fight Devils*

aid programs include: scholarships and grants · general need-based awards · Federal Pell grants · state scholarships and grants · college-based scholarships and grants · private scholarships and grants · Federal Nursing scholarships. *Non-Need-based aid programs include:* scholarships and grants · state scholarships and grants · creative arts and performance awards · special achievements and activities awards · special characteristics awards · athletic scholarships · ROTC scholarships · tribal scholarships.

AUBURN UNIVERSITY

108 Mary Martin Hall, Auburn, AL 36849
Admissions: 800-282-8769 · Financial Aid: 334-844-4634
Email: admissions@auburn.edu · Website: http://www.auburn.edu

From the College

"Auburn University has provided instruction, research and outreach for more than 150 years, and is among a distinctive group of universities designated as Land, Sea, and Space Grant institutions. AU has more than 250,000 graduates and provides 130 degree programs to more than 24,000 graduate and undergraduate students. Graduates include six NASA astronauts, the head of the Kennedy Space Center, the nation's first and only class of undergraduate wireless engineers, dozens of CEOs, world-famous architects and several authors and journalists. AU emphasizes international education, is at the forefront of engineering, transportation technology and veterinary medicine, achieves global impact through modern agricultural, extension and forestry/wildlife programs, and fulfills critical research and national shortages through pharmaceutical, sciences, mathematics, education, nursing and human sciences offerings."

Campus Setting

Auburn is a public, multipurpose, land-grant university. It was founded as a private, liberal arts institution in 1856, came under state control in 1872, and began admitting women in 1892. Its 1,871-acre campus is located in Auburn. A four-year public institution, Auburn University has an enrollment of 24,530 students. Although not originally co-educational college, Auburn University has been co-ed since 1892. In addition to a large, well-stocked library, the campus facilities include: art museum · herbarium · research center · research institute · flight simulators · animal clinics · special centers · laboratories. Auburn University provides on-campus housing that can accommodate 4,048 students. Housing options: co-ed dorms · women's dorms · fraternity housing · single-student apartments · special housing for disabled students. Recreation and sports facilities include: aquatic center · coliseum · fitness and weight rooms · golf course · track · racquetball and tennis courts.

Student Life and Activities

Most students (87 percent) live off campus, which does impact the on-campus social scene. Nevertheless, like any college, students find time to create their own recreational outlets. Popular campus events include A-Day, Freshman Convocation, Greek Recruitment, Greek Sing, Splash Into Spring, University Program Council-sponsored entertainment, Holiday Tree Lighting, Tiger Nights, Burn the (Georgia) Bulldogs, Homecoming Week, student government elections, outdoor and international movies, Rolling Toomer's Corner, athletics events, Step Shows & Tiger-Stomp, Beat Bama Parade, Beat Bama Food Drive, and Black History Month. Auburn University has 300 official student organizations. The most popular are: G.A.N.G. Student Ministries · Gay Straight Alliance · Historic Preservation Guild · Agriculture Ambassadors · American Institute of Chemical Engineers · Association of Certified Fraud Examiners · Mock Trial Competition Team · Public Relations Council of Alabama. For those interested in sports, there are intramural teams such as: badminton · cycling · lacrosse · rowing · rugby · sailing · soccer · table tennis · tennis · volleyball · water polo · water skiing · wrestling. Auburn University is a member of the Southeastern Conference (Division I, Football I-A).

AUBURN UNIVERSITY

Auburn University
Auburn/Opelika, AL (Pop. 71,000)
Location: Large town
Website: http://www.auburn.edu

Students
Total enrollment: 24,530
Undergrads: 10,288
Freshmen: 3,984
Part-time students: 8%
From out-of-state: 43%
Male/Female: 51%/49%
Live on-campus: 13%
In fraternities: 22%
In sororities: 31%
Off-campus employment rating: Excellent
Caucasian: 86%
African American: 8%
Hispanic: 2%
Asian or Pacific Islander: 2%
Native American: 1%
International: 1%

Academics
Student/faculty ratio: 18:1
Class size 9 or fewer: 37%
Class size 10-29: 63%
Class size 30-49: 15%
Class size 50-99: 6%
Class size 100 or more: 5%
Returning freshmen: 87%
Six-year graduation rate: 64%

Most Popular Fields of Study
Business, Finance, Sales and Marketing
Biological and Life Sciences
Agriculture, Aquaculture and Animal Sciences
Visual and Performing Arts
Social Sciences, History, Economics, Political Science
Protective Services, Criminal Justice and Public Administration
Family and Consumer Sciences, Nutrition and Home Economics
Computer and Information Sciences
Communications, Journalism, Advertising and Comm. Technologies
Philosophy, Religion and Theology

98

Academics and Learning Environment

For the B student, the learning environment of a college is just as important as the quality of its academic program. Auburn University has 1,176 full-time and 149 part-time faculty members, offering a student-to-faculty ratio of 18:1. Auburn University offers 271 majors with the most popular being finance, marketing and biomedical sciences and least popular being German, international trade-German, botany, medical technology and religious studies. The school has a general core requirement. Cooperative education is available. All first-year students must maintain a 1.50 GPA or higher to avoid academic probation, and a minimum overall GPA of 2.0 is required to graduate. Other special academic programs that would appeal to a B student: independent study · double majors · dual degrees · accelerated study · honors program · Phi Beta Kappa · internships · distance learning certificate programs.

B Student Support and Success

Auburn's network of academic advisors is by department or major. Advisors assist students with selecting classes and career planning, and they also give general advice. Some department heads provide information about their departments to prospective applicants as well. Learning Communities bring together first-year students in the same major to take certain required classes as a group. This enables students to easily form study groups and to navigate classes cooperatively. Departments also offer help that is basic to a student's field of study. For example, the Auburn Office of Engineering Student Services provides tutoring for freshmen and transfer engineering students who need assistance in entry-level math, chemistry and physics classes. The tutoring is done by volunteer upperclassmen in group or one-on-one sessions.

Auburn University provides a variety of support programs including dedicated guidance for: academic · career · personal · psychological · minority students · military · veterans · non-traditional students · family planning. Additional counseling services include: sexual assault. The average freshman year GPA is 2.6, and 87 percent of freshmen students return for their sophomore year. Among students who enter the work force, approximately 80 percent enter a field related to their major within six months of graduation. Companies that most frequently hire graduates from Auburn University include: Alabama Power · AmSouth Bank · Baptist Health System · Cargill Steel Corp.· Chevron · Colonial Bank · DMJM Harris · Ernst & Young · Exxon Mobil · Georgia Pacific · Honeywell · IBM · Kimley-Horn & Associates · KMPG · Lockheed Martin · Lennar Homes · Merrill Lynch · Michelin North America · Milliken & Co. · Northrop Grumman · Pepsico · PricewaterhouseCooper · Proctor & Gamble · Regions Bank · Sony · Southern Co. · Weyerhaeuser.

Support for Students with Learning Disabilities

Students with learning disabilities may take advantage of specific support programs offered by Auburn University. If necessary, the college will grant additional time to students with learning disabilities to complete their degree. Also, a lightened course load may be granted to LD students. According to the school, The Program for Students with Disabilities offers a variety of Assistive Technology for students with learning disabilities. Text-to-speech software and electronic text are available for students with reading disabilities. Kurweil 3000, a scanning and reading software, and Dragon Naturally Speaking, a speech-to-text software, are available for student use in two locations on campus. Individual training is offered for students that may benefit from the use of assistive technology. Students with learning disabilities will find the following programs at Auburn University extremely useful: tutors · learning center · testing accommodations · extended time for tests · oral tests · readers · typist/scribe · note-taking services · reading machines · early syllabus · diagnostic testing service · priority registration · waiver of math degree requirement. Individual or small group tutorials are also available in: time management · organizational skills · learning strategies · specific subject areas · writing labs · math labs · study skills. An advisor/advocate from the Program for Students with Disabilities is available to students.

How to Get Admitted

For admissions decisions, non-academic factors considered: extracurricular activities · special talents, interests, abilities · character/personal qualities · volunteer work · work experience · geographical location · alumni relationship. A high school diploma is required, although a GED is also accepted for admissions consideration. SAT or ACT test scores are required of all applicants. SAT Subject Test scores are recommended but not required. *According to the admissions office:* Math units must include algebra I, algebra II, and one unit of analysis, calculus, geometry or trigonometry. Science units must include biology and a physical science. Minimum composite ACT score of 18 and minimum 2.5 GPA required of in-state applicants; minimum composite ACT score of 22 and minimum 2.5 GPA required of out-of-state applicants. *Academic units recommended:* 4 English, 3 Math, 3 Science, 4 Social Studies, 1 Foreign Language.

How to Pay for College

To apply for financial aid, students should submit the following: Free Application for Federal Student Aid (FAFSA). Auburn University participates in the Federal Work Study program. *Need-based aid programs include:* scholarships and grants · general need-based awards · Federal Pell grants · state scholarships and grants · college-based scholarships and grants · private scholarships and grants. *Non-Need-based aid programs include:* scholarships and grants · general need-based awards · state scholarships and grants · athletic scholarships · ROTC scholarships.

AUBURN UNIVERSITY

Highlights

Admissions
Applicants: 17,068
Accepted: 12,085
Acceptance rate: 70.8%
Average GPA: 3.7
ACT range: 23-28
SAT Math range: 550-650
SAT Reading range: 520-620
SAT Writing range: 520-620
Top 10% of class: 31%
Top 25% of class: 60%
Top 50% of class: 91%

Deadlines
Early Action: October 1
Early Decision: No
Regular Action: February 1 (priority)
Common Application: Not accepted

Financial Aid
In-state tuition: $5,880
Out-of-state tuition: $17,640
Room: $3,772
Board: $4,488
Books: $1,100
Freshmen receiving need-based aid: 28%
Undergrads receiving need-based aid: 29%
Avg. % of need met by financial aid: 57%
Avg. aid package (freshmen): $8,648
Avg. aid package (undergrads): $8,565
Freshmen receiving merit-based aid: 17%
Undergrads receiving merit-based aid: 10%
Avg. student debt upon graduation: $34,398

Prominent Alumni
Kathy Thornton, astronaut; Millard Fuller, founder/president, Habitat for Humanity - International; Don Logan, chairman of board, Time Warner Cable.

School Spirit
Mascot: Tigers
Colors: Burnt orange and navy blue
Song: *War Eagle*

AUGSBURG COLLEGE

2211 Riverside Avenue S, Minneapolis, MN 55454
Admissions: 800-788-5678 · Financial Aid: 800-788-5678
Email: admissions@augsburg.edu · Website: http://www.augsburg.edu

From the College

"As the Evangelical Lutheran Church in America's (ELCA) most diverse and only urban institution, Augsburg strives to educate both traditional and non-traditional students, offering undergraduate degrees in over 50 major areas of study. The college also grants six graduate degrees, among them the Master of Science in Physician Assistant Studies, the state's only Physician Assistant training program. Augsburg's 3,700 students come from diverse religious, cultural and ethnic backgrounds. The college also is a nationally recognized leader in providing services to students with physical and learning disabilities. This on-campus diversity is enhanced by Augsburg's location at the crossroads of the Twin Cities' most diverse neighborhoods. The college's location also provides access for Augsburg's students to participate in community service and internship experiences."

Campus Setting

Augsburg, founded in 1869, is a church-affiliated, liberal arts college. Its 23-acre campus is located one mile from downtown Minneapolis. A four-year private institution, Augsburg College has an enrollment of 3,898 students. Although not originally co-educational college, Augsburg College has been co-ed since 1874. In addition to a large, well-stocked library, the campus facilities include: art gallery · auditorium · chapel. Augsburg College provides on-campus housing with 525 units that can accommodate 950 students. Housing options: co-ed dorms · single-student apartments · special housing for disabled students. Recreation and sports facilities include: athletic · baseball · football · soccer and softball fields · basketball and volleyball courts · cross-country park · ice arena · stadium.

Student Life and Activities

Most students (60 percent) live off campus, which does impact the on-campus social scene. Nevertheless, like any college, students find time to create their own recreational outlets. Popular events include: Daily Chapel, Annual Homecoming Weekend, Velkommen Jule and Campus Kitchens. Augsburg College has 40 official student organizations. The most popular are: Association for Computing Machinery · Augsburg Chemistry Society · Augsburg Art Club · Augsburg Business Organization · Goliard Society of Medievalists · International Student Organization · Queer and Straight in Unity · Augsburg College Democrats · Augsburg College Republicans. For those interested in sports, there are intramural teams such as: basketball · broomball · fantasy football · flag football · hockey/skating · kickball · pickleball · powderpuff football · soccer · softball · ultimate Frisbee · volleyball. Augsburg College is a member of the Minnesota Intercollegiate Athletic Conference (Division III).

Academics and Learning Environment

For the B student, the learning environment of a college is just as important as the quality of its academic program. Augsburg College has 185 full-time and 214 part-time faculty members, offering a student-to-faculty ratio of 14:1. The most common course size is 10 to 19 students. Augsburg College offers 51 majors with the most popular being business administration, elementary education and communications and least popular being American Indian studies, physics and art history. The school has a general core requirement as well as a religion requirement Cooperative education is not offered. All first-year students must maintain a 2.0 GPA or higher to avoid academic probation, and a minimum overall GPA of 2.0 is required to graduate. Other special academic programs that would appeal to a B student: self-designed majors · pass/fail grading option · independent study · double majors · dual degrees · accelerated study · honors program · Phi Beta Kappa · internships · weekend college.

B Student Support and Success

Support for academic success is provided through tutoring, academic skills coaching, supplemental instruction and the math, public speaking and writing labs. Augsburg's TRiO/Student Support Services program helps students who are 1) low-income, 2) first-generation enrollees or 3) disabled (learning or physical) to achieve their bachelor's degrees.

StepUp provides ongoing support to students in chemical recovery who are willing and able to progress toward an academic degree while remaining clean and sober. Students live together in separate, chemical-free housing.

The Center for Learning and Adaptive Student Services (CLASS) assists academically qualified students with learning, attention, psychiatric or other cognitive disabilities reach their individual potential through services and accommodations, while the Access Center supports students with documented physical disabilities.

Augsburg College provides a variety of support programs including dedicated guidance for: academic · career · personal · psychological · minority students · religious. The average freshman year GPA is 2.8, and 80 percent of freshmen students return for their sophomore year. Among students who enter the work force, approximately 85 percent enter a field related to their major within six months of graduation. Companies that most frequently hire graduates from Augsburg College include: Target Corp. · Cargill · KPMG International · Best Buy Corp · Anoka Hennepin School District · Hennepin County Social Services · Wells Fargo Bank.

Support for Students with Learning Disabilities

Students with learning disabilities may take advantage of specific support programs. If necessary, the college will grant additional time to students with learning disabilities to complete their degree. According to the school, the Center for Learning and Adaptive Student Services (CLASS) provides accommodations and academic support to students with any of a broad range of specific cognitive and psychological disabilities, including dyslexia, ADHD and Asperger syndrome. CLASS also serves students with psychiatric disabilities such as anxiety disorder, depression and PTSD, and those with acquired or developmental neurological conditions in which the primary impact is on cognitive function. Students with learning disabilities will find the following programs extremely useful: tutors · learning center · testing accommodations · extended time for tests · take-home exam · oral tests · readers · note-taking services · reading machines · tape recorders · waiver of math degree requirement. Individual or small group tutorials are also available in: time management · organizational skills · learning strategies · writing labs · math labs · study skills. An advisor/advocate from the Center for Learning and Adaptive Student Services is available.

AUGSBURG COLLEGE

Highlights

Augsburg College
Minneapolis (Pop. 380,000)
Location: Major city
Website: http://www.augsburg.edu

Students
Total enrollment: 3,898
Undergrads: 1,353
Freshmen: 440
Part-time students: 18%
From out-of-state: 14%
Male/Female: 44%/56%
Live on-campus: 40%
Off-campus employment rating: Excellent
Caucasian: 74%
African American: 6%
Hispanic: 2%
Asian or Pacific Islander: 4%
Native American: 1%
International: 1%

Academics
Student/faculty ratio: 14:1
Class size 9 or fewer: 33%
Class size 10-29: 64%
Class size 30-49: 2%
Class size 50-99: -
Class size 100 or more: 5%
Returning freshmen: 80%
Six-year graduation rate: 58%

Most Popular Fields of Study
Business, Finance, Sales and Marketing
Protective Services, Criminal Justice and Public Administration
Visual and Performing Arts
English and Literature
Philosophy, Religion and Theology
Computer and Information Sciences
Mathematics
Physical Sciences, Chemistry, Physics and Astronomy
Health Professions, Medicine and Related Sciences
Foreign Languages, Literature and Linguistics

College Profiles

AUGSBURG COLLEGE

Admissions
Applicants: 1,938
Accepted: 1,082
Acceptance rate: 55.8%
Average GPA: 3.2
ACT range: 20-25
SAT Math range: 500-635
SAT Reading range: 510-640
SAT Writing range: Not reported
Top 10% of class: 12%
Top 25% of class: 32%
Top 50% of class: 61%

Deadlines
Early Action: No
Early Decision: No
Regular Action: Rolling admissions
Common Application: Accepted

Financial Aid
In-state tuition: $27,020
Out-of-state tuition: $27,020
Room: $3,768
Board: $3,740
Books: $1,000
Freshmen receiving need-based aid: 84%
Undergrads receiving need-based aid: 80%
Avg. % of need met by financial aid: 55%
Avg. aid package (freshmen): $7,736
Avg. aid package (undergrads): $9,164
Freshmen receiving merit-based aid: 13%
Undergrads receiving merit-based aid: 9%
Avg. student debt upon graduation: $24,096

Prominent Alumni
Lute Olson, NCAA national champion basketball coach University of Arizona; Devean George, professional basketball player Dallas Mavericks

School Spirit
Mascot: Auggies
Colors: Maroon and Gray
Song: *Auggie War Song*

How to Get Admitted

For admissions decisions, non-academic factors considered: interview · extracurricular activities · special talents, interests, abilities · character/personal qualities · volunteer work · work experience · state of residency · minority affiliation · alumni relationship. A high school diploma is required, although a GED is also accepted for admissions consideration. SAT or ACT test scores are required of all applicants. SAT Subject Test scores are considered, if submitted, but are not required. *According to the admissions office:* Minimum composite ACT score of 22, rank in top half of secondary school class, and minimum 2.5 GPA recommended.

Insight

"At Augsburg, we realize that grades are only one measure of success," says Bethany Bierman, assistant director of the Office of Undergraduate Admissions. She notes that one of the college's graduates received a D in high school chemistry and went on to receive a Nobel Prize in chemistry! The college is an intentionally diverse community, and with that comes students from a range of academic backgrounds. The admissions officers do a thorough review of an application, but grades are not the only basis on which students are accepted. Applicants can demonstrate that they are qualified for Augsburg by the extracurricular activities in which they are involved, including work positions or volunteer work. The difficulty of courses a student has selected in high school is also considered. Additionally, letters of recommendation that focus on the character of the student tell the admissions officers a great deal. "Ultimately, Augsburg seeks to accept students who want to use their gifts to make a difference in the world," she says. Bierman states that the school's overall philosophy is that it is "more concerned with the quality and character of the alumni we produce than the incoming GPA of our students. As long as we know that students are working to their full potential, taking their academic work seriously and are seeking to make a difference in their community, we are proud of them, regardless of grades that are B's or C's."

How to Pay for College

To apply for financial aid, students should submit the following: Free Application for Federal Student Aid (FAFSA). Augsburg College participates in the Federal Work Study program. *Need-based aid programs include:* scholarships and grants · general need-based awards · Federal Pell grants · state scholarships and grants · college-based scholarships and grants · private scholarships and grants. *Non-Need-based aid programs include:* scholarships and grants · state scholarships and grants · special achievements and activities awards.

AUGUSTA STATE UNIVERSITY

2500 Walton Way, Augusta, GA 30904-2200
Admissions: 800-341-4373 · Financial Aid: 706-737-1431
Email: admissions@aug.edu · Website: http://www.aug.edu

From the College

"ASU is a public metropolitan university with the atmosphere of a small liberal arts college. A supportive staff and a diverse student body. Or the personal one-on-one attention given by faculty. Or maybe it's the friendliness of a supportive staff who care about student success. Perhaps it's the beauty of a historic campus with new technology-rich academic buildings. It's all of these and the more than 200 faculty, 300 dedicated staff, and 6,300 diverse students that make Augusta State University a truly unique place to be."

Campus Setting

Augusta is a public, comprehensive university. Founded as a post-graduate academy in 1783, it became a junior college in 1925, was incorporated into the state university system in 1958 and began granting four-year degrees in 1967. Its 72-acre campus is located on a former plantation in Augusta. A four-year public institution, Augusta State University has an enrollment of 6,689 students. In addition to a large, well-stocked library, the campus facilities include: history museum · golf course. Augusta State University provides on-campus housing with 162 units that can accommodate 508 students. Housing options: single-student apartments.

Student Life and Activities

Most students (93 percent) live off campus, which does impact the on-campus social scene. Nevertheless, like any college, students find time to create their own recreational outlets. Popular campus event includes Homecoming. Augusta State University has 66 official student organizations. The most popular are: Choir · concert and pep bands · jazz ensemble · drama guild · team managers. Augusta State University is a member of the Peach Bell Conference (Division II).

Academics and Learning Environment

For the B student, the learning environment of a college is just as important as the quality of its academic program. Augusta State University has 236 full-time and 166 part-time faculty members, offering a student-to-faculty ratio of 18:1. The most common course size is 20 to 29 students. Augusta State University offers 49 majors with the most popular being biology, psychology and early childhood education and least popular being Spanish, art and music performance. The school has a general core requirement. Cooperative education is available. All first-year students must maintain a 1.3 GPA or higher to avoid academic probation. Other special academic programs that would appeal to a B student: independent study · double majors · honors program · Phi Beta Kappa · internships · distance learning certificate programs.

AUGUSTA STATE UNIVERSITY

Admissions
Applicants: 2,418
Accepted: 1,383
Acceptance rate: 57.2%
Average GPA: 2.9
ACT range: Not reported
SAT Math range: 430-540
SAT Reading range: 440-540
SAT Writing range: Not reported

Deadlines
Early Action: No
Early Decision: No
Regular Action: July 1 (priority)
Common Application: Not accepted

Financial Aid
In-state tuition: $3,098
Out-of-state tuition: $12,390
Room: -
Board: -
Books: -
Freshmen receiving need-based aid: 45%
Undergrads receiving need-based aid: 51%
Avg. % of need met by financial aid: 70%
Avg. aid package (freshmen): $3,289
Avg. aid package (undergrads): $3,522
Freshmen receiving merit-based aid: 3%
Undergrads receiving merit-based aid: 12%
Avg. student debt upon graduation: $5,914

School Spirit
Mascot: Jaguars

B Student Support and Success

Augusta offers an extensive First Year Experience to help new students transition to college life. Its goal is "to increase retention and help students successfully progress toward graduation". Participants take classes with other first year students, live together at University Village, have a close support group with mentors, get together for study sessions, attend campus social and athletic events, be a part of a social support system to help students meet others and share experiences with others.

Augusta State University provides a variety of support programs including dedicated guidance for: academic · career · personal · minority students · military · veterans. Recognizing that some students may need extra preparation, Augusta State University offers remedial and refresher courses in: reading · writing · math · study skills. Annually, 69 percent of freshmen students return for their sophomore year.

Support for Students with Learning Disabilities

Students with learning disabilities may take advantage of specific support programs offered by Augusta State University. If necessary, the college will grant additional time to students with learning disabilities to complete their degree. Also, a lightened course load may be granted to LD students. Students with learning disabilities will find the following programs at Augusta State University extremely useful: remedial math · remedial English · remedial reading · learning center · testing accommodations · extended time for tests · take-home exam · oral tests · readers · typist/scribe · note-taking services · reading machines · tape recorders · diagnostic testing service · priority registration. Individual or small group tutorials are also available in: time management · organizational skills · learning strategies · writing labs · math labs · study skills. An advisor/advocate from the Testing and Disability Service is available to students.

How to Get Admitted

For admissions decisions, non-academic factors considered: state of residency. A high school diploma is required, although a GED is also accepted for admissions consideration. SAT or ACT test scores are required of all applicants. SAT Subject Test scores are recommended but not required. *According to the admissions office:* Admission based on eligibility index of standardized test scores and GPA; minimum eligibility index of 1830 required.

How to Pay for College

To apply for financial aid, students should submit the following: Free Application for Federal Student Aid (FAFSA) · institution's own financial aid forms. Augusta State University participates in the Federal Work Study program. *Need-based aid programs include:* scholarships and grants · general need-based awards · Federal Pell grants · state scholarships and grants · college-based scholarships and grants · private scholarships and grants. *Non-Need-based aid programs include:* scholarships and grants · general need-based awards · state scholarships and grants · creative arts and performance awards · special achievements and activities awards · special characteristics awards · athletic scholarships · ROTC scholarships.

BELLARMINE UNIVERSITY

2001 Newburg Road, Louisville, KY 40205
Admissions: 800-274-4723 · Financial Aid: 800-274-4723
Email: admissions@bellarmine.edu · Website: http://www.bellarmine.edu

From the College

"Bellarmine University is an independent Catholic university educating students of many faiths, ages, nations and cultures ... through undergraduate and graduate programs in the liberal arts and professional studies.

"Here we seek to foster a thoughtful, informed consideration of serious ideas, values and issues, time-honored and contemporary, across a broad range of compelling concerns that are regional, national and international. Thus we strive to be worthy of our foundational motto: In Veritatis Amore, In the Love of Truth.

"Our lush 137-acre campus currently comprises more than 30 buildings including the W.L. Lyons Brown Library, the Norton Health Science Center and halls that are home to the nursing, education, and the arts and sciences. Bellarmine has six residence halls (with a seventh currently under construction), a chapel, campus center and university quadrangle. Our recreational facilities include indoor and outdoor tennis courts; fitness center; golf course and athletic fields including a state-of-the-art Frazier Stadium that's home to lacrosse, soccer, field hockey and track and field. Our campus on three hills and our award-winning architecture evoke the beautiful Italian hill towns of Tuscany, birthplace of our patron."

Campus Setting

Bellarmine opened in 1950, under the sponsorship of the Roman Catholic Archdiocese of Louisville and with the special assistance of the Conventual Franciscan Fathers. The new school became one of the first in the Commonwealth of Kentucky open to all races. In 1968, Bellarmine merged with Ursuline College, a Catholic college for women established by the Ursuline Sisters. It was at the time of merger that the traditional student body became co-educational and Bellarmine became independent with a self-perpetuating governing board. In 2000, the Board of Trustees voted to change the name of the institution from Bellarmine College to Bellarmine University to reflect its true status as a Masters I university. Colleges/Schools include Bellarmine College of Arts and Sciences, the Donna and Allan Lansing School of Nursing and Health Sciences, the W. Fielding Rubel School of Business, the Annsley Frazier Thornton School of Education, and the School of Continuing and Professional School. BU is located on a 135-acre campus. A four-year private institution, Bellarmine University has an enrollment of 3,020 students. Bellarmine University has been co-ed since 1968. The school is also affiliated with the Roman Catholic Church. Bellarmine University provides on-campus housing with 6 units that can accommodate 716 students. Housing options: co-ed dorms · women's dorms · men's dorms · special housing for disabled students. Recreation and sports facilities include: baseball and softball fields · golf course · gymnasium · recreation and fitness center · soccer stadium · tennis courts · track.

Student Life and Activities

Most students (61 percent) live off campus, which does impact the on-campus social scene. Nevertheless, like any college, students find time to create their own recreational outlets. Popular gathering spots include Campus Center, SAC, and Bardstown Road. Popular campus events include Hillside, Relay for Life, Family Weekend, Ball on the Bell, Homecoming, Pioneer Dance, Senior Week and Flow Hip-Hop Dance Show. Bellarmine University has 70 official student organizations. The most popular are:

BELLARMINE UNIVERSITY

Bellarmine University

Louisville, KY (Pop. 1,000,000)
Location: Major city
Website: http://www.bellarmine.edu

Students

Total enrollment: 3,020
Undergrads: 832
Freshmen: 572
Part-time students: 16%
From out-of-state: 41%
Male/Female: 35%/65%
Live on-campus: 39%
In fraternities: 1%
In sororities: 1%
Off-campus employment rating: Excellent
Caucasian: 82%
African American: 3%
Hispanic: 2%
Asian or Pacific Islander: 3%
Native American: 0%
International: 2%

Academics

Student/faculty ratio: 13:1
Class size 9 or fewer: 16%
Class size 10-29: 70%
Class size 30-49: 13%
Class size 50-99: 1%
Class size 100 or more: 5%
Returning freshmen: 80%
Six-year graduation rate: 63%

Most Popular Fields of Study

Business, Finance, Sales and Marketing
Protective Services, Criminal Justice and
    Public Administration
Psychology
English and Literature
Philosophy, Religion and Theology
Mathematics
Engineering and Engineering Technologies
Interdisciplinary Studies
Health Professions, Medicine and Related
    Sciences
Liberal Arts, Humanities and General
    Studies

Jazz club · student theatre · Student Ambassadors · Students for Social Justice · The Concord · The Lance · Bellarmine Students for Life · University Radio Association · Dance Team · Colleges Against Cancer · Students for Organ Donation · education club · Friendly English Society · philosophy club. For those interested in sports, there are intramural teams such as: basketball · flag football · golf · soccer · tennis · volleyball. Bellarmine University is a member of the Great Western Lacrosse League (Division I), Great Lakes Valley Conference (Division II).

Academics and Learning Environment

For the B student, the learning environment of a college is just as important as the quality of its academic program. Bellarmine University has 141 full-time and 147 part-time faculty members, offering a student-to-faculty ratio of 13:1. The most common course size is 10 to 19 students. Bellarmine University offers 39 majors with the most popular being nursing, psychology and business administration and least popular being theology, philosophy and sociology. The school has a general core requirement as well as a religion requirement Cooperative education is not offered. All first-year students must maintain a 2.0 GPA or higher to avoid academic probation. Other special academic programs that would appeal to a B student: self-designed majors · independent study · double majors · dual degrees · accelerated study · honors program · internships · certificate programs.

B Student Support and Success

This college's Academic Resource Center is the place for help with your classes and college career. There are tutors available for the 100- and 200-level classes, both in individual and group study sessions. The staff at ARC will help analyze your essays to improve grammar, style and formatting.

Bellarmine also offers a one-hour credit course called Freshman Focus. It helps freshmen make the transition to college. This program includes reading, writing, discussion and out-of-class activities. The focus of the course is increasing a student's self-awareness and sense of purpose when it comes to his/her education and making important decisions about academic and social lives. Students are graded (A to F) in this class.

Bellarmine University provides a variety of support programs including dedicated guidance for: academic · career · personal · psychological · religious. The average freshman year GPA is 2.9, and 80 percent of freshmen students return for their sophomore year. What do students do after college? While many enter the work force, approximately 22 percent pursue a graduate degree immediately after graduation, and another 23 percent enter graduate school within two years. Among students who enter the work force, approximately 80 percent enter a field related to their major within six months of graduation. Companies that most frequently hire graduates from Bellarmine University include: Abercrombie and Fitch · AIG · Americorps · Baptist East Hospital · Bellarmine University · Deloitte & Touche · Department of the Navy · Ernst and Young · Evanston Hospital · Frazier Arms Museum · GE Industrial · Girl Scouts of Kentuckiana · Hardin Memorial Hospital · Heaven Hills Distillery · Kessler Co. · Kosair Hospital · Jefferson County

Public Schools · Jewish Hospital · Mayor of Louisville · Norton Hospital · Old Towne Mortgage · Rescare · Saint Xavier High School · Sherman Williams · Strothman and Co. · United Parcel Service · U.S. Bank · Wells Fargo · William M. Mercer Co..

Support for Students with Learning Disabilities

Students with learning disabilities may take advantage of specific support programs offered by Bellarmine University. According to the school, LD advisor/advocate can meet with faculty on an individual basis. Students with learning disabilities will find the following programs at Bellarmine University extremely useful: tutors · learning center · untimed tests · extended time for tests · take-home exam · oral tests · readers · note-taking services · reading machines · tape recorders · texts on tape · videotaped classes · early syllabus. Individual or small group tutorials are also available in: time management · organizational skills · learning strategies · specific subject areas · writing labs · math labs · study skills. An advisor/advocate from the Counseling Center is available to students.

How to Get Admitted

For admissions decisions, non-academic factors considered: interview · extracurricular activities · special talents, interests, abilities · character/personal qualities · volunteer work · work experience · geographical location · minority affiliation · alumni relationship. A high school diploma is required, although a GED is also accepted for admissions consideration. SAT or ACT test scores are required of all applicants. SAT Subject Test scores are not required. *According to the admissions office:* Minimum combined SAT Reasoning score of 1000 (composite ACT score of 21), rank in top half of secondary school class, and minimum 2.5 GPA recommended. *Academic units recommended:* 4 English, 4 Math, 4 Science, 3 Social Studies, 2 Foreign Language.

How to Pay for College

To apply for financial aid, students should submit the following: Free Application for Federal Student Aid (FAFSA). Bellarmine University participates in the Federal Work Study program. *Need-based aid programs include:* scholarships and grants · general need-based awards · Federal Pell grants · state scholarships and grants · college-based scholarships and grants · private scholarships and grants. *Non-Need-based aid programs include:* scholarships and grants · general need-based awards · state scholarships and grants · creative arts and performance awards · special achievements and activities awards · special characteristics awards · athletic scholarships · ROTC scholarships.

BELLARMINE UNIVERSITY

Highlights

Admissions
Applicants: 4,336
Accepted: 2,534
Acceptance rate: 58.4%
Average GPA: 3.5
ACT range: 22-26
SAT Math range: 510-600
SAT Reading range: 500-600
SAT Writing range: Not reported
Top 10% of class: 22%
Top 25% of class: 55%
Top 50% of class: 83%

Deadlines
Early Action: November 1
Early Decision: No
Regular Action: February 1 (priority)
August 15 (final)
Common Application: Accepted

Financial Aid
In-state tuition: $27,800
Out-of-state tuition: $27,800
Room: $4,960
Board: $3,450
Books: $764
Freshmen receiving need-based aid: 75%
Undergrads receiving need-based aid: 70%
Avg. % of need met by financial aid: 71%
Avg. aid package (freshmen): $22,285
Avg. aid package (undergrads): $21,278
Freshmen receiving merit-based aid: 24%
Undergrads receiving merit-based aid: 29%
Avg. student debt upon graduation: $19,055

Prominent Alumni
Dr. James Heck, inventor of drug Cancidas; Angela Mason, co-founder ITS Services; Joseph P. Clayton, Former CEO/Chairman Sirius Satellite Radio.

School Spirit
Mascot: Knights
Colors: Scarlet and silver
Song: *On Knights of Bellarmine*

Bowie State University
Bowie, MD (Pop. 50,000)
Location: Large town
Website: http://www.bowiestate.edu

Students
Total enrollment: 6,653
Undergrads: 3,339
Freshmen: 781
Part-time students: 50%
From out-of-state: 11%
Male/Female: 60%/40%
Live on-campus: Not reported
Off-campus employment rating: Fair
Caucasian: 4%
African American: 90%
Hispanic: 2%
Asian or Pacific Islander: 1%
Native American: 0%
International: 1%

Academics
Student/faculty ratio: Not reported
Class size 9 or fewer: 8%
Class size 10-29: 81%
Class size 30-49: 11%
Class size 50-99: 1%
Class size 100 or more: 5%
Returning freshmen: 73%
Six-year graduation rate: 37%

Most Popular Fields of Study
Business, Finance, Sales and Marketing
Protective Services, Criminal Justice and
    Public Administration
Psychology
English and Literature
Computer and Information Sciences
Mathematics
Interdisciplinary Studies
Health Professions, Medicine and Re-
    lated Sciences
Liberal Arts, Humanities and General
    Studies
Communications, Journalism, Advertising
    and Comm. Technologies

BOWIE STATE UNIVERSITY

14000 Jericho Park Road, Bowie, MD 20715-9465
Admissions: 877-772-6943 · Financial Aid: 301-860-3540
Email: ugradadmissions@bowiestate.edu
Website: http://www.bowiestate.edu

From the College

"Building on its image as a student-centered institution, Bowie State University will provide its diverse student population with a course of study that ensures a broad scope of knowledge and understanding that is deeply rooted in expanded research activities. The university excels in teacher education and will become the premier teacher of teachers."

Campus Setting

Bowie State, founded in 1865, is a public university of liberal arts and technology studies. Its 312-acre campus is located in Bowie, 22 miles from Washington, DC. A four-year public institution, Bowie State University is a historically black university with 6,653 students. In addition to a large, well-stocked library, the campus also has an art gallery. Bowie State University provides on-campus housing with 1,350 units. Housing options: co-ed dorms · women's dorms · men's dorms · single-student apartments. Recreation and sports facilities include a gymnasium.

Student Life and Activities

Most students live off campus, which does impact the on-campus social scene. Nevertheless, like any college, students find time to create their own recreational outlets. Bowie State University has 71 official student organizations. The most popular are: Gospel choir · university singers · jazz ensemble · concert · marching and pep bands · departmental and political clubs · honor societies · team managers. Bowie State University is a member of the Central Intercollegiate Athletic Association (Division II).

Academics and Learning Environment

For the B student, the learning environment of a college is just as important as the quality of its academic program. Bowie State University has 206 full-time and 142 part-time faculty members. The most common course size is 20 to 29 students. Bowie State University offers 37 majors with the most popular being business administration, computer science and education and least popular being English, mathematics and fine/performing arts. The school has a general core requirement. Cooperative education is not offered. All first-year students must maintain a 2.0 GPA or higher to avoid academic probation, and a minimum overall GPA of 2.0 is required to graduate. Other special academic programs that would appeal to a B student: pass/fail grading option · independent study · double majors · dual degrees · honors program · internships · distance learning certificate programs.

B Student Support and Success

Bowie's Writing Center helps students with English class assignments. The school also has a Student Success and Retention Center. The center assists students through programs and activities that "foster student academic, social and personal development." It is focused on helping freshmen transition into college life with the aid of placement testing, mentoring and tutorial services.

In addition to these services, Bowie State sponsors the Freshman Seminar course. It is designed to help each student pursue academic excellence and includes lessons about the college's history and its contribution to Maryland. Students learn to critically analyze specific readings that introduce them to concepts in liberal arts and to broaden their understanding of global awareness, critical thinking and oral and written communication skills. According to the college, "The goal is for students to become academically, personally and socially successful within and beyond the intellectual community."

Mentoring is popular at Bowie State. Mentors are matched with students to help foster a strong relationship that "promotes academic success, retention and the successful graduation of students." Peer mentors are paired with six freshmen based on academic majors.

KEAP, or Knowledge Enriched through Academic Performance, helps students with issues like poor grades and poor attendance. Students with a GPA of 2.0 or lower are required to take part in KEAP.

Bowie State University provides a variety of support programs including dedicated guidance for: academic · career · personal · psychological · minority students · military. Recognizing that some students may need extra preparation, Bowie State University offers remedial and refresher courses in: reading · writing · math · study skills. The average freshman year GPA is 2.5, and 73 percent of freshmen students return for their sophomore year.

Support for Students with Learning Disabilities

Students with learning disabilities may take advantage of specific support programs offered by Bowie State University. If necessary, the college will grant additional time to students with learning disabilities to complete their degree. Also, a lightened course load may be granted to LD students. Students with learning disabilities will find the following programs at Bowie State University extremely useful: tutors · learning center · testing accommodations · extended time for tests · take-home exam · oral tests · typist/scribe · note-taking services · reading machines · tape recorders · early syllabus · priority registration. Individual or small group tutorials are also available in: time management · organizational skills · writing labs · math labs. An advisor/advocate from the Disability Support Services is available to students.

How to Get Admitted

For admissions decisions, non-academic factors considered: extracurricular activities · state of residency. A high school diploma is required, although a GED is also accepted for admissions consideration. SAT or ACT test scores are required of all applicants. *According to the admissions office:* Minimum combined SAT Reasoning score of 900 and minimum 2.2 GPA required of in-state applicants; minimum

BOWIE STATE UNIVERSITY

Highlights

Admissions
Applicants: 5,099
Accepted: 2,168
Acceptance rate: 42.5%
Average GPA: Not reported
ACT range: Not reported
SAT Math range: 495-599
SAT Reading range: 490-590
SAT Writing range: Not reported

Deadlines
Early Action: No
Early Decision: No
Regular Action: Rolling admissions
Common Application: Not accepted

Financial Aid
In-state tuition: $4,286
Out-of-state tuition: $14,724
Room: $2,715
Board: $2,705
Books: $1,388
Freshmen receiving need-based aid: 77%
Undergrads receiving need-based aid: 78%
Avg. % of need met by financial aid: 48%
Avg. aid package (freshmen): $7,157
Avg. aid package (undergrads): $7,402
Freshmen receiving merit-based aid: 1%
Undergrads receiving merit-based aid: 1%
Avg. student debt upon graduation: $14,399

School Spirit
Mascot: Bulldog
Colors: Black and gold

College Profiles

combined SAT Reasoning score of 950 and minimum 2.6 GPA required of out-of-state applicants.

How to Pay for College

To apply for financial aid, students should submit the following: Free Application for Federal Student Aid (FAFSA) · institution's own financial aid forms. Bowie State University participates in the Federal Work Study program. *Need-based aid programs include:* scholarships and grants · general need-based awards · Federal Pell grants · state scholarships and grants · college-based scholarships and grants · private scholarships and grants. *Non-Need-based aid programs include:* scholarships and grants · general need-based awards · state scholarships and grants · creative arts and performance awards · athletic scholarships · ROTC scholarships.

BOWLING GREEN STATE UNIVERSITY

110 McFall Center, Bowling Green, OH 43403
Admissions: 419-372-2478 · Financial Aid: 419-372-2651
Email: admissions@bgsu.edu · Website: http://www.bgsu.edu

From the College

"Bowling Green State University is passionate about offering a nurturing atmosphere where values exploration, critical thinking and character development flourish. The university emphasizes a culture of respect, celebrates diversity and provides the personal attention typical of a small, private college. Smaller residential learning communities, undergraduate research, first-year transition programs, interdisciplinary collaborations and an expectation of campus and community involvement reinforce learning both in and out of the classroom."

Campus Setting

Bowling Green State is a public university. Founded as a teacher-training institution in 1910, it began granting bachelor's degrees in 1929. Programs are offered through the Colleges of Arts and Sciences, Business Administration, Education and Human Development, Health and Human Services, Musical Arts, and Technology. Its 1,338-acre campus is located in Bowling Green, 25 miles south of Toledo. A four-year public institution, Bowling Green State University has an enrollment of 17,874 students. Although not originally a co-educational college, Bowling Green State University has been co-ed since 1910. In addition to a large, well-stocked library, the campus facilities include: musical arts building · planetarium · life science building. Bowling Green State University provides on-campus housing with 52 units that can accommodate 6,671 students. Housing options: co-ed dorms · sorority housing · fraternity housing · single-student apartments · special housing for disabled students · special housing for International students. Recreation and sports facilities include: field house · golf course · ice arena · outdoor and indoor recreation centers.

Student Life and Activities

Most students (59 percent) live off campus, which does impact the on-campus social scene. Nevertheless, like any college, students find time to create their own recreational outlets. Homecoming, Dance Marathon, All campus picnic and Family Weekend are a few examples of popular events. Bowling Green State University has 300 official student organizations. The most popular are: Music · theatre · political · service and special-interest groups.. For those interested in sports, there are intramural teams such as: badminton · basketball · broomball · curling · dodgeball · flag football · indoor soccer · racquetball · softball · tennis · ultimate Frisbee · volleyball · wallyball · water polo · wiffle ball. Bowling Green State University is a member of the Central Collegiate Hockey Association (Division I), Mid-America Conference (Division I, Football I-A).

Academics and Learning Environment

For the B student, the learning environment of a college is just as important as the quality of its academic program. Bowling Green State University has 851 full-time and 171 part-time faculty members, offering a student-to-faculty ratio of 18:1. The most common course size is 20 to 29 students. Bowling Green State University offers 215 majors with the most popular being Kindergarten/Preschool Education and Teaching, Speech and Rhetorical Studies and Accounting. The school has a general core requirement. Cooperative education is available. All first-year students must

BOWLING GREEN STATE UNIVERSITY

Highlights

Bowling Green State University
Bowling Green, OH (Pop. 30,000)
Location: Large town
Website: http://www.bgsu.edu

Students
Total enrollment: 17,874
Undergrads: 6,903
Freshmen: 6,765
Part-time students: 7%
From out-of-state: 12%
Male/Female: 46%/54%
Live on-campus: 41%
In fraternities: 11%
In sororities: 12%
Off-campus employment rating: Good
Caucasian: 81%
African American: 10%
Hispanic: 3%
Asian or Pacific Islander: 1%
Native American: 1%
International: 2%

Academics
Student/faculty ratio: 18:1
Class size 9 or fewer: 9%
Class size 10-29: 66%
Class size 30-49: 19%
Class size 50-99: 5%
Class size 100 or more: 1%
Returning freshmen: 73%
Six-year graduation rate: 58%

Most Popular Fields of Study
Business, Finance, Sales and Marketing
Visual and Performing Arts
Social Sciences, History, Economics,
   Political Science
Protective Services, Criminal Justice and
   Public Administration
Biological and Life Sciences
Family and Consumer Sciences, Nutrition
   and Home Economics
Computer and Information Sciences
Communications, Journalism, Advertising
   and Comm. Technologies
Liberal Arts, Humanities and General
   Studies

maintain a 2.0 GPA or higher to avoid academic probation. Other special academic programs that would appeal to a B student: self-designed majors · pass/fail grading option · independent study · double majors · dual degrees · accelerated study · honors program · Phi Beta Kappa · internships · distance learning.

B Student Support and Success

Bowling Green offers the Office of Academic Enhancement (ACEN), which is dedicated to providing advice and academic support to new students so that they can make a smooth transition from high school to college. Students can find tutoring, mentoring and individualized academic assistance through ACEN, so that they can achieve academic success.

In addition to this, Bowling Green has a Study Skills Center that features computer software, course content video cassettes, a "How to Succeed in…"series of manuals, study tips brochures and charts and tests from various classes. Mentor groups are available for students who are struggling in their coursework. These groups meet once a week for 50-minute sessions. The mentors are students who have earned an A in the course he/she is helping with. Students who are enrolled in a Math or Statistics course are also encouraged to utilize the Math and Stats Tutoring Center. Students can get help on any course writing needed through the Writing Center.

The school offers a class called ACEN 100, which is a College Reading/Learning Skills course. It is designed to improve the basic reading and learning habits of students in topics like vocabulary, note taking, comprehension, time management, test taking and critical thinking.

Bowling Green State University provides a variety of support programs including dedicated guidance for: academic · career · personal · psychological · minority students · military · veterans · non-traditional students · family planning. Recognizing that some students may need extra preparation, Bowling Green State University offers remedial and refresher courses in: reading · writing · math · study skills. The average freshman year GPA is 2.7, and 73 percent of freshmen students return for their sophomore year.

Support for Students with Learning Disabilities

Students with learning disabilities may take advantage of specific support programs offered by Bowling Green State University. If necessary, the college will grant additional time to students with learning disabilities to complete their degree. High school foreign language waivers are accepted. High school math waivers are also accepted. According to the school, all services are provided on the basis of documented need to ensure equal access. Students with learning disabilities will find the following programs at Bowling Green State University extremely useful: tutors · learning center · testing accommodations · extended time for tests · take-home exam · oral tests · exam on tape or computer · readers · typist/scribe · note-taking services · reading machines · tape recorders · texts on tape · early syllabus · priority registration · waiver of math degree requirement. Individual or small group tutorials are also available in: time management · organizational skills · specific subject areas · writing labs · math labs · study skills. An advisor/advocate from the Office of Disability Services is available to students.

How to Get Admitted

For admissions decisions, non-academic factors considered: interview · extracurricular activities · special talents, interests, abilities · character/personal qualities · volunteer work · work experience · state of residency · minority affiliation · alumni relationship. A high school diploma is required, although a GED is also accepted for admissions consideration. SAT or ACT test scores are required of all applicants. *According to the admissions office:* Minimum composite ACT score of 20 (combined SAT score of 920) and minimum 2.5 GPA required. *Academic units recommended:* 4 English, 3 Math, 3 Science, 3 Social Studies, 2 Foreign Language.

How to Pay for College

To apply for financial aid, students should submit the following: Free Application for Federal Student Aid (FAFSA). Bowling Green State University participates in the Federal Work Study program. *Need-based aid programs include:* scholarships and grants · general need-based awards · Federal Pell grants · state scholarships and grants · college-based scholarships and grants · private scholarships and grants. *Non-Need-based aid programs include:* scholarships and grants · general need-based awards · state scholarships and grants · creative arts and performance awards · special achievements and activities awards · special characteristics awards · athletic scholarships · ROTC scholarships.

BOWLING GREEN STATE UNIVERSITY

Highlights

Admissions
Applicants: 11,111
Accepted: 9,712
Acceptance rate: 87.4%
Average GPA: 3.2
ACT range: 19-24
SAT Math range: 450-550
SAT Reading range: 440-560
SAT Writing range: 435-535
Top 10% of class: 12%
Top 25% of class: 33%
Top 50% of class: 70%

Deadlines
Early Action: No
Early Decision: No
Regular Action: Rolling admissions
Common Application: Not accepted

Financial Aid
In-state tuition: $7,778
Out-of-state tuition: $15,086
Room: -
Board: -
Books: $1,174
Freshmen receiving need-based aid: 67%
Undergrads receiving need-based aid: 63%
Avg. % of need met by financial aid: 74%
Avg. aid package (freshmen): $11,514
Avg. aid package (undergrads): $12,274
Freshmen receiving merit-based aid: 10%
Undergrads receiving merit-based aid: 11%
Avg. student debt upon graduation: $26,860

School Spirit
Mascot: Falcons

BRADLEY UNIVERSITY

1501 West Bradley Avenue, Peoria, IL 61625
Admissions: 800-447-6460 · Financial Aid: 309-677-3089
Email: admissions@bradley.edu · Website: http://www.bradley.edu

From the College

"Bradley University is a private, independent university offering undergraduate and graduate programs in the liberal and fine arts, the sciences, business, communications, education, engineering and the health sciences. This residential campus of 5,000 students blends large-school opportunities with a small-school personality. Bradley students experience a balance of academic and co-curricular opportunities that emphasize collaboration, teamwork and active learning. This experience provides an integration of a liberal arts education, professional preparation and personal and social development. Located just three hours from Chicago and St. Louis, Bradley is committed to serving central Illinois through its research, creative production, and outreach programs."

Campus Setting

Bradley, founded in 1897, is a private, co-educational, comprehensive university. Programs are offered through the Foster Colleges of Business Administration, the Slane College Communications and Fine Arts, the College of Education and Health Sciences, the College of Engineering and Technology and the College of Liberal Arts and Sciences and the Graduate School. Its 85-acre campus is located in a residential area of Peoria, Illinois. A four-year private institution, Bradley University has an enrollment of 5,872 students. In addition to a large, well-stocked library, the campus also has a global communications center. Bradley University provides on-campus housing with 30 units that can accommodate 2,850 students. Housing options: co-ed dorms · sorority housing · fraternity housing · single-student apartments · married-student apartments. Recreation and sports facilities include a recreation center.

Student Life and Activities

With 63 percent of students living on campus, there are plenty of social activities. According to the school, Bradley has an active calendar of theatre and musical performances. The new Markin Student Recreation Center and Greek houses are favorite gathering spots. Popular campus events include Late Night BU, Homecoming, Sibling's Weekend, Parents' Weekends and Welcome Week activities. Bradley University has 249 official student organizations. Popular groups on campus include Student Activities Council, student government, men's basketball team and Greek life. For those interested in sports, there are intramural teams such as: 5K run · badminton · basketball · billiards · bowling · diving · flag football · golf · indoor soccer · racquetball · soccer · softball · swimming · table tennis · volleyball · wallyball · wrestling. Bradley University is a member of the Missouri Valley Conference (Division I).

Academics and Learning Environment

For the B student, the learning environment of a college is just as important as the quality of its academic program. Bradley University has 337 full-time and 222 part-time faculty members, offering a student-to-faculty ratio of 14:1. The most common course size is 20 to 29 students. Bradley University offers 99 majors with the most popular being nursing, mechanical engineering and psychology and least popular being business, economics and engineering physics. The school has a general core requirement. Cooperative education is available. All first-year students must maintain a 2.0 GPA or higher to avoid academic probation. Other special academic programs that would appeal to a B student: self-designed majors · pass/fail grading option · independent study · double majors · dual degrees · honors program · internships · certificate programs.

B Student Support and Success

Bradley's website states, "We encourage students to apply who feel that they can demonstrate both the academic ability to succeed and the potential to contribute to the total educational experience at Bradley. While our students perform above national averages in strong college preparation curriculums, we do not have a stated minimum rank, grade point average (GPA), or ACT or SAT score. We also recognize that rank and GPA can only be considered meaningful in the context of the quality of the high school attended and the classes that a student takes. It is also very important to our admissions review committee that our students balance academic ability with the other qualities that lead to success at Bradley. Social skills, communications skills, leadership, community service and unique experiences are important qualities in our admission and scholarship review. Finally, different academic areas have different admission requirements."

Bradley University provides a variety of support programs including dedicated guidance for: academic · career · psychological · minority students. The average freshman year GPA is 2.9, and 89 percent of freshmen students return for their sophomore year. What do students do after college? While many enter the work force, approximately 16 percent pursue a graduate degree immediately after graduation. Among students who enter the work force, approximately 94 percent enter a field related to their major within six months of graduation. Companies that most frequently hire graduates from Bradley University include: Accenture · Caterpillar Inc. · Enterprise Rent-A-Car · eServLLC · LaSalle Bank Corp. · Liberty Mutual Insurance Co. · Loyola Medical Center · Peoria Public School District · Target Corp. · United States Patent and Trademark Office.

Support for Students with Learning Disabilities

Students with learning disabilities may take advantage of specific support programs offered by Bradley University. The Center for Learning Assistance can assist those students with certain learning disabilities by providing "select coordinated accommodations" as defined by standardized national service-delivery models. This includes the provision of a contact person, generic support services, peer tutors and student referral service for off-campus testing resources. These services are available only during the academic year. Students with learning disabilities will find the following programs at Bradley University extremely useful: tutors · learning center · untimed tests · extended time for tests · tape recorders · videotaped classes · early syllabus. Individual or small group tutorials are also available in: time management · organizational skills · learning strategies · writing labs · math labs · study skills. An advisor/advocate from the LD program is available to students.

How to Get Admitted

For admissions decisions, non-academic factors considered: interview · extracurricular activities · special talents, interests, abilities · char-

BRADLEY UNIVERSITY

Bradley University
Peoria, IL (Pop. 350,000)
Location: Medium city
Website: http://www.bradley.edu

Students
Total enrollment: 5,872
Undergrads: 2,339
Freshmen: 1,032
Part-time students: 6%
From out-of-state: 14%
Male/Female: 46%/54%
Live on-campus: 63%
In fraternities: 33%
In sororities: 27%
Off-campus employment rating: Fair
Caucasian: 83%
African American: 7%
Hispanic: 3%
Asian or Pacific Islander: 4%
Native American: 0%
International: 1%

Academics
Student/faculty ratio: 14:1
Class size 9 or fewer: 21%
Class size 10-29: 57%
Class size 30-49: 12%
Class size 50-99: 3%
Class size 100 or more: 1%
Returning freshmen: 89%
Six-year graduation rate: 76%

Most Popular Fields of Study
Business, Finance, Sales and Marketing
Protective Services, Criminal Justice and
    Public Administration
English and Literature
Philosophy, Religion and Theology
Computer and Information Sciences
Psychology
Engineering and Engineering Technologies
Health Professions, Medicine and Related Sciences
Family and Consumer Sciences, Nutrition
    and Home Economics
Foreign Languages, Literature and Linguistics

115

BRADLEY UNIVERSITY

Admissions
Applicants: 5,932
Accepted: 3,817
Acceptance rate: 64.3%
placed on wait list: 74
Average GPA: 3.6
ACT range: 23-27
SAT Math range: 520-650
SAT Reading range: 500-630
SAT Writing range: Not reported
Top 10% of class: 29%
Top 25% of class: 65%
Top 50% of class: 92%

Deadlines
Early Action: No
Early Decision: No
Regular Action: Rolling admissions
Common Application: Accepted

Financial Aid
In-state tuition: $23,950
Out-of-state tuition: $23,950
Room: -
Board: -
Books: $1,050
Freshmen receiving need-based aid: 69%
Undergrads receiving need-based aid:
    72%
Avg. % of need met by financial aid: 66%
Avg. aid package (freshmen): $14,032
Avg. aid package (undergrads): $13,798
Freshmen receiving merit-based aid: 18%
Undergrads receiving merit-based aid:
    23%
Avg. student debt upon graduation:
    $17,116

Prominent Alumni
Ray LaHood '71, U.S. Secretary of Transportation; Aaron Schock '02, member U.S. House of Representatives, Illinois,18th District; Rene C. Byer '80, winner of the Pulitzer Prize, senior photographer, Sacramento Bee.

School Spirit
Colors: Red and white
Song: *Hail Red and White*

acter/personal qualities · volunteer work · work experience · state of residency · geographical location · minority affiliation · alumni relationship. A high school diploma is required, although a GED is also accepted for admissions consideration. SAT or ACT test scores are required of all applicants. SAT Subject Test scores are not required. *Academic units recommended:* 5 English, 4 Math, 3 Science, 3 Social Studies, 2 Foreign Language.

How to Pay for College
To apply for financial aid, students should submit the following: Free Application for Federal Student Aid (FAFSA). Bradley University participates in the Federal Work Study program. *Need-based aid programs include:* scholarships and grants · general need-based awards · Federal Pell grants · state scholarships and grants · college-based scholarships and grants · private scholarships and grants. *Non-Need-based aid programs include:* scholarships and grants · state scholarships and grants · creative arts and performance awards · special achievements and activities awards · special characteristics awards · athletic scholarships.

BRIDGEWATER STATE COLLEGE

Boyden Hall, Bridgewater, MA 02325
Admissions: 508-531-1237 · Financial Aid: 508-531-1341
Email: admission@bridgew.edu
Website: http://www.bridgew.edu

From the College

"Bridgewater State College is the comprehensive public college of Southeastern Massachusetts and has a dual mission: to educate the residents of Southeastern Massachusetts and the Commonwealth, and to use its intellectual, scientific and technological resources to support and advance the economic and cultural life of the region. While maintaining its historical focus on the preparation of teachers, Bridgewater today provides a broad range of baccalaureate degree programs through its School of Arts and Sciences, its School of Education and Allied Studies and new School of Management and Aviation Science, which includes the only four-year Aviation program at a public college in New England."

Campus Setting

Bridgewater, founded in 1840, is a public college of liberal arts and professional studies. Its 235-acre campus is located in Bridgewater, 28 miles south of Boston. A four-year public institution, Bridgewater State College has an enrollment of 9,934 students. The school also has a library with 292,292 books. Bridgewater State College provides on-campus housing that can accommodate 2,065 students. Housing options: co-ed dorms · single-student apartments. Recreation and sports facilities include: athletic and football fields · baseball and softball parks · gymnasium · tennis courts.

Student Life and Activities

Most students (71 percent) live off campus, which does impact the on-campus social scene. Nevertheless, like any college, students find time to create their own recreational outlets. Popular gathering spots include the campus center, the Rat and Cenzio's. Popular campus activities are Winterfest, Springfest, Homecoming and spring break. Bridgewater State College has 67 official student organizations. Popular groups include: Circle K, WBIM, the Program Committee and the Student Government Association. Bridgewater State College is a member of the ECAC (Division I, Football I-AA), Little East Conference (Division III), Massachusetts State College Athletic Conference (Division III), New England Football Conference (Division III), New England Women's Lacrosse Alliance (Division III), Pilgrim League (Division III).

Academics and Learning Environment

For the B student, the learning environment of a college is just as important as the quality of its academic program. Bridgewater State College has 299 full-time and 288 part-time faculty members, offering a student-to-faculty ratio of 20:1. The most common course size is 10 to 19 students. Bridgewater State College offers 44 majors with the most popular being business/marketing, elementary educa-

BRIDGEWATER STATE COLLEGE

Highlights

Admissions
Applicants: 6,498
Accepted: 4,507
Acceptance rate: 69.4%
Average GPA: 3.0
ACT range: 19-24
SAT Math range: 460-560
SAT Reading range: 450-550
SAT Writing range: Not reported
Top 10% of class: 7%
Top 25% of class: 27%
Top 50% of class: 69%

Deadlines
Early Action: November 15
Early Decision: No
Regular Action: Rolling admissions
Common Application: Accepted

Financial Aid
In-state tuition: $910
Out-of-state tuition: $7,050
Room: -
Board: -
Freshmen receiving need-based aid: 46%
Undergrads receiving need-based aid: 49%
Avg. % of need met by financial aid: Not reported
Avg. aid package (freshmen): $3,040
Avg. aid package (undergrads): $6,496
Freshmen receiving merit-based aid: 1%
Undergrads receiving merit-based aid: 1%
Avg. student debt upon graduation: Not reported

School Spirit
Mascot: Bears
Colors: Crimson and white

America's
Best Colleges for
B Students

tion and psychology and least popular being physics, economics and philosophy. The school has a general core requirement. Cooperative education is not offered. All first-year students must maintain a 2.0 GPA or higher to avoid academic probation, and a minimum overall GPA of 2.0 is required to graduate. Other special academic programs that would appeal to a B student: independent study · double majors · accelerated study · honors program · internships · distance learning.

B Student Support and Success

Bridgewater offers the Academic Achievement Center (AAC), which features learning assistance programs and is home to Second Language Services, the Office of Disability Resources, Tutoring Services, the Writing Studio, Mathematics Services, Study and Research Services and the Communication Laboratory. The college also provides a Core Curriculum that is a skill centered, outcomes-based general education course, designed to help all students prepare for learning in their chosen fields. It is made up of four areas: skills requirements (writing, logical reasoning, mathematical reasoning and spoken communication); core distribution requirements (arts, humanities, natural and social and behavioral sciences, global culture, multiculturalism, quantitative reasoning and the U.S. Constitution); seminars (writing/speaking intensive courses) and requirements in the major (connecting the core curriculum to each major).

Bridgewater State College provides a variety of support programs including dedicated guidance for: academic · career · personal · psychological · minority students · family planning · religious. Annually, 74 percent of freshmen students return for their sophomore year.

Support for Students with Learning Disabilities

Students with learning disabilities may take advantage of specific support programs offered by Bridgewater State College. If necessary, the college will grant additional time to students with learning disabilities to complete their degree. Also, a lightened course load may be granted to LD students. Students with learning disabilities will find the following programs at Bridgewater State College extremely useful: tutors · learning center · testing accommodations · untimed tests · extended time for tests · take-home exam · oral tests · readers · note-taking services · tape recorders · early syllabus · priority registration · waiver of math degree requirement. Individual or small group tutorials are also available in: time management · organizational skills · learning strategies · specific subject areas · writing labs · math labs · study skills. An advisor/advocate from the Disability Resources is available to students.

How to Get Admitted

For admissions decisions, non-academic factors considered: extracurricular activities · special talents, interests, abilities · character/personal qualities · volunteer work · work experience · state of residency · minority affiliation · alumni relationship. A high school diploma is required, although a GED is also accepted for admissions consideration. SAT or ACT test scores are required of all applicants. SAT Subject Test scores are considered, if submitted, but are not required. *Academic units recommended:* 4 English, 3 Math, 3 Science, 1 Social Studies, 2 Foreign Language.

How to Pay for College

To apply for financial aid, students should submit the following: Free Application for Federal Student Aid (FAFSA). Bridgewater State College participates in the Federal Work Study program. *Need-based aid programs include:* scholarships and grants · general need-based awards · Federal Pell grants · state scholarships and grants · college-based scholarships and grants · private scholarships and grants. *Non-Need-based aid programs include:* scholarships and grants · state scholarships and grants.

BRIDGEWATER STATE COLLEGE

BRYANT UNIVERSITY

1150 Douglas Pike, Smithfield, RI 02917-1291
Admissions: 800-622-7001 · Financial Aid: 800-248-4036
Email: admission@bryant.edu · Website: http://www.bryant.edu

From the College

"Bryant was established in 1863, and is a small, private university in New England that focuses on helping students build knowledge, develop character and achieve success—as they define it. The College of Arts and Sciences and the College of Business integrate business, liberal arts and technology to distinguish the Bryant educational experience. This integration ensures that students become well-rounded individuals with the analytical, problem-solving, business, and communication skills to successfully compete and contribute in a complex, global environment.

"Bryant enrolls 3,200 undergraduate and more than 400 graduate students with 112 tenured and tenure-track, full-time faculty. More than 3,000 individuals and businesses benefit on an annual basis from professional education and consulting services offered by Bryant's Executive Development Center and the John H. Chafee Center for International Business.

"Bryant offers undergraduate programs in actuarial mathematics, business administration with seven concentrations available, communication, economics, environmental science, global studies, history, information technology, international business, literary and cultural studies, mathematics and statistics, politics and law, psychology and sociology. Bryant's Graduate School of Business offers master's degrees in business administration (MBA), information systems (MSIS), taxation (MST) and professional accountancy (MPAc). All of Bryant's academic programs are accredited by the New England Association of Schools and Colleges (NEASC). The College of Business is accredited by AACSB International-The Association to Advance Collegiate Schools of Business, a distinction earned by less than 10 percent of business colleges worldwide."

Campus Setting

Bryant is a university of business studies. Its 420-acre campus is located in Smithfield, 12 miles from Providence. Bryant University has an enrollment of 3,733 students. In addition to a library, the campus facilities include: theatre · food court. Bryant University provides on-campus housing with 1,036 units that can accommodate 2,882 students. Housing options: co-ed dorms · women's dorms · special housing for disabled students. Recreation and sports facilities include: athletic fields · baseball and softball complex · gymnasium · natatorium · recreation and wellness center · rugby field · sports arena · stadium · weight room.

Student Life and Activities

Most students live off campus, which does impact the on-campus social scene. Nevertheless, like any college, students find time to create their own recreational outlets. According to the editor of the student newspaper, the student organization try to increase the social aspect of college life. Popular gathering places are Lupo's, The Living Room, The Strand, Thayer Street, The Junction and Parente's. Popular events on campus are semi-formals, MSU Extravaganza Night, commencement, convocation, ISO UN Festival, Parents' Weekend, Spring Weekend, Special Olympics and the Festival of Lights. Bryant University has 83 official student organizations. Influential groups on campus are the Student Programming Board, rugby teams, Student Senate and Greek organizations. For those interested in sports, there are intramural teams such as: basketball · flag football · floor hockey · indoor soccer · inner-tube water polo · softball · volleyball. Bryant University is a member of the Northeast Conference (Division I).

Academics and Learning Environment

For the B student, the learning environment of a college is just as important as the quality of its academic program. Bryant University has 155 full-time and 96 part-time faculty members, offering a student-to-faculty ratio of 17:1. The most common course size is 30 to 39 students. Bryant University offers 31 majors with the most popular being marketing, finance and management and least popular being history, economics and literary/cultural studies. The school has a general core requirement. Cooperative education is not offered. All first-year students must maintain a 2.0 GPA or higher to avoid academic probation, and a minimum overall GPA of 2.0 is required to graduate. Other special academic programs that would appeal to a B student: independent study · double majors · dual degrees · honors program · internships.

B Student Support and Success

Bryant College provides extra help to students through the Academic Center for Excellence (ACE). Each year, more than 1,600 students use its services to help with class performance. ACE's philosophy is that college students are not born with good study skills and habits, and like anything else in life, they require practice on a regular basis. Even students who have great study skills in high school may find that they need extra help in college. According to the college, ACE's primary goal is to "help students become self-reliant, independent, confident learners so that they may successfully meet the demands of their chosen academic curricula." They do this through both a tutoring program and study skills instruction in group sessions provided by a combination of staff, peer tutors and faculty. Along with ACE, Bryant offers a Writing Center. Here you can learn and polish the skills of written communication through one-on-one consultations with staff and tutors. Access is provided through ACE to workshops and printed materials that are helpful tools in honing writing skills.

Bryant University provides a variety of support programs including dedicated guidance for: academic · career · personal · psychological · minority students · non-traditional students · family planning · religious. The average freshman year GPA is 2.8, and 88 percent of freshmen students return for their sophomore year. What do students do after college? While many enter the work force, approximately 5 percent pursue a graduate degree immediately after graduation. Among students who enter the work force, approximately 94 percent enter a field related to their major within six months of graduation. Companies that most frequently hire graduates from Bryant University include: State Street Bank · Tech Target · TJX · DiSanto · Priest & Co. · Lightolier · St. Paul's Travelers · PricewaterhouseCoopers · The Hartford Life · Fidelity Investments · CVS · Ernst & Young · Meditech · Liberty Mutual · Target · Hanover Insurance · Travelers · Cambridge Associates · Bank of America · Wolfe & Co. · Brown Brothers Harriman · EMC Corp.· Mercier · Amica Insurance.

BRYANT UNIVERSITY

BRYANT UNIVERSITY

Highlights

Admissions
Average GPA: 3.4
ACT range: Not reported
SAT Math range: 560-630
SAT Reading range: 520-600
SAT Writing range: Not reported
Top 10% of class: 25%
Top 25% of class: 64%
Top 50% of class: 95%

Deadlines
Early Action: No
Early Decision: November 16 and January 4
Regular Action: February 1 (final)
Common Application: Accepted

Financial Aid
In-state tuition: $29,021
Out-of-state tuition: $29,021
Room: $6,735
Board: $4,363
Books: $1,200
Freshmen receiving need-based aid: 64%
Undergrads receiving need-based aid: 66%
Avg. % of need met by financial aid: 73%
Avg. aid package (freshmen): $16,731
Avg. aid package (undergrads): $15,707
Freshmen receiving merit-based aid: 13%
Undergrads receiving merit-based aid: 11%
Avg. student debt upon graduation: $29,128

Prominent Alumni
Kristian P. Moor, '81, Executive Vice President, American International Group; Thomas Hewitt, '68, CEO, Interstate Hotels & Resorts; Joseph Puishys, '81, President, Division of Honeywell.

School Spirit
Mascot: Bulldogs
Colors: Black, gold and white

Support for Students with Learning Disabilities

Students with learning disabilities may take advantage of specific support programs offered by Bryant University. Students with learning disabilities will find the following programs at Bryant University extremely useful: tutors · learning center · testing accommodations · extended time for tests · take-home exam · reading machines · tape recorders. Individual or small group tutorials are also available in: time management · organizational skills · learning strategies · specific subject areas · writing labs · math labs · study skills. An advisor/advocate from the LD program is available to students.

How to Get Admitted

For admissions decisions, non-academic factors considered: interview · extracurricular activities · special talents, interests, abilities · character/personal qualities · volunteer work · work experience · geographical location · minority affiliation · alumni relationship. A high school diploma is required, although a GED is also accepted for admissions consideration. SAT or ACT test scores are required of all applicants. SAT Subject Test scores are not required. *According to the admissions office:* The average GPA of admitted students is 3.4 and the average SAT Reasoning score is 1150 (composite ACT score is 25). *Academic units recommended:* 4 English, 4 Math, 4 Science, 4 Foreign Language.

How to Pay for College

To apply for financial aid, students should submit the following: Free Application for Federal Student Aid (FAFSA). Bryant University participates in the Federal Work Study program. *Need-based aid programs include:* scholarships and grants · general need-based awards · Federal Pell grants · state scholarships and grants · college-based scholarships and grants · private scholarships and grants. *Non-Need-based aid programs include:* scholarships and grants · state scholarships and grants · athletic scholarships · ROTC scholarships · minority scholarships.

CALDWELL COLLEGE

9 Ryerson Avenue, Caldwell, NJ 07006
Admissions: 888-864-9516 · Financial Aid: 973-618-3221
Email: admissions@caldwell.edu · Website: http://www.caldwell.edu

From the College

"Founded in 1939 by the Sisters of St. Dominic, Caldwell College is a Catholic institution in the Judeo-Christian tradition with a heritage of over seven centuries of Dominican commitment to higher education. Serving a diverse population of all ages, Caldwell College provides a liberal arts education which promotes spiritual, aesthetic and intellectual growth. Upon this foundation, the college offers career-related programs which prepare its graduates to take advantage of opportunities in a complex society."

Campus Setting

Founded as a college for women in 1939, it adopted co-education in 1986. Its 70-acre campus is located in Caldwell, 20 miles from New York City. A four-year private institution, Caldwell College has an enrollment of 2,291 students. Although not originally co-educational college, Caldwell College has been co-ed since 1986. The school is also affiliated with the Roman Catholic Church. In addition to a large, well-stocked library, the campus also has an art gallery. Caldwell College provides on-campus housing with 191 units that can accommodate 380 students. Housing options: co-ed dorms.

Student Life and Activities

Most students (57 percent) live off campus, which does impact the on-campus social scene. Nevertheless, like any college, students do find time to create their own recreational outlets. Popular events include: Diversity Day, Homecoming and Founder's Day. Caldwell College has 21 official student organizations. The most popular are: Choral groups · drama club · jazz and pep bands · music ensembles · musical theatre · resident and commuter councils · service groups · Spanish club · business club · team managers. Caldwell College is a member of the Central Atlantic Collegiate Conference (Division II).

Academics and Learning Environment

For the B student, the learning environment of a college is just as important as the quality of its academic program. Caldwell College has 80 full-time and 113 part-time faculty members, offering a student-to-faculty ratio of 12:1. The most common course size is 10 to 19 students. Caldwell College offers 39 majors with the most popular being business administration, psychology and elementary education and least popular being medical technology, political science and French. The school has a general core requirement as well as a religion requirement Cooperative education is not offered. All first-year students must maintain a 2.0 GPA or higher to avoid academic probation. Other special academic programs that would appeal to a B student: self-designed majors · pass/fail grading option · independent study · double majors · accelerated study · honors program · internships · weekend college · distance learning certificate programs.

B Student Support and Success

A variety of support services are available through Caldwell's Academic Support Center. Individual and group tutoring is offered on both a scheduled and drop-in basis. The Writing Center has regular hours also and focuses on helping students become

CALDWELL COLLEGE

Caldwell College
Caldwell, NJ (Pop. 11,000)
Location: Large town
Website: http://www.caldwell.edu

Students
Total enrollment: 2,291
Undergrads: 546
Freshmen: 284
Part-time students: 35%
From out-of-state: 5%
Male/Female: 32%/68%
Live on-campus: 43%
Off-campus employment rating: Excellent
Caucasian: 61%
African American: 16%
Hispanic: 12%
Asian or Pacific Islander: 2%
Native American: 0%
International: 5%

Academics
Student/faculty ratio: 12:1
Class size 9 or fewer: 32%
Class size 10-29: 65%
Class size 30-49: 4%
Class size 50-99: 1%
Class size 100 or more: 1%
Returning freshmen: 73%
Six-year graduation rate: 52%

Most Popular Fields of Study
Business, Finance, Sales and Marketing
Biological and Life Sciences
Protective Services, Criminal Justice and
    Public Administration
Visual and Performing Arts
English and Literature
Philosophy, Religion and Theology
Computer and Information Sciences
Mathematics
Foreign Languages, Literature and Lin-
    guistics
Communications, Journalism, Advertising
    and Comm. Technologies

independent critical thinkers and writers. In addition, an online writing lab is another option students may access. Students work with peer or professional tutors and there is no charge for these sessions. A supplemental instruction program is offered during the year in courses that serve large numbers of freshman or sophomores. This course focuses on skills needed to better understand lectures, develop study strategies and prepare for exams. Workshops on note taking, textbook reading, time management and test taking strategies are offered throughout the year.

Caldwell College provides a variety of support programs including dedicated guidance for: academic · personal · minority students · non-traditional students · religious. Additional counseling services include: Alcohol/substance abuse counseling. Recognizing that some students may need extra preparation, Caldwell College offers remedial and refresher courses in: reading · writing · math · study skills. The average freshman year GPA is 2.8, and 73 percent of freshmen students return for their sophomore year. What do students do after college? While many enter the work force, approximately 20 percent pursue a graduate degree immediately after graduation. Among students who enter the work force, approximately 70 percent enter a field related to their major within six months of graduation. Companies that most frequently hire graduates from Caldwell College include: Xerox · Ricoh · Cosmair Inc. · Horizon Blue Cross/Blue Shield · Boards of Education.

Support for Students with Learning Disabilities

Students with learning disabilities may take advantage of specific support programs offered by Caldwell College. If necessary, the college will grant additional time to students with learning disabilities to complete their degree. Also, a lightened course load may be granted to LD students. High school foreign language waivers are accepted. High school math waivers are also accepted. Students with learning disabilities will find the following programs at Caldwell College extremely useful: remedial math · remedial English · remedial reading · special classes · tutors · learning center · untimed tests · extended time for tests · oral tests · readers · note-taking services · reading machines · tape recorders. Individual or small group tutorials are also available in: time management · organizational skills · learning strategies · writing labs · math labs.

How to Get Admitted

For admissions decisions, non-academic factors considered: interview · extracurricular activities · special talents, interests, abilities · character/personal qualities · volunteer work · work experience · state of residency · alumni relationship. A high school diploma is required, although a GED is also accepted for admissions consideration. SAT or ACT test scores are required of all applicants. SAT Subject Test scores are considered, if submitted, but are not required. *According to the admissions office:* Minimum combined SAT Reasoning score of 900, rank in top half of secondary school class and minimum 2.5 GPA recommended.

How to Pay for College

To apply for financial aid, students should submit the following: Free Application for Federal Student Aid (FAFSA) · institution's own financial aid forms · state aid form. Caldwell College participates in the Federal Work Study program. *Need-based aid programs include:* scholarships and grants · general need-based awards · Federal Pell grants · state scholarships and grants · college-based scholarships and grants · private scholarships and grants. *Non-Need-based aid programs include:* scholarships and grants · state scholarships and grants · creative arts and performance awards · special achievements and activities awards · special characteristics awards · athletic scholarships.

CALDWELL COLLEGE

Highlights

Admissions
Applicants: 1,442
Accepted: 957
Acceptance rate: 66.4%
Average GPA: 3.0
ACT range: Not reported
SAT Math range: 420-540
SAT Reading range: 430-530
SAT Writing range: Not reported
Top 10% of class: 7%
Top 25% of class: 18%
Top 50% of class: 53%

Deadlines
Early Action:
Early Decision: No
Regular Action: Rolling admissions
Common Application: Accepted

Financial Aid
In-state tuition: $23,800
Out-of-state tuition: $23,800
Room: $4,535
Board: $4,455
Books: $1,200
Freshmen receiving need-based aid: 71%
Undergrads receiving need-based aid: 64%
Avg. % of need met by financial aid: 51%
Avg. aid package (freshmen): $15,638
Avg. aid package (undergrads): $15,690
Freshmen receiving merit-based aid: 11%
Undergrads receiving merit-based aid: 6%
Avg. student debt upon graduation: $18,733

School Spirit
Mascot: Cougars

CAMPBELL UNIVERSITY

P.O. Box 546, Buies Creek, NC 27506
Admissions: 800-334-4111, extension 1290 · Financial Aid: 800-334-4111, extension 1310
Email: buildyourfuture@campbell.edu · Website: http://www.campbell.edu

From the College

"Campbell University is a university of the liberal arts, sciences and professions that is committed to helping students develop an integrated Christian personality characterized by a wholeness of body, mind and spirit. Campbell is a Baptist university affiliated with the Baptist State Convention of North Carolina. Both in and out of the classroom, the university endeavors to present Christian principles to students and to foster their application to daily life.

"Located in Buies Creek, a rural, residential community in Harnett County, Campbell University has an 850-acre campus. Raleigh, the state's capital, and Fayetteville are less than thirty miles from campus. Within about an hour's driving time students can enjoy the benefits of the Research Triangle Park, the cities of Durham and Chapel Hill. Campbell has been named 'The Safest Campus in North Carolina,' by *USA Today*.

"Campbell is fully accredited by the Southern Association of Colleges and Schools (SACS), Commission on Colleges, as a Level V Institution. Campbell also has accredited and nationally recognized graduate programs in business, divinity, education, law and pharmacy.

"Affiliated with the Atlantic Sun Conference, Campbell features enjoys competitive Division I Varsity athletics. The Fighting Camels men's sports include: basketball, baseball, cross-country, golf, soccer, tennis, track, wrestling and football. Campbell's women's sports include: basketball, cheerleading, cross-country, golf, soccer, softball, tennis, track, volleyball and swimming.

"Campbell's total enrollment is over 2,600 undergraduate and 1,500 graduate students. In an average year, the student body comes from over 90 North Carolina counties, all 49 other states and 50 countries. Seventy-five percent of the student body comes from North Carolina."

Campus Setting

Campbell was founded as an academy in 1887, became a four-year college in 1961 and gained university status in 1979. A four-year private institution, Campbell University has an enrollment of 6,033 students. The school is also affiliated with the Baptist Church. In addition to a large, well-stocked library, the campus facilities include: drug information center · museum and exhibit hall · nature trail · golf course. Campbell University provides on-campus housing with 28 units that can accommodate 1,500 students. Housing options: women's dorms · men's dorms · single-student apartments · married-student apartments · special housing for disabled students.

Student Life and Activities

Buies Creek is a small town, still quiet and safe, according to the student newspaper. In fact, there are no stop signs. Chele's Place (a coffeehouse), the student center and Faces are favorite gathering spots for students. Popular events include: Welcome Week, Homecoming/Parent's Weekend, Spring Fling, Mr. Campbell Pageant and Spring Formal. Campbell University has 50 official student organizations. The Baptist Student Union, the Student Government Association, men's and women's basketball and soccer teams and Kappa Psi (pharmacy fraternity) are popular groups on campus. Campbell University is a member of the Atlantic Sun Conference (Division I),

Colonial Athletic Association (Division I), Northeast Conference (Division I, Football I-AA).

Academics and Learning Environment

For the B student, the learning environment of a college is just as important as the quality of its academic program. Campbell University has 188 full-time and 148 part-time faculty members, offering a student-to-faculty ratio of 14:1. The most common course size is 2 to 9 students. Campbell University offers 100 majors with the most popular being business administration, government and mass communication and least popular being dramatic art. The school has a general core requirement as well as a religion requirement Cooperative education is not offered. All first-year students must maintain a 1.4 GPA or higher to avoid academic probation, and a minimum overall GPA of 2.0 is required to graduate. Other special academic programs that would appeal to a B student: independent study · double majors · accelerated study · honors program · internships · distance learning.

B Student Support and Success

Both group and peer tutoring are available at Campbell University, and the school also has a Writing Center. Student support services include workshops on study skills, test taking skills, time management and test anxiety. The school has a program known as the Early Alert System, which puts students in contact with the appropriate campus resources in order to help them to meet their educational goals. Faculty and staff members refer students who are struggling in their academic work, as well as those who are missing class often or who are having trouble adjusting to campus life. The Early Alert System helps to make sure that every student is able to take full advantage of the educational opportunities available at Campbell.

Campbell University provides a variety of support programs including dedicated guidance for: academic · career · personal · psychological · veterans · non-traditional students · religious. The average freshman year GPA is 2.5, and among students who enter the work force, approximately 85 percent enter a field related to their major within six months of graduation. Companies that most frequently hire graduates from Campbell University include: Wachovia · Merrill Lynch · BB&T · Bank of America · Enterprise Rental Cars.

Support for Students with Learning Disabilities

Students with learning disabilities may take advantage of specific support programs offered by Campbell University. Also, a lightened course load may be granted to LD students. Students with learning disabilities will find the following programs at Campbell University extremely useful: remedial math · remedial English · tutors · testing accommodations · untimed tests · extended time for tests · take-home exam · oral tests · readers · note-taking services · tape recorders · texts on tape · early syllabus · priority registration. Individual or small group tutorials are also available in: time management · organizational skills · learning strategies · specific subject areas · writing labs · study skills. An advisor/advocate from the Student Support Services is available to students.

CAMPBELL UNIVERSITY

Highlights

Campbell University
Buies Creek, NC
Location: Rural
Website: http://www.campbell.edu

Students
Total enrollment: 6,033
Undergrads: 2,083
Freshmen: 826
Part-time students: 30%
From out-of-state: 32%
Male/Female: 48%/52%
Live on-campus: Not reported
Off-campus employment rating: Fair
Caucasian: 71%
African American: 15%
Hispanic: 5%
Native American: 1%
International: 4%

Academics
Student/faculty ratio: 14:1
Class size 9 or fewer: 32%
Class size 10-29: 45%
Class size 30-49: 13%
Class size 50-99: 10%
Class size 100 or more: 1%
Returning freshmen: Not reported
Six-year graduation rate: Not reported

Most Popular Fields of Study
Business, Finance, Sales and Marketing
English and Literature
Philosophy, Religion and Theology
Computer and Information Sciences
Psychology
Law and Legal Studies
Health Professions, Medicine and Related
    Sciences
Foreign Languages, Literature and Linguistics
Communications, Journalism, Advertising
    and Comm. Technologies
Education

127

CAMPBELL UNIVERSITY

Admissions

Applicants: 3,014
Accepted: 1,800
Acceptance rate: 59.7%
Average GPA: Not reported
ACT range: Not reported
SAT Math range: Not reported
SAT Reading range: Not reported
SAT Writing range: Not reported
Top 10% of class: 38%
Top 25% of class: 80%
Top 50% of class: 92%

Deadlines

Early Action: No
Early Decision: No
Regular Action: Rolling admissions
Common Application: Accepted

Financial Aid

In-state tuition: $19,650
Out-of-state tuition: $19,650
Room: $3,250
Board: $3,580
Books: $1,200
Freshmen receiving need-based aid: 73%
Undergrads receiving need-based aid: 65%
Avg. % of need met by financial aid: 100%
Avg. aid package (freshmen): Not reported
Avg. aid package (undergrads): Not reported
Freshmen receiving merit-based aid: 23%
Undergrads receiving merit-based aid: 17%
Avg. student debt upon graduation: $21,703

School Spirit

Mascot: Fighting Camels

How to Get Admitted

For admissions decisions, non-academic factors considered: interview · extracurricular activities · special talents, interests, abilities · character/personal qualities · volunteer work · work experience · state of residency · alumni relationship. A high school diploma is required, although a GED is also accepted for admissions consideration. SAT or ACT test scores are required of all applicants. SAT Subject Test scores are recommended but not required. *According to the admissions office:* Math units must include 2 units of algebra and 1 unit of geometry. Social studies units must include 1 unit of U.S. history. Minimum combined SAT score of 900 and minimum 2.5 GPA required.

How to Pay for College

To apply for financial aid, students should submit the following: Free Application for Federal Student Aid (FAFSA). Campbell University participates in the Federal Work Study program. *Need-based aid programs include:* scholarships and grants · general need-based awards · Federal Pell grants · state scholarships and grants · college-based scholarships and grants · private scholarships and grants. *Non-Need-based aid programs include:* scholarships and grants · general need-based awards · state scholarships and grants · athletic scholarships · ROTC scholarships.

CARROLL COLLEGE

1601 North Benton Avenue, Helena, MT 59625-0002
Admissions: 800-992-3648 · Financial Aid: 800-992-3648
Email: enroll@carroll.edu · Website: http://www.carroll.edu

From the College

"Carroll College is a Catholic diocesean liberal arts college dedicated to making a difference. Most Carroll faculty, staff and students choose to volunteer their time to help others. It's called service learning, and it's a foundation of the Carroll College experience. The commitment to selfless service naturally extends to the classroom. Because of faculty support, Carroll students enjoy high acceptance rates to medical schools and law and business graduate programs. The philosophy of putting students first applies to every department on campus, from student housing and community life to class registration and financial aid. Carroll ensures a student's education is "Non scholae sed vitae—not for school alone but for life.""

Campus Setting

Carroll's 63-acre campus is located in central Helena, on the eastern slope of the Rocky Mountains. A four-year private institution, Carroll College has an enrollment of 1,409 students. Carroll College has been co-ed since 1944. The school is also affiliated with the Roman Catholic Church. In addition to a large, well-stocked library, the campus facilities include: performing arts center · arts lab · dance studio · engineering lab · observatory · seismograph station · science labs · nursing lab · fitness center. Carroll College provides on-campus housing with 435 units that can accommodate 830 students. Housing options: co-ed dorms · single-student apartments.

Student Life and Activities

With 65 percent of students living on campus, there are plenty of social activities. Popular events include: Search Weekend, Senior Retreat, Community Halloween Events for Children, Jr./Sr. Banquet and Softball Weekend. Carroll College has 37 official student organizations. The most popular are: Astronomy · Gay-Straight Alliance · Health Services · Music · Psychology · SAVE · Student Ambassadors · Students for a Just Society · Outdoor Club · Cadet Corps · CC Student Nurses Association · Circle K · College Democrats · College Republicans · Dance Team · Education · Engineers without Borders. Carroll College is a member of the Frontier Conference (NAIA).

Academics and Learning Environment

For the B student, the learning environment of a college is just as important as the quality of its academic program. Carroll College has 84 full-time and 73 part-time faculty members, offering a student-to-faculty ratio of 12:1. The most common course size is 10 to 19 students. Carroll College offers 31 majors with the most popular being business administration, elementary education and biology and least popular being foreign languages, computer science and arts. The school has a general core requirement as well as a religion requirement Cooperative education is not offered. All first-year students must maintain a 2.0 GPA or higher to avoid academic probation, and a minimum overall GPA of 2.0 is required to graduate. Other special academic programs that would appeal to a B student: self-designed majors · pass/fail grading option · independent study · double majors · dual degrees · accelerated study · honors program · internships.

CARROLL COLLEGE

B Student Support and Success

The Learning Commons exists to provide students with free opportunities to strengthen their academic skills through peer tutoring and study skills assistance. Carroll also offers supplemental instruction in some of the most difficult courses, and Writing Center assistants help tutor anyone struggling in English classes. Carroll's philosophy is based on the Four Pillars: Integrated Knowledge, Lifelong Skills, Enduring Values and Gateway Experiences. In addition, the Walter Young Center offers personal counseling for emotional challenges facing students. Anyone needing assistance in a class can also be matched with an academic coach for additional help and resources.

Carroll College provides a variety of support programs including dedicated guidance for: academic · career · personal · psychological · religious. Recognizing that some students may need extra preparation, Carroll College offers remedial and refresher courses in: reading · writing · math · study skills. The average freshman year GPA is 3.2, and 80 percent of freshmen students return for their sophomore year. What do students do after college? While many enter the work force, approximately 22 percent pursue a graduate degree immediately after graduation, and another 3 percent enter graduate school within two years. Among students who enter the work force, approximately 35 percent enter a field related to their major within six months of graduation. Companies that most frequently hire graduates from Carroll College include: Galusha Higgins Galusha · Anderson ZurMuehlen · Helena School District · Mountain West Bank · DA Davidson.

Support for Students with Learning Disabilities

Students with learning disabilities may take advantage of specific support programs. If necessary, the college will grant additional time to students with learning disabilities to complete their degree. Also, a lightened course load may be granted to LD students. Students with learning disabilities will find the following programs extremely useful: tutors · learning center · extended time for tests · oral tests · readers · note-taking services · waiver of math degree requirement. Tutorials are also available in: writing labs · math labs. An advisor/advocate from the LD program is available to students.

How to Get Admitted

For admissions decisions, non-academic factors considered: interview · extracurricular activities · special talents, interests, abilities · character/personal qualities · volunteer work · work experience · state of residency · religious affiliation/commitment · alumni relationship. A high school diploma is required, although a GED is also accepted for admissions consideration. SAT or ACT test scores are required of all applicants. SAT Subject Test scores are required for some applicants. *According to the admissions office:* Minimum composite ACT score of 21 (combined SAT Reasoning score of 1000) and minimum 2.5 GPA recommended. *Academic units recommended:* 4 English, 3 Math, 2 Science, 1 Social Studies, 2 Foreign Language.

How to Pay for College

To apply for financial aid, students should submit the following: Free Application for Federal Student Aid (FAFSA). Carroll College participates in the Federal Work Study program. *Need-based aid programs include:* scholarships and grants · general need-based awards · Federal Pell grants · state scholarships and grants · college-based scholarships and grants · private scholarships and grants. *Non-Need-based aid programs include:* scholarships and grants · state scholarships and grants · athletic scholarships · ROTC scholarships.

CARROLL COLLEGE

Admissions
Applicants: 1,174
Accepted: 895
Acceptance rate: 76.2%
Average GPA: 3.5
ACT range: 21-26
SAT Math range: 500-610
SAT Reading range: 490-590
SAT Writing range: 480-580
Top 10% of class: 26%
Top 25% of class: 59%
Top 50% of class: 87%

Deadlines
Early Action: No
Early Decision: No
Regular Action: Rolling admissions
Common Application: Accepted

Financial Aid
In-state tuition: $22,252
Out-of-state tuition: $22,252
Room: $3,670
Board: $3,448
Books: $800
Freshmen receiving need-based aid: 60%
Undergrads receiving need-based aid: 61%
Avg. % of need met by financial aid: 79%
Avg. aid package (freshmen): $17,292
Avg. aid package (undergrads): $17,133
Freshmen receiving merit-based aid: 22%
Undergrads receiving merit-based aid: 15%
Avg. student debt upon graduation: $25,246

Prominent Alumni
Archbishop Raymond Hunthausen, retired Seattle Archdiocese; Marc Racicot, former Governor of Montana

School Spirit
Mascot: Fighting Saints
Colors: Purple/Vegas gold

CHAMPLAIN COLLEGE

163 South Willard Street, Burlington, VT 05401
Admissions: 800-570-5858 · Financial Aid: 800-570-5858
Email: admission@champlain.edu · Website: http://www.champlain.edu

From the College

"Champlain College overlooks the city of Burlington, Vermont, and Lake Champlain, and has provided a career-oriented education for 125 years. Champlain reacts quickly to changes in the business world to offer up-to-date academic programs—the latest include Broadcasting, Electronic Game and Interactive Development, Marketing (with concentrations in Advertising and Marketing Management), Mass Communication, Middle School Education and Secondary School Education. Champlain's curriculum allows freshmen to begin right away taking courses in their field of interest, while internship and community service opportunities enhance the hands-on learning. 97 percent of Champlain students seeking employment find jobs within four months of graduation. Students also enjoy recreational opportunities in Vermont's Green Mountains."

Campus Setting

Champlain has introduced new fields of study, like Game Design and Computer and Digital Forensics, and offer majors with a specific focus, like e-Business Management, Digital Filmmaking and Public Relations. Champlain's three-dimensional education programs integrate relevant, professionally focused studies with a rigorous Core curriculum and practical Life Skills program. A four-year private institution, Champlain College has an enrollment of 2,763 students. In addition to a small library, the campus also has a business and technology center. Champlain College provides on-campus housing with 318 units that can accommodate 780 students. Housing options: co-ed dorms · women's dorms · special housing for International students. Recreation and sports facilities include: fitness center · gymnasium.

Student Life and Activities

Most students (60 percent) live off campus, which does impact the on-campus social scene. Nevertheless, like any college, students find time to create their own recreational outlets. According to the editor of the student newspaper, Burlington is a small but active college town along the shore of Lake Champlain. Five colleges are in town, and there are lots of clubs, activities, skiing, hiking and water sports in the area. A popular gathering place on campus is the IDX Student Life Center. Champlain College has 30 official student organizations. The most popular are: Get Real (service club) · World Drummers Club · book club · children's club · criminal justice club · e-gaming club · Heritage Society · psychology club · software engineering club · social work club · computer forensics club · international club · URGE · Speak Easy · Student Alumni Association · MusicMakers. For those interested in sports, there are intramural teams such as: basketball · crew · dance · golf · hiking · ice hockey · indoor soccer · lacrosse · rock climbing · running · sailing · skiing · snowboarding · ultimate Frisbee · volleyball.

Academics and Learning Environment

For the B student, the learning environment of a college is just as important as the quality of its academic program. Champlain College has 88 full-time and 225 part-time faculty members, offering a student-to-faculty ratio of 17:1. The most common course size is 10 to 19 students. Champlain College offers 52 majors with the most popular being business, multimedia/graphic design and professional studies. The school has a general core requirement. Cooperative education is not offered. All first-year students must maintain a 2.0 GPA or higher to avoid academic probation, and a minimum overall GPA of 2.0 is required to graduate. Other special academic programs that would appeal to a B student: self-designed majors · independent study · double majors · dual degrees · accelerated study · honors program · internships · distance learning certificate programs.

B Student Support and Success

Champlain offers a number of different centers to help students become and stay academically strong. At the Advising and Registration Center, or ARC, academic advisors provide one-on-one help to students who are choosing courses and planning their majors. At the Student Life Office, various academic support labs in accounting/math, writing and computers are offered as well as peer tutoring and counseling. The school also has Career Services and Health Services departments to help with planning and to give support.

Champlain College provides a variety of support programs including dedicated guidance for: academic · career · personal · minority students · non-traditional students. The average freshman year GPA is 2.8, and 73 percent of freshmen students return for their sophomore year. What do students do after college? While many enter the work force, approximately 8 percent pursue a graduate degree immediately after graduation. Among students who enter the work force, approximately 85 percent enter a field related to their major within six months of graduation. Companies that most frequently hire graduates from Champlain College include: IBM · KPMG · IDX Systems Corp. · Chittenden Bank · General Dynamics · Marsh Management · U.S. Immigration and Naturalization Services (INS).

Support for Students with Learning Disabilities

Students with learning disabilities may take advantage of specific support programs offered by Champlain College. Students with learning disabilities will find the following programs at Champlain College extremely useful: tutors · testing accommodations · untimed tests · extended time for tests · oral tests · note-taking services · early syllabus · priority registration.

How to Get Admitted

For admissions decisions, non-academic factors considered: interview · extracurricular activities · special talents, interests, abilities · character/personal qualities · volunteer work · work experience · state of residency · geographical location · alumni relationship. A high school diploma is required, although a GED is also accepted for admissions consideration. SAT or ACT test scores are required of all applicants. SAT Subject Test scores are required for some applicants. *According to the admissions office:* Minimum 2.0 GPA and essay required. *Academic units recommended:* 4 English, 4 Math, 4 Science, 3 Social Studies, 2 Foreign Language.

How to Pay for College

To apply for financial aid, students should submit the following: Free Application for Federal Student Aid (FAFSA) · institution's own financial aid forms · state aid form · Non-custodian (Divorced/

CHAMPLAIN COLLEGE

Highlights

Champlain College
Burlington, VT (Pop. 40,000)
Location: Medium city
Website: http://www.champlain.edu

Students
Total enrollment: 2,763
Undergrads: 1,506
Freshmen: 732
Part-time students: 20%
From out-of-state: 78%
Male/Female: 57%/43%
Live on-campus: 40%
Off-campus employment rating: Excellent
Caucasian: 63%
African American: 1%
Hispanic: 1%
Asian or Pacific Islander: 2%
Native American: 0%
International: 0%

Academics
Student/faculty ratio: 17:1
Class size 9 or fewer: 11%
Class size 10-29: 84%
Class size 30-49: 6%
Class size 50-99: 1%
Class size 100 or more: 1%
Returning freshmen: 73%
Six-year graduation rate: 72%

Most Popular Fields of Study
Business, Finance, Sales and Marketing
Computer and Information Sciences
Health Professions, Medicine and Related
 Sciences
Education
Communications, Journalism, Advertising
 and Comm. Technologies
Protective Services, Criminal Justice and
 Public Administration
Liberal Arts, Humanities and General
 Studies

CHAMPLAIN COLLEGE

Admissions
Applicants: 2,980
Accepted: 2,189
Acceptance rate: 73.5%
Average GPA: Not reported
ACT range: 20-25
SAT Math range: 510-610
SAT Reading range: 500-590
SAT Writing range: Not reported
Top 10% of class: 10%
Top 25% of class: 15%
Top 50% of class: 85%

Deadlines
Early Action: No
Early Decision: November 15
Regular Action: November 15 (priority)
January 31 (final)
Common Application: Accepted

Financial Aid
In-state tuition: $24,355
Out-of-state tuition: $24,355
Room: $6,770
Board: $4,440
Books: $600
Freshmen receiving need-based aid: 66%
Undergrads receiving need-based aid:
    68%
Avg. % of need met by financial aid: 68%
Avg. aid package (freshmen): $13,029
Avg. aid package (undergrads): $12,703
Freshmen receiving merit-based aid: 12%
Undergrads receiving merit-based aid:
    22%
Avg. student debt upon graduation: Not
    reported

School Spirit
Colors: Blue and white

Separated) Parent's Statement. Champlain College participates in the Federal Work Study program. *Need-based aid programs include:* scholarships and grants · general need-based awards · Federal Pell grants · state scholarships and grants · college-based scholarships and grants · private scholarships and grants. *Non-Need-based aid programs include:* state scholarships and grants.

CHOWAN UNIVERSITY

One University Place, Murfreesboro, NC 27855
Admissions: 800-488-4101 · Financial Aid: 252-398-1229
Email: enroll@chowan.edu
Website: http://www.chowan.edu

From the College

"Chowan University offers a personal liberal arts education in a rural, church-related setting, with regionally acclaimed programs in graphics communication, business, teacher education, history and physical education. Personal attention from faculty and staff gives each student his or her best opportunity for success."

Campus Setting

Chowan, founded in 1848, is a private, liberal arts college. Its 300-acre campus is located in Murfreesboro, 60 miles from Norfolk. A four-year private institution, Chowan University has an enrollment of 886 students. Chowan University has been co-ed since 1931. The school is also affiliated with the Baptist Church. The school also has a library with 120,000 books. Chowan University provides on-campus housing with 800 units that can accommodate 1,020 students. Housing options: women's dorms · men's dorms · special housing for disabled students.

Student Life and Activities

With 85 percent of students living on campus, there are plenty of social activities. Popular campus events include Homecoming and the Snow Ball. The most popular student organizations are: Chorus · singing group · concert · jazz · marching and pep bands · Chowan Players · athletic training · creative writing · education · history · imaging technology · physical education · psychology and science clubs · ambassadors · campus program board · inter-club council · off-campus student group · orientation team · team managers · women's club · Circle K · College Democrats · Future Sisters · Order of the Silver Feather · Rotaract Club. For those interested in sports, there are intramural teams such as: basketball · dodgeball · flag football · football · in-line hockey · indoor soccer · indoor volleyball · roller hockey · ultimate Frisbee. Chowan University is a member of the South Atlantic Conference (Division II).

Academics and Learning Environment

For the B student, the learning environment of a college is just as important as the quality of its academic program. Chowan University has 47 full-time and 26 part-time faculty members, offering a student-to-faculty ratio of 15:1. The most common course size is 2 to 9 students. Chowan University offers 25 majors with the most popular being business administration, physical education and graphic communication and least popular being religion, music and mathematics. The school has a general core requirement as well as a religion requirement Cooperative education is not offered. All first-year students must maintain a 1.4 GPA or higher to avoid academic probation, and a minimum overall GPA of 2.0 is required

Highlights

Chowan University
Murfreesboro, NC (Pop. 2,000)
Location: Rural
Website: http://www.chowan.edu

Students
Total enrollment: 886
Undergrads: 478
Freshmen: 351
Part-time students: 3%
From out-of-state: 60%
Male/Female: 54%/46%
Live on-campus: 85%
In fraternities: 10%
In sororities: 10%
Off-campus employment rating: Good
Caucasian: 50%
African American: 42%
Hispanic: 2%
Asian or Pacific Islander: 1%
Native American: 1%
International: 1%

Academics
Student/faculty ratio: 15:1
Class size 9 or fewer: 37%
Class size 10-29: 49%
Class size 30-49: 14%
Class size 50-99: 1%
Class size 100 or more: 1%
Returning freshmen: 53%
Six-year graduation rate: 26%

Admissions
Applicants: 2,385
Accepted: 1,464
Acceptance rate: 61.4%
Average GPA: Not reported
ACT range: Not reported
SAT Math range: 380-490
SAT Reading range: 380-480
SAT Writing range: Not reported
Top 10% of class: 4%
Top 25% of class: 18%
Top 50% of class: 34%

CHOWAN UNIVERSITY

Deadlines
Early Action: No
Early Decision: No
Regular Action: March 1 (priority)
Common Application: Not accepted

Financial Aid
In-state tuition: $18,850
Out-of-state tuition: $18,850
Room: $3,460
Board: $3,314
Books: $864
Freshmen receiving need-based aid: 86%
Undergrads receiving need-based aid: 88%
Avg. % of need met by financial aid: 60%
Avg. aid package (freshmen): $12,162
Avg. aid package (undergrads): $11,697
Freshmen receiving merit-based aid: 12%
Undergrads receiving merit-based aid: 11%
Avg. student debt upon graduation: Not reported

School Spirit
Mascot: Hawks
Colors: Blue and white

to graduate. Other special academic programs that would appeal to a B student: self-designed majors · independent study · double majors · honors program · internships · distance learning.

B Student Support and Success

Chowan offers its entire student body a tutoring program located in the campus library. Students request a tutor in any area of study by filling out an online tutor request form. Student tutors work one on one with students to provide this service four nights a week at no cost. Chowan also has Camp 121, a tutoring center that gives students a quiet space for individual studying between the hours of 9 and 5. Individual and group study sessions are frequently held at Camp 121 as well.

Chowan University provides a variety of support programs including dedicated guidance for: academic · career · religious. The average freshman year GPA is 2.4, and 53 percent of freshmen students return for their sophomore year.

Support for Students with Learning Disabilities

Students with learning disabilities may take advantage of specific support programs offered by Chowan University. Students with learning disabilities will find the following programs at Chowan University extremely useful: remedial math · tutors · learning center · untimed tests · extended time for tests · oral tests · note-taking services · tape recorders · early syllabus · priority registration. Individual or small group tutorials are also available in: time management · organizational skills · learning strategies · specific subject areas · writing labs · math labs · study skills. An advisor/advocate from the Learning Center is available to students.

How to Get Admitted

For admissions decisions, non-academic factors considered: interview · extracurricular activities · special talents, interests, abilities · character/personal qualities · volunteer work · work experience · state of residency · geographical location. A high school diploma is required, although a GED is also accepted for admissions consideration. SAT or ACT test scores are required of all applicants. SAT Subject Test scores are not required. *Academic units recommended:* 4 English, 3 Math, 2 Science, 3 Social Studies.

How to Pay for College

To apply for financial aid, students should submit the following: Free Application for Federal Student Aid (FAFSA). Chowan University participates in the Federal Work Study program. *Need-based aid programs include:* scholarships and grants · general need-based awards · Federal Pell grants · state scholarships and grants · college-based scholarships and grants · private scholarships and grants. *Non-Need-based aid programs include:* scholarships and grants · general need-based awards · state scholarships and grants · athletic scholarships · church-related scholarships · leadership scholarships · regional scholarships.

CHRISTOPHER NEWPORT UNIVERSITY

1 University Place, Newport News, VA 23606
Admissions: 800-333-4268 · Financial Aid: 800-333-4268
Email: admit@cnu.edu · Website: http://www.cnu.edu

From the College

"CNU is a public school that offers a private school experience—small classes that average only 25 students and a sense of community. Led by former U.S. Senator Paul Trible, Christopher Newport University has more than doubled the size of its freshman class and substantially increased the number of its faculty. CNU continues to build as a small academically selective public university dedicated to liberal learning, scholarship and service.

"CNU is nearing completion of a $500 million building campaign that has created a campus with new residential facilities; CNU Village, a residential and commercial complex housing apartments for upper-classmen and a variety of restaurants and stores; the Freeman Center, a $16 million sports and convocation center; the newly opened David Student Union, a 116,000 square foot 'one-stop shop' for students and the $60 million Ferguson Center for the Arts. Construction will soon begin on a new academic center providing state-of-the-art facilities including additional classrooms, seminar rooms and faculty offices.

"Christopher Newport University has one of the most successful NCAA Division III programs in the nation producing more than 70 individual and team championships and more than 500 All-Americans. In addition to The Freeman Center, home to basketball and indoor track, CNU's sports facilities include football's POMOCO Stadium, the Erwin Belk Track, and new baseball and softball stadiums."

Campus Setting

Christopher Newport, founded in 1960, is a comprehensive, public university. Programs are offered through the College of Liberal Arts and Science and the College of Business and Leadership. Its 150-acre campus is located in Newport News, midway between Williamsburg and Norfolk. A four-year public institution, Christopher Newport University has an enrollment of 4,904 students. In addition to a large, well-stocked library, the campus facilities include: museum · arts and sports/convocation centers. Christopher Newport University provides on-campus housing with 963 units that can accommodate 2,893 students. Housing options: co-ed dorms · single-student apartments. Recreation and sports facilities include: artificial turf field · field house · fitness center · grass field · tennis courts.

Student Life and Activities

With 58 percent of students living on campus, there are plenty of social activities. The David Student Center is a popular gathering spot. Popular events include Ella Fitzgerald Jazz Festival and Ferguson Center for the Arts concerts/performances. Christopher Newport University has 130 official student organizations. The most popular are: Citizens of the World · Campus Girl Scouts · Animal Welfare Coalition · Ballroom Dancing Society · Association for Computing Machinery · Roleplaying Guild · Virginia Association of Teachers of English · College Music Educators National Conference · Direct Marketing Association · Fine Arts Society · Graduate Student Association · Gay-Straight Student Union · Institute of Electric and Electronic Engineers · Model UN. For those interested in sports, there are intramural teams such as: badminton · basketball · dodgeball · flag football · free-throw shooting · soccer · softball · tennis · volleyball. Christopher Newport University is a member of the USA South Athletic Conference (Division III).

CHRISTOPHER NEWPORT UNIVERSITY

Christopher Newport University
Newport News, VA (Pop. 180,150)
Location: Medium city
Website: http://www.cnu.edu

Students
Total enrollment: 4,904
Undergrads: 2,143
Freshmen: 1,541
Part-time students: 4%
From out-of-state: 7%
Male/Female: 45%/55%
Live on-campus: 58%
In fraternities: 10%
In sororities: 14%
Off-campus employment rating: Excellent
Caucasian: 83%
African American: 8%
Hispanic: 3%
Asian or Pacific Islander: 3%
Native American: 1%
International: 0%

Academics
Student/faculty ratio: 17:1
Class size 9 or fewer: 8%
Class size 10-29: 71%
Class size 30-49: 19%
Class size 50-99: 2%
Class size 100 or more: -
Returning freshmen: 80%
Six-year graduation rate: 49%

Most Popular Fields of Study
Business, Finance, Sales and Marketing
Visual and Performing Arts
English and Literature
Philosophy, Religion and Theology
Computer and Information Sciences
Mathematics
Engineering and Engineering Technologies
Foreign Languages, Literature and Linguistics
Communications, Journalism, Advertising and Comm. Technologies
Social Sciences, History, Economics, Political Science

138

Academics and Learning Environment

For the B student, the learning environment of a college is just as important as the quality of its academic program. Christopher Newport University has 239 full-time and 125 part-time faculty members, offering a student-to-faculty ratio of 17:1. The most common course size is 20 to 29 students. Christopher Newport University offers 31 majors with the most popular being business administration, political science and psychology and least popular being German, economics and finance. The school has a general core requirement. Cooperative education is not offered. All first-year students must maintain a 2.0 GPA or higher to avoid academic probation, and a minimum overall GPA of 2.0 is required to graduate. Other special academic programs that would appeal to a B student: self-designed majors · independent study · double majors · dual degrees · honors program · internships.

B Student Support and Success

Christopher Newport College provides academic advising and counseling/career services to their students. Their Writing Center offers help to students who are writing papers or projects.

In addition, the school has a Learning Communities program for first-year students. This program involves 18 to 24 students who live together, take two classes together and build strong relationships with the community. This arrangement provides support for the transition from home to college, while also giving each participant a peer mentor to learn from as well as help with setting up study groups, test review sessions, informal group tutoring and more.

Christopher Newport University provides a variety of support programs including dedicated guidance for: academic · career · personal · minority students · religious. The average freshman year GPA is 2.8, and 80 percent of freshmen students return for their sophomore year.

Support for Students with Learning Disabilities

Students with learning disabilities may take advantage of specific support programs offered by Christopher Newport University. Students with learning disabilities will find the following programs at Christopher Newport University extremely useful: extended time for tests · oral tests · note-taking services · tape recorders.

How to Get Admitted

For admissions decisions, non-academic factors considered: extracurricular activities · special talents, interests, abilities · volunteer work · work experience · state of residency · alumni relationship. A high school diploma is required, although a GED is also accepted for admissions consideration. SAT or ACT test scores are required for some applicants. SAT Subject Test scores are not required. *According to the admissions office:* Rank in top half of secondary school class and minimum 3.0 GPA required. *Academic units recommended:* 4 English, 4 Math, 4 Science, 4 Foreign Language.

How to Pay for College

To apply for financial aid, students should submit the following: Free Application for Federal Student Aid (FAFSA). Christopher Newport University participates in the Federal Work Study program.

Need-based aid programs include: scholarships and grants · general need-based awards · Federal Pell grants · state scholarships and grants · college-based scholarships and grants · private scholarships and grants. *Non-Need-based aid programs include:* scholarships and grants · state scholarships and grants · creative arts and performance awards · ROTC scholarships.

CHRISTOPHER NEWPORT UNIVERSITY

Highlights

Admissions
Applicants: 7,174
Accepted: 3,984
Acceptance rate: 55.5%
placed on wait list: 330
Average GPA: 3.6
ACT range: 22-26
SAT Math range: 550-630
SAT Reading range: 5540-630
SAT Writing range: Not reported
Top 10% of class: 20%
Top 25% of class: 58%
Top 50% of class: 95%

Deadlines
Early Action: December 1
Early Decision: No
Regular Action: Rolling admissions
Common Application: Accepted

Financial Aid
In-state tuition: $7,550
Out-of-state tuition: $14,930
Room: $5,780
Board: $3,120
Books: $870
Freshmen receiving need-based aid: 40%
Undergrads receiving need-based aid: 36%
Avg. % of need met by financial aid: 75%
Avg. aid package (freshmen): $7,346
Avg. aid package (undergrads): $7,534
Freshmen receiving merit-based aid: 10%
Undergrads receiving merit-based aid: 8%
Avg. student debt upon graduation: $17,752

School Spirit
Mascot: Captain Chris
Colors: Royal blue and silver
Song: *Go Captains*

COASTAL CAROLINA UNIVERSITY

P.O. Box 261954, Conway, SC 29528-6054
Admissions: 800-277-7000 · Financial Aid: 843-349-2313
Email: admissions@coastal.edu · Website: http://www.coastal.edu

From the College

"Coastal Carolina University is a public, comprehensive, liberal arts institution. The university offers baccalaureate programs to approximately 8,000 students in 40 fields of study including acclaimed programs in marine science, resort tourism and professional golf management. Graduate programs include an M.B.A. Waties Island, 1,062 acres of pristine barrier island on the Atlantic coast, provides a natural laboratory for extensive study in the sciences. Students enjoy a nationally competitive NCAA I athletic program that includes football, an inspiring cultural calendar, and a tradition of community interaction fueled by more than 100 student clubs and organizations."

Campus Setting

Coastal Carolina University, founded in 1954, has a 307-acre campus located in Conway, nine miles from Myrtle Beach. A four-year public institution, Coastal Carolina University has an enrollment of 8,154 students. In addition to a large, well-stocked library, the campus also has a marine science and wetland biology lab. Coastal Carolina University provides on-campus housing with 732 units that can accommodate 2,250 students. Housing options: co-ed dorms · single-student apartments · special housing for disabled students. Recreation and sports facilities include: athletic fields · basketball and volleyball courts · weight room.

Student Life and Activities

Most students (70 percent) live off campus, which does impact the on-campus social scene. Nevertheless, like any college, students find time to create their own recreational outlets. As reported by a school representative, "'Cliques' are prominent, social and cultural life is up and coming. OSAL, Residence Life, and Multicultural Student Services are working to enhance cultural diversity and awareness." Popular gathering spots include the CINO Grille, Student Center game room, volleyball court in front of the Woods community, campus recreation center, Broadway at the Beach, Coastal Ale House and the beach. Popular campus events include football games/tailgating, late night bingo in the commons, Casino Night in the Fall, CINO Day in the Spring, Homecoming week events, Greek week events, Greek formals, step shows, diversity programs, intramural sports, basketball games, baseball games and game show nights. Coastal Carolina University has 63 official student organizations. Popular groups on campus include Greeks, athletes, STAR members, Leadership Challenge members, Coastal Productions Board, honor societies, the Chanticleer, CCU Customs, gospel choir and intramural teams. For those interested in sports, there are intramural teams such as: basketball · football · soccer · softball · volleyball · water polo. Coastal Carolina University is a member of the Big South Conference (Division I).

Academics and Learning Environment

For the B student, the learning environment of a college is just as important as the quality of its academic program. Coastal Carolina University has 299 full-time and 262 part-time faculty members, offering a student-to-faculty ratio of 18:1. The most common course size is 20 to 29 students. Coastal Carolina University offers 56 majors with the most popular being marketing, management and health promotion and least popular being philosophy, musical theatre and Spanish. The school has a general core requirement. Cooperative education is available. All first-year students must maintain a 2.0 GPA or higher to avoid academic probation, and a minimum overall GPA of 2.0 is required to graduate. Other special academic programs that would appeal to a B student: self-designed majors · pass/fail grading option · independent study · double majors · dual degrees · accelerated study · honors program · Phi Beta Kappa · internships · distance learning certificate programs.

B Student Support and Success

At Coastal Carolina, professional academic advising and peer mentoring are available. The school also has a course called UNIV 110, which is designed to develop critical thinking and research skills, to provide community support during the first semester of enrollment, and to acquaint students with the school's resources. Tutoring sessions are offered and there is even a Grammar Hotline to call.

The UNIV 110 course, also known as a "First Year Experience," involves peers, faculty and staff and other members within the community. Students play an active part in forums, workshops, discussions, readings, case studies and community service projects. This includes assignments that might come in various forms, ranging from quizzes, tests and journals to presentations, portfolios and writing projects. In the end, UNIV 110 helps students to develop a clearer and more comprehensive academic and career development plan for the future.

Coastal Carolina University provides a variety of support programs including dedicated guidance for: academic · career · personal · psychological · minority students · veterans · non-traditional students · family planning. The average freshman year GPA is 2.9, and 71 percent of freshmen students return for their sophomore year. What do students do after college? While many enter the work force, approximately 18 percent pursue a graduate degree immediately after graduation. Among students who enter the work force, approximately 83 percent enter a field related to their major within six months of graduation. Companies that most frequently hire graduates from Coastal Carolina University include: City of Myrtle Beach · Coastal Carolina University · Horry County Government · Horry County Schools · Horry Telephone.

Support for Students with Learning Disabilities

Students with learning disabilities may take advantage of specific support programs offered by Coastal Carolina University. Also, a lightened course load may be granted to LD students. High school foreign language waivers are accepted. According to the school, all students who register are requested to participate in a coaching relationship with the counselor where an academic plan is developed and followed, and there are meetings with the student throughout the first semester. Meetings include time management, organization, specific areas of weakness (i.e. reading, math, writing), tutoring and study group. Students with learning disabilities will find the following programs at Coastal Carolina University extremely useful: remedial math · special classes · tutors · learning center · testing accommodations · untimed tests · extended time for tests · take-home exam · oral tests · readers · typist/scribe · note-taking services · reading machines · tape recorders · texts on tape · videotaped classes · early syllabus · priority registration · priority seating. Individual or small group tutorials are also available in: time management ·

COASTAL CAROLINA UNIVERSITY

Coastal Carolina University
Conway, SC (Pop. 12,200)
Location: Large town
Website: http://www.coastal.edu

Students
Total enrollment: 8,154
Undergrads: 3,565
Freshmen: 2,270
Part-time students: 9%
From out-of-state: 54%
Male/Female: 47%/53%
Live on-campus: 30%
In fraternities: 6%
In sororities: 10%
Off-campus employment rating: Excellent
Caucasian: 82%
African American: 13%
Hispanic: 2%
Asian or Pacific Islander: 1%
Native American: 1%
International: 1%

Academics
Student/faculty ratio: 18:1
Class size 9 or fewer: 14%
Class size 10-29: 55%
Class size 30-49: 26%
Class size 50-99: 5%
Class size 100 or more: -
Returning freshmen: 71%
Six-year graduation rate: 47%

Most Popular Fields of Study
Business, Finance, Sales and Marketing
Biological and Life Sciences
Visual and Performing Arts
English and Literature
Computer and Information Sciences
Mathematics
Parks, Recreation and Fitness
Health Professions, Medicine and Related Sciences
Liberal Arts, Humanities and General Studies
Foreign Languages, Literature and Linguistics

141

COASTAL CAROLINA
UNIVERSITY

Admissions
Applicants: 7,514
Accepted: 5,215
Acceptance rate: 69.4%
Average GPA: 3.4
ACT range: 20-23
SAT Math range: 480-560
SAT Reading range: 460-540
SAT Writing range: Not reported
Top 10% of class: 9%
Top 25% of class: 34%
Top 50% of class: 73%

Deadlines
Early Action: No
Early Decision: No
Regular Action: March 1 (priority)
August 15 (final)
Common Application: Accepted

Financial Aid
In-state tuition: $8,570
Out-of-state tuition: $18,010
Room: $4,630
Board: $2,450
Books: $1,044
Freshmen receiving need-based aid: 60%
Undergrads receiving need-based aid:
   56%
Avg. % of need met by financial aid: 51%
Avg. aid package (freshmen): $8,141
Avg. aid package (undergrads): $8,094
Freshmen receiving merit-based aid: 22%
Undergrads receiving merit-based aid:
   21%
Avg. student debt upon graduation:
   $24,856

Prominent Alumni
Tyler Thigpen, quarterback, Kansas City
Chiefs; Dustin Johnson, professional
golfer, PGA; Michael Kelly, actor, The
Changeling.

School Spirit
Mascot: Chanticleers
Colors: Bronze and coastal teal

organizational skills · learning strategies · specific subject areas · writing labs · math labs · study skills. An advisor/advocate from the LD program is available to students.

How to Get Admitted

For admissions decisions, non-academic factors considered: interview · extracurricular activities · special talents, interests, abilities · character/personal qualities · work experience · geographical location. A high school diploma is required, although a GED is also accepted for admissions consideration. SAT or ACT test scores are required of all applicants. SAT Subject Test scores are recommended but not required. *According to the admissions office:* Minimum combined SAT Reasoning score of 960 (composite ACT score of 20) and minimum 2.5 GPA required.

How to Pay for College

To apply for financial aid, students should submit the following: Free Application for Federal Student Aid (FAFSA). Coastal Carolina University participates in the Federal Work Study program. *Need-based aid programs include:* scholarships and grants · general need-based awards · Federal Pell grants · state scholarships and grants · college-based scholarships and grants · private scholarships and grants. *Non-Need-based aid programs include:* scholarships and grants · general need-based awards · state scholarships and grants · creative arts and performance awards · athletic scholarships.

COE COLLEGE

1220 First Avenue, NE, Cedar Rapids, IA 52402
Admissions: 877-225-5863 · Financial Aid: 877-225-5863
Email: admission@coe.edu · Website: http://www.coe.edu

From the College

"Coe College believes that a liberal arts education allows students to discover their real talents and interests, while developing the skills, abilities and habits of mind that will make possible a successful career in any field of endeavor, including ones that do not yet exist. The Coe Plan, a unique program grounded in the liberal arts, is designed to ensure that Coe students make an effective transition from college to career. Coe makes practical experience—internships, off-campus study or research—a requirement for graduation."

Campus Setting

Coe, founded in 1851, is a church-affiliated college. Its 60-acre campus is located a mile from downtown Cedar Rapids. A four-year private institution, Coe College has been co-ed since 1853. The school is also affiliated with the Presbyterian Church. In addition to a large, well-stocked library, the campus facilities include: music studio · GIS/GPS lab. Coe College provides on-campus housing that can accommodate 1,040 students. Housing options: co-ed dorms · women's dorms · men's dorms · sorority housing · fraternity housing · single-student apartments. Recreation and sports facilities include: baseball · soccer and softball fields · basketball courts · cross-country course · field house · football and volleyball stadiums · racquetball center · swimming pool.

Student Life and Activities

With 88 percent of students living on campus, there are plenty of social activities. Hot spots on and off campus include the Pub, the Piano Lounge, Library Quad, TKE House, Mahoney's, Moose McDuffies and Brewed Awakenings. Blindspot, athletic events, plays, Presidential Ball, Homecoming are the most popular social events of the year. Coe College has 74 official student organizations. Student groups that influence campus life include Greeks, Cosmos, athletes and the Senate. For those interested in sports, there are intramural teams such as: basketball · flag football · floor hockey · racquetball · soccer · softball · squash · tennis · ultimate Frisbee · volleyball. Coe College is a member of the Iowa Intercollegiate Athletic Conference (Division III).

Academics and Learning Environment

For the B student, the learning environment of a college is just as important as the quality of its academic program. Coe College has 81 full-time and 78 part-time faculty members, offering a student-to-faculty ratio of 11:1. The most common course size is 10 to 19 students. Coe College offers 49 majors with the most popular being business administration, psychology and nursing and least popular being environmental studies, Asian studies and African American studies. The school has a general core requirement. Cooperative education is available. All first-year students must maintain a 2.0 GPA or higher to avoid academic probation. Other special academic programs that would appeal to a B student: self-designed majors · pass/fail grading option · independent study · double majors · accelerated study · honors program · Phi Beta Kappa · internships.

B Student Support and Success

Like a growing number of colleges today, Coe offers a First Year Seminar to help students transition from high school to college. This program emphasizes learning

COE COLLEGE

Coe College
Cedar Rapids, IA (Pop. 175,000)
Location: Medium city
Website: http://www.coe.edu

Students
Total enrollment: 1,326
Undergrads: 590
Freshmen: 342
Part-time students: 5%
From out-of-state: 40%
Male/Female: 45%/55%
Live on-campus: 88%
In fraternities: 21%
In sororities: 21%
Off-campus employment rating: Excellent
Caucasian: 85%
African American: 2%
Hispanic: 2%
Asian or Pacific Islander: 1%
Native American: 0%
International: 4%

Academics
Student/faculty ratio: 11:1
Class size 9 or fewer: 24%
Class size 10-29: 69%
Class size 30-49: 6%
Class size 50-99: 1%
Class size 100 or more: -
Returning freshmen: 80%
Six-year graduation rate: 69%

Most Popular Fields of Study
Business, Finance, Sales and Marketing
Psychology
Visual and Performing Arts
English and Literature
Philosophy, Religion and Theology
Physical Sciences, Chemistry, Physics
 and Astronomy
Mathematics
Parks, Recreation and Fitness
Interdisciplinary Studies
Health Professions, Medicine and Re-
 lated Sciences

basic writing skills and offers a number of different classes to take to get these skills. To support this, the college has a Writing Center plus a Speaking Center for stronger oral presentations. The college also provides an Academic Achievement Program that offers an umbrella of services. Academic assistance includes tutoring, advising, helping with study skills, getting supplemental instruction, reading assistance and math help. Several types of counseling are offered, including peer, personal, career and substance abuse. In addition, Coe offers the TRANSITIONS program, a half-credit course that helps students "improve skills necessary for successful performance in college," including the topics of study skills, time management, self motivation and personal responsibility.

Coe College provides a variety of support programs including dedicated guidance for: academic · career · personal · psychological · minority students · family planning · religious. Recognizing that some students may need extra preparation, Coe College offers remedial and refresher courses in: reading · writing · math · study skills. Annually, 80 percent of freshmen students return for their sophomore year. What do students do after college? While many enter the work force, approximately 20 percent pursue a graduate degree immediately after graduation. Among students who enter the work force, approximately 73 percent enter a field related to their major within six months of graduation. Companies that most frequently hire graduates from Coe College include: Aegon USA · branch offices of McGladry and Pullen · Deloitte & Touche · Principal Financial Group · Rockwell-Collins · U.S. Department of Labor · University of Iowa Hospitals and Clinics · various school districts throughout the region.

Support for Students with Learning Disabilities

Students with learning disabilities may take advantage of specific support programs offered by Coe College. If necessary, the college will grant additional time to students with learning disabilities to complete their degree. Also, a lightened course load may be granted to LD students. Students with learning disabilities will find the following programs at Coe College extremely useful: remedial reading · tutors · learning center · testing accommodations · untimed tests · extended time for tests · take-home exam · oral tests · note-taking services · tape recorders · early syllabus. Individual or small group tutorials are also available in: time management · organizational skills · learning strategies · specific subject areas · writing labs · math labs · study skills. An advisor/advocate from the Academic Achievement Program is available to students. This member also sits on the admissions committee.

How to Get Admitted

For admissions decisions, non-academic factors considered: interview · extracurricular activities · special talents, interests, abilities · character/personal qualities · volunteer work · work experience · state of residency · alumni relationship. A high school diploma is required, although a GED is also accepted for admissions consideration. SAT or ACT test scores are required of all applicants. *According to the admissions office:* Minimum composite ACT score of 20 or SAT score of 1000 (verbal and math), rank in top two-fifths of secondary school class, and minimum 3.0 GPA recommended. *Academic*

units recommended: 4 English, 3 Math, 3 Science, 3 Social Studies, 2 Foreign Language.

How to Pay for College

To apply for financial aid, students should submit the following: Free Application for Federal Student Aid (FAFSA). Coe College participates in the Federal Work Study program. *Need-based aid programs include:* scholarships and grants · general need-based awards · Federal Pell grants · state scholarships and grants · college-based scholarships and grants · private scholarships and grants. *Non-Need-based aid programs include:* scholarships and grants · general need-based awards · state scholarships and grants · creative arts and performance awards · special achievements and activities awards · special characteristics awards · ROTC scholarships.

COE COLLEGE

Highlights

Admissions
Applicants: 1,943
Accepted: 1,224
Acceptance rate: 63.0%
Average GPA: 3.7
ACT range: 23-28
SAT Math range: 550-670
SAT Reading range: 560-680
SAT Writing range: 540-650
Top 10% of class: 30%
Top 25% of class: 66%
Top 50% of class: 94%

Deadlines
Early Action: December 10
Early Decision: No
Regular Action: Rolling admissions
Common Application: Accepted

Financial Aid
In-state tuition: $28,950
Out-of-state tuition: $28,950
Room: $3,210
Board: $3,940
Books: $1,000
Freshmen receiving need-based aid: 73%
Undergrads receiving need-based aid: 74%
Avg. % of need met by financial aid: 92%
Avg. aid package (freshmen): $24,455
Avg. aid package (undergrads): $23,972
Freshmen receiving merit-based aid: 26%
Undergrads receiving merit-based aid: 24%

School Spirit
Mascot: Kohawks
Colors: Crimson and Vegas gold

COLLEGE OF IDAHO

2112 Cleveland Boulevard, Caldwell, ID 83605
Admissions: 800-224-3246 · Financial Aid: 800-224-3246
Email: admission@collegeofidaho.edu
Website: http://www.collegeofidaho.edu

From the College

"The College of Idaho is a place where you can complete your degree in four years, with a high job placement rate. If you plan to attend graduate school, the College of Idaho has a very positive record for acceptance and placement rates at some of the most reputable programs in the country. We offer small classes (11:1 student to faculty ratio), faculty who care about you as a person, internships, an academic calendar which encourages international travel, and opportunities to participate in community-based classes and projects. The college was recently ranked the 20th best college in the U.S. for "More Things to Do on Campus" by the Princeton Review and is regularly ranked in various publications as a top college in the Pacific Northwest. The College of Idaho's location in "the Treasure Valley" allows for outdoor opportunities that include skiing, hiking, climbing, rafting, kayaking and exploring the desert. Located minutes from metropolitan Boise, the college is easily accessible by air or automobile."

Campus Setting

The College of Idaho is a liberal arts institution founded in 1891. Its 50-acre campus is located in Caldwell, 25 miles west of Boise. A four-year private institution, the College of Idaho has an enrollment of 944 students. In addition to a large, well-stocked library, the campus facilities include: fine arts center · movie theatre · activities center · chapel · gem and mineral collection · museum of natural history · planetarium · herbarium. The College of Idaho provides on-campus housing with 347 units that can accommodate 571 students. Housing options: co-ed dorms · fraternity housing · single-student apartments · special housing for disabled students. Recreation and sports facilities include: activities center · stadium.

Student Life and Activities

With 62 percent of students living on campus, there are plenty of social activities. According to the school, there are many activities going on during the school year. The Student Involvement Office helps students discover how to get involved in activities on campus and in the community. From athletics to theater or music, the opportunities are limitless for students to be involved. Students gather at McCain Student Union, Simplot Dining Hall, local coffee shops, restaurants, and businesses including Albertson's Athletic Center and Center on the Grove in Boise. Home Coming, Caldwell Fine Art Programs, Theater Productions, Langroise Trio, Greek Formal, Liberal Art Lectures, Potters Clay, A.L.A.S. Cultural Dinners, Late Night Campus Ministry, Finals Breakfasts , Berger's Bench, Spring Fling, Rosenthal Art Gallery, student government activities, C of I Student Research Conference, Cinco de Mayo Celebration, Comedy in the Pub, Phreakin' Phrenzies, Film Festivales, Greek Week, Winter Fest, sporting activities, intramural activities, and Outdoor Program are popular events. The College of Idaho has 60 official student organizations. The most popular are: Music · theatre · political · service and special-interest groups. For those interested in sports, there are intramural teams such as: badminton · baseball · basketball · bowling · dodgeball · flag football · Frisbee · lacrosse · soccer · softball · volleyball. The College of Idaho is a member of the Cascade Collegiate Conference (NAIA).

Academics and Learning Environment

For the B student, the learning environment of a college is just as important as the quality of its academic program. The College of Idaho has 65 full-time and 50 part-time faculty members, offering a student-to-faculty ratio of 11:1. The most common course size is 2 to 9 students. The College of Idaho offers 36 majors with the most popular being biology, business and psychology and least popular being pre-engineering, religion and philosophy. The school has a general core requirement. Cooperative education is available. All first-year students must maintain a 2.0 GPA or higher to avoid academic probation, and a minimum overall GPA of 2.0 is required to graduate. Other special academic programs that would appeal to a B student: self-designed majors · pass/fail grading option · independent study · double majors · dual degrees · honors program · internships.

B Student Support and Success

At the College of Idaho, new students participate in the First Year Experience, which is geared to provide "living and learning experiences that facilitates a successful transition to a college community centered on exacting scholarship and life-long learning." The program includes a First Year Theme and Book in which a theme is chosen and then a book supporting that theme is read before the fall semester begins. From there, discussions of the book are held, as well as guest speakers, films, debates, theatrical productions and even special tie in menus in the dining halls.

The College of Idaho provides a variety of support programs including dedicated guidance for: academic · career · personal · psychological · minority students · military · non-traditional students · family planning · religious. Additional counseling services include: peer counseling. Recognizing that some students may need extra preparation, the College of Idaho offers remedial and refresher courses in: reading · writing · math · study skills. Annually, 80 percent of freshmen students return for their sophomore year.

Support for Students with Learning Disabilities

Students with learning disabilities may take advantage of specific support programs. If necessary, the college will grant additional time to students with learning disabilities to complete their degree. Also, a lightened course load may be granted to LD students. Students with learning disabilities will find the following programs extremely useful: remedial math · tutors · learning center · testing accommodations · untimed tests · extended time for tests · take-home exam · oral tests · readers · note-taking services · reading machines · tape recorders · early syllabus · diagnostic testing service · priority registration · waiver of math degree requirement. Tutorials are also available in: time management · organizational skills · learning strategies · specific subject areas · study skills. An advisor/advocate from the Learning Support and Disability Services is available to students. This member also sits on the admissions committee.

How to Get Admitted

For admissions decisions, non-academic factors considered: interview · extracurricular activities · special talents, interests, abilities · character/personal qualities · volunteer work · state of residency · alumni

COLLEGE OF IDAHO

COLLEGE OF IDAHO

Admissions
Applicants: 1,275
Accepted: 756
Acceptance rate: 59.3%
Average GPA: 3.6
ACT range: 22-27
SAT Math range: 490-630
SAT Reading range: 470-623
SAT Writing range: 460-570
Top 10% of class: 29%
Top 25% of class: 68%
Top 50% of class: 91%

Deadlines
Early Action: December 15
Early Decision: No
Regular Action: Rolling admissions
Common Application: Accepted

Financial Aid
In-state tuition: $19,300
Out-of-state tuition: $19,300
Room: $3,450
Board: $4,028
Books: $900
Freshmen receiving need-based aid: 66%
Undergrads receiving need-based aid: 61%
Avg. % of need met by financial aid: 88%
Avg. aid package (freshmen): $17,364
Avg. aid package (undergrads): $16,324
Freshmen receiving merit-based aid: 34%
Undergrads receiving merit-based aid: 36%
Avg. student debt upon graduation: $24,919

Prominent Alumni
Loretta Warner Holway, first Idaho woman accepted by Harvard Law School; Dr. Mary Shorb, co-discoverer of vitamin B-12; Joe Albertson, founder of Albertsons grocery stores; Kris McDivitt, co-founder of Patagonia Outerwear.

School Spirit
Mascot: Coyotes
Colors: Purple and gold
Song: *Hail College of Idaho*

relationship. A high school diploma is required, although a GED is also accepted for admissions consideration. SAT or ACT test scores are required of all applicants. SAT Subject Test scores are not required. *According to the admissions office:* Minimum 3.0 GPA and SAT of 1000 or ACT of 22 for regular admission. Provisional admission also considered. *Academic units recommended:* 4 English, 4 Math, 3 Science, 2 Social Studies, 3 Foreign Language.

How to Pay for College

To apply for financial aid, students should submit the following: Free Application for Federal Student Aid (FAFSA) · institution's own financial aid forms. The College of Idaho participates in the Federal Work Study program. *Need-based aid programs include:* scholarships and grants · general need-based awards · Federal Pell grants · state scholarships and grants · college-based scholarships and grants · private scholarships and grants. *Non-Need-based aid programs include:* scholarships and grants · general need-based awards · state scholarships and grants · creative arts and performance awards · special achievements and activities awards · athletic scholarships · ROTC scholarships.

COLLEGE OF NOTRE DAME OF MARYLAND

4701 North Charles Street, Baltimore, MD 21210
Admissions: 800-435-0300 · Financial Aid: 410-532-5369
Email: admiss@ndm.edu · Website: http://www.ndm.edu

From the College

"The College of Notre Dame of Maryland educates women to strive for intellectual and professional excellence, to build inclusive communities, to engage in service to others and promote social responsibility."

Campus Setting

The College of Notre Dame of Maryland, founded in 1873, is a private, church-affiliated, liberal arts college for women. Its 58-acre campus is located inside city limits in northern Baltimore. A four-year college, the College of Notre Dame of Maryland has an enrollment of 3,259 students. The school is also affiliated with the Roman Catholic Church. The school also has a library with 426,000 books. The College of Notre Dame of Maryland provides on-campus housing with 2 units that can accommodate 406 students. Housing options: women's dorms. Recreation and sports facilities include: athletic complex · fields · fitness center · gymnasium · racquetball courts · tennis courts · track.

Student Life and Activities

With 52 percent of students living on campus, there are plenty of social activities. The Connection (an eatery) is a popular on-campus hangout and students often gather off-campus at other local college campuses. Popular campus events include the Advent Service, Tree Trim and Christmas Dinner, Family Weekend, Winter Ball, Notre Dame Day, 100 Nights, Lantern Chain, Winterfest, Spring Formal and Alternative Spring Break. The College of Notre Dame of Maryland has 30 official student organizations. Some groups with a strong social presence on campus include the Senate and the Interorganizational Council (IOC). The College of Notre Dame of Maryland is a member of the Atlantic Women's Colleges Conference (Division III).

Academics and Learning Environment

For the B student, the learning environment of a college is just as important as the quality of its academic program. The College of Notre Dame of Maryland has 80 full-time and 12 part-time faculty members, offering a student-to-faculty ratio of 12:1. The most common course size is 10 to 19 students. The College of Notre Dame of Maryland offers 36 majors with the most popular being business, nursing and education and least popular being economics, chemistry and music. The school has a general core requirement as well as a religion requirement Cooperative education is not offered. All first-year students must maintain a 2.0 GPA or higher to avoid academic probation. Other special academic programs that would appeal to a B student: self-designed majors · pass/fail grading op-

COLLEGE OF NOTRE DAME OF MARYLAND

Admissions
Applicants: 501
Accepted: 356
Acceptance rate: 71.1%
Average GPA: 3.4
ACT range: Not reported
SAT Math range: 440-550
SAT Reading range: 470-600
SAT Writing range: Not reported
Top 10% of class: 18%
Top 25% of class: 45%
Top 50% of class: 77%

Deadlines
Early Action: No
Early Decision: No
Regular Action: February 15 (priority)
Common Application: Accepted

Financial Aid
In-state tuition: $26,500
Out-of-state tuition: $26,500
Room: -
Board: -
Books: $1,200
Freshmen receiving need-based aid: 87%
Undergrads receiving need-based aid: 76%
Avg. % of need met by financial aid: 72%
Avg. aid package (freshmen): $20,505
Avg. aid package (undergrads): $17,950
Freshmen receiving merit-based aid: 10%
Undergrads receiving merit-based aid: 8%
Avg. student debt upon graduation: $21,681

Prominent Alumni
Kathleen Beres, finalist in teacher in space program, aerospace industry; Eileen O'Neill, senior vice president and general manager, Discovery Health.

School Spirit
Mascot: Gators
Colors: Royal blue and white

tion · independent study · double majors · dual degrees · accelerated study · honors program · internships · weekend college.

B Student Support and Success

College of Notre Dame's campus-wide peer tutoring program is known as Each One, Teach One. It is designed to achieve "increases in the success rate of students in courses that have historically proved to be extremely challenging." A Writing Center is also available to all students either by appointment or on a drop-in basis.

The College of Notre Dame of Maryland provides a variety of support programs including dedicated guidance for: academic · career · personal · psychological · non-traditional students. Annually, 71 percent of freshmen students return for their sophomore year.

Support for Students with Learning Disabilities

Students with learning disabilities may take advantage of specific support programs offered by the College of Notre Dame of Maryland. If necessary, the college will grant additional time to students with learning disabilities to complete their degree. Also, a lightened course load may be granted to LD students. Students with learning disabilities will find the following programs at the College of Notre Dame of Maryland extremely useful: tutors · testing accommodations · untimed tests · extended time for tests · take-home exam · oral tests · reading machines · tape recorders · early syllabus · priority registration. Individual or small group tutorials are also available in: time management · organizational skills · learning strategies · writing labs · study skills. An advisor/advocate from the Disability Support Services is available to students.

How to Get Admitted

For admissions decisions, non-academic factors considered: interview · extracurricular activities · special talents, interests, abilities · character/personal qualities · volunteer work · work experience · state of residency · alumni relationship. A high school diploma is required, although a GED is also accepted for admissions consideration. SAT or ACT test scores are required of all applicants. SAT Subject Test scores are not required. *According to the admissions office:* Minimum combined SAT Reasoning score of 950, minimum 2.5 GPA in college-preparatory courses, and strong recommendations required.

How to Pay for College

To apply for financial aid, students should submit the following: Free Application for Federal Student Aid (FAFSA) · institution's own financial aid forms. The College of Notre Dame of Maryland participates in the Federal Work Study program. *Need-based aid programs include:* scholarships and grants · general need-based awards · Federal Pell grants · state scholarships and grants · college-based scholarships and grants · private scholarships and grants. *Non-Need-based aid programs include:* scholarships and grants · state scholarships and grants · creative arts and performance awards · special achievements and activities awards · special characteristics awards · ROTC scholarships.

COLLEGE OF SANTA FE

1600 St. Michael's Drive, Santa Fe, NM 87505
Admissions: 800-456-2673 · Financial Aid: 800-456-2673
Email: admissions@csf.edu · Website: http://www.csf.edu

From the College

"The College of Santa Fe offers an interdisciplinary arts education grounded in the liberal arts. Some of our most popular majors include film, theater, creative writing, visual arts and contemporary music. Programs in documentary studies, politics and psychology are growing. Close faculty-student interaction promotes active class discussion and artistic activities, and there are frequent guest appearances by internationally renowned artists and writers on campus and in the community. Small classes and studios characterize the academic experience. We are located in one of the most scenic areas in the American Southwest. The Christian Brother/Lasallian heritage of College of Santa Fe calls for attention to the values of service and high ethical standards in the pursuit of educational goals."

Campus Setting

The College of Santa Fe is a private college with strengths in the arts, founded in 1874. Inspired by its Lasallian heritage and enhanced by its location in the culturally rich Southwest, College of Santa Fe is guided in its mission by the core values of student centeredness, creativity, character, culture, civic capacity and shared governance. A four-year institution, the College of Santa Fe has an enrollment of 672 students. The College of Santa Fe has been co-ed since 1966. In addition to a large, well-stocked library, the campus facilities include: fine arts galleries · contemporary music building · center for photographic arts · art history center · theatre center · film education center · professional film studios · fitness center · tennis center. The College of Santa Fe provides on-campus housing with 5 units that can accommodate 499 students. Housing options: co-ed dorms · women's dorms · men's dorms · single-student apartments · special housing for disabled students. Recreation and sports facilities include: baseball · soccer and softball fields · fitness center · tennis courts.

Student Life and Activities

With 68 percent of students living on campus, there are plenty of social activities. "The arts are central to life on campus and in the city of Santa Fe," reports one student leader. "People are laid back and open-minded. It is a haven for those who have always been a little different, hence the name for Santa Fe, 'The City Different.' Our school is filled with artists, actors, filmmakers, musicians and writers; therefore, most activities are those in which students' works can be viewed or experience." Popular gathering spots include: art gallery openings, Center for Contemporary Arts, pd bean coffee house, Lensic Performing Art Center and the Cowgirl Hall of Fame. Popular events include: Fiesta de Santa Fe, Day of Service, Quadstock, World Music Day, Battle of the Bands, Pancake Flip, Valentine's Day Date Auction, Semi-formal, theatrical productions and the Lannan Foundation speaker series. The College of Santa Fe has 18 official student organizations. Popular groups on campus are U.S. Institute for Theater Technology, Apple Miner Colony, Student Programming Board and COLORS For those interested in sports, there are intramural teams such as: basketball · cycling · jousting · racquetball · volleyball. The College of Santa Fe is a member of the NAIA.

Academics and Learning Environment

For the B student, the learning environment of a college is just as important as the

COLLEGE OF SANTA FE

College of Santa Fe
Santa Fe, NM (Pop. 66,000)
Location: Large town
Website: http://www.csf.edu

Students
Total enrollment: 672
Undergrads: 340
Freshmen: Not reported
Part-time students: 9%
From out-of-state: 87%
Male/Female: 51%/49%
Live on-campus: 68%
Off-campus employment rating: Excellent
Caucasian: 67%
African American: 2%
Hispanic: 12%
Asian or Pacific Islander: 3%
Native American: 2%
International: 0%

Academics
Student/faculty ratio: 7:1
Class size 9 or fewer: 34%
Class size 10-29: 65%
Class size 30-49: 14%
Class size 50-99: -
Class size 100 or more: -
Returning freshmen: 68%
Six-year graduation rate: 47%

Most Popular Fields of Study
Psychology
English and Literature
Philosophy, Religion and Theology
Interdisciplinary Studies
Liberal Arts, Humanities and General
    Studies
Communications, Journalism, Advertising
    and Comm. Technologies
Social Sciences, History, Economics,
    Political Science
Natural Resources and Environmental
    Science
Visual and Performing Arts

quality of its academic program. The College of Santa Fe has 73 full-time and 105 part-time faculty members, offering a student-to-faculty ratio of 7:1. The most common course size is 10 to 19 students. The College of Santa Fe offers 24 majors with the most popular being moving image arts, theatre and studio art. The school has a general core requirement. Cooperative education is available. All first-year students must maintain a 2.0 GPA or higher to avoid academic probation. Other special academic programs that would appeal to a B student: self-designed majors · pass/fail grading option · independent study · double majors · internships.

B Student Support and Success

CSF has a First Year Seminar that is essentially a 9-week introductory course to help ease students into the college life. The class meets for 90 minutes each week during the fall semester.

TRiO Student Support Services (SSS) and the Center for Academic Excellence (CAE) are available to students who need academic assistance. Workshops are offered that deal with learning strategies such as reading, study skills, note taking, test taking, time management and memory improvement. Tutoring is available through the center and can be arranged by contacting support personnel. Coordinators help students find the right tutor, sustain motivation, learn stress reduction techniques and "journey wisely through academic and social situations."

The College of Santa Fe provides a variety of support programs including dedicated guidance for: academic · career · personal · psychological · veterans · non-traditional students · family planning · religious. Recognizing that some students may need extra preparation, the College of Santa Fe offers remedial and refresher courses in: reading · writing · math · study skills. Annually, 68 percent of freshmen students return for their sophomore year. What do students do after college? While many enter the work force, approximately 21 percent pursue a graduate degree immediately after graduation. Among students who enter the work force, approximately 84 percent enter a field related to their major within six months of graduation.

Support for Students with Learning Disabilities

Students with learning disabilities may take advantage of specific support programs offered by the College of Santa Fe. If necessary, the college will grant additional time to students with learning disabilities to complete their degree. Also, a lightened course load may be granted to LD students. Students with learning disabilities will find the following programs at the College of Santa Fe extremely useful: special classes · tutors · learning center · untimed tests · extended time for tests · take-home exam · oral tests · substitution of courses · readers · note-taking services · reading machines · tape recorders · texts on tape · videotaped classes · early syllabus · diagnostic testing service. Individual or small group tutorials are also available in: time management · organizational skills · learning strategies · specific subject areas · writing labs · math labs · study skills. An advisor/advocate from the Academic Resource Center is available to students.

How to Get Admitted

For admissions decisions, non-academic factors considered: interview · extracurricular activities · special talents, interests, abilities · character/personal qualities · volunteer work · work experience · state of residency · alumni relationship. A high school diploma is required, although a GED is also accepted for admissions consideration. SAT or ACT test scores are required of all applicants. SAT Subject Test scores are considered, if submitted, but are not required. *Academic units recommended:* 4 English, 3 Math, 3 Science, 2 Social Studies, 2 Foreign Language.

How to Pay for College

To apply for financial aid, students should submit the following: Free Application for Federal Student Aid (FAFSA). The College of Santa Fe participates in the Federal Work Study program. *Need-based aid programs include:* scholarships and grants · general need-based awards · Federal Pell grants · state scholarships and grants · college-based scholarships and grants · private scholarships and grants. *Non-Need-based aid programs include:* scholarships and grants · state scholarships and grants · creative arts and performance awards · special achievements and activities awards · special characteristics awards · athletic scholarships.

COLLEGE OF SANTA FE

Highlights

Admissions
Applicants: 624
Accepted: 516
Acceptance rate: 82.7%
Average GPA: 3.2
ACT range: 21-27
SAT Math range: 470-590
SAT Reading range: 540-640
SAT Writing range: 510-620
Top 10% of class: 12%
Top 25% of class: 40%
Top 50% of class: 73%

Deadlines
Early Action: No
Early Decision: No
Regular Action: Rolling admissions
Common Application: Accepted

Financial Aid
In-state tuition: $27,358
Out-of-state tuition: $27,358
Room: $3,692
Board: $3,644
Books: $1,180
Avg. % of need met by financial aid: Not reported
Avg. aid package (freshmen): Not reported
Avg. aid package (undergrads): Not reported
Avg. student debt upon graduation: Not reported

School Spirit
Mascot: Prairie Dogs
Colors: Mouton red and sweeney gold

COLLEGE OF ST. MARY

7000 Mercy Road, Omaha, NE 68106
Admissions: 800-926-5534 · Financial Aid: 800-926-5534
Email: enroll@csm.edu · Website: http://www.csm.edu

From the College

"The only women's university in a five-state Midwestern region, College of Saint Mary (CSM) is a Catholic college dedicated to the education of women in an environment that calls forth potential and fosters leadership. College of Saint Mary offers 30 programs of study, including education, nursing, applied psychology, forensic science and women's studies, with divisions in professional studies, arts and sciences and health professions. Since 1923, CSM has remained dedicated to its original mission: the education of women for leadership, service and success. While CSM is committed to undergraduate education, graduate programs in education, the health professions and organizational leadership enable professionals in the area to reach their career and personal goals while still working full-time.

"College of Saint Mary offers innovative programs unavailable elsewhere in the region. A specially designed residence hall, Mothers Living and Learning, allows single mothers and their children to live on campus while the mother pursues her degree. Education students directly teach at-risk children while learning to instruct math and science effectively in our Operation SMART program, a partnership with Girls, Inc. of Omaha. An agreement with the Peter Kiewit Institute encourages women studying math and science at CSM to enter into the engineering profession. This '2 + 3' program allows a CSM student to receive a CSM bachelor's degree in Math or Science and a Master's Degree from the University of Nebraska in engineering in just five years.

"Over 90 percent of CSM students receive financial aid, and CSM has several unique scholarship programs. Through donor support, the McAuley Scholarship program provides full tuition and fees for 15 women at any one time who are currently receiving public assistance, such as food stamps or housing subsidies. The Marie Curie Scholars Program, funded by a grant from the National Science Foundation, provides significant financial support for academically talented, but financially challenged, students who plan to study biology, chemistry, or mathematics.

"Campus life is rich and exciting. CSM fields competitive NAIA teams in basketball, cross country, softball, volleyball, and soccer. The new Hixson-Lied Commons offers a coffee shop, chairs for studying or chatting, wireless internet and rooms where student organizations can meet. The Achievement Center, also located in the Commons, is a place where students can build study skills, receive tutoring in a variety of subjects and find help searching for internships and jobs.

"Omaha's midtown development, Aksarben Village, is emerging just across the street from campus; soon students will close to new restaurants, retail stores and a movie theatre. Our Lied Fitness Center offers free, on campus workout facilities including a swimming pool, and the Keystone Trail and Papio Creek winds across the edge of campus, offering a place to run, walk or bike.

"In the classroom, students combine a liberal arts core with practical learning opportunities, career-specific skills, leadership development and community service. Our service learning program sponsors annual winter, spring and summer break trips where students travel to locations such as the U.S.-Mexico border and Costa Rica to learn while serving."

Campus Setting

The College of Saint Mary, founded in 1923, is a private college for women. Its 25-

acre campus is located in a suburban section of Omaha. A four-year college, College of St. Mary has an enrollment of 953 students. The school is also affiliated with the Roman Catholic Church. The school also has a library with 68,313 books. College of St. Mary provides on-campus housing with 168 units that can accommodate 275 students. Housing options: women's dorms. Recreation and sports facilities include: fitness center · parks.

Student Life and Activities

Most students (81 percent) live off campus, which does impact the on-campus social scene. Nevertheless, like any college, students find time to create their own recreational outlets. A popular gathering place on campus is the Hixson-Lied Commons. Popular events include Welcome Days, Queen of Hearts Celebration, Annual Powder Puff Football Competition followed by bonfire and hayrack ride, Spirit of Service Day and Hypnotist. College of St. Mary has 21 official student organizations. The most popular are: Residence Hall Council (RHC) · Student Education Association of Nebraska (SEAN) · Student Nurses Association (SNA) · Student Occupational Therapy Association (SOTA) · Student Paralegal Association · Student Senate · Collegiate Association of Professionals (CAP) · Campus Activities Board (CAB) · Cheerleading and Dance Team · Do Unto Others (DUO) Board · Golden S · Graduate Legacy Council · Math and Science Club. For those interested in sports, there are intramural teams such as: basketball · swimming · volleyball. College of St. Mary is a member of the Midlands Collegiate Athletic Conference (NAIA).

Academics and Learning Environment

For the B student, the learning environment of a college is just as important as the quality of its academic program. College of St. Mary has 57 full-time and 103 part-time faculty members, offering a student-to-faculty ratio of 11:1. The most common course size is 2 to 9 students. College of St. Mary offers 34 majors with the most popular being nursing, business and education and least popular being English, theology and chemistry. The school has a general core requirement as well as a religion requirement Cooperative education is not offered. All first-year students must maintain a 2.0 GPA or higher to avoid academic probation. Other special academic programs that would appeal to a B student: pass/fail grading option · independent study · double majors · dual degrees · accelerated study · honors program · internships · weekend college · certificate programs.

B Student Support and Success

The Achievement Center at the College of Saint Mary helps students develop self-confidence, effective study skills, a strong resume, job search strategies and "unique gifts and talents". Tutoring and testing services are available and the website offers multiple support links to developing a variety of skills in multiple subjects.

College of St. Mary provides a variety of support programs including dedicated guidance for: academic · career · personal · psychological · minority students · non-traditional students · religious. Recognizing that some students may need extra preparation, College of St. Mary offers remedial and refresher courses in:

COLLEGE OF ST. MARY

Highlights

College of St. Mary
Omaha, NE (Pop. 424,000)
Location: Major city
Website: http://www.csm.edu

Students
Total enrollment: 953
Undergrads: 3
Freshmen: 133
Part-time students: 24%
From out-of-state: 11%
Male/Female: 0%/100%
Live on-campus: 19%
Off-campus employment rating: Good
Caucasian: 79%
African American: 11%
Hispanic: 8%
Asian or Pacific Islander: 1%
Native American: 1%
International: 0%

Academics
Student/faculty ratio: 11:1
Class size 9 or fewer: 46%
Class size 10-29: 50%
Class size 30-49: 3%
Class size 50-99: 1%
Class size 100 or more: -
Returning freshmen: 60%
Six-year graduation rate: 51%

Most Popular Fields of Study
Business, Finance, Sales and Marketing
Biological and Life Sciences
Psychology
English and Literature
Philosophy, Religion and Theology
Mathematics
Law and Legal Studies
Health Professions, Medicine and Related Sciences
Liberal Arts, Humanities and General Studies
Education

COLLEGE OF ST. MARY

Admissions
Applicants: 506
Accepted: 228
Acceptance rate: 45.1%
Average GPA: 3.4
ACT range: 18-23
SAT Math range: Not reported
SAT Reading range: Not reported
SAT Writing range: Not reported
Top 10% of class: 12%
Top 25% of class: 35%
Top 50% of class: 67%

Deadlines
Early Action: No
Early Decision: No
Regular Action: Rolling admissions
Common Application: Not accepted

Financial Aid
In-state tuition: $21,780
Out-of-state tuition: $21,780
Room: $3,200
Board: $3,200
Books: $1,200
Freshmen receiving need-based aid: 92%
Undergrads receiving need-based aid: 92%
Avg. % of need met by financial aid: 60%
Avg. aid package (freshmen): $18,380
Avg. aid package (undergrads): $15,018
Freshmen receiving merit-based aid: 8%
Undergrads receiving merit-based aid: 7%
Avg. student debt upon graduation: $26,244

Prominent Alumni
Sharon Kava (pen name Alex Kava), Writer; Dr. Bridget Brosnihan Simmons, Surgical Science, Pharmicology and Physiology Professor.

School Spirit
Mascot: Flames
Colors: Blue and gold

reading · writing · math · study skills. The average freshman year GPA is 2.9, and 60 percent of freshmen students return for their sophomore year. What do students do after college? While many enter the work force, approximately 50 percent pursue a graduate degree immediately after graduation. Among students who enter the work force, approximately 78 percent enter a field related to their major within six months of graduation. Companies that most frequently hire graduates from College of St. Mary include: Alegent Healthcare · Bergan Mercy Medical Center · Children's Hospital · Creighton Medical Center · Immanuel Hospital · Omaha Public Schools · Union Pacific Railroad.

Support for Students with Learning Disabilities

Students with learning disabilities may take advantage of specific support programs offered by College of St. Mary. If necessary, the college will grant additional time to students with learning disabilities to complete their degree. Also, a lightened course load may be granted to LD students. Students with learning disabilities will find the following programs at College of St. Mary extremely useful: remedial math · remedial English · tutors · learning center · testing accommodations · extended time for tests · take-home exam · oral tests · readers · note-taking services · reading machines · tape recorders · videotaped classes · early syllabus · diagnostic testing service · priority registration. Individual or small group tutorials are also available in: time management · organizational skills · learning strategies · specific subject areas · study skills. An advisor/advocate from the LD program is available to students.

How to Get Admitted

For admissions decisions, non-academic factors considered: interview · extracurricular activities · special talents, interests, abilities · character/personal qualities · state of residency · alumni relationship. A high school diploma is required, although a GED is also accepted for admissions consideration. SAT or ACT test scores are required for some applicants. SAT Subject Test scores are not required. *According to the admissions office:* Minimum composite ACT score of 18 and one of the following: rank in top half of secondary school class or have a minimum 2.0 GPA. *Academic units recommended:* 4 English, 3 Math, 3 Science, 2 Social Studies, 1 Foreign Language.

How to Pay for College

To apply for financial aid, students should submit the following: Free Application for Federal Student Aid (FAFSA). College of St. Mary participates in the Federal Work Study program. *Need-based aid programs include:* scholarships and grants · general need-based awards · Federal Pell grants · state scholarships and grants · college-based scholarships and grants · private scholarships and grants. *Non-Need-based aid programs include:* scholarships and grants · state scholarships and grants · athletic scholarships.

COLLEGE OF THE ATLANTIC

105 Eden Street, Bar Harbor, ME 04609
Admissions: 800-528-0025 · Financial Aid: 800-528-0025
Email: inquiry@ecology.coa.edu
Website: http://www.coa.edu

From the College

"Located between the Atlantic Ocean and Acadia National Park, College of the Atlantic offers two degrees: a BA and MPhil, both in Human Ecology. In pursuit of this degree, students consider their individual passions to create their own academic trajectories, integrating knowledge from all academic disciplines and personal experience to fulfill the mission of Human Ecology: investigating and improving relationships between humans and our social, natural, built and virtual communities. COA's small size and individualized curriculum encourages tutorials, intensive seminar-style classes and frequent faculty-student interchanges.

"Having one major means that COA has no departments and no departmental requirements; classes are interdisciplinary. Coursework consists of readings, usually from primary sources, as well as active investigation. These efforts culminate in a term-long senior project. As part of coursework and/or senior projects, recent students have participated in international meetings on climate change, investigated the impact of big box stores (resulting in first-in-the-nation legislation for Maine), used GIS maps to educate local towns on impending planning decisions and prepared an emergency system for a California town, and more.

"Beyond this, COA is a democratic institution, with students involved on all levels of governance and a weekly campus meeting to discuss current campus issues and decisions. Major decisions must be brought to this All-College Meeting; committees that filter into the governance structure include participation by students. Opportunities for travel abound; students must complete a one-term internship, which usually takes them off-campus and often abroad. The college offers a residency term in Mexico and another in Quebec. International connections on campus are extensive, as COA has one of the highest percentages of international students of any college.

"COA is the first college to become carbon neutral; new student residences are outfitted with composting toilets; the kitchen serves food from the college's organic farm. Now, COA offers one of the very few undergraduate green and socially responsible business programs and a Food Systems Program that connects COA's organic farm to an organic research center in the United Kingdom and a graduate school in Germany."

Campus Setting

College of the Atlantic was founded in 1969 on the premise that education should go beyond understanding the world as it is, to enabling students to actively shape its future. Classes focus on understanding the relationships between humans and our environment—and improving those relationships: in policy, the arts, science and a multitude of category-defying fields. We call this Human Ecology. Classes are interdisciplinary, learning hands-on and active, relationships are emphasized. Students are expected to shape their own individual path to their degree, and are encouraged to go to the source and do their own creative thinking in the hopes that they may help shape a more sustainable and just future. A four-year private institution, College of the Atlantic has an enrollment of 327 students. In addition to a small library, the campus facilities include: art gallery · natural history museum · GIS Laboratory · green graphics lab · applied human ecology center · watershed coalition · media design studio · video editing lab. College of the Atlantic provides on-campus hous-

COLLEGE OF THE ATLANTIC

College of the Atlantic
Bar Harbor, ME (Pop. 2,680)
Location: Rural
Website: http://www.coa.edu

Students
Total enrollment: 327
Undergrads: 116
Freshmen: 97
Part-time students: 6%
From out-of-state: 82%
Male/Female: 36%/64%
Live on-campus: 43%
Off-campus employment rating: Fair
Caucasian: 29%
African American: 0%
Hispanic: 1%
Asian or Pacific Islander: 1%
International: 13%

Academics
Student/faculty ratio: 11:1
Class size 9 or fewer: 37%
Class size 10-29: 63%
Class size 30-49: 15%
Class size 50-99: 6%
Class size 100 or more: 5%
Returning freshmen: 82%
Six-year graduation rate: 62%

Admissions
Applicants: 314
Accepted: 217
Acceptance rate: 69.1%
Average GPA: 3.5
ACT range: 25-29
SAT Math range: 500-650
SAT Reading range: 600-690
SAT Writing range: 550-580
Top 10% of class: 31%
Top 25% of class: 62%
Top 50% of class: 96%

ing with 15 units that can accommodate 150 students. Housing options: co-ed dorms.

Student Life and Activities

Most students (57 percent) live off campus, which does impact the on-campus social scene. Nevertheless, like any college, students find time to create their own recreational outlets. Students hang out at Take-A-Break, and elsewhere on campus, but often tend to make their own social life at various homes, since half the students live off campus. On campus during the afternoons, there's frequently a pick-up game –hockey in winter, frisbee, soccer, cricket and others during the warmer months. Acadia National Park is in our backyard, so students often go hiking, kayaking, biking or skiing in the park. We're right on the ocean and a group of students swim year-round. Several musical groups operate on campus at all times - currently they include a number of rock bands, a bluegrass band, several jazz ensembles and a few classical music groups. All find venues at which to perform during the year. Popular gathering spots include Take-A-Break, student homes, the dock and the Shrine, as well as Deering Common, the new campus center. Popular campus events include Bar Island Swim, The Nature of Halloween, Annual National Toboggan Championships, Coffeehouse performances, Ultimate Frisbee, 24-hour plays, Film festivals, Aurora Ball-ealis –a staff-created party for students, staff and faculty –cricket, soccer, ice hockey, Fandango—international cultural show with humor, music, dance; also a philanthropic fundraiser, Faculty-Staff-Senior Tug of War, Winter Carnival and Green Graduation. College of the Atlantic has 9 official student organizations. Popular groups on campus range from SustainUS, to the international cultural organization that creates Fandango, to a meditation group. For those interested in sports, there are intramural teams such as: bicycling · climbing · cricket · diving · hiking · ice hockey · sailing · skiing/cross-country · snowshoeing · soccer · softball · volleyball · water polo · ultimate Frisbee.

Academics and Learning Environment

For the B student, the learning environment of a college is just as important as the quality of its academic program. College of the Atlantic has 24 full-time and 14 part-time faculty members, offering a student-to-faculty ratio of 11:1. The most common course size is 10 to 19 students. College of the Atlantic offers 23 majors with the most popular being human ecology. The school does not have a general core requirement. Cooperative education is available. Other special academic programs that would appeal to a B student: self-designed majors · pass/fail grading option · independent study · internships.

B Student Support and Success

"At COA, we focus on a student's creativity, desire to do something, as well as their innate interest in learning." From there, they have a lot of advice on how to become a part of this college.
College of the Atlantic provides a variety of support programs including dedicated guidance for: academic · career · personal · psychological · minority students · family planning · religious. Annually, 82 percent of freshmen students return for their sopho-

more year. What do students do after college? While many enter the work force, approximately 5 percent pursue a graduate degree immediately after graduation. Among students who enter the work force, approximately 85 percent enter a field related to their major within six months of graduation. Companies that most frequently hire graduates from College of the Atlantic include: New England Aquarium · Maine State Department of Education · National Park Service.

Support for Students with Learning Disabilities

Students with learning disabilities may take advantage of specific support programs offered by College of the Atlantic. If necessary, the college will grant additional time to students with learning disabilities to complete their degree. Also, a lightened course load may be granted to LD students. Credit is given for remedial courses taken. High school foreign language waivers are accepted. According to the school, Rooms for disabled students located within student housing. Students with learning disabilities will find the following programs at College of the Atlantic extremely useful: remedial English · remedial reading · special classes · tutors · testing accommodations · untimed tests · extended time for tests · take-home exam · oral tests · readers · note-taking services · reading machines · tape recorders · texts on tape · early syllabus · priority registration. Individual or small group tutorials are also available in: time management · organizational skills · learning strategies · specific subject areas · writing labs · math labs · study skills. An advisor/advocate from the LD program is available to students. This member also sits on the admissions committee.

How to Get Admitted

For admissions decisions, non-academic factors considered: interview · extracurricular activities · special talents, interests, abilities · character/personal qualities · volunteer work · work experience · geographical location · minority affiliation · alumni relationship. A high school diploma is required, although a GED is also accepted for admissions consideration. SAT or ACT test scores are considered, if submitted, but are not required. SAT Subject Test scores are considered, if submitted, but are not required. *According to the admissions office:* Rank in top quarter of secondary school class or minimum 3.0 GPA recommended. *Academic units recommended:* 4 Math, 3 Science, 2 Foreign Language.

How to Pay for College

To apply for financial aid, students should submit the following: Free Application for Federal Student Aid (FAFSA) · institution's own financial aid forms · Non-custodian (Divorced/Separated) Parent's Statement. College of the Atlantic participates in the Federal Work Study program. *Need-based aid programs include:* scholarships and grants · general need-based awards · Federal Pell grants · state scholarships and grants · college-based scholarships and grants · private scholarships and grants. *Non-Need-based aid programs include:* scholarships and grants · state scholarships and grants.

COLLEGE OF THE ATLANTIC

Highlights

Deadlines
Early Action: No
Early Decision: December 1
Regular Action: February 15 (priority)
February 15 (final)
Common Application: Accepted

Financial Aid
In-state tuition: $32,580
Out-of-state tuition: $21,580
Room: $5,400
Board: $3,090
Books: $600
Freshmen receiving need-based aid: 80%
Undergrads receiving need-based aid: 82%
Avg. % of need met by financial aid: 96%
Avg. aid package (freshmen): $33,029
Avg. aid package (undergrads): $28,020
Avg. student debt upon graduation: $16,926

Prominent Alumni
Chellie Pingree, First District Congresswoman from Maine; Greg Stone, VP of Global Marine Programs at the New England Aquarium, influential in creating the world's largest marine sanctuary in Kiribati, the Phoenix Islands; Nell Newman, founder Newman's Own Organics.

COLORADO STATE UNIVERSITY

1062 Campus Delivery, Fort Collins, CO 80523
Admissions: 970-491-6909 · Financial Aid: 970-491-6321
Email: admissions@colostate.edu · Website: http://www.colostate.edu

From the College

"Founded in 1870 and established as a land-grant institution, Colorado State is a fully accredited public university recognized for its excellence in academic programs from the baccalaureate to the postgraduate level. Our land-grant mission of teaching, research, and outreach means that we're dedicated to service - serving you, our students, first. Colorado State offers more than 150 programs of study within eight colleges allowing you to shape a course of study that best meets your personal and professional goals. The university emphasizes the importance of active learning providing opportunities for field experience, laboratory research, internships and study abroad. As a student at Colorado State, you will learn side by side with faculty mentors who are recognized internationally as leaders in their fields."

"Colorado State University is located in the center of Fort Collins, a city of about 131,000 people. Fort Collins provides a unique blend of big city advantages and small town friendliness. There are several shopping malls, hundreds of restaurants, multiple movie complexes, a regional cultural center, natural areas and miles of bike trails. Close to campus are Rocky Mountain National Park, the Poudre River and Horsetooth Reservoir. These recreation areas, as well as many others close by, offer endless opportunities for outdoor activities - such as skiing, snowboarding, hiking, camping, white water rafting, and boating. And the city's agreeable climate of 300 days of sunshine a year enables you to take year-round advantage of the spectacular surroundings."

Campus Setting

Colorado State University became a land-grant college in 1879 and was granted university status in 1957. Its 581-acre main campus is located in Fort Collins, Colorado, at the foot of the Rocky Mountains, 65 miles north of Denver. A four-year public institution, Colorado State University has an enrollment of 27,800 students. In addition to a large, well-stocked library, the campus facilities include: art gallery · center for the arts · historic costume and textile museum. Colorado State University provides on-campus housing with 3,797 units that can accommodate 6,477 students. Housing options: co-ed dorms · single-student apartments · married-student apartments · special housing for disabled students · special housing for International students. Recreation and sports facilities include: arena · basketball and recreational centers · lacrosse · soccer and softball fields · gymnasium · stadium · tennis courts.

Student Life and Activities

Most students (75 percent) live off campus, which does impact the on-campus social scene. Nevertheless, like any college, students find time to create their own recreational outlets. CSU Rams maintain an active social life; whether enjoying live music in the vibrant local nightlife, or attending one of the many cultural events held on campus, there's no shortage of opportunities to unwind. The hot spots for students are Lory Student Center, Morgan Library, Mugs Coffee Lounge, and any of the numerous bars and restaurants in Old Town Fort Collins. CSU/CU (football) Rocky Mountain Showdown , Homecoming, Commencement, Ag day, Monfort lecture series, President's Fall Address and University Picnic, Spring Career Fair, and Business Day are popular events. Colorado State University has 331 official student organizations. Student Government has a widespread influence on campus, as do many other academic and social groups. For those interested in sports, there are intramural teams such as: basketball · bowling · disc golf · dodgeball · flag football · golf · kickball · indoor triathlon · paintball · poker · racquetball · running · skiing · snowboarding · soccer · softball · ultimate Frisbee · volleyball · Inner tube water polo · wiffle ball · Wii Sports tournament. Colorado State University is a member of the Mountain West Conference (Division I, Football I-A), Western Water Polo Association.

Academics and Learning Environment

For the B student, the learning environment of a college is just as important as the quality of its academic program. Colorado State University has 925 full-time and 43 part-time faculty members, offering a student-to-faculty ratio of 17:1. The most common course size is 10 to 19 students. Colorado State University offers 192 majors with the most popular being business administration, psychology and construction management and least popular being botany, agricultural economics and chemical and biological engineering. The school has a general core requirement. Cooperative education is available. All first-year students must maintain a 2.0 GPA or higher to avoid academic probation. Other special academic programs that would appeal to a B student: pass/fail grading option · independent study · double majors · dual degrees · accelerated study · honors program · Phi Beta Kappa · internships · distance learning certificate programs.

B Student Support and Success

Colorado State's Academic Advancement Center is available for low income and/or first generation backgrounds or have disabilities. These students are also eligible for the Mentoring for Leadership Program. A peer mentoring program, it connects students with upper class mentors and campus resources. Tutoring is available through the Center and is built around the philosophy that "with the right study strategies and resources to clarify content any student can raise their course grade." Tutors assist students with finding study strategies that work for their course and explain content that students may have not completely understood in lecture.

Colorado State University provides a variety of support programs including dedicated guidance for: academic · career · personal · psychological · minority students · military · veterans · non-traditional students · family planning · religious. The average freshman year GPA is 2.8, and 82 percent of freshmen students return for their sophomore year.

Support for Students with Learning Disabilities

Students with learning disabilities may take advantage of specific support programs offered by Colorado State University. If necessary, the college will grant additional time to students with learning disabilities to complete their degree. Also, a lightened course load may be granted to LD students. Students with learning disabilities will find the following programs at Colorado State University extremely useful: tutors · testing accommodations · extended time for tests · take-home exam · exam on tape or computer · readers · typist/scribe · note-taking services · reading machines · tape recorders · early syllabus · diagnostic testing service · waiver of math degree

COLORADO STATE UNIVERSITY

Colorado State University
Fort Collins, CO (Pop. 131,000)
Location: Medium city
Website: http://www.colostate.edu

Students
Total enrollment: 27,800
Undergrads: 10,493
Freshmen: 6,117
Part-time students: 10%
From out-of-state: 20%
Male/Female: 48%/52%
Live on-campus: 25%
In fraternities: 6%
In sororities: 7%
Off-campus employment rating: Excellent
Caucasian: 80%
African American: 2%
Hispanic: 6%
Asian or Pacific Islander: 3%
Native American: 2%
International: 2%

Academics
Student/faculty ratio: 17:1
Class size 9 or fewer: 11%
Class size 10-29: 51%
Class size 30-49: 21%
Class size 50-99: 10%
Class size 100 or more: 7%
Returning freshmen: 82%
Six-year graduation rate: 63%

Most Popular Fields of Study
Business, Finance, Sales and Marketing
Biological and Life Sciences
Agriculture, Aquaculture and Animal Sciences
Visual and Performing Arts
Social Sciences, History, Economics, Political Science
Protective Services, Criminal Justice and Public Administration
Family and Consumer Sciences, Nutrition and Home Economics
Computer and Information Sciences
Communications, Journalism, Advertising and Comm. Technologies
Philosophy, Religion and Theology

161

COLORADO STATE UNIVERSITY

Admissions
Applicants: 12,494
Accepted: 10,688
Acceptance rate: 85.5%
Average GPA: 3.5
ACT range: 22-26
SAT Math range: 510-620
SAT Reading range: 500-610
SAT Writing range: 480-590
Top 10% of class: 20%
Top 25% of class: 49%
Top 50% of class: 87%

Deadlines
Early Action: No
Early Decision: No
Regular Action: Rolling admissions
Common Application: Accepted

Financial Aid
In-state tuition: $4,424
Out-of-state tuition: $20,140
Room: $4,114
Board: $4,020
Books: $1,126
Freshmen receiving need-based aid: 33%
Undergrads receiving need-based aid: 40%
Avg. % of need met by financial aid: 71%
Avg. aid package (freshmen): $7,710
Avg. aid package (undergrads): $8,776
Freshmen receiving merit-based aid: 5%
Undergrads receiving merit-based aid: 8%
Avg. student debt upon graduation: $18,607

Prominent Alumni
Bill Ritter, Jr., governor, Colorado; Mary Cleave, astronaut and associate administrator, Science Mission Directorate, NASA; Yusef Komunyakaa, Pulitzer Prize winning poet.

School Spirit
Mascot: Rams
Colors: Green and gold

requirement. Individual or small group tutorials are also available in: time management · organizational skills · learning strategies · specific subject areas · writing labs · math labs · study skills. An advisor/advocate from the Resources for Disabled Students is available to students.

How to Get Admitted

For admissions decisions, non-academic factors considered: interview · extracurricular activities · special talents, interests, abilities · character/personal qualities · volunteer work · work experience · geographical location · alumni relationship. A high school diploma is required, although a GED is also accepted for admissions consideration. SAT or ACT test scores are required of all applicants. *According to the admissions office:* Priority consideration is given to those with a minimum 3.25 GPA and 18 recommended high school credits. Applicants who have a GPA below 3.25 and/or who do not meet the recommended high school units are encouraged to apply as all applicants receive a careful, holistic review. An essay (minimum 250 words) and one recommendation required. *Academic units recommended:* 4 English, 4 Math, 3 Science, 2 Social Studies, 2 Foreign Language.

How to Pay for College

To apply for financial aid, students should submit the following: Free Application for Federal Student Aid (FAFSA). Colorado State University participates in the Federal Work Study program. *Need-based aid programs include:* scholarships and grants · general need-based awards · Federal Pell grants · state scholarships and grants · college-based scholarships and grants · private scholarships and grants. *Non-Need-based aid programs include:* scholarships and grants · general need-based awards · state scholarships and grants · creative arts and performance awards · special characteristics awards · athletic scholarships · ROTC scholarships.

COPPIN STATE UNIVERSITY

2500 West North Avenue, Baltimore, MD 21216-3698
Admissions: 800-635-3674 · Financial Aid: 410-951-3636
Email: admissions@coppin.edu
Website: http://www.coppin.edu

From the College

"A comprehensive, urban, liberal arts institution with a commitment to teaching, research and continuing service to its community, Coppin State University provides educational access and diverse opportunities for students with a high potential for success and for students whose promise may have been hindered by a lack of social, personal or financial opportunity. Powered by information technology as the centerpiece for achieving its institutional goals, Coppin State University embodies urban education and public service."

Campus Setting

Coppin State, founded in 1900, is a public university. Its 33-acre campus is located in Baltimore. A four-year public institution, Coppin State University is a historically black university with 4,051 students. The school also has a library. Coppin State University provides on-campus housing with 2 units that can accommodate 650 students. Housing options: co-ed dorms · special housing for disabled students. Recreation and sports facilities include: center · tennis courts.

Student Life and Activities

Coppin State University has 28 official student organizations. The most popular are: Gospel choir · Coppin Dancers · Coppin Models · Coppin Players · Thurgood Marshall club · history club · mathematics and computer science club · criminal justice club · psychology club · Social Work Association · Student Recruitment Team. For those interested in sports, there are intramural teams such as: basketball · flag football · softball · tennis · volleyball. Coppin State University is a member of the NCAA, Eastern College Athletic Conference (Division I, Football I-AA), Mid-Eastern Athletic Conference (Division I, Football I-AA).

Academics and Learning Environment

For the B student, the learning environment of a college is just as important as the quality of its academic program. Coppin State University has 162 full-time and 139 part-time faculty members, offering a student-to-faculty ratio of 18:1. Coppin State University offers 28 majors with the most popular being psychology, management science and criminal justice and least popular being history and philosophy. The school has a general core requirement. Cooperative education is available. All first-year students must maintain a 1.2 GPA or higher to avoid academic probation. Other special academic programs that would appeal to a B student: independent study · double majors · dual degrees · accelerated study · honors program · internships · weekend college · distance learning.

Highlights

Coppin State University
Baltimore, MD (Pop. 628,670)
Location: Major city
Website: http://www.coppin.edu

Students
Total enrollment: 4,051
Undergrads: 734
Freshmen: 675
Part-time students: 22%
From out-of-state: 16%
Male/Female: 22%/78%
Live on-campus: Not reported
Off-campus employment rating: Fair
Caucasian: 1%
African American: 87%
Hispanic: 0%
Asian or Pacific Islander: 0%
Native American: 0%
International: 4%

Academics
Student/faculty ratio: 18:1
Class size 9 or fewer: 11%
Class size 10-29: 51%
Class size 30-49: 21%
Class size 50-99: 10%
Class size 100 or more: 7%
Returning freshmen: 58%
Six-year graduation rate: 16%

Admissions
Applicants: 5,138
Accepted: 2,197
Acceptance rate: 42.8%
Average GPA: Not reported
ACT range: Not reported
SAT Math range: 380-460
SAT Reading range: 400-470
SAT Writing range: Not reported

Deadlines
Early Action: No
Early Decision: No
Regular Action: July 15 (final)
Common Application: Accepted

COPPIN STATE UNIVERSITY

America's
Best Colleges for
B Students

B Student Support and Success

Coppin offers a variety of Student Support Services with one-on-one help. They also require that each new student take a one-semester Freshman Seminar course. Students may receive help at the Academic Resource Center, which features four labs with basic, intermediate and advanced levels of instruction and tutoring at no cost. Coppin's Student Support Services includes academic advising with assistance in course selection and career planning. It also offers individual and group tutoring services, computer-assisted instruction and informational workshops on topics like study skills, computer literacy, test taking and note taking. Coppin also has a series of video-assisted instruction in courses like algebra and writing.

Coppin State University provides a variety of support programs including dedicated guidance for: academic · career · personal · psychological · minority students. Additional counseling services include: financial aid, substance abuse counseling and veterans' counseling. Recognizing that some students may need extra preparation, Coppin State University offers remedial and refresher courses in: reading · writing · math · study skills. The average freshman year GPA is 2.0, and 58 percent of freshmen students return for their sophomore year. Among students who enter the work force, approximately 70 percent enter a field related to their major within six months of graduation. Companies that most frequently hire graduates include: Baltimore City Public Schools · Social Security Administration · Baltimore City Department of Social Services.

Support for Students with Learning Disabilities

Students with learning disabilities may take advantage of specific support programs offered by Coppin State University. Students with learning disabilities will find the following programs at Coppin State University extremely useful: remedial math · remedial English · remedial reading · learning center · untimed tests · extended time for tests.

How to Get Admitted

For admissions decisions, non-academic factors considered: interview · extracurricular activities · special talents, interests, abilities · character/personal qualities · volunteer work · work experience · geographical location · minority affiliation · alumni relationship. A high school diploma is required, although a GED is also accepted for admissions consideration. SAT or ACT test scores are required of all applicants. *According to the admissions office:* Minimum composite ACT score of 18 (combined SAT Reasoning score of 900) and minimum 2.5 GPA required.

How to Pay for College

To apply for financial aid, students should submit the following: Free Application for Federal Student Aid (FAFSA). Coppin State University participates in the Federal Work Study program. *Need-based aid programs include:* scholarships and grants · general need-based awards · Federal Pell grants · state scholarships and grants · college-based scholarships and grants · private scholarships and grants · Federal Nursing scholarships · United Negro College Fund. *Non-Need-based aid programs include:* scholarships and grants · general need-based awards · state scholarships and grants · athletic scholarships.

CORNELL COLLEGE

600 First Street Southwest, Mount Vernon, IA 52314-1098
Admissions: 800-747-1112 · Financial Aid: 877-579-4049
Email: admissions@cornellcollege.edu
Website: http://www.cornellcollege.edu

From the College

"Cornell College is a private, liberal arts college recognized for its personalized and intellectually engaging undergraduate education. Our distinctiveness begins in the classroom with our One Course at a Time (OCAAT) academic calendar and extends onto the campus where there is a strong sense of community, mentoring relationships between faculty and students and opportunities to lead and volunteer. Cornell College was founded in 1853, and the historic 129-acre campus is home of a diverse student body of 1,121 who come from 48 states and 20 countries. The academic calendar provides students with creativity and depth in each course where students and their professor spend 3 1/2 weeks focusing their time and effort. Instead of balancing 4-6 courses, Cornell students delve deeply into the material exploring a range of perspectives and taking advantage of the flexibility, which provides time for extended discussions, lab experience virtually every day in the sciences and field work whenever possible.

"In addition to the engagement in the classroom, Cornell students find OCAAT also provides them with the flexibility to be fully engaged outside of class through more than 100 clubs and organizations, varsity athletics and an array of performing arts organizations. The flexibility also provides students with a breadth of study abroad opportunities (students typically study in more than 20 countries each year), internships (which may be done virtually anywhere), research on and off campus within students major fields of interests, and through independent study."

Campus Setting

Cornell College is a four-year college located in Mount Vernon, Iowa. The 129-acre campus is situated 15 miles east of Cedar Rapids, 20 miles north of Iowa City and approximately 200 miles west of Chicago. Cornell was the first college in the country to have the entire campus listed with the National Register of Historic Places. Cornell was also the second college in the country to adopt the block plan, or One Course at a Time, an academic calendar in which students devote themselves to just one subject for 3½-week course terms. A four-year private institution, Cornell College has an enrollment of 1,115 students. Cornell College has been co-ed since 1853. The school is also affiliated with the United Methodist Church. In addition to a large, well-stocked library, the campus facilities include: theatre · museum · geology center. Cornell College provides on-campus housing with 12 units that can accommodate 1,083 students. Housing options: co-ed dorms · women's dorms · men's dorms · single-student apartments. Recreation and sports facilities include: athletic fields · baseball diamond · football · soccer and softball fields · basketball and volleyball courts · gymnasium · indoor and outdoor track · multi-sports center · racquetball courts · strength training center · wrestling facility · weight room.

Student Life and Activities

With 92 percent of students living on campus, there are plenty of social activities. In addition to the events scheduled at Cornell, students take advantage of performances, bands and more that visit the Cedar Rapids and Iowa City area. Students also use "block breaks" for visits to many of the regional cities including Chicago, Minneapolis, St. Louis, Kansas City and Indianapolis. Student organization such as the mountain-

CORNELL COLLEGE

Cornell College
Mount Vernon, IA (Pop. 4,400)
Location: Small town
Website: http://www.cornellcollege.edu

Students
Total enrollment: 1,115
Undergrads: 553
Freshmen: 344
Part-time students: 1%
From out-of-state: 83%
Male/Female: 50%/50%
Live on-campus: 92%
In fraternities: 23%
In sororities: 31%
Off-campus employment rating: Fair
Caucasian: 80%
African American: 3%
Hispanic: 3%
Asian or Pacific Islander: 2%
Native American: 1%
International: 4%

Academics
Student/faculty ratio: 11:1
Class size 9 or fewer: 21%
Class size 10-29: 79%
Class size 30-49: 21%
Class size 50-99: 10%
Class size 100 or more: 7%
Returning freshmen: 81%
Six-year graduation rate: 71%

Most Popular Fields of Study
Biological and Life Sciences
Area, Ethnic and Gender Studies
Business, Finance, Sales and Marketing

eering and outdoors clubs will also use these extended weekends for trips to the Rockies or to nearby states for camping and hiking Favorite gathering spots include the Ratt, the Commons, Pfeiffer Lounge and Scores Sports Bar and Grill. Student Symposium, Music Mondays, Homecoming, Knock Your Block Off, New Student Orientation Events, music and theatre concerts, athletic contests for most sports are the most popular social events of the school year. Cornell College has 122 official student organizations. Groups that influence student life include the media, PAAC - Performing Arts and Activities Council, the non-national fraternities and sororities, athletics multicultural groups and theatre and music organizations. For those interested in sports, there are intramural teams such as: badminton · bowling · basketball · dodge ball · floor hockey · football · indoor soccer · racquetball · softball · ultimate Frisbee · volleyball · wallyball · wrestling. Cornell College is a member of the Iowa Intercollegiate Athletic Conference (Division III).

Academics and Learning Environment

For the B student, the learning environment of a college is just as important as the quality of its academic program. Cornell College has 92 full-time and 8 part-time faculty members, offering a student-to-faculty ratio of 11:1. The most common course size is 10 to 19 students. Cornell College offers 37 majors with the most popular being psychology, economics/business and English and least popular being Russian, Latin American studies and German. The school has a general core requirement. Cooperative education is available. All first-year students must maintain a 2.0 GPA or higher to avoid academic probation. Other special academic programs that would appeal to a B student: self-designed majors · independent study · double majors · Phi Beta Kappa · internships · certificate programs.

B Student Support and Success

Cornell has a first-year-only course that helps new students acclimate to doing college-level work. It includes a writing emphasis course, student mentors and a full advising system. Instructors help students develop skills in writing, reading comprehension, oral communication, information literacy, creativity, research and mathematics. They also show students how to build independent work habits.

A lot of personal attention is given to help students be successful in a rather intense program.

Cornell College provides a variety of support programs including dedicated guidance for: academic · career · personal · psychological · minority students · non-traditional students · family planning · religious. The average freshman year GPA is 3.0, and 81 percent of freshmen students return for their sophomore year. What do students do after college? While many enter the work force, approximately 35 percent pursue a graduate degree immediately after graduation. Among students who enter the work force, approximately 50 percent enter a field related to their major within six months of graduation. Companies that most frequently hire graduates from Cornell College include: GE Healthcare · Department of Defense · Country Insurance · National Student Leadership Council · University of Iowa · San Francisco Ballet ·

Toyota Financial Services · Van Meter Industrial Inc. · NSC Pearson · Mercy Hospital · Denver Public Schools · Chicago Public Schools · Integrated DNA Technologies · Target Corp.· Bank One · AEGON/Life Investors · Allied Insurance · Ernst & Young · Iowa Dept of Natural Resources · KPMG LLP · Mutual of Omaha · Principal Financial Group · Rockwell Collins · Wells Fargo.

Support for Students with Learning Disabilities

Students with learning disabilities may take advantage of specific support programs offered by Cornell College. According to the school, Cornell College does not have an LD program. We provide an Academic Learning Center which supports all students in areas of writing, tutoring, etc. For students with documented Learning Differences we are able to provide minimal support such as individual tutoring, extended time on tests, books on tape, etc. Students with learning disabilities will find the following programs at Cornell College extremely useful: tutors · learning center · testing accommodations · untimed tests · extended time for tests · take-home exam · exam on tape or computer · typist/scribe · tape recorders · early syllabus · priority registration · waiver of math degree requirement. Individual or small group tutorials are also available in: time management · organizational skills · learning strategies · specific subject areas · writing labs · math labs · study skills. An advisor/advocate from the Registrar's Office is available to students.

How to Get Admitted

For admissions decisions, non-academic factors considered: interview · extracurricular activities · special talents, interests, abilities · character/ personal qualities · volunteer work · work experience · geographical location · minority affiliation · alumni relationship. A high school diploma is required, although a GED is also accepted for admissions consideration. SAT or ACT test scores are required of all applicants. SAT Subject Test scores are considered, if submitted, but are not required. *According to the admissions office:* Cornell College does not have cut-offs or requirements for admission. The Admissions Committee takes a holistic approach to application review considering: high school courses, grade point average, class rank, competitiveness of school, essays, recommendations, leadership and involvement, seriousness about college and motivation, the ACT or SAT score and an optional interview. *Academic units recommended:* 4 English, 3 Math, 3 Science, 3 Social Studies, 2 Foreign Language.

How to Pay for College

To apply for financial aid, students should submit the following: Free Application for Federal Student Aid (FAFSA) · institution's own financial aid forms · Non-custodian (Divorced/Separated) Parent's Statement. Cornell College participates in the Federal Work Study program. *Need-based aid programs include:* scholarships and grants · general need-based awards · Federal Pell grants · state scholarships and grants · college-based scholarships and grants · private scholarships and grants · AC Grants · SMART Grants and TEACH Grant. *Non-Need-based aid programs include:* scholarships and grants · general need-based awards · state scholarships and grants · creative arts and performance awards.

CORNELL COLLEGE

Highlights

Admissions
Applicants: 2,917
Accepted: 1,279
Acceptance rate: 43.8%
placed on wait list: 104
Average GPA: 3.4
ACT range: 24-29
SAT Math range: 570-670
SAT Reading range: 550-660
SAT Writing range: Not reported
Top 10% of class: 29%
Top 25% of class: 53%
Top 50% of class: 85%

Deadlines
Early Action: December 1
Early Decision: November 1
Regular Action: December 1 (priority)
February 1 (final)
Common Application: Accepted

Financial Aid
In-state tuition: $29,400
Out-of-state tuition: $29,400
Room: $3,500
Board: $4,000
Books: $810
Freshmen receiving need-based aid: 69%
Undergrads receiving need-based aid: 68%
Avg. % of need met by financial aid: 92%
Avg. aid package (freshmen): $26,875
Avg. aid package (undergrads): $23,720
Freshmen receiving merit-based aid: 26%
Undergrads receiving merit-based aid: 26%
Avg. student debt upon graduation: $29,825

Prominent Alumni
Christopher Carney, Representative, U.S. Congress; Dr. Lawrence Dorr, director of Dorr Arthritis Institute at Centinela Hospital, California; Dr. Campbell McConnell, economist, educator and author.

School Spirit
Mascot: Rams
Colors: Purple and white

167

DEAN COLLEGE

99 Main Street, Franklin, MA 02038
Admissions: 877-879-3326 · Financial Aid: 508-541-1518
Email: admission@dean.edu · Website: http://www.dean.edu

From the College

"Dean College offers what you expect to find—safe, residential campus, athletic programs, clubs and activities, wireless network, scholarships and financial aid—but with an atmosphere that is a little more patient, a bit more nurturing. The college bridges the leap between high school and university by offering two- or four-year degrees from a New England campus guided by a passionate faculty."

Campus Setting

Dean College, founded in 1865, is a private, co-ed institution. The 140-acre campus is located in Franklin. A four-year private institution, Dean College has an enrollment of 1,302 students. The school also has a library with 44,795 books. Dean College provides on-campus housing with 507 units that can accommodate 935 students. Housing options: co-ed dorms · women's dorms · special housing for disabled students. Recreation and sports facilities include: field · fitness center · golf course · gymnasium.

Student Life and Activities

With 87 percent of students living on campus, there are plenty of social activities. A popular on-campus gathering spot is the Campus Center. Popular campus events include Cabaret Night, Spring Weekend, Dance Team and Dance Company shows and Family Weekend. Dean College has 25 official student organizations. The most popular are: Dance Team · Drama Club · Criminal Justice Club · SORT Leaders · Community Advisors · Student Ambassadors · Dean Community Outreach · Emerging Leaders · Orientation and Welcome Leaders. For those interested in sports, there are intramural teams such as: badminton · basketball · soccer · softball · volleyball. Dean College is a member of the NJCAA, Northeast Football Conference.

Academics and Learning Environment

For the B student, the learning environment of a college is just as important as the quality of its academic program. Dean College has 34 full-time and 84 part-time faculty members, offering a student-to-faculty ratio of 18:1. The most common course size is 10 to 19 students. Dean College offers 14 majors with the most popular being dance. The school has a general core requirement. Cooperative education is not offered. All first-year students must maintain a 1.75 GPA or higher to avoid academic probation. Other special academic programs that would appeal to a B student: independent study · accelerated study · honors program · internships.

B Student Support and Success

A quote from Dean College offers these words regarding their staff and programs: "Dean College provides a level of academic support that goes above and beyond the norm found in higher education today. Our full-time academic advisors are completely dedicated to helping students through their time at Dean and thus do not have any faculty responsibilities. Faculty, meanwhile, are required to submit progress reports on every student periodically during the semester. In addition, Dean offers a comprehensive learning center that provides students with opportunities for personalized, drop-in or peer-tutoring services according to their academic needs."

Dean College provides a variety of support programs including dedicated guidance for: academic · personal · psychological · veterans · non-traditional students ·

family planning. Recognizing that some students may need extra preparation, Dean College offers remedial and refresher courses in: reading · writing · math · study skills. The average freshman year GPA is 2.7, and 66 percent of freshmen students return for their sophomore year.

Support for Students with Learning Disabilities

Students with learning disabilities may take advantage of specific support programs. If necessary, the college will grant additional time to students with learning disabilities to complete their degree. Also, a lightened course load may be granted to LD students. High school foreign language waivers are accepted. Students with learning disabilities will find the following programs extremely useful: special classes · tutors · learning center · extended time for tests · oral tests · readers · note-taking services · reading machines · tape recorders · texts on tape. Individual or small group tutorials are also available in: time management · organizational skills · learning strategies · specific subject areas · writing labs · math labs · study skills. An advisor/advocate from the Dean Arch Program is available to students. This member also sits on the admissions committee.

How to Get Admitted

For admissions decisions, non-academic factors considered: interview · extracurricular activities · special talents, interests, abilities · character/personal qualities · volunteer work · work experience · state of residency · geographical location · alumni relationship. A high school diploma is required, although a GED is also accepted for admissions consideration. SAT or ACT test scores are required of all applicants. SAT Subject Test scores are considered, if submitted, but are not required. *Academic units recommended:* 4 English, 3 Math, 2 Science, 3 Social Studies, 2 Foreign Language.

Insight

"Dean College is more focused on a student's future than we are on his/her past. While we are not about open enrollment, we are about providing students with opportunity and helping them to reposition their academic profile in the hopes of transferring to the school of choice. Applicants need to show us academic potential in the admissions process. If we can identify academic potential (be it through improving grades, SAT scores, recommendations, etc.) we feel that Dean's supportive learning environment and structure can help harness that potential and position students for what is near in their academic lives.

"Dean College helps students get into four-year schools and more often than not, we help them get into four-year schools that academically are at least one level higher than what their profile would have allowed them to get into as incoming freshmen. Dean College is made for the B or C student who aspires to transfer to a higher level school as we foster the type of initial accomplishment, growth and confidence necessary for them to ultimately pursue and complete a bachelor's degree at a four-year institution."

How to Pay for College

To apply for financial aid, students should submit the following: Free Application for Federal Student Aid (FAFSA). Dean College partici-

DEAN COLLEGE

Highlights

Dean College
Franklin, MA (Pop. 32,000)
Location: Large town
Website: http://www.dean.edu

Students
Total enrollment: 1,302
Undergrads: 637
Freshmen: 540
Part-time students: 22%
From out-of-state: 48%
Male/Female: 49%/51%
Live on-campus: 87%
Off-campus employment rating: Good
Caucasian: 51%
African American: 10%
Hispanic: 3%
Asian or Pacific Islander: 10%
Native American: 1%
International: 10%

Academics
Student/faculty ratio: 18:1
Class size 9 or fewer: 14%
Class size 10-29: 71%
Class size 30-49: 15%
Class size 50-99: 10%
Class size 100 or more: 7%
Returning freshmen: 66%
Six-year graduation rate: 91%

Admissions
Applicants: 2,155
Accepted: 1,491
Acceptance rate: 69.2%
Average GPA: 2.2
ACT range: 15-19
SAT Math range: 380-490
SAT Reading range: 390-490
SAT Writing range: Not reported

169

DEAN COLLEGE

Highlights

Deadlines
Early Action: No
Early Decision: No
Regular Action: Rolling admissions
Common Application: Accepted

Financial Aid
In-state tuition: $26,944
Out-of-state tuition: $26,944
Room: $7,346
Board: $4,270
Books: $1,000
Freshmen receiving need-based aid: 62%
Undergrads receiving need-based aid: 84%
Avg. % of need met by financial aid: 93%
Avg. aid package (freshmen): $21,255
Avg. aid package (undergrads): $21,194
Freshmen receiving merit-based aid: 38%
Undergrads receiving merit-based aid: 38%
Avg. student debt upon graduation: $9,984

Prominent Alumni
William Green, CEO, Accenture; Richard Belzer, actor; Jay T. Jenkins, Broadway choreographer.

School Spirit
Mascot: Bulldogs
Colors: Cardinal red, black, and white

pates in the Federal Work Study program. *Need-based aid programs include:* scholarships and grants · general need-based awards · Federal Pell grants · state scholarships and grants · college-based scholarships and grants · private scholarships and grants. *Non-Need-based aid programs include:* scholarships and grants · state scholarships and grants · athletic scholarships.

DEPAUL UNIVERSITY

1 East Jackson Boulevard, Chicago, IL 60604-2287
Admissions: 800-433-7285 · Financial Aid: 312-362-8091
Email: admission@depaul.edu · Website: http://www.depaul.edu

From the College

"DePaul is dedicated to teaching, research and public service. Among these three fundamental responsibilities, this university places highest priority on programs of instruction and learning. Research at the university entails not only the discovery and dissemination of new knowledge, but also the creation and interpretation of artistic works, application of expertise to enduring societal issues and development of methodologies that improve inquiry, teaching and professional practice. In meeting its public service responsibility, the university encourages faculty, staff and students to apply specialized expertise in ways that contribute to the social, economic, cultural and ethical quality of life."

Campus Setting

DePaul University is the nation's largest Catholic university, with over 25,000 students and about 275 degree programs. Its partnerships throughout Chicago enable DePaul to provide an exceptional educational experience that is vibrant, pragmatic and socially engaged. Classes are small and taught by faculty members who take full advantage of Chicago's corporate, cultural and community resources. DePaul is nationally recognized for incorporating service learning throughout its curriculum and for the academic rigor and prominence of its programs. Founded in 1898 by the Congregation of the Mission (Vincentians), DePaul's tradition of providing a quality education to students from a broad range of backgrounds, with particular attention to first-generation students, has resulted in one of the nation's most diverse student bodies. With nine colleges and schools, DePaul has campuses in Chicago's Loop and Lincoln Park neighborhoods, four suburban locations, and degree programs in six nations. A four-year private institution, DePaul University has an enrollment of 23,149 students. DePaul University has been co-ed since 1911. The school is also affiliated with the Roman Catholic Church. In addition to a large, well-stocked library, the campus facilities include: art gallery · performing arts center · theatre · recording studio · marketing research center · science center · fitness center. DePaul University provides on-campus housing with 1,164 units that can accommodate 2,641 students. Housing options: co-ed dorms · single-student apartments.

Student Life and Activities

Most students (81 percent) live off campus, which does impact the on-campus social scene. Nevertheless, like any college, students find time to create their own recreational outlets. DePaul University has 179 official student organizations. In sports, DePaul University is a member of the Big East Conference (Division I).

Academics and Learning Environment

For the B student, the learning environment of a college is just as important as the quality of its academic program. DePaul University has 850 full-time and 847 part-time faculty members, offering a student-to-faculty ratio of 16:1. The most common course size is 20 to 29 students. DePaul University offers 233 majors with the most popular being accountancy, finance and communication and least popular being dramaturgy/criticism, costume design and theatre technology. The school has a general core requirement as well as a religion requirement Cooperative education is not offered. All first-year students must maintain a 2.0 GPA or higher to avoid

DEPAUL UNIVERSITY

DePaul University
Chicago, IL (Pop. 2,896,016)
Location: Major city
Website: http://www.depaul.edu

Students
Total enrollment: 23,149
Undergrads: 6,555
Freshmen: 2,537
Part-time students: 21%
From out-of-state: 10%
Male/Female: 44%/56%
Live on-campus: 19%
In sororities: 1%
Off-campus employment rating: Excellent
Caucasian: 61%
African American: 9%
Hispanic: 13%
Asian or Pacific Islander: 9%
Native American: 0%
International: 1%

Academics
Student/faculty ratio: 16:1
Class size 9 or fewer: 19%
Class size 10-29: 50%
Class size 30-49: 30%
Class size 50-99: 1%
Class size 100 or more: 7%
Returning freshmen: 83%
Six-year graduation rate: 64%

Most Popular Fields of Study
Business, Finance, Sales and Marketing
Psychology
English and Literature
Computer and Information Sciences
Mathematics
Liberal Arts, Humanities and General
    Studies
Communications, Journalism, Advertising
    and Comm. Technologies
Education
Social Sciences, History, Economics,
    Political Science
Visual and Performing Arts

academic probation. Other special academic programs that would appeal to a B student: self-designed majors · pass/fail grading option · independent study · double majors · dual degrees · accelerated study · honors program · internships · weekend college · distance learning.

B Student Support and Success

Student Support Services at DePaul is a program that is open to students who demonstrate a need for academic support and meet one of the following three requirements: 1) a low income as defined by the U.S. Department of Education, 2) from a family from which neither parent has a bachelor's degree or 3) has a documented physical or learning disability.

SSS provides advising, academic assistance and mentoring to undergrads meeting the above requirements. Students are assigned an advisor who will help develop an educational plan, select courses and find resources to help with financing the student's education. SSS also offers individual tutoring and group study opportunities in a variety of subjects. Workshops are offered each quarter to help with learning on topics such as memory, active learning, note taking and test preparation.

DePaul University provides a variety of support programs including dedicated guidance for: academic · career · personal · psychological · minority students · military · veterans · non-traditional students · family planning · religious. Annually, 83 percent of freshmen students return for their sophomore year. Among students who enter the work force, approximately 84 percent enter a field related to their major within six months of graduation. Companies that most frequently hire graduates from DePaul University include: DePaul University · CNA Insurance · Chicago Public Schools · Northern Trust · Bank of America · City of Chicago.

Support for Students with Learning Disabilities

Students with learning disabilities may take advantage of specific support programs offered by DePaul University. Also, a lightened course load may be granted to LD students. Credit is given for remedial courses taken. High school foreign language waivers are accepted. According to the school, PLuS (Productive Learning Strategies) serves all LD and/or AD/HD students with a diagnosis within the last 3 years. All students receive extended time on exams, priority registration and advocacy. Weekly meetings with LD specialists who will monitor progress, and work on time management, organization, reading comprehension and written language skills and strategies, are available for a fee. Availability is limited, and a student may be temporarily placed on a waiting list. Students with learning disabilities will find the following programs at DePaul University extremely useful: remedial math · remedial English · remedial reading · tutors · untimed tests · extended time for tests · take-home exam · readers · typist/scribe · tape recorders · waiver of math degree requirement. Individual or small group tutorials are also available in: time management · organizational skills · learning strategies · writing labs · study skills. An advisor/advocate from the PLuS is available to students.

How to Get Admitted

For admissions decisions, non-academic factors considered: interview · extracurricular activities · special talents, interests, abilities · character/personal qualities · volunteer work · work experience · geographical location · religious affiliation/commitment · minority affiliation · alumni relationship. A high school diploma is required, although a GED is also accepted for admissions consideration. SAT or ACT test scores are required of all applicants.

How to Pay for College

To apply for financial aid, students should submit the following: Free Application for Federal Student Aid (FAFSA). DePaul University participates in the Federal Work Study program. *Need-based aid programs include:* scholarships and grants · general need-based awards · Federal Pell grants · state scholarships and grants · college-based scholarships and grants · private scholarships and grants. *Non-Need-based aid programs include:* scholarships and grants · state scholarships and grants · creative arts and performance awards · athletic scholarships · ROTC scholarships.

DEPAUL UNIVERSITY

Highlights

Admissions
Applicants: 10,414
Accepted: 7,308
Acceptance rate: 70.2%
Average GPA: 3.4
ACT range: 21-26
SAT Math range: 510-620
SAT Reading range: 510-630
SAT Writing range: Not reported
Top 10% of class: 19%
Top 25% of class: 47%
Top 50% of class: 79%

Deadlines
Early Action:
Early Decision: No
Regular Action: Rolling admissions
Common Application: Accepted

Financial Aid
In-state tuition: $25,490
Room: $5,829
Board: $1,460
Books: $1,000
Freshmen receiving need-based aid: 62%
Undergrads receiving need-based aid: 59%
Avg. % of need met by financial aid: 66%
Avg. aid package (freshmen): $17,601
Avg. aid package (undergrads): $16,990
Freshmen receiving merit-based aid: 6%
Undergrads receiving merit-based aid: 3%
Avg. student debt upon graduation: $18,053

School Spirit
Mascot: Blue Demons
Colors: Royal blue and scarlet
Song: *DePaul Fight Song*

DREW UNIVERSITY

36 Madison Avenue, Madison, NJ 07940-1493
Admissions: 973-408-3739 · Financial Aid: 973-408-3112
Email: cadm@drew.edu · Website: http://www.drew.edu

From the College

"Drew, a traditional small liberal arts college, combines the classic liberal arts tradition with innovative programming across the curriculum and upholds the highest intellectual standards. Drew seeks to promote diversity, civic engagement and social responsibility both in and out of the classroom. Located on nearly 200 acres known by students as "the Forest," Drew's campus is 30 miles west of midtown Manhattan. Students take advantage of this location by studying in New York City on programs like the Wall Street Semester, the Art Semester and the United Nations Semester, all directed by Drew faculty. Drew offers the full range of traditional majors in the liberal arts, along with several cutting-edge interdisciplinary and area-studies programs, as well as many opportunities for study abroad, including the unique and popular Drew International Seminars and semester-long programs in London and Brussels run by Drew's own faculty. Because of Drew's location, students benefit from internship opportunities at corporate headquarters, research laboratories, foundations, charitable organizations and government agencies. Drew's low student-to-faculty ratio and small class size enable its faculty to develop close mentoring relationships with students."

Campus Setting

Drew, founded in 1867, is a private university. Its 186-acre campus is located in Madison, 27 miles from New York City. Many of its buildings date from the 19th and early 20th centuries. A four-year private institution, Drew University has an enrollment of 2,605 students. Drew University has been co-ed since 1943. The school is also affiliated with the Methodist Church. In addition to a large, well-stocked library, the campus also has the archives of the United Methodist Church. Drew University provides on-campus housing with 761 units that can accommodate 1,424 students. Housing options: co-ed dorms · special housing for disabled students. Recreation and sports facilities include: athletic center · baseball and softball fields · stadium.

Student Life and Activities

With 86 percent of students living on campus, there are plenty of social activities. Drew students frequent The Other End Coffee House and The Pub. Popular campus events include Drew Forum Lecture Series, Community Day, First Annual Picnic, Winter Ball, Winter Fest, Block Party, Family Weekend, Fall Sports Weekend and Alumni Reunion. Drew University has 62 official student organizations. The University Programming Board, Women's Concerns and Kuumba are major influences on student life. For those interested in sports, there are intramural teams such as: basketball · billiards · flag football · indoor soccer · soccer · softball · tennis. Drew University is a member of the Landmark Conference (Division III).

Academics and Learning Environment

For the B student, the learning environment of a college is just as important as the quality of its academic program. Drew University has 159 full-time and 74 part-time faculty members, offering a student-to-faculty ratio of 11:1. The most common course size is 10 to 19 students. Drew University offers 47 majors with the most popular being political science, economics and psychology and least popular being Russian, mathematics and mathematics/computer science. The school has a general core requirement. Cooperative education is available. All first-year students must maintain a 2.0 GPA or higher to avoid academic probation. Other special academic programs that would appeal to a B student: self-designed majors · pass/fail grading option · independent study · double majors · accelerated study · honors program · Phi Beta Kappa · internships.

B Student Support and Success

Peer tutors are available for all courses taught in any given semester at Drew University. The campus also features a Writing Center where students can learn more about the writing process and bring reports, papers and other written material to receive feedback in the form of impartial and helpful responses. At the center, students can find out more about organizing papers, the process of revisions, grammar techniques, writing speeches and resumes and looking at proper word choice.

Drew University provides a variety of support programs including dedicated guidance for: academic · career · personal · psychological · minority students · non-traditional students · family planning · religious. The average freshman year GPA is 3.1, and 83 percent of freshmen students return for their sophomore year. What do students do after college? While many enter the work force, approximately 29 percent pursue a graduate degree immediately after graduation.

Support for Students with Learning Disabilities

Students with learning disabilities may take advantage of specific support programs offered by Drew University. If necessary, the college will grant additional time to students with learning disabilities to complete their degree. Also, a lightened course load may be granted to LD students. Students with learning disabilities will find the following programs at Drew University extremely useful: tutors · extended time for tests · take-home exam · note-taking services · tape recorders · early syllabus. Individual or small group tutorials are also available in: time management · organizational skills · learning strategies · writing labs · study skills.

How to Get Admitted

For admissions decisions, non-academic factors considered: interview · extracurricular activities · special talents, interests, abilities · character/personal qualities · volunteer work · work experience · state of residency · geographical location · minority affiliation · alumni relationship. A high school diploma is not required for admissions consideration. SAT or ACT test scores are considered, if submitted, but are not required. SAT Subject Test scores are considered, if submitted, but are not required. *Academic units recommended:* 4 English, 3 Math, 2 Science, 2 Social Studies, 2 Foreign Language.

How to Pay for College

To apply for financial aid, students should submit the following: Free Application for Federal Student Aid (FAFSA) · CSS/Financial Aid PROFILE. Drew University participates in the Federal Work Study program. *Need-based aid programs include:* scholarships and grants · general need-based awards · Federal Pell grants · state scholarships and grants · college-based scholarships and grants · private scholarships and grants. *Non-Need-based aid programs include:*

DREW UNIVERSITY

Drew University
Madison, NJ (Pop. 16,000)
Location: Small town
Website: http://www.drew.edu

Students
Total enrollment: 2,605
Undergrads: 626
Freshmen: 390
Part-time students: 6%
From out-of-state: 44%
Male/Female: 38%/62%
Live on-campus: 86%
Off-campus employment rating: Fair
Caucasian: 61%
African American: 7%
Hispanic: 9%
Asian or Pacific Islander: 5%
Native American: 0%
International: 2%

Academics
Student/faculty ratio: 11:1
Class size 9 or fewer: 21%
Class size 10-29: 68%
Class size 30-49: 10%
Class size 50-99: 1%
Class size 100 or more: 7%
Returning freshmen: 83%
Six-year graduation rate: 77%

Most Popular Fields of Study
Biological and Life Sciences
Area, Ethnic and Gender Studies

Admissions
Applicants: 5,219
Accepted: 3,531
Acceptance rate: 67.7%
Average GPA: 3.3
ACT range: 23-28
SAT Math range: 510-620
SAT Reading range: 520-650
SAT Writing range: 510-640
Top 10% of class: 36%
Top 25% of class: 68%
Top 50% of class: 90%

DREW UNIVERSITY

Highlights

Deadlines
Early Action: No
Early Decision: December 1
Regular Action: February 15 (final)
Common Application: Accepted

Financial Aid
In-state tuition: $37,310
Out-of-state tuition: $37,310
Room: $6,702
Board: $3,666
Books: $1,228
Freshmen receiving need-based aid: 54%
Undergrads receiving need-based aid: 53%
Avg. % of need met by financial aid: 81%
Avg. aid package (freshmen): $28,828
Avg. aid package (undergrads): $27,675
Freshmen receiving merit-based aid: 44%
Undergrads receiving merit-based aid: 35%
Avg. student debt upon graduation: $16,640

Prominent Alumni
Leo H. Grohowski, chief investment officer, Bank of New York Mellon; Amy Introcaso-Davis, senior vice president for original programming and development, Oxygen Media; Tim Rothwell, chairman, Sanofi-Aventis

School Spirit
Mascot: Rangers
Colors: Green and blue

scholarships and grants · general need-based awards · state scholarships and grants · creative arts and performance awards · special characteristics awards.

DREXEL UNIVERSITY

3141 Chestnut Street, Philadelphia, PA 19104-2875
Admissions: 800-2-DREXEL · Financial Aid: 215-895-2537
Email: enroll@drexel.edu · Website: http://www.drexel.edu

From the College

"Drexel, as Philadelphia's technological, cooperative education university, was the first university to mandate students to own computers and the first to operate a fully wireless campus. Technology is integrated into every aspect of the university. Drexel focuses on experiential learning through its cooperative education program, one of the nation's largest and oldest. The service-learning initiative complements cooperative education by allowing students to utilize the resources of Philadelphia as a "living laboratory." Drexel's thriving multidisciplinary research enterprise has erased boundaries between academic specialties. As a comprehensive university, Drexel includes the nation's largest private medical school and newest law school. As a comprehensive university, Drexel includes the nation's largest private medical school and newest law school."

Campus Setting

Drexel is a comprehensive national research university founded in 1891 to provide educational opportunities to women and men from all walks of life. Drexel offers 73 undergraduate majors in disciplines including arts and sciences, business, education, engineering and biomedicine, information science and technology, media arts, nursing and health professions. The university's 13,000-plus undergraduates comprise traditional students, adult students and online students around the world. Undergraduate studies at Drexel are distinguished by the Drexel Co-op, in which most students alternate classroom study with up to three 6-month periods of full-time professional employment in their field of interest. A four-year private institution, Drexel University has an enrollment of 20,649 students. In addition to a large, well-stocked library, the campus also has galleries. Drexel University provides on-campus housing that can accommodate 3,053 students. Housing options: co-ed dorms · sorority housing · fraternity housing · special housing for disabled students · special housing for International students. Recreation and sports facilities include: athletic center · fields and tennis courts.

Student Life and Activities

Most students (65 percent) live off campus, which does impact the on-campus social scene. Nevertheless, like any college, students find time to create their own recreational outlets. Drexel University has 135 official student organizations. The most popular are: Concert · jazz and pep bands · glee club · Varsity Singers · musical theatre · music ensembles · drama club · dance club · film society · chess club · Jewish heritage program · Amnesty International · commuter coalition · College Republicans · team managers. For those interested in sports, there are intramural teams such as: aerobics · badminton · basketball · billiards · darts · flag football · floor hockey · horseback riding · rock climbing · soccer · softball · skiing · squash · table tennis · tennis · ultimate Frisbee · volleyball · wiffle ball. Drexel University is a member of the Colonial Athletic Association (Division I).

Academics and Learning Environment

For the B student, the learning environment of a college is just as important as the quality of its academic program. Drexel University has 826 full-time and 490 part-time faculty members, offering a student-to-faculty ratio of 9:1. The most common course

DREXEL UNIVERSITY

Highlights

Drexel University
Philadelphia, PA (Pop. 1,449,000)
Location: Major city
Website: http://www.drexel.edu

Students
Total enrollment: 20,649
Undergrads: 7,440
Freshmen: 2,396
Part-time students: 20%
From out-of-state: 54%
Male/Female: 56%/44%
Live on-campus: 35%
In fraternities: 3%
In sororities: 3%
Off-campus employment rating: Excellent
Caucasian: 63%
African American: 8%
Hispanic: 3%
Asian or Pacific Islander: 12%
Native American: 0%
International: 7%

Academics
Student/faculty ratio: 9:1
Class size 9 or fewer: 31%
Class size 10-29: 56%
Class size 30-49: 8%
Class size 50-99: 3%
Class size 100 or more: 1%
Returning freshmen: 83%
Six-year graduation rate: 64%

Most Popular Fields of Study
Business, Finance, Sales and Marketing
Biological and Life Sciences
Architecture
Area, Ethnic and Gender Studies

size is 10 to 19 students. Drexel University offers 147 majors with the most popular being business administration, nursing and information systems and least popular being appropriate technology, unified science and anthropology. The school does not have a general core requirement. Cooperative education is available. Other special academic programs that would appeal to a B student: self-designed majors · pass/fail grading option · independent study · double majors · dual degrees · accelerated study · honors program · internships · weekend college · distance learning certificate programs.

B Student Support and Success

Free tutoring is available to all students of the College of Nursing and Health Professions, the School of Public Health and non-medical students of the College of Medicine. Some tutoring is individualized, while other situations include group settings.

The Student Counseling Center helps students with personal issues, including making the adjustment to university life. At different times throughout the year, workshops on study skills, stress management, assertiveness training and sexual health are offered. The center provides academic skills testing, and counselors can help students to establish an individualized time-management system to improve study skills and test taking abilities and to reduce test anxiety.

Drexel University provides a variety of support programs including dedicated guidance for: academic · career · personal · psychological · minority students · non-traditional students. Additional counseling services include: General Psychotherapy for range of psychological disorders. Recognizing that some students may need extra preparation, Drexel University offers remedial and refresher courses in: reading · writing · math · study skills. The average freshman year GPA is 2.9, and 83 percent of freshmen students return for their sophomore year. Among students who enter the work force, approximately 71 percent enter a field related to their major within six months of graduation. Companies that most frequently hire graduates from Drexel University include: Lockheed Martin · Glaxosmithkline · the Vanguard Group · Unisys · DuPont · Boeing · Deloitte and Touche · Independence Blue Cross · Merck · Rohm and Haas · PSE&G · Susquehanna International · PECO.

Support for Students with Learning Disabilities

Students with learning disabilities may take advantage of specific support programs offered by Drexel University. If necessary, the college will grant additional time to students with learning disabilities to complete their degree. Also, a lightened course load may be granted to LD students. According to the school, Drexel University does not have a specific learning disability program, but accommodation and services are provided for all students with documented disabilities through the office of Disability Services. The professional staff works with the students with disabilities to insure they have the opportunity to participate fully in Drexel University's programs and activities. Students need to self disclose and request accommodations from the office of Disability Services. Students with learning disabilities will find the following programs at Drexel University extremely useful: tutors · learning center · testing accommodations · extended time for tests · take-home exam

· oral tests · readers · typist/scribe · note-taking services · reading machines · tape recorders · texts on tape · early syllabus · diagnostic testing service · priority registration. Individual or small group tutorials are also available in: time management · organizational skills · learning strategies · specific subject areas · writing labs · math labs · study skills.

How to Get Admitted

For admissions decisions, non-academic factors considered: interview · extracurricular activities · special talents, interests, abilities · character/personal qualities · volunteer work · work experience · state of residency · alumni relationship. A high school diploma is required, although a GED is also accepted for admissions consideration. SAT or ACT test scores are required of all applicants. SAT Subject Test scores are recommended but not required. *Academic units recommended:* 1 Foreign Language.

How to Pay for College

To apply for financial aid, students should submit the following: Free Application for Federal Student Aid (FAFSA). Drexel University participates in the Federal Work Study program. *Need-based aid programs include:* scholarships and grants · general need-based awards · Federal Pell grants · state scholarships and grants · college-based scholarships and grants · private scholarships and grants · United Negro College Fund. *Non-Need-based aid programs include:* scholarships and grants · state scholarships and grants · creative arts and performance awards · athletic scholarships · ROTC scholarships.

DREXEL UNIVERSITY

Highlights

Admissions
Applicants: 16,867
Accepted: 12,097
Acceptance rate: 71.7%
Average GPA: 3.5
ACT range: 23-28
SAT Math range: 560-670
SAT Reading range: 530-630
SAT Writing range: Not reported
Top 10% of class: 31%
Top 25% of class: 65%
Top 50% of class: 92%

Deadlines
Early Action: No
Early Decision: No
Regular Action: Rolling admissions
Common Application: Accepted

Financial Aid
In-state tuition: $28,500
Out-of-state tuition: $28,500
Room: $7,275
Board: $4,860
Books: $1,800
Freshmen receiving need-based aid: 64%
Undergrads receiving need-based aid: 64%
Avg. % of need met by financial aid: 87%
Avg. aid package (freshmen): $20,791
Avg. aid package (undergrads): $16,876
Freshmen receiving merit-based aid: 1%
Undergrads receiving merit-based aid: 1%
Avg. student debt upon graduation: $35,082

School Spirit
Mascot: Dragons
Colors: Blue and gold

DUQUESNE UNIVERSITY

600 Forbes Avenue, Pittsburgh, PA 15282
Admissions: 800-456-0590 · Financial Aid: 412-396-6607
Email: admissions@duq.edu · Website: http://www.duq.edu

From the College

"Duquesne is consistently ranked among America's top Catholic universities for its faculty and 131-year tradition of academic excellence. A co-educational university on a self-contained campus with views of Pittsburgh's skyline and rivers, the university has 10,106 students representing nearly every state and 80 nations. Some 87 percent of incoming freshman are drawn from the top half of their high school class. Duquesne offers undergraduate and graduate degree programs in natural and environmental sciences, leadership, business, nursing, health sciences, pharmacy, law, education, music and the liberal arts."

Campus Setting

Duquesne, founded in 1878, is a church-affiliated university. Its 49-acre campus overlooks downtown Pittsburgh. A four-year private institution, Duquesne University has an enrollment of 10,106 students. Duquesne University has been co-ed since 1909. The school is also affiliated with the Roman Catholic Church. In addition to a large, well-stocked library, the campus facilities include: music technology · academic research in pharmaceutical information · pharmaceutical technology · phenomenology · computational sciences liberal arts international nursing and nurse managed wellness centers · recording complex · recital hall · electronic studio · keyboard lab · pharmacy manufacturing lab · phenomenology center · health sciences cadaver lab. Duquesne University provides on-campus housing with 1,764 units that can accommodate 3,428 students. Housing options: co-ed dorms · sorority housing · fraternity housing · single-student apartments · married-student apartments · special housing for disabled students. Recreation and sports facilities include: basketball · tennis and volleyball courts · football · lacrosse and soccer fields · aerobics and yoga studios · weight training and cardio equipment centers · hockey rink · swimming pool · indoor and outdoor tracks.

Student Life and Activities

With 59 percent of students living on campus, there are plenty of social activities. Popular gathering spots include Nite Spot, Starbucks, Power Recreation Center, the Red Ring, the South Side, the Carnegie Museum and music venues, Heinz Field, PNC Park, Warhol Museum, Heinz Hall, Benedum, Cultural District and Station Square. Popular events include Orientation, Carnival, International Student Week, Christmas Ball, Freshman Parent Weekend, Greek Week, Bluffstock, Light Up the Night, Multi-Cultural Unity Banquet, Commuter Day, Spotlight Musical Theater Shows, Program Council Major Concert and Nightspot Late Night Programs. Duquesne University has 150 official student organizations. Student Government, Campus Ministry and Greeks influence student life. For those interested in sports, there are intramural teams such as: badminton · basketball · indoor soccer · non-tackle football · racquetball · soccer · softball · skiing · swimming · table tennis · tennis · track and field · volleyball. Duquesne University is a member of the Atlantic 10 Conference (Division I), Northeast Conference (Division I for football).

Academics and Learning Environment

For the B student, the learning environment of a college is just as important as the quality of its academic program. Duquesne University has 463 full-time and 483 part-time faculty members, offering a student-to-faculty ratio of 16:1. The most common course size is 10 to 19 students. Duquesne University offers 183 majors with the most popular being nursing, accounting and psychology and least popular being broadcast journalism, multimedia development and advertising. The school has a general core requirement as well as a religion requirement Cooperative education is not offered. All first-year students must maintain a 1.8 GPA or higher to avoid academic probation, and a minimum overall GPA of 2.0 is required to graduate. Other special academic programs that would appeal to a B student: self-designed majors · pass/fail grading option · independent study · double majors · dual degrees · accelerated study · honors program · internships · weekend college · distance learning certificate programs.

B Student Support and Success

At Duquesne's Michael P. Weber Learning Skills Center, students will find three programs that are designed to help them achieve academic success: Individualized Study Skills Assistance, College Success Credit Courses and tutoring.

Individualized Study Skills Assistance teaches students about reading, note taking, organizing information, listening, test taking and more. The program is designed to assist students in understanding how to learn more effectively and efficiently. Tutoring is done on a one-to-one basis on in small-group settings and is free for all students. Study skills classes can also be taken for college course credit.

Duquesne University provides a variety of support programs including dedicated guidance for: academic · career · personal · psychological · minority students · non-traditional students · religious. Recognizing that some students may need extra preparation, Duquesne University offers remedial and refresher courses in: reading · writing · math · study skills. Other remedial services include test prep, foreign language training, ESL tutorials. The average freshman year GPA is 3.3, and 88 percent of freshmen students return for their sophomore year. What do students do after college? While many enter the work force, approximately 8 percent pursue a graduate degree immediately after graduation. Among students who enter the work force, approximately 57 percent enter a field related to their major within six months of graduation. Companies that most frequently hire graduates from Duquesne University include: Deloitte and Touche · Ernst & Young · Pricewaterhouse Coopers · Alcoa · PNC Financial Services Group · CVS · Enterprise · KPMG · National City Corp. · Walgreens · Giant Eagle · Bechtel Plant Machinery Inc. · UPMC (University of Pittsburgh Medical Center) · Schneider Downs & · LL Co · U.S. Steel · Kennemetal Inc. · Bank of New York Mellon.

Support for Students with Learning Disabilities

Students with learning disabilities may take advantage of specific support programs offered by Duquesne University. If necessary, the college will grant additional time to students with learning disabilities to complete their degree. Also, a lightened course load may be granted to LD students. Students with learning disabilities will find the following programs at Duquesne University extremely useful: tutors · learning center · testing accommodations · extended time

DUQUESNE UNIVERSITY

Highlights

Duquesne University
Pittsburgh, PA (Pop. 311,218)
Location: Major city
Website: http://www.duq.edu

Students
Total enrollment: 10,106
Undergrads: 2,391
Freshmen: 1,438
Part-time students: 5%
From out-of-state: 26%
Male/Female: 42%/58%
Live on-campus: 59%
In fraternities: 11%
In sororities: 8%
Off-campus employment rating: Good
Caucasian: 83%
African American: 4%
Hispanic: 1%
Asian or Pacific Islander: 2%
Native American: 0%
International: 2%

Academics
Student/faculty ratio: 16:1
Class size 9 or fewer: 15%
Class size 10-29: 54%
Class size 30-49: 24%
Class size 50-99: 4%
Class size 100 or more: 3%
Returning freshmen: 88%
Six-year graduation rate: 72%

Most Popular Fields of Study
Business, Finance, Sales and Marketing
Protective Services, Criminal Justice and Public Administration
Visual and Performing Arts
English and Literature
Philosophy, Religion and Theology
Computer and Information Sciences
Mathematics
Health Professions, Medicine and Related Sciences
Liberal Arts, Humanities and General Studies
Foreign Languages, Literature and Linguistics

181

College Profiles

DUQUESNE UNIVERSITY

Admissions

Applicants: 5,715
Accepted: 4,320
Acceptance rate: 75.6%
Average GPA: 3.6
ACT range: 22-26
SAT Math range: 520-610
SAT Reading range: 510-600
SAT Writing range: 510-600
Top 10% of class: 23%
Top 25% of class: 55%
Top 50% of class: 87%

Deadlines

Early Action: December 1
Early Decision: November 1
Regular Action: Rolling admissions
Common Application: Accepted

Financial Aid

In-state tuition: $23,470
Out-of-state tuition: $23,470
Room: $4,848
Board: $4,040
Books: $600
Freshmen receiving need-based aid: 71%
Undergrads receiving need-based aid: 69%
Avg. % of need met by financial aid: 87%
Avg. aid package (freshmen): $19,046
Avg. aid package (undergrads): $18,949
Freshmen receiving merit-based aid: 26%
Undergrads receiving merit-based aid: 24%
Avg. student debt upon graduation: $29,616

Prominent Alumni

General Michael V. Hayden, CIA director; John Clayton, NFL analyst, ESPN; Marianne Cornetti, opera singer.

School Spirit

Mascot: Duke
Colors: Red and blue
Song: *The Victory Song*

for tests · oral tests · readers · typist/scribe · note-taking services · tape recorders · texts on tape · early syllabus · priority registration. Individual or small group tutorials are also available in: time management · organizational skills · learning strategies · specific subject areas · writing labs · math labs · study skills.

How to Get Admitted

For admissions decisions, non-academic factors considered: interview · extracurricular activities · special talents, interests, abilities · character/personal qualities · volunteer work · work experience · state of residency · minority affiliation · alumni relationship. A high school diploma is required, although a GED is also accepted for admissions consideration. SAT or ACT test scores are required of all applicants. SAT Subject Test scores are considered, if submitted, but are not required. *According to the admissions office:* Minimum combined SAT Reasoning score of 1000 (minimum composite ACT score of 22) and minimum 3.0 GPA recommended. *Academic units recommended:* 4 English, 2 Math, 2 Science, 2 Social Studies, 2 Foreign Language.

How to Pay for College

To apply for financial aid, students should submit the following: Free Application for Federal Student Aid (FAFSA) · institution's own financial aid forms. Duquesne University participates in the Federal Work Study program. *Need-based aid programs include:* scholarships and grants · general need-based awards · Federal Pell grants · state scholarships and grants · college-based scholarships and grants · private scholarships and grants · United Negro College Fund. *Non-Need-based aid programs include:* scholarships and grants · state scholarships and grants · athletic scholarships · ROTC scholarships · music and drama scholarships.

America's
Best Colleges for
B Students

EARLHAM COLLEGE

801 National Road West, Richmond, IN 47374
Admissions: 800-327-5426 · Financial Aid: 765-983-1217
Email: admission@earlham.edu · Website: http://www.earlham.edu

From the College

"Earlham's international character makes it special—the college was awarded the 2006 Senator Paul Simon Award for Campus Internationalization by NAFSA: Association of International Educators. Internationalism is woven into the fabric of Earlham, where classroom learning goes hand-in-hand with experiencing the diversity of the world. Ten percent of all Earlham students and 15 percent of the faculty are international in background. More than 70 percent of Earlham students and 60 percent of the faculty have participated in study off-campus. As a part of the college's general education program, students complete an international diversity requirement, including proficiency in a second language. More than 200 courses throughout Earlham's curriculum include international themes and content. The college recently celebrated the 50th anniversary of study overseas."

Campus Setting

Earlham, founded in 1847, is a church-affiliated, liberal arts college. Its 800-acre campus is located in Richmond, 45 miles west of Dayton, Ohio. A four-year private institution, Earlham College has an enrollment of 1,319 students. The school is also affiliated with the Society of Friends Church. In addition to a large, well-stocked library, the campus also has a natural history museum. Earlham College provides on-campus housing with 507 units that can accommodate 1,015 students. Housing options: co-ed dorms · women's dorms · men's dorms · special housing for disabled students · special housing for International students.

Student Life and Activities

With 81 percent of students living on campus, there are plenty of social activities. Popular events on campus include Sunsplash, Homecoming, Parent's Weekend, Little Sibs Weekend, Air Guitar, Springfest, Africa fest, Latino fest and Kwanzaa. Earlham College has 70 official student organizations. The most popular are: Action Against Rape · The Committee for Justice in the Middle East · Dance Alloy · Earlham College Democrats · Earlham Environmental Action Coalition · Earlham Equestrian Program · Earlham Literary Magazine · Earlham Progressive Union · Earlham Volunteer Exchange · Earlham Young Friends · Economic Club · Active Minds · Figure Drawing · Gamers United · Geology Club · Hunt Seat Equestrian Team · Mock Trial · Model UN · Outdoors Club. For those interested in sports, there are intramural teams such as: basketball · non-tackle football · racquetball · soccer. Earlham College is a member of the North Coast Athletic Conference (Division III).

Academics and Learning Environment

For the B student, the learning environment of a college is just as important as the quality of its academic program. Earlham College has 94 full-time and 10 part-time faculty members, offering a student-to-faculty ratio of 12:1. The most common course size is 10 to 19 students. Earlham College offers 36 majors with the most popular being psychology, biology and history and least popular being studies in education, African/African American studies and international studies. The school has a general core requirement. Cooperative education is not offered. All first-year students must maintain a 2.0 GPA or higher to avoid academic probation, and a minimum overall GPA of 2.0 is required to graduate. Other special academic programs that would

EARLHAM COLLEGE

Earlham College
Richmond, IN (Pop. 40,000)
Location: Large town
Website: http://www.earlham.edu

Students
Total enrollment: 1,319
Undergrads: 522
Freshmen: 325
Part-time students: 1%
From out-of-state: 71%
Male/Female: 44%/56%
Live on-campus: 81%
Off-campus employment rating: Good
Caucasian: 66%
African American: 6%
Hispanic: 3%
Asian or Pacific Islander: 3%
Native American: 0%
International: 12%

Academics
Student/faculty ratio: 12:1
Class size 9 or fewer: 18%
Class size 10-29: 70%
Class size 30-49: 9%
Class size 50-99: 3%
Class size 100 or more: 3%
Returning freshmen: 85%
Six-year graduation rate: 73%

Most Popular Fields of Study
Biological and Life Sciences
Area, Ethnic and Gender Studies
Business, Finance, Sales and Marketing

appeal to a B student: self-designed majors · independent study · double majors · dual degrees · accelerated study · Phi Beta Kappa · internships.

B Student Support and Success

Based on Quaker traditions and orientation, Earlham College is considered a high-level liberal arts school. Class discussions are more common than lectures here. The Center for Academic Enrichment offers free peer tutoring to all students and has regular information on study skills. A Writing Lab is available for those having trouble with any aspect of the writing process, from brainstorming the initial idea to making the final edits. The Office of Student Development centers its programs and policies on the belief that "life outside the classroom influences a student's growth and development as much as the academic experience." According to the college's website, "Student Development designs, implements and evaluates programs and services in the following areas: student success, wellness, recreational sports, career development, counseling, athletics, residence life, student activities, campus safety and security, health services, service learning, alcohol and drug education and conduct."

Earlham College provides a variety of support programs including dedicated guidance for: academic · career · personal · psychological · minority students · family planning · religious. The average freshman year GPA is 2.8, and 85 percent of freshmen students return for their sophomore year. What do students do after college? While many enter the work force, approximately 41 percent pursue a graduate degree immediately after graduation.

Support for Students with Learning Disabilities

Students with learning disabilities may take advantage of specific support programs offered by Earlham College. If necessary, the college will grant additional time to students with learning disabilities to complete their degree. Also, a lightened course load may be granted to LD students. According to the school, it doesn't track by disability. An advisor from the LD program is available to students on an as-needed basis to meet with faculty and/or students—usually 3-5 times a semester. Students with learning disabilities will find the following programs at Earlham College extremely useful: extended time for tests · take-home exam · exam on tape or computer · note-taking services · reading machines · tape recorders · priority registration · waiver of math degree requirement. Individual or small group tutorials are also available in: time management · organizational skills · learning strategies · specific subject areas · writing labs · study skills. An advisor/advocate from the Center for Academic Enrichment is available to students.

How to Get Admitted

For admissions decisions, non-academic factors considered: interview · extracurricular activities · special talents, interests, abilities · character/personal qualities · volunteer work · work experience · state of residency. A high school diploma is required, although a GED is also accepted for admissions consideration. SAT or ACT test scores are required of all applicants. SAT Subject Test scores are not required. *According to the admissions office:* Minimum SAT scores of

500 in both verbal and math and minimum 3.0 GPA recommended. *Academic units recommended:* 4 English, 4 Math, 4 Science, 4 Social Studies, 4 Foreign Language.

How to Pay for College

To apply for financial aid, students should submit the following: Free Application for Federal Student Aid (FAFSA) · institution's own financial aid forms. Earlham College participates in the Federal Work Study program. *Need-based aid programs include:* scholarships and grants · general need-based awards · Federal Pell grants · state scholarships and grants · college-based scholarships and grants · private scholarships and grants. *Non-Need-based aid programs include:* scholarships and grants · state scholarships and grants · minority student scholarships.

EARLHAM COLLEGE

Highlights

Admissions
Applicants: 1,825
Accepted: 1,376
Acceptance rate: 75.4%
placed on wait list: 21
Average GPA: 3.5
ACT range: 24-29
SAT Math range: 540-660
SAT Reading range: 570-690
SAT Writing range: 560-680
Top 10% of class: 32%
Top 25% of class: 70%
Top 50% of class: 90%

Deadlines
Early Action: January 1
Early Decision: December 1
Regular Action: January 1 (priority)
February 15 (final)
Common Application: Accepted

Financial Aid
In-state tuition: $33,274
Out-of-state tuition: $33,274
Room: $3,424
Board: $3,390
Books: $850
Freshmen receiving need-based aid: 58%
Undergrads receiving need-based aid: 57%
Avg. % of need met by financial aid: 87%
Avg. aid package (freshmen): $26,889
Avg. aid package (undergrads): $24,146
Freshmen receiving merit-based aid: 21%
Undergrads receiving merit-based aid: 32%
Avg. student debt upon graduation: $20,287

Prominent Alumni
Michael C. Hall, star of the Showtime series *Dexter*; Frances Moore Lappe, author of *Diet for a Small Planet.*

School Spirit
Mascot: Quakers
Colors: Maroon and white

ECKERD COLLEGE

4200 54th Avenue South, St. Petersburg, FL 33711
Admissions: 800-456-9009 · Financial Aid: 800-456-9009
Email: admissions@eckerd.edu · Website: http://www.eckerd.edu

From the College

"Eckerd College is the only private, national, liberal arts college in Florida that is located on a waterfront setting in St. Petersburg. It offers a commitment to teaching and mentoring and innovative educational programs attracting students of all ages from a rich international diversity of cultural and ethnic backgrounds. Eckerd students are engaged in their education through small classes, independent and collaborative research, internships, study abroad, volunteer service and campus activities. The mission of the college is to assist students to develop a disciplined intellect, trained imagination and a motivation to lead."

Campus Setting

Eckerd, founded in 1958, is a church-affiliated college of liberal arts and sciences. Its 188-acre campus is located on Boca Ciega Bay in St. Petersburg, 25 miles from Tampa. A four-year institution, Eckerd College has an enrollment of 1,819 students. The school is also affiliated with the Presbyterian Church. In addition to a large, well-stocked library, the campus facilities include: chapel auditorium · marine science laboratory · art and music centers. Eckerd College provides on-campus housing with 788 units that can accommodate 1,408 students. Housing options: co-ed dorms · women's dorms · single-student apartments · special housing for disabled students. Recreation and sports facilities include: baseball and softball fields · tennis courts.

Student Life and Activities

With 78 percent of students living on campus, there are plenty of social activities. Popular campus events include Festival of Cultures, Chinese New Year, Festival of Hope, Family Weekend, Kappa Karnival, Fall Ball, Spring Cruise, Earth Day Celebration, Take Back the Night, Givers Banquet, Health Fair and Career Day. Eckerd College has 82 official student organizations. The most popular are: Association of Environmental Professionals · Bipedal Society · Creative Writing Club · Association for Computing Machinery · marketing club · Herpetological Society · law club · management club · pre-health club · psychology club · Students in Free Enterprise · Triton Software · art club · anime club · cinema club · dance squad · Ale Connoisseurs · ECapella · jazz club · Palmetto Productions · SAVEGAME · Spirit Bank · sewing club · Theatre Troupe. For those interested in sports, there are intramural teams such as: basketball · cricket · disc golf · dodgeball · equestrian sports · field hockey · flag football · kayaking · kickball · kiteboarding · martial arts · sand volleyball · soccer · softball · surfing · swimming club · tennis club · ultimate Frisbee · wakeboarding. Eckerd College is a member of the Sunshine State Conference (Division II).

Academics and Learning Environment

For the B student, the learning environment of a college is just as important as the quality of its academic program. Eckerd College has 112 full-time and 48 part-time faculty members, offering a student-to-faculty ratio of 13:1. The most common course size is 20 to 29 students. Eckerd College offers 37 majors with the most popular being environmental studies, marine science and management and least popular being French, German and music. The school has a general core requirement. Cooperative education is not offered. All first-year students must maintain a 1.8 GPA or higher to avoid academic probation, and a minimum overall GPA of 2.0 is required to graduate.

Other special academic programs that would appeal to a B student: self-designed majors · pass/fail grading option · independent study · double majors · dual degrees · accelerated study · honors program · Phi Beta Kappa · internships.

B Student Support and Success

Eckerd believes in support for struggling students. Faculty advisors are like mentors and provide continuing support and counsel through the student's years. Freshmen choose a mentor from a list of professionals who lead what is called Autumn Term at Eckerd. First-year students report to the school three weeks before returning students and take part in a course (for credit) that provides a thorough introduction to the campus and its resources as well as academic requirements and policies. Following the freshman year, students can choose a new mentor who specializes in their area of academic interest. Graduates receive more than the official academic transcript. They also get a co-curricular transcript that includes all of the out-of-class activities in which the student has been involved, including volunteer work, sports, leadership positions and club involvement. This transcript can be used to supplement applications for jobs, graduate work or other postgraduate plans.

Eckerd College provides a variety of support programs including dedicated guidance for: academic · career · personal · psychological · minority students · family planning · religious. The average freshman year GPA is 2.9, and 80 percent of freshmen students return for their sophomore year. Among students who enter the work force, approximately 33 percent enter a field related to their major within six months of graduation. Companies that most frequently hire graduates from Eckerd College include: Apple · Bank of America · Discovery Channel · Ernst & Young · Federal Trade Commission · Florida Department of Environmental Protection · Florida Humanities Council · Franklin Templeton · Lab Corp. · Morgan Stanley · National Institute on Aging · National Park Service · National Science Foundation · Peace Corps · Raymond James Financial · Sierra Club · Southern DataCOMM · Tampa Bay Devil Rays · Tech Data · Toronto Raptors · Tropicana-Pepsi · United States Geological Survey · UPS · Verizon · Wachovia Securities · Walt Disney World.

How to Get Admitted

For admissions decisions, non-academic factors considered: interview · extracurricular activities · special talents, interests, abilities · character/personal qualities · volunteer work · work experience · state of residency · alumni relationship. A high school diploma is required, although a GED is also accepted for admissions consideration. SAT or ACT test scores are required of all applicants. *According to the admissions office:* Minimum combined SAT Reasoning score of 1000 (composite ACT score of 22) and minimum 2.5 GPA recommended. *Academic units recommended:* 4 English, 3 Math, 3 Science, 2 Social Studies, 2 Foreign Language.

How to Pay for College

To apply for financial aid, students should submit the following: Free Application for Federal Student Aid (FAFSA). Eckerd College participates in the Federal Work Study program. *Need-based aid*

ECKERD COLLEGE

Highlights

Eckerd College
St. Petersburg, FL (Pop. 250,000)
Location: Medium city
Website: http://www.eckerd.edu

Students
Total enrollment: 1,819
Undergrads: 756
Freshmen: 489
Part-time students: 1%
From out-of-state: 74%
Male/Female: 42%/58%
Live on-campus: 78%
Off-campus employment rating: Excellent
Caucasian: 75%
African American: 3%
Hispanic: 5%
Asian or Pacific Islander: 2%
Native American: 0%
International: 3%

Academics
Student/faculty ratio: 13:1
Class size 9 or fewer: 14%
Class size 10-29: 76%
Class size 30-49: 9%
Class size 50-99: -
Class size 100 or more: 3%
Returning freshmen: 80%
Six-year graduation rate: 58%

Most Popular Fields of Study
Business, Finance, Sales and Marketing
Biological and Life Sciences
Visual and Performing Arts
English and Literature
Philosophy, Religion and Theology
Computer and Information Sciences
Psychology
Foreign Languages, Literature and Linguistics
Communications, Journalism, Advertising and Comm. Technologies
Social Sciences, History, Economics, Political Science

ECKERD COLLEGE

Admissions
Applicants: 3,398
Accepted: 2,227
Acceptance rate: 65.5%
placed on wait list: 142
Average GPA: 3.3
ACT range: 22-27
SAT Math range: 510-610
SAT Reading range: 510-615
SAT Writing range: 500-600
Top 10% of class: 16%
Top 25% of class: 48%
Top 50% of class: 85%

Deadlines
Early Action: No
Early Decision: No
Regular Action: Common Application:
   Accepted

Financial Aid
In-state tuition: $31,818
Out-of-state tuition: $31,818
Room: $4,624
Board: $4,434
Books: $1,000
Freshmen receiving need-based aid: 57%
Undergrads receiving need-based aid:
   56%
Avg. % of need met by financial aid: 91%
Avg. aid package (freshmen): $25,450
Avg. aid package (undergrads): $26,150
Freshmen receiving merit-based aid: 36%
Undergrads receiving merit-based aid:
   33%
Avg. student debt upon graduation:
   $28,219

School Spirit
Mascot: Triton
Colors: Teal, black, navy, and white

programs include: scholarships and grants · general need-based awards · Federal Pell grants · state scholarships and grants · college-based scholarships and grants · private scholarships and grants. *Non-Need-based aid programs include:* scholarships and grants · state scholarships and grants · creative arts and performance awards · special achievements and activities awards · athletic scholarships · ROTC scholarships.

ELMIRA COLLEGE

One Park Place, Elmira, NY 14901
Admissions: 800-935-6472 · Financial Aid: 800-935-6472
Email: admissions@elmira.edu · Website: http://www.elmira.edu

From the College

"Elmira College is a traditional, fully residential liberal arts college with a historical association with Mark Twain. In all majors, even several pre-professional programs, students complete a foundation in liberal arts and sciences. Ninety percent of students are traditional college age and live on campus in dormitories, apartments and houses. Forty percent of students study abroad. Intensive study is required in six-week spring term in April and May. Numerous student traditions bring students and faculty together. In coursework, emphasis is on writing; on campus, strong emphasis is on activities, including 26 athletic teams. All students attend performing arts events, and complete community service and internships."

Campus Setting

Elmira is a private, liberal arts college. Founded as a women's college in 1855, it adopted co-education in 1969. Its 42-acre campus is located in a residential area of Elmira. A four-year private institution, Elmira College has an enrollment of 1,859 students. The school also has a library with 391,038 books. Elmira College provides on-campus housing with 16 units that can accommodate 1,082 students. Housing options: co-ed dorms · women's dorms · single-student apartments. Recreation and sports facilities include: ice Arena · 2 gymnasiums · 4 indoor tennis courts · racquetball courts · recreational pool · fitness center · 6 squash courts · 3 playing fields (one with lights) · Eldridge Park Stadium (softball) · Elmira Country Club (golf).

Student Life and Activities

With 90 percent of students living on campus, there are plenty of social activities. "The entertainment-based organizations do an excellent job of bringing fun and educational acts to campus," reports the editor of the student newspaper. "There is always something going on around campus every weekend. If you are looking for a college where everyone knows your name, this is the one you are looking for!" Mackenzies, the Branch, Kingsbury's, Sheehans, the Arnot Mall and Harris Hill are favorite hang-outs. Popular events include: May Days, Holiday Weekend, Honors and Recognition Banquet, Octagon Fair and Mountain Day. Elmira College has 103 official student organizations. Student Association, Residence Life, the Octagon, Student Activities Board, Big Event Committee and the Guys & Girls House have widespread influence on campus life. For those interested in sports, there are intramural teams such as: basketball · bowling · flag football · racquetball · softball · step aerobics · turkey trot · volleyball · water aerobics. Elmira College is a member of the Empire Eight (Division III).

Academics and Learning Environment

For the B student, the learning environment of a college is just as important as the quality of its academic program. Elmira College has 83 full-time and 19 part-time faculty members, offering a student-to-faculty ratio of 12:1. The most common course size is 2 to 9 students. Elmira College offers 36 majors with the most popular being elementary education, psychology and business administration and least popular being sociology/anthropology, classical studies and philosophy/religion. The school has a general core requirement. Cooperative education is not offered. All first-year students must maintain a 2.0 GPA or higher to avoid academic probation, and a minimum

ELMIRA COLLEGE

Elmira College
Elmira, NY (Pop. 35,000)
Location: Medium city
Website: http://www.elmira.edu

Students
Total enrollment: 1,859
Undergrads: 447
Freshmen: 375
Part-time students: 18%
From out-of-state: 55%
Male/Female: 30%/70%
Live on-campus: 90%
Off-campus employment rating: Fair
Caucasian: 82%
African American: 2%
Hispanic: 1%
Asian or Pacific Islander: 1%
Native American: 0%
International: 2%

Academics
Student/faculty ratio: 12:1
Class size 9 or fewer: 55%
Class size 10-29: 42%
Class size 30-49: 6%
Class size 50-99: -
Class size 100 or more: 3%
Returning freshmen: 75%
Six-year graduation rate: 61%

Most Popular Fields of Study
Business, Finance, Sales and Marketing
Biological and Life Sciences
Area, Ethnic and Gender Studies

overall GPA of 2.0 is required to graduate. Other special academic programs that would appeal to a B student: self-designed majors · pass/fail grading option · independent study · double majors · dual degrees · accelerated study · honors program · Phi Beta Kappa · internships · distance learning certificate programs.

B Student Support and Success

In addition to small class sizes (12 or less usually), Elmira also offers a special writing class during the fall term of a student's first year. It is held on Saturdays and comes with a tutor. Elmira states that the class is designed to "hone one of the most important skills you will ever develop in your life: the ability to communicate clearly in writing." The college holds that this special program will help students develop good academic habits by making studying a part of weekend plans. Their final comment says it all: "And finally, we care enough about your academic development to get up and teach on Saturday."

Elmira College provides a variety of support programs including dedicated guidance for: academic · career · personal · psychological · family planning · religious. The average freshman year GPA is 3.0, and 75 percent of freshmen students return for their sophomore year. What do students do after college? While many enter the work force, approximately 40 percent pursue a graduate degree immediately after graduation. Among students who enter the work force, approximately 83 percent enter a field related to their major within six months of graduation. Companies that most frequently hire graduates from Elmira College include: Blackbaud · Cornell University · Blue Shield · Tribune Television Co. · Bose Inc. · Federal Bureau of Investigation · U.S. Armed Forces · National Cancer Institute · Americorps · Ford Motor Co. · Fidelity Investments · CIGNA · NYS Inspector General · Deloitte & Touche · MCI-North America · Delta Airlines · Morgan Stanley · Merrill Lynch · Panasonic · Wyeth Labs · Newell-Rubbermaid · Wells Fargo Financial Services · Unilever · Maersk · HSBC Financial Services · Pfizer Inc. · Corning Inc. · Walt Disney World · Xerox Corp.· Deutsch Bank NY · Federal Reserve Bank of New York.

Support for Students with Learning Disabilities

Students with learning disabilities may take advantage of specific support programs offered by Elmira College. If necessary, the college will grant additional time to students with learning disabilities to complete their degree. Also, a lightened course load may be granted to LD students. Students with learning disabilities will find the following programs at Elmira College extremely useful: tutors · testing accommodations · untimed tests · extended time for tests · take-home exam · oral tests · readers · note-taking services · reading machines · tape recorders · early syllabus · diagnostic testing service · waiver of math degree requirement · waiver of foreign language degree requirement. Individual or small group tutorials are also available in: time management · organizational skills · learning strategies · specific subject areas · writing labs · math labs · study skills. An advisor/advocate from the Disability Services is available to students.

How to Get Admitted

For admissions decisions, non-academic factors considered: interview · extracurricular activities · special talents, interests, abilities · character/personal qualities · volunteer work · work experience · state of residency · geographical location · minority affiliation · alumni relationship. A high school diploma is required, although a GED is also accepted for admissions consideration. SAT or ACT test scores are required of all applicants. SAT Subject Test scores are not required. *Academic units recommended:* 2 Foreign Language.

How to Pay for College

To apply for financial aid, students should submit the following: Free Application for Federal Student Aid (FAFSA) · state aid form. Elmira College participates in the Federal Work Study program. *Need-based aid programs include:* scholarships and grants · general need-based awards · Federal Pell grants · state scholarships and grants · college-based scholarships and grants · private scholarships and grants. *Non-Need-based aid programs include:* scholarships and grants · state scholarships and grants · special achievements and activities awards · special characteristics awards · ROTC scholarships.

ELMIRA COLLEGE

Highlights

Admissions
Applicants: 1,996
Accepted: 1,431
Acceptance rate: 71.7%
placed on wait list: 48
Average GPA: 3.4
ACT range: 23-27
SAT Math range: 500-630
SAT Reading range: 510-630
SAT Writing range: Not reported
Top 10% of class: 29%
Top 25% of class: 68%
Top 50% of class: 96%

Deadlines
Early Action: No
Early Decision: November 15
Regular Action: February 1 (priority)
March 1 (final)
Common Application: Accepted

Financial Aid
In-state tuition: $33,500
Out-of-state tuition: $33,500
Room: $6,000
Board: $4,800
Books: $450
Freshmen receiving need-based aid: 76%
Undergrads receiving need-based aid: 76%
Avg. % of need met by financial aid: 81%
Avg. aid package (freshmen): $24,400
Avg. aid package (undergrads): $23,500
Freshmen receiving merit-based aid: 24%
Undergrads receiving merit-based aid: 21%
Avg. student debt upon graduation: $27,058

School Spirit
Mascot: Soaring Eagle
Colors: Purple and Gold

ENDICOTT COLLEGE

376 Hale Street, Beverly, MA 01915
Admissions: 800-325-1114 · Financial Aid: 800-325-1114 (out-of-state)
Email: admissio@endicott.edu · Website: http://www.endicott.edu

From the College

"Endicott College is the first college in the nation to require all students to complete yearly internships. Today, Endicott remains dedicated to that vision and every student completes a first-year seminar, three work-experience internships, senior seminar and a senior thesis. Endicott's competency-based curriculum exposes students to their field of study early in the program. Students select from 23 bachelor's programs and 27 concentrations. Master's programs are offered in business, education and computer science. The core emphasizes research, communication, creative and analytic skills. The mission emphasizes values, community service, technological competency, diversity, international awareness and ultimately, lives open to change."

Campus Setting

Endicott is a private, liberal and professional studies institution that offers baccalaureate and graduate-level programs. Founded in 1939 as a women's college, it became co-educational in 1994. Its 231-acre campus is located in Beverly, 20 miles north of Boston. A four-year private institution, Endicott College has an enrollment of 3,947 students. In addition to a large, well-stocked library, the campus facilities include: museum · performing arts center · student-run restaurant · cyber-cafe. Endicott College provides on-campus housing with 807 units that can accommodate 1,689 students. Housing options: co-ed dorms · women's dorms · single-student apartments · special housing for disabled students · special housing for International students. Recreation and sports facilities include: baseball and softball fields · climbing walls · field house · fitness center · gymnasium · practice fields · racquetball and tennis courts · stadium · track · skating rink (off campus) · aerobics studio · nature trails.

Student Life and Activities

With 86 percent of students living on campus, there are plenty of social activities. Popular gathering spots include the Callahan Center (student center), the Post Center (athletic facilities), the Visual and Performing Arts Center and private beaches. Popular campus events include Homecoming/Family Weekend, Annual Regatta and the Festival of Lights. Endicott College has 44 official student organizations. The most popular are: Chorus · Student Arts Council · drama club · dance team · film society · book club · C.O.A.L. · E.C.T.V. · Musicians Collective · education club · International Interior Design Association · Gay-Straight Alliance · hall councils · Commuter Student Association · athletic training club · Outdoor Adventure Club · environmental club · investment club · Student Senate · Law & Justice · Leadership Advisory Board · Amnesty International · Best Buddies · Colleges Against Cancer · Rotaract Service Club. For those interested in sports, there are intramural teams such as: baseball · dodge ball · flag football · floor hockey · kickball · racquetball · soccer · volleyball. Endicott College is a member of the NCAA, Commonwealth Coast Conference (Division III), ECAC, Intercollegiate Horse Show Association, New England Football Conference (Division III), North Eastern Collegiate Volleyball Association (Division III), North Eastern Collegiate Hockey Association.

Academics and Learning Environment

For the B student, the learning environment of a college is just as important as the quality of its academic program. Endicott College has 76 full-time and 97 part-time faculty members, offering a student-to-faculty ratio of 16:1. The most common course size is 20 to 29 students. Endicott College offers 27 majors with the most popular being business administration, sport management and communication. The school has a general core requirement. Cooperative education is not offered. All first-year students must maintain a 1.8 GPA or higher to avoid academic probation. Other special academic programs that would appeal to a B student: self-designed majors · independent study · accelerated study · honors program · internships · distance learning certificate programs.

B Student Support and Success

Endicott offers students access to an extensive computer lab, plus the availability of the Scangas Center for Media and Learning where workshops and training sessions are taught throughout the year. The Academic Technology Workshops provide tips on common software packages. The college also offers FYE 101 (first year experience), which is a one-credit class taught by faculty and staff, addressing the challenges incoming students face and strategies on how to meet them. This course helps students to learn and use social skills, to find academic resources, to become familiar with college policies and to follow procedures. According to the website, "The program is designed to promote student learning and development, improve student satisfaction and success and encourage engagement in the life of the college which is fostered by connections with the Endicott community. Ultimately, we expect that by the end of the first year, students will have increased self-confidence, stronger academic and professional skills, and will be involved and committed to the 'Endicott Experience'."

Endicott College provides a variety of support programs including dedicated guidance for: academic · career · personal · psychological · minority students · family planning · religious. Annually, 81 percent of freshmen students return for their sophomore year. What do students do after college? While many enter the work force, approximately 15 percent pursue a graduate degree immediately after graduation.

Support for Students with Learning Disabilities

Students with learning disabilities may take advantage of specific support programs offered by Endicott College. Students with learning disabilities will find the following programs at Endicott College extremely useful: tutors · learning center · testing accommodations · untimed tests · extended time for tests · take-home exam · oral tests · readers · note-taking services · tape recorders · priority registration. Individual or small group tutorials are also available in: time management · organizational skills · learning strategies · specific subject areas · writing labs · math labs · study skills. An advisor/advocate from the LD program is available to students.

How to Get Admitted

For admissions decisions, non-academic factors considered: interview · extracurricular activities · special talents, interests, abilities · character/personal qualities · volunteer work · work experience · geographical location · minority affiliation · alumni relationship. A high school diploma is required, although a GED is also accepted

ENDICOTT COLLEGE

Highlights

Endicott College
Beverly, MA (Pop. 40,166)
Location: Large town
Website: http://www.endicott.edu

Students
Total enrollment: 3,947
Undergrads: 1,016
Freshmen: 642
Part-time students: 8%
From out-of-state: 53%
Male/Female: 44%/56%
Live on-campus: 86%
Off-campus employment rating: Good
Caucasian: 76%
African American: 1%
Hispanic: 1%
Asian or Pacific Islander: 1%
Native American: 0%
International: 3%

Academics
Student/faculty ratio: 16:1
Class size 9 or fewer: 10%
Class size 10-29: 86%
Class size 30-49: 7%
Class size 50-99: -
Class size 100 or more: 3%
Returning freshmen: 81%
Six-year graduation rate: 67%

Most Popular Fields of Study
Business, Finance, Sales and Marketing
Protective Services, Criminal Justice and
    Public Administration
Psychology
English and Literature
Computer and Information Sciences
Parks, Recreation and Fitness
Interdisciplinary Studies
Health Professions, Medicine and Related Sciences
Liberal Arts, Humanities and General
    Studies

ENDICOTT COLLEGE

Admissions
Applicants: 4,032
Accepted: 1,958
Acceptance rate: 48.6%
placed on wait list: 374
Average GPA: Not reported
ACT range: 20-25
SAT Math range: 500-590
SAT Reading range: 500-570
SAT Writing range: 500-580
Top 10% of class: 10%
Top 25% of class: 38%
Top 50% of class: 83%

Deadlines
Early Action: No
Early Decision: No
Regular Action: Rolling admissions
Common Application: Accepted

Financial Aid
In-state tuition: $24,130
Out-of-state tuition: $24,130
Room: $7,930
Board: $3,450
Books: $1,000
Freshmen receiving need-based aid: 48%
Undergrads receiving need-based aid: 56%
Avg. % of need met by financial aid: 60%
Avg. aid package (freshmen): $14,385
Avg. aid package (undergrads): $15,615
Freshmen receiving merit-based aid: 16%
Undergrads receiving merit-based aid: 17%
Avg. student debt upon graduation: $28,022

School Spirit
Mascot: Gulls
Colors: Blue and green

for admissions consideration. SAT or ACT test scores are required of all applicants. SAT Subject Test scores are recommended but not required. *Academic units recommended:* 4 English, 3 Math, 2 Science, 2 Social Studies.

How to Pay for College

To apply for financial aid, students should submit the following: Free Application for Federal Student Aid (FAFSA) · institution's own financial aid forms · Non-custodian (Divorced/Separated) Parent's Statement. Endicott College participates in the Federal Work Study program. *Need-based aid programs include:* scholarships and grants · general need-based awards · Federal Pell grants · state scholarships and grants · college-based scholarships and grants · private scholarships and grants. *Non-Need-based aid programs include:* scholarships and grants · general need-based awards · state scholarships and grants · creative arts and performance awards · special achievements and activities awards · special characteristics awards · ROTC scholarships.

EVERGREEN STATE COLLEGE

2700 Evergreen Parkway NW, Olympia, WA 98505
Admissions: 360-867-6170 · Financial Aid: 360-867-6205
Email: admissions@evergreen.edu · Website: http://www.evergreen.edu

From the College

"Evergreen State College in Olympia, Washington is a public, liberal arts college where coordinated, team-taught, interdisciplinary programs—combining a range of topics around a central theme—replace disconnected courses. Faculty members write narrative evaluations to assess student work, rather than reducing performance and progress to a letter grade. The curriculum promotes engagement and collaboration, rather than competition. Students have the freedom, and accountability, to design their education to meet their personal and career goals, without the limits of formalized majors or rigid requirements. The curriculum is redesigned every year, and upper division students can propose individual learning contracts to further customize their learning experience.

"While in many ways Evergreen breaks the mold of traditional higher education—and in doing so opens up opportunities for students with a wide range of learning styles and career goals—the college delivers a high level of academic rigor. The National Survey of Student Engagement, sponsored by the Pew Charitable Trusts, notes that Evergreen students tend to read more, prepare more extensively for class, make more presentations and engage more actively with faculty and each other than at the vast majority of colleges and universities nationwide. Students have opportunities for research, hands-on field study, community service, internships and study abroad. Evergreen is one of just three institutions on the West Coast included in the book *Colleges That Change Lives* by former New York Times education editor Loren Pope.

"Evergreen is located in the state capital of Olympia. Students can easily access the urban life of Seattle or Portland, or the recreational opportunities of the Pacific Ocean, Mount Rainier and the Olympic National Park, all within a one- to two-hour drive. Evergreen's forested 1,000-acre campus features a half-mile of saltwater beach on Puget Sound, a Native American longhouse, an organic farm, and award winning, environmentally friendly architecture in its newest classroom and office complex. With a strong commitment to sustainability in operations, curriculum and policy, Evergreen has been noted as one of the nation's top 'green' colleges.

"The vast majority of Evergreen's 4,300 students are undergraduates studying the liberal arts and the sciences, including natural and physical sciences. The college also offers graduate programs in education, environmental study, Public administration and teaching."

Campus Setting

Evergreen State College, founded in 1967, is a four-year, public institution, Evergreen State College has an enrollment of 4,696 students. In addition to a large, well-stocked library, the campus facilities include: gallery · animation and design studio · art annex · ceramics studio · metal shop · photography studios and darkrooms · wood shop · education and cultural center · organic farm and community gardens · science labs. Evergreen State College provides on-campus housing with 965 units that can accommodate 990 students. Housing options: co-ed dorms · single-student apartments · married-student apartments · special housing for disabled students · special housing for International students. Recreation and sports facilities include: aerobic room · dance rooms · fields · gymnasium · outdoor and indoor climbing walls · racquetball courts · sports pavilion · swimming pool · weight rooms.

EVERGREEN STATE COLLEGE

Evergreen State College
Olympia, WA (Pop. 44,925)
Location: Medium city
Website: http://www.evergreen.edu

Students
Total enrollment: 4,696
Undergrads: 1,973
Freshmen: 844
Part-time students: 10%
From out-of-state: 49%
Male/Female: 45%/55%
Live on-campus: 22%
Off-campus employment rating: Good
Caucasian: 70%
African American: 5%
Hispanic: 5%
Asian or Pacific Islander: 5%
Native American: 3%
International: 1%

Academics
Student/faculty ratio: 22:1
Class size 9 or fewer: 11%
Class size 10-29: 56%
Class size 30-49: 22%
Class size 50-99: 12%
Class size 100 or more: 3%
Returning freshmen: 70%
Six-year graduation rate: 63%

Admissions
Applicants: 1,989
Accepted: 1,876
Acceptance rate: 94.3%
Average GPA: 3.1
ACT range: 22-27
SAT Math range: 470-600
SAT Reading range: 530-660
SAT Writing range: Not reported
Top 10% of class: 9%
Top 25% of class: 22%
Top 50% of class: 61%

Student Life and Activities

Most students (78 percent) live off campus, which does impact the on-campus social scene. Nevertheless, like any college, students find time to create their own recreational outlets. "There's an independent streak at Evergreen," explains one junior. "The academic approach—interdisciplinary programs, freedom to create your own academic pathway, individual learning contracts—attracts people who like to take a different approach to things. There's a definite 'green' and activist feel on campus, and there's a lot less concern about who's wearing what or who belongs to what group than you'd see at some schools. Beyond campus, lots of students hang out in downtown Olympia, where there are more restaurants, coffee shops and brew pubs. And yes, it rains a lot here." Popular on-campus gathering spots include Red Square, the CAB, the library and (when the weather's good) the field. Popular off-campus gathering spots include Old School Pizza, Darby's, Café Vita, the New Moon Café, Last Word Books, Vic's Pizza, and Batdorf & Bronson. Popular campus events include Synergy (Sustainability Conference), Graduation, Harvest Festival, Day of Presence/Day of Absence, Longhouse Native Arts Fair, and Lunar New Year Festival. Evergreen State College has 61 official student organizations. Groups that have a strong presence in Evergreen's social life include the Geoduck Student Union, KAOS, Hip Hop Congress, the Women's Resource Center, S&A Productions and the Folk Dance Alliance. For those interested in sports, there are intramural teams such as: badminton · basketball · soccer · softball · tennis · ultimate Frisbee · volleyball. Evergreen State College is a member of the Cascade Collegiate Conference (NAIA).

Academics and Learning Environment

For the B student, the learning environment of a college is just as important as the quality of its academic program. Evergreen State College has 164 full-time and 79 part-time faculty members, offering a student-to-faculty ratio of 22:1. The most common course size is 20 to 29 students. Evergreen State College offers 56 majors with the most popular being. The school does not have a general core requirement. Cooperative education is not offered. Other special academic programs that would appeal to a B student: self-designed majors · independent study · double majors · dual degrees · accelerated study · internships · weekend college.

B Student Support and Success

Evergreen has a unique style of teaching that will appeal to students who do not excel in traditional classrooms that are facilitated by the typical lecture/listen methods. This college designs classes so that there is a balance between seminars, hands-on learning and off-campus exploration. Weeklong field trips are not uncommon here. The college also offers a program called Individual Learning Contracts. This allows students to do advanced academic study in an area they already have a background in, working independently and meeting weekly with a sponsor. Evergreen also has an extensive study abroad program for students.

Evergreen State College provides a variety of support programs including dedicated guidance for: academic · career · personal · psychological · minority students · veterans · family planning. Additional counseling services include: addictive behavior specialist. Annually, 70 percent of freshmen students return for their sophomore year.

Support for Students with Learning Disabilities

Students with learning disabilities may take advantage of specific support programs offered by Evergreen State College. If necessary, the college will grant additional time to students with learning disabilities to complete their degree. Also, a lightened course load may be granted to LD students. According to the school, Depending on the nature of your disability and how it impact your educational experience, services and accommodations provided on an individually determined basis, may include: accessible facilities, alternative testing, accessible parking, sign language interpreters/CART, note takers, priority registration, adaptive equipment/assistive technology, books on tape, tutorial assistance from KEY Student Services and the Learning Resource Center, counseling referrals and peer support and advocacy. Students with learning disabilities will find the following programs at Evergreen State College extremely useful: tutors · learning center · testing accommodations · extended time for tests · take-home exam · typist/scribe · note-taking services · reading machines · tape recorders · priority registration · waiver of math degree requirement. Individual or small group tutorials are also available in: time management · organizational skills · learning strategies · specific subject areas · writing labs · math labs · study skills. An advisor/advocate from the Access Services is available to students.

How to Get Admitted

For admissions decisions, non-academic factors considered: interview · extracurricular activities · volunteer work · work experience · state of residency. A high school diploma is required, although a GED is also accepted for admissions consideration. SAT or ACT test scores are required of all applicants. SAT Subject Test scores are not required. *According to the admissions office:* Minimum 2.0 GPA required.

How to Pay for College

To apply for financial aid, students should submit the following: Free Application for Federal Student Aid (FAFSA) · institution's own financial aid forms. Evergreen State College participates in the Federal Work Study program. *Need-based aid programs include:* scholarships and grants · general need-based awards · Federal Pell grants · state scholarships and grants · college-based scholarships and grants · private scholarships and grants. *Non-Need-based aid programs include:* scholarships and grants · state scholarships and grants · special achievements and activities awards · special characteristics awards · athletic scholarships.

EVERGREEN STATE COLLEGE

Highlights

Deadlines
Early Action: No
Early Decision: No
Regular Action: Rolling admissions
Common Application: Not accepted

Financial Aid
In-state tuition: $5,133
Out-of-state tuition: $16,440
Room: -
Board: -
Books: $924
Freshmen receiving need-based aid: 41%
Undergrads receiving need-based aid: 52%
Avg. % of need met by financial aid: 75%
Avg. aid package (freshmen): $6,481
Avg. aid package (undergrads): $7,221
Freshmen receiving merit-based aid: 3%
Undergrads receiving merit-based aid: 1%
Avg. student debt upon graduation: $15,597

Prominent Alumni
Matt Groening, cartoonist, creator of *Life in Hell*, *The Simpsons*, and *Futurama*; Rosalund Jenkins, executive director, Washington State Commission on African American Affairs; Lynda Barry, graphic novelist and cartoonist.

School Spirit
Mascot: Geoducks
Colors: Forest and white
Song: *The Geoduck Fight Song*

FAIRMONT STATE UNIVERSITY

1201 Locust Avenue, Fairmont, WV 26554
Admissions: 800-641-5678 · Financial Aid: 800-641-5678, extension 3
Email: admit@fairmontstate.edu · Website: http://www.fairmontstate.edu

From the College

"Fairmont State University, including Pierpont Community and Technical College, which is a division of the university, offers a wide variety of graduate, bachelor's and associate degrees. The mission of FSU is to provide opportunities for individuals to achieve their professional and personal goals and discover roles for responsible citizenship that promote the common good. The mission of Pierpont C&TC is to provide opportunities for learning, training and further education that enrich the lives of individuals and promote the economic growth of our service region and state. With a 120-acre main campus in Fairmont, West Virginia, FSU is part of the state's growing high technology corridor, including a metro area of about 50,000 residents. The FSU main campus is within a short drive of larger cities such as Pittsburgh, Pennsylvania, and opportunities for outdoor recreation in West Virginia. FSU serves a 13-county region with facilities including the Robert C. Byrd National Aerospace Education Center in Bridgeport, West Virginia. The main campus is home to the West Virginia Folklife Center. A recent project between Pierpont C&TC and Braxton County High School has created the nation's first rural Early College High School, allowing students to earn a certificate or an associate degree while they are in high school. FSU offers many evening and online classes to accommodate non-traditional students."

Campus Setting

Fairmont State, founded in 1865, is a public university of the arts and sciences. It was founded as a private teacher training school, became state-supported in 1867 and began offering bachelor's degrees in 1943. Programs are offered through the Schools of Business and Economics, Education and Health and Human Performance, Fine Arts, Health Careers, Languages and Literatures, Science and Mathematics, Social Science, and Technology. Its campus is located in Fairmont, 75 miles south of Pittsburgh. A four-year public institution, Fairmont State University has an enrollment of 4,547 students. In addition to a large, well-stocked library, the campus also has the West Virginia folklife center. Fairmont State University provides on-campus housing with 424 units that can accommodate 1,068 students. Housing options: co-ed dorms · women's dorms · men's dorms · single-student apartments · married-student apartments. Recreation and sports facilities include: arena · center · fields · tracks.

Student Life and Activities

Most students (79 percent) live off campus, which does impact the on-campus social scene. Nevertheless, like any college, students find time to create their own recreational outlets. Popular campus events include Celebration of Ideas Lecture Series, Live at Lunch Music Series, Women of WV Art Expo, annual blood drive, activities fair, majors fair, career fair, education career fair, Banned Book Week, Alcohol, Substance Abuse, and Sexuality Awareness Week and the talent contest series. Fairmont State University has 81 official student organizations. The most popular are: Collegiate Singers · ballroom dancing club · American Choral Directors Association · Percussion Ensemble · Music Educators National Conference · Spanish club · Student Graphics Organization · American Institute of Architecture Students · Student Historical Society · Masquers Club · Bisexual Gay and Lesbian Students and Friends · Honors Association. For those interested in sports, there are intramural teams such as: baseball · basketball · billiards · football · horseshoes · softball · table tennis · tennis. Fairmont

State University is a member of the West Virginia Intercollegiate Athletic Conference (Division II), Blue Grass Conference.

Academics and Learning Environment

For the B student, the learning environment of a college is just as important as the quality of its academic program. Fairmont State University has 165 full-time and 169 part-time faculty members, offering a student-to-faculty ratio of 17:1. The most common course size is 20 to 29 students. Fairmont State University offers 83 majors with the most popular being business administration, criminal justice and education and least popular being English and history. The school has a general core requirement. Cooperative education is available. All first-year students must maintain a 2.0 GPA or higher to avoid academic probation, and a minimum overall GPA of 2.0 is required to graduate. Other special academic programs that would appeal to a B student: self-designed majors · independent study · double majors · accelerated study · honors program · internships · weekend college · distance learning.

B Student Support and Success

Fairmont is two schools in one. Here you can earn an associate degree through Fairmont State Community and Technical College; then get a bachelor's degree at the university. The student-to-faculty ratio at Fairmont is about 17:1, and average class size is 22 students. Tutoring is free for all students through the Tutorial Services Program, although the majority of students are limited to 10 hours per semester. (Students with documented learning disabilities may get additional sessions.) Virtually all subject areas are covered. Fairmont also offers a cutting-edge program called Supplemental Instruction. It is based on the experience of past students and is designed to help enrollees with courses that have been historically proven to be the most difficult. The course is free and is taught by faculty-recommended students.

Fairmont State University provides a variety of support programs including dedicated guidance for: academic · career · personal · psychological · minority students · military · veterans. Recognizing that some students may need extra preparation, Fairmont State University offers remedial and refresher courses in: reading · writing · math · study skills. The average freshman year GPA is 2.6, and 67 percent of freshmen students return for their sophomore year. What do students do after college? While many enter the work force, approximately 17 percent pursue a graduate degree immediately after graduation. Among students who enter the work force, approximately 80 percent enter a field related to their major within six months of graduation. Companies that most frequently hire graduates from Fairmont State University include: AEGiS · BB&T · Fastenal · federal and state government · KeyLogic Systems · Marion County Board of Education · Prologic · WesBanco.

Support for Students with Learning Disabilities

Students with learning disabilities may take advantage of specific support programs offered by Fairmont State University. If necessary, the college will grant additional time to students with learning disabilities to complete their degree. Also, a lightened course load may be granted to LD students. Students with learning disabilities will

FAIRMONT STATE UNIVERSITY

Highlights

Fairmont State University
Fairmont, WV (Pop. 20,000)
Location: Medium town
Website: http://www.fairmontstate.edu

Students
Total enrollment: 4,547
Undergrads: 1,842
Freshmen: 771
Part-time students: 14%
From out-of-state: 10%
Male/Female: 45%/55%
Live on-campus: 21%
In fraternities: 2%
In sororities: 2%
Off-campus employment rating: Good
Caucasian: 91%
African American: 4%
Hispanic: 1%
Asian or Pacific Islander: 1%
Native American: 0%
International: 2%

Academics
Student/faculty ratio: 17:1
Class size 9 or fewer: 19%
Class size 10-29: 60%
Class size 30-49: 15%
Class size 50-99: 6%
Class size 100 or more: 2%
Returning freshmen: 67%
Six-year graduation rate: 36%

Most Popular Fields of Study
Business, Finance, Sales and Marketing
Protective Services, Criminal Justice and
    Public Administration
Psychology
English and Literature
Computer and Information Sciences
Mathematics
Engineering and Engineering Technologies
Parks, Recreation and Fitness
Health Professions, Medicine and Related
    Sciences
Liberal Arts, Humanities and General
    Studies

199

College Profiles

FAIRMONT STATE UNIVERSITY

Admissions

Applicants: 3,072
Accepted: 2,690
Acceptance rate: 87.6%
Average GPA: 3.1
ACT range: 18-23
SAT Math range: 420-540
SAT Reading range: 410-530
SAT Writing range: Not reported
Top 10% of class: 9%
Top 25% of class: 30%
Top 50% of class: 67%

Deadlines

Early Action: No
Early Decision: No
Regular Action: Common Application:
    Accepted

Financial Aid

In-state tuition: $5,024
Out-of-state tuition: $10,590
Room: $3,280
Board: $3,004
Books: $1,000
Freshmen receiving need-based aid: 54%
Undergrads receiving need-based aid:
    66%
Avg. % of need met by financial aid: Not
    reported
Avg. aid package (freshmen): $6,866
Avg. aid package (undergrads): $7,364
Freshmen receiving merit-based aid: 12%
Undergrads receiving merit-based aid:
    8%

School Spirit

Mascot: Falcon
Colors: Maroon, tan, and white
Song: *College on the Hill*

find the following programs at Fairmont State University extremely useful: remedial math · remedial English · remedial reading · tutors · learning center · testing accommodations · extended time for tests · oral tests · readers · typist/scribe · note-taking services · reading machines · tape recorders · texts on tape · early syllabus · diagnostic testing service · special bookstore section · priority registration. Individual or small group tutorials are also available in: time management · organizational skills · learning strategies · specific subject areas · writing labs · math labs · study skills. An advisor/advocate from the LD program is available to students. This member also sits on the admissions committee.

How to Get Admitted

For admissions decisions, non-academic factors considered: state of residency. A high school diploma is required, although a GED is also accepted for admissions consideration. SAT or ACT test scores are required of all applicants. *According to the admissions office:* Minimum composite ACT score of 19 and minimum 2.25 GPA required.

How to Pay for College

To apply for financial aid, students should submit the following: Free Application for Federal Student Aid (FAFSA). Fairmont State University participates in the Federal Work Study program. *Need-based aid programs include:* scholarships and grants · general need-based awards · Federal Pell grants · state scholarships and grants · college-based scholarships and grants · private scholarships and grants. *Non-Need-based aid programs include:* scholarships and grants · state scholarships and grants · creative arts and performance awards · athletic scholarships.

FISK UNIVERSITY

1000 17th Avenue North, Nashville, TN 37208-3051
Admissions: 800-443-FISK · Financial Aid: 615-329-8585
Email: admit@fisk.edu · Website: http://www.fisk.edu

From the College

"Founded in 1866, the university is co-educational, private, and one of America's premier historically black universities. The first black college to be granted a chapter of Phi Beta Kappa Honor Society, Fisk serves a diverse student body with students from 40 states and 6 foreign countries. The focal point of the 40-acre campus and architectural symbol of the university is Jubilee Hall, the first permanent building for the education of blacks in the South, named for the internationally renowned Fisk Jubilee Singers. From its earliest days, Fisk faculty and alumni have been among America's intellectual leaders providing leadership in several fields including medicine, science, art, humanities, religion, literature, sociology and philosophy. Fisk alumni include W. E. B. Du Bois, the first black Ph.D. from Harvard, great social critic and co-founder of the NAACP. In proportion to its size, Fisk continues to contribute a higher percentage of African American alumni to the ranks of scholars pursuing doctoral degrees than any other institution in the United States."

Campus Setting

Fisk, founded as the Fisk School in 1866, is a church-affiliated, liberal arts university. Its 40-acre campus, listed with the National Register of Historical Landmarks, is located on a hill overlooking downtown Nashville. A four-year private institution, Fisk University is a historically black university with 726 students. The school is also affiliated with the Church of Christ. In addition to a large, well-stocked library, the campus also has galleries. Fisk University provides on-campus housing with 460 units that can accommodate 850 students. Housing options: co-ed dorms · women's dorms · men's dorms.

Student Life and Activities

With 61 percent of students living on campus, there are plenty of social activities and exposure to diverse cultures (Caribbean, South American, African). The Campus Grove is a popular on-campus gathering spot. Popular campus events include Homecoming, Greek Step Show and Competition and the Spring Arts Festival. Fisk University has 85 official student organizations. Popular groups on campus include Greek fraternities and sororities and the Jubilee Singers. Fisk University is a member of the Great South Athletic Conference (Division III).

Academics and Learning Environment

For the B student, the learning environment of a college is just as important as the quality of its academic program. Fisk University has 58 full-time and 30 part-time faculty members, offering a student-to-faculty ratio of 11:1. The most common course size is 2 to 9 students. Fisk University offers 25 majors with the most popular being psychology, business administration and biology and least popular being mathematics, music and music performance. The school has a general core requirement. Cooperative education is not offered. All first-year students must maintain a 1.5 GPA or higher to avoid academic probation, and a minimum overall GPA of 2.0 is required to graduate. Other special academic programs that would appeal to a B student: self-designed majors · pass/fail grading option · independent study · double majors · honors program · Phi Beta Kappa · internships.

FISK UNIVERSITY

Highlights

Fisk University
Nashville, TN (Pop. 1,000,000)
Location: Major city
Website: http://www.fisk.edu

Students
Total enrollment: 726
Undergrads: 218
Freshmen: 138
Part-time students: 4%
From out-of-state: 71%
Male/Female: 32%/68%
Live on-campus: 61%
In fraternities: 18%
In sororities: 23%
Off-campus employment rating: Excellent
Caucasian: 0%
African American: 82%
Hispanic: 0%
Asian or Pacific Islander: 1%
International: 12%

Academics
Student/faculty ratio: 11:1
Class size 9 or fewer: 46%
Class size 10-29: 46%
Class size 30-49: 6%
Class size 50-99: 1%
Class size 100 or more: 2%
Returning freshmen: 73%
Six-year graduation rate: 53%

Most Popular Fields of Study
Business, Finance, Sales and Marketing
Biological and Life Sciences

B Student Support and Success

The Core Curriculum is really the heart of Fisk's education program. It centers around eight multicultural and interdisciplinary courses and is designed to help students grasp oral and written communication skills, logical and critical thinking, knowledge of the arts, history and literature and the processes and methods of science.

Fisk University provides a variety of support programs including dedicated guidance for: academic · personal · psychological · religious. Recognizing that some students may need extra preparation, Fisk University offers remedial and refresher courses in: reading · writing · math · study skills. The average freshman year GPA is 2.8, and 73 percent of freshmen students return for their sophomore year. What do students do after college? While many enter the work force, approximately 28 percent pursue a graduate degree immediately after graduation. Among students who enter the work force, approximately 12 percent enter a field related to their major within six months of graduation. Companies that most frequently hire graduates from Fisk University include: Baptist Hospital · Vanderbilt Hospital.

Support for Students with Learning Disabilities

Students with learning disabilities may take advantage of specific support programs offered by Fisk University. High school foreign language waivers are accepted. High school math waivers are also accepted. Students with learning disabilities will find the following programs at Fisk University extremely useful: tutors · learning center · untimed tests · extended time for tests · oral tests · readers. Individual or small group tutorials are also available in: time management · organizational skills · learning strategies · specific subject areas · writing labs · math labs · study skills.

How to Get Admitted

For admissions decisions, non-academic factors considered: interview · extracurricular activities · special talents, interests, abilities · character/personal qualities · volunteer work · work experience · state of residency · geographical location · alumni relationship. A high school diploma is required, although a GED is also accepted for admissions consideration. SAT or ACT test scores are required of all applicants. SAT Subject Test scores are considered, if submitted, but are not required. *According to the admissions office:* Math units should include algebra and plane geometry. *Academic units recommended:* 4 English, 3 Math, 1 Science, 3 Social Studies, 1 Foreign Language.

How to Pay for College

To apply for financial aid, students should submit the following: Free Application for Federal Student Aid (FAFSA) · student eligibility report. Fisk University participates in the Federal Work Study program. *Need-based aid programs include:* scholarships and grants · general need-based awards · Federal Pell grants · state scholarships and grants · college-based scholarships and grants · private scholarships and grants · United Negro College Fund. *Non-Need-based aid programs include:* scholarships and grants · state scholarships and grants.

FISK UNIVERSITY

Highlights

Admissions
Applicants: 1,418
Accepted: 844
Acceptance rate: 59.5%
Average GPA: 3.1
ACT range: 19-23
SAT Math range: 440-540
SAT Reading range: 450-550
SAT Writing range: Not reported
Top 25% of class: 52%
Top 50% of class: 77%

Deadlines
Early Action: No
Early Decision: No
Regular Action: June 1 (priority)
June 1 (final)
Common Application: Accepted

Financial Aid
In-state tuition: $15,140
Out-of-state tuition: $15,140
Room: $4,480
Board: $3,245
Books: $1,400
Freshmen receiving need-based aid: 88%
Undergrads receiving need-based aid: 87%
Avg. % of need met by financial aid: 75%
Avg. aid package (freshmen): $11,573
Avg. aid package (undergrads): $13,625
Avg. student debt upon graduation: $5,963

Prominent Alumni
Dr. W.E.B. Du Bois; Nikki Giovanni, poet and writer; Dr. John Hope Franklin, historian and scholar.

School Spirit
Mascot: Bulldogs

FLAGLER COLLEGE

74 King Street, St. Augustine, FL 32085
Admissions: 800-304-4208, extension 220
Financial Aid: 800-304-4208, extension 225
Email: admiss@flagler.edu · Website: http://www.flagler.edu

From the College

Flagler College is best described as a traditional liberal arts college. A founding principle was to provide a quality education at a reasonable cost; consequently, tuition and fees are approximately half the national average of comparable institutions. Faculty are selected and appointed on the basis of their commitment to the teaching and advising of students. Emphasis is placed upon class attendance, and a zero-tolerance policy on the use of illegal drugs is strictly enforced. The college offers over 30 student organizations, 13 intercollegiate athletic teams and encourages community service."

Campus Setting

Flagler, founded in 1968, is a private, liberal arts college. Its 42-acre campus is located in the center of St. Augustine. Its administration building is located in the former Ponce de Leon Hotel, a Spanish-style former luxury resort now listed on the National Register of Historic Places. A four-year institution, Flagler College has an enrollment of 2,653 students. Flagler College has been co-ed since 1971. In addition to a large, well-stocked library, the campus facilities include: art gallery · art building · hotel. Flagler College provides on-campus housing with 4 units that can accommodate 710 students. Housing options: women's dorms · men's dorms. Recreation and sports facilities include: baseball · soccer and softball fields · gymnasium · tennis courts.

Student Life and Activities

Most students (59 percent) live off campus, which does impact the on-campus social scene. Nevertheless, like any college, students find time to create their own recreational outlets. According to a school official, Flagler is close to Anastais State Beach Park and Pier. Popular gathering spots include the student center, West Lawn, Ponce Hall breezeway, local coffee shops, cafes and beaches. Popular campus events include Midnight Breakfast, Mu Fest, Spring and Winter Formal, sports team competitions, surfing, speaker forums and literary presentations. Flagler College has 37 official student organizations. Popular groups on campus include the artistic organizations and theatre groups. For those interested in sports, there are intramural teams such as: badminton · bowling · football · tennis · ultimate Frisbee · volleyball · surfing. Flagler College is a member of the NCAA (Division II).

Academics and Learning Environment

For the B student, the learning environment of a college is just as important as the quality of its academic program. Flagler College has 86 full-time and 94 part-time faculty members, offering a student-to-faculty ratio of 21:1. The most common course size is 20 to 29 students. Flagler College offers 23 majors with the most popular being elementary education, business administration and communication and least popular being philosophy/religion, Latin American studies/Spanish and history. The school has a general core requirement. Cooperative education is not offered. All first-year students must maintain a 2.0 GPA or higher to avoid academic probation. Other special academic programs that would appeal to a B student: independent study · double majors · dual degrees · internships.

B Student Support and Success

Flagler College was established as a memorial to Henry M. Flagler, and in accordance with his high standards, the college adheres to strict requirements on values. They have a strong attendance policy, prohibit alcohol and inter-dorm visitation and put a heavy emphasis on social justice and service. According to their website, "The objectives of the student life program at Flagler are to establish appropriate standards of conduct and to promote activities that will contribute to the development of self-discipline, integrity and leadership."

Flagler College provides a variety of support programs including dedicated guidance for: academic · career · personal · psychological. The average freshman year GPA is 2.6, and 78 percent of freshmen students return for their sophomore year.

Support for Students with Learning Disabilities

Students with learning disabilities may take advantage of specific support programs offered by Flagler College. If necessary, the college will grant additional time to students with learning disabilities to complete their degree. Also, a lightened course load may be granted to LD students. According to the school, Services for students with disabilities are determined on an individual basis according to the documented significant limitation of the disability. The admission process, while allowing for reasonable accommodations, still looks for students who are otherwise qualified. Students with learning disabilities will find the following programs at Flagler College extremely useful: remedial math · remedial English · remedial reading · tutors · testing accommodations · extended time for tests · take-home exam · oral tests · readers · typist/scribe · note-taking services · reading machines · tape recorders · early syllabus. Individual or small group tutorials are also available in: learning strategies · writing labs · math labs · study skills. An advisor/advocate from the Office of Services for Students with Disabilities is available to students.

How to Get Admitted

For admissions decisions, non-academic factors considered: interview · extracurricular activities · special talents, interests, abilities · character/personal qualities · volunteer work · state of residency · alumni relationship. A high school diploma is required, although a GED is also accepted for admissions consideration. SAT or ACT test scores are not considered or required. SAT Subject Test scores are recommended but not required. *According to the admissions office:* Minimum SAT Reasoning scores of 500 in both verbal and math (composite ACT score of 21), rank in top half of secondary school class, and minimum 2.8 unweighted GPA recommended. *Academic units recommended:* 4 English, 4 Math, 3 Science, 3 Social Studies, 2 Foreign Language.

How to Pay for College

To apply for financial aid, students should submit the following: Free Application for Federal Student Aid (FAFSA) · institution's own financial aid forms · state aid form. Flagler College participates in the Federal Work Study program. *Need-based aid programs include:* scholarships and grants · general need-based awards · Federal Pell

FLAGLER COLLEGE

Highlights

Flagler College
St. Augustine, FL (Pop. 20,000)
Location: Small town
Website: http://www.flagler.edu

Students
Total enrollment: 2,653
Undergrads: 1,099
Freshmen: 618
Part-time students: 3%
From out-of-state: 33%
Male/Female: 41%/59%
Live on-campus: 40%
Off-campus employment rating: Excellent
Caucasian: 88%
African American: 2%
Hispanic: 4%
Asian or Pacific Islander: 1%
Native American: 0%
International: 1%

Academics
Student/faculty ratio: 21:1
Class size 9 or fewer: 6%
Class size 10-29: 81%
Class size 30-49: 13%
Class size 50-99: -
Class size 100 or more: 2%
Returning freshmen: 78%
Six-year graduation rate: 59%

Most Popular Fields of Study
Business, Finance, Sales and Marketing
Protective Services, Criminal Justice and
    Public Administration
Psychology
English and Literature
Philosophy, Religion and Theology
Liberal Arts, Humanities and General
    Studies
Foreign Languages, Literature and Linguistics
Communications, Journalism, Advertising
    and Comm. Technologies
Education

FLAGLER COLLEGE

Admissions
Applicants: 2,368
Accepted: 1,065
Acceptance rate: 45.0%
placed on wait list: 484
Average GPA: 3.3
ACT range: 21-25
SAT Math range: 510-580
SAT Reading range: 520-580
SAT Writing range: 500-600
Top 10% of class: 18%
Top 25% of class: 49%
Top 50% of class: 90%

Deadlines
Early Action: No
Early Decision: December 1
Regular Action: January 15 (priority)
March 1 (final)
Common Application: Accepted

Financial Aid
In-state tuition: $13,300
Out-of-state tuition: $13,300
Room: $3,500
Board: $3,690
Books: $1,100
Freshmen receiving need-based aid: 42%
Undergrads receiving need-based aid:
    48%
Avg. % of need met by financial aid: 89%
Avg. aid package (freshmen): $16,711
Avg. aid package (undergrads): $15,963
Freshmen receiving merit-based aid: 7%
Undergrads receiving merit-based aid:
    11%
Avg. student debt upon graduation:
    $18,414

Prominent Alumni
Robert Strang, founder of Decision Strategies; Laura Neal Hill, director of communications, PGA; John Kreiger, attorney, U.S. Public Interest Research Group.

School Spirit
Mascot: Saints/Lady
Colors: Red and gold

grants · state scholarships and grants · college-based scholarships and grants · private scholarships and grants. *Non-Need-based aid programs include:* scholarships and grants · general need-based awards · state scholarships and grants · creative arts and performance awards · special characteristics awards · athletic scholarships.

FLORIDA A&M UNIVERSITY

Foote Hilyer Administration Center, Suite G9, Tallahassee, FL 32307
Admissions: 850-599-3796 · Financial Aid: 866-238-2318
Email: ugrdadmissions@famu.edu · Website: http://www.famu.edu

From the College

"Florida A&M University is a student-centered institution of higher learning whose main mission is to provide an enriched academic and intellectual experience conducive to the development of highly qualified individuals. The university offers a variety of academic, professional, cultural and athletic programs that draw students from more than 80 countries all over the world. At Florida A&M University, both teaching and learning occur in the context of Excellence with Caring."

Campus Setting

Florida Agricultural and Mechanical University, founded in 1887, is a public, historically black university. Its 419-acre campus is located in Tallahassee. A four-year institution, Florida A&M University has 11,907 students. The school also has a library with 879,458 books. Florida A&M University provides on-campus housing with 11 units that can accommodate 2,356 students. Housing options: co-ed dorms · women's dorms · men's dorms · single-student apartments · married-student apartments.

Student Life and Activities

With 75 percent of students living on campus, there are plenty of social activities. Popular campus events include Be Out Day, SGA campaign rallies Rattler Cinema, Game Night, drive-in movies, Homecoming, Rattler Pride Award, Make a Difference, Volunteer Day and the Essence Fashion Show. Florida A&M University has 160 official student organizations. The most popular are: Marching and pep bands · musical and drama groups · drill team · literary guild · team managers · academic and special-interest groups. Florida A&M University is a member of the Mid-Eastern Athletic Conference (Division I, Football I-AA), Northeast Conference (Division I, Football I-AA).

Academics and Learning Environment

For the B student, the learning environment of a college is just as important as the quality of its academic program. Florida A&M University has 610 full-time and 176 part-time faculty members, offering a student-to-faculty ratio of 17:1. The most common course size is 2 to 9 students. Florida A&M University offers 120 majors with the most popular being business administration and least popular being animal science, chemistry and physics. The school has a general core requirement. Cooperative education is not offered. All first-year students must maintain a 2.0 GPA or higher to avoid academic probation. Other special academic programs that would appeal to a B student: pass/fail grading option · independent study · double majors · honors program · internships · weekend college · distance learning.

B Student Support and Success

While academics are very important at Florida A&M, the school also seeks students with diverse backgrounds, believing that other skills and talents students may possess can benefit the university. Applicants may demonstrate their strengths through the admission essay.

Florida A&M University provides a variety of support programs including dedicated guidance for: academic · career · personal · psychological · minority students · military · veterans · non-traditional students. Recognizing that some students may

FLORIDA A&M UNIVERSITY

Highlights

Florida A&M University
Tallahassee, FL (Pop. 153,938)
Location: Medium city
Website: http://www.famu.edu

Students
Total enrollment: 11,907
Undergrads: 4,278
Freshmen: 1,733
Part-time students: 10%
From out-of-state: 36%
Male/Female: 42%/58%
Live on-campus: 75%
Off-campus employment rating: Good
Caucasian: 3%
African American: 94%
Hispanic: 1%
Asian or Pacific Islander: 1%
Native American: 0%
International: 1%

Academics
Student/faculty ratio: 17:1
Class size 9 or fewer: 29%
Class size 10-29: 44%
Class size 30-49: 20%
Class size 50-99: 6%
Class size 100 or more: 2%
Returning freshmen: Not reported
Six-year graduation rate: Not reported

Admissions
Applicants: 5,313
Accepted: 3,016
Acceptance rate: 56.8%
Average GPA: 3.0
ACT range: 19-22
SAT Math range: 440-550
SAT Reading range: 440-550
SAT Writing range: Not reported

need extra preparation, Florida A&M University offers remedial and refresher courses in: reading · writing · math · study skills. The average freshman year GPA is 2.3. What do students do after college? While many enter the work force, approximately 20 percent pursue a graduate degree immediately after graduation. Among students who enter the work force, approximately 25 percent enter a field related to their major within six months of graduation.

Support for Students with Learning Disabilities

Students with learning disabilities may take advantage of specific support programs offered by Florida A&M University. If necessary, the college will grant additional time to students with learning disabilities to complete their degree. Also, a lightened course load may be granted to LD students. High school foreign language waivers are accepted. High school math waivers are also accepted. According to the school, The Center of Disability Accessibility and Resources (CeDAR) at Florida A & M University provides unique and comprehensive services and accommodations for students with learning and physical disabilities who desire to pursue college level studies. We identify participants' level of abilities and provide services that include assessment, prescriptive plans of study, academic advisement, and individualized counseling. Students with learning disabilities will find the following programs at Florida A&M University extremely useful: remedial math · remedial English · remedial reading · special classes · tutors · learning center · testing accommodations · extended time for tests · oral tests · exam on tape or computer · readers · note-taking services · reading machines · tape recorders · texts on tape · early syllabus · special bookstore section · priority registration · waiver of math degree requirement · waiver of foreign language degree requirement. Individual or small group tutorials are also available in: time management · organizational skills · learning strategies · specific subject areas · writing labs · math labs · study skills. An advisor/advocate from the CeDAR-Center of Disability Accessibility and Resources is available to students. This member also sits on the admissions committee.

How to Get Admitted

For admissions decisions, non-academic factors considered: extracurricular activities · special talents, interests, abilities · character/personal qualities · volunteer work · work experience · minority affiliation · alumni relationship. A high school diploma is required, although a GED is also accepted for admissions consideration. SAT or ACT test scores are required of all applicants. SAT Subject Test scores are not required. *According to the admissions office:* Minimum combined SAT Reasoning score of 1450 (composite ACT score of 21) and minimum 2.5 GPA required. *Academic units recommended:* 4 English, 3 Math, 3 Science, 3 Social Studies, 2 Foreign Language.

How to Pay for College

To apply for financial aid, students should submit the following: Free Application for Federal Student Aid (FAFSA). Florida A&M University participates in the Federal Work Study program. *Need-based aid programs include:* scholarships and grants · general need-based awards · Federal Pell grants · state scholarships and grants · college-based scholarships and grants · private scholarships and grants · Federal

Nursing scholarships · United Negro College Fund. *Non-Need-based aid programs include:* scholarships and grants · state scholarships and grants · creative arts and performance awards · athletic scholarships · ROTC scholarships.

FLORIDA A&M UNIVERSITY

Deadlines
Early Action: No
Early Decision: No
Regular Action: January 1 (priority)
May 10 (final)
Common Application: Accepted

Financial Aid
In-state tuition: $9,486
Out-of-state tuition: $21,426
Room: $3,600
Board: $750
Books: $700
Freshmen receiving need-based aid: 79%
Undergrads receiving need-based aid: 78%
Avg. % of need met by financial aid: 74%
Avg. aid package (freshmen): $8,668
Avg. aid package (undergrads): $10,290
Freshmen receiving merit-based aid: 5%
Undergrads receiving merit-based aid: 5%
Avg. student debt upon graduation: $27,640

School Spirit
Mascot: Rattlers

FLORIDA SOUTHERN COLLEGE

111 Lake Hollingsworth Drive, Lakeland, FL 33801-5698
Admissions: 800-274-4131 · Financial Aid: 863-680-4140
Email: fscadm@flsouthern.edu · Website: http://www.flsouthern.edu

From the College

"Florida Southern College is a comprehensive college with a liberal arts core offering 39 undergraduate majors and distinctive graduate programs in business administration, education and nursing. The college's mission is to prepare students to make positive and consequential contributions to our world, and our 13:1 student-faculty ratio allows for the personalized instruction and mentoring relationships that reflect our "engaged learning" approach to educational preparation. Engaged learning at Florida Southern refers to a range of pedagogical practices oriented around the student as an active, creative participant in academic endeavors.

We require our 2,200 undergraduate and graduate students to contribute significantly to the learning process in and out of the classroom. Engaged learning encompasses an array of student-faculty collaborative research, performance, service learning, study abroad and internship opportunities. Numerous fine and performing arts options are available to our students as well. Students' performances and gallery exhibitions enhance cultural life throughout Central Florida. Our students are also service-oriented, logging more than 10,000 hours of community service annually.

Forty percent of our undergraduates study abroad, and this year's offerings include summer programs in 10 countries (e.g. China, New Zealand, and Austria); and semester programs in England, Northern Ireland and Spain. Students enrolled in May Option for the international business and international financial management courses will study multinational and local corporations in China for three weeks.

Campus Setting

Florida Southern, founded in 1883, is a church-affiliated college of liberal arts and sciences. Its 100-acre campus, containing buildings designed by Frank Lloyd Wright, is listed with the National Register of Historic Places. It is located in Lakeland, 45 miles from both Tampa and Orlando. A four-year private institution, Florida Southern College has an enrollment of 1,818 students. The school is also affiliated with the Methodist Church. In addition to a large, well-stocked library, the campus facilities include: art gallery · performing arts center · planetarium. Florida Southern College provides on-campus housing with 744 units that can accommodate 1,251 students. Housing options: women's dorms · men's dorms · sorority housing · fraternity housing · single-student apartments · married-student apartments · special housing for disabled students. Recreation and sports facilities include: gymnasium · wellness center.

Student Life and Activities

With 74 percent of students living on campus, there are plenty of social activities. Popular campus events include Festival of Fine Arts, Melvin Gallery Art Shows, and Florida Lecture Series. Florida Southern College has 69 official student organizations. The most popular are: Allies · history club · Mathematic Association · Multicultural Students Council · Physical Education Majors · Residence Hall Association · The Mechanicals · Toastmasters International · Vagabonds · American Chemical Society · Advertising Federation · Citrus and Horticulture Club · Florida Public Relations Association. For those interested in sports, there are intramural teams such as: basketball · bowling · flag football · rugby · soccer · softball · volleyball. Florida Southern College is a member of the Sunshine State Conference (Division II).

Academics and Learning Environment

For the B student, the learning environment of a college is just as important as the quality of its academic program. Florida Southern College has 107 full-time and 74 part-time faculty members, offering a student-to-faculty ratio of 13:1. The most common course size is 10 to 19 students. Florida Southern College offers 48 majors with the most popular being biology, elementary education and psychology and least popular being biochemistry and molecular biology, dramatic art and landscape horticulture production. The school has a general core requirement as well as a religion requirement Cooperative education is not offered. All first-year students must maintain a 2.0 GPA or higher to avoid academic probation. Other special academic programs that would appeal to a B student: self-designed majors · pass/fail grading option · independent study · double majors · honors program · internships.

B Student Support and Success

The Academic Support Services at Florida Southern College hopes to "foster the development of life skills and habits of academic excellence". It helps students make the transition to college life through offering specific orientation programs, customizing help sessions to identify needs and provide resources and supplying referrals.

Florida Southern College provides a variety of support programs including dedicated guidance for: academic · career · personal · psychological · minority students · religious. Additional counseling services include: non-traditional student. The average freshman year GPA is 2.8, and 71 percent of freshmen students return for their sophomore year. What do students do after college? While many enter the work force, approximately 27 percent pursue a graduate degree immediately after graduation. Among students who enter the work force, approximately 76 percent enter a field related to their major within six months of graduation. Companies that most frequently hire graduates from Florida Southern College include: Enterprise Rent-A-Car · GEICO Direct · Lakeland Regional Health Systems · Polk County Public Schools · Publix Super Markets · Pulte Homes · State of Florida · U.S. Army · Walt Disney World · Watson Clinic.

Support for Students with Learning Disabilities

Students with learning disabilities may take advantage of specific support programs offered by Florida Southern College. According to the school, Florida Southern College does not modify any courses or requirement for LD students. Students with learning disabilities will find the following program at Florida Southern College extremely useful: extended time for tests.

How to Get Admitted

For admissions decisions, non-academic factors considered: interview · extracurricular activities · special talents, interests, abilities · character/personal qualities · volunteer work · work experience · state of residency · religious affiliation/commitment · minority affiliation · alumni relationship. A high school diploma is required, although a GED is also accepted for admissions consideration. SAT or ACT test scores are required of all applicants. SAT Subject Test scores are not required. *According to the admissions office:* Minimum combined

FLORIDA SOUTHERN COLLEGE

Highlights

Florida Southern College
Lakeland, FL (Pop. 90,000)
Location: Large town
Website: http://www.flsouthern.edu

Students
Total enrollment: 1,818
Undergrads: 685
Freshmen: 424
Part-time students: 4%
From out-of-state: 19%
Male/Female: 40%/60%
Live on-campus: 74%
In fraternities: 30%
In sororities: 35%
Off-campus employment rating: Excellent
Caucasian: 82%
African American: 7%
Hispanic: 6%
Asian or Pacific Islander: 1%
Native American: 0%
International: 4%

Academics
Student/faculty ratio: 13:1
Class size 9 or fewer: 22%
Class size 10-29: 65%
Class size 30-49: 13%
Class size 50-99: 6%
Class size 100 or more: 2%
Returning freshmen: 71%
Six-year graduation rate: 55%

Most Popular Fields of Study
Business, Finance, Sales and Marketing
Visual and Performing Arts
Computer and Information Sciences
Communications, Journalism, Advertising and Comm. Technologies
Philosophy, Religion and Theology
Liberal Arts, Humanities and General Studies
English and Literature
Parks, Recreation and Fitness
Health Professions, Medicine and Related Sciences

211

FLORIDA SOUTHERN COLLEGE

Admissions
Applicants: 2,559
Accepted: 1,490
Acceptance rate: 58.2%
Average GPA: 3.5
ACT range: 20-26
SAT Math range: 470-600
SAT Reading range: 480-600
SAT Writing range: 460-570
Top 10% of class: 25%
Top 25% of class: 50%
Top 50% of class: 83%

Deadlines
Early Action: No
Early Decision: December 1
Regular Action: Rolling admissions
Common Application: Accepted

Financial Aid
In-state tuition: $21,620
Out-of-state tuition: $21,620
Room: $4,350
Board: $2,350
Books: $1,150
Freshmen receiving need-based aid: 62%
Undergrads receiving need-based aid: 62%
Avg. % of need met by financial aid: 72%
Avg. aid package (freshmen): $17,154
Avg. aid package (undergrads): $15,987
Freshmen receiving merit-based aid: 35%
Undergrads receiving merit-based aid: 33%
Avg. student debt upon graduation: $8,914

Prominent Alumni
James C. France, CEO, Daytona International Speedway Corp.; Joseph B. McCormick, president, NASCAR; James H. Steele, professor of epidemiology, University of Texas Health Science.

School Spirit
Mascot: Moccasins
Colors: Red and black

SAT Reasoning score of 950 (composite ACT score of 20), rank in top half of secondary school class, and minimum 2.5 GPA recommended. *Academic units recommended:* 2 Foreign Language.

How to Pay for College

To apply for financial aid, students should submit the following: Free Application for Federal Student Aid (FAFSA) · institution's own financial aid forms. Florida Southern College participates in the Federal Work Study program. *Need-based aid programs include:* scholarships and grants · general need-based awards · Federal Pell grants · state scholarships and grants · college-based scholarships and grants · private scholarships and grants. *Non-Need-based aid programs include:* scholarships and grants · general need-based awards · state scholarships and grants · creative arts and performance awards · special achievements and activities awards · special characteristics awards · athletic scholarships · ROTC scholarships · community service and leadership scholarships.

FLORIDA STATE UNIVERSITY

211 Westcott Building, Tallahassee, FL 32306
Admissions: 850-644-3420 · Financial Aid: 850-644-5871
Email: admissions@admin.fsu.edu · Website: http://www.fsu.edu

From the College

"Florida State University is a comprehensive, national graduate research university with both law and medical schools. The faculty include Nobel Laureates, Pulitzer Prize winners and fellows of the American Academy of Arts and Sciences. Our 200 degree programs are enhanced by thousands of opportunities in international programs and world-class research centers, including the National High Magnetic Field Laboratory, Reading Research Center and School for Computational Science. With a wide range of highly ranked academic programs and excellence in the visual and performing arts, this university offers an opportunity for interdisciplinary learning in a diverse and caring environment."

Campus Setting

Florida State, founded in 1851, has a 463-acre campus is located within a mile of downtown Tallahassee. A four-year public institution, Florida State University has an enrollment of 38,682 students. Florida State University has been co-ed since 1947. In addition to a large, well-stocked library, the campus facilities include: conservatory · museums · marine laboratory · oceanographic institute · magnetic field laboratory · developmental research school · Challenger space center · planetarium · accelerators · super computers. Florida State University provides on-campus housing with 3,407 units that can accommodate 6,111 students. Housing options: co-ed dorms · women's dorms · sorority housing · fraternity housing · single-student apartments · married-student apartments · special housing for disabled students. Recreation and sports facilities include: football · lacrosse · soccer and softball fields · racquetball and tennis courts · swimming pool · indoor and outdoor tracks.

Student Life and Activities

Most students (79 percent) live off campus, which does impact the on-campus social scene. Nevertheless, like any college, students find time to create their own recreational outlets. Popular on-campus gathering spots include the Student Union, Student Life Center and Landis Green. Popular campus events include Seven Days of Opening Nights, Market Wednesday, LEAD - In at the Rez, President's Retreat, speakers series, FSUnity Day, Earth Day, Dance Marathon, Flying High Circus, Parents' Weekend, Homecoming Festivities and Parade, PowWow, President's Ice Cream Social, Last Call Before Fall and Seminole Sensation Week. Florida State University has 500 official student organizations. The most popular are: Music ensembles · marching and pep bands · baton twirling · drill team · theatre and dance groups · debate groups · team managers · other academic and special-interest groups. For those interested in sports, there are intramural teams such as: basketball · beach volleyball · billiards · bowling · disc golf · flag football · homerun derby · horseshoes · kickball · racquetball · speedball · soccer · softball · swimming · table tennis · tennis · volleyball · wallyball · wiffleball. Florida State University is a member of the Atlantic Coast Conference (Division I, Football I-A).

Academics and Learning Environment

For the B student, the learning environment of a college is just as important as the quality of its academic program. Florida State University has 1,298 full-time and 368 part-time faculty members, offering a student-to-faculty ratio of 21:1. The most com-

FLORIDA STATE UNIVERSITY

Highlights

Florida State University
Tallahassee, FL (Pop. 176,336)
Location: Medium city
Website: http://www.fsu.edu

Students
Total enrollment: 38,682
Undergrads: 13,295
Freshmen: 5,027
Part-time students: 12%
From out-of-state: 9%
Male/Female: 45%/55%
Live on-campus: 21%
In fraternities: 18%
In sororities: 18%
Off-campus employment rating: Good
Caucasian: 72%
African American: 10%
Hispanic: 12%
Asian or Pacific Islander: 3%
Native American: 1%
International: 0%

Academics
Student/faculty ratio: 21:1
Class size 9 or fewer: 12%
Class size 10-29: 52%
Class size 30-49: 21%
Class size 50-99: 10%
Class size 100 or more: 7%
Returning freshmen: 89%
Six-year graduation rate: 70%

Most Popular Fields of Study
Business, Finance, Sales and Marketing
Biological and Life Sciences
Area, Ethnic and Gender Studies

mon course size is 20 to 29 students. Florida State University offers 505 majors with the most popular being criminology, psychology and finance. The school has a general core requirement. Cooperative education is available. All first-year students must maintain a 2.0 GPA or higher to avoid academic probation, and a minimum overall GPA of 2.0 is required to graduate. Other special academic programs that would appeal to a B student: pass/fail grading option · independent study · double majors · dual degrees · accelerated study · honors program · Phi Beta Kappa · internships · distance learning certificate programs.

B Student Support and Success

Although this is a rather large college, its staff and faculty care about the students and their success. FSU's Center for Academic Retention and Enhancement provides preparation, orientation and academic support programming for students who may be facing unique challenges because of cultural, economic of educational circumstances. A program called SSSMO, or Student Supporting Students Mentoring Organization, offers mentors that help students in becoming acclimated to the school. They also act as role models in academic areas and in leadership.

Florida State University provides a variety of support programs including dedicated guidance for: academic · career · personal · psychological · minority students · military · veterans · non-traditional students · family planning · religious. Recognizing that some students may need extra preparation, Florida State University offers remedial and refresher courses in: reading · writing · math · study skills. The average freshman year GPA is 3.0, and 89 percent of freshmen students return for their sophomore year. What do students do after college? While many enter the work force, approximately 35 percent pursue a graduate degree immediately after graduation. Among students who enter the work force, approximately 70 percent enter a field related to their major within six months of graduation. Companies that most frequently hire graduates from Florida State University include: Abercrombie & Fitch · Ameriprise Financial Services · Babies R Us · City Furniture · CSX Transportation · Deloitte & Touche · Dirt Devil/Hoover · E & J GALLO · Ernst & Young · Florida Auditor General · GEICO · Harris Corp. · IBM · KPMG · Lockheed Martin · Macy's Florida · Marriott International Corp. · NOAA · Northwestern Mutual Financial Network · Pulte Homes · Protivit · Rachlin Cohen & Holtz · Regions Financial Organization · Schlumberger · Sears Holdings Corp. · Shell Oil · Software Architects · State of Florida · Target Corp. · Teach for America · U.S. Armed Forces · Wachovia · Woseley North America.

Support for Students with Learning Disabilities

Students with learning disabilities may take advantage of specific support programs offered by Florida State University. If necessary, the college will grant additional time to students with learning disabilities to complete their degree. Also, a lightened course load may be granted to LD students. Students with learning disabilities will find the following programs at Florida State University extremely useful: testing accommodations · extended time for tests · take-home exam · oral tests · exam on tape or computer · readers · typist/scribe

· note-taking services · reading machines · tape recorders · texts on tape · early syllabus · diagnostic testing service · priority registration · priority seating · waiver of math degree requirement. Individual or small group tutorials are also available in: time management · organizational skills · learning strategies · writing labs · math labs · study skills. An advisor/advocate from the Student Disability Resource Center is available to students.

How to Get Admitted

For admissions decisions, non-academic factors considered: extracurricular activities · special talents, interests, abilities · character/personal qualities · volunteer work · work experience · geographical location · alumni relationship. A high school diploma is required, although a GED is also accepted for admissions consideration. SAT or ACT test scores are required of all applicants. SAT Subject Test scores are not required. *Academic units recommended:* 4 English, 4 Math, 4 Science, 2 Social Studies, 4 Foreign Language.

How to Pay for College

To apply for financial aid, students should submit the following: Free Application for Federal Student Aid (FAFSA). Florida State University participates in the Federal Work Study program. *Need-based aid programs include:* scholarships and grants · general need-based awards · Federal Pell grants · state scholarships and grants · college-based scholarships and grants · private scholarships and grants. *Non-Need-based aid programs include:* scholarships and grants · general need-based awards · state scholarships and grants · athletic scholarships.

FLORIDA STATE UNIVERSITY

Highlights

Admissions
Applicants: 25,485
Accepted: 11,901
Acceptance rate: 46.7%
placed on wait list: 1,907
Average GPA: 3.7
ACT range: 24-28
SAT Math range: 560-650
SAT Reading range: 550-640
SAT Writing range: Not reported
Top 10% of class: 31%
Top 25% of class: 71%
Top 50% of class: 96%

Deadlines
Early Action: No
Early Decision: No
Regular Action: January 21 (final)
Common Application: Accepted

Financial Aid
In-state tuition: $3,987
Out-of-state tuition: $18,432
Room: $4,936
Board: $3,466
Books: $1,000
Freshmen receiving need-based aid: 34%
Undergrads receiving need-based aid: 35%
Avg. % of need met by financial aid: 78%
Avg. aid package (freshmen): $10,133
Avg. aid package (undergrads): $10,632
Freshmen receiving merit-based aid: 10%
Undergrads receiving merit-based aid: 5%
Avg. student debt upon graduation: $16,927

Prominent Alumni
Charlie Crist, governor, Florida; Brigadier General Franklin Hagenbeck, superintendent, United States Military Academy; Meg Crofton, president, Walt Disney World.

School Spirit
Mascot: Seminoles
Colors: Garnet and gold
Song: *Alma Mater - High over Towering Pines*

215

Fort Lewis College
Durango, CO (Pop. 15,254)
Location: Rural
Website: http://www.fortlewis.edu

Students
Total enrollment: 3,746
Undergrads: 1,930
Freshmen: Not reported
Part-time students: 9%
From out-of-state: 36%
Male/Female: 52%/48%
Live on-campus: 36%
Off-campus employment rating: Fair
Caucasian: 63%
African American: 1%
Hispanic: 5%
Asian or Pacific Islander: 1%
Native American: 21%
International: 1%

Academics
Student/faculty ratio: 17:1
Class size 9 or fewer: 27%
Class size 10-29: 59%
Class size 30-49: 12%
Class size 50-99: 1%
Class size 100 or more: -
Returning freshmen: 59%
Six-year graduation rate: 30%

Most Popular Fields of Study
Business, Finance, Sales and Marketing
Biological and Life Sciences
Area, Ethnic and Gender Studies

Admissions
Applicants: 3,434
Accepted: 2,074
Acceptance rate: 60.4%
Average GPA: 3.1
ACT range: 19-24
SAT Math range: 470-590
SAT Reading range: 470-573
SAT Writing range: 450-560
Top 10% of class: 7%
Top 25% of class: 23%
Top 50% of class: 57%

FORT LEWIS COLLEGE

1000 Rim Drive, Durango, CO 81301
Admissions: 970-247-7184 · Financial Aid: 970-247-7142
Email: admission@fortlewis.edu
Website: http://www.fortlewis.edu

From the College

"Fort Lewis College is a public liberal arts and sciences college focused on preparing students for leadership in their careers and communities. The college offers over 96 academic options in the School of Natural and Behavioral Sciences, the School of Arts, Humanities and Social Sciences and the School of Business Administration. Students pursue academic excellence in a thought-provoking setting. Located in Durango, at the crossroads of the San Juan Mountains and the desert Southwest, Fort Lewis College uses its location and heritage as educational resources, with faculty who give a high degree of attention to individual students."

Campus Setting

Fort Lewis, founded in 1911, is a public, liberal arts college. Its 350-acre campus is located southwest of Durango's business district, in southern Colorado. A four-year institution, Fort Lewis College has an enrollment of 3,746 students. In addition to a large, well-stocked library, the campus also has a museum. Fort Lewis College provides on-campus housing with 744 units that can accommodate 1,486 students. Housing options: co-ed dorms · single-student apartments · married-student apartments · special housing for disabled students. Recreation and sports facilities include: center · fields · gymnasium · outdoor track.

Student Life and Activities

Most students (64 percent) live off campus, which does impact the on-campus social scene. Nevertheless, like any college, students find time to create their own recreational outlets. "Fort Lewis brags of its cultural diversity but recognizes that it needs to improve racial relationships. Because of the nearby Native American population and our Native American students, we know the importance of acceptance and appreciation of different cultures," reports the student newspaper. Students gather at the snack bar on campus and at the Steamin' Bean Coffee Company, Carver's Bakery and various bars in Durango. Popular events include: Hozhoni Days and Homecoming. Fort Lewis College has 71 official student organizations. The most popular are: Dance Co-Motion Club · Service Tree · Uniting Students through Wellness · Engineers without Borders · Outdoor Pursuits. For those interested in sports, there are intramural teams such as: baseball · cycling · dance · flag football · indoor soccer · kickball · lacrosse · skiing · soccer · softball · track and field · triathlon · ultimate Frisbee · volleyball · wrestling. Fort Lewis College is a member of the Rocky Mountain Athletic Conference (Division II).

Academics and Learning Environment

For the B student, the learning environment of a college is just as important as the quality of its academic program. Fort Lewis College has 189 full-time and 80 part-time faculty members, offering a student-to-faculty ratio of 17:1. The most common course size is 10 to 19 students. Fort Lewis College offers 30 majors with the most popular being business administration and psychology and least popular being physics, economics and music. The school has a general core requirement. Cooperative education is not offered. All first-year students must maintain a 2.0 GPA or higher to avoid academic probation. Other special academic programs that would appeal to a B student: self-designed majors · independent study · double majors · accelerated study · honors program · internships · distance learning.

B Student Support and Success

The Academic Success Program at Fort Lewis is free to all college students. It allows students to network with other learning support programs on campus and offers fall and winter symposiums to help first-year students acclimate to college life. An Early Alert System is available for students who are struggling and small study groups are set up across campus. The Algebra Alcove helps students in their math classes, including the provision of problem-solving classes and supplemental instruction. A Writing Center is offered for "building better writers."

Fort Lewis College provides a variety of support programs including dedicated guidance for: academic · career · personal · psychological · minority students · veterans · non-traditional students · family planning · religious. The average freshman year GPA is 2.5, and 59 percent of freshmen students return for their sophomore year.

Support for Students with Learning Disabilities

Students with learning disabilities may take advantage of specific support programs offered by Fort Lewis College. Students with learning disabilities will find the following programs at Fort Lewis College extremely useful: extended time for tests · oral tests · readers · note-taking services · tape recorders. Individual or small group tutorials are also available in: specific subject areas · writing labs · math labs. An advisor/advocate from the Academic Success Program is available to students.

How to Get Admitted

For admissions decisions, non-academic factors considered: interview · extracurricular activities · special talents, interests, abilities · character/personal qualities · volunteer work · work experience · state of residency · alumni relationship. A high school diploma is required, although a GED is also accepted for admissions consideration. SAT or ACT test scores are required of all applicants. SAT Subject Test scores are not required. *According to the admissions office:* Computer science and modern languages courses recommended. Admissions based on an index of standardized test scores and GPA.

FORT LEWIS COLLEGE

Highlights

Deadlines
Early Action: No
Early Decision: No
Regular Action: Rolling admissions
Common Application: Accepted

Financial Aid
In-state tuition: $5,606
Out-of-state tuition: $15,162
Room: $3,842
Board: $3,036
Books: $1,000
Freshmen receiving need-based aid: 49%
Undergrads receiving need-based aid: 48%
Avg. % of need met by financial aid: 70%
Avg. aid package (freshmen): $6,877
Avg. aid package (undergrads): $7,571
Freshmen receiving merit-based aid: 29%
Undergrads receiving merit-based aid: 12%
Avg. student debt upon graduation: $17,962

School Spirit
Mascot: Skyhawks
Colors: Blue and gold

217

FORT LEWIS COLLEGE

How to Pay for College

To apply for financial aid, students should submit the following: Free Application for Federal Student Aid (FAFSA). Fort Lewis College participates in the Federal Work Study program. *Need-based aid programs include:* scholarships and grants · general need-based awards · Federal Pell grants · state scholarships and grants · college-based scholarships and grants · private scholarships and grants. *Non-Need-based aid programs include:* scholarships and grants · general need-based awards · state scholarships and grants · creative arts and performance awards · athletic scholarships.

GEORGE MASON UNIVERSITY

4400 University Drive, Fairfax, VA 22030
Admissions: 703-993-2400 · Financial Aid: 703-993-2353
Email: admissions@gmu.edu · Website: http://www.gmu.edu

From the College

"Founded in 1972, George Mason University has earned a reputation as an innovative, entrepreneurial institution that has gained national distinction in a range of academic fields. In 2008, *U.S. News & World Report* named Mason the number one national university to watch on its list of "Up-and-Coming Schools." Mason was cited as an institution that has recently made the most promising and innovative changes in academics, faculty, students, campus or facilities.

"Opportunities for students abound both inside and outside the classroom in areas such as internships at nationally and internationally recognized organizations, from Fortune 500 companies to the Kennedy Center. Many Mason graduates continue employment with places they interned, or remain in the area to take advantage of the job market. The university has recently partnered with the Smithsonian Institution to create the Smithsonian Semester, which allows students to live on-site at the Conservation and Research Center of the Smithsonian's National Zoo and study global-scale conservation issues and civic concerns. Mason has one of the largest global education programs in the world, ranking second among U.S. doctoral institutions by the Institution of International Education for the number of students who study abroad. Mason has programs in more than 30 countries, with reciprocal relationships with universities in Russia, Korea, China and Germany.

"Mason's undergraduates come from all 50 states and 125 countries. In 2008, the university opened a 40,000 square-foot state-of-the-art sustainable dining facility, designed to exceed "green" standards, with an emphasis on recycling and the use of biodegradable products. Mason is in the midst of a building boom, investing more than $500 million between 2002 and 2013. Currently under construction are multiple new academic buildings, an on-campus conference center and hotel and a residential community."

Campus Setting

George Mason, founded in 1972, is a public university. Programs are offered through the College of Humanities and Social Sciences, the College of Education and Human Development, the Volgenau School of Information Technology and Engineering, the College of Visual and Performing Arts, the Institute for Conflict Analysis and Resolution, the College of Health and Human Services, the College of Science, the School of Management, the School of Public Policy and the School of Law. Its 677-acre main campus is located in Fairfax, 18 miles from Washington, DC. A four-year institution, George Mason University has an enrollment of 30,714 students. In addition to a large, well-stocked library, the campus facilities include: astronomy observatory · research buildings · biomedical research lab · performing arts and conservation and research centers. George Mason University provides on-campus housing with 1,802 units that can accommodate 4,834 students. Housing options: co-ed dorms · single-student apartments · special housing for disabled students. Recreation and sports facilities include: aquatics and fitness center · field house · gymnasium · stadium.

Student Life and Activities

Although 75 percent of freshmen live on campus, most students (75 percent) live off campus, which does impact the on-campus social scene. Nevertheless, like any college, students find time to create their own recreational outlets. Mason students

GEORGE MASON UNIVERSITY

George Mason University
Fairfax, VA (Pop. 21,498)
Location: Large town
Website: http://www.gmu.edu

Students
Total enrollment: 30,714
Undergrads: 8,815
Freshmen: 3,645
Part-time students: 24%
From out-of-state: 22%
Male/Female: 47%/53%
Live on-campus: 25%
In fraternities: 1%
In sororities: 1%
Off-campus employment rating: Excellent
Caucasian: 43%
African American: 7%
Hispanic: 6%
Asian or Pacific Islander: 16%
Native American: 0%
International: 3%

Academics
Student/faculty ratio: 15:1
Class size 9 or fewer: 11%
Class size 10-29: 52%
Class size 30-49: 24%
Class size 50-99: 11%
Class size 100 or more: 3%
Returning freshmen: 84%
Six-year graduation rate: 61%

Most Popular Fields of Study
Business, Finance, Sales and Marketing
Biological and Life Sciences
Area, Ethnic and Gender Studies

Admissions
Applicants: 12,943
Accepted: 8,112
Acceptance rate: 62.7%
Average GPA: 3.5
ACT range: Not reported
SAT Math range: 520-610
SAT Reading range: 500-600
SAT Writing range: 500-590
Top 10% of class: 18%
Top 25% of class: 52%
Top 50% of class: 93%

220

have a wide range of places to go, including Old Towne Fairfax and Washington D.C. Mason also has a variety of student organizations and activities. Favorite gathering places include the Student Union, the Johnson Center, Damon's, Jazzman's Cafe, and Fat Tuesday's. Popular campus events include Welcome Week, New Student Days, Patriot Days, Homecoming, Mason Day, International Week, Mason Madness and Pride Week. George Mason University has 238 official student organizations. Influential groups include Greeks, Campus Ministries, Student Government, International Clubs and various athletic groups. For those interested in sports, there are intramural teams such as: basketball · golf · martial arts · water polo · racquetball · soccer · softball · tennis · volleyball. George Mason University is a member of the Colonial Athletic Association (Division I), Eastern College Athletic Conference (Division I, Football I-AA), Eastern Intercollegiate Volleyball Association (Division I).

Academics and Learning Environment

For the B student, the learning environment of a college is just as important as the quality of its academic program. George Mason University has 1,123 full-time and 950 part-time faculty members, offering a student-to-faculty ratio of 15:1. The most common course size is 20 to 29 students. George Mason University offers 153 majors with the most popular being psychology, political science and government and speech and rhetorical studies and least popular being Latin American studies, business administration and management and astronomy. The school has a general core requirement. Cooperative education is available. All first-year students must maintain a 2.0 GPA or higher to avoid academic probation, and a minimum overall GPA of 2.0 is required to graduate. Other special academic programs that would appeal to a B student: self-designed majors · pass/fail grading option · independent study · double majors · dual degrees · accelerated study · honors program · internships · distance learning certificate programs.

B Student Support and Success

Learning Services at George Mason encompasses many different methods to help support students who are struggling academically. Study skills workshops are offered on topics such as concentration, procrastination, academic skills, motivation and goal setting. Tutor Referral matches students with peer tutors (which charge varying fees). Services are confidential, and use of these services does not become part of the student's academic record.

George Mason University provides a variety of support programs including dedicated guidance for: academic · career · personal · psychological · minority students · military · veterans · non-traditional students · family planning · religious. Additional counseling services include: international student advising, alcohol, drug, and health and sexual assault. Recognizing that some students may need extra preparation, George Mason University offers remedial and refresher courses in: reading · writing · math · study skills. Other remedial services include miscellaneous life skills. The average freshman year GPA is 2.8, and 84 percent of freshmen students return for their sophomore year. What do students do after college? While many enter the work force, approximately 14 percent pursue a graduate degree immediately after graduation. Among students who enter the work force, approximately 71 percent enter a field related to their major within six months of graduation. Companies that most frequently hire graduates from George Mason University include: the federal government · Fannie Mae · Commonwealth Consultants · Computer Business Methods · Computer Sciences Corp.· Corporate Risk International · Cotton & Co. · Covance Laboratories · Crate&Barrel · ICF International · Defense Intelligence Agency · Up with People · National Public Radio · Abercrombie & Fitch · ACF Solutions LLC · Department of The Navy · Aerospace Corp.· Aerotek · AFLAC.

Support for Students with Learning Disabilities

Students with learning disabilities may take advantage of specific support programs offered by George Mason University. If necessary, the college will grant additional time to students with learning disabilities to complete their degree. Also, a lightened course load may be granted to LD students. Students with learning disabilities will find the following programs at George Mason University extremely useful: learning center · testing accommodations · extended time for tests · take-home exam · oral tests · readers · typist/scribe · note-taking services · proofreading services · reading machines · tape recorders · texts on tape · early syllabus · priority registration · priority seating. Individual or small group tutorials are also available in: time management · organizational skills · learning strategies · writing labs · math labs · study skills. An advisor/advocate from the Office of Disability Services is available to students.

How to Get Admitted

For admissions decisions, non-academic factors considered: extracurricular activities · special talents, interests, abilities · character/personal qualities · volunteer work · work experience · state of residency · alumni relationship. A high school diploma is required, although a GED is also accepted for admissions consideration. SAT or ACT test scores are required for some applicants. SAT Subject Test scores are considered, if submitted, but are not required. *Academic units recommended:* 4 English, 4 Math, 4 Science, 4 Social Studies, 3 Foreign Language.

How to Pay for College

To apply for financial aid, students should submit the following: Free Application for Federal Student Aid (FAFSA). George Mason University participates in the Federal Work Study program. *Need-based aid programs include:* scholarships and grants · general need-based awards · Federal Pell grants · state scholarships and grants · college-based scholarships and grants · private scholarships and grants. *Non-Need-based aid programs include:* scholarships and grants · general need-based awards · state scholarships and grants · athletic scholarships · ROTC scholarships.

GEORGE MASON UNIVERSITY

Highlights

Deadlines
Early Action: November 1
Early Decision: No
Regular Action: December 1 (priority)
January 15 (final)
Common Application: Accepted

Financial Aid
In-state tuition: $5,526
Out-of-state tuition: $20,490
Room: $4,200
Board: $3,160
Books: $900
Freshmen receiving need-based aid: 41%
Undergrads receiving need-based aid: 38%
Avg. % of need met by financial aid: 70%
Avg. aid package (freshmen): $9,894
Avg. aid package (undergrads): $9,738
Freshmen receiving merit-based aid: 4%
Undergrads receiving merit-based aid: 2%
Avg. student debt upon graduation: $16,705

Prominent Alumni
Carolyn Kreiter-Foronda, Virginia poetl-Laureate; Zainab Salbi, president and founder, Women for Women International; Anousheh Ansari, vice president and general manager, Intelligent IP Division of Sonus Networks.

School Spirit
Mascot: Patriots/Gunston
Colors: Green and gold
Song: *GMU Alma Mater*

GOUCHER COLLEGE

1021 Dulaney Valley Road, Baltimore, MD 21204
Admissions: 410-337-6100 · Financial Aid: 410-337-6141
Email: admissions@goucher.edu · Website: http://www.goucher.edu

From the College

"Goucher College is a small college with a big view of the world and intellectual community without boundaries. Here, students are prepared to embark on a life of inquiry and discovery, creativity and analytical thinking. Goucher students are able to put their learning into action through collaborative research in the natural sciences, guest residencies of renowned professors, service-learning programs that support local communities, internships and international study.

"Building on these strengths, our vision for a liberal arts education grows from the understanding that in the 21st century, every academic inquiry and intellectual endeavor has a global context. In all of our 18 undergraduate departments, we encourage our students to explore their intellectual interests in ways that transcend the boundaries of traditional disciplines. Goucher's well-known study-abroad requirement comes with a great deal of curricular flexibility and a $1,200 stipend to help defray travel costs.

"Another asset is its soon-to-open Athenaeum: Part high-tech library, part public forum, part art gallery, part café, and many others. The Athenaeum assumes an integrated, harmonious place within a pedestrian-friendly, architecturally unified campus. The world-class lecturers who visit this campus every year give our students the opportunity to step up and ask important questions of important people.

"The college's environmental initiatives, both curricular and extracurricular, have derived much of their direction and momentum from the suggestions and activities of our students. Representing 43 states and 10 countries, our students arrive at Goucher prepared to excel academically and eager to take advantage of the many resources offered on campus and in nearby Baltimore and Washington, DC. Our 287-acre campus boasts comfortable residence halls, a modern athletic complex and playing fields, stables and miles of wooded trails."

Campus Setting

Goucher is a selective, independent, co-educational institution dedicated to the interdisciplinary traditions of the liberal arts and a broad international perspective on education. Founded as a college for women in 1885, it adopted co-education in 1987. Its 287-acre campus is located in Towson, eight miles north of the center of Baltimore. A four-year private institution, Goucher College has a large, well-stocked library. Goucher College provides on-campus housing with 750 units that can accommodate 1,220 students. Housing options: co-ed dorms · women's dorms · men's dorms · special housing for disabled students.

Student Life and Activities

With 84 percent of students living on campus, there are plenty of social activities. As reported by a school official, "Goucher is more than just a residential college. It's a living and learning community in which the lines between those two key elements—living and learning—become blurred by design. Many of our residence halls have classrooms built into them. Some of the houses within them are centered on themes that unite their residents around common areas where you'll frequently find students coming together to study, hold club meetings, participate in activities and just enjoy each other's company. Once you are here, you won't have to go far to find a stellar array of cultural, social and education events." Goucher offers lectures, readings and performances by international renowned guests and homegrown talent alike. There are more than 60 student-run clubs here, 17 varsity sports teams, language clubs, political organizations, music groups and religious and art organizations. Popular gathering spots include the Gopher Hole on campus and the Inner Harbor and Fells Point off campus. Popular campus events include The Kratz Center for Creative Writing Guest Speaker and Writer-in-Residence, Blind Date Ball, Spring Gala, Fusion Diversity Celebration, The Henry and Ruth Blaustein Rosenberg Lecture-Performance, The Janet and Avery Fisher Music Residency, Get into Goucher Day (GIG), The Women Writing About Women Symposium and Dancers in Action Concerts. The Women's Interest Group, Umoja-African American group, Quindecim and the Student Government Association have a strong presence in the school social life. For those interested in sports, there are intramural teams such as: basketball · lightweight football · racquetball · softball · ultimate Frisbee. Goucher College is a member of the Landmark Athletic Conference (Division III).

Academics and Learning Environment

For the B student, the learning environment of a college is just as important as the quality of its academic program. Goucher College has 130 full-time and 79 part-time faculty members, offering a student-to-faculty ratio of 9:1. The most common course size is 10 to 19 students. Goucher College offers 34 majors with the most popular being communication, psychology and English and least popular being historic preservation and American studies. The school has a general core requirement. Cooperative education is not offered. Other special academic programs that would appeal to a B student: self-designed majors · pass/fail grading option · independent study · double majors · dual degrees · Phi Beta Kappa · internships · distance learning.

B Student Support and Success

Goucher's Academic Center for Excellence (ACE) is for all students and is based on the premise that each student has the ability to learn and successfully complete all college course work. Individual help in study skills is provided by mentors who are successful students that have been trained in peer counseling. They meet with students one or two times a week. Others work with students on issues like time management, procrastination prevention, organizational skills, memory and concentration, note and test taking strategies and test preparation. Study Skills Workshops are offered repeatedly on these same subjects. In addition to these services, Goucher offers supplemental instruction in the sciences and humanities. Study groups meet regularly with an instructor and work together as a team to better understand the material. A drop-in Math Lab is offered on campus Sunday through Thursday, and a Writing Center, although not part of ACE, is available to help students at all stages of the writing process.

Goucher College provides a variety of support programs including dedicated guidance for: academic · career · personal · psychological · minority students · non-traditional students · family planning · religious. The average freshman year GPA is 3.0, and 83 percent of freshmen students return for their sophomore year. Among students who enter the work force, approximately 80 percent enter a field

GOUCHER COLLEGE

Goucher College
Towson, MD (Pop. 65,000)
Location: Large town
Website: http://www.goucher.edu

Students
Total enrollment: 2,319
Undergrads: 459
Freshmen: 422
Part-time students: 2%
From out-of-state: 76%
Male/Female: 32%/68%
Live on-campus: 84%
Off-campus employment rating: Excellent
Caucasian: 68%
African American: 6%
Hispanic: 4%
Asian or Pacific Islander: 3%
Native American: 0%
International: 1%

Academics
Student/faculty ratio: 9:1
Class size 9 or fewer: 15%
Class size 10-29: 80%
Class size 30-49: 4%
Class size 50-99: 1%
Class size 100 or more: -
Returning freshmen: 83%
Six-year graduation rate: 67%

Most Popular Fields of Study
Visual and Performing Arts
English and Literature
Philosophy, Religion and Theology
Computer and Information Sciences
Mathematics
Interdisciplinary Studies
Physical Sciences, Chemistry, Physics and Astronomy
Foreign Languages, Literature and Linguistics
Communications, Journalism, Advertising and Comm. Technologies
Education

GOUCHER COLLEGE

Admissions
Applicants: 4,077
Accepted: 2,591
Acceptance rate: 63.6%
placed on wait list: 171
Average GPA: 3.2
ACT range: Not reported
SAT Math range: 490-620
SAT Reading range: 530-660
SAT Writing range: 530-650
Top 10% of class: 28%
Top 25% of class: 55%
Top 50% of class: 87%

Deadlines
Early Action: December 1
Early Decision: No
Regular Action: February 1 (final)
Common Application: Accepted

Financial Aid
In-state tuition: $33,294
Out-of-state tuition: $33,294
Room: $6,156
Board: $3,042
Books: $800
Freshmen receiving need-based aid: 53%
Undergrads receiving need-based aid: 54%
Avg. % of need met by financial aid: 80%
Avg. aid package (freshmen): $25,779
Avg. aid package (undergrads): $24,213
Freshmen receiving merit-based aid: 18%
Undergrads receiving merit-based aid: 22%
Avg. student debt upon graduation: $16,729

School Spirit
Mascot: Gophers
Colors: Blue and gold

related to their major within six months of graduation. Companies that most frequently hire graduates from Goucher College include: Americorps · Baltimore city public schools · Baltimore County public schools · Goucher College · Johns Hopkins University · Lockheed Martin · Office of Senators/Representatives · Pierce Promotions and Event Management · University of Maryland.

Support for Students with Learning Disabilities

Students with learning disabilities may take advantage of specific support programs offered by Goucher College. If necessary, the college will grant additional time to students with learning disabilities to complete their degree. Also, a lightened course load may be granted to LD students.

How to Get Admitted

For admissions decisions, non-academic factors considered: interview · extracurricular activities · special talents, interests, abilities · character/personal qualities · volunteer work · work experience · geographical location · minority affiliation · alumni relationship. A high school diploma is required, although a GED is also accepted for admissions consideration. SAT or ACT test scores are considered, if submitted, but are not required. SAT Subject Test scores are considered, if submitted, but are not required. *Academic units recommended:* 4 English, 4 Math, 3 Science, 3 Social Studies, 4 Foreign Language.

How to Pay for College

To apply for financial aid, students should submit the following: Free Application for Federal Student Aid (FAFSA) · CSS/Financial Aid PROFILE · Non-custodian (Divorced/Separated) Parent's Statement · Business/Farm Supplement. Goucher College participates in the Federal Work Study program. *Need-based aid programs include:* scholarships and grants · general need-based awards · Federal Pell grants · state scholarships and grants · college-based scholarships and grants · private scholarships and grants. *Non-Need-based aid programs include:* scholarships and grants · state scholarships and grants · creative arts and performance awards.

GRAND CANYON UNIVERSITY

3300 West Camelback Road, Phoenix, AZ 85017
Admissions: · Financial Aid: 800-800-9776, extension 6600
Website: http://www.gcu.edu

From the College

"Grand Canyon University, founded in 1949, is a private, accredited, non-denominational Christian university located in Phoenix, Arizona. The university offers online and campus-based bachelor's and master's degree programs through the Ken Blanchard College of Business, College of Education, College of Nursing and Health Sciences and College of Liberal Arts and Sciences and supports both traditional undergraduate students as well as the working professional."

Campus Setting

Grand Canyon University is big enough to offer a wide variety of bachelor's and master's degrees, Ed.D. program, NCAA athletics, ministry, life-long friendships and an active, safe campus and yet small enough to be personally invested in its students. The school is also affiliated with the Christian Church. The school also has a library with 78,571 books. Grand Canyon University provides on-campus housing with 300 units that can accommodate 723 students. Housing options: co-ed dorms · single-student apartments · married-student apartments. Recreation and sports facilities include: baseball and soccer complex · gymnasium · softball field · stadium · tennis center · training and weight center.

Student Life and Activities

Popular on-campus gathering spots include the Student Union, stadium and the theatre. Popular campus events include Division II intercollegiate and intramural sports, contemporary chapel services and ministries, GCU Sampler, careers in Science, Medicine and Nursing Day, Preview Days, Canyon Institute, campus tours, lip Sync Contest and Mr. GCU. Popular campus groups include the Associated Students of Grand Canyon University, Fellowship for Christian Athletes, Student Nurses Association, International Student Organization and Student Ministries. For those interested in sports, there are intramural teams such as: basketball · bowling · chess · flag football · laser tag · soccer · softball · tennis · ultimate Frisbee · volleyball. Grand Canyon University is a member of the California Collegiate Athletic Conference (Division II), Pacific West Conference (Division II), Rocky Mountain Athlete Conference (Division II).

Academics and Learning Environment

For the B student, the learning environment of a college is just as important as the quality of its academic program. Grand Canyon University has 135 full-time and 1,154 part-time faculty members, offering a student-to-faculty ratio of 20:1. The most common course size is 20 to 29 students. Grand Canyon University offers 67 majors with the most popular being nursing, psychology and elementary

Grand Canyon University
Phoenix, AZ (Pop. 3,000,000)
Location: Major city
Website: http://www.gcu.edu

Students
Total enrollment: 21,738
Undergrads: 2,526
Freshmen: Not reported
Part-time students: 71%
From out-of-state: 89%
Male/Female: 26%/74%
Live on-campus: Not reported
Off-campus employment rating: Good

Academics
Student/faculty ratio: 13:1
Class size 9 or fewer: 15%
Class size 10-29: 62%
Class size 30-49: 2%
Class size 50-99: -
Class size 100 or more: -
Returning freshmen: Not reported
Six-year graduation rate: 49%

Most Popular Fields of Study
Business, Finance, Sales and Marketing
Protective Services, Criminal Justice and
    Public Administration
Psychology
English and Literature
Philosophy, Religion and Theology
Health Professions, Medicine and Related
    Sciences
Liberal Arts, Humanities and General
    Studies
Communications, Journalism, Advertising
    and Comm. Technologies
Education
Biological and Life Sciences

GRAND CANYON UNIVERSITY

Admissions
Average GPA: Not reported
ACT range: Not reported
SAT Math range: Not reported
SAT Reading range: Not reported
SAT Writing range: Not reported

Deadlines
Early Action: No
Early Decision: No
Regular Action: Rolling admissions
Common Application: Not accepted

Financial Aid
In-state tuition: $15,480
Out-of-state tuition: $15,480
Room: $3,640
Board: $4,424
Books: $2,800
Freshmen receiving need-based aid: 57%
Undergrads receiving need-based aid: 64%
Avg. % of need met by financial aid: Not reported
Avg. aid package (freshmen): $3,350
Avg. aid package (undergrads): $3,371

Prominent Alumni
Tim Salmon, major league baseball player; Jim Rice, superintendent, Alhambra (AZ) District, 2007 superintendent of the year.

School Spirit
Mascot: Antelopes
Colors: Purple, white, and black
Song: *Antelope Fight Song, Our Director*

education and least popular being corporate fitness/wellness: athletic coaching, human resource development and music education: instructional conducting. The school has a general core requirement as well as a religion requirement Cooperative education is not offered. All first-year students must maintain a 2.0 GPA or higher to avoid academic probation. Other special academic programs that would appeal to a B student: independent study · double majors · dual degrees · accelerated study · honors program · internships · distance learning certificate programs.

B Student Support and Success

While the college features open admissions, it has some minimal standards. A minimum GPA of 2.25, a combined SAT score of 920 or above or a composite ACT score of 19 or above are required. The school does have a strong Christian focus and bills itself as the "University with a Heart" because of its strong commitment to the student-teacher relationship.

Grand Canyon University provides a variety of support programs including dedicated guidance for: academic · career · personal · military · veterans · family planning · religious. The average freshman year GPA is 3.0.

Support for Students with Learning Disabilities

Students with learning disabilities may take advantage of specific support programs. If necessary, the college will grant additional time to students with learning disabilities to complete their degree. Students with learning disabilities will find the following programs extremely useful: testing accommodations · untimed tests · extended time for tests · take-home exam · oral tests · substitution of courses · readers · early syllabus · priority registration · priority seating. Individual or small group tutorials are also available in: specific subject areas · writing labs · math labs · study skills. An advisor/advocate from the LD program is available to students.

How to Get Admitted

For admissions decisions, non-academic factors considered: interview · extracurricular activities · special talents, interests, abilities · character/personal qualities · volunteer work · work experience · state of residency · alumni relationship. A high school diploma is required, although a GED is also accepted for admissions consideration. SAT or ACT test scores are recommended but not required. SAT Subject Test scores are not required. *According to the admissions office:* Minimum 2.75 GPA or minimum GED score of 520 required.

How to Pay for College

To apply for financial aid, students should submit the following: Free Application for Federal Student Aid (FAFSA). Grand Canyon University participates in the Federal Work Study program. *Need-based aid programs include:* scholarships and grants · general need-based awards · Federal Pell grants · state scholarships and grants · college-based scholarships and grants · private scholarships and grants · ACG · Smart Grants. *Non-Need-based aid programs include:* scholarships and grants · state scholarships and grants · creative arts and performance awards · special characteristics awards · athletic scholarships · ROTC scholarships.

GRANITE STATE COLLEGE

8 Old Suncook Road, Concord, NH 03301
Admissions: 888-228-3000 · Financial Aid: 888-228-3000
Email: ruth.nawn@granite.edu
Website: http://www.granite.edu

From the College

"Granite State College is the University System of New Hampshire's statewide college for adults of all ages. Innovative programs and flexible scheduling make it possible for students to balance responsibilities such as work and family while earning a college degree. Nine centers, many satellite classroom locations and an online Virtual Center make higher education accessible, engaging, and convenient. GSC faculty are experienced teachers with years of practical experience in their fields. Self-design Bachelor of Arts and Bachelor of Science degrees, along with a strong independent study program, match educational outcomes to students' individual interests and backgrounds."

Campus Setting

Founded in 1972, the mission of the college is to provide the citizens of the state with access to public higher education. Access is achieved in a number of ways. Granite State College operates nine centers located throughout the state and offers classes, advising and administrative services to students who live and work in each area. GSC delivers its programs and courses in formats that meet the needs of part-time students who are balancing family and work with their educational responsibilities. This includes classes offered in the evenings, during the weekends, totally online and through a hybrid or blended format. A four-year public institution, Granite State College has an enrollment of 1,542 students. The school also has a library. Granite State College does not have on-campus housing for students.

Student Life and Activities

All students live off campus. Most students are adults and have established ties to the community and are not interested in social events or activities. Students tend to remain focused on degree goals until graduation. Granite State College has one official student organization, the Alumni-Learner Association.

Academics and Learning Environment

For the B student, the learning environment of a college is just as important as the quality of its academic program. Granite State College has no full-time and 147 part-time faculty members, offering a student-to-faculty ratio of 10:1. The most common course size is 2 to 9 students. Granite State College offers 16 majors with the most popular being self-designed, business and behavioral science and least popular being information technology, criminal justice and early childhood education. The school has a general core requirement. Cooperative education is available. All first-year students must maintain a 2.0 GPA or higher to avoid academic probation,

Granite State College
Nine New Hampshire locations statewide
Location: Small towns
Website: http://www.granite.edu

Students
Total enrollment: 1,542
Undergrads: 362
Freshmen: 267
Part-time students: 59%
From out-of-state: 8%
Male/Female: 27%/73%
Live on-campus: Not reported
Off-campus employment rating: Good
Caucasian: 94%
African American: 1%
Hispanic: 1%
Asian or Pacific Islander: 1%
Native American: 1%

Academics
Student/faculty ratio: 10:1
Class size 9 or fewer: 56%
Class size 10-29: 44%
Class size 30-49: 2%
Class size 50-99: -
Class size 100 or more: -
Returning freshmen: 76%
Six-year graduation rate: 58%

Most Popular Fields of Study
Business, Finance, Sales and Marketing

Admissions
Applicants: 93
Accepted: 93
Acceptance rate: 100%
Average GPA: Not reported
ACT range: Not reported
SAT Math range: Not reported
SAT Reading range: Not reported
SAT Writing range: Not reported

GRANITE STATE COLLEGE

Deadlines
Early Action: No
Early Decision: No
Regular Action: Rolling admissions
Common Application: Not accepted

Financial Aid
In-state tuition: $5,712
Out-of-state tuition: $6,048
Room: -
Board: -
Books: $900
Avg. % of need met by financial aid: Not reported
Avg. aid package (freshmen): Not reported
Avg. aid package (undergrads): Not reported

and a minimum overall GPA of 2.0 is required to graduate. Other special academic programs that would appeal to a B student: self-designed majors · independent study · double majors · dual degrees · accelerated study · internships · distance learning.

B Student Support and Success

At this college, recently renamed Granite State, students can design their own bachelor's degree programs. Orientation sessions are offered year round, and academic advisors focus on helping enrollees prepare for tests, study and take notes. Academic Resource Coordinators provide additional academic services. The college's Academic Resource Center offers students computers, books, study sheets and multiple resources. In addition, skills assessments help students choose the best courses in writing and math. Regular workshops are offered throughout the year and cover the professional focus to personal support. Granite focuses on a set of core values in order to meet the educational needs of its students.

Granite State College provides a variety of support programs including dedicated guidance for: academic · career · veterans · non-traditional students. Additional counseling services include: Financial aid counseling. Annually, 76 percent of freshmen students return for their sophomore year. Among students who enter the work force, approximately 94 percent enter a field related to their major within six months of graduation.

Support for Students with Learning Disabilities

Students with learning disabilities may take advantage of specific support programs offered by Granite State College. If necessary, the college will grant additional time to students with learning disabilities to complete their degree. Students with learning disabilities will find the following programs at Granite State College extremely useful: tutors · extended time for tests · take-home exam · readers · note-taking services · tape recorders · texts on tape · early syllabus · waiver of math degree requirement. An advisor/advocate from the Accommodations for Disabilities is available to students.

How to Get Admitted

For admissions decisions, non-academic factors considered: interview · state of residency. A high school diploma is required, although a GED is also accepted for admissions consideration. SAT or ACT test scores

How to Pay for College

To apply for financial aid, students should submit the following: Free Application for Federal Student Aid (FAFSA) · institution's own financial aid forms. Granite State College participates in the Federal Work Study program. *Need-based aid programs include:* scholarships and grants · general need-based awards · Federal Pell grants · state scholarships and grants · college-based scholarships and grants · private scholarships and grants · NH Adult Student Aid Program. *Non-Need-based aid programs include:* scholarships and grants · state scholarships and grants.

GREEN MOUNTAIN COLLEGE

1 Brennan Circle, Poultney, VT 05764-1199
Admissions: 800-776-6675 · Financial Aid: 800-776-6675
Email: admiss@greenmtn.edu · Website: http://www.greenmtn.edu

From the College

"Green Mountain College takes the environment as the unifying theme underlying the academic and social experience of the campus. Through a broad range of liberal arts and career-focused majors and a service-oriented student affairs program, the college fosters ideals of environmental responsibility, public service, international understanding, and life-long intellectual, physical and spiritual development."

Campus Setting

Green Mountain, founded in 1834, is a private college offering specialized programs in the fields of business and education. Its 155-acre campus is located in Poultney, 20 miles from Rutland. A four-year institution, Green Mountain College has an enrollment of 867 students. Green Mountain College has been co-ed since 1974. The school is also affiliated with the United Methodist Church. In addition to a medium-sized library, the campus also has an art center. Green Mountain College provides on-campus housing with 370 units that can accommodate 605 students. Housing options: co-ed dorms · single-student apartments · cooperative housing. Recreation and sports facilities include: gymnasium · playing fields · soccer and softball fields · swimming pool · weight room.

Student Life and Activities

With 81 percent of students living on campus, there are plenty of social activities. Off-campus gathering spots include the Pub House, the Lake House and A.J.'s. Popular campus events include the spring concert. Green Mountain College has 20 official student organizations. The most popular are: America Reads · chorus · Do Everything Club (substance-free group) · drama and dance groups · educational policy committee · education and psychology clubs · judicial board · music guild · research groups · student life committee · volunteer groups · business association · New England Explorers · outing club. For those interested in sports, there are intramural teams such as: basketball · floor hockey · golf · rugby · snowboarding · soccer · softball · ultimate Frisbee · volleyball.

Academics and Learning Environment

For the B student, the learning environment of a college is just as important as the quality of its academic program. Green Mountain College has 49 full-time and 33 part-time faculty members, offering a student-to-faculty ratio of 14:1. The most common course size is 20 to 29 students. Green Mountain College offers 23 majors with the most popular being recreation, elementary education and business and least popular being writing and history. The school has a general core requirement. Cooperative education is not offered. All first-year students must maintain a 1.7 GPA or higher to avoid academic probation, and a minimum overall GPA of 2.0 is required to graduate. Other special academic programs that would appeal to a B student: self-designed majors · pass/fail grading option · independent study · double majors · dual degrees · honors program · internships · distance learning certificate programs.

GREEN MOUNTAIN COLLEGE

Highlights

Green Mountain College
Poultney, VT (Pop. 3,000)
Location: Rural
Website: http://www.greenmtn.edu

Students
Total enrollment: 867
Undergrads: 380
Freshmen: 221
Part-time students: 3%
From out-of-state: Not reported
Male/Female: 49%/51%
Live on-campus: 81%
Off-campus employment rating: Excellent
Caucasian: 70%
African American: 3%
Hispanic: 2%
Asian or Pacific Islander: 1%
Native American: 1%
International: 0%

Academics
Student/faculty ratio: 14:1
Class size 9 or fewer: 16%
Class size 10-29: 77%
Class size 30-49: 7%
Class size 50-99: -
Class size 100 or more: -
Returning freshmen: Not reported
Six-year graduation rate: 40%

Most Popular Fields of Study
Psychology
Visual and Performing Arts
English and Literature
Philosophy, Religion and Theology
Parks, Recreation and Fitness
Interdisciplinary Studies
Liberal Arts, Humanities and General
    Studies
Communications, Journalism, Advertising
    and Comm. Technologies
Social Sciences, History, Economics,
    Political Science
Natural Resources and Environmental
    Science

B Student Support and Success

Green Mountain College provides a variety of support programs including dedicated guidance for: academic · career · personal · psychological · minority students · family planning · religious. Recognizing that some students may need extra preparation, Green Mountain College offers remedial and refresher courses in: reading · writing · math · study skills.

Support for Students with Learning Disabilities

Students with learning disabilities may take advantage of specific support programs offered by Green Mountain College. If necessary, the college will grant additional time to students with learning disabilities to complete their degree. Also, a lightened course load may be granted to LD students. Students with learning disabilities will find the following programs at Green Mountain College extremely useful: remedial math · tutors · learning center · extended time for tests · take-home exam · oral tests · readers · note-taking services · reading machines · tape recorders · texts on tape · early syllabus · priority registration · waiver of math degree requirement. Individual or small group tutorials are also available in: time management · organizational skills · learning strategies · specific subject areas · writing labs · math labs · study skills.

How to Get Admitted

For admissions decisions, non-academic factors considered: interview · extracurricular activities · special talents, interests, abilities · character/personal qualities · volunteer work · work experience · state of residency. A high school diploma is required, although a GED is also accepted for admissions consideration. SAT or ACT test scores are recommended but not required. SAT Subject Test scores are considered, if submitted, but are not required. *Academic units recommended:* 4 Math, 4 Science, 3 Social Studies, 3 Foreign Language.

Insight

Sandra Bartholomew is the dean of enrollment management at Green Mountain College. She says the average GPA for incoming classes is about 3.0 and that GMC students are "passionate, committed and highly functioning young people who place a high value on interactive experiences that connect classroom learning with the real world." Academic programs are field-based and interdisciplinary. With small class sizes and a "talented, experienced" faculty (over 90 percent of professors at GMC have terminal degrees) students thrive on a campus that "values individuality and community." Results from the 2008 National Survey of Students Engagement (NSSE) show that students give GMC high marks compared to peer institutions in level of academic challenge, degree of active and collaborative learning, number of enriching educational experiences and degree of student/faculty interaction.

How to Pay for College

To apply for financial aid, students should submit the following: Free Application for Federal Student Aid (FAFSA) · state aid form · scholarship forms. Green Mountain College participates in the Federal Work Study program. *Need-based aid programs include:* scholarships and grants · general need-based awards · Federal Pell grants · state scholarships and grants · college-based scholarships and grants · private scholarships and grants. *Non-Need-based aid programs include:* scholarships and grants · general need-based awards · state scholarships and grants · creative arts and performance awards · special achievements and activities awards.

GREEN MOUNTAIN COLLEGE

Admissions
Applicants: 1,431
Accepted: 1,008
Acceptance rate: 70.4%
Average GPA: Not reported
ACT range: Not reported
SAT Math range: Not reported
SAT Reading range: Not reported
SAT Writing range: Not reported

Deadlines
Early Action: No
Early Decision: No
Regular Action: March 1 (priority)
Common Application: Accepted

Financial Aid
In-state tuition: $25,910
Out-of-state tuition: $25,910
Room: $5,704
Board: $3,966
Books: $1,000
Freshmen receiving need-based aid: 68%
Undergrads receiving need-based aid: 73%
Avg. % of need met by financial aid: 92%
Avg. aid package (freshmen): $18,937
Avg. aid package (undergrads): $20,207
Freshmen receiving merit-based aid: 20%
Undergrads receiving merit-based aid: 16%
Avg. student debt upon graduation: $32,448

School Spirit
Mascot: Eagle
Colors: Green and gold
Song: *This Green Place*

GUILFORD COLLEGE

5800 W. Friendly Avenue, Greensboro, NC 27410
Admissions: 800-992-7759 · Financial Aid: 336-316-2165
Email: admission@guilford.edu · Website: http://www.guilford.edu

From the College

"Guilford College draws on Quaker and liberal arts traditions to produce lifelong learners and agents of change in the world. Student-centered instruction nurtures each individual amid an intentionally diverse community. A values-rich educational experience explores the ethical dimension of knowledge and promotes honesty, compassion, integrity, courage and respect for the individual. A challenging academic program fosters critical and creative thinking through analysis, inquiry, communication, consensus building, problem solving and leadership. A global perspective values people of other cultures and the natural environment in which we all live. Service opportunities forge a connection between thought and action."

Campus Setting

Guilford, founded in 1837, is a church-affiliated college. Its 340-acre campus is located in northwest Greensboro in the Piedmont section of North Carolina. A four-year private institution, Guilford College has an enrollment of 2,687 students. The school is also affiliated with the Society of Friends Church. In addition to a large, well-stocked library, the campus facilities include: art gallery · language lab · science center · observatory. Guilford College provides on-campus housing with 9 units that can accommodate 1,069 students. Housing options: co-ed dorms · women's dorms · men's dorms · single-student apartments · special housing for International students. Recreation and sports facilities include: athletic center · fields · field house · golf club · gymnasium · park · physical education center · swimming pool · tennis courts.

Student Life and Activities

With 77 percent of students living on campus, there are plenty of social activities. Guilford College has 33 official student organizations. The most popular are: Archery club · Campus Activities Board · College Democrats · Community Aids Awareness Project · Community Senate · Cooking Club · Expressions in Dance · Fancy Feet and Fingers · Forensic Biology Club · Forevergreen · French club · Gender Equality Now · German club · GPeace · Health Science Club · History club · Organic Gardening · Outdoors club · Photo club · Poetry club · Pride · Project Community · Psychology club. For those interested in sports, there are intramural teams such as: baseball · basketball · bowling · cheerleading · non-tackle football · rugby · soccer · softball · table tennis · tennis · volleyball · water polo. Guilford College is a member of the Old Dominion Athletic Conference (Division III).

Academics and Learning Environment

For the B student, the learning environment of a college is just as important as the quality of its academic program. Guilford College has 135 full-time and 83 part-time faculty members, offering a student-to-faculty ratio of 16:1. The most common course size is 10 to 19 students. Guilford College offers 39 majors with the most popular being business management, psychology and forensic biology. The school has a general core requirement. Cooperative education is available. All first-year students must maintain a 2.0 GPA or higher to avoid academic probation. Other special academic programs that would appeal to a B student: self-designed majors · pass/fail grading option · independent study · double majors · dual degrees · honors program · internships · weekend college · certificate programs.

B Student Support and Success

At Guilford, the SAT is optional. Writing samples and an interview are required when a student does not submit standardized test scores. It is home to a high school preparation school with 100 students. In a required first-year class, students are taken on campus tours, shown various resources and helped to transition to college life.

Guilford College provides a variety of support programs including dedicated guidance for: academic · career · personal · psychological · minority students · veterans · non-traditional students · family planning · religious. Additional counseling services include: first-year transitional counseling. Recognizing that some students may need extra preparation, Guilford College offers remedial and refresher courses in: reading · writing · math · study skills. Other remedial services include science. The average freshman year GPA is 3.1, and 72 percent of freshmen students return for their sophomore year.

Support for Students with Learning Disabilities

Students with learning disabilities may take advantage of specific support programs offered by Guilford College. If necessary, the college will grant additional time to students with learning disabilities to complete their degree. Also, a lightened course load may be granted to LD students. High school foreign language waivers are accepted. High school math waivers are also accepted. The school only offers LD services not a stand-alone LD program. Students with learning disabilities will find the following programs at Guilford College extremely useful: special classes · tutors · learning center · testing accommodations · untimed tests · extended time for tests · take-home exam · oral tests · readers · note-taking services · reading machines · tape recorders. Individual or small group tutorials are also available in: time management · organizational skills · learning strategies · specific subject areas · study skills. An advisor/advocate from the Disability Services is available to students. This member also sits on the admissions committee.

How to Get Admitted

For admissions decisions, non-academic factors considered: interview · extracurricular activities · special talents, interests, abilities · character/personal qualities · volunteer work · work experience · geographical location · religious affiliation/commitment · minority affiliation · alumni relationship. A high school diploma is required, although a GED is also accepted for admissions consideration. SAT or ACT test scores are recommended but not required. SAT Subject Test scores are recommended but not required. *According to the admissions office:* Minimum 2.0 GPA required. *Academic units recommended:* 4 English, 3 Math, 3 Science, 2 Foreign Language.

Insight

"We have a multi-layer approach to student success," says the Guilford staff. The First Year Program addresses the needs of first year Guilford students from the time they are admitted to the college until they declare their major. To assist the students in their transition into college life, the First Year Program coordinates all contact with the students during the summer prior to their first year.

GUILFORD COLLEGE

Highlights

Guilford College
Greensboro, NC (Pop. 240,955)
Location: Large city
Website: http://www.guilford.edu

Students
Total enrollment: 2,687
Undergrads: 1,018
Freshmen: 444
Part-time students: 17%
From out-of-state: 71%
Male/Female: 38%/62%
Live on-campus: 77%
Off-campus employment rating: Fair

Academics
Student/faculty ratio: 16:1
Class size 9 or fewer: 15%
Class size 10-29: 80%
Class size 30-49: 4%
Class size 50-99: -
Class size 100 or more: -
Returning freshmen: 72%
Six-year graduation rate: 57%

Most Popular Fields of Study
Business, Finance, Sales and Marketing
Biological and Life Sciences
Area, Ethnic and Gender Studies

Admissions
Applicants: 3,493
Accepted: 2,019
Acceptance rate: 57.8%
placed on wait list: 172
Average GPA: 3.1
ACT range: 22-26
SAT Math range: 500-610
SAT Reading range: 490-630
SAT Writing range: Not reported
Top 10% of class: 20%
Top 25% of class: 50%
Top 50% of class: 79%

GUILFORD COLLEGE

Through CHAOS (Guilford College's Orientation Program), First Year Experience classes and the FYE lab, the First Year Program steers students to target issues of diversity, academic success and the new student experience.

"The Learning Commons is ready to help students become more efficient and self-directed learners," says the college staff. The LC offers faculty tutors and peer tutors, in group or individual sessions. Faculty tutors help students with quantitative skills, writing, reading, study skills, test taking and time management. Students are active in three peer tutoring groups: Writing Studio peer tutors (students can help brainstorm a paper, discuss the focus and support in a paper a student has written or give feedback on a draft); Chemistry 911 (students can get help with intro-level chemistry courses); and a large Student Tutoring Service (tutoring in specific courses across the curriculum).

While Guilford doesn't have a special program for students with disabilities, the college does have useful services for these students. "Many students do well academically in spite of frustrating 'glitches,'" says the staff. The retention rate for students with learning disabilities is approximately the same as that of the college in general. The staff reports that students who do best are generally those who work hard, who consult with advisors to carefully plan/balance classes and schedules and who are good self-advocates. The staff also says that students with learning differences often know themselves well as learners and so they regularly "offer us new ideas and strategies and fresh insights into methods that work."

According to the college, Guilford is looking for students who have challenged themselves academically, who have been involved in their high school and home communities and who have shown leadership and the potential to be successful in the college's academic environment. Students should show a desire to be successful in college. "Drive to succeed goes a long way to making us feel that a student can make a difference in our environment," says the staff. Grades are relative to the school environment. The college wants to see that a student has given a strong effort in a challenging course setting. "The grade alone does not tell the whole story. We look at the school setting, the course title and level. We want hard-working students who have the desire to be successful at Guilford and to graduate," says the staff.

How to Pay for College

To apply for financial aid, students should submit the following: Free Application for Federal Student Aid (FAFSA). Guilford College participates in the Federal Work Study program. *Need-based aid programs include:* scholarships and grants · general need-based awards · Federal Pell grants · state scholarships and grants · college-based scholarships and grants · private scholarships and grants. *Non-Need-based aid programs include:* scholarships and grants · state scholarships and grants · special achievements and activities awards.

GUSTAVUS ADOLPHUS COLLEGE

800 West College Avenue, St. Peter, MN 56082
Admissions: 800-487-8288 · Financial Aid: 507-933-7527
Email: admission@gac.edu · Website: http://www.gac.edu

From the College

"The oldest Lutheran college in Minnesota, Gustavus was founded in 1862 by Swedish Lutheran immigrants and named for Swedish King Gustav II Adolf. Gustavus Adolphus College is affiliated with the Evangelical Lutheran Church in America. Throughout its history, it has valued its Lutheran and Swedish heritages. The Gustavus culture derives from our founding traditions and offers a distinctiveness of feeling and deed on the campus and in the greater world.

"At Gustavus, students receive personal attention in small-sized classes and engage in collaborative research with their professors. The college is fully accredited and known for its strong music, science, writing, athletics, study-abroad and service-learning programs. We maintain a chapter of Phi Beta Kappa and our annual Mayday! Peace Conference, an event devoted to topics relating to human rights and social justice. Gustavus is internationally recognized for its annual Nobel Conference. This signature event was launched in 1965 following a gathering on campus of 26 Nobel laureates for the dedication of the Nobel Hall of Science in 1963. The conference brings cutting-edge science issues to the attention of the public, engages world-renowned science speakers and provides opportunities to explore the moral and societal impact of scientific issues.

"Gustavus holds the conviction that religious faith enriches and informs learning and is a fundamental notion underpinning our emphasis on community, ethics and service. While strongly Lutheran in tradition and character, conformity to that specific faith tradition is not expected.

"We embrace the notion that true leadership expresses itself in service to others, and affirm the classical ideal of a liberating education, an education that frees one to serve God and humanity to the best of one's ability."

Campus Setting

Gustavus Adolphus, founded in 1862, is a private, liberal arts college. Its 340-acre campus is located in St. Peter, 60 miles southwest of Minneapolis-St. Paul. A four-year institution, Gustavus Adolphus College has an enrollment of 2,578 students. The school is also affiliated with the Lutheran Church. In addition to a large, well-stocked library, the campus also has an art museum. Gustavus Adolphus College provides on-campus housing with 20 units that can accommodate 2,081 students. Housing options: co-ed dorms · single-student apartments. Recreation and sports facilities include: arboretum · baseball · soccer and softball field · basketball · volleyball and indoor/outdoor tennis courts · country club · football stadium · gymnastics studio · ice rink · natatorium · track complex.

Student Life and Activities

With 80 percent of students living on campus, there are plenty of social activities. According to the student newspaper, campus organizations try to make up for Gustavus' small-town atmosphere, and their success is apparent in how few students leave for the weekend. Greek events and successful varsity sports offer many reasons to stick around. The favorite on-campus gathering spot is The Dive, a non-alcoholic dance club. Off campus, students frequent local bars and house parties. Popular events on campus include Nobel Conference, MayDay! Peace Conference, Christmas in Christ Chapel, Honors Day and Building Bridges. Gustavus Adolphus College has 120 of-

GUSTAVUS ADOLPHUS COLLEGE

Gustavus Adolphus College
Saint Peter, MN (Pop. 10,500)
Location: Rural
Website: http://www.gac.edu

Students
Total enrollment: 2,578
Undergrads: 1,107
Freshmen: 635
Part-time students: 2%
From out-of-state: 17%
Male/Female: 43%/57%
Live on-campus: 80%
In fraternities: 11%
In sororities: 12%
Off-campus employment rating: Excellent
Caucasian: 89%
African American: 2%
Hispanic: 2%
Asian or Pacific Islander: 5%
Native American: 0%
International: 1%

Academics
Student/faculty ratio: 12:1
Class size 9 or fewer: 13%
Class size 10-29: 65%
Class size 30-49: 20%
Class size 50-99: 3%
Class size 100 or more: -
Returning freshmen: 91%
Six-year graduation rate: 81%

Most Popular Fields of Study
Business, Finance, Sales and Marketing
Protective Services, Criminal Justice and
    Public Administration
Visual and Performing Arts
Computer and Information Sciences
Communications, Journalism, Advertising
    and Comm. Technologies
Philosophy, Religion and Theology
English and Literature
Parks, Recreation and Fitness
Health Professions, Medicine and Re-
    lated Sciences

ficial student organizations. Greeks and athletes have a widespread influence on campus life. For those interested in sports, there are intramural teams such as: badminton · basketball · broomball · flag football · golf · hockey · racquetball · soccer · softball · tennis · ultimate Frisbee · volleyball · wallyball. Gustavus Adolphus College is a member of the Minnesota Intercollegiate Athletic Conference (Division III).

Academics and Learning Environment

For the B student, the learning environment of a college is just as important as the quality of its academic program. Gustavus Adolphus College has 200 full-time and 51 part-time faculty members, offering a student-to-faculty ratio of 12:1. The most common course size is 10 to 19 students. Gustavus Adolphus College offers 48 majors with the most popular being business administration, biology and education and least popular being Russian studies, German and Japanese studies. The school has a general core requirement as well as a religion requirement Cooperative education is not offered. All first-year students must maintain a 1.75 GPA or higher to avoid academic probation. Other special academic programs that would appeal to a B student: self-designed majors · independent study · double majors · dual degrees · honors program · Phi Beta Kappa · internships.

B Student Support and Success

Gustavus Adolphus offers a Writing Center for one-on-one consultation and help with reading and interpreting assignments. The Advising Center helps coordinate meetings between students, advisors and professors to make the most of career help.

Gustavus Adolphus College provides a variety of support programs including dedicated guidance for: academic · career · personal · psychological · minority students · family planning · religious. The average freshman year GPA is 3.3, and 91 percent of freshmen students return for their sophomore year. What do students do after college? While many enter the work force, approximately 26 percent pursue a graduate degree immediately after graduation. Among students who enter the work force, approximately 31 percent enter a field related to their major within six months of graduation. Companies that most frequently hire graduates from Gustavus Adolphus College include: Federated Insurance · Liberty Mutual · Mayo Clinic · Target.

Support for Students with Learning Disabilities

Students with learning disabilities may take advantage of specific support programs offered by Gustavus Adolphus College. According to the school, Disability Services offers counseling and accommodations to all students who self-identify and provide documentation. Students must also meet with the Disability Services Coordinator and register with Disability Services. One-on-one peer tutoring is also available as well as designated tutors to serve students with LD in the Writing Center. Additional services include a computer with the Kurzweil system installed. Students with learning disabilities will find the following programs at Gustavus Adolphus College extremely useful: tutors · learning center · testing accommodations · extended time for tests · take-home exam · oral tests · exam on tape or computer · readers · typist/scribe · note-taking services · proofreading services · reading machines · tape recorders · texts on tape · early syllabus · special bookstore section · priority registration · waiver of foreign language degree requirement. Individual or small group tutorials are also available in: time management · organizational skills · learning strategies · specific subject areas · writing labs · math labs · study skills. An advisor/advocate from the Disability Services/Advising and Counseling is available to students.

How to Get Admitted

For admissions decisions, non-academic factors considered: interview · extracurricular activities · special talents, interests, abilities · character/personal qualities · volunteer work · work experience · geographical location · religious affiliation/commitment · minority affiliation · alumni relationship. A high school diploma is required, although a GED is also accepted for admissions consideration. SAT or ACT test scores are recommended but not required. *According to the admissions office:* Rank in top third of secondary school class recommended. *Academic units recommended:* 4 English, 4 Math, 3 Science, 2 Social Studies, 2 Foreign Language.

How to Pay for College

To apply for financial aid, students should submit the following: Free Application for Federal Student Aid (FAFSA) · institution's own financial aid forms · CSS/Financial Aid PROFILE. Gustavus Adolphus College participates in the Federal Work Study program. *Need-based aid programs include:* scholarships and grants · general need-based awards · Federal Pell grants · state scholarships and grants · college-based scholarships and grants · private scholarships and grants. *Non-Need-based aid programs include:* scholarships and grants · general need-based awards · state scholarships and grants · creative arts and performance awards · special achievements and activities awards · special characteristics awards · ROTC scholarships.

GUSTAVUS ADOLPHUS COLLEGE

Highlights

Admissions
Applicants: 3,128
Accepted: 2,343
Acceptance rate: 74.9%
Average GPA: 3.6
ACT range: 24-29
SAT Math range: 580-690
SAT Reading range: Not reported
SAT Writing range: Not reported
Top 10% of class: 34%
Top 25% of class: 69%
Top 50% of class: 97%

Deadlines
Early Action: November 1
Early Decision: No
Regular Action: Rolling admissions
Common Application: Accepted

Financial Aid
In-state tuition: $31,460
Out-of-state tuition: $31,460
Room: $5,000
Board: $2,900
Books: $750
Freshmen receiving need-based aid: 70%
Undergrads receiving need-based aid: 65%
Avg. % of need met by financial aid: 90%
Avg. aid package (freshmen): $25,665
Avg. aid package (undergrads): $23,656
Freshmen receiving merit-based aid: 30%
Undergrads receiving merit-based aid: 32%
Avg. student debt upon graduation: $24,297

Prominent Alumni
James M. McPherson, American Civil War historian; Peter Krause, actor, Six Feet Under; Margaret Anderson Kelliher, Minnesota House of Representatives.

School Spirit
Mascot: Gus the Lion
Colors: Black and gold
Song: *Gustie Rouser*

HAMPDEN-SYDNEY COLLEGE

P.O. Box 667, Hampden-Sydney, VA 23943
Admissions: 800-755-0733 · Financial Aid: 434-223-6119
Email: hsapp@hsc.edu · Website: http://www.hsc.edu

From the College

"Hampden-Sydney College's spirit lies in its sense of community and its preservation of tradition. HSC is all about seeking to form good men and good citizens in an atmosphere of sound learning. Challenged by the curriculum and guided by the professors, students can get help when they need it because classes are small. The greatest advantage of small-college life is that everyone can be involved. Athletics, debating, publications, fraternity life—all are part of the education process. Many students enjoy the outdoors: hunting, fishing, camping and hiking. Public service, leadership and volunteerism are developed through opportunities to participate in the HSC Volunteer Fire Department, The Wilson Center for Leadership, community service projects with the local community and 'Beyond the Hill' community service trips to Belize, Honduras, and other service-oriented trips abroad. In addition to the college's own study abroad programs, HSC students are eligible to participate and earn academic credit in approved foreign-study programs in Europe, Central and South America, South and East Asia, the Middle East and the Virginia program at Oxford. In addition, the HSC faculty develops May Term Abroad programs in special topics in their discipline. Past programs have included European Union Studies in France, Economics/Political Science/Culture studies in Eastern Europe, Tropical Biology in Mexico, Theatre in Scotland, Language Immersion in Spain and Area Studies in Egypt. The total experience at the college produces a man well-suited for the challenges of a job, the demands of social service, and the pleasure of personal endeavors."

Campus Setting

Hampden-Sydney, founded in 1776, is a private, liberal arts college for men. Its 660-acre campus is located 65 miles southwest of Richmond. A four-year college, Hampden-Sydney College has an enrollment of 1,120 students. The school is also affiliated with the Presbyterian Church. In addition to a large, well-stocked library, the campus facilities include: museum · center for leadership · athletic hall of fame. Hampden-Sydney College provides on-campus housing with 51 units that can accommodate 1,122 students. Housing options: men's dorms · fraternity housing · single-student apartments · married-student apartments · special housing for International students. Recreation and sports facilities include: field house · gymnasium.

Student Life and Activities

With 95 percent of students living on campus, there are plenty of social activities. Popular gathering spots include The Tiger Inn, Kirby Field House, Main Street Lanes, and Macado's. Popular campus events include Family Weekend, Homecoming Concert, Symposium, Music Festival, Greek Week, ODAC Basketball and Signing of the Honor Code. Hampden-Sydney College has 43 official student organizations. The most popular are: Film · French · philosophy · psychology · Spanish Club · Animation Society · WWHS-FM · Pre-Business Society · Pre-Healthy Society · Pre-Law Society · College Democrats · College Republicans · Tiger Athletic Club · Outsiders Club · Madisonian Society · Ambassadorial Committee · Volunteer Fire Department · Good Men Good Citizens · Student Admissions Committee. For those interested in sports, there are intramural teams such as: clay target · fly-fishing · lacrosse · rugby · soccer · skiing · snowboarding. Hampden-Sydney College is a member of the Old Dominion Athletic Conference (Division III).

Academics and Learning Environment

For the B student, the learning environment of a college is just as important as the quality of its academic program. Hampden-Sydney College has 97 full-time and 24 part-time faculty members, offering a student-to-faculty ratio of 10:1. The most common course size is 10 to 19 students. Hampden-Sydney College offers 29 majors with the most popular being economics, history and political science and least popular being biochemistry, French and Spanish. The school has a general core requirement. Cooperative education is available. All first-year students must maintain a 1.5 GPA or higher to avoid academic probation, and a minimum overall GPA of 2.0 is required to graduate. Other special academic programs that would appeal to a B student: independent study · double majors · dual degrees · honors program · Phi Beta Kappa · internships.

B Student Support and Success

Hampden-Sydney College offers a number of services for the B student. The Advising Program is for all freshmen. They are assigned an Academic Advisor who, in turn, helps with class selection, study skills development and transitioning to college life. Pre Term Workshops are offered before the fall semester begins to help students develop and improve academic skills and Tutoring is available in a number of different courses, Academic Skills Workshops are offered weekly on topics such as goal setting, time management, note taking, reading skills, active learning, test taking and preparation, charting academic progress and dealing with stress.

Hampden-Sydney College provides a variety of support programs including dedicated guidance for: academic · career · personal · psychological · minority students · religious. The average freshman year GPA is 2.6, and 79 percent of freshmen students return for their sophomore year. What do students do after college? While many enter the work force, approximately 26 percent pursue a graduate degree immediately after graduation. Among students who enter the work force, approximately 22 percent enter a field related to their major within six months of graduation, while a further 20 percent enter a related career within two years of graduation. Companies that most frequently hire graduates from Hampden-Sydney College include: AIG SunAmerica Securities · Anhueser-Busch · Blue Ridge Outdoors Magazine · Ferguson Enterprises · HomeTown Realty · JP Morgan · McGuire Woods · Merrill Lynch · Morgan Stanley · Signature Government Solutions · Suntrust · Swiss Finance Academy · U.S. Senate · Congress and Representatives · Wachovia · the White House · Youth Service International.

Support for Students with Learning Disabilities

Students with learning disabilities may take advantage of specific support programs offered by Hampden-Sydney College. According to the school, most services of the Academic Success office are available to all students, regardless of whether a disability has been identified (testing and course accommodations excluded). Students with learning disabilities will find the following programs at Hampden-Sydney College extremely useful: tutors · learning center · extended time for tests · oral tests · note-taking services · reading machines · tape recorders · texts on tape · videotaped classes · waiver of math degree requirement. Individual or small group

HAMPDEN-SYDNEY COLLEGE

Highlights

Hampden-Sydney College
Hampden-Sydney, VA (Pop. 400)
Location: Rural
Website: http://www.hsc.edu

Students
Total enrollment: 1,120
Undergrads: 1,119
Freshmen: 314
Part-time students: 0%
From out-of-state: 24%
Male/Female: 100%/ 0%
Live on-campus: 95%
In fraternities: 25%
Off-campus employment rating: Fair
Caucasian: 87%
African American: 5%
Hispanic: 1%
Asian or Pacific Islander: 1%
Native American: 0%
International: 2%

Academics
Student/faculty ratio: 10:1
Class size 9 or fewer: 30%
Class size 10-29: 66%
Class size 30-49: 9%
Class size 50-99: 3%
Class size 100 or more: -
Returning freshmen: 79%
Six-year graduation rate: 62%

Most Popular Fields of Study
Business, Finance, Sales and Marketing
Biological and Life Sciences

HAMPDEN-SYDNEY COLLEGE

Highlights

Admissions
Applicants: 1,553
Accepted: 987
Acceptance rate: 63.6%
Average GPA: 3.2
ACT range: 20-26
SAT Math range: 515-610
SAT Reading range: 500-610
SAT Writing range: 480-590
Top 10% of class: 9%
Top 25% of class: 17%
Top 50% of class: 78%

Deadlines
Early Action: December 15
Early Decision: November 15
Regular Action: March 1 (final)
Common Application: Accepted

Financial Aid
In-state tuition: $29,518
Out-of-state tuition: $29,518
Room: -
Board: -
Books: $1,200
Freshmen receiving need-based aid: 53%
Undergrads receiving need-based aid: 48%
Avg. % of need met by financial aid: 83%
Avg. aid package (freshmen): $22,799
Avg. aid package (undergrads): $22,412
Freshmen receiving merit-based aid: 51%
Undergrads receiving merit-based aid: 50%
Avg. student debt upon graduation: $17,277

Prominent Alumni
Dr. Eugene Hickcock, U.S. deputy secretary of Education; Dr. Randall Chitwood, chairman of surgery, East Carolina University.

School Spirit
Mascot: Tiger
Colors: Garmet and gray

tutorials are also available in: time management · organizational skills · learning strategies · specific subject areas · writing labs · math labs · study skills. An advisor/advocate from the LD program is available to students.

How to Get Admitted

For admissions decisions, non-academic factors considered: interview · extracurricular activities · special talents, interests, abilities · character/personal qualities · volunteer work · work experience · state of residency · minority affiliation · alumni relationship. A high school diploma is required, although a GED is also accepted for admissions consideration. SAT or ACT test scores are required of all applicants. SAT Subject Test scores are recommended but not required. *According to the admissions office:* Rank in top two-fifths of secondary school class and minimum grade average of B- recommended. *Academic units recommended:* 4 Math, 3 Science, 3 Foreign Language.

How to Pay for College

To apply for financial aid, students should submit the following: Free Application for Federal Student Aid (FAFSA) · CSS/Financial Aid PROFILE · state aid form. Hampden-Sydney College participates in the Federal Work Study program. *Need-based aid programs include:* scholarships and grants · general need-based awards · Federal Pell grants · state scholarships and grants · college-based scholarships and grants · private scholarships and grants. *Non-Need-based aid programs include:* scholarships and grants · general need-based awards · state scholarships and grants · special achievements and activities awards · ROTC scholarships.

HAMPTON UNIVERSITY

Tyler Street, Hampton, VA 23668
Admissions: 800-624-3328 · Financial Aid: 800-624-3341
Email: admissions@hamptonu.edu
Website: http://www.hamptonu.edu

From the College

"Hampton University is a comprehensive institution of higher education, dedicated to the promotion of learning, building of character and preparation of promising students for positions of leadership and service. Its curricular emphasis is scientific and professional, with a strong liberal arts undergirding. In carrying out its mission, the university requires that everything that it does be done of highest quality."

Campus Setting

Hampton, founded in 1868, is a historically black, private, liberal arts university. Programs are offered through the Schools of Business, Engineering and Technology, Liberal Arts and Education, Nursing, Pharmacy and Science, and through the College of Continuing Education and the Graduate College. Its 285-acre campus, including buildings listed with the National Register of Historic Places, is located within 40 miles of Jamestown, Yorktown, and Williamsburg. A four-year private institution, Hampton University has 6,152 students. In addition to a large, well-stocked library, the campus facilities include: museum · chapel. Hampton University provides on-campus housing with 19 units that can accommodate 3,080 students. Housing options: women's dorms · men's dorms. Recreation and sports facilities include a gymnasium.

Student Life and Activities

With 68 percent of students living on campus, there are plenty of social activities. The social and cultural atmosphere of the Hampton University community is one characterized by African American unity. In addition, Hampton encourages academic as well as social development and the importance of reaching out to the community surrounding the campus. On campus, students gather at the student union and the library; off campus, Ogden Circle and Hampden Harbor are popular hangouts. Popular annual events include Homecoming, the Black Family Conference, the Mass Media Arts Symposium and Career Day. Hampton University has 85 official student organizations. Student Government Association, Student Christian Association and the Greek community are among the groups that have a widespread influence on campus life. For those interested in sports, there are intramural teams such as: basketball. Hampton University is a member of the Mid-Eastern Athletic Conference (Division I, Football I-AA).

Academics and Learning Environment

For the B student, the learning environment of a college is just as important as the quality of its academic program. Hampton University offers a student-to-faculty ratio of 16:1. The most com-

HAMPTON UNIVERSITY

Admissions
Applicants: 5,401
Accepted: 2,433
Acceptance rate: 45.0%
Average GPA: 3.2
ACT range: 17-26
SAT Math range: 464-606
SAT Reading range: 481-552
SAT Writing range: Not reported
Top 10% of class: 20%
Top 25% of class: 45%
Top 50% of class: 90%

Deadlines
Early Action:
Early Decision: No
Regular Action: Rolling admissions
Common Application: Accepted

Financial Aid
In-state tuition: $15,464
Room: -
Board: -
Books: -
Freshmen receiving need-based aid: 96%
Undergrads receiving need-based aid: 44%
Avg. % of need met by financial aid: 28%
Avg. aid package (freshmen): $20,146
Avg. aid package (undergrads): $20,146
Freshmen receiving merit-based aid: 8%
Undergrads receiving merit-based aid: 8%
Avg. student debt upon graduation: $17,125

School Spirit
Mascot: Pirates
Colors: Royal blue and white

mon course size is 20 to 29 students. Hampton University offers 74 majors with the most popular being biology, psychology and management. The school has a general core requirement. Cooperative education is available. All first-year students must maintain a 2.0 GPA or higher to avoid academic probation, and a minimum overall GPA of 2.0 is required to graduate. Other special academic programs that would appeal to a B student: independent study · double majors · dual degrees · accelerated study · honors program · internships · distance learning.

B Student Support and Success

Student Support Services is a federally funded program that, like many others, helps to support students as long as they meet one or more of three criteria: 1) come from a family where neither parent has a college degree, 2) come from a low-income family or 3) have a documented learning or physical disability. This program provides educational support service through counseling, tutoring and educational and career seminars. The overall goal is to develop and implement educational services and activities that will motivate and assist students toward the achievement of their academic, career, social and personal goals.

Hampton University provides a variety of support programs including dedicated guidance for: academic · career · personal · military · veterans · non-traditional students · religious. Recognizing that some students may need extra preparation, Hampton University offers remedial and refresher courses in: reading · writing · math · study skills. Annually, 85 percent of freshmen students return for their sophomore year. Among students who enter the work force, approximately 44 percent enter a field related to their major within six months of graduation. Companies that most frequently hire graduates from Hampton University include: Johnson and Johnson · Daimler Chrysler · Lockheed Martin.

Support for Students with Learning Disabilities

Students with learning disabilities may take advantage of specific support programs offered by Hampton University. Also, a lightened course load may be granted to LD students. Students with learning disabilities will find the following programs at Hampton University extremely useful: remedial math · remedial English · remedial reading · tutors · untimed tests · extended time for tests · oral tests · readers · note-taking services · tape recorders. An advisor/advocate from the LD program is available to students.

How to Get Admitted

For admissions decisions, non-academic factors considered: extracurricular activities · special talents, interests, abilities · character/personal qualities · volunteer work · work experience · state of residency · alumni relationship. A high school diploma is required, although a GED is also accepted for admissions consideration. SAT or ACT test scores are required of all applicants. *According to the admissions office:* Minimum ACT scores of 20 in both English and math (minimum combined SAT Reasoning score of 920), rank in top half of secondary school class, and minimum 2.0 GPA required. *Academic units recommended:* 2 Foreign Language.

How to Pay for College

To apply for financial aid, students should submit the following: Free Application for Federal Student Aid (FAFSA). Hampton University participates in the Federal Work Study program. *Need-based aid programs include:* scholarships and grants · general need-based awards · Federal Pell grants · state scholarships and grants · college-based scholarships and grants · private scholarships and grants. *Non-Need-based aid programs include:* scholarships and grants · state scholarships and grants · athletic scholarships · ROTC scholarships.

Students
Total enrollment: 569
Undergrads: Not reported
Freshmen: Not reported
Male/Female: 56%/44%
Live on-campus: 0%

Academics
Student/faculty ratio: 9:1
Class size 9 or fewer: 26%
Class size 10-29: 51%
Class size 30-49: 18%
Class size 50-99: 4%
Class size 100 or more: 1%
Returning freshmen: Not reported
Six-year graduation rate: Not reported

Admissions
Average GPA: Not reported
ACT range: Not reported
SAT Math range: Not reported
SAT Reading range: Not reported
SAT Writing range: Not reported

Deadlines
Early Action: No
Early Decision: No
Regular Action: Common Application: Not
    accepted

Financial Aid
In-state tuition: $14,750
Out-of-state tuition: $14,750
Room: -
Board: -
Books: $2,200
Avg. % of need met by financial aid: Not
    reported
Avg. aid package (freshmen): Not re-
    ported
Avg. aid package (undergrads): Not
    reported

HARRISBURG UNIVERSITY OF SCIENCE AND TECHNOLOGY

326 Market Street, Harrisburg, PA 17101, Harrisburg, PA 17101
Admissions: 717-901-5152 · Financial Aid: 717-901-5115
Email: admissions@harrisburgu.net
Website: http://www.harrisburgu.net

Campus Setting

A four-year, private (for-profit) institution, Harrisburg University of Science and Technology has an enrollment of 569 students. It does not have on-campus housing for students.

Student Life and Activities

All students live off campus. Nevertheless, like any college, students find time to create their own recreational outlets.

Academics and Learning Environment

For the B student, the learning environment of a college is just as important as the quality of its academic program. Harrisburg University of Science and Technology has a student-to-faculty ratio of 9:1. It offers majors in biotechnology, integrative sciences, computer and information services, management and eBusiness and geography and geospatial imaging. The school does not have a general core requirement. Cooperative education is not offered.

B Student Support and Success

Harrisburg University offers a small-school setting, which makes it is easy to get one-on-one attention for any academic needs. The school emphasizes connecting school with work through their Business Mentor Program. During the first semester, students are paired with a business mentor in their field of study. They also offer internships and projects and a corporate faculty.

How to Get Admitted

For admissions decisions, non-academic factors considered: interview · extracurricular activities · special talents, interests, abilities · character/personal qualities · volunteer work · work experience · geographical location · religious affiliation/commitment · minority affiliation · alumni relationship. A high school diploma is for admissions consideration. SAT or ACT test scores are recommended.

How to Pay for College

To apply for financial aid, students should submit the following: Free Application for Federal Student Aid (FAFSA). Harrisburg University of Science and Technology does not participate in the Federal Work Study program. *Need-based aid programs include:* scholarships and grants · general need-based awards · Federal Pell grants · state scholarships and grants · college-based scholarships and grants · private scholarships and grants. *Non-Need-based aid programs include:* scholarships and grants · state scholarships and grants.

HARTWICK COLLEGE

1 Hartwick Drive, Oneonta, NY 13820-4020
Admissions: 888-HARTWICK · Financial Aid: 888-HARTWICK
Email: admissions@hartwick.edu · Website: http://www.hartwick.edu

From the College

"As a small, private, liberal arts college, Hartwick College focuses on fostering collaborative student-faculty relationships: Our faculty bring the latest insights from the world into the classroom to deepen student learning. The college's setting upon a hill overlooking Oneonta, New York, features the close relationships expected from a college of 1,480 students with a student-to-faculty ratio of 11:1.

"Our Connecting the Classroom to the World philosophy puts an emphasis on experiential learning so that students are prepared to continuously shape and reshape their future. When our students study abroad, complete an internship, collaborate with a professor on a research project or work in the local community, their learning translates into an education that changes lives. More than 60 percent of Hartwick students gain first-hand experience either studying off-campus or completing an internship. Hartwick faculty lead off-campus programs all over the world during our January Term, which allows students to broaden their horizons. Our academic calendar, centered on the four-week January Term, not only enables students to travel the world, but also offers opportunities to undertake a topic-focused class, do an internship, perform directed research or complete a senior capstone project.

"Our nearby Pine Lake Environmental Campus has also provided residential and curricular opportunities for students to investigate the importance of sustainability since 1972. The entire Hartwick community from academic to residential life and athletics now embraces a longstanding commitment to experiential learning through our Connecting the Classroom to the World approach to a liberal arts education."

Campus Setting

Hartwick, founded in 1797, has a 425-acre campus is located in Oneonta, 75 miles from Albany. In addition to a large, well-stocked library, the campus also has an art and culture museum. Hartwick College provides on-campus housing with 16 units that can accommodate 1,300 students. Housing options: co-ed dorms · sorority housing · fraternity housing · single-student apartments. Recreation and sports facilities include: grass and turf fields · gymnasium · racquetball and squash courts · stable (off-campus) · stadium · swimming pool · fitness room.

Student Life and Activities

With 85 percent of students living on campus, there are plenty of social activities. Popular gathering spots include the Dewar Student Union and the Yager Hall foyer by the entrance to the library. Popular campus events include Taste of Hartwick, Holiday Ball, Time to Unwind during Exam Week, Habitat for Humanity Spring Break Challenge, OH Fest-Oneonta State/Hartwick concert and fair, Last Day of Clash Bash, Midnight Madness and Breakfast of Champions. Hartwick College has 70 official student organizations. The most popular are: BiGala+ · International Club · Circle K · SOSU/BU · Pluralism Associates League for Students · Women's Center. For those interested in sports, there are intramural teams such as: basketball · dodgeball · flag football · volleyball · soccer · softball. Hartwick College is a member of the Mid-American Conference (Division I for soccer), Collegiate Water Polo Association (Division I), Empire Eight (Division III).

HARTWICK COLLEGE

Hartwick College
Oneonta, NY (Pop. 14,000)
Location: Small town
Website: http://www.hartwick.edu

Students
Total enrollment: 1,493
Undergrads: 642
Freshmen: 446
Part-time students: 4%
From out-of-state: 34%
Male/Female: 43%/57%
Live on-campus: 85%
In fraternities: 5%
In sororities: 4%
Off-campus employment rating: Fair
Caucasian: 61%
African American: 4%
Hispanic: 4%
Asian or Pacific Islander: 2%
Native American: 0%
International: 4%

Academics
Student/faculty ratio: 11:1
Class size 9 or fewer: 23%
Class size 10-29: 69%
Class size 30-49: 8%
Class size 50-99: -
Class size 100 or more: -
Returning freshmen: 70%
Six-year graduation rate: 57%

Most Popular Fields of Study
Business, Finance, Sales and Marketing
Biological and Life Sciences

Academics and Learning Environment

For the B student, the learning environment of a college is just as important as the quality of its academic program. Hartwick College has 181 full-time and 87 part-time faculty members, offering a student-to-faculty ratio of 11:1. The most common course size is 10 to 19 students. Hartwick College offers 35 majors with the most popular being business, English and political science and least popular being physics, French and German. The school has a general core requirement. Cooperative education is available. All first-year students must maintain a 2.0 GPA or higher to avoid academic probation. Other special academic programs that would appeal to a B student: self-designed majors · independent study · double majors · dual degrees · accelerated study · honors program · internships.

B Student Support and Success

Hartwick's Academic Center for Excellence assigns each incoming student to a professional advisor. Together they discuss academic progress and course selection. Other ACE staff members are available to advise students in related areas such as schedule changes and degree planning. Tutoring is available in most subject areas simply by filling out a request form. Supplemental instructors also help with courses that are considered especially challenging. They organize group tutoring sessions and work one on one inside the classroom. If a student's overall GPA falls below 2.0, he/she must sign a probationary agreement. All students on probation are to be involved in one of three programs: Close Scrutiny (a weekly one on one with a professional staff member); College Success (a small group weekly meeting to discuss issues of concern and develop strategies for academic success); or regular meetings with professional staff (to ensure students are staying on track).

Hartwick College provides a variety of support programs including dedicated guidance for: academic · career · personal · psychological · family planning. Annually, 70 percent of freshmen students return for their sophomore year.

Support for Students with Learning Disabilities

Students with learning disabilities may take advantage of specific support programs offered by Hartwick College. If necessary, the college will grant additional time to students with learning disabilities to complete their degree. Also, a lightened course load may be granted to LD students. High school foreign language waivers are accepted. High school math waivers are also accepted. According to the school, all applicants are encouraged to visit campus and meet with a counselor. If the student self-identifies and requests assistance, the office of disability services will meet individually with the student to discuss available services and academic support. Students with learning disabilities will find the following programs at Hartwick College extremely useful: tutors · learning center · extended time for tests · readers · typist/scribe · note-taking services · tape recorders. Individual or small group tutorials are also available in: time management · organizational skills · learning strategies · specific subject areas · writing labs · study skills. An advisor/advocate from the Office of Disability Services is available to students.

How to Get Admitted

For admissions decisions, non-academic factors considered: interview · extracurricular activities · special talents, interests, abilities · character/personal qualities · volunteer work · work experience · geographical location · alumni relationship. A high school diploma is required, although a GED is also accepted for admissions consideration. SAT or ACT test scores are required for some applicants. SAT Subject Test scores are considered, if submitted, but are not required. *According to the admissions office:* Grades, strength of curriculum, and rank in class are all considered. *Academic units recommended:* 4 English, 3 Math, 3 Science, 2 Social Studies, 3 Foreign Language.

How to Pay for College

To apply for financial aid, students should submit the following: Free Application for Federal Student Aid (FAFSA) · institution's own financial aid forms · CSS/Financial Aid PROFILE · state aid form. Hartwick College participates in the Federal Work Study program. *Need-based aid programs include:* scholarships and grants · general need-based awards · Federal Pell grants · state scholarships and grants · college-based scholarships and grants · private scholarships and grants. *Non-Need-based aid programs include:* scholarships and grants · state scholarships and grants · creative arts and performance awards · special achievements and activities awards · athletic scholarships.

HARTWICK COLLEGE

Highlights

Admissions
Applicants: 2,532
Accepted: 2,101
Acceptance rate: 83.0%
placed on wait list: 199
Average GPA: 86.3
ACT range: 22-26
SAT Math range: 500-500
SAT Reading range: 490-590
SAT Writing range: 480-580
Top 10% of class: 17%
Top 25% of class: 46%
Top 50% of class: 80%

Deadlines
Early Action: No
Early Decision: November 15, January 15
Regular Action: February 15 (priority)
February 15 (final)
Common Application: Accepted

Financial Aid
In-state tuition: $32,550
Out-of-state tuition: $32,550
Room: $4,700
Board: $4,375
Books: $700
Freshmen receiving need-based aid: 74%
Undergrads receiving need-based aid: 73%
Avg. % of need met by financial aid: 78%
Avg. aid package (freshmen): $24,857
Avg. aid package (undergrads): $22,955
Freshmen receiving merit-based aid: 24%
Undergrads receiving merit-based aid: 25%
Avg. student debt upon graduation: $30,802

Prominent Alumni
Scott Adams, creator of Dilbert comic strip; John Johnstone, CEO of Olin Corporation; Cyrus Mehri, founding partner of the law firm Mehri & Skalet

School Spirit
Mascot: Hawks
Colors: Blue and white

HIGH POINT UNIVERSITY

833 Montlieu Avenue, High Point, NC 27262-3598
Admissions: 800-345-6993 · Financial Aid: 336-841-9128
Email: admiss@highpoint.edu · Website: http://www.highpoint.edu

From the College

"Situated on 135 acres in the heart of North Carolina's Piedmont Triad, High Point University combines the warmth and intimacy of a small liberal arts college with the academic offerings and amenities of a large state university. With nearly 3,000 students representing 41 states and 50 countries, the High Point University student body is both diverse and dynamic. Most classes have enrollments of less than 20, allowing students to interact with instructors who are well-trained career teachers, not graduate assistants. Students may earn academic credit by participating in internships or by traveling abroad and studying in such locations as England, Mexico, Scotland and China. High Point University also offers 14 NCAA Division I athletic programs and numerous extracurricular opportunities, and is one of only 100 colleges and universities nationwide to be named to the Templeton Foundation's Honor Roll for Character-Building Colleges."

Campus Setting

The campus is open and spacious, and the cities of High Point, Greensboro and Winston-Salem form the Piedmont Triad, a metropolitan area with a population of 1.9 million. The university is located within twenty minutes of the Piedmont Triad International Airport. Fourteen colleges and universities are found within a 60-mile radius, including Duke, the University of North Carolina at Chapel Hill and Wake Forest. High Point University is a four-year, co-educational, liberal arts university related to the United Methodist Church. It offers 50 majors in a traditional day format. It also offers non-traditional evening programs and five master's programs. A private institution, High Point University has an enrollment of 3,064 students. In addition to a large, well-stocked library, the campus facilities include: gallery · fine arts center · athletic/convocation center. High Point University provides on-campus housing with 700 units that can accommodate 1,515 students. Housing options: co-ed dorms · women's dorms · men's dorms · sorority housing · fraternity housing · single-student apartments. Recreation and sports facilities include: baseball and soccer fields · stadium.

Student Life and Activities

With 70 percent of students living on campus, there are plenty of social activities. Popular events include: New Student Orientation, Homecoming, Snow Ball Dance, Spring Fling, Greek Week, Campus Life Award Ceremony, Derby Day and Panther Palooza. High Point University has 109 official student organizations. The most popular are: Community Affairs Board · University Singers · American Humanics · Craven Investment Club · Interior Design Club · Panhellenic Council · Intrafraternity Council · Pre-Law Club · Judicial Board · Psychology Club · Student Senate · Student Activities Board · Art League · Cabaret · Spotlight Players · Wind Ensemble · Tower Players. For those interested in sports, there are intramural teams such as: basketball · flag football · soccer · ultimate Frisbee · volleyball. High Point University is a member of the Big South Conference (Division I).

Academics and Learning Environment

For the B student, the learning environment of a college is just as important as the quality of its academic program. High Point University has 129 full-time and 137 part-time faculty members, offering a student-to-faculty ratio of 14:1. The most common course size is 10 to 19 students. High Point University offers 56 majors with the most popular being business administration/economics, computer information systems and elementary education. The school has a general core requirement as well as a religion requirement Cooperative education is not offered. All first-year students must maintain a 2.0 GPA or higher to avoid academic probation. Other special academic programs that would appeal to a B student: self-designed majors · pass/fail grading option · independent study · double majors · dual degrees · honors program · internships · distance learning.

B Student Support and Success

The Academic Services Center at High Point "strives to foster the academic growth and development" of its students, according to its website. Tutoring is available at no charge year round. Walk-in tutoring promotes group tutoring, while individual tutoring can be scheduled with a simple request form. In addition, supplemental instruction puts a tutor in classrooms to listen and take notes and then help students with those classes. For communication classes, Writing Fellows review students' essays to help them improve their work.

High Point University provides a variety of support programs including dedicated guidance for: academic · career · personal · psychological · minority students · military · veterans · non-traditional students · family planning · religious. Recognizing that some students may need extra preparation, High Point University offers remedial and refresher courses in: reading · writing · math · study skills. The average freshman year GPA is 2.8, and 79 percent of freshmen students return for their sophomore year. Among students who enter the work force, approximately 80 percent enter a field related to their major within six months of graduation. Companies that most frequently hire graduates from High Point University include: Bank of America · United Airlines · Wachovia · Barnes and Nobles · BB&T · BellSouth · CIGNA Government Services · Citi Group · Coca-Cola Consolidated · MassMutual Financial Group · Novant Health.

Support for Students with Learning Disabilities

Students with learning disabilities may take advantage of specific support programs offered by High Point University. If necessary, the college will grant additional time to students with learning disabilities to complete their degree. Also, a lightened course load may be granted to LD students. Credit is given for remedial courses taken. High school foreign language waivers are accepted. High school math waivers are also accepted. According to the school, the program remains flexible to meet the needs of students with all types of disabilities. Audio textbooks conversion completed on campus. Students may meet individually with the program director to address areas not covered by their disability accommodations (self-advocacy, study and social skills, campus involvement, etc.). Student employment opportunities are available. Students with learning disabilities will find the following programs at High Point University extremely useful: remedial math · remedial English · remedial reading · tutors · learning center · testing accommodations ·

HIGH POINT UNIVERSITY

Highlights

High Point University
High Point, NC (Pop. 95,000)
Location: Medium city
Website: http://www.highpoint.edu

Students
Total enrollment: 3,064
Undergrads: 1,054
Freshmen: 890
Part-time students: 10%
From out-of-state: 70%
Male/Female: 38%/62%
Live on-campus: 70%
In fraternities: 15%
In sororities: 25%
Off-campus employment rating: Good
Caucasian: 71%
African American: 20%
Hispanic: 2%
Asian or Pacific Islander: 3%
Native American: 0%
International: 3%

Academics
Student/faculty ratio: 14:1
Class size 9 or fewer: 39%
Class size 10-29: 57%
Class size 30-49: 3%
Class size 50-99: 5%
Class size 100 or more: -
Returning freshmen: 79%
Six-year graduation rate: 56%

Most Popular Fields of Study
Business, Finance, Sales and Marketing
Biological and Life Sciences
Protective Services, Criminal Justice and
    Public Administration
Visual and Performing Arts
English and Literature
Computer and Information Sciences
Mathematics
Health Professions, Medicine and Related
    Sciences
Foreign Languages, Literature and Linguistics

HIGH POINT UNIVERSITY

Admissions
Applicants: 2,546
Accepted: 1,857
Acceptance rate: 72.9%
Average GPA: 3.2
ACT range: 19-24
SAT Math range: 460-570
SAT Reading range: 460-570
SAT Writing range: Not reported
Top 10% of class: 17%
Top 25% of class: 38%
Top 50% of class: 71%

Deadlines
Early Action: November 17
Early Decision: November 7
Regular Action: Rolling admissions
Common Application: Accepted

Financial Aid
Room: -
Board: -
Books: $1,200
Freshmen receiving need-based aid: 62%
Undergrads receiving need-based aid: 55%
Avg. % of need met by financial aid: 74%
Avg. aid package (freshmen): $13,567
Avg. aid package (undergrads): $15,675
Freshmen receiving merit-based aid: 5%
Undergrads receiving merit-based aid: 9%
Avg. student debt upon graduation: $16,871

Prominent Alumni
Tubby Smith, Kentucky basketball coach; James Doolittle, Time-Warner Cable (CEO emeritus); Dr. Nido R. Qubein, motivational speaker, businessman, university president

School Spirit
Mascot: Panthers
Colors: Purple and white

extended time for tests · take-home exam · oral tests · exam on tape or computer · readers · typist/scribe · note-taking services · reading machines · tape recorders · priority registration · priority seating. Individual or small group tutorials are also available in: time management · organizational skills · learning strategies · specific subject areas · writing labs · math labs · study skills. An advisor/advocate from the Academic Services Center is available to students. This member also sits on the admissions committee.

How to Get Admitted

For admissions decisions, non-academic factors considered: interview · extracurricular activities · special talents, interests, abilities · character/personal qualities · volunteer work · work experience · state of residency. A high school diploma is required, although a GED is also accepted for admissions consideration. SAT or ACT test scores are required of all applicants. SAT Subject Test scores are not required. *According to the admissions office:* Minimum combined SAT score of 820, rank in top half of secondary class, and minimum 2.0 GPA in college-preparatory courses recommended.

How to Pay for College

To apply for financial aid, students should submit the following: Free Application for Federal Student Aid (FAFSA). High Point University participates in the Federal Work Study program. *Need-based aid programs include:* scholarships and grants · general need-based awards · Federal Pell grants · state scholarships and grants · college-based scholarships and grants · private scholarships and grants. *Non-Need-based aid programs include:* scholarships and grants · general need-based awards · state scholarships and grants · creative arts and performance awards · athletic scholarships.

HILBERT COLLEGE

5200 South Park Avenue, Hamburg, NY 14075-1597
Admissions: 800-649-8003 · Financial Aid: 716-649-7900
Email: admissions@hilbert.edu · Website: http://www.hilbert.edu

From the College

"A private, four-year institution in the Catholic, Franciscan tradition, Hilbert encourages personal and organizational change through vision and hope, and creates a meaningful undergraduate educational experience based in the liberal arts. Hilbert's challenging academic programs are taught by professors who bring in-depth theoretical and practical experience to the classroom, which is balanced with student internship opportunities. New academic concentrations have been added in family violence, forensic investigation, rehabilitation services and sports management. Known for its law and justice programs, Hilbert's new economic crime investigation lab is one of only a few computer crime and forensic training labs for undergraduates in the country to give students hands-on training in the field."

Campus Setting

Founded in 1957, it adopted co-education in 1969. Its 49-acre campus is located in the town of Hamburg, 10 miles from Buffalo. Hilbert College has an enrollment of 997 students. The school is also affiliated with the Franciscans. In addition to a small library, the campus also has a legal research lab. Hilbert College provides on-campus housing with 116 units that can accommodate 166 students. Housing options: co-ed dorms · single-student apartments.

Student Life and Activities

Popular gathering spots include the campus center pool room, the commuter locker room and the campus pond. Social events include Wellness Week, Parent's Weekend Homecoming, Halloween Dance and Medieval Dinner. Hilbert College has 20 official student organizations. Student Government, C.I.B. (Color is Blind) and the Wellness Club influence student life. Hilbert College is a member of the Allegheny Mountain Collegiate Conference (Division III), ECAC (Division I, Football I-AA) and North Eastern Collegiate Volleyball Association (Division III).

Academics and Learning Environment

For the B student, the learning environment of a college is just as important as the quality of its academic program. Hilbert College has 46 full-time and 68 part-time faculty members, offering a student-to-faculty ratio of 14:1. Hilbert College offers 21 majors with the most popular being criminal justice, business administration and paralegal studies and least popular being liberal studies, accounting and English. The school has a general core requirement. Cooperative education is not offered. All first-year students must maintain a 1.74 GPA or higher to avoid academic probation, and a minimum overall GPA of 2.0 is required to graduate. Other special academic programs that would appeal to a B student: independent study · double majors · honors program · internships · distance learning.

B Student Support and Success

Hilbert College provides a variety of support programs including dedicated guidance for: academic · career · personal · minority students · veterans · non-traditional students · religious. Recognizing that some students may need extra preparation, Hilbert College offers remedial and refresher courses in: reading · writing · math · study skills. The average freshman year GPA is 2.4, and What do students do after college? While

HILBERT COLLEGE

Hilbert College
Hamburg, NY
Location: Large town
Website: http://www.hilbert.edu

Students
Total enrollment: 997
Undergrads: 380
Freshmen: 449
Part-time students: 29%
From out-of-state: 3%
Male/Female: 38%/62%
Live on-campus: Not reported
Off-campus employment rating: Good

Academics
Student/faculty ratio: 14:1
Class size 9 or fewer: 39%
Class size 10-29: 57%
Class size 30-49: 3%
Class size 50-99: 5%
Class size 100 or more: -
Returning freshmen: Not reported
Six-year graduation rate: Not reported

Most Popular Fields of Study
Business, Finance, Sales and Marketing

Admissions
Applicants: 941
Accepted: 827
Acceptance rate: 87.9%
Average GPA: 83.0
ACT range: Not reported
SAT Math range: Not reported
SAT Reading range: Not reported
SAT Writing range: Not reported
Top 10% of class: 4%
Top 25% of class: 14%
Top 50% of class: 45%

many enter the work force, approximately 17 percent pursue a graduate degree immediately after graduation. Among students who enter the work force, approximately 70 percent enter a field related to their major within six months of graduation, while 75 percent enter a related career within two years of graduation. Companies that most frequently hire graduates from Hilbert College include: Federal government agencies (U.S. Customs · INS · Border Patrol · FBI · Secret Service); local and state government courts and police agencies; M&T Bank; HSBC · Fleet Bank · National Fuel · Fisher-Price · Carlton Technologies and other businesses · numerous law firms and human services agencies.

Support for Students with Learning Disabilities

Students with learning disabilities may take advantage of specific support programs offered by Hilbert College. If necessary, the college will grant additional time to students with learning disabilities to complete their degree. Also, a lightened course load may be granted to LD students. According to the school, Hilbert does not have a separate program for students with learning disabilities. All students with disabilities who have self-identified and requested academic accommodations receive services through the Department of Academic Services. To be eligible, students need to provide official documentation supporting their request for services. Students with learning disabilities will find the following programs at Hilbert College extremely useful: remedial math · remedial English · tutors · extended time for tests · oral tests · readers · note-taking services · tape recorders. Individual or small group tutorials are also available in: time management · organizational skills · learning strategies · specific subject areas · writing labs · math labs · study skills. An advisor/advocate from the LD program is available to students.

How to Get Admitted

For admissions decisions, non-academic factors considered: interview · extracurricular activities · special talents, interests, abilities · character/personal qualities · volunteer work · work experience · state of residency. A high school diploma is required, although a GED is also accepted for admissions consideration. SAT or ACT test scores are recommended but not required. SAT Subject Test scores are not required. *According to the admissions office:* Minimum 2.0 GPA required. *Academic units recommended:* 4 English, 3 Math, 3 Science, 3 Social Studies, 1 Foreign Language.

Insight

Paula Witherell, public relations director, says that Hilbert offers a supportive campus where every student matters. Its philosophy is that since it was founded by the Franciscan Sisters of St. Joseph congregation, it "embraces the values of St. Francis of Assisi: respect, service, hope, vision, joy, integrity, compassion and peace."

252

America's
Best Colleges for
B Students

How to Pay for College

To apply for financial aid, students should submit the following: Free Application for Federal Student Aid (FAFSA). Hilbert College participates in the Federal Work Study program. *Need-based aid programs include:* scholarships and grants · general need-based awards · Federal Pell grants · state scholarships and grants · college-based scholarships and grants · private scholarships and grants. *Non-Need-based aid programs include:* scholarships and grants · state scholarships and grants.

HILBERT COLLEGE

Highlights

Deadlines
Early Action: No
Early Decision: No
Regular Action: Rolling admissions
Common Application: Not accepted

Financial Aid
In-state tuition: $17,950
Out-of-state tuition: $17,950
Room: -
Board: -
Books: -
Avg. % of need met by financial aid: Not reported
Avg. aid package (freshmen): Not reported
Avg. aid package (undergrads): Not reported
Avg. student debt upon graduation: Not reported

School Spirit
Mascot: Hawks

HIRAM COLLEGE

P.O. Box 67, Hiram, OH 44234
Admissions: 800-362-5280 · Financial Aid: 330-569-5107
Email: admission@hiram.edu
Website: http://www.hiram.edu

Hiram College
Hiram, OH (Pop. 1,500)
Location: Rural
Website: http://www.hiram.edu

Students
Total enrollment: 1,357
Undergrads: 611
Freshmen: 369
Part-time students: 14%
From out-of-state: 26%
Male/Female: 46%/54%
Live on-campus: 94%
Off-campus employment rating: Good

Academics
Student/faculty ratio: 12:1
Class size 9 or fewer: 39%
Class size 10-29: 57%
Class size 30-49: 3%
Class size 50-99: 5%
Class size 100 or more: -
Returning freshmen: 80%
Six-year graduation rate: 62%

Most Popular Fields of Study
Business, Finance, Sales and Marketing
Biological and Life Sciences
English and Literature
Philosophy, Religion and Theology
Computer and Information Sciences
Psychology
Interdisciplinary Studies
Health Professions, Medicine and Related
    Sciences
Liberal Arts, Humanities and General
    Studies
Foreign Languages, Literature and Lin-
    guistics

From the College

"Hiram College offers distinctive programs. About half of Hiram's students study abroad at some point during their four years. Recently, a group of 17 students led by two faculty members traveled around the world to study climate change, stopping in nine different locations. Common study abroad destinations include France, China, Mexico, Guatemala, Costa Rica, the Galapagos Islands and several African countries. Because Hiram students receive credits for the courses taught by Hiram faculty on these trips, studying abroad will not impede progress in their majors or delay graduation. Another unique aspect of a Hiram education is our academic calendar, known as the Hiram Plan. Our semesters are divided into 12-week and 3-week periods. Students usually enroll in three courses during each 12-week period, and one intensive course during the 3-week period. Many students spend the 3-week on study abroad trips or taking unusual courses not typically offered during the 12-week period. Our small classes encourage interaction between students and their professors. Students can work with professors on original research projects and often participate in musical groups and intramural sports teams alongside faculty members."

Campus Setting

Hiram College, founded in 1850, is a private, residential, liberal arts college located in Hiram, Ohio, southeast of Cleveland. A private institution, Hiram College has an enrollment of 1,357 students. The school is also affiliated with the Christian Church (Disciples of Christ). The school has a library with 516,297 books. Housing options: co-ed dorms · women's dorms · special housing for disabled students.

Student Life and Activities

With 94 percent of students living on campus, there are plenty of social activities. Popular events include Celebrating Excellence at Hiram and Education that Works Conference. Hiram College has a number of official student organizations. The most popular are: Chemistry club · education club · investment club · marching band · chamber orchestra · jazz ensemble · Democratic club · Republican club · students against social injustice · Hiram Christian outreach · Newman club · dance team. Hiram College is a member of the North Coast Athletic Conference (Division III).

Academics and Learning Environment

For the B student, the learning environment of a college is just as important as the quality of its academic program. Hiram College has 74 full-time and 110 part-time faculty members, offering a student-to-faculty ratio of 12:1. Hiram College offers 33 majors with the most popular being biology, management and biomedical humanities. The school has a general core requirement. Cooperative education is not offered. All first-year students must maintain a 2.0 GPA or higher to avoid academic probation. Other special academic programs that would appeal to a B student: self-designed majors · pass/fail grading option · independent study · double majors · dual degrees · accelerated study · Phi Beta Kappa · internships · weekend college.

B Student Support and Success

Hiram offers hands-on experiences in academics as well as off-campus study programs. Student Academic Services provides a variety of assistance programs including online time management tips and free peer tutoring with fellow students who excel in the class the student finds to be a challenge.

The Writing Center offers information, services and programs to help students write more efficiently and effectively, as well as to foster a love and respect for language. Trained writing assistants are available by appointment. Along with these services, the college provides test-taking tips.

Hiram College provides a variety of support programs including dedicated guidance for: academic · career · personal · psychological · minority students · veterans · non-traditional students · family planning · religious. Annually, 80 percent of freshmen students return for their sophomore year. What do students do after college? While many enter the work force, approximately 20 percent pursue a graduate degree immediately after graduation, and 40 percent enter graduate school within two years. Among students who enter the work force, approximately 50 percent enter a field related to their major within six months of graduation, while 75 percent enter a related career within two years of graduation. Companies that most frequently hire graduates from Hiram College include: Case Western Reserve Medical Research Laboratories · Progressive Insurance · KeyLink · Berea Childrens' Home · Enterprise · Penske.

Support for Students with Learning Disabilities

Students with learning disabilities may take advantage of specific support programs offered by Hiram College. Students with learning disabilities will find the following programs at Hiram College extremely useful: tutors · testing accommodations · extended time for tests · take-home exam · oral tests · note-taking services · early syllabus. Individual or small group tutorials are also available in: time management · organizational skills · learning strategies · specific subject areas · writing labs · math labs · study skills. An advisor/advocate from the LD program is available to students.

How to Get Admitted

For admissions decisions, non-academic factors considered: interview · extracurricular activities · special talents, interests, abilities · character/personal qualities · volunteer work · state of residency · alumni relationship. A high school diploma is required, although a GED is also accepted for admissions consideration. SAT or ACT test scores are required of all applicants. *Academic units recommended:* 4 English, 4 Math, 3 Science, 2 Social Studies, 2 Foreign Language.

HIRAM COLLEGE

Highlights

Admissions
Applicants: 1,513
Accepted: 1,138
Acceptance rate: 75.2%
Average GPA: 3.3
ACT range: 20-25
SAT Math range: 470-590
SAT Reading range: 480-610
SAT Writing range: Not reported
Top 10% of class: 18%
Top 25% of class: 42%
Top 50% of class: 79%

Deadlines
Early Action: No
Early Decision: No
Regular Action: February 15 (priority)
April 15 (final)
Common Application: Accepted

Financial Aid
In-state tuition: $26,435
Out-of-state tuition: $26,435
Room: $4,400
Board: $4,610
Books: $0
Avg. % of need met by financial aid: Not reported
Avg. aid package (freshmen): Not reported
Avg. aid package (undergrads): Not reported
Avg. student debt upon graduation: $21,247

School Spirit
Mascot: Terriers

HIRAM COLLEGE

How to Pay for College

To apply for financial aid, students should submit the following: Free Application for Federal Student Aid (FAFSA). Hiram College participates in the Federal Work Study program. *Need-based aid programs include:* scholarships and grants · general need-based awards · Federal Pell grants · state scholarships and grants · college-based scholarships and grants · private scholarships and grants. *Non-Need-based aid programs include:* scholarships and grants · general need-based awards · state scholarships and grants · creative arts and performance awards · special achievements and activities awards · special characteristics awards.

HOLLINS UNIVERSITY

P.O. Box 9707, Roanoke, VA 24020
Admissions: 800-456-9595 · Financial Aid: 540-362-6332
Email: huadm@hollins.edu
Website: http://www.hollins.edu

From the College

"Founded in 1842, Hollins was the first chartered women's college in Virginia. Today it is a small university with an undergraduate program for women and an array of graduate programs for men and women. Some of Hollins' distinctions include a nationally ranked creative writing program, one of the oldest study abroad programs in the country and extensive opportunities for internships and faculty/student research. Through the university's Batten Leadership Institute, students can earn a certificate in leadership studies through a program that combines classes, skills-building groups and leadership projects on and off campus. Hollins' program of seminars for first-year students is designed to encourage creative problem solving and to introduce students to the university's collaborative learning environment."

Campus Setting

Hollins' 475-acre campus is located in Roanoke. A four-year, private, women's college, Hollins University has an enrollment of 1,058 students. In addition to a large, well-stocked library, the campus facilities include: visual arts center · museum · fitness center · equestrian center · science building · swim center · climbing wall. Hollins University provides on-campus housing with 448 units that can accommodate 725 students. Housing options: women's dorms · single-student apartments · special housing for disabled students · special housing for International students. Recreation and sports facilities include: aerobics studio · climbing wall · fields · gymnasium · riding ring · swimming pool · tennis court · weight room.

Student Life and Activities

With 89 percent of students living on campus, there are plenty of social activities. "Many students spend a majority of their time at other colleges," reports the editor of the student newspaper. "Most students road trip and participate in other school's activities." Popular on-campus gathering spots include the Moody Student Center, Front Quad and Tinker Beach. Off-campus, students gather at the Roanoke City Market and Grandin Village. Popular campus events include fall and spring theatre and dance productions, Ring Night, Fall Formal, Tinker Day, Spring Cotillion and MayFest. Hollins University has 40 official student organizations. Hollins Activities Board is an influential group on campus. For those interested in sports, there are intramural teams such as: outdoor program. Hollins University is a member of the Old Dominion Athletic Conference (Division III).

HOLLINS UNIVERSITY

Deadlines
Early Action: No
Early Decision: December 1
Regular Action: February 1 (priority)
Common Application: Accepted

Financial Aid
In-state tuition: $27,550
Out-of-state tuition: $27,550
Room: $5,965
Board: $4,075
Books: $1,000
Freshmen receiving need-based aid: 78%
Undergrads receiving need-based aid: 66%
Avg. % of need met by financial aid: 71%
Avg. aid package (freshmen): $24,419
Avg. aid package (undergrads): $21,407
Freshmen receiving merit-based aid: 25%
Undergrads receiving merit-based aid: 39%
Avg. student debt upon graduation: $22,161

Prominent Alumni
Annie Dillard, author and Pulitzer Prize winner; Ann Compton, ABC News Washington correspondent; Sally Mann, photographer.

School Spirit
Colors: Green and gold
Song: *The Green and the Gold*

Academics and Learning Environment

For the B student, the learning environment of a college is just as important as the quality of its academic program. Hollins University has 73 full-time and 35 part-time faculty members, offering a student-to-faculty ratio of 10:1. The most common course size is 10 to 19 students. Hollins University offers 34 majors with the most popular being English, business and studio art and least popular being economics, art history and chemistry. The school has a general core requirement. Cooperative education is not offered. All first-year students must maintain a 1.8 GPA or higher to avoid academic probation, and a minimum overall GPA of 2.0 is required to graduate. Other special academic programs that would appeal to a B student: self-designed majors · pass/fail grading option · independent study · double majors · dual degrees · accelerated study · honors program · Phi Beta Kappa · internships.

B Student Support and Success

While Hollins is listed as an all-women college, men do account for 4 percent of the student body. Help for students is available through the Center for Learning Excellence, which is made up of a Writing Center and a Quantitative Reasoning Center.

Hollins University provides a variety of support programs including dedicated guidance for: academic · career · personal · psychological · minority students · non-traditional students · family planning · religious. Recognizing that some students may need extra preparation, Hollins University offers remedial and refresher courses in: reading · writing · math · study skills. The average freshman year GPA is 3.0, and 74 percent of freshmen students return for their sophomore year.

Support for Students with Learning Disabilities

Students with learning disabilities may take advantage of specific support programs offered by Hollins University. If necessary, the college will grant additional time to students with learning disabilities to complete their degree. Also, a lightened course load may be granted to LD students. According to the school, a student requesting accommodation and support services needs to provide a diagnostic report that clearly identifies a learning disability based on testing and evaluation. Students with learning disabilities will find the following programs at Hollins University extremely useful: tutors · learning center · testing accommodations · untimed tests · extended time for tests · take-home exam · oral tests · readers · note-taking services · tape recorders · waiver of math degree requirement. Individual or small group tutorials are also available in: time management · organizational skills · learning strategies · specific subject areas · writing labs · math labs · study skills. An advisor/advocate from the Academic Services is available to students.

How to Get Admitted

For admissions decisions, non-academic factors considered: interview · extracurricular activities · special talents, interests, abilities · character/personal qualities · volunteer work · work experience · state of residency · alumni relationship. A high school diploma is required, although a GED is also accepted for admissions consideration. SAT or ACT test scores are required of all applicants. *According to the admissions office:* Minimum combined SAT Reasoning score of 1000, rank in top two-fifths of secondary school class, and minimum 3.0 GPA recommended.

How to Pay for College

To apply for financial aid, students should submit the following: Free Application for Federal Student Aid (FAFSA) · state aid form. Hollins University participates in the Federal Work Study program. *Need-based aid programs include:* scholarships and grants · general need-based awards · Federal Pell grants · state scholarships and grants · college-based scholarships and grants · private scholarships and grants. *Non-Need-based aid programs include:* scholarships and grants · general need-based awards · state scholarships and grants · creative arts and performance awards.

HOOD COLLEGE

401 Rosemont Avenue, Frederick, MD 21701
Admissions: 800-922-1599 · Financial Aid: 301-696-3411
Email: admissions@hood.edu · Website: http://www.hood.edu

From the College

"Hood College was founded in 1893, and is an independent, liberal arts college providing a residential experience for undergraduate women and men, and a professionally oriented graduate school. Located on 50 acres in the middle of historic Frederick, Maryland, and within an hour's drive of Washington, DC, and Baltimore, Hood is consistently ranked as one of the nation's best and most affordable colleges. In this closely-knit community, students and professors know each other by name. Hood maintains a vibrant community that responds to the intellectual, professional and personal goals of individual students of diverse races, ethnicities and ages. Stressing high-quality undergraduate research and internship opportunities, Hood provides a university-like education in a small college setting."

Campus Setting

A four-year institution, Hood College has an enrollment of 2,533 students. Hood College has been co-ed since 2003. In addition to a large, well-stocked library, the campus facilities include: observatory · child development laboratory school. Hood College provides on-campus housing with 380 units that can accommodate 663 students. Housing options: co-ed dorms · women's dorms · special housing for disabled students.

Student Life and Activities

With 54 percent of students living on campus, there are plenty of social activities. Popular gathering spots include the Whitaker Student Union on campus and Baker Park or Cunningham Falls off campus. Popular campus events include the Messiah performed by the Hood Choir, Policies for Dollars, Liberation of the Black Mind Weekend, May Madness Week, Crab Feast, Midnight Breakfast, Weekend Blockbuster Movies, Junior Ring Dinner, Strawberry Breakfast and Welcome Back Week featuring the Foam Bash. Hood College has 79 official student organizations. Popular groups on campus include the Student Government Association, the Campus Activities Board and the House Forum. For those interested in sports, there are intramural teams such as: basketball · billiards · football · soccer · table tennis · volleyball. Hood College is a member of the Capital Athletic Conference (Division III).

Academics and Learning Environment

For the B student, the learning environment of a college is just as important as the quality of its academic program. Hood College has 80 full-time and 180 part-time faculty members, offering a student-to-faculty ratio of 13:1. The most common course size is 10 to 19 students. Hood College offers 43 majors with the most popular being psychology, management and history and least popular being French/German, Latin American studies and religion. The school has a general core requirement. Cooperative education is not offered. All first-year students must maintain a 2.0 GPA or higher to avoid academic probation. Other special academic programs that would appeal to a B student: self-designed majors · pass/fail grading option · independent study · double majors · dual degrees · honors program · internships · certificate programs.

B Student Support and Success

Student-to-faculty ratios are 10:1 for undergrads. Class sizes are also small.

Academic Services focuses on helping students who are having trouble in specific courses as well as those who want to be more effective learners. Freshmen and sophomores are advised by a special group of faculty. Once a major is declared they are reassigned to an advisor in that subject.

Assessment of skills and knowledge is available through a Basic Skills Inventory. The results are studied so that students can be encouraged to take remedial courses before entering the college classroom. For example, should a student find that he/she would benefit from a review of math foundations before enrolling in a college math course, algebra review classes are available. In addition, classroom teaching, tutoring, videos, computer software and printed materials are provided. Individualized programs are also sometimes offered.

Hood College provides a variety of support programs including dedicated guidance for: academic · career · personal · psychological · minority students · military · veterans · non-traditional students · family planning · religious. Recognizing that some students may need extra preparation, Hood College offers remedial and refresher courses in: reading · writing · math · study skills. Other remedial services include workshops for time management and research papers. The average freshman year GPA is 2.8, and 79 percent of freshmen students return for their sophomore year. What do students do after college? While many enter the work force, approximately 32 percent pursue a graduate degree immediately after graduation. Among students who enter the work force, approximately 77 percent enter a field related to their major within six months of graduation. Companies that most frequently hire graduates from Hood College include: Bechtel Corp.· Booz Allen Hamilton · Frederick County Public Schools · Invitrogen/Life Technologies · National Cancer Institute · NSA · USARIMIID.

Support for Students with Learning Disabilities

Students with learning disabilities may take advantage of specific support programs offered by Hood College. If necessary, the college will grant additional time to students with learning disabilities to complete their degree. Also, a lightened course load may be granted to LD students. According to the school, Lighter course load recommended; services provided on an individual basis. Students with learning disabilities will find the following programs at Hood College extremely useful: remedial math · remedial English · special classes · tutors · testing accommodations · untimed tests · extended time for tests · oral tests · note-taking services · reading machines · tape recorders · priority registration · waiver of math degree requirement. Individual or small group tutorials are also available in: time management · organizational skills · learning strategies · specific subject areas · writing labs · math labs · study skills. An advisor/advocate from the LD program is available to students.

How to Get Admitted

For admissions decisions, non-academic factors considered: interview · extracurricular activities · state of residency · alumni relationship.

HOOD COLLEGE

Highlights

Hood College
Frederick, MD (Pop. 57,907)
Location: Medium city
Website: http://www.hood.edu

Students
Total enrollment: 2,533
Undergrads: 454
Freshmen: 321
Part-time students: 11%
From out-of-state: 27%
Male/Female: 31%/69%
Live on-campus: 54%
Off-campus employment rating: Excellent
Caucasian: 74%
African American: 10%
Hispanic: 3%
Asian or Pacific Islander: 3%
Native American: 0%
International: 2%

Academics
Student/faculty ratio: 13:1
Class size 9 or fewer: 18%
Class size 10-29: 72%
Class size 30-49: 9%
Class size 50-99: 1%
Class size 100 or more: -
Returning freshmen: 79%
Six-year graduation rate: 65%

Most Popular Fields of Study
Business, Finance, Sales and Marketing
Biological and Life Sciences
Psychology
Protective Services, Criminal Justice and
    Public Administration
Visual and Performing Arts
English and Literature
Philosophy, Religion and Theology
Computer and Information Sciences
Mathematics
Interdisciplinary Studies

261

HOOD COLLEGE

Admissions

Applicants: 1,570
Accepted: 1,227
Acceptance rate: 78.2%
placed on wait list: 17
Average GPA: 3.5
ACT range: 18-25
SAT Math range: 480-580
SAT Reading range: 470-600
SAT Writing range: 480-590
Top 10% of class: 22%
Top 25% of class: 53%
Top 50% of class: 87%

Deadlines

Early Action: December 15
Early Decision: No
Regular Action: Rolling admissions
Common Application: Accepted

Financial Aid

In-state tuition: $27,770
Out-of-state tuition: $27,770
Room: $4,930
Board: $4,510
Books: $1,000
Freshmen receiving need-based aid: 74%
Undergrads receiving need-based aid: 76%
Avg. % of need met by financial aid: 83%
Avg. aid package (freshmen): $20,894
Avg. aid package (undergrads): $20,854
Freshmen receiving merit-based aid: 22%
Undergrads receiving merit-based aid: 22%
Avg. student debt upon graduation: $19,038

Prominent Alumni

Patricia Chapple Wright, professor/anthropologist, SUNY; Laura Lee Miller, president of licensing and marketing, Vera Wang; Tina Wells, CEO, Buzz Marketing Group.

School Spirit

Mascot: Blazers
Colors: Navy and gray

A high school diploma is required, although a GED is also accepted for admissions consideration. SAT or ACT test scores are required of all applicants. SAT Subject Test scores are considered, if submitted, but are not required. *According to the admissions office:* Minimum combined SAT Reasoning score of 1000 (500 in both verbal and math), rank in top fifth of secondary school class, and minimum 3.0 GPA required.

How to Pay for College

To apply for financial aid, students should submit the following: Free Application for Federal Student Aid (FAFSA). Hood College participates in the Federal Work Study program. *Need-based aid programs include:* scholarships and grants · general need-based awards · Federal Pell grants · state scholarships and grants · college-based scholarships and grants · private scholarships and grants. *Non-Need-based aid programs include:* scholarships and grants · general need-based awards · state scholarships and grants · creative arts and performance awards · special characteristics awards · ROTC scholarships.

HOWARD UNIVERSITY

2400 Sixth Street, NW, Washington, DC 20059
Admissions: 800-822-6363 · Financial Aid: 800-433-3243
Email: admission@howard.edu · Website: http://www.howard.edu

From the College

"Howard University is a comprehensive, research-oriented, predominantly African American university providing an educational experience at reasonable cost to students of high academic potential. Particular emphasis is placed upon providing educational opportunities for African Americans, and for other historically disenfranchised groups. It is a place where students come to study, free of oppression of any type, stripe or kind; and a university which engenders and nurtures an environment that celebrates African American culture in all its diversity. It educates students and prepares them for important leadership positions and responsibility in an increasingly complex world."

Campus Setting

Howard, founded in 1867, is a private, comprehensive university with high research activity. Programs are offered through the Colleges of Arts and Sciences; Dentistry; Engineering, Architecture and Computer Sciences; Medicine; and Pharmacy, Nursing and Allied Health Sciences; through the Schools of Business, Communications, Divinity, Education, Law and Social Work; and through the Graduate School of Arts and Sciences. Its main campus is located in Washington, DC. A four-year institution, Howard University is a historically black university with 10,288 students. In addition to a large, well-stocked library, the campus facilities include: art gallery · hospital · museum · international affairs and research centers. Howard University provides on-campus housing with 5,000 units that can accommodate 6,500 students. Housing options: co-ed dorms · women's dorms · men's dorms · single-student apartments · married-student apartments.

Student Life and Activities

With 55 percent of students living on campus, there are plenty of social activities. A popular gathering spot is the Punchout. Popular campus events include the Homecoming Program, Spring Black Arts Festival, Week-end at the Mecca, Commencement Week, Convocation, Residence Hall Week, International Student Night, Howard's Musical Productions and the James Porter Colloquium. Howard University has 225 official student organizations. The most popular are: Gospel choir · marching and pep bands · string ensemble · jazz society · dance group · drama groups · chess club · debate group · team managers · state and city geographical clubs · other academic and professional clubs. For those interested in sports, there are intramural teams such as: badminton · basketball · bowling · soccer · softball · table tennis. Howard University is a member of the NCAA.

Academics and Learning Environment

For the B student, the learning environment of a college is just as important as the quality of its academic program. Howard University has 1,064 full-time and 456 part-time faculty members, offering a student-to-faculty ratio of 8:1. The most common course size is 2 to 9 students. Howard University offers 187 majors with the most popular being biology, psychology and journalism and least popular being German, classical civilization and French. The school has a general core requirement. Cooperative education is available. All first-year students must maintain a 2.0 GPA or higher to avoid academic probation. Other special academic programs that would appeal to

HOWARD UNIVERSITY

Howard University
Washington, DC (Pop. 607,000)
Location: Major city
Website: http://www.howard.edu

Students
Total enrollment: 10,288
Undergrads: 2,432
Freshmen: 1,464
Part-time students: 6%
From out-of-state: 98%
Male/Female: 34%/66%
Live on-campus: 55%
In fraternities: 2%
In sororities: 1%
Off-campus employment rating: Good
Caucasian: 2%
African American: 84%
Hispanic: 1%
Asian or Pacific Islander: 2%
Native American: 1%
International: 10%

Academics
Student/faculty ratio: 8:1
Class size 9 or fewer: 37%
Class size 10-29: 44%
Class size 30-49: 15%
Class size 50-99: 3%
Class size 100 or more: 1%
Returning freshmen: 84%
Six-year graduation rate: 68%

Most Popular Fields of Study
Business, Finance, Sales and Marketing
Foreign Languages, Literature and Linguistics
Visual and Performing Arts
English and Literature
Computer and Information Sciences
Mathematics
Engineering and Engineering Technologies
Physical Sciences, Chemistry, Physics and Astronomy
Health Professions, Medicine and Related Sciences
Family and Consumer Sciences, Nutrition and Home Economics

America's
Best Colleges for
B Students

a B student: self-designed majors · pass/fail grading option · independent study · double majors · dual degrees · accelerated study · honors program · Phi Beta Kappa · internships · distance learning certificate programs.

B Student Support and Success

Howard assigns undergraduates an academic advisor during their first week of school.

The Center for Academic Reinforcement assists students with academic difficulties, conducts pre-orientation programs for entering freshmen, offers three-credit-hour courses in mathematics, verbal, study skills and reading and recently provided 2,000 tutoring and laboratory assistance sessions.

Howard University provides a variety of support programs including dedicated guidance for: academic · career · personal · psychological · minority students · veterans · non-traditional students · family planning · religious. Recognizing that some students may need extra preparation, Howard University offers remedial and refresher courses in: reading · writing · math · study skills. Annually, 84 percent of freshmen students return for their sophomore year. What do students do after college? While many enter the work force, approximately 40 percent pursue a graduate degree immediately after graduation. Among students who enter the work force, approximately 65 percent enter a field related to their major within six months of graduation. Companies that most frequently hire graduates from Howard University include: ABC Disney · Allstate Insurance · American Power Conversion · Ameriprise Financial · Booz Allen & Hamilton · Cardinal Health · Carrier Corp. · Central Intelligence Agency · CGI · Cintas Corp. · CISCO · Ford Motor Co. · Freddie Mac · Gap Inc. · Geico · Northern Trust · Northrop Grumman Corp · Pepsi Bottling Group · Prudential Mortgage Capital Group · The Walt Disney Co. · U.S. Department of Health and Human Services · U.S. Department of State · U.S. Secret Service.

Support for Students with Learning Disabilities

Students with learning disabilities may take advantage of specific support programs offered by Howard University. According to the school, Admission requirements for LD student are the same as those for regular students. Students with learning disabilities will find the following programs at Howard University extremely useful: testing accommodations · extended time for tests · take-home exam · substitution of courses · readers · note-taking services · tape recorders · texts on tape · early syllabus · priority registration · waiver of math degree requirement. An advisor/advocate from the Special Students Services is available to students.

How to Get Admitted

For admissions decisions, non-academic factors considered: extracurricular activities · special talents, interests, abilities · volunteer work · work experience · state of residency · alumni relationship. A high school diploma is required, although a GED is also accepted for admissions consideration. SAT or ACT test scores are required of all applicants. SAT Subject Test scores are considered, if submitted, but are not required. *Academic units recommended:* 4 English, 2 Math, 3 Science, 2 Social Studies, 2 Foreign Language.

How to Pay for College

To apply for financial aid, students should submit the following: Free Application for Federal Student Aid (FAFSA) · institution's own financial aid forms. Howard University participates in the Federal Work Study program. *Need-based aid programs include:* scholarships and grants · general need-based awards · Federal Pell grants · state scholarships and grants · college-based scholarships and grants · private scholarships and grants · Federal Nursing scholarships. *Non-Need-based aid programs include:* scholarships and grants · general need-based awards · state scholarships and grants · creative arts and performance awards · athletic scholarships · ROTC scholarships.

HOWARD UNIVERSITY

Highlights

Admissions
Applicants: 9,750
Accepted: 4,731
Acceptance rate: 48.5%
Average GPA: Not reported
ACT range: 19-29
SAT Math range: 460-680
SAT Reading range: 470-670
SAT Writing range: 430-670
Top 10% of class: 26%
Top 25% of class: 55%
Top 50% of class: 84%

Deadlines
Early Action: November 1
Early Decision: November 1
Regular Action: Rolling admissions
Common Application: Not accepted

Financial Aid
In-state tuition: $15,270
Out-of-state tuition: $15,270
Room: -
Board: -
Books: $1,300
Freshmen receiving need-based aid: 82%
Undergrads receiving need-based aid: 60%
Avg. % of need met by financial aid: Not reported
Avg. aid package (freshmen): $16,109
Avg. aid package (undergrads): $5,641
Freshmen receiving merit-based aid: 8%
Undergrads receiving merit-based aid: 10%
Avg. student debt upon graduation: $16,798

Prominent Alumni
Edward Brooke, senator; Douglas Wilder, governor, former U.S. senator, former governor of Virginia, mayor of Richmond.

School Spirit
Mascot: Bison
Colors: Red, white, and blue
Song: *Alma Mater*

INDIANA STATE UNIVERSITY

200 North Seventh Street, Terre Haute, IN 47809-9989
Admissions: 800-742-0891 · Financial Aid: 800-841-4744
Email: admissions@indstate.edu · Website: http://www.indstate.edu

From the College

"Indiana State University integrates teaching and research for high-achieving, goal-oriented students who seek opportunities for personal, professional and intellectual growth on a diverse, civically engaged campus. From their first day, our students are challenged by high-quality, experiential academic programs and are supported by personal attention from our faculty and staff who inspire students to create and apply knowledge through dynamic partnerships with the community and the world. Our graduates are valued for their demonstrated knowledge and expertise, active citizenship and leadership qualities."

Campus Setting

Indiana State, founded in 1865, is a public university. Programs are offered through the Colleges of Arts and Sciences; Business; Education; Nursing, Health and Human Services; Technology; and School of Graduate Studies. Its 92-acre campus is located on the north side of Terre Haute's downtown business district, 71 miles from Indianapolis. A four-year institution, Indiana State University has an enrollment of 10,457 students. In addition to a large, well-stocked library, the campus facilities include: art gallery · music hall · museum · civic center · observatory. Indiana State University provides on-campus housing with 2,397 units that can accommodate 3,761 students. Housing options: co-ed dorms · women's dorms · men's dorms · sorority housing · fraternity housing · single-student apartments · married-student apartments · special housing for disabled students. Recreation and sports facilities include: arena · cross country course · softball and soccer complex · tennis club and complex.

Student Life and Activities

Most students (62 percent) live off campus, which does impact the on-campus social scene. Nevertheless, like any college, students find time to create their own recreational outlets. Because Terre Haute is a rural community, students often have to make their own fun. The Student Union Board sponsors movies, bands and lectures. There's a strong music scene in the Midwest, so a lot of great acts pass through. Bloomington and Indianapolis are each an hour away and are further repositories of culture. For night life, students head to the 4th Quarter or the Verve (for live music), the Indiana Theatre (a historic movie house), Sonka's Irish Pub, The Coffee Grounds and the Ballyhoo. The most popular events on campus are: Homecoming, men's and women's basketball, Battle of the Bands, Theatrefest, the Convocation Series, International Film Series, Trike Race in fall and Tandem Race in spring. Indiana State University has 96 official student organizations. Greeks, international students, Union Board and the Afro-American Cultural Center influence life on campus. For those interested in sports, there are intramural teams such as: badminton · basketball · bowling · soccer · softball · swimming · table tennis · tennis · track and field · volleyball. Indiana State University is a member of the Gateway Football Conference (Division I, Football I-AA); Missouri Valley Conference (Division I).

Academics and Learning Environment

For the B student, the learning environment of a college is just as important as the quality of its academic program. Indiana State University has 436 full-time and 191 part-time faculty members, offering a student-to-faculty ratio of 18:1. The most common course size is 2 to 9 students. Indiana State University offers 129 majors with the most popular being elementary education, early childhood education and criminology. The school has a general core requirement. Cooperative education is available. All first-year students must maintain a 2.0 GPA or higher to avoid academic probation, and a minimum overall GPA of 2.5 is required to graduate. Other special academic programs that would appeal to a B student: independent study · double majors · dual degrees · accelerated study · honors program · internships · distance learning.

B Student Support and Success

The Student Academic Services Center at Indiana State helps in several ways. The Mentoring Program's primary goal, according to the college, is to "assist first-year students so that they may benefit from additional support, encouragement and services." Staff members are updated weekly on each student's progress and adjustment to college life. Students sign a Mentoring Contract at the beginning of the process.

A professional advisement staff is always available for help or advice. The school offers a tutoring program for all general studies classes on either a drop-in or appointment basis. Additionally, students are invited to take University 101-Learning in the University Community, a two-credit hour elective that helps with the transition to the college. Students can learn study strategies, critical thinking and writing skills while being introduced to campus resources and services. The course also discusses the history of the school and the community around it.

Indiana State University provides a variety of support programs including dedicated guidance for: academic · career · personal · psychological · minority students. Annually, 66 percent of freshmen students return for their sophomore year. What do students do after college? While many enter the work force, approximately 10 percent pursue a graduate degree immediately after graduation, and another 17 percent enter graduate school within two years.

Support for Students with Learning Disabilities

Students with learning disabilities may take advantage of specific support programs offered by Indiana State University. If necessary, the college will grant additional time to students with learning disabilities to complete their degree. Also, a lightened course load may be granted to LD students. Students with learning disabilities will find the following programs at Indiana State University extremely useful: tutors · learning center · testing accommodations · extended time for tests · take-home exam · oral tests · exam on tape or computer · readers · note-taking services · tape recorders · texts on tape · early syllabus · waiver of math degree requirement. Individual or small group tutorials are also available in: time management · organizational skills · learning strategies · specific subject areas · writing labs · math labs · study skills. An advisor/advocate from the Student Support Services is available to students.

How to Get Admitted

For admissions decisions, non-academic factors considered: interview · extracurricular activities · special talents, interests, abilities · character/personal qualities · state of residency. A high school diploma

INDIANA STATE UNIVERSITY

Highlights

Indiana State University
Terre Haute, IN (Pop. 59,614)
Location: Medium city
Website: http://www.indstate.edu

Students
Total enrollment: 10,457
Undergrads: 4,030
Freshmen: 3,179
Part-time students: 14%
From out-of-state: 10%
Male/Female: 48%/52%
Live on-campus: 38%
In fraternities: 12%
In sororities: 10%
Off-campus employment rating: Excellent
Caucasian: 78%
African American: 13%
Hispanic: 1%
Asian or Pacific Islander: 1%
Native American: 0%
International: 2%

Academics
Student/faculty ratio: 18:1
Class size 9 or fewer: 27%
Class size 10-29: 49%
Class size 30-49: 19%
Class size 50-99: 4%
Class size 100 or more: 1%
Returning freshmen: 66%
Six-year graduation rate: 41%

Most Popular Fields of Study
Business, Finance, Sales and Marketing
Visual and Performing Arts
Social Sciences, History, Economics, Political Science
Protective Services, Criminal Justice and Public Administration
Family and Consumer Sciences, Nutrition and Home Economics
Computer and Information Sciences
Communications, Journalism, Advertising and Comm. Technologies
Philosophy, Religion and Theology
Liberal Arts, Humanities and General Studies

267

College Profiles

INDIANA STATE UNIVERSITY

Admissions
Applicants: 7,575
Accepted: 5,024
Acceptance rate: 66.3%
Average GPA: 3.0
ACT range: 17-22
SAT Math range: 410-530
SAT Reading range: 410-510
SAT Writing range: 400-500
Top 10% of class: 10%
Top 25% of class: 28%
Top 50% of class: 65%

Deadlines
Early Action: No
Early Decision: No
Regular Action: July 1 (priority)
August 15 (final)
Common Application: Not accepted

Financial Aid
In-state tuition: $7,226
Out-of-state tuition: $15,802
Room: $3,878
Board: $3,094
Books: $1,170
Freshmen receiving need-based aid: 68%
Undergrads receiving need-based aid: 63%
Avg. % of need met by financial aid: 83%
Avg. aid package (freshmen): $9,579
Avg. aid package (undergrads): $9,234
Freshmen receiving merit-based aid: 14%
Undergrads receiving merit-based aid: 11%
Avg. student debt upon graduation: $22,961

Prominent Alumni
Anton 'Tony' Hulman George, president of Indianapolis Motor Speedway; Bruce Baumgartner, Olympic wrestler and coach; Larry Bird, Boston Celtics basketball player, Olympic gold medalist and president of the Indiana Pacers.

School Spirit
Mascot: Sycamore Sam
Colors: Blue and white
Song: *March On*

is required, although a GED is also accepted for admissions consideration. SAT or ACT test scores are required of all applicants. SAT Subject Test scores are considered, if submitted, but are not required. *According to the admissions office:* Indiana Core 40 curriculum required. Rank in top half of secondary school class and minimum 2.0 GPA required; minimum combined SAT score of 800 recommended. *Academic units recommended:* 8 English, 6 Math, 6 Science, 4 Social Studies, 2 Foreign Language.

How to Pay for College

To apply for financial aid, students should submit the following: Free Application for Federal Student Aid (FAFSA). Indiana State University participates in the Federal Work Study program. *Need-based aid programs include:* scholarships and grants · general need-based awards · Federal Pell grants · state scholarships and grants · college-based scholarships and grants · private scholarships and grants. *Non-Need-based aid programs include:* scholarships and grants · general need-based awards · state scholarships and grants · creative arts and performance awards · athletic scholarships · ROTC scholarships · alumni affiliation scholarships · art scholarships · minority scholarships · state and district residency scholarships.

INDIANA UNIVERSITY BLOOMINGTON

107 South Indiana Avenue, Bloomington, IN 47405-7000
Admissions: 812-855-0661 · Financial Aid: 812-855-0321
Email: iuadmit@indiana.edu · Website: http://www.iub.edu

From the College

"Indiana University Bloomington finds that the most common response for students choosing IU over similar schools are the reputation of our academic and extracurricular opportunities; flexibility in curricula, especially for exploratory students; a variety of academic and extracurricular opportunities; access to faculty and current technology; beauty of campus; an institutional philosophy of personal attention; a friendly and diverse college town; and the promise of a true college experience."

Campus Setting

Indiana University Bloomington, founded in 1820, is a public, comprehensive institution. Programs are offered through the College of Arts and Sciences, the Division of Labor Studies, Henry Radford Hope School of Fine Arts, Hutton Honors College, Jabobs School of Music, Kelley School of Business, School of Continuing Studies, School of Education, School of Health, Physical Education, and Recreation, School of Informatics, School of Journalism, School of Law, School of Library and Information Science, School of Nursing, School of Optometry, School of Public and Environmental Affairs, School of Social Work, University Division and the University Graduate School. Its 1,878-acre campus is located in the city of Bloomington, 45 miles from Indianapolis. A four-year institution, Indiana University Bloomington has an enrollment of 40,354 students. Indiana University Bloomington has been co-ed since 1867. In addition to a large, well-stocked library, the campus facilities include: anthropology · art, folklore and history museums · musical arts center · auditorium · arboretum · outdoor educational center · observatories. Housing options: co-ed dorms · women's dorms · men's dorms · sorority housing · fraternity housing · single-student apartments · married-student apartments · special housing for disabled students · special housing for International students · cooperative housing. Recreation and sports facilities include: baseball · field hockey · football · soccer and softball fields · basketball and volleyball courts · football and soccer stadium · cross-country course · field house · golf course · gymnasium · indoor track and field complex · rowing center · tennis center · volleyball court · wrestling facility · water polo · swimming and diving facility.

Student Life and Activities

Most students (64 percent) live off campus, which does impact the on-campus social scene. Nevertheless, like any college, students find time to create their own recreational outlets. Some popular on-campus gathering spots include the Memorial Union and the recreational sports center, while off-campus students gather at the Bloomington Bagel Company and the Village Deli. Popular events include: IU Little 500 Bicycle race, Homecoming Parade and IU Dance Marathon. Indiana University Bloomington has a number of official student organizations. The most popular are: AIESEC student organization · Apparel Merchandising Organization · French and Italian Graduate Student Organization · Indiana University Mongolian Student Organization · NELC Graduate Student Organization · Graduate Employees Organization · Cinephile Film Arts Organization · Student Philanthropy Organization · IU Cigarette Clean Up Organization. Indiana University Bloomington is a member of the Big Ten Conference (Division I, Football I-A); Collegiate Water Polo Association (Division I).

INDIANA UNIVERSITY BLOOMINGTON

Highlights

Indiana University Bloomington
Bloomington, IN (Pop. 70,000)
Location: Medium city
Website: http://www.iub.edu

Students
Total enrollment: 40,354
Undergrads: 15,706
Freshmen: 8,132
Part-time students: 5%
From out-of-state: 36%
Male/Female: 50%/50%
Live on-campus: 36%
In fraternities: 16%
In sororities: 18%
Off-campus employment rating: Good
Caucasian: 82%
African American: 5%
Hispanic: 2%
Asian or Pacific Islander: 4%
Native American: 0%
International: 5%

Academics
Student/faculty ratio: 18:1
Class size 9 or fewer: 11%
Class size 10-29: 56%
Class size 30-49: 14%
Class size 50-99: 12%
Class size 100 or more: 7%
Returning freshmen: 90%
Six-year graduation rate: 73%

Most Popular Fields of Study
Business, Finance, Sales and Marketing
Biological and Life Sciences
Protective Services, Criminal Justice and
    Public Administration
Visual and Performing Arts
Family and Consumer Sciences, Nutrition
    and Home Economics
Computer and Information Sciences
Social Sciences, History, Economics,
    Political Science
Philosophy, Religion and Theology
Liberal Arts, Humanities and General
    Studies

Academics and Learning Environment

For the B student, the learning environment of a college is just as important as the quality of its academic program. Indiana University Bloomington has 2,007 full-time and 354 part-time faculty members, offering a student-to-faculty ratio of 18:1. The most common course size is 20 to 29 students. Indiana University Bloomington offers 522 majors with the most popular being business/marketing, education and communications/journalism. The school has a general core requirement. Cooperative education is not offered. All first-year students must maintain a 2.0 GPA or higher to avoid academic probation. Other special academic programs that would appeal to a B student: self-designed majors · pass/fail grading option · independent study · double majors · dual degrees · accelerated study · honors program · Phi Beta Kappa · internships · distance learning.

B Student Support and Success

The Student Academic Center of Indiana University is focused on helping with any problems students might have. According to the college, its philosophy is "student support, student respect and student success."

Study Smarter Workshops cover a wide field of topics, including learning from returned exams, improving reading speed and catching up in a course when all hope seems gone.

Supplemental Instruction offers small group study sessions guided by fellow students who have already taken the same course and have been recommended by the professor. Here, students can review content, ask questions, discuss issues and learn effective reading and study strategies.

The Phoenix Program serves students who have been put on academic probation. It offers several courses to help these individuals get back on track. Those that do are later offered the chance to serve as peer mentors to others.

Individualized Academic Assessment and Assistance is offered to students who are not sure about their strengths and weaknesses or exactly what kind of help they need. This free assessment program is done on a walk-in or appointment basis.

Outreach Services is a program of mini-workshops or presentations that are offered in the residence halls, fraternity houses, classes or organizations on topics such as test taking and time management.

Non-Credit Programs and Services is an hour-long, individual session that can help students identify and target areas causing academic stress.

The Right Start Program is for freshmen who are not familiar with campus/college life (first-generation students, or students from small towns or high schools, etc.). It offers an orientation to the college life and culture of IU through resources in small seminar groups. This is a full semester course that earns the student two credit hours and teaches lessons about the campus, college lifestyles and study skills.

Indiana University Bloomington provides a variety of support programs including dedicated guidance for: academic · career · personal · psychological · minority students · military · veterans · non-traditional students · family planning · religious. Recognizing that some students may need extra preparation, Indiana University Bloomington offers remedial and refresher courses in: reading · writing · math · study skills. Annually, 90 percent of freshmen students return for their sophomore year.

Support for Students with Learning Disabilities

Students with learning disabilities may take advantage of specific support programs offered by Indiana University Bloomington. Also, a lightened course load may be granted to LD students. According to the school, Disability Services for Students (DSS) provides a welcoming and supportive environment for students with disabilities at Indiana University Bloomington and ensures they have equal access to all available opportunities. DSS coordinates the implementation of support services, empowers students to achieve their personal and academic goals, and promotes awareness by educating the university community. Students with learning disabilities will find the following programs at Indiana University Bloomington extremely useful: testing accommodations · extended time for tests · take-home exam · oral tests · readers · typist/scribe · note-taking services · reading machines · tape recorders · priority registration · waiver of math degree requirement. Individual or small group tutorials are also available in: time management · organizational skills · learning strategies · study skills. An advisor/advocate from the Learning Disability Services/Disability Services for Students is available to students.

How to Get Admitted

For admissions decisions, non-academic factors considered: interview · extracurricular activities · special talents, interests, abilities · character/personal qualities · volunteer work · work experience · geographical location · minority affiliation · alumni relationship. A high school diploma is required, although a GED is also accepted for admissions consideration. SAT or ACT test scores are required of all applicants. SAT Subject Test scores are recommended but not required. *According to the admissions office:* Rank in top third of secondary school class recommended. At least three year-long courses in different subjects taken during senior year required of in-state applicants; 16 units and at least four year-long courses required of out-of-state applicants. *Academic units recommended:* 4 Math, 3 Science, 3 Social Studies, 3 Foreign Language.

How to Pay for College

To apply for financial aid, students should submit the following: Free Application for Federal Student Aid (FAFSA). Indiana University Bloomington participates in the Federal Work Study program. *Need-based aid programs include:* scholarships and grants · general need-based awards · Federal Pell grants · state scholarships and grants · college-based scholarships and grants · private scholarships and grants. *Non-Need-based aid programs include:* scholarships and grants · state scholarships and grants · creative arts and performance awards · special achievements and activities awards · special characteristics awards · athletic scholarships.

INDIANA UNIVERSITY BLOOMINGTON

Highlights

Admissions
Applicants: 31,160
Accepted: 22,030
Acceptance rate: 70.7%
Average GPA: 3.6
ACT range: 23-29
SAT Math range: 530-640
SAT Reading range: 510-620
SAT Writing range: Not reported
Top 10% of class: 31%
Top 25% of class: 69%
Top 50% of class: 97%

Deadlines
Early Action: No
Early Decision: No
Regular Action: Rolling admissions
Common Application: Not accepted

Financial Aid
In-state tuition: $8,613
Out-of-state tuition: $26,160
Room: -
Board: -
Books: $790
Freshmen receiving need-based aid: 41%
Undergrads receiving need-based aid: 37%
Avg. % of need met by financial aid: 89%
Avg. aid package (freshmen): $10,549
Avg. aid package (undergrads): $10,206
Freshmen receiving merit-based aid: 25%
Undergrads receiving merit-based aid: 20%
Avg. student debt upon graduation: $22,013

School Spirit
Mascot: Hoosiers
Colors: Cream and crimson
Song: *Indiana, Our Indiana*

271

College Profiles

Indiana University of Pennsylvania
Indiana, PA (Pop. 30,000)
Location: Large town
Website: http://www.iup.edu

Students
Total enrollment: 14,310
Undergrads: 5,363
Freshmen: 4,578
Part-time students: 8%
From out-of-state: 7%
Male/Female: 45%/55%
Live on-campus: 35%
In fraternities: 9%
In sororities: 7%
Off-campus employment rating: Good
Caucasian: 78%
African American: 11%
Hispanic: 2%
Asian or Pacific Islander: 1%
Native American: 0%
International: 1%

Academics
Student/faculty ratio: 16:1
Class size 9 or fewer: 15%
Class size 10-29: 48%
Class size 30-49: 24%
Class size 50-99: 10%
Class size 100 or more: 2%
Returning freshmen: 73%
Six-year graduation rate: 51%

Most Popular Fields of Study
Business, Finance, Sales and Marketing
English and Literature
Computer and Information Sciences
Mathematics
Engineering and Engineering Technologies
Parks, Recreation and Fitness
Interdisciplinary Studies
Health Professions, Medicine and Related Sciences
Family and Consumer Sciences, Nutrition and Home Economics
Foreign Languages, Literature and Linguistics

America's
Best Colleges for
B Students

INDIANA UNIVERSITY OF PENNSYLVANIA

1011 South Drive, Indiana, PA 15705
Admissions: 800-442-6830 · Financial Aid: 724-357-2218
Email: admissions-inquiry@iup.edu
Website: http://www.iup.edu

From the College

"With its original 1875 building at the heart of campus, Indiana University of Pennsylvania receives frequent national accolades and recognition. IUP is home to more than 13,000 students and provides special academic challenges through the Robert E. Cook Honors College. IUP is the largest institution in Pennsylvania's System of Higher Education and the only university authorized to confer doctoral degrees. IUP has more than 100 majors, varied internship and study abroad programs, 40 master's degree programs and eight doctoral degrees. IUP is home to the John Murtha Center for Homeland Security and is a center of excellence in Information Assurance."

Campus Setting

Indiana University of Pennsylvania, founded in 1875, is a public, comprehensive institution. Programs are offered through the Colleges of Business, Education, Fine Arts, Health and Human Services, Humanities and Social Sciences, and Natural Sciences and Mathematics and the School of Continuing Education. Its 350-acre campus is located in western Pennsylvania, 65 miles from Pittsburgh. A four-year institution, Indiana University of Pennsylvania has an enrollment of 14,310 students. In addition to a large, well-stocked library, the campus facilities include: art museum · natural history museum · lodge · farm · co-generation plant · sailing base. Indiana University of Pennsylvania provides on-campus housing with 1,979 units that can accommodate 3,800 students. Housing options: co-ed dorms · single-student apartments · special housing for disabled students · special housing for International students. Recreation and sports facilities include: field house · natatorium · stadium.

Student Life and Activities

Most students (66 percent) live off campus, which does impact the on-campus social scene. Nevertheless, like any college, students find time to create their own recreational outlets. Indiana University of Pennsylvania has 210 official student organizations. The most popular are: Choral and instrumental ensembles · jazz · marching and pep bands · residence hall association · drill team · team managers · departmental · service and special-interest groups. For those interested in sports, there are intramural teams such as: basketball · bench press · bowling · flag football · golf · racquetball · soccer · softball · volleyball · wallyball · water polo · wrestling. Indiana University of Pennsylvania is a member of the Pennsylvania State Athletic Conference (Division II).

Academics and Learning Environment

For the B student, the learning environment of a college is just as important as the quality of its academic program. Indiana University of Pennsylvania has 648 full-time and 64 part-time faculty members, offering a student-to-faculty ratio of 16:1. The most common course size is 20 to 29 students. Indiana University of Pennsylvania offers 149 majors with the most popular being elementary education, criminology and communications media and least popular being consumer affairs, nuclear medicine technology and government/public service. The school has a general core requirement. Cooperative education is not offered. All first-year students must maintain a 2.0 GPA or higher to avoid academic probation, and a minimum overall GPA of 2.0 is required to graduate. Other special academic programs that would appeal to a B student: pass/fail grading option · independent study · double majors · dual degrees · accelerated study · honors program · internships · weekend college · distance learning.

B Student Support and Success

IU offers credit courses that help students cope with the demands of college. Through the Learning Enhancement Center, a student can take classes on such topics as learning strategies, vocabulary expansion, reading skills for college study and introduction to college math. The center provides tutoring, supplemental instruction, workshops and a campus-wide academic support program to help all levels of students.

The Writing Center offers tutoring by other students on a drop-in basis. The center also sponsors writing workshops with subjects such Internet use in research and resume writing.

If a student's GPA falls below 2.0, he/she is placed on academic probation and must implement an Academic Recovery Plan, which is designed to help students make progress toward academic good standing.

Indiana University of Pennsylvania provides a variety of support programs including dedicated guidance for: academic · career · personal · psychological · minority students · military · veterans · non-traditional students · family planning. Recognizing that some students may need extra preparation, Indiana University of Pennsylvania offers remedial and refresher courses in: reading · writing · math · study skills. Annually, 73 percent of freshmen students return for their sophomore year.

Support for Students with Learning Disabilities

Students with learning disabilities may take advantage of specific support programs offered by Indiana University of Pennsylvania. Students with learning disabilities will find the following programs at Indiana University of Pennsylvania extremely useful: remedial math · remedial reading · learning center · testing accommodations · extended time for tests · take-home exam · oral tests · readers · note-taking services · reading machines · tape recorders · priority registration. Individual or small group tutorials are also available in: time management · organizational skills · learning strategies · specific subject areas · writing labs · math labs · study skills. An advisor/advocate from the LD program is available to students.

INDIANA UNIVERSITY OF PENNSYLVANIA

Highlights

Admissions
Applicants: 11,030
Accepted: 7,065
Acceptance rate: 64.1%
Average GPA: Not reported
ACT range: Not reported
SAT Math range: 440-540
SAT Reading range: 440-540
SAT Writing range: Not reported
Top 10% of class: 8%
Top 25% of class: 28%
Top 50% of class: 59%

Deadlines
Early Action: No
Early Decision: No
Regular Action: December 31 (priority)
Common Application: Accepted

Financial Aid
In-state tuition: $5,358
Out-of-state tuition: $13,396
Room: -
Board: -
Books: $1,100
Freshmen receiving need-based aid: 68%
Undergrads receiving need-based aid: 65%
Avg. % of need met by financial aid: 75%
Avg. aid package (freshmen): $10,135
Avg. aid package (undergrads): $9,002
Freshmen receiving merit-based aid: 4%
Undergrads receiving merit-based aid: 3%
Avg. student debt upon graduation: $23,265

School Spirit
Mascot: Crimson Hawks
Colors: Crimson and grey
Song: *Hail Indiana*

INDIANA UNIVERSITY OF PENNSYLVANIA

How to Get Admitted

For admissions decisions, non-academic factors considered: extracurricular activities · special talents, interests, abilities · state of residency. A high school diploma is required, although a GED is also accepted for admissions consideration. SAT or ACT test scores are required of all applicants. SAT Subject Test scores are recommended but not required. *Academic units recommended:* 3 English, 3 Math, 3 Science, 3 Social Studies, 2 Foreign Language.

How to Pay for College

To apply for financial aid, students should submit the following: Free Application for Federal Student Aid (FAFSA). Indiana University of Pennsylvania participates in the Federal Work Study program. *Need-based aid programs include:* scholarships and grants · general need-based awards · Federal Pell grants · state scholarships and grants · college-based scholarships and grants · private scholarships and grants · United Negro College Fund. *Non-Need-based aid programs include:* scholarships and grants · general need-based awards · state scholarships and grants · creative arts and performance awards · athletic scholarships · ROTC scholarships.

LAKE FOREST COLLEGE

555 North Sheridan Road, Lake Forest, IL 60045
Admissions: 800-828-4751 · Financial Aid: 847-735-5104
Email: admissions@lakeforest.edu · Website: http://www.lakeforest.edu

From the College

"A highly selective, undergraduate, liberal arts institution, the 107-acre campus is located 30 miles north of downtown Chicago in a suburb along Lake Michigan. The college takes full advantage of its proximity to one of the world's most dynamic cities, offering unmatched academic, cultural, internship, mentorship and employment resources. Its faculty is committed to teaching and, as the college's mission statement reads, 'We know our students by name.' Lake Forest College prepares students to become responsible citizens of the global community and celebrates the personal growth that accompanies the quest for excellence."

Campus Setting

Lake Forest, founded in 1857, is a church-affiliated college. A four-year, private institution, Lake Forest College has an enrollment of 1,448 students. The school is also affiliated with the Presbyterian Church. The school has a library with 378,556 books. Lake Forest College provides on-campus housing with 593 units that can accommodate 1,126 students. Housing options: co-ed dorms · women's dorms · single-student apartments. Recreation and sports facilities include: basketball · handball and racquetball courts · ice rink · softball field · swimming pool · weight rooms.

Student Life and Activities

With 81 percent of students living on campus, there are plenty of social activities. Popular events include: Ra Fest and Homecoming. Lake Forest College has 82 official student organizations. The most popular are: Entrepreneur Group · Star Gazers Society · Student Alumni Association · Students Educating Students · Future Health Professionals · College Democrats · College Republicans · Chess Club · Debate Club · Film Society · French Club · Spanish Club. For those interested in sports, there are intramural teams such as: basketball · flag football · indoor soccer · racquetball · tennis · volleyball. Lake Forest College is a member of the Midwest Conference (Division III);Northern Collegiate Hockey Association (Division III).

Academics and Learning Environment

For the B student, the learning environment of a college is just as important as the quality of its academic program. Lake Forest College has 88 full-time and 71 part-time faculty members, offering a student-to-faculty ratio of 12:1. The most common course size is 10 to 19 students. Lake Forest College offers 30 majors with the most popular being economics, business and psychology and least popular being German, Asian studies and area studies. The school has a general core requirement. Cooperative education is not offered. All first-year students must maintain a 1.5 GPA or higher to avoid academic probation. Other special academic programs that would appeal to a B student: self-designed majors · pass/fail grading option · independent study · double majors · accelerated study · honors program · Phi Beta Kappa · internships.

B Student Support and Success

Insight from Lake Forest College includes the following: "We offer a comprehensive Academic Resource Center, which provides tutorial support open to all students. The program is coordinated by a Learning Resource Specialist. The college also supports

LAKE FOREST COLLEGE

Lake Forest College
Lake Forest, IL (Pop. 20,000)
Location: Large town
Website: http://www.lakeforest.edu

Students
Total enrollment: 1,448
Undergrads: 599
Freshmen: 386
Part-time students: 1%
From out-of-state: 57%
Male/Female: 42%/58%
Live on-campus: 81%
In fraternities: 7%
In sororities: 18%
Off-campus employment rating: Excellent
Caucasian: 78%
African American: 4%
Hispanic: 7%
Asian or Pacific Islander: 5%
Native American: 0%
International: 7%

Academics
Student/faculty ratio: 12:1
Class size 9 or fewer: 14%
Class size 10-29: 79%
Class size 30-49: 7%
Class size 50-99: 10%
Class size 100 or more: 6%
Returning freshmen: 79%
Six-year graduation rate: 69%

Most Popular Fields of Study
Business, Finance, Sales and Marketing
Visual and Performing Arts
English and Literature
Philosophy, Religion and Theology
Computer and Information Sciences
Mathematics
Interdisciplinary Studies
Physical Sciences, Chemistry, Physics
    and Astronomy
Foreign Languages, Literature and Lin-
    guistics
Communications, Journalism, Advertising
    and Comm. Technologies

a strong Writing Center, seminars in time management and study skills development.

"The personal interview is strongly recommended and is the best resource for assessing a student's potential to flourish at Lake Forest. We value students who are committed to community and campus involvement, who have a clear understanding of why they have applied to Lake Forest and whose needs are well matched with the college. In addition to the interview, students should strive to take a challenging high school curriculum, including honors or advanced placement courses when possible.

"We consider the rigor of a student's high school curriculum in contest to the grade point average and we read transcripts carefully. In this regard, we can appreciate strengths and weaknesses of each individual student, including a consideration of B or even C grades. There is a 'story' behind each transcript and we seek to understand a student's academic journey through the personal interview."

Lake Forest College provides a variety of support programs including dedicated guidance for: academic · career · personal · psychological · minority students · veterans · non-traditional students · family planning · religious. The average freshman year GPA is 2.5, and 79 percent of freshmen students return for their sophomore year. What do students do after college? While many enter the work force, approximately 35 percent pursue a graduate degree immediately after graduation. Among students who enter the work force, approximately 87 percent enter a field related to their major within six months of graduation. Companies that most frequently hire graduates from Lake Forest College include: Abbott Laboratories · Accenture · Brunswick · Enterprise Rental Car · SBC · IMC Global · Chicago Historical Society · Bank One · LaSalle Financial · Northern Trust · Wells Fargo Financial · Medline.

Support for Students with Learning Disabilities

Students with learning disabilities may take advantage of specific support programs offered by Lake Forest College. Also, a lightened course load may be granted to LD students. Students with learning disabilities will find the following programs at Lake Forest College extremely useful: tutors · learning center · testing accommodations · untimed tests · extended time for tests · take-home exam · oral tests · typist/scribe · note-taking services · reading machines · tape recorders · texts on tape · early syllabus · priority registration · waiver of foreign language degree requirement. Individual or small group tutorials are also available in: time management · organizational skills · learning strategies · specific subject areas · writing labs · math labs · study skills. An advisor/advocate from the LD program is available to students.

How to Get Admitted

For admissions decisions, non-academic factors considered: interview · extracurricular activities · special talents, interests, abilities · character/personal qualities · volunteer work · work experience · state of residency · geographical location · alumni relationship. A high school diploma is required, although a GED is also accepted for admissions consideration. SAT or ACT test scores are considered, if submitted, but are not required. SAT Subject Test scores are recommended but not required. *According to the admissions office:* Accelerated courses recommended. *Academic units recommended:* 4 English, 4 Math, 4 Science, 2 Social Studies, 4 Foreign Language.

How to Pay for College

To apply for financial aid, students should submit the following: Free Application for Federal Student Aid (FAFSA) · institution's own financial aid forms. Lake Forest College participates in the Federal Work Study program. *Need-based aid programs include:* scholarships and grants · general need-based awards · Federal Pell grants · state scholarships and grants · college-based scholarships and grants · private scholarships and grants. *Non-Need-based aid programs include:* scholarships and grants · general need-based awards · state scholarships and grants · creative arts and performance awards · special characteristics awards.

LAKE FOREST COLLEGE

Highlights

Admissions
Applicants: 2,197
Accepted: 1,390
Acceptance rate: 63.3%
placed on wait list: 61
Average GPA: 3.5
ACT range: 24-28
SAT Math range: Not reported
SAT Reading range: Not reported
SAT Writing range: Not reported
Top 10% of class: 32%
Top 25% of class: 59%
Top 50% of class: 88%

Deadlines
Early Action:
Early Decision: December 1
Regular Action: February 15 (priority)
May 1 (final)
Common Application: Accepted

Financial Aid
In-state tuition: $34,206
Out-of-state tuition: $34,206
Room: $3,966
Board: $4,040
Books: $800
Freshmen receiving need-based aid: 77%
Undergrads receiving need-based aid: 76%
Avg. % of need met by financial aid: 100%
Avg. aid package (freshmen): $21,963
Avg. aid package (undergrads): $23,024
Freshmen receiving merit-based aid: 12%
Undergrads receiving merit-based aid: 15%
Avg. student debt upon graduation: $19,976

School Spirit
Mascot: Black Bear
Colors: Red and black

277

Longwood University

Farmville, VA (Pop. 10,000)
Location: Small town
Website: http://www.whylongwood.com

Students

Total enrollment: 4,727
Undergrads: 1,392
Freshmen: 1,049
Part-time students: 5%
From out-of-state: 10%
Male/Female: 35%/65%
Live on-campus: 70%
In fraternities: 15%
In sororities: 19%
Off-campus employment rating: Good
Caucasian: 87%
African American: 6%
Hispanic: 2%
Asian or Pacific Islander: 2%
Native American: 1%
International: 0%

Academics

Student/faculty ratio: 20:1
Class size 9 or fewer: 16%
Class size 10-29: 66%
Class size 30-49: 16%
Class size 50-99: 1%
Class size 100 or more: 6%
Returning freshmen: 79%
Six-year graduation rate: 65%

Most Popular Fields of Study

Business, Finance, Sales and Marketing
Biological and Life Sciences
Protective Services, Criminal Justice and
    Public Administration
Visual and Performing Arts
English and Literature
Computer and Information Sciences
Mathematics
Parks, Recreation and Fitness
Health Professions, Medicine and Related
    Sciences

LONGWOOD UNIVERSITY

201 High Street, Farmville, VA 23909
Admissions: 800-281-4677 · Financial Aid: 800-281-4677
Email: admissions@longwood.edu
Website: http://www.whylongwood.com

From the College

"Longwood University offers the opportunities, diversity and affordability of a public university, along with the warmth and spirit of a smaller college. All students participate in internships or research projects to gain relevant work-related experience. Over 90 percent of our graduates have found successful careers or have entered graduate school within three months of graduation. Longwood is committed to providing students with the technological, communication and human relation skills necessary to succeed."

Campus Setting

Longwood, founded in 1839, has a 160-acre campus located in Farmville, 60 miles west of Richmond. A four-year institution, Longwood University has an enrollment of 4,727 students. Longwood University has been co-ed since 1976. In addition to a large, well-stocked library, the campus also has a center for the visual arts. Longwood University provides on-campus housing that can accommodate 2,910 students. Housing options: co-ed dorms · women's dorms · sorority housing · single-student apartments · special housing for disabled students · special housing for International students. Recreation and sports facilities include: basketball · racquetball and tennis courts · field hockey · lacrosse · softball and soccer fields · gymnasium · weight room.

Student Life and Activities

With 70 percent of students living on campus, there are plenty of social activities. Popular on-campus gathering spots include Stubbs Lawn or Wheeler Lawn. Popular campus events include October Fest, Spring Weekend and Theme Mixers. Longwood University has 125 official student organizations. The most popular are: Camerata Singers · Gospel Choir · Lancer Productions · Longwood Company of Dancers · Blue Heat (Dancers) · Ambassadors · Longwood Players · cheerleading · Music Educators National Conference · modern foreign language club · National Student Speech/Language/Hearing Association · history club · Honor Board · Campus Safety Escort Service · Groups and Individuals Volunteering Efforts (GIVE) · Habitat for Humanity. For those interested in sports, there are intramural teams such as: air hockey · basketball · bowling · flag football · indoor soccer · indoor volleyball · sand volleyball · softball · spades · table tennis. Longwood University is a member of the Atlantic Soccer Conference (Division I), Northern Pacific Field Hockey Conference (Division I).

Academics and Learning Environment

For the B student, the learning environment of a college is just as important as the quality of its academic program. Longwood University has 211 full-time and 76 part-time faculty members, offering a student-to-faculty ratio of 20:1. The most common course size is 20 to 29 students. Longwood University offers 33 majors with the most popular being liberal studies, business administration and psychology and least popular being modern foreign languages, economics and chemistry. The school has a general core requirement. Cooperative education is not offered. All first-year students must maintain a 2.0 GPA or higher to avoid academic probation, and a minimum overall GPA of 2.0 is required to graduate. Other special academic programs that would appeal to a B student: pass/fail grading option · independent study · double majors · dual degrees · accelerated study · honors program · internships · distance learning.

B Student Support and Success

Longwood College offers a Learning Center that is located in the Greenwood Library. It features a speaking center, as well as a writing center and open labs. There is no charge for any of the services offered, and sessions are on a drop-in basis.

Longwood University provides a variety of support programs including dedicated guidance for: academic · career · personal · psychological · family planning · religious. The average freshman year GPA is 2.6, and 79 percent of freshmen students return for their sophomore year. Among students who enter the work force, approximately 90 percent enter a field related to their major within six months of graduation. Companies that most frequently hire graduates from Longwood University include: America Online · AT&T · BB&T · Capital One · Circuit City · Deloitte & Touce · Dominion Virginia Power · DuPont · Federal Reserve Bank · Goodman & Co. · Johnson & Johnson · Kraft Foods · KPMG · Microsoft Corp.· Philip Morris · State Farm Insurance · SunTrust · Wachovia.

Support for Students with Learning Disabilities

Students with learning disabilities may take advantage of specific support programs offered by Longwood University. If necessary, the college will grant additional time to students with learning disabilities to complete their degree. Also, a lightened course load may be granted to LD students. Students with learning disabilities will find the following programs at Longwood University extremely useful: tutors · learning center · testing accommodations · extended time for tests · take-home exam · readers · typist/scribe · note-taking services · reading machines · tape recorders · texts on tape · priority seating · waiver of math degree requirement. Individual or small group tutorials are also available in: time management · organizational skills · learning strategies · specific subject areas · writing labs · math labs · study skills. An advisor/advocate from the Office of Disability Support Services is available to students.

How to Get Admitted

For admissions decisions, non-academic factors considered: extracurricular activities · special talents, interests, abilities · character/personal qualities · volunteer work · work experience · geographical location · minority affiliation · alumni relationship. A high school diploma is required, although a GED is also accepted for admissions consideration. SAT or ACT test scores are required of all applicants.

LONGWOOD UNIVERSITY

Highlights

Admissions
Applicants: 4,197
Accepted: 2,879
Acceptance rate: 68.6%
placed on wait list: 200
Average GPA: 3.3
ACT range: Not reported
SAT Math range: 480-570
SAT Reading range: 490-570
SAT Writing range: Not reported
Top 10% of class: 11%
Top 25% of class: 39%
Top 50% of class: 84%

Deadlines
Early Action: December 1
Early Decision: No
Regular Action: March 1 (priority)
Common Application: Accepted

Financial Aid
In-state tuition: $9,192
Out-of-state tuition: $17,112
Room: $4,300
Board: $2,208
Books: $800
Freshmen receiving need-based aid: 45%
Undergrads receiving need-based aid: 44%
Avg. % of need met by financial aid: 68%
Avg. aid package (freshmen): $7,814
Avg. aid package (undergrads): $8,004
Freshmen receiving merit-based aid: 2%
Undergrads receiving merit-based aid: 2%
Avg. student debt upon graduation: $14,934

School Spirit
Mascot: Lancers
Colors: Blue and white
Song: *Alma Mater*

LONGWOOD UNIVERSITY

SAT Subject Test scores are not required. *According to the admissions office:* Minimum combined SAT Reasoning score of 990, rank in top half of secondary school class, and minimum 2.6 GPA required. *Academic units recommended:* 4 Math, 4 Science, 2 Social Studies, 3 Foreign Language.

How to Pay for College

To apply for financial aid, students should submit the following: Free Application for Federal Student Aid (FAFSA). Longwood University participates in the Federal Work Study program. *Need-based aid programs include:* scholarships and grants · general need-based awards · Federal Pell grants · state scholarships and grants · college-based scholarships and grants · private scholarships and grants. *Non-Need-based aid programs include:* scholarships and grants · general need-based awards · state scholarships and grants · creative arts and performance awards · athletic scholarships · ROTC scholarships.

LUTHER COLLEGE

700 College Drive, Decorah, IA 52101-1045
Admissions: 800-458-8437 · Financial Aid: 800-458-8437
Email: admissions@luther.edu · Website: http://www.luther.edu

From the College

"A Phi Beta Kappa institution of 2,423 students, Luther College is a community of faith and learning in which creative scholarship, personal growth, worship and social relationships are interwoven. Students, faculty and staff work together for the development of a living and learning environment which encourages caring relationships and an understanding of the wholeness of life. Forty states and 44 countries are represented in the student body; co-curricular activities include 16 music ensembles and 19 intercollegiate sports for men and women. The campus has scenic vistas of the Oneota Valley and the Upper Iowa River."

Campus Setting

Luther is a church-affiliated, liberal arts college. Founded as a college for men in 1861, it adopted co-education in 1936. Its 800-acre campus is located in Decorah, 15 miles south of the Minnesota border. A four-year private institution, the school is also affiliated with the Lutheran Church. The school has a library with more than 300,000 books. Luther College provides on-campus housing that can accommodate 2,144 students. Housing options: co-ed dorms · single-student apartments · married-student apartments. Recreation and sports facilities include: center · fitness center.

Student Life and Activities

With 88 percent of students living on campus, there are plenty of social activities. Popular events include: Homecoming, Flamingo Ball, Family Weekend, Christmas at Luther, Ethnic Arts Festival, Center Stage Series, major concerts and guest speakers. Luther College has 120 official student organizations. The most popular are: Nordic Choir · Collegiate Chorale · Cathedral Choir · Aurora (women's choir) · Norsemen (men's choir) · Cantorei · Student Activities Council · Performing Arts Council · Concert Band · Entrepreneurship Club · Environmental Concerns · Student Senate · Health Sciences Club · Chemistry Club · Pre-Registered Nurses · Luther Republicans · Luther Democrats. Luther College is a member of the Iowa Intercollegiate Athletic Conference (Division III).

Academics and Learning Environment

For the B student, the learning environment of a college is just as important as the quality of its academic program. Luther College has 178 full-time and 70 part-time faculty members, offering a student-to-faculty ratio of 12:1. The most common course size is 10 to 19 students. Luther College offers 37 majors with the most popular being biology, management and music and least popular being German, Greek and classical studies. The school has a general core requirement as well as a religion requirement Cooperative education is not offered. All first-year students must maintain a 1.75 GPA or higher to avoid academic probation, and a minimum overall GPA of 2.0 is required to graduate. Other special academic programs that would appeal to a B student: self-designed majors · pass/fail grading option · independent study · double majors · dual degrees · honors program · Phi Beta Kappa · internships · certificate programs.

B Student Support and Success

This Lutheran college has a Student Academic Support Center. The goals of the center include assisting students in becoming self-confident critical thinkers and learners,

LUTHER COLLEGE

Luther College
Decorah, IA (Pop. 8,210)
Location: Small town
Website: http://www.luther.edu

Students
Total enrollment: 2,423
Undergrads: 1,024
Freshmen: 630
Part-time students: 2%
From out-of-state: 65%
Male/Female: 42%/58%
Live on-campus: 88%
In fraternities: 3%
In sororities: 4%
Off-campus employment rating: Good
Caucasian: 84%
African American: 1%
Hispanic: 2%
Asian or Pacific Islander: 2%
Native American: 0%
International: 4%

Academics
Student/faculty ratio: 12:1
Class size 9 or fewer: 17%
Class size 10-29: 75%
Class size 30-49: 6%
Class size 50-99: 2%
Class size 100 or more: -
Returning freshmen: 85%
Six-year graduation rate: 72%

Most Popular Fields of Study
Business, Finance, Sales and Marketing
Biological and Life Sciences
Psychology
Protective Services, Criminal Justice and
    Public Administration
Visual and Performing Arts
English and Literature
Philosophy, Religion and Theology
Computer and Information Sciences
Mathematics
Physical Sciences, Chemistry, Physics
    and Astronomy

helping with peer tutoring, linking students to helpful resources and meeting the needs of all students who need any kind of academic assistance. Luther offers a class called Critical Reading and Learning Strategies (GS110) that helps students become better readers through the description, interpretation and evaluation of different texts. Additionally, the Learning and Study Skills Inventory (LASSI) is a diagnostic measure to help students discover the areas in which they need help. This assessment measures everything from attitude and motivation to test anxiety and information processing. The college's Academic Support Services includes independent tutoring and group sessions, as well as learning skills workshops, academic advising and access to a series of helpful hand-outs.

Luther College provides a variety of support programs including dedicated guidance for: academic · career · personal · psychological · minority students · non-traditional students · family planning · religious. The average freshman year GPA is 3.0, and 85 percent of freshmen students return for their sophomore year. What do students do after college? While many enter the work force, approximately 19 percent pursue a graduate degree immediately after graduation. Among students who enter the work force, approximately 66 percent enter a field related to their major within six months of graduation. Companies that most frequently hire graduates from Luther College include: Mayo Clinic · Wells Fargo · Thrivent · Gunderson Lutheran · Fastenal Co. · Target · Jeld Wenn · IBM · Epic Systems · Accenture · Hormel · University of Iowa Hospital and Research Center · Securian Financial Group · Best Buy · Weber Shandwick.

Support for Students with Learning Disabilities
Students with learning disabilities may take advantage of specific support programs offered by Luther College. If necessary, the college will grant additional time to students with learning disabilities to complete their degree. Credit is given for remedial courses taken. High school foreign language waivers are accepted. High school math waivers are also accepted. Students with learning disabilities will find the following programs at Luther College extremely useful: tutors · learning center · testing accommodations · extended time for tests · take-home exam · oral tests · typist/scribe · note-taking services · tape recorders · waiver of math degree requirement. Individual or small group tutorials are also available in: time management · organizational skills · learning strategies · specific subject areas · writing labs · math labs · study skills. An advisor/advocate from the Student Academic Support Center is available to students.

How to Get Admitted
For admissions decisions, non-academic factors considered: interview · extracurricular activities · special talents, interests, abilities · character/personal qualities · volunteer work · state of residency · geographical location · minority affiliation · alumni relationship. A high school diploma is required, although a GED is also accepted for admissions consideration. SAT or ACT test scores are required of all applicants. *According to the admissions office:* Class rank and ACT/SAT scores which show the potential for success at Luther College. *Academic units recommended:* 4 English, 3 Math, 2 Science, 3 Social Studies, 2 Foreign Language.

How to Pay for College

To apply for financial aid, students should submit the following: Free Application for Federal Student Aid (FAFSA) · institution's own financial aid forms. Luther College participates in the Federal Work Study program. *Need-based aid programs include:* scholarships and grants · general need-based awards · Federal Pell grants · state scholarships and grants · college-based scholarships and grants · private scholarships and grants. *Non-Need-based aid programs include:* scholarships and grants · state scholarships and grants · creative arts and performance awards.

LUTHER COLLEGE

Highlights

Admissions
Applicants: 2,053
Accepted: 1,648
Acceptance rate: 80.3%
Average GPA: 3.7
ACT range: 23-29
SAT Math range: 510-670
SAT Reading range: 492-647
SAT Writing range: Not reported
Top 10% of class: 39%
Top 25% of class: 69%
Top 50% of class: 92%

Deadlines
Early Action: No
Early Decision: No
Regular Action: Rolling admissions
Common Application: Accepted

Financial Aid
In-state tuition: $32,140
Out-of-state tuition: $32,140
Room: $2,580
Board: $2,800
Books: $910
Freshmen receiving need-based aid: 68%
Undergrads receiving need-based aid: 70%
Avg. % of need met by financial aid: 87%
Avg. aid package (freshmen): $25,205
Avg. aid package (undergrads): $23,487
Freshmen receiving merit-based aid: 18%
Undergrads receiving merit-based aid: 12%
Avg. student debt upon graduation: $29,770

Prominent Alumni
Arne Sorenson, Executive vice president and chief financial officer, Marriott Corp.; Brian Andreas, creator of StoryPeople.

School Spirit
Mascot: Norse
Colors: Blue and white

Lycoming College

Williamsport, PA (Pop. 40,000)
Location: Medium city
Website: http://www.lycoming.edu

Students

Total enrollment: 1,348
Undergrads: 606
Freshmen: 340
Part-time students: 2%
From out-of-state: 37%
Male/Female: 45%/55%
Live on-campus: 85%
In fraternities: 8%
In sororities: 12%
Off-campus employment rating: Good
Caucasian: 93%
African American: 3%
Hispanic: 2%
Asian or Pacific Islander: 1%
Native American: 0%
International: 1%

Academics

Student/faculty ratio: 13:1
Class size 9 or fewer: 26%
Class size 10-29: 60%
Class size 30-49: 13%
Class size 50-99: 1%
Class size 100 or more: -
Returning freshmen: 79%
Six-year graduation rate: 71%

Most Popular Fields of Study

Business, Finance, Sales and Marketing
Biological and Life Sciences
Area, Ethnic and Gender Studies

Admissions

Applicants: 1,601
Accepted: 111
Acceptance rate: 6.9%
Average GPA: Not reported
ACT range: 20-27
SAT Math range: 470-580
SAT Reading range: 470-580
SAT Writing range: 460-570
Top 10% of class: 19%
Top 25% of class: 43%
Top 50% of class: 80%

284

LYCOMING COLLEGE

700 College Place, Williamsport, PA 17701
Admissions: 800-345-3920 · Financial Aid: 800-345-3920
Email: admissions@lycoming.edu
Website: http://www.lycoming.edu

From the College

"The mission of Lycoming College is to offer students a distinguished education in the traditional liberal arts and sciences. The college has sought to accomplish that goal by gathering a strong faculty with a primary focus on teaching and a strong secondary focus on research. The college has established a teaching effectiveness program to focus on new strategies for the classroom including those involving the most recent technology. Lycoming features an extensive writing program for students in which they are expected to have a specific writing component in all their general education courses and to take an additional three courses designated as writing intensive. The college has encouraged student research across the curriculum with a particular focus in the sciences. Lycoming has also introduced capstone courses in most departments featuring an opportunity for students to bring their academic work together in some form of major research project or artistic presentation. In order to accomplish the close work between faculty and students required by our mission, the college has sustained a full-time faculty of approximately 90y percent of the total."

Campus Setting

Lycoming is a private, four-year, liberal arts college. Founded in 1812, it is one of the 50 oldest colleges in the United States. There are 1,500 undergraduate students from 28 states and 12 foreign countries. Students living on campus are guaranteed housing all four years. In the past few years, Lycoming has seen a new Recreation Center built and the restoration of a building that is now called Honors Hall. The school is also affiliated with the Methodist Church. In addition to a large, well-stocked library, the campus has an art gallery. Lycoming College that can accommodate 1,245 students. Housing options: co-ed dorms · women's dorms · sorority housing · fraternity housing · single-student apartments · special housing for disabled students. Recreation and sports facilities include: athletic complex · intramural fields · recreation center.

Student Life and Activities

With 85 percent of students living on campus, there are plenty of social activities. Popular gathering spots include Wertz Student Center, residence halls, Pennington Lounge, The Pub, and The Coffee and Tea Room. Popular campus events include Homecoming Weekend, Little Sibs Weekend, Carnival and concerts. Lycoming College has 81 official student organizations. The most popular are: Amnesty International · Creative Arts Society · Equestrian Club · FLOAT Tutoring Program · Gays · Lesbians · Or BiSexuals and Allies at Lycoming (GLOBAL) · Habitat for Humanity · juggling club · Leadership Education Advancement Project (LEAP) · dance program · College Democrats · fly fishing club (FLYCO) · College Republicans · Environmental Awareness Foundation · Raging Stitches · Recreation Board · Student Senate (SSLC) · Best Buddies. For those interested in sports, there are intramural teams such as: basketball · dodgeball · flag football · fly fishing · soccer · volleyball · wiffle ball. Lycoming College is a member of the Commonwealth Conference (Division III), Middle Atlantic States Collegiate Athletic Conference (Division III).

Academics and Learning Environment

For the B student, the learning environment of a college is just as important as the quality of its academic program. Lycoming College has 89 full-time and 37 part-time faculty members, offering a student-to-faculty ratio of 13:1. The most common course size is 10 to 19 students. Lycoming College offers 31 majors with the most popular being business administration, psychology and biology. The school has a general core requirement. Cooperative education is not offered. All first-year students must maintain a 1.8 GPA or higher to avoid academic probation, and a minimum overall GPA of 3.0 is required to graduate. Other special academic programs that would appeal to a B student: self-designed majors · pass/fail grading option · independent study · double majors · dual degrees · accelerated study · honors program · internships.

B Student Support and Success

Lycoming has an Academic Resource Center that offers subject tutors, writing consultants, study groups, study skills workshops and support services for learning disabilities. In addition, the school provides a program called Writing across the Curriculum, which helps students develop their ability to communicate clearly.

Lycoming College provides a variety of support programs including dedicated guidance for: academic · career · personal · psychological · minority students · non-traditional students · family planning · religious. The average freshman year GPA is 2.8, and 79 percent of freshmen students return for their sophomore year. What do students do after college? While many enter the work force, approximately 20 percent pursue a graduate degree immediately after graduation. Among students who enter the work force, approximately 72 percent enter a field related to their major within six months of graduation. Companies that most frequently hire graduates from Lycoming College include: Merck · Kimberly Clark · Merrill Lynch · American Express · Vanguard Group · Marsh-McLennan.

Support for Students with Learning Disabilities

Students with learning disabilities may take advantage of specific support programs offered by Lycoming College. If necessary, the college will grant additional time to students with learning disabilities to complete their degree. Also, a lightened course load may be granted to LD students. Credit is given for remedial courses taken. According to the school, the director of the Academic Resources Center and the assistant dean for freshmen work closely with students with learning disabilities to ensure a personalized plan for success at the college. Students with learning disabilities will find the following programs at Lycoming College extremely useful:

LYCOMING COLLEGE

Deadlines
Early Action: No
Early Decision: No
Regular Action: Rolling admissions
Common Application: Accepted

Financial Aid
In-state tuition: $29,344
Out-of-state tuition: $29,344
Room: $4,150
Board: $3,984
Books: $900
Freshmen receiving need-based aid: 85%
Undergrads receiving need-based aid: 81%
Avg. % of need met by financial aid: 78%
Avg. aid package (freshmen): $22,525
Avg. aid package (undergrads): $21,298
Freshmen receiving merit-based aid: 14%
Undergrads receiving merit-based aid: 16%
Avg. student debt upon graduation: $27,179

Prominent Alumni
Deidre Connelly, CEO of Lilly USA; Tom Woodruff Jr., Oscar-winning special-effects artist and actor.

School Spirit
Mascot: Warriors
Colors: Blue and gold

remedial math · special classes · tutors · learning center · testing accommodations · untimed tests · extended time for tests · oral tests · readers · note-taking services · reading machines · tape recorders · videotaped classes · priority seating. Individual or small group tutorials are also available in: time management · organizational skills · learning strategies · specific subject areas · writing labs · math labs · study skills. An advisor/advocate from the Academic Resource Center is available to students.

How to Get Admitted

For admissions decisions, non-academic factors considered: interview · extracurricular activities · special talents, interests, abilities · character/personal qualities · volunteer work · work experience · geographical location · religious affiliation/commitment · minority affiliation · alumni relationship. A high school diploma is required, although a GED is also accepted for admissions consideration. SAT or ACT test scores are required of all applicants. SAT Subject Test scores are recommended but not required. *Academic units recommended:* 4 English, 4 Math, 4 Science, 4 Social Studies, 4 Foreign Language.

How to Pay for College

To apply for financial aid, students should submit the following: Free Application for Federal Student Aid (FAFSA) · institution's own financial aid forms · state aid form. Lycoming College participates in the Federal Work Study program. *Need-based aid programs include:* scholarships and grants · general need-based awards · Federal Pell grants · state scholarships and grants · college-based scholarships and grants · private scholarships and grants. *Non-Need-based aid programs include:* scholarships and grants · state scholarships and grants · creative arts and performance awards · special achievements and activities awards · ROTC scholarships.

LYNN UNIVERSITY

3601 North Military Trail, Boca Raton, FL 33431
Admissions: 800-888-5966 · Financial Aid: 800-544-8035
Email: admission@lynn.edu · Website: http://www.lynn.edu

From the College

"Lynn University was founded in 1962 and is a private, co-educational institution with a solid reputation for academic quality and educational innovation, providing academic programs that reflect societal needs and encourage collaborative approaches to the challenges our students will face in the workplace and in the world. The student body is comprised of students from 84 countries and 46 states."

Campus Setting

Lynn University is a four-year, liberal arts university with a 123-acre campus located in Boca Raton, 23 miles from Fort Lauderdale and Palm Beach and 50 miles from Miami. Lynn University has an enrollment of 2,410 students. Lynn University has been co-ed since 1971. The school also has a library with 110,000 books. Lynn University provides on-campus housing with 497 units that can accommodate 1,138 students. Housing options: co-ed dorms · women's dorms · special housing for disabled students · special housing for International students. Recreation and sports facilities include: basketball court · fields · fitness and sports center · tennis complex.

Student Life and Activities

Most students (58 percent) live off campus, which does impact the on-campus social scene. Nevertheless, like any college, students find time to create their own recreational outlets. Lynn University has 31 official student organizations. The most popular are: Music of the Knights · theatre improv group · team managers · Knights of the Roundtable · hospitality club · Students in Free Enterprise · Best Buddies · environmental club · residence hall councils · student judicial board · service groups. For those interested in sports, there are intramural teams such as: basketball · equestrian sports · flag football · golf · tennis. Lynn University is a member of the Sunshine State Conference (Division II).

Academics and Learning Environment

For the B student, the learning environment of a college is just as important as the quality of its academic program. Lynn University has 98 full-time and 59 part-time faculty members, offering a student-to-faculty ratio of 18:1. The most common course size is 10 to 19 students. Lynn University offers 25 majors with the most popular being business administration, hospitality administration and communication. The school has a general core requirement. Cooperative education is available. All first-year students must maintain a 2.0 GPA or higher to avoid academic probation. Other special academic programs that would appeal to a B student: independent study · double majors · dual degrees · accelerated study · honors program · internships · distance learning.

B Student Support and Success

Lynn's Institute for Achievement and Learning focuses on personalized education. The college states that the institute "embraces, empowers and engages its students to offer opportunities for greater accomplishments in higher education and career realization." Programs include First Year Experience, the Tutoring Center, Discovery Writing Center, Metamorphosis Coaching, Probationary Support and Academic Status Support.

LYNN UNIVERSITY

Lynn University
Boca Raton, FL (Pop. 74,764)
Location: Large town
Website: http://www.lynn.edu

Students
Total enrollment: 2,410
Undergrads: 1,023
Freshmen: 375
Part-time students: 12%
From out-of-state: 70%
Male/Female: 50%/50%
Live on-campus: 42%
Off-campus employment rating: Excellent
Caucasian: 49%
African American: 4%
Hispanic: 6%
Asian or Pacific Islander: 0%
Native American: 0%
International: 14%

Academics
Student/faculty ratio: 18:1
Class size 9 or fewer: 17%
Class size 10-29: 74%
Class size 30-49: 9%
Class size 50-99: 1%
Class size 100 or more: -
Returning freshmen: 60%
Six-year graduation rate: 37%

Most Popular Fields of Study
Business, Finance, Sales and Marketing
Liberal Arts, Humanities and General
    Studies
Visual and Performing Arts
Education
Psychology
Communications, Journalism, Advertising
    and Comm. Technologies
Protective Services, Criminal Justice and
    Public Administration
Biological and Life Sciences

First Year Experience is required of all freshmen. This two-semester academic program connects new students with peers, campus resources and faculty. In the first class (FYE-1), students focus on the nature of education, including units on time management, test taking, communication skills, study techniques, university policies and procedures, resources and services, health and wellness issues and personal issues. FYE-1 also includes a pre-orientation to Academic Adventure, a faculty-led program in which the entire freshman class spends five days in the Caribbean on a ship studying the region's cultures and people. In FYE-2, students explore multicultural and diversity awareness, educational planning, career development, leadership, community service and learning potential—plus reflect upon their Academic Adventure.

The Discovery Writing Center offers one-on-one tutoring for all levels of writing skills. The Hannifan Center for Career Development and Internships provides personalized career counseling, group career workshops, internships and job-placement assistance.

Academic Status Support assists students who are on academic probation. This no-cost program includes advising and learning strategy suggestions to help students improve their grades. Probationary Support is similar and offers free advising, group tutoring, social activities, counseling sessions and workshops.

Metamorphosis Coaching is geared to students who learn best from hands-on experience rather than traditional classroom methods. It takes students out of the classroom and into such settings as the campus butterfly garden or a local nature center as they learn observation skills logged into journals. According to the college, this program is not just about studying nature, but it also is "a study of life and the nature of our own selves. The 'lessons' learned through this reflective process will provide valuable insights about the way you learn best—and yourself." The program also includes group dinners and guest lecturers as well as private tutoring and field trips. (There is a charge for this program.)

Lynn University provides a variety of support programs including dedicated guidance for: academic · career · personal. The average freshman year GPA is 2.6, and 60 percent of freshmen students return for their sophomore year. Among students who enter the work force, approximately 82 percent enter a field related to their major within six months of graduation. Companies that most frequently hire graduates from Lynn University include: Applied Card Systems · Boca Raton Resort and Club · Enterprise Rent-A-Car · Five-Star Productions · Four Seasons Resort · Lynn University · Nickelodeon · Palm Beach School System · Target Stores.

Support for Students with Learning Disabilities

Students with learning disabilities may take advantage of specific support programs offered by Lynn University. If necessary, the college will grant additional time to students with learning disabilities to complete their degree. Students with learning disabilities will find the following programs at Lynn University extremely useful: special classes · tutors · learning center · testing accommodations · untimed tests · extended time for tests · oral tests · readers · reading machines · tape recorders · texts on tape · videotaped classes · early syllabus · diagnostic testing service · waiver of foreign language degree requirement. Individual or small group tutorials are also available in: time management · organizational skills · learning strategies · specific subject areas · writing labs · math labs · study skills. An advisor/advocate from the Comprehensive Support Program is available to students.

How to Get Admitted

For admissions decisions, non-academic factors considered: interview · extracurricular activities · special talents, interests, abilities · character/personal qualities · volunteer work · work experience · alumni relationship. A high school diploma is required, although a GED is also accepted for admissions consideration. SAT or ACT test scores are required of all applicants.

How to Pay for College

To apply for financial aid, students should submit the following: Free Application for Federal Student Aid (FAFSA) · institution's own financial aid forms. Lynn University participates in the Federal Work Study program. *Need-based aid programs include:* scholarships and grants · general need-based awards · Federal Pell grants · state scholarships and grants · college-based scholarships and grants · private scholarships and grants. *Non-Need-based aid programs include:* scholarships and grants · general need-based awards · state scholarships and grants · creative arts and performance awards · special achievements and activities awards · special characteristics awards · athletic scholarships.

LYNN UNIVERSITY

Highlights

Admissions
Applicants: 2,657
Accepted: 1,636
Acceptance rate: 61.6%
Average GPA: 2.8
ACT range: 17-21
SAT Math range: 410-520
SAT Reading range: 370-510
SAT Writing range: Not reported
Top 10% of class: 7%
Top 25% of class: 16%
Top 50% of class: 43%

Deadlines
Early Action: No
Early Decision: No
Regular Action: Rolling admissions
Common Application: Accepted

Financial Aid
In-state tuition: $27,800
Out-of-state tuition: $27,800
Room: -
Board: $2,180
Books: $1,000
Freshmen receiving need-based aid: 34%
Undergrads receiving need-based aid: 34%
Avg. % of need met by financial aid: 61%
Avg. aid package (freshmen): $19,838
Avg. aid package (undergrads): $19,444
Freshmen receiving merit-based aid: 33%
Undergrads receiving merit-based aid: 25%
Avg. student debt upon graduation: $30,175

School Spirit
Mascot: Fighting Knights
Colors: Blue and white
Song: *Lynn University Fight Song*

MANHATTANVILLE COLLEGE

2900 Purchase Street, Purchase, NY 10577
Admissions: 800-32-VILLE · Financial Aid: 800-32-VILLE
Email: admissions@mville.edu · Website: http://www.mville.edu

From the College

"At Manhattanville College, we offer a rigorous academic experience within a nurturing environment. Every one of our 1,600 undergraduate students is able to make his or her own personal contribution to our community. With more than 40 areas of study and 50 campus clubs, our students discover who they are while they are here. This richly diverse community embodies the college's mission to educate ethically and socially responsible leaders for the global community. This commitment to saving the community is demonstrated by the 23,000 hours of service provided by Manhattanville undergraduates in a year. Students come to our 100-acre campus from more than 39 states and 59 countries. Set in prosperous and thriving Westchester County, New York, our campus offers the spaciousness and leisurely pace of a suburban location along with the resources of New York City, which is just 30 minutes away. Many students choose to spend a semester abroad living, interning and studying in NYC."

Campus Setting

Manhattanville is a private, liberal arts college. Founded as an academy for girls in 1841, it adopted co-education in 1971. Its campus is located in Purchase, 25 miles from New York City. A four-year institution, Manhattanville College has an enrollment of 2,821 students. In addition to a large, well-stocked library, the campus also has an environmental science building. Manhattanville College provides on-campus housing with 744 units that can accommodate 1,263 students. Housing options: co-ed dorms.

Student Life and Activities

With 80 percent of students living on campus, there are plenty of social activities. According to the editor of the school newspaper, social life has traditionally been slow and people usually went off-campus for activities, but this past year, there have been improvements aimed at keeping students on campus for the weekend. It's worth staying now. Popular on-campus hangouts include Reid Castle, Manhattanville Cafe, the quad and the commuter lounge. Off campus, students frequent Ivy, O'Henry's and 7 Willow Street. Popular events include Shakespeare Events, Community Service Trips, the Living Theatre, Fair Trade Week, Vagina Monologues, Cymbeline, Quad Jam, the Global Pot, Dance Concerts, Shabbat Dinners, Latin Bash, India Art Exhibit, Hispanic Summit and Kwaanza Celebration. Manhattanville College has 57 official student organizations. The Student Programming Board, Quad Jam Committees, Student Government and the Clubs' Council are influential on-campus groups. Manhattanville College is a member of the Eastern College Athletic Conference (Division I, Football I-AA), Freedom Conference (Division III), Knickerbocker Lacrosse Conference (Division III, men's only) and Middle Atlantic Conference (Division III).

Academics and Learning Environment

For the B student, the learning environment of a college is just as important as the quality of its academic program. Manhattanville College has 102 full-time and 194 part-time faculty members, offering a student-to-faculty ratio of 12:1. The most common course size is 10 to 19 students. Manhattanville College offers 32 majors with the most popular being management, psychology and art and least popular being American studies, art history and philosophy. The school has a general core requirement. Cooperative education is not offered. All first-year students must maintain a 1.8 GPA or higher to avoid academic probation, and a minimum overall GPA of 2.0 is required to graduate. Other special academic programs that would appeal to a B student: self-designed majors · pass/fail grading option · independent study · double majors · dual degrees · accelerated study · honors program · internships · weekend college · distance learning certificate programs.

B Student Support and Success

Manhattanville's Academic Resource Center offers individual tutoring, group supplemental instruction and a variety of workshops. ARC has full-time professional instructors in writing, math and study strategies and part-time tutors in subjects that include accounting, foreign languages, math, music theory, statistics for social sciences and economic statistics. Special credit-bearing courses are offered to help students learn science, math and the humanities.

According to the college, the philosophy of the ARC is one of "fostering independence in the students who seek help. We are equipped to deal with many types of academic difficulties and to offer personal assistance in a relaxed and supportive atmosphere."

Manhattanville College provides a variety of support programs including dedicated guidance for: academic · career · personal · psychological · minority students · family planning · religious. Recognizing that some students may need extra preparation, Manhattanville College offers remedial and refresher courses in: reading · writing · math · study skills. The average freshman year GPA is 3.0, and 76 percent of freshmen students return for their sophomore year. What do students do after college? While many enter the work force, approximately 18 percent pursue a graduate degree immediately after graduation, and another 17 percent enter graduate school within two years. Among students who enter the work force, approximately 68 percent enter a field related to their major within six months of graduation. Companies that most frequently hire graduates from Manhattanville College include: PepsiCo · Mastercard International · MBIA · Salomon Smith Barney · Diversified Investment Advisors · NYC Board of Education · Bank of New York · Goldman Sachs · New York Rangers · New York Jets · Sesame Street Trips · Lincoln Center · Teach for America · Greenwich Hospital · MCI.

Support for Students with Learning Disabilities

Students with learning disabilities may take advantage of specific support programs offered by Manhattanville College. If necessary, the college will grant additional time to students with learning disabilities to complete their degree. Also, a lightened course load may be granted to LD students. Students with learning disabilities will find the following programs at Manhattanville College extremely useful: remedial math · remedial English · tutors · learning center · testing accommodations · untimed tests · extended time for tests · take-home exam · oral tests · readers · note-taking services · reading machines · tape recorders · early syllabus · priority registration · waiver of math degree requirement · waiver of foreign language degree requirement. Individual or small group tutorials are also

MANHATTANVILLE COLLEGE

Highlights

Manhattanville College
Purchase, NY (Pop. 8,000)
Location: Large town
Website: http://www.mville.edu

Students
Total enrollment: 2,821
Undergrads: 588
Freshmen: 555
Part-time students: 6%
From out-of-state: 35%
Male/Female: 33%/67%
Live on-campus: 80%
Off-campus employment rating: Excellent

Academics
Student/faculty ratio: 12:1
Class size 9 or fewer: 31%
Class size 10-29: 64%
Class size 30-49: 6%
Class size 50-99: 10%
Class size 100 or more: 3%
Returning freshmen: 76%
Six-year graduation rate: 58%

Most Popular Fields of Study
Business, Finance, Sales and Marketing
Biological and Life Sciences
Area, Ethnic and Gender Studies

Admissions
Applicants: 4,556
Accepted: 2,350
Acceptance rate: 51.6%
Average GPA: 3.0
ACT range: 22-26
SAT Math range: 500-610
SAT Reading range: 500-620
SAT Writing range: Not reported
Top 10% of class: 21%
Top 25% of class: 47%
Top 50% of class: 80%

MANHATTANVILLE
COLLEGE

Deadlines
Early Action: No
Early Decision: December 1
Regular Action: Rolling admissions
Common Application: Accepted

Financial Aid
In-state tuition: $31,490
Out-of-state tuition: $31,490
Room: $8,000
Board: $5,500
Books: $800
Freshmen receiving need-based aid: 73%
Undergrads receiving need-based aid:
   68%
Avg. % of need met by financial aid: 79%
Avg. aid package (freshmen): $25,039
Avg. aid package (undergrads): $25,548
Freshmen receiving merit-based aid: 20%
Undergrads receiving merit-based aid:
   22%
Avg. student debt upon graduation:
   $23,253

School Spirit
Mascot: Valiants

available in: time management · organizational skills · learning strategies · specific subject areas · writing labs · math labs · study skills. An advisor/advocate from the Office of Disability Services, HELP Center is available to students.

How to Get Admitted

For admissions decisions, non-academic factors considered: interview · extracurricular activities · special talents, interests, abilities · character/personal qualities · volunteer work · work experience · state of residency · geographical location · alumni relationship. A high school diploma is required, although a GED is also accepted for admissions consideration. SAT or ACT test scores are required of all applicants. SAT Subject Test scores are required for some applicants. *According to the admissions office:* Minimum grade average of B required.

How to Pay for College

To apply for financial aid, students should submit the following: Free Application for Federal Student Aid (FAFSA) · state aid form. Manhattanville College participates in the Federal Work Study program. *Need-based aid programs include:* scholarships and grants · general need-based awards · Federal Pell grants · state scholarships and grants · college-based scholarships and grants · private scholarships and grants. *Non-Need-based aid programs include:* scholarships and grants · state scholarships and grants · creative arts and performance awards.

MARIETTA COLLEGE

215 Fifth Street, Marietta, OH 45750
Admissions: 800-331-7896 · Financial Aid: 800-331-2709
Email: admit@marietta.edu · Website: http://www.marietta.edu

From the College

"Marietta College's mission revolves around nine core values. The central value reflects our belief that 'the liberal arts are the best preparation for any career' and expresses our 'equal commitment to practical experience as a necessary prerequisite for the world of work.' Every Marietta student receives a liberal arts foundation and in-depth study in their major, and each of our graduates is 'prepared to succeed in a technological society…and to thrive in a diverse, global society.' In addition, all graduates understand 'the role of the citizen-leader…in a livable, sustainable, ethical future.'"

Campus Setting

Marietta, founded in 1835, is a private college. Its 120-acre campus is located in Marietta, 115 miles southwest of Columbus. The campus's oldest building, of Greek Revival design, is listed in the National Register of Historic Places. A four-year institution, Marietta College has been co-ed since 1897. In addition to a large, well-stocked library, the campus facilities include: dinosaur exhibit · planetarium. Marietta College provides on-campus housing that can accommodate 1,199 students. Housing options: co-ed dorms · women's dorms · men's dorms · sorority housing · fraternity housing · single-student apartments · special housing for disabled students. Recreation and sports facilities include: athletic fields · recreation center · stadium · tennis courts.

Student Life and Activities

With 73 percent of students living on campus, there are plenty of social activities. Popular events include Homecoming, Family Weekend, Little Sibs Weekend, Community Service Day and Make a Difference Day. Marietta College has 60 official student organizations. The most popular are: Concert choir · concert · jazz and pep bands. Jazz/rock ensemble · dance team · theatrical group · forensics team · team managers · environmental awareness group · computer club · Circle K · tournaments · Great Outdoors Club · Rainbow Alliance · Young Democrats · Young Republicans · Model UN · Philanthropy Connection · teacher education association · Society of Petroleum Engineers · marketing club · service and special-interest groups. For those interested in sports, there are intramural teams such as: basketball · football · handball · racquetball · soccer · softball · table tennis · volleyball. Marietta College is a member of the Ohio Athletic Conference (Division III).

Academics and Learning Environment

For the B student, the learning environment of a college is just as important as the quality of its academic program. Marietta College has 103 full-time and 42 part-time faculty members, offering a student-to-faculty ratio of 13:1. The most common course size is 10 to 19 students. Marietta College offers 42 majors with the most popular being marketing, management and advertising/public relations and least popular being music, chemistry and computer science. The school has a general core requirement. Cooperative education is available. All first-year students must maintain a 2.0 GPA or higher to avoid academic probation. Other special academic programs that would appeal to a B student: self-designed majors · pass/fail grading option · independent study · double majors · dual degrees · honors program · Phi Beta Kappa · internships · certificate programs.

MARIETTA COLLEGE

Highlights

Marietta College
Marietta, OH (Pop. 18,000)
Location: Medium city
Website: http://www.marietta.edu

Students
Total enrollment: 1,602
Undergrads: 740
Freshmen: 493
Part-time students: 6%
From out-of-state: 33%
Male/Female: 50%/50%
Live on-campus: 73%
In fraternities: 15%
In sororities: 23%
Off-campus employment rating: Excellent
Caucasian: 83%
African American: 4%
Hispanic: 2%
Asian or Pacific Islander: 1%
Native American: 0%
International: 9%

Academics
Student/faculty ratio: 13:1
Class size 9 or fewer: 34%
Class size 10-29: 62%
Class size 30-49: 4%
Class size 50-99: -
Class size 100 or more: 3%
Returning freshmen: 73%
Six-year graduation rate: 65%

Most Popular Fields of Study
Business, Finance, Sales and Marketing
Social Sciences, History, Economics, Political Science
Visual and Performing Arts
Computer and Information Sciences
Communications, Journalism, Advertising and Comm. Technologies
Liberal Arts, Humanities and General Studies
English and Literature
Health Professions, Medicine and Related Sciences
Psychology
Engineering and Engineering Technologies

B Student Support and Success

At Marietta, the Academic Resource Center offers individualized academic support for students by means of several different avenues. Students are advised early on when their performance assessment may be dangerously low through the use of the college's early warning system. Help is available to struggling students through individual and small group tutoring and study skills assistance. Additionally, students have access to computers and educational technology, personal development workshops on topics like study skills and time management, a resource library and referral to additional resources.

Marietta College provides a variety of support programs including dedicated guidance for: academic · career · personal · psychological · minority students · family planning. Recognizing that some students may need extra preparation, Marietta College offers remedial and refresher courses in: reading · writing · math · study skills. The average freshman year GPA is 2.9, and 73 percent of freshmen students return for their sophomore year. What do students do after college? While many enter the work force, approximately 30 percent pursue a graduate degree immediately after graduation, and another 20 percent enter graduate school within two years. Among students who enter the work force, approximately 65 percent enter a field related to their major within six months of graduation. Companies that most frequently hire graduates from Marietta College include: Chevron · Unocal · Marathon · Anadarko · Exxon-Mobil · Deloitte & Touche · Cleveland Clinic.

Support for Students with Learning Disabilities

Students with learning disabilities may take advantage of specific support programs offered by Marietta College. If necessary, the college will grant additional time to students with learning disabilities to complete their degree. High school foreign language waivers are accepted. High school math waivers are also accepted. According to the school, recent documentation, guidelines, criteria requirements are available for specific disabilities. Services are individualized based on the disability, and progress is monitored. Students with learning disabilities will find the following programs at Marietta College extremely useful: remedial math · remedial English · tutors · learning center · testing accommodations · untimed tests · extended time for tests · take-home exam · oral tests · readers · note-taking services · reading machines · tape recorders · texts on tape · early syllabus · priority registration · waiver of math degree requirement. Individual or small group tutorials are also available in: time management · organizational skills · learning strategies · specific subject areas · writing labs · math labs · study skills. An advisor/advocate from the Academic Resource Center is available to students.

How to Get Admitted

For admissions decisions, non-academic factors considered: interview · extracurricular activities · special talents, interests, abilities · character/personal qualities · volunteer work · work experience · geographical location · minority affiliation · alumni relationship. A high school diploma is required, although a GED is also accepted for admissions consideration. SAT or ACT test scores are required of all applicants. SAT Subject Test scores are considered, if submitted, but are not required. *Academic units recommended:* 4 English, 4 Math, 4 Science, 2 Social Studies, 4 Foreign Language.

How to Pay for College

To apply for financial aid, students should submit the following: Free Application for Federal Student Aid (FAFSA) · institution's own financial aid forms. Marietta College participates in the Federal Work Study program. *Need-based aid programs include:* scholarships and grants · general need-based awards · Federal Pell grants · state scholarships and grants · college-based scholarships and grants · private scholarships and grants. *Non-Need-based aid programs include:* scholarships and grants · general need-based awards · state scholarships and grants · creative arts and performance awards · special achievements and activities awards.

MARIETTA COLLEGE

Highlights

Admissions
Applicants: 2,440
Accepted: 1,883
Acceptance rate: 77.2%
Average GPA: 3.4
ACT range: 20-26
SAT Math range: 490-630
SAT Reading range: 500-600
SAT Writing range: Not reported
Top 10% of class: 27%
Top 25% of class: 50%
Top 50% of class: 85%

Deadlines
Early Action: No
Early Decision: No
Regular Action: Rolling admissions
Common Application: Accepted

Financial Aid
In-state tuition: $26,386
Out-of-state tuition: $26,386
Room: $4,400
Board: $3,646
Books: $720
Freshmen receiving need-based aid: 84%
Undergrads receiving need-based aid: 78%
Avg. % of need met by financial aid: 90%
Avg. aid package (freshmen): $21,683
Avg. aid package (undergrads): $20,605
Freshmen receiving merit-based aid: 22%
Undergrads receiving merit-based aid: 17%
Avg. student debt upon graduation: $22,123

Prominent Alumni
Charles Gates Dawes, U.S. vice president, Nobel Prize winner; Story Musgrave, scientist, physician, astronaut; Jim Tracy, manager, Colorado Rockies baseball team

School Spirit
Mascot: Pioneers
Colors: Navy blue and white

Marymount Manhattan College

New York, NY (Pop. 9,000,000)
Location: Major city
Website: http://www.mmm.edu

Students

Total enrollment: 1,938
Undergrads: 453
Freshmen: 454
Part-time students: 18%
From out-of-state: 50%
Male/Female: 23%/77%
Live on-campus: 44%
Off-campus employment rating: Fair
Caucasian: 71%
African American: 12%
Hispanic: 10%
Asian or Pacific Islander: 4%
Native American: 1%
International: 3%

Academics

Student/faculty ratio: 12:1
Class size 9 or fewer: 27%
Class size 10-29: 72%
Class size 30-49: 1%
Class size 50-99: 4%
Class size 100 or more: -
Returning freshmen: 69%
Six-year graduation rate: 41%

Most Popular Fields of Study

Business, Finance, Sales and Marketing
Social Sciences, History, Economics,
  Political Science
Visual and Performing Arts
Liberal Arts, Humanities and General
  Studies
Psychology
Communications, Journalism, Advertising
  and Comm. Technologies
English and Literature
Biological and Life Sciences

MARYMOUNT MANHATTAN COLLEGE

221 East 71st Street, New York, NY 10021
Admissions: 800-MARYMOU · Financial Aid: 212-517-0480
Email: admissions@mmm.edu
Website: http://www.mmm.edu

From the College

"Commitment to intercultural dialogue; commitment to complementary career preparation courses and liberal arts courses; strong programs in biology, English, psychology, international studies, communication arts, business, theatre, and dance."

Campus Setting

Marymount Manhattan, founded in 1936, is a private, liberal arts college. Founded as a branch of Marymount College of Tarrytown, N.Y., it became an independent institution in 1961. Its one-acre campus is located in midtown Manhattan. A four-year private institution, Marymount Manhattan College has been co-ed since 1989. The school also has a library with 70,000 books. Marymount Manhattan College provides on-campus housing with 3 units that can accommodate 675 students.

Student Life and Activities

Most students (56 percent) live off campus, which does impact the on-campus social scene. Nevertheless, like any college, students find time to create their own recreational outlets. Popular events include: Snow Ball, 100 Nights Celebration, Earth Day, Leadership Awards Reception, Charter Day and Strawberry Festival. Marymount Manhattan College has 43 official student organizations. The most popular are: Advocates for Animals · Amnesty International · Art Fusion · Campus Activities Board · dance club · Expressions of Grace · Feminist Majority Leadership Alliance · French club · international studies club · literary society · Marymount Outreach · Nutz and Boltz of Comedy · philosophy club · Poptards 101 · psychology club. Marymount Manhattan does not offer athletic programs.

Academics and Learning Environment

For the B student, the learning environment of a college is just as important as the quality of its academic program. Marymount Manhattan College has 91 full-time and 217 part-time faculty members, offering a student-to-faculty ratio of 12:1. The most common course size is 10 to 19 students. Marymount Manhattan College offers 18 majors with the most popular being communication arts, theatre and business management and least popular being history, speech/language pathology/audiology and international studies. The school has a general core requirement. Cooperative education is not offered. Other special academic programs that would appeal to a B student: pass/fail grading option · independent study · double majors · accelerated study · honors program · internships · distance learning certificate programs.

B Student Support and Success

Marymount's students may find assistance with coursework at a tutoring center that provides full support to walk-ins through student tutors as well as trained staff. The Center for Academic Advancement (formerly known as College Skills) has courses for students who need to reinforce their skills in reading comprehension, vocabulary, grammar and basic writing. According to the college, "It is our mission to provide these services in any reasonable manner in order to secure student futures. Our main objective is to assure each student who passes through our doors that they can and will succeed in college."

Marymount Manhattan College provides a variety of support programs including dedicated guidance for: academic · career · personal · psychological · minority students · non-traditional students. Recognizing that some students may need extra preparation, Marymount Manhattan College offers remedial and refresher courses in: reading · writing · math · study skills. The average freshman year GPA is 3.2, and 69 percent of freshmen students return for their sophomore year. What do students do after college? While many enter the work force, approximately 31 percent pursue a graduate degree immediately after graduation.

Support for Students with Learning Disabilities

Students with learning disabilities may take advantage of specific support programs offered by Marymount Manhattan College. High school foreign language waivers are accepted. High school math waivers are also accepted. Students with learning disabilities will find the following programs at Marymount Manhattan College extremely useful: remedial math · remedial English · remedial reading · tutors · extended time for tests · tape recorders · diagnostic testing service. Individual or small group tutorials are also available in: time management · organizational skills · learning strategies · specific subject areas · writing labs · math labs · study skills. An advisor/advocate from the Access Program is available to students. This member also sits on the admissions committee.

How to Get Admitted

For admissions decisions, non-academic factors considered: interview · extracurricular activities · special talents, interests, abilities · character/personal qualities · volunteer work · work experience · state of residency · alumni relationship. A high school diploma is required, although a GED is also accepted for admissions consideration. SAT or ACT test scores are required for some applicants. SAT Subject Test scores are considered, if submitted, but are not required. *According to the admissions office:* Minimum SAT scores of 450 in both verbal and math and minimum 2.0 GPA recommended. *Academic units recommended:* 1 Science, 3 Foreign Language.

How to Pay for College

To apply for financial aid, students should submit the following: Free Application for Federal Student Aid (FAFSA). Marymount Manhattan College participates in the Federal Work Study program. *Need-based aid programs include:* scholarships and grants · general need-based awards · Federal Pell grants · state scholarships and grants · college-based scholarships and grants · private scholarships and grants.

MARYMOUNT MANHATTAN COLLEGE

Highlights

Admissions
Applicants: 2,255
Accepted: 1,710
Acceptance rate: 75.8%
Average GPA: 3.1
ACT range: 20-25
SAT Math range: 460-570
SAT Reading range: 500-600
SAT Writing range: Not reported
Top 10% of class: 25%
Top 25% of class: 75%
Top 50% of class: 89%

Deadlines
Early Action: No
Early Decision: No
Regular Action: March 15 (priority)
Common Application: Accepted

Financial Aid
In-state tuition: $21,578
Out-of-state tuition: $21,578
Room: $10,874
Board: $2,000
Books: $1,000
Freshmen receiving need-based aid: 61%
Undergrads receiving need-based aid: 60%
Avg. % of need met by financial aid: 52%
Avg. aid package (freshmen): $11,278
Avg. aid package (undergrads): $10,849
Freshmen receiving merit-based aid: 20%
Undergrads receiving merit-based aid: 11%
Avg. student debt upon graduation: $17,125

MARYMOUNT MANHATTAN COLLEGE

Non-Need-based aid programs include: scholarships and grants · state scholarships and grants · creative arts and performance awards · special achievements and activities awards.

McDANIEL COLLEGE

2 College Hill, Westminster, MD 21157
Admissions: 800-638-5005 · Financial Aid: 410-857-2233
Email: admissions@mcdaniel.edu
Website: http://www.mcdaniel.edu

From the College

"McDaniel College students become involved, connected and confident. First-year seminars, a January mini-mester of uncommon courses, and options for self-designed majors provide learning opportunities. Less than an hour's drive from Washington, DC, students take advantage of all the career and cultural possibilities of the nation's capital while honing leadership skills on campus as faculty-research assistants across all majors, as volunteers directing over 100 student clubs or as teammates on the playing fields of 24 intercollegiate sports. A nine-hole golf course doubles as both a place to practice your swing or snowboard downhill in winter."

Campus Setting

McDaniel, founded in 1867, is a private, liberal arts college. Its 160-acre campus is located in Westminster, 35 miles northwest of Baltimore. A four-year institution, McDaniel College has an enrollment of 3,896 students. The campus also has a gallery. McDaniel College provides on-campus housing with 763 units that can accommodate 1,318 students. Housing options: co-ed dorms · women's dorms · men's dorms · sorority housing · fraternity housing · single-student apartments. Recreation and sports facilities include: baseball · football · lacrosse and softball fields · fitness center · gymnasium · golf course · tennis courts · outdoor track.

Student Life and Activities

With 75 percent of students living on campus, there are plenty of social activities. The editor of the student newspaper observes that "because the campus is small, it is possible to get to know just about everyone—and the campus is beautiful, with beautiful sunsets over the hill." On campus, students gather at Gazebo, Harvey Stone Park, Upper Decker and the Game Room. Popular off-campus haunts include Ernie's, Westminster Inn, Champs and Maggie's. Popular social events include Spring Fling, Homecoming, Jazz Night, Performance Concerts, BSU Fashion Show, International Student Dinner, Soul Food Dinner and Unity Week. McDaniel College has 132 official student organizations. Influential groups on campus include Greeks, Christian Fellowship, CAPBoard, the football team, BACCHUS, SEAC, Residence Life and the International Club. For those interested in sports, there are intramural teams such as: badminton · basketball · flag football · floor hockey · soccer · tennis · volleyball. McDaniel College is a member of the Centennial Conference (Division III).

Academics and Learning Environment

For the B student, the learning environment of a college is just as important as the quality of its academic program. McDaniel Col-

McDaniel College
Westminster, MD (Pop. 17,000)
Location: Large town
Website: http://www.mcdaniel.edu

Students
Total enrollment: 3,896
Undergrads: 797
Freshmen: 487
Part-time students: 5%
From out-of-state: 41%
Male/Female: 45%/55%
Live on-campus: 75%
In fraternities: 12%
In sororities: 12%
Off-campus employment rating: Fair
Caucasian: 77%
African American: 5%
Hispanic: 2%
Asian or Pacific Islander: 3%
Native American: 1%
International: 0%

Academics
Student/faculty ratio: 12:1
Class size 9 or fewer: 22%
Class size 10-29: 74%
Class size 30-49: 3%
Class size 50-99: -
Class size 100 or more: 9%
Returning freshmen: 87%
Six-year graduation rate: 72%

Most Popular Fields of Study
Business, Finance, Sales and Marketing
Psychology
Protective Services, Criminal Justice and
    Public Administration
Visual and Performing Arts
English and Literature
Philosophy, Religion and Theology
Mathematics
Parks, Recreation and Fitness
Foreign Languages, Literature and Lin-
    guistics

McDANIEL COLLEGE

Admissions

Applicants: 2,651
Accepted: 2,050
Acceptance rate: 77.3%
placed on wait list: 38
Average GPA: 3.4
ACT range: 21-26
SAT Math range: 510-610
SAT Reading range: 500-620
SAT Writing range: Not reported
Top 10% of class: 28%
Top 25% of class: 57%
Top 50% of class: 88%

Deadlines

Early Action: December 1
Early Decision: No
Regular Action: February 1 (final)
Common Application: Accepted

Financial Aid

In-state tuition: $30,780
Out-of-state tuition: $30,780
Room: $3,300
Board: $2,850
Books: $1,200
Freshmen receiving need-based aid: 68%
Undergrads receiving need-based aid: 66%
Avg. % of need met by financial aid: 93%
Avg. aid package (freshmen): $22,446
Avg. aid package (undergrads): $23,576
Freshmen receiving merit-based aid: 32%
Undergrads receiving merit-based aid: 34%
Avg. student debt upon graduation: $25,345

Prominent Alumni

Alan Rabinowitz, director of science and exploration, Wildlife Conservation Society, founder of jaguar preserve in Belize; David Carrasco, world-renowned scholar, Mesoamerican religions; Neil L. Rudenstine, professor of the study of Latin America, Harvard

School Spirit

Mascot: Green Terror
Colors: Green and gold

lege has 135 full-time and 244 part-time faculty members, offering a student-to-faculty ratio of 12:1. The most common course size is 10 to 19 students. McDaniel College offers 41 majors with the most popular being psychology, sociology and business administration/economics and least popular being environmental policy and science, physics and mathematics. The school has a general core requirement. Cooperative education is not offered. All first-year students must maintain a 1.5 GPA or higher to avoid academic probation, and a minimum overall GPA of 2.0 is required to graduate. Other special academic programs that would appeal to a B student: self-designed majors · pass/fail grading option · independent study · double majors · dual degrees · accelerated study · honors program · Phi Beta Kappa · internships · certificate programs.

B Student Support and Success

McDaniel offers a variety of academic support for students. It has tutoring services, as well as faculty advising for choosing courses. The Writing Center works one on one with students to become "better, more confident writers" through peer tutoring. Students can get assistance with ideas, notes, rough drafts and final drafts. Computer resources are available and the College also has a range of services for any students with disabilities.

McDaniel College provides a variety of support programs including dedicated guidance for: academic · career · personal · minority students · family planning. The average freshman year GPA is 2.9, and 87 percent of freshmen students return for their sophomore year.

Support for Students with Learning Disabilities

Students with learning disabilities may take advantage of specific support programs offered by McDaniel College. High school foreign language waivers are accepted. Students with learning disabilities will find the following programs at McDaniel College extremely useful: remedial math · remedial English · tutors · learning center · extended time for tests · take-home exam · readers · note-taking services · reading machines · tape recorders. Individual or small group tutorials are also available in: time management · organizational skills · learning strategies · writing labs · study skills. An advisor/advocate from the Academic Skills Program is available to students.

How to Get Admitted

For admissions decisions, non-academic factors considered: interview · extracurricular activities · special talents, interests, abilities · character/personal qualities · volunteer work · work experience · state of residency · alumni relationship. A high school diploma is required, although a GED is also accepted for admissions consideration. SAT or ACT test scores are required for some applicants. SAT Subject Test scores are considered, if submitted, but are not required. *According to the admissions office:* Minimum combined SAT Reasoning score of 1000 and minimum 2.5 GPA required. SAT Reasoning/ACT scores optional for applicants with minimum 3.5 GPA. *Academic units recommended:* 4 English, 4 Math, 4 Science, 3 Social Studies, 4 Foreign Language.

How to Pay for College

To apply for financial aid, students should submit the following: Free Application for Federal Student Aid (FAFSA) · institution's own financial aid forms · state aid form. McDaniel College participates in the Federal Work Study program. *Need-based aid programs include:* scholarships and grants · general need-based awards · Federal Pell grants · state scholarships and grants · college-based scholarships and grants · private scholarships and grants. *Non-Need-based aid programs include:* scholarships and grants · general need-based awards · state scholarships and grants · special achievements and activities awards · ROTC scholarships.

McKENDREE UNIVERSITY

701 College Road, Lebanon, IL 62254-1299
Admissions: 800-BEAR CAT, extension 6831
Financial Aid: 800-BEAR CAT, extension 6828
Email: inquiry@mckendree.edu · Website: http://www.mckendree.edu

From the College

"McKendree University provides students a peaceful, residential campus in a small, friendly town, yet is just minutes away from St. Louis. McKendree students receive a broad-based, liberal arts-oriented education while also developing skills in preparation for a career or graduate studies. The college's philosophy reflects concern for individual development of its students and its commitment to personalized education. Co-curricular programs are also of importance, as McKendree students participate in community service, voluntary spiritual development, athletics and a wide variety of clubs and organizations meeting student needs and interests."

Campus Setting

McKendree, founded in 1828, has a 110-acre campus located in Lebanon, 15 miles east of St. Louis. A four-year private institution, McKendree University has an enrollment of 3,212 students. The school is also affiliated with the Methodist Church. The school has a library with 97,265 books. McKendree University provides on-campus housing with 260 units that can accommodate 690 students. Housing options: co-ed dorms · single-student apartments.

Student Life and Activities

With 55 percent of students living on campus, there are plenty of social activities. But "off-campus is more popular for the small campus community," reports the student newspaper. "Visiting area malls and trips into St. Louis are frequent. Most students go home on weeks, so weekly social activities are better attended." Hot spots on- and off-campus include Deneen center, Ron's, Olive Garden, Hideout, Schiappa's Pizza, Applebee's, St. Clair Square, the dorm and commuters lounge. Popular events include: Technos International Week , McKendree Idol and the George E. McCammon Memorial Distinguished Speaker Series. McKendree University has 62 official student organizations. Campus Christian Fellowship, Greeks, Students Against Social Injustice, baseball, basketball, soccer, softball and volleyball teams have influence on student life. McKendree University is a member of the American Midwest Conference (NAIA).

Academics and Learning Environment

For the B student, the learning environment of a college is just as important as the quality of its academic program. McKendree University has 86 full-time and 220 part-time faculty members, offering a student-to-faculty ratio of 15:1. The most common course size is 10 to 19 students. McKendree University offers 44 majors with the most popular being business administration and least popular being religious studies and art. The school has a general core requirement. Cooperative education is not offered. All first-year students must maintain a 1.75 GPA or higher to avoid academic probation, and a minimum overall GPA of 2.0 is required to graduate. Other special academic programs that would appeal to a B student: self-designed majors · pass/fail grading option · independent study · double majors · dual degrees · honors program · internships · distance learning.

B Student Support and Success

The college features small classes, is eager to accept students who are really trying and is dedicated to not letting any of them "slip through the cracks."

McKendree University provides a variety of support programs including dedicated guidance for: academic · career · personal · psychological · minority students · veterans · religious. Recognizing that some students may need extra preparation, McKendree University offers remedial and refresher courses in: reading · writing · math · study skills. The average freshman year GPA is 3.0, and 77 percent of freshmen students return for their sophomore year. What do students do after college? While many enter the work force, approximately 21 percent pursue a graduate degree immediately after graduation. Among students who enter the work force, approximately 89 percent enter a field related to their major within six months of graduation. Companies that most frequently hire graduates from McKendree University include: Catholic Charities · Scott Air Force Base · Clinton County Sheriff · Judevine Center for Autism · Better Business Bureau · Stifel · Nicolaus · Springfield Police Department · Boeing · Evangelical Childrens Home · CHASI · National Childrens Cancer Society · May Department Stores · Attorney Generals Office · Standard Lab · Edward Jones · CitiFinancial · Jims Formal Wear · Gliks · SBC · St. Louis Childrens Hospital · Behavioral Intervention · Fuehne & Fuehne Anders · Minkler and Diehl · University of Illinois Extension · Celsis Lab · Allsup · Campus Crusade for Christ · D.C. Lobbying Firm · US Bank · Big Brothers Big Sisters · First Community Credit · Tri-National Inc · UHY Advisors · American Water.

Support for Students with Learning Disabilities

Students with learning disabilities may take advantage of specific support programs offered by McKendree University. If necessary, the college will grant additional time to students with learning disabilities to complete their degree. Also, a lightened course load may be granted to LD students. High school foreign language waivers are accepted. Students with learning disabilities will find the following programs at McKendree University extremely useful: remedial math · remedial English · tutors · learning center · untimed tests · extended time for tests · take-home exam · oral tests · reading machines · tape recorders · priority registration. Individual or small group tutorials are also available in: time management · organizational skills · learning strategies · specific subject areas · writing labs · math labs · study skills.

How to Get Admitted

For admissions decisions, non-academic factors considered: interview · extracurricular activities · special talents, interests, abilities · character/personal qualities · volunteer work · work experience · state of residency · alumni relationship. A high school diploma is required, although a GED is also accepted for admissions consideration. SAT or ACT test scores are required of all applicants. SAT Subject Test scores are recommended but not required. *According to the admissions office:* Minimum composite ACT score of 20, rank in top half of secondary school class, and minimum 2.5 GPA required. *Academic*

McKENDREE UNIVERSITY

Highlights

McKendree University
Lebanon, IL (Pop. 4,000)
Location: Large town
Website: http://www.mckendree.edu

Students
Total enrollment: 3,212
Undergrads: 1,046
Freshmen: 343
Part-time students: 26%
From out-of-state: 14%
Male/Female: 44%/56%
Live on-campus: 55%
In fraternities: 6%
In sororities: 8%
Off-campus employment rating: Fair
Caucasian: 79%
African American: 13%
Hispanic: 2%
Asian or Pacific Islander: 1%
Native American: 0%
International: 3%

Academics
Student/faculty ratio: 15:1
Class size 9 or fewer: 31%
Class size 10-29: 60%
Class size 30-49: 9%
Class size 50-99: -
Class size 100 or more: 9%
Returning freshmen: 77%
Six-year graduation rate: 57%

Most Popular Fields of Study
Business, Finance, Sales and Marketing
Psychology
English and Literature
Computer and Information Sciences
Mathematics
Health Professions, Medicine and Related Sciences
Liberal Arts, Humanities and General Studies
Communications, Journalism, Advertising and Comm. Technologies
Education
Social Sciences, History, Economics, Political Science

McKENDREE UNIVERSITY

Highlights

Admissions
Applicants: 1,076
Accepted: 808
Acceptance rate: 75.1%
Average GPA: 3.3
ACT range: 20-25
SAT Math range: 530-600
SAT Reading range: 530-650
SAT Writing range: Not reported
Top 10% of class: 22%
Top 25% of class: 49%
Top 50% of class: 76%

Deadlines
Early Action: No
Early Decision: No
Regular Action: March 1 (priority)
Common Application: Accepted

Financial Aid
In-state tuition: $20,570
Out-of-state tuition: $20,570
Room: -
Board: -
Books: $1,200
Freshmen receiving need-based aid: 86%
Undergrads receiving need-based aid:
    78%
Avg. % of need met by financial aid: 82%
Avg. aid package (freshmen): $17,910
Avg. aid package (undergrads): $15,361
Freshmen receiving merit-based aid: 13%
Undergrads receiving merit-based aid:
    19%
Avg. student debt upon graduation:
    $18,956

Prominent Alumni
Harry Statham 1960, men's basketball
coach McKendree University; Andrew
McChesney 1997, editor of the *Moscow
Times*.

School Spirit
Mascot: Bearcats
Colors: Purple/White

units recommended: 4 English, 3 Math, 3 Science, 2 Social Studies, 2 Foreign Language.

Insight

McKendree is the only place in southern Illinois where you have an average class size of 15 and all classes are under 50 according to Mark Campbell, vice president for enrollment management. The more intimate classes help students to feel less anonymous. "We do not evaluate students with multiple-choice tests," he adds. "Instead, we want to see how they write. There is a real gray area between students who are easy to admit and those who are easy to deny. The key is in the students' strength in English. How do they read, write and comprehend?" All students who are admitted must submit a writing sample before they are placed in an English class. All potential students are invited to write an essay for the university—even graded papers from school are allowed. "In the end, we are obligated to not admit students who will not do well. We simply focus on a student's determination to succeed," says Campbell.

How to Pay for College

To apply for financial aid, students should submit the following: Free Application for Federal Student Aid (FAFSA). McKendree University participates in the Federal Work Study program. *Need-based aid programs include:* scholarships and grants · general need-based awards · Federal Pell grants · state scholarships and grants · college-based scholarships and grants · private scholarships and grants. *Non-Need-based aid programs include:* scholarships and grants · state scholarships and grants · creative arts and performance awards · athletic scholarships · ROTC scholarships.

MENLO COLLEGE

1000 El Camino Real, Atherton, CA 94027
Admissions: 800-556-3656 · Financial Aid: 800-556-3656
Email: admissions@menlo.edu · Website: http://www.menlo.edu

From the College

"Menlo College offers an integrative four-year curriculum in our traditional under-graduate program and an innovative accelerated degree program for working adults, both of which support the mission of the college to educate women and men to 'think critically, manage resources responsibly, communicate effectively, and incorporate a multicultural and international perspective' into their lives and work. Menlo's faculty are consistently rated by students at the college's greatest strength because of their commitment to their students' education and the range and breadth of expertise that they bring to the classroom. In addition, in their role as student advisors, faculty mentor students and advise them on careers and on ways that they can make the most of their Menlo education."

Campus Setting

Menlo, founded in 1927, is a private business school. Its 62-acre campus is located in Atherton, 30 miles south of San Francisco. Menlo College has an enrollment of 680 students. Menlo College has been co-ed since 1971. The school also has a library with 81,600 books. Menlo College provides on-campus housing with 286 units that can accommodate 424 students. Housing options: co-ed dorms · men's dorms. Recreation and sports facilities include: pavilion · fields.

Student Life and Activities

With 53 percent of students living on campus, there are plenty of social activities. Popular gathering spots include the Student Union, Dutch Goose, The Oasis and the Stanford Mall. Popular campus events include the BSU's Apollo Night Talent Show, Powder Puff Football Game, Homecoming Football Game, Homecoming Dance, Women's Luncheon, International Week, Menlo Madness, Halloween Party, BSU's Poetry Slam, the Oakies, Rites of Spring, Hawai'i Club Annual Luau, Women's Club Annual Women's Luncheon, Mystery Dance and the LSU's Latin Dance Classes and Competition. Menlo College has 28 official student organizations. The most popular are: International Club · Old Oak Tavern · Hole in One Club · Mass Communication Club · Music Club · Newspaper Club · Outdoor Club · Psychology Club · Women's Club · Rize Hip Hop Dance · Student Athlete Leadership · Sixth Man Band · Video Game Appreciation · Video Production Club · Baywatch · Black Sunday Film Club · Menlo Cheerleaders · Disc-O-Fever · Gay Straight Alliance · Business Club · Contender's Club. Menlo College is a member of the Northwest Conference (Division III, football) and California Pacific Conference (NAIA).

Academics and Learning Environment

For the B student, the learning environment of a college is just as important as the quality of its academic program. Menlo College has 29 full-time and 72 part-time faculty members, offering a student-to-faculty ratio of 6:1. The most common course size is 10 to 19 students. Menlo College offers 3 majors with the most popular being management and least popular being mass communication. The school has a general core requirement. Cooperative education is not offered. All first-year students must maintain a 2.0 GPA or higher to avoid academic probation. Other special academic programs that would appeal to a B student: self-designed majors · independent study · double majors · accelerated study · honors program · internships · weekend college.

MENLO COLLEGE

Menlo College
Atherton, CA (Pop. 7,194)
Location: Large town
Website: http://www.menlo.edu

Students
Total enrollment: 680
Undergrads: 404
Freshmen: 159
Part-time students: 8%
From out-of-state: 31%
Male/Female: 59%/41%
Live on-campus: 53%
Off-campus employment rating: Good
Caucasian: 40%
African American: 7%
Hispanic: 15%
Asian or Pacific Islander: 11%
Native American: 0%
International: 10%

Academics
Student/faculty ratio: 6:1
Class size 9 or fewer: 18%
Class size 10-29: 76%
Class size 30-49: 10%
Class size 50-99: 2%
Class size 100 or more: 2%
Returning freshmen: 56%
Six-year graduation rate: 24%

Most Popular Fields of Study
Business, Finance, Sales and Marketing
Liberal Arts, Humanities and General
    Studies ·
Communications, Journalism, Advertising
    and Comm. Technologies

B Student Support and Success

Menlo offers an Academic Success Center, which includes a great deal of information and support on changing careers, and advising on what courses to take to fulfill a degree. The Writing Center is available to all students on both a drop-in and appointment basis and helps them with any writing assignment at any stage of the writing process.

Menlo College provides a variety of support programs including dedicated guidance for: academic · career · psychological. The average freshman year GPA is 2.2, and 56 percent of freshmen students return for their sophomore year. What do students do after college? While many enter the work force, approximately 5 percent pursue a graduate degree immediately after graduation, and another 9 percent enter graduate school within two years. Among students who enter the work force, approximately 47 percent enter a field related to their major within six months of graduation. Companies that most frequently hire graduates from Menlo College include: Accenture · Alain Pinel Realtors · Apex Systems · CB Richard Ellis Realtors · Champion Development · ClearChannel Communications · Coldwell Banker Real Estate · Collier's International · Com-Global Systems · Electronic Arts · Enterprise Rent-a-Car · Fathom Online · Intuit · Merrill Lynch Financial Services · Morgan Stanley Investments · MSNBC · Oracle Corp.· San Francisco Giants · San Jose State University · Siebel Systems · Stanford University.

Support for Students with Learning Disabilities

Students with learning disabilities may take advantage of specific support programs offered by Menlo College. If necessary, the college will grant additional time to students with learning disabilities to complete their degree. Also, a lightened course load may be granted to LD students. Students with learning disabilities will find the following programs at Menlo College extremely useful: remedial math · remedial English · special classes · tutors · learning center · testing accommodations · extended time for tests · exam on tape or computer · note-taking services · tape recorders · early syllabus · waiver of math degree requirement. Individual or small group tutorials are also available in: time management · organizational skills · learning strategies · specific subject areas · writing labs · study skills. An advisor/advocate from the LD program is available to students.

How to Get Admitted

For admissions decisions, non-academic factors considered: interview · extracurricular activities · special talents, interests, abilities · character/personal qualities · volunteer work · work experience · state of residency · geographical location · alumni relationship. A high school diploma is required, although a GED is also accepted for admissions consideration. SAT or ACT test scores are required of all applicants. SAT Subject Test scores are considered, if submitted, but are not required. *Academic units recommended:* 4 English, 3 Math, 3 Science, 3 Social Studies, 3 Foreign Language.

How to Pay for College

To apply for financial aid, students should submit the following: Free Application for Federal Student Aid (FAFSA) · state aid form. Menlo

College participates in the Federal Work Study program. *Need-based aid programs include:* scholarships and grants · general need-based awards · Federal Pell grants · state scholarships and grants · college-based scholarships and grants. *Non-Need-based aid programs include:* scholarships and grants · state scholarships and grants.

MENLO COLLEGE

Highlights

Admissions
Applicants: 978
Accepted: 407
Acceptance rate: 41.6%
Average GPA: 2.9
ACT range: 14-21
SAT Math range: 420-520
SAT Reading range: 400-510
SAT Writing range: 400-440
Top 10% of class: 8%
Top 25% of class: 27%
Top 50% of class: 66%

Deadlines
Early Action: February 1
Early Decision: December 1
Regular Action: Rolling admissions
Common Application: Accepted

Financial Aid
In-state tuition: $31,720
Out-of-state tuition: $31,720
Room: -
Board: -
Books: $1,566
Freshmen receiving need-based aid: 55%
Undergrads receiving need-based aid: 57%
Avg. % of need met by financial aid: 71%
Avg. aid package (freshmen): $21,472
Avg. aid package (undergrads): $21,294
Freshmen receiving merit-based aid: 32%
Undergrads receiving merit-based aid: 29%
Avg. student debt upon graduation: $17,625

Prominent Alumni
Bud Adams, owner, Tennessee Titans; Daniel Crown, real estate, Crown Theaters.

School Spirit
Mascot: Oaks
Colors: Navy and white

MICHIGAN STATE UNIVERSITY

Administration Building, East Lansing, MI 48824
Admissions: 517-355-8332 · Financial Aid: 517-353-5940
Email: admis@msu.edu · Website: http://www.msu.edu

From the College

"Michigan State University has been advancing knowledge and transforming lives through innovative teaching, research and outreach for 150 years, and is known worldwide as a major public university with global reach and impact. MSU's degree-granting colleges and affiliated law college offer top-ranked academic programs in a park-like Big Ten campus and community setting. Undergraduate students can choose from more than 150 programs of study and have the opportunity to work with faculty on research projects. MSU distinctions include one of the largest study abroad programs and one of the largest career placement services in the nation."

Campus Setting

Michigan State, founded in 1855, is a comprehensive, land-grant university. Programs are offered through the Colleges of Agriculture and Natural Resources, Arts and Letters, Communication Arts and Sciences, Education, Engineering, Human Ecology, Natural Science, Nursing, Osteopathic Medicine, Social Science, Veterinary Medicine, Eli Broad College of Business and James Madison College. Its 5,315-acre campus is located in East Lansing, 80 miles northwest of Detroit. A four-year institution, Michigan State University has an enrollment of 46,648 students. In addition to a large, well-stocked library, the campus facilities include: museums · art center · center for performing arts · superconducting cyclotron · hotel · planetarium · chapel · magnetic resonance imaging center · veterinary medical center · clinical center · athletic academic center. Michigan State University provides on-campus housing with 10,948 units that can accommodate 22,200 students. Housing options: co-ed dorms · women's dorms · sorority housing · fraternity housing · single-student apartments · married-student apartments · special housing for disabled students · special housing for International students · cooperative housing.

Student Life and Activities

Most students (58 percent) live off campus, which does impact the on-campus social scene. Nevertheless, like any college, students find time to create their own recreational outlets. Students enjoy gathering at football games, basketball games, concerts and bars. Popular campus events include home football and basketball games (particularly against University of Michigan), Homecoming Parade and concerts. Michigan State University has 500 official student organizations. Greek organizations are influential on campus. For those interested in sports, there are intramural teams such as: baseball · basketball · billiards · cross-country · cycling · fencing · football · golf · ice hockey · lacrosse · martial arts · racquetball · rugby · sailing · scuba diving · skiing · soccer · softball · swimming · tennis · track and field · volleyball · water polo. Michigan State University is a member of the Big Ten Conference (Division I, Football I-A) and Central Collegiate Hockey Association (Division I).

Academics and Learning Environment

For the B student, the learning environment of a college is just as important as the quality of its academic program. Michigan State University has 2,616 full-time and 381 part-time faculty members, offering a student-to-faculty ratio of 16:1. The most common course size is 20 to 29 students. Michigan State University offers 458 majors with the most popular being psychology, accounting and finance. The school has a general core requirement. Cooperative education is available. All first-year students must maintain a 2.0 GPA or higher to avoid academic probation. Other special academic programs that would appeal to a B student: self-designed majors · pass/fail grading option · independent study · double majors · dual degrees · accelerated study · honors program · Phi Beta Kappa · internships · weekend college · distance learning certificate programs.

B Student Support and Success

MSU's Learning Resource Center offers help to students who are looking to improve their grades, to develop study strategies and to boost their overall scholastic performance. The center features a professional staff, interactive learning lab and tutoring services in the residence halls. Daytime tutoring is offered in one-hour individual sessions at no cost, and evening tutoring is available for math groups twice a week. Seminars and workshops are also offered on topics such as test taking and preparing for finals.

Insight from the school includes this advice: "Great, dynamic learning environment highlighted by extremely helpful and accessible professors and great on campus resources, including the Learning Resource Center, the English Language Center and the Office of Supportive Services.

"Apply before November 1. Complete a challenging curriculum in high school. Complete a well written personal statement, required as part of the application. Use it to show how well rounded you are as a student and person. Be involved in activities."

Michigan State University provides a variety of support programs including dedicated guidance for: academic · career · personal · psychological · minority students · military · veterans · non-traditional students · family planning · religious. Recognizing that some students may need extra preparation, Michigan State University offers remedial and refresher courses in: reading · writing · math · study skills. Annually, 91 percent of freshmen students return for their sophomore year. Among students who enter the work force, approximately 95 percent enter a field related to their major within six months of graduation. Companies that most frequently hire graduates from Michigan State University include: 3M · Abbott Labs · ABC Group · ABN Amro · Accenture.

Support for Students with Learning Disabilities

Students with learning disabilities may take advantage of specific support programs offered by Michigan State University. Students with learning disabilities will find the following programs at Michigan State University extremely useful: remedial math · remedial English · tutors · learning center · testing accommodations · untimed tests · extended time for tests · take-home exam · readers · typist/scribe · reading machines · tape recorders · texts on tape · early syllabus · priority registration · waiver of math degree requirement. Individual or small group tutorials are also available in: time management · organizational skills · learning strategies · specific subject areas · writing labs · math labs · study skills. An advisor/advocate from the Resource Center for Persons with Disabilities is available to students.

MICHIGAN STATE UNIVERSITY

Highlights

Michigan State University
East Lansing, MI (Pop. 50,000)
Location: Medium city
Website: http://www.msu.edu

Students
Total enrollment: 46,648
Undergrads: 17,073
Freshmen: 9,417
Part-time students: 8%
From out-of-state: 12%
Male/Female: 47%/53%
Live on-campus: 42%
In fraternities: 8%
In sororities: 7%
Off-campus employment rating: Excellent
Caucasian: 77%
African American: 8%
Hispanic: 3%
Asian or Pacific Islander: 5%
Native American: 1%
International: 5%

Academics
Student/faculty ratio: 16:1
Class size 9 or fewer: 6%
Class size 10-29: 51%
Class size 30-49: 22%
Class size 50-99: 9%
Class size 100 or more: 12%
Returning freshmen: 91%
Six-year graduation rate: 75%

Most Popular Fields of Study
Business, Finance, Sales and Marketing
Visual and Performing Arts
Social Sciences, History, Economics, Political Science
Protective Services, Criminal Justice and Public Administration
Family and Consumer Sciences, Nutrition and Home Economics
Computer and Information Sciences
Communications, Journalism, Advertising and Comm. Technologies
Law and Legal Studies
Liberal Arts, Humanities and General Studies

309

College Profiles

MICHIGAN STATE UNIVERSITY

Admissions
Applicants: 25,589
Accepted: 17,919
Acceptance rate: 70%
Average GPA: 3.6
ACT range: 23-27
SAT Math range: 540-660
SAT Reading range: 480-620
SAT Writing range: 480-610
Top 10% of class: 31%
Top 25% of class: 72%
Top 50% of class: 97%

Deadlines
Early Action: October 6
Early Decision: No
Regular Action: Common Application:
   Accepted

Financial Aid
In-state tuition: $10,410
Out-of-state tuition: $26,850
Room: $3,997
Board: $4,126
Books: $944
Freshmen receiving need-based aid: 45%
Undergrads receiving need-based aid:
   43%
Avg. % of need met by financial aid: 70%
Avg. aid package (freshmen): $10,789
Avg. aid package (undergrads): $10,308
Freshmen receiving merit-based aid: 5%
Undergrads receiving merit-based aid:
   4%
Avg. student debt upon graduation:
   $19,488

Prominent Alumni
Richard Ford, author and Pulitzer Prize winner; Kay Koplovitz, founder of the USA Network.

School Spirit
Mascot: Spartans
Colors: Green and White
Song: *MSU Fight Song*

How to Get Admitted

For admissions decisions, non-academic factors considered: extracurricular activities · special talents, interests, abilities · character/personal qualities · volunteer work · work experience · state of residency · geographical location · alumni relationship. A high school diploma is required, although a GED is also accepted for admissions consideration. SAT or ACT test scores are required of all applicants. SAT Subject Test scores are considered, if submitted, but are not required. *According to the admissions office:* Minimum composite ACT score of 21 and minimum grade average of B- recommended. *Academic units recommended:* 2 Social Studies, 2 Foreign Language.

How to Pay for College

To apply for financial aid, students should submit the following: Free Application for Federal Student Aid (FAFSA). Michigan State University participates in the Federal Work Study program. *Need-based aid programs include:* scholarships and grants · general need-based awards · Federal Pell grants · state scholarships and grants · college-based scholarships and grants · private scholarships and grants · United Negro College Fund. *Non-Need-based aid programs include:* scholarships and grants · general need-based awards · state scholarships and grants · creative arts and performance awards · special achievements and activities awards · special characteristics awards · athletic scholarships · ROTC scholarships.

MILLS COLLEGE

5000 MacArthur Boulevard, Oakland, CA 94613
Admissions: 800-87-MILLS · Financial Aid: 510-430-2000
Email: admission@mills.edu · Website: http://www.mills.edu

From the College

"Mills College offers women the opportunity to study and grow in a dynamic environment that supports intellectual exploration and a thoughtful approach to life. Working closely with faculty members and diverse students in intimate, collaborative classes, Mills women explore, debate and challenge conventional thinking both inside and outside the classroom. Students work with faculty members on meaningful real-world projects and engage with distinguished professors, thinkers, writers, and artists. Set on a 135-acre park-like campus, Mills provides a home with convenient access to the thriving cultural, artistic, social and professional worlds of the metropolitan San Francisco Bay Area."

Campus Setting

Mills, founded in 1852, is a private, liberal arts college for women. Its is located in Oakland, 18 miles east of San Francisco. A four-year college, Mills College has an enrollment of 1,476 students. In addition to a large, well-stocked library, the campus facilities include: art museum · theatres · contemporary music center · studios. Mills College provides on-campus housing that can accommodate 650 students. Housing options: co-ed dorms · women's dorms · single-student apartments · married-student apartments · special housing for disabled students · cooperative housing. Recreation and sports facilities include: activity room · aquatic center with therapy spa · fitness center · fitness trail · gymnasium · jogging track · tennis courts · soccer field · boat house for rowing team.

Student Life and Activities

With 56 percent of students living on campus, there are plenty of social activities. "Oakland is a wonderful multi-cultural community with theater, museums and a world-class ballet," reports the student newspaper. "A small campus with woods and a running stream, Mills is an oasis in the city—quiet and peaceful, but with easy access to everything." Popular gathering spots include San Francisco, Berkeley, Oakland, Peet's Coffee, cafes, clubs, bookstores, clothes shops, video arcades, movies and restaurants. Popular campus events include Black and White Ball, Literary Salon Series, Fetish Ball, speakers, colloquium, basketball games, volleyball games, health fairs, dorm parties and the annual celebrity tennis invitational. Mills College has 42 official student organizations. Influential groups include Black Women's Collective, Earth C.O.R.P.S., Asian Pacific Islander Sisterhood Alliance, Jewish Students Association, Muslim Student Association, Mouthing Off!, Commuter Student Association, Resumer Student Association, Mujeres Unidas, South Asian and Middle Eastern Cultural Awareness Organization and the Campanil. Mills College is a member of the Member of California Pacific Conference (NAIA) and NCAA Association of Division III Independents.

Academics and Learning Environment

For the B student, the learning environment of a college is just as important as the quality of its academic program. Mills College has 96 full-time and 103 part-time faculty members, offering a student-to-faculty ratio of 11:1. The most common course size is 10 to 19 students. Mills College offers 52 majors with the most popular being English, political/legal/economic analysis and psychology and least popular being

MILLS COLLEGE

Mills College
Oakland, CA (Pop. 399,444)
Location: Major city
Website: http://www.mills.edu
Students
Total enrollment: 1,476
Undergrads: 969
Freshmen: 260
Part-time students: 6%
From out-of-state: 27%
Male/Female: 0%/100%
Live on-campus: 56%
Off-campus employment rating: Excellent
Caucasian: 44%
African American: 9%
Hispanic: 14%
Asian or Pacific Islander: 8%
Native American: 1%
International: 3%

Academics
Student/faculty ratio: 11:1
Class size 9 or fewer: 37%
Class size 10-29: 57%
Class size 30-49: 5%
Class size 50-99: 1%
Class size 100 or more: -
Returning freshmen: 74%
Six-year graduation rate: 58%
Most Popular Fields of Study
Area, Ethnic and Gender Studies
Biological and Life Sciences
Business, Finance, Sales and Marketing
Psychology
Protective Services, Criminal Justice and
    Public Administration
Visual and Performing Arts
English and Literature
Philosophy, Religion and Theology
Computer and Information Sciences
Mathematics

history, mathematics and philosophy. The school has a general core requirement. Cooperative education is not offered. All first-year students must maintain a 2.0 GPA or higher to avoid academic probation, and a minimum overall GPA of 2.0 is required to graduate. Other special academic programs that would appeal to a B student: self-designed majors · independent study · double majors · Phi Beta Kappa · internships · certificate programs.

B Student Support and Success

The Writing Center at Mills College provides assistance for students who need help in developing communication skills. It is staffed by graduate students from the English Department, and one-on-one tutoring is available. In addition, workshops on writing are offered throughout the entire school year. Classes are commonly 20 students or less, and the student-to-faculty ratio is 10:1.

Mills College provides a variety of support programs including dedicated guidance for: academic · career · personal · psychological · minority students · non-traditional students · religious. The average freshman year GPA is 3.3, and 74 percent of freshmen students return for their sophomore year. What do students do after college? While many enter the work force, approximately 40 percent pursue a graduate degree immediately after graduation. Among students who enter the work force, approximately 40 percent enter a field related to their major within six months of graduation. Companies that most frequently hire graduates from Mills College include: Cultural organizations · Enterprise · school districts · State of California · U.S. Government · Wells Fargo.

Support for Students with Learning Disabilities

Students with learning disabilities may take advantage of specific support programs offered by Mills College. If necessary, the college will grant additional time to students with learning disabilities to complete their degree. Also, a lightened course load may be granted to LD students. High school foreign language waivers are accepted. Students with learning disabilities will find the following programs at Mills College extremely useful: tutors · extended time for tests · take-home exam · oral tests · substitution of courses · readers · note-taking services · proofreading services · reading machines · tape recorders · texts on tape · early syllabus · priority registration · waiver of foreign language degree requirement. Individual or small group tutorials are also available in: time management · organizational skills · learning strategies · writing labs · math labs · study skills. An advisor/advocate from the Services for Students with Disabilities is available to students.

How to Get Admitted

For admissions decisions, non-academic factors considered: interview · extracurricular activities · special talents, interests, abilities · character/personal qualities · volunteer work · work experience · state of residency · alumni relationship. A high school diploma is required, although a GED is also accepted for admissions consideration. SAT or ACT test scores are required of all applicants. SAT Subject Test scores are recommended but not required. *According to the admissions office:* Minimum 3.0 GPA required. *Academic units recommended:* 4 English, 4 Math, 4 Science, 4 Social Studies, 4 Foreign Language.

How to Pay for College

To apply for financial aid, students should submit the following: Free Application for Federal Student Aid (FAFSA) · institution's own financial aid forms · state aid form · Non-custodian (Divorced/Separated) Parent's Statement. Mills College participates in the Federal Work Study program. *Need-based aid programs include:* scholarships and grants · general need-based awards · Federal Pell grants · state scholarships and grants · college-based scholarships and grants · private scholarships and grants. *Non-Need-based aid programs include:* scholarships and grants · state scholarships and grants · creative arts and performance awards · special achievements and activities awards · special characteristics awards.

MILLS COLLEGE

Highlights

Admissions
Applicants: 1,177
Accepted: 776
Acceptance rate: 65.9%
Average GPA: 3.7
ACT range: 20-27
SAT Math range: 490-590
SAT Reading range: 520-650
SAT Writing range: 520-620
Top 10% of class: 43%
Top 25% of class: 78%
Top 50% of class: 98%

Deadlines
Early Action: November 15
Early Decision: No
Regular Action: Rolling admissions
Common Application: Accepted

Financial Aid
In-state tuition: $35,196
Out-of-state tuition: $35,196
Room: $5,310
Board: $4,774
Books: $1,400
Freshmen receiving need-based aid: 86%
Undergrads receiving need-based aid: 89%
Avg. % of need met by financial aid: 85%
Avg. aid package (freshmen): $34,127
Avg. aid package (undergrads): $30,184
Freshmen receiving merit-based aid: 11%
Undergrads receiving merit-based aid: 8%
Avg. student debt upon graduation: $24,255

Prominent Alumni
Barbara Lee, Congresswoman; Thoraya Ahmed Obaid, undersecretary general of UN Population Fund; April Glaspie, first woman ambassador to the Middle East.

School Spirit
Mascot: Cyclones
Colors: Yellow, white, and blue
Song: *Fires of Wisdom*

313

MITCHELL COLLEGE

437 Pequot Avenue, New London, CT 06320
Admissions: 800-443-2811 · Financial Aid: 800-443-2811
Email: admissions@mitchell.edu · Website: http://www.mitchell.edu

From the College

"Mitchell College is a private institution, providing a transforming educational experience culminating in a bachelor's or associate's degree. Within a diverse and student-centered community and with an emphasis on holistic student development, Mitchell College supports individual learning differences, nurtures untapped academic potential and instills the professional knowledge and skills needed for students to contribute to an ever-changing world. Mitchell offers premier programs for students with diagnosed learning disabilities or ADHD within a mainstream college. A one year pre-college experience allows students to earn up to 18 credits while strengthening academic preparedness. Each academic major provides students with internships tailored to their interests and career goals. Mitchell is located half-way between New York and Boston on a 68-acre waterfront campus with two private beaches, pond and nature preserve."

Campus Setting

Mitchell College, founded in 1938, is a private college located in New London. It provides a transforming educational experience. A four-year institution, Mitchell College has an enrollment of 805 students. The school also has a library with 73,590 books. Housing options: co-ed dorms · women's dorms · men's dorms.

Student Life and Activities

With 80 percent of students living on campus, there are plenty of social activities. Popular campus events include Applefest, Strawberryfest, Evening of International Song and Dance, Lighthouse Idol, Campus Luau, Late Night Breakfast and Mitchell Idol. Mitchell College has 20 official student organizations. The most popular are: Campus Activities Board · Class Officers · Commuter Students Association · Early Childhood Education Club · Dance Club · Choir · Drama Society · Gaming Club · Recreation Club · Behavior Science Club · Business Club · Thames Log. Mitchell College is a member of the Independents (Division III), EACC.

Academics and Learning Environment

For the B student, the learning environment of a college is just as important as the quality of its academic program. Mitchell College has 32 full-time and 53 part-time faculty members, offering a student-to-faculty ratio of 12:1. Mitchell College offers 27 majors with the most popular being business, education and liberal studies. The school has a general core requirement. Cooperative education is not offered. All first-year students must maintain a 1.5 GPA or higher to avoid academic probation, and a minimum overall GPA of 2.0 is required to graduate. Other special academic programs that would appeal to a B student: self-designed majors · independent study · Phi Beta Kappa · internships · certificate programs.

B Student Support and Success

This statement from Mitchell College gives insight into its facilities and programs: "Mitchell College prides itself on the fact that its greatest success and satisfaction comes from working with students who have yet to realize their full academic potential." The college embraces student differences and provides the following resources and strategies that can help B students achieve success:

Free professional content tutoring; learning and writing specialists; LD support program; five-week summer transition enrichment program; post-grad transitional year certificate; Freshman Interest Groups mentoring program; Discovery program for undecided students.

Mitchell College provides a variety of support programs including dedicated guidance for: academic · career · personal · minority students · veterans · family planning.

Support for Students with Learning Disabilities

Students with learning disabilities may take advantage of specific support programs offered by Mitchell College. If necessary, the college will grant additional time to students with learning disabilities to complete their degree. Also, a lightened course load may be granted to LD students. High school foreign language waivers are accepted. According to the school, Mitchell College's Learning Resource Center includes a staff of trained learning and writing specialists as well as three levels of support. Level I: Learning and writing specialists arrange up to four weekly sessions of academic support on an individual and small group basis. Level 2: Learning and writing specialists arrange up to two weekly sessions of academic support designed to sustain students academic efforts. Level 3: Consultations provided on a student-initiated basis. Students with learning disabilities will find the following programs at Mitchell College extremely useful: tutors · learning center · testing accommodations · extended time for tests · take-home exam · oral tests · readers · note-taking services · reading machines · tape recorders · texts on tape · videotaped classes · early syllabus · priority registration. Individual or small group tutorials are also available in: time management · organizational skills · learning strategies · specific subject areas · writing labs · math labs · study skills. An advisor/advocate from the Learning Resource Center is available to students.

How to Get Admitted

For admissions decisions, non-academic factors considered: interview · extracurricular activities · special talents, interests, abilities · character/personal qualities · volunteer work · work experience · state of residency · alumni relationship. A high school diploma is required, although a GED is also accepted for admissions consideration. SAT or ACT test scores are not considered or required. SAT Subject Test scores are not required. *Academic units recommended:* 4 English, 3 Math, 3 Science, 3 Social Studies.

Insight

"You are more than just your grade point average. While admission to Mitchell College is based on a comprehensive appraisal of your entire academic record, a huge part of that is also your personal character, aptitude, motivation and above all, your potential for academic success. We welcome the B student who recognizes his/her strengths and weaknesses and wants to be in an environment that will challenge him/her to improve and succeed.

"We would encourage B students to showcase their talents—those within the classroom and outside the classroom. Community and club involvement, volunteer and work experience, as well as

MITCHELL COLLEGE

Highlights

Mitchell College
New London, CT (Pop. 27,000)
Location: Large town
Website: http://www.mitchell.edu

Students
Total enrollment: 805
Undergrads: 403
Freshmen: 297
Part-time students: 7%
From out-of-state: 47%
Male/Female: 50%/50%
Live on-campus: 80%
Off-campus employment rating: Excellent
Caucasian: 70%
African American: 14%
Hispanic: 9%
Asian or Pacific Islander: 1%
Native American: 3%
International: 1%

Academics
Student/faculty ratio: 12:1
Class size 9 or fewer: 18%
Class size 10-29: 53%
Class size 30-49: 14%
Class size 50-99: 11%
Class size 100 or more: 3%
Returning freshmen: Not reported
Six-year graduation rate: Not reported

Admissions
Applicants: 1,600
Accepted: 651
Acceptance rate: 40.7%
Average GPA: 2.7
ACT range: Not reported
SAT Math range: Not reported
SAT Reading range: Not reported
SAT Writing range: Not reported
Top 10% of class: 1%

315

College Profiles

MITCHELL COLLEGE

Deadlines
Early Action: No
Early Decision: November 15
Regular Action: Rolling admissions
Common Application: Accepted

Financial Aid
In-state tuition: $22,846
Out-of-state tuition: $22,846
Room: $5,708
Board: $5,269
Books: $1,500
Avg. % of need met by financial aid: Not reported
Avg. aid package (freshmen): Not reported
Avg. aid package (undergrads): Not reported
Avg. student debt upon graduation: Not reported

School Spirit
Mascot: Mariner
Colors: Red, black, and white

hobbies and leadership opportunities, are a great way to show that a student has more to offer than just grades alone.

"Mitchell College has always been a college that focuses on asset development rather than deficit management. Our mission says it well when it states that we 'support individual learning differences and nurture untapped academic potential.' We welcome B and C students and find it very rewarding to have the privilege to be able to work with them to realize their full potential.

"Mitchell College's educational philosophy is one that is based on five distinctive values called C.A.R.E.S.—Character, Achievement, Respect, Engagement and Self-Discovery. It is a learning experience that provides students with the foundation and knowledge base they need for the education and life they wish to pursue. This partnership enables students to take their classroom instruction and apply it directly to the real world through a variety of unique internship and service learning opportunities—experiences that enable students to make a difference locally, nationally and globally."

How to Pay for College

To apply for financial aid, students should submit the following: Free Application for Federal Student Aid (FAFSA) · institution's own financial aid forms. Mitchell College participates in the Federal Work Study program. *Need-based aid programs include:* scholarships and grants · general need-based awards · Federal Pell grants · state scholarships and grants · college-based scholarships and grants · private scholarships and grants. *Non-Need-based aid programs include:* scholarships and grants · general need-based awards · state scholarships and grants · creative arts and performance awards · special achievements and activities awards · leadership scholarships.

MONTANA TECH OF
THE UNIVERSITY OF MONTANA

1300 West Park Street, Butte, MT 59701
Admissions: 800-445-TECH · Financial Aid: 800-445-TECH
Email: enrollment@mtech.edu · Website: http://www.mtech.edu

From the College

"Montana Tech can be characterized by listening to what employers say. They tell us Tech graduates stand out due to their work ethic and skills. Last year, 151 employers came to our campus competing for Tech students and graduates. Montana Tech has had a 10-year annual average placement rate of 97 percent or above with exceptional starting salaries. Learning takes place in a personalized environment, in first-class academic facilities, and in the heart of the Rocky Mountains."

Campus Setting

Montana Tech, founded in 1896 as Montana College of Mineral Science and Technology, is a public, multipurpose institution. Its 56-acre campus is located in Butte, south of Great Falls. A four-year public institution, Montana Tech of the University of Montana has an enrollment of 2,402 students. In addition to a large, well-stocked library, the campus also has a mining and mineral museums. Montana Tech of the University of Montana provides on-campus housing with 5 units that can accommodate 400 students. Housing options: co-ed dorms · single-student apartments · married-student apartments · special housing for disabled students. Recreation and sports facilities include: cardio room · gymnasium · racquetball and tennis courts · trails.

Student Life and Activities

Most students (83 percent) live off campus, which does impact the on-campus social scene. Nevertheless, like any college, students find time to create their own recreational outlets. Orientation, Homecoming (Parade, Bed Races, Games), M-Days, Holiday Stroll, Talent Show, Digger Hunt, Mulletfest, Career Fair, Late Night Breakfast, Montana Tech Ski Day, and Mining and Mucking Contest are popular events. Montana Tech of the University of Montana has 53 official student organizations. The most popular are: Society Of Petroleum Engineers · Biology Club · Business Activities Club · Chemistry Club · Chess Club of Montana Tech · Circle K · Club Met · Copper Guard · Dance Club · American Association of Drilling Engineers · Environmental Engineers of Montana Tech · Fly Fishing Club · Geology Club · Healthcare Informatics Club · Inst. of Electrical and Electronic Engineers · Liberal Studies Club · Marcus Daly Mining Club · Math Club. For those interested in sports, there are intramural teams such as: basketball · biking · fishing · football · hiking · racquetball · rugby · skiing · snowboarding · softball · swimming · volleyball. Montana Tech of the University of Montana is a member of the Member of Frontier Conference (NAIA).

Academics and Learning Environment

For the B student, the learning environment of a college is just as important as the quality of its academic program. Montana Tech of the University of Montana has 121 full-time and 61 part-time faculty members, offering a student-to-faculty ratio of 14:1. The most common course size is 2 to 9 students. Montana Tech of the University of Montana offers 49 majors with the most popular being general engineering, petroleum engineering and business/information technology and least popular being software engineering and geophysical engineering. The school has a general core requirement. Cooperative education is available. All first-year students must maintain a 2.0 GPA

MONTANA TECH OF THE UNIVERSITY OF MONTANA

**Montana Tech of
the University of Montana**
Butte, MT (Pop. 33,000)
Location: Large town
Website: http://www.mtech.edu
Students
Total enrollment: 2,402
Undergrads: 1,381
Freshmen: 1,120
Part-time students: 17%
From out-of-state: 11%
Male/Female: 60%/40%
Live on-campus: 17%
Off-campus employment rating: Good
Caucasian: 83%
African American: 1%
Hispanic: 2%
Asian or Pacific Islander: 1%
Native American: 2%
International: 7%

Academics
Student/faculty ratio: 14:1
Class size 9 or fewer: 35%
Class size 10-29: 45%
Class size 30-49: 10%
Class size 50-99: 9%
Class size 100 or more: 1%
Returning freshmen: 69%
Six-year graduation rate: 38%

Admissions
Applicants: 577
Accepted: 522
Acceptance rate: 90.5%
Average GPA: 3.2
ACT range: 20-25
SAT Math range: 490-620
SAT Reading range: 440-580
SAT Writing range: 430-560
Top 10% of class: 17%
Top 25% of class: 37%
Top 50% of class: 70%

or higher to avoid academic probation. Other special academic programs that would appeal to a B student: pass/fail grading option · independent study · double majors · dual degrees · honors program · internships · distance learning certificate programs.

B Student Support and Success

A quote about Montana Tech explains the services that the college provides to its students: "Montana Tech has a great learning center. This is a place where all students can get help with any of their courses. Tech also has very attentive professors that are always available for personal help.

"Montana Tech admits students that are in the top half of their graduating class or who have a 2.5 or higher. You do not need to have straight A's to get admitted or to get scholarships here. All B students are accepted to Montana Tech! Any student above a 2.5 is accepted in good academic standing. Students with lower GPAs than 2.5 are accepted on academic probation. They will be in college success courses and monitored carefully."

Montana Tech of the University of Montana provides a variety of support programs including dedicated guidance for: academic · career · personal · minority students · military · veterans · non-traditional students. Annually, 69 percent of freshmen students return for their sophomore year. What do students do after college? While many enter the work force, approximately 18 percent pursue a graduate degree immediately after graduation.

Support for Students with Learning Disabilities

Students with learning disabilities may take advantage of specific support programs offered by Montana Tech of the University of Montana. If necessary, the college will grant additional time to students with learning disabilities to complete their degree. Also, a lightened course load may be granted to LD students. Students with learning disabilities will find the following programs at Montana Tech of the University of Montana extremely useful: remedial math · remedial English · tutors · learning center · testing accommodations · extended time for tests · oral tests · readers · reading machines · priority registration. Individual or small group tutorials are also available in: time management · organizational skills · learning strategies · specific subject areas · writing labs · math labs · study skills. An advisor/advocate from the Disability Services is available to students.

How to Get Admitted

For admissions decisions, non-academic factors considered: state of residency. A high school diploma is required, although a GED is also accepted for admissions consideration. SAT or ACT test scores are required for some applicants. *According to the admissions office:* Minimum composite ACT score of 22 (combined SAT score of 1530), rank in top half of secondary school class, or minimum 2.5 GPA required. *Academic units recommended:* 4 English, 4 Math, 2 Science, 3 Social Studies.

How to Pay for College

To apply for financial aid, students should submit the following: Free Application for Federal Student Aid (FAFSA) · scholarship application. Montana Tech of the University of Montana participates in the Federal Work Study program. *Need-based aid programs include:* scholarships and grants · general need-based awards · Federal Pell grants · state scholarships and grants · college-based scholarships and grants · private scholarships and grants. *Non-Need-based aid programs include:* scholarships and grants · general need-based awards · state scholarships and grants · athletic scholarships.

MONTANA TECH OF THE UNIVERSITY OF MONTANA

Highlights

Deadlines
Early Action: No
Early Decision: No
Regular Action: Rolling admissions
Common Application: Not accepted

Financial Aid
In-state tuition: $5,772
Out-of-state tuition: $16,049
Room: $2,788
Board: $3,658
Books: $1,000
Freshmen receiving need-based aid: 60%
Undergrads receiving need-based aid: 55%
Avg. % of need met by financial aid: 76%
Avg. aid package (freshmen): $7,366
Avg. aid package (undergrads): $8,418
Freshmen receiving merit-based aid: 11%
Undergrads receiving merit-based aid: 12%
Avg. student debt upon graduation: $21,000

School Spirit
Mascot: Orediggers
Colors: Green and copper
Song: *Forward Tech*

MOREHOUSE COLLEGE

830 Westview Drive, SW, Atlanta, GA 30314
Admissions: 404-215-2632 · Financial Aid: 800-873-9041
Email: admissions@morehouse.edu · Website: http://www.morehouse.edu

From the College

"Morehouse, a historically black liberal arts college for men, assumes a special responsibility for teaching students about the history and culture of black people. The college seeks to develop men with disciplined minds, emphasizing the continuing search for truth as a liberating force. Morehouse prepares its students for leadership and service through instructional programs and extracurricular activities that: develop skills in oral and written communications, analytical and critical thinking and interpersonal relationships; foster an understanding and appreciation of the elements and evolution of various cultures and the nature of the physical universe; foster an understanding and appreciation of the specific knowledge and skills needed for the pursuit of professional careers and/or graduate study; cultivate the personal attributes of self-confidence, tolerance, morality, ethical behavior, humility, a global perspective and a commitment to a social justice."

Campus Setting

Morehouse, founded in 1867, is a private, liberal arts, historically black, men's college. Its 61-acre campus is located in downtown Atlanta. Morehouse College has 2,796 students. In addition to a large, well-stocked library, the campus facilities include: leadership center · technology tower. Morehouse College provides on-campus housing that can accommodate 1,500 students. Housing options: men's dorms · special housing for international students.

Student Life and Activities

With 55 percent of students living on campus, there are plenty of social activities. Popular campus events include New Student Orientation, Homecoming, Martin Luther King Celebration, Founder's Day, Prospective Student Seminar, Africa Awareness Week, Public Health Awareness Conference, Science and Spiritual Awareness Week and Annual Family Institute. Morehouse College has 78 official student organizations. Morehouse College is a member of the Southern Intercollegiate Athletic Conference (Division II).

Academics and Learning Environment

For the B student, the learning environment of a college is just as important as the quality of its academic program. Morehouse College has 161 full-time and no part-time faculty members, offering a student-to-faculty ratio of 15:1. The most common course size is 20 to 29 students. Morehouse College offers 34 majors with the most popular being business administration, psychology and biology and least popular being French, urban studies and education. The school has a general core requirement. Cooperative education is available. All first-year students must maintain a 2.0 GPA or higher to avoid academic probation, and a minimum overall GPA of 2.0 is required to graduate. Other special academic programs that would appeal to a B student: double majors · dual degrees · honors program · Phi Beta Kappa · internships.

B Student Support and Success

The Wellness Resource Center offers personal counseling to help students "resolve personal difficulties and acquire the skills, attitudes and knowledge that will enable them to take full advantage of their experiences at Morehouse College."

Morehouse College provides a variety of support programs including dedicated guidance for: academic · career · personal · psychological · non-traditional students · family planning. The average freshman year GPA is 2.6, and 83 percent of freshmen students return for their sophomore year. What do students do after college? While many enter the work force, approximately 29 percent pursue a graduate degree immediately after graduation. Among students who enter the work force, approximately 68 percent enter a field related to their major within six months of graduation. Companies that most frequently hire graduates from Morehouse College include: Bank of America · Deloitte and Touche · Goldman Sachs · JP Morgan Chase · Lehman Brothers · Merrill Lynch · McKinsey & Co. · Morgan Stanley · PricewaterhouseCoopers · UBS · Wachovia.

Support for Students with Learning Disabilities

Students with learning disabilities may take advantage of specific support programs offered by Morehouse College. If necessary, the college will grant additional time to students with learning disabilities to complete their degree. Also, a lightened course load may be granted to LD students. High school foreign language waivers are accepted. High school math waivers are also accepted. Students with learning disabilities will find the following programs at Morehouse College extremely useful: remedial math · remedial English · remedial reading · tutors · learning center · testing accommodations · untimed tests · extended time for tests · take-home exam · oral tests · exam on tape or computer · readers · typist/scribe · note-taking services · proofreading services · reading machines · tape recorders · texts on tape · early syllabus · diagnostic testing service · special bookstore section · priority registration · priority seating · waiver of math degree requirement · waiver of foreign language degree requirement. Individual or small group tutorials are also available in: time management · organizational skills · learning strategies · specific subject areas · writing labs · math labs · study skills. An advisor/advocate from the Disability Service Office is available to students.

How to Get Admitted

For admissions decisions, non-academic factors considered: interview · extracurricular activities · special talents, interests, abilities · character/personal qualities · volunteer work · state of residency · geographical location · minority affiliation · alumni relationship. A high school diploma is required, although a GED is also accepted for admissions consideration. SAT or ACT test scores are required of all applicants. *According to the admissions office:* Minimum combined SAT Reasoning score of 1500 (composite ACT score of 22), rank in top half of secondary school class, and minimum 2.8 GPA required.

How to Pay for College

To apply for financial aid, students should submit the following: Free Application for Federal Student Aid (FAFSA) · institution's own financial aid forms · CSS/Financial Aid PROFILE · state aid form. Morehouse College participates in the Federal Work Study program. *Need-based aid programs include:* scholarships and grants ·

MOREHOUSE COLLEGE

Highlights

Morehouse College
Atlanta, GA (Pop. 416,474)
Location: Major city
Website: http://www.morehouse.edu

Students
Total enrollment: 2,796
Undergrads: 2,796
Freshmen: 800
Part-time students: 6%
From out-of-state: 72%
Male/Female: 100%/ 0%
Live on-campus: 55%
In fraternities: 10%
Off-campus employment rating: Good
Caucasian: 0%
African American: 95%
Hispanic: 0%
Native American: 0%
International: 3%

Academics
Student/faculty ratio: 15:1
Class size 9 or fewer: 23%
Class size 10-29: 65%
Class size 30-49: 10%
Class size 50-99: 1%
Class size 100 or more: 1%
Returning freshmen: 83%
Six-year graduation rate: 54%

Most Popular Fields of Study
Business, Finance, Sales and Marketing
Biological and Life Sciences
Area, Ethnic and Gender Studies

MOREHOUSE COLLEGE

Admissions
Applicants: 2,369
Accepted: 1,399
Acceptance rate: 59.1%
Average GPA: Not reported
ACT range: 20-24
SAT Math range: 480-590
SAT Reading range: 480-580
SAT Writing range: Not reported
Top 10% of class: 14%
Top 25% of class: 45%
Top 50% of class: 77%

Deadlines
Early Action: November 1
Early Decision: No
Regular Action: November 1 (priority)
February 15 (final)
Common Application: Accepted

Financial Aid
In-state tuition: $19,424
Out-of-state tuition: $19,424
Room: $4,708
Board: $6,238
Books: $1,500
Freshmen receiving need-based aid:
    101%
Undergrads receiving need-based aid:
    95%
Avg. % of need met by financial aid: 47%
Avg. aid package (freshmen): $8,725
Avg. aid package (undergrads): $12,500
Freshmen receiving merit-based aid: 33%
Undergrads receiving merit-based aid:
    32%
Avg. student debt upon graduation:
    $35,000

Prominent Alumni
Martin Luther King. Jr, Nobel Peace Prize
laureate and civil rights leader; Sandford
D. Bishop, U.S. Congressman, Georgia.

School Spirit
Mascot: Maroon Tigers
Colors: Maroon and white
Song: *Dear Old Morehouse*

general need-based awards · Federal Pell grants · state scholarships and grants · college-based scholarships and grants · private scholarships and grants · United Negro College Fund. *Non-Need-based aid programs include:* scholarships and grants · general need-based awards · state scholarships and grants · special achievements and activities awards · athletic scholarships · ROTC scholarships.

MUSKINGUM COLLEGE

163 Stormont Street, New Concord, OH 43762
Admissions: 800-752-6082 · Financial Aid: 800-752-6082
Email: adminfo@muskingum.edu · Website: http://www.muskingum.edu

From the College

"At a recent Muskingum College commencement, the graduating class student representative talked about Muskingum this way: Muskingum has always been a small liberal arts school in rural Ohio with about 1,000 students at any given time (until the past ten years). Despite this amount of former graduates, compared to larger universities, Muskingum has produced a senator and astronaut, John Glenn, as many people know us for. But Muskingum has also provided the United States with an ambassador to Mexico and an editor of the Wall Street Journal. Muskingum has produced a vice president or president of the three largest corporations in the world: a former chairman and CEO of Ford Motor Co.; an executive vice president of AT&T, and a vice president for General Motors. The list could go on and on. We have already seen major impacts by our fellow graduates. One of today's graduates is at the forefront of city management with a job he has held several months before his actual graduation. Another graduate helped with a wildlife population project in Kenya. What mark will we have put on Ohio, the United States and the world? It is the same challenge that previous Muskingum graduates have had and they have gone beyond all expectations."

Campus Setting

Muskingum, founded in 1837, is a private, church-affiliated, liberal arts college. Its 215-acre campus is located in New Concord, 80 miles east of Columbus. A four-year institution, Muskingum College has an enrollment of 2,135 students. Muskingum College has been co-ed since 1854. The school is also affiliated with the Presbyterian Church. In addition to a large, well-stocked library, the campus also has the John & Annie Glenn Historic Site and Exploration Center. Muskingum College provides on-campus housing with 674 units that can accommodate 1,200 students. Housing options: co-ed dorms · women's dorms · men's dorms · sorority housing · fraternity housing · single-student apartments. Recreation and sports facilities include: artificial turf football field · baseball · soccer and softball fields · cross-country trail · recreation center · tennis courts.

Student Life and Activities

With 85 percent of students living on campus, there are plenty of social activities. Popular events include: Muskiepalooza, Casino Night, Relay for Life, Coffee house events, comedians and musical artists. Muskingum College has 96 official student organizations. The most popular are: AGORA · GLASS · Residence Hall Advisors · Habitat for Humanity · Student Senate · Spirit Band · Bacchus · Circle K · Muskie Greens · Centerboard · Council for Exceptional Children · Peer Educators · Dance Team · Forensics · Democrat Students · Republican Students · CARE (vegetarian club) · MESA (environmental student activists) · Wellness Club. For those interested in sports, there are intramural teams such as: basketball · bowling · flag football · golf · racquetball · softball · volleyball · wallyball. Muskingum College is a member of the Ohio Athletic Conference (Division III).

Academics and Learning Environment

For the B student, the learning environment of a college is just as important as the quality of its academic program. Muskingum College has 102 full-time and 34 part-

MUSKINGUM COLLEGE

Muskingum College
New Concord, OH (Pop. 2,500)
Location: Rural
Website: http://www.muskingum.edu

Students
Total enrollment: 2,135
Undergrads: 811
Freshmen: 602
Part-time students: 7%
From out-of-state: 8%
Male/Female: 48%/52%
Live on-campus: 85%
In fraternities: 20%
In sororities: 21%
Off-campus employment rating: Fair
Caucasian: 87%
African American: 5%
Hispanic: 1%
Asian or Pacific Islander: 1%
Native American: 0%
International: 1%

Academics
Student/faculty ratio: 16:1
Class size 9 or fewer: 34%
Class size 10-29: 58%
Class size 30-49: 7%
Class size 50-99: -
Class size 100 or more: 1%
Returning freshmen: 67%
Six-year graduation rate: 53%

Most Popular Fields of Study
Business, Finance, Sales and Marketing
Protective Services, Criminal Justice and
    Public Administration
Visual and Performing Arts
English and Literature
Philosophy, Religion and Theology
Computer and Information Sciences
Mathematics
Interdisciplinary Studies
Liberal Arts, Humanities and General
    Studies
Foreign Languages, Literature and Lin-
    guistics

time faculty members, offering a student-to-faculty ratio of 16:1. The most common course size is 2 to 9 students. Muskingum College offers 46 majors with the most popular being business and education and least popular being philosophy and religion. The school has a general core requirement as well as a religion requirement. Cooperative education is not offered. All first-year students must maintain a 2.0 GPA or higher to avoid academic probation. Other special academic programs that would appeal to a B student: self-designed majors · pass/fail grading option · independent study · double majors · accelerated study · internships · distance learning certificate programs.

B Student Support and Success

The Center for Advancement of Learning at Muskingum provides assistance to students in a number of different ways. Their PLUS program is a complex system for students with significant learning disabilities. There is also a Learning Strategies and Resources Program that helps at-risk students through weekly workshops, weekly strategy sessions, and more. In addition, their First Step Transition Program provides an intensive and comprehensive summer orientation for students before they begin their undergraduate studies.

Muskingum College provides a variety of support programs including dedicated guidance for: academic · career · personal · psychological · minority students · family planning · religious. The average freshman year GPA is 2.7, and 67 percent of freshmen students return for their sophomore year. What do students do after college? While many enter the work force, approximately 15 percent pursue a graduate degree immediately after graduation. Among students who enter the work force, approximately 73 percent enter a field related to their major within six months of graduation. Companies that most frequently hire graduates from Muskingum College include: CED · Groveport Madison Schools · Nationwide Insurance · National City Bank · Resource Systems · State of Ohio Auditor's Office · Wal-Mart · Southeastern Equipment · Sherwin Williams · State Farm Insurance · The Longaberger Co. · Verizon Wireless · Wells Fargo · Zanesville · Upper Arlington Schools.

Support for Students with Learning Disabilities

Students with learning disabilities may take advantage of specific support programs offered by Muskingum College. If necessary, the college will grant additional time to students with learning disabilities to complete their degree. Also, a lightened course load may be granted to LD students. High school foreign language waivers are accepted. High school math waivers are also accepted. According to the school, degree requirements for LD students are the same as those for all students. Students with learning disabilities will find the following programs at Muskingum College extremely useful: tutors · learning center · testing accommodations · untimed tests · extended time for tests · take-home exam · oral tests · readers · note-taking services · reading machines · tape recorders · texts on tape · waiver of foreign language degree requirement. Individual or small group tutorials are also available in: time management · organizational skills · learning strategies · specific subject areas · writing labs · study skills. An advisor/advocate from the PLUS Program is available to students. This member also sits on the admissions committee.

How to Get Admitted

For admissions decisions, non-academic factors considered: interview · extracurricular activities · special talents, interests, abilities · character/personal qualities · work experience · state of residency · geographical location · minority affiliation · alumni relationship. A high school diploma is required, although a GED is also accepted for admissions consideration. SAT or ACT test scores are required of all applicants. SAT Subject Test scores are considered, if submitted, but are not required. *According to the admissions office:* Minimum 2.5 GPA in college-preparatory courses required. *Academic units recommended:* 4 English, 3 Math, 3 Science, 1 Social Studies, 2 Foreign Language.

How to Pay for College

To apply for financial aid, students should submit the following: Free Application for Federal Student Aid (FAFSA) · state aid form. Muskingum College participates in the Federal Work Study program. *Need-based aid programs include:* scholarships and grants · general need-based awards · Federal Pell grants · state scholarships and grants · college-based scholarships and grants · private scholarships and grants. *Non-Need-based aid programs include:* scholarships and grants · general need-based awards · state scholarships and grants · creative arts and performance awards · special achievements and activities awards.

Highlights

Admissions
Applicants: 2,051
Accepted: 1,607
Acceptance rate: 78.4%
Average GPA: 3.2
ACT range: 19-25
SAT Math range: 480-590
SAT Reading range: 460-580
SAT Writing range: 450-590
Top 10% of class: 24%
Top 25% of class: 49%
Top 50% of class: 76%

Deadlines
Early Action: No
Early Decision: No
Regular Action: Rolling admissions
Common Application: Accepted

Financial Aid
In-state tuition: $19,190
Out-of-state tuition: $19,190
Room: $3,990
Board: $3,750
Books: $1,000
Freshmen receiving need-based aid: 83%
Undergrads receiving need-based aid: 78%
Avg. % of need met by financial aid: 84%
Avg. aid package (freshmen): $17,290
Avg. aid package (undergrads): $18,865
Freshmen receiving merit-based aid: 14%
Undergrads receiving merit-based aid: 22%
Avg. student debt upon graduation: $23,405

Prominent Alumni
John Glenn, U.S. Senator, astronaut (ret.); Jack Hanna, zoologist; Philip Caldwell, CEO, Ford Motor Co. (ret.)

School Spirit
Mascot: Fighting Muskies
Colors: Black and magenta

325

Norwich University
Northfield, VT (Pop. 6,500)
Location: Rural
Website: http://www.norwich.edu

Students
Total enrollment: 3,309
Undergrads: 1,997
Freshmen: Not reported
Live on-campus: Not reported
Off-campus employment rating: Good

Academics
Student/faculty ratio: 14:1
Class size 9 or fewer: 19%
Class size 10-29: 56%
Class size 30-49: 15%
Class size 50-99: 10%
Class size 100 or more: 3%
Returning freshmen: Not reported
Six-year graduation rate: Not reported

Admissions
Average GPA: Not reported
ACT range: Not reported
SAT Math range: Not reported
SAT Reading range: Not reported
SAT Writing range: Not reported
Top 10% of class: 16%
Top 25% of class: 34%
Top 50% of class: 66%

Deadlines
Early Action: No
Early Decision: No
Regular Action: February 1 (priority)
Common Application: Not accepted

NORWICH UNIVERSITY

158 Harmon Drive, Northfield, VT 05663
Admissions: 800-468-6679 · Financial Aid: 800-468-6679
Email: nuadm@norwich.edu
Website: http://www.norwich.edu

From the College
"Vision: Norwich University will be a learning community, American in character yet global in perspective, engaged in personal and intellectual transformation and dedicated to knowledge, mutual respect, creativity and service."

Campus Setting
Norwich, including the Military College of Vermont and Vermont College, is a private, multipurpose university. Founded in 1819, it adopted co-education in 1972. The Military College of Vermont, in Northfield, is a co-educational Corps of Cadets organized in a military lifestyle. Vermont College, in Montpelier, is a co-educational, undergraduate, non-military college. The two campuses are 12 miles apart. A four-year institution, Norwich University has an enrollment of 3,309 students. In addition to a large, well-stocked library, the campus also has a museum. Norwich University provides on-campus housing that can accommodate 1,593 students. Recreation and sports facilities include: arena · armory · field house.

Student Life and Activities
Norwich University has 80 official student organizations. The most popular are: Choir · music ensembles · orchestra · regimental and stage bands · symphonic band · marching and pep bands · drill team · artillery platoon · cavalry troop · drill team · military police · mountain rescue team · parachute club · team managers · departmental · service and special-interest groups. For those interested in sports, there are intramural teams such as: basketball · dodgeball · football · hockey · softball · wiffle ball. Norwich University is a member of the ECAC Hockey (Division III), Freedom Football Conference (Division III), Great Northeast Athletic Conference (Division III), New England College Wrestling Association (Division III) and Pilgrim League (Division III).

Academics and Learning Environment
For the B student, the learning environment of a college is just as important as the quality of its academic program. Norwich University has 125 full-time and 137 part-time faculty members, offering a student-to-faculty ratio of 14:1. Norwich University offers 36 majors with the most popular being criminal justice and architecture and least popular being physics, mathematics and biomedical technology. The school has a general core requirement. Cooperative education is not offered. All first-year students must maintain a 1.45 GPA or higher to avoid academic probation. Other special academic programs that would appeal to a B student: pass/fail grading option · independent study · double majors · dual degrees · internships · distance learning.

B Student Support and Success

Norwich's Learning Support Services (LSC) offers assistance to those students who need it. LSC provides support for students who need help in planning, organizing and managing their responsibilities as well as assessing best ways of learning in different environments. Support services are also available in areas of reading, writing, note taking and exam-taking strategies. Additionally, students are afforded opportunities to receive tutoring and to participate in review sessions in selected course subject areas. Students may request counseling and coaching for specific academic problems such as probation status and learning disorders.

Norwich University provides a variety of support programs including dedicated guidance for: academic · career · personal · psychological · military · veterans · religious. The average freshman year GPA is 2.0. Among students who enter the work force, approximately 93 percent enter a field related to their major within six months of graduation. Companies that most frequently hire graduates from Norwich University include: Army, Navy and Air Force; Homeland Security; General Electric; Goodrich; Dartmouth-Hitchcock Medical center; Cap World; many state and local police departments; Bectal and Metcalf & Eddy.

Support for Students with Learning Disabilities

Students with learning disabilities may take advantage of specific support programs. If necessary, the college will grant additional time to students with learning disabilities to complete their degree. Students with learning disabilities will find the following programs extremely useful: remedial math · remedial English · tutors · learning center · testing accommodations · extended time for tests · take-home exam · oral tests · readers · typist/scribe. Individual or small group tutorials are also available in: time management · organizational skills · learning strategies · specific subject areas · math labs · study skills.

How to Get Admitted

For admissions decisions, non-academic factors considered: interview · extracurricular activities · special talents, interests, abilities · character/personal qualities · volunteer work · work experience · state of residency · geographical location · minority affiliation · alumni relationship. A high school diploma is required, although a GED is also accepted for admissions consideration. SAT or ACT test scores are required of all applicants. *Academic units recommended:* 4 English, 3 Math, 3 Science, 2 Foreign Language.

How to Pay for College

To apply for financial aid, students should submit the following: Free Application for Federal Student Aid (FAFSA) · institution's own financial aid forms · CSS/Financial Aid PROFILE. Norwich University participates in the Federal Work Study program. *Need-based aid programs include:* scholarships and grants · general need-based awards · Federal Pell grants · state scholarships and grants · college-based scholarships and grants · private scholarships and grants. *Non-Need-based aid programs include:* scholarships and grants · state scholarships and grants · special achievements and activities awards · ROTC scholarships.

NORWICH UNIVERSITY

Highlights

Financial Aid
In-state tuition: $24,722
Out-of-state tuition: $24,722
Room: -
Board: -
Books: -
Avg. % of need met by financial aid: Not reported
Avg. aid package (freshmen): Not reported
Avg. aid package (undergrads): Not reported
Avg. student debt upon graduation: Not reported

School Spirit
Mascot: Cadets
Colors: Maroon and gold
Song: *Norwich Forever*

OHIO NORTHERN UNIVERSITY

525 S. Main Street, Ada, OH 45810
Admissions: 888-408-4668 · Financial Aid: 888-408-4668
Email: admissions-ug@onu.edu · Website: http://www.onu.edu

From the College

"Ohio Northern University seeks to educate and graduate students accomplished in scholastic achievement, prepared for a useful life and meaningful career, inspired with a desire to contribute to the good of mankind consistent with Judeo-Christian ideals and committed to a quality of life that will result in maximum personal and social worth. Ohio Northern University offers the heritage of a liberal arts tradition within the College of Arts and Sciences and the diversity of four professional colleges: the College of Business Administration, the College of Engineering, the College of Pharmacy and the College of Law."

Campus Setting

Ohio Northern University is a private, United Methodist-related institution. ONU was founded in 1871. The 300-acre campus is located in Ada, a small rural village in northwestern Ohio. A four-year private institution, Ohio Northern University has an enrollment of 3,721 students. In addition to a large, well-stocked library, the campus facilities include: art gallery · pharmacy museum. Housing options: co-ed dorms · women's dorms · men's dorms · sorority housing · fraternity housing · single-student apartments · married-student apartments · special housing for disabled students. Recreation and sports facilities include: baseball · soccer and softball fields · basketball · volleyball and tennis courts · stadium · swimming pool · track and field complex · wrestling center.

Student Life and Activities

With 71 percent of students living on campus, there are plenty of social activities. Athletic events, performing arts events, Regal Beagle (local tavern) are all popular hot spots. The Hypnotist, Comedians, all athletic events, various concerts and performing arts programs are all popular events for students. Ohio Northern University has 150 official student organizations. Popular groups on campus are Greeks, athletes, Student Planning Committee and Student Senate. For those interested in sports, there are intramural teams such as: basketball · roller hockey · ski club · soccer · ultimate Frisbee · volleyball. Ohio Northern University is a member of the Ohio Athletic Conference (Division III).

Academics and Learning Environment

For the B student, the learning environment of a college is just as important as the quality of its academic program. Ohio Northern University has 235 full-time and 87 part-time faculty members, offering a student-to-faculty ratio of 13:1. The most common course size is 20 to 29 students. Ohio Northern University offers 63 majors with the most popular being engineering, biology and business and least popular being philosophy/religion, international studies and physics. The school has a general core requirement as well as a religion requirement Cooperative education is available. All first-year students must maintain a 2.0 GPA or higher to avoid academic probation. Other special academic programs that would appeal to a B student: pass/fail grading option · independent study · double majors · dual degrees · honors program · internships · distance learning certificate programs.

B Student Support and Success

Admission to Ohio Northern is based on class rank and SAT or ACT scores, but there is a strong willingness to look beyond the numbers. Letters of recommendation are not required but will be read if submitted. Extracurricular activities are considered, as well as recent academic trends. A special program helps with college transition.

Ohio Northern University provides a variety of support programs including dedicated guidance for: academic · career · personal · psychological · minority students · family planning · religious. Recognizing that some students may need extra preparation, Ohio Northern University offers remedial and refresher courses in: reading · writing · math · study skills. Annually, 86 percent of freshmen students return for their sophomore year.

Support for Students with Learning Disabilities

Students with learning disabilities may take advantage of specific support programs offered by Ohio Northern University. If necessary, the college will grant additional time to students with learning disabilities to complete their degree. Also, a lightened course load may be granted to LD students. According to the school, each undergraduate college has a representative that works with disability resources. Students with learning disabilities will find the following programs at Ohio Northern University extremely useful: remedial math · remedial English · remedial reading · special classes · tutors · untimed tests · extended time for tests · oral tests · readers · note-taking services · tape recorders · waiver of math degree requirement. Individual or small group tutorials are also available in: time management · organizational skills · learning strategies · specific subject areas · writing labs · math labs · study skills.

How to Get Admitted

For admissions decisions, non-academic factors considered: interview · extracurricular activities · special talents, interests, abilities · character/personal qualities · volunteer work · geographical location · alumni relationship. A high school diploma is required, although a GED is also accepted for admissions consideration. SAT or ACT test scores are required of all applicants. SAT Subject Test scores are considered, if submitted, but are not required. *According to the admissions office:* Minimum composite ACT score of 20, rank in top half of secondary school class, and minimum 2.5 GPA required. *Academic units recommended:* 4 English, 4 Math, 3 Science, 3 Social Studies, 2 Foreign Language.

Insight

According to Karen Condeni, vice president and dean of enrollment, the school makes a real effort to look past the standard statistics to the student behind them. "A strong number of students show potential but not number-wise," she says. "We look at their high school records overall as a whole picture and we look at trends." The school also considers personal information that might affect grades. "We look to see if students were working while going to school or if they had a single parent they had to help. We are looking for students who show determination," she says.

OHIO NORTHERN UNIVERSITY

Admissions
Applicants: 3,032
Accepted: 2,662
Acceptance rate: 87.8%
Average GPA: 3.6
ACT range: 23-28
SAT Math range: 530-650
SAT Reading range: 500-620
SAT Writing range: 490-620
Top 10% of class: 41%
Top 25% of class: 69%
Top 50% of class: 89%

Deadlines
Early Action: No
Early Decision: No
Regular Action: Rolling admissions
Common Application: Accepted

Financial Aid
In-state tuition: $30,555
Out-of-state tuition: $30,555
Room: $3,945
Board: $3,945
Books: $1,800
Freshmen receiving need-based aid: 82%
Undergrads receiving need-based aid: 76%
Avg. % of need met by financial aid: 82%
Avg. aid package (freshmen): $26,490
Avg. aid package (undergrads): $25,084
Freshmen receiving merit-based aid: 15%
Undergrads receiving merit-based aid: 14%
Avg. student debt upon graduation: $45,753

Prominent Alumni
Clayton Mathile, former CEO and owner of Campbell Soup; Mike DeWine, former Republican senator from Ohio; Floyd Keith, executive director, Black Coaches and Administrators Association.

School Spirit
Mascot: Polar Bears
Colors: Burnt Orange and black
Song: *Sons of Dear Old ONU*

Ohio Northern University has a support program called College Transition that is not remedial work but helps students that need extra attention. For example, students in this program do not take a full load of classes (17 to 18 hours) but average 12 to 14 hours or three classes. The students are monitored more closely and meet regularly with an advisor. Tutors are also available.

How to Pay for College

To apply for financial aid, students should submit the following: Free Application for Federal Student Aid (FAFSA). Ohio Northern University participates in the Federal Work Study program. *Need-based aid programs include:* scholarships and grants · general need-based awards · Federal Pell grants · state scholarships and grants · college-based scholarships and grants · private scholarships and grants. *Non-Need-based aid programs include:* scholarships and grants · general need-based awards · state scholarships and grants · creative arts and performance awards · special achievements and activities awards · special characteristics awards · ROTC scholarships.

OHIO UNIVERSITY

120 Chubb Hall, Athens, OH 45701
Admissions: 740-593-4100 · Financial Aid: 740-593-4141
Email: admissions@ohio.edu · Website: http://www.ohio.edu

From the College

"Ohio University holds as its central purpose the intellectual and personal development of its students. Distinguished by its rich history, diverse campus, international community and beautiful Appalachian setting, Ohio University is known as well for its faculty whose research and creative activity advance knowledge across many disciplines."

Campus Setting

Ohio University, founded in 1804, is a public, comprehensive institution. Programs are offered through the Colleges of Arts and Sciences, Business, Communication, Education, Engineering and Technology, Fine Arts, Health and Human Services, Honors Tutorial and University College. One of its campus buildings has been designated a National Historic Landmark. The 1,700-acre campus is located in Athens, 75 miles southeast of Columbus. A four-year public institution, Ohio University has been co-ed since 1870. In addition to a large, well-stocked library, the campus also has an art museum. Ohio University provides on-campus housing with 43 units that can accommodate 8,087 students. Housing options: co-ed dorms · women's dorms · sorority housing · fraternity housing · married-student apartments. Recreation and sports facilities include: centers · fields · softball track and stadiums.

Student Life and Activities

Most students (55 percent) live off campus, which does impact the on-campus social scene. Nevertheless, like any college, students find time to create their own recreational outlets. Ohio University has 321 official student organizations. The most popular are: Comedy for the Masses · Hip-hop Congress · Jitterbug Club · Stand up Comedian Club. For those interested in sports, there are intramural teams such as: air hockey · badminton · basketball · billiards · bowling · broomball · disc golf · dodgeball · flag football · floor hockey · foosball · golf · horseshoes · indoor soccer · racquetball · sandball · soccer · squash · table tennis · tennis · volleyball · wallyball. Ohio University is a member of the Mid-America Conference (Division I, Football I-A).

Academics and Learning Environment

For the B student, the learning environment of a college is just as important as the quality of its academic program. Ohio University has 881 full-time and 297 part-time faculty members, offering a student-to-faculty ratio of 19:1. The most common course size is 10 to 19 students. Ohio University offers 146 majors with the most popular being recreation and sport sciences, journalism and psychology and least popular being women and gender studies, classics and film. The school has a general core requirement. Cooperative education is available. All first-year students must maintain a 2.0 GPA or higher to avoid academic probation. Other special academic programs that would appeal to a B student: self-designed majors · pass/fail grading option · independent study · double majors · dual degrees · accelerated study · honors program · Phi Beta Kappa · internships · distance learning certificate programs.

B Student Support and Success

Ohio University's Academic Advancement Center helps prepare students for college-level work through a variety of student services that focus on computer, writing,

OHIO UNIVERSITY

Ohio University
Athens, OH (Pop. 22,000)
Location: Large town
Website: http://www.ohio.edu

Students
Total enrollment: 21,337
Undergrads: 8,730
Freshmen: 3,985
Part-time students: 7%
From out-of-state: 10%
Male/Female: 50%/50%
Live on-campus: 45%
In fraternities: 13%
In sororities: 16%
Off-campus employment rating: Good
Caucasian: 89%
African American: 5%
Hispanic: 2%
Asian or Pacific Islander: 1%
Native American: 0%
International: 2%

Academics
Student/faculty ratio: 19:1
Class size 9 or fewer: 13%
Class size 10-29: 59%
Class size 30-49: 18%
Class size 50-99: 6%
Class size 100 or more: 4%
Returning freshmen: 80%
Six-year graduation rate: 71%

Most Popular Fields of Study
Protective Services, Criminal Justice and
    Public Administration
Visual and Performing Arts
Family and Consumer Sciences, Nutrition
    and Home Economics
Computer and Information Sciences
Communications, Journalism, Advertising
    and Comm. Technologies
Liberal Arts, Humanities and General
    Studies
English and Literature
Parks, Recreation and Fitness
Health Professions, Medicine and Re-
    lated Sciences
Psychology

reading and study skills. A brief overview of areas in which help is offered follows:

Computer Skills: The computer lab offers equipment such as digital cameras, zip drives, scanners and more. A one-credit hour course for freshmen is available that provides detailed instruction in basic computer skills needed for college work.

Writing Support: The Writing Center gives free assistance to all undergrad and graduate students through peer tutoring. Help is given at all steps of the process from writing an outline to final revisions. Tutoring is available on a walk-in and appointment basis.

Reading Skills: Reading instructors help students develop comprehension and vocabulary skills. They also explain how to draw conclusions, make inferences and recognize tone. A two-credit course called College Reading Skills is offered.

Study Skills: A two-credit course called Learning Strategies teaches note taking, time management, exam preparation and other study habits. Private tutoring is available (at a cost) for students, and the college has a referral service to match tutors with students.

Supplemental Instruction: Extra sessions in which students review lecture notes outside of class, clarify text materials, discuss ideas, organize material, evaluate and improve study skills are available for certain courses. These are free and led by students who have already completed the course.

College Adjustment Program: Ohio University also offers assistance to students who are struggling with the adjustment to college life. Services include free tutoring, academic advising and study skills instruction.

Ohio University provides a variety of support programs including dedicated guidance for: academic · career · personal · psychological · minority students · military · veterans · family planning. Recognizing that some students may need extra preparation, Ohio University offers remedial and refresher courses in: reading · writing · math · study skills. The average freshman year GPA is 3.0, and 80 percent of freshmen students return for their sophomore year. Among students who enter the work force, approximately 75 percent enter a field related to their major within six months of graduation, while 85 percent enter a related career within two years of graduation. Companies that most frequently hire graduates from Ohio University include: Cardinal Health · KPMG LLP · Target · JP Morgan Chase · Deloitte & Touche LLP & Progressive Insurance.

Support for Students with Learning Disabilities

Students with learning disabilities may take advantage of specific support programs offered by Ohio University. If necessary, the college will grant additional time to students with learning disabilities to complete their degree. Also, a lightened course load may be granted to LD students. Students with learning disabilities will find the following programs at Ohio University extremely useful: remedial math · remedial English · remedial reading · tutors · learning center · testing accommodations · extended time for tests · take-home exam · oral tests · readers · typist/scribe · note-taking services · reading machines · tape recorders · texts on tape · diagnostic testing service · priority registration. Individual or small group tutorials are also available in: time management · organizational skills · learning strategies · specific subject areas · writing labs ·

math labs · study skills. An advisor/advocate from the LD program is available to students.

How to Get Admitted

For admissions decisions, non-academic factors considered: extracurricular activities · special talents, interests, abilities · character/personal qualities · volunteer work · work experience · state of residency · minority affiliation · alumni relationship. A high school diploma is required, although a GED is also accepted for admissions consideration. SAT or ACT test scores are required of all applicants. *According to the admissions office:* Rank in top half of secondary school class recommended.

How to Pay for College

To apply for financial aid, students should submit the following: Free Application for Federal Student Aid (FAFSA). Ohio University participates in the Federal Work Study program. *Need-based aid programs include:* scholarships and grants · general need-based awards · Federal Pell grants · state scholarships and grants · college-based scholarships and grants · private scholarships and grants. *Non-Need-based aid programs include:* scholarships and grants · state scholarships and grants · athletic scholarships · ROTC scholarships.

OHIO UNIVERSITY

Highlights

Admissions
Applicants: 14,046
Accepted: 10,931
Acceptance rate: 77.8%
placed on wait list: 346
Average GPA: 3.4
ACT range: 21-26
SAT Math range: 490-600
SAT Reading range: 480-600
SAT Writing range: Not reported
Top 10% of class: 15%
Top 25% of class: 44%
Top 50% of class: 85%

Deadlines
Early Action: No
Early Decision: No
Regular Action: Rolling admissions
Common Application: Not accepted

Financial Aid
In-state tuition: $8,907
Out-of-state tuition: $17,871
Room: $4,857
Board: $4,089
Books: $873
Freshmen receiving need-based aid: 55%
Undergrads receiving need-based aid: 50%
Avg. % of need met by financial aid: 59%
Avg. aid package (freshmen): $7,891
Avg. aid package (undergrads): $8,247
Freshmen receiving merit-based aid: 18%
Undergrads receiving merit-based aid: 11%
Avg. student debt upon graduation: $23,041

Prominent Alumni
George Voinovich, U.S. Senator, Ohio; Clarence Page, journalist, *The Chicago Tribune*; Matt Lauer, host, *The Today Show*.

School Spirit
Mascot: Bobcats
Colors: Hunter green and white
Song: *Stand Up and Cheer*

333

OHIO WESLEYAN UNIVERSITY

61 South Sandusky Street, Delaware, OH 43015
Admissions: 800-922-8953 · Financial Aid: 800-922-8953
Email: owuadmit@owu.edu · Website: http://web.owu.edu

From the College

"Founded in 1842, Ohio Wesleyan is a selective, diverse, national, liberal arts university in Delaware, Ohio. Students obtain a wide breadth of knowledge through rigorous study of the arts, humanities, natural sciences and social sciences. Personalized honors study offers opportunities to talented students, while internships and research are encouraged of all students. Small classes afford personalized attention from professors, all of whom hold the Ph.D. or highest degree attainable in their field. Students come to the university from 43 states and 45 countries. Housing options include six large residence halls with special-interest corridors; a number of smaller special-interest units, ranging from the Creative Arts House to the Peace and Justice House; and 11 fraternity houses. The five sorority houses are non-residential. Students can participate in more than 100 campus organizations as well as 23 NCAA Division III men's and women's athletic teams. OWU's distinctive commitment to public service is reflected in annual student mission trips across the U.S. and abroad, the Sagan National Colloquium lecture series, and extensive community service opportunities. In 2007, the Ohio Wesleyan Department of Education was granted accreditation without provision by the National Council for Accreditation of Teacher Education (NCATE), a benchmark for high standards not easily achieved by smaller universities."

Campus Setting

Ohio Wesleyan, founded in 1842, is a church-affiliated university. Its 200-acre campus is located in Delaware, 20 miles north of Columbus. A four-year, private institution, Ohio Wesleyan University has an enrollment of 1,960 students. The university has been co-ed since 1877. The school is also affiliated with the Methodist Church. In addition to a large, well-stocked library, the campus facilities include: art museum · observatories · scanning electron microscope · nine-inch refractor telescope · science center · nature preserve. Center for economics, business and entrepreneurship. Ohio Wesleyan University provides on-campus housing with 26 units that can accommodate 1,695 students. Housing options: co-ed dorms · women's dorms · fraternity housing · single-student apartments · special housing for disabled students · special housing for International students.

Student Life and Activities

With 71 percent of students living on campus, there are plenty of social activities. Students gather at fraternities on campus and at local bars and theatres off campus. Popular events include: Homecoming Weekend, Performing Arts Series, Spring Fest, Unity Through Music and Sagan National Colloquium. Ohio Wesleyan University has 95 official student organizations. According to the student newspaper, Greeks are the most influential group on campus. Ohio Wesleyan University is a member of the North Coast Athletic Conference (Division III).

Academics and Learning Environment

For the B student, the learning environment of a college is just as important as the quality of its academic program. Ohio Wesleyan University has 135 full-time and 69 part-time faculty members, offering a student-to-faculty ratio of 12:1. The most common course size is 10 to 19 students. Ohio Wesleyan University offers 61 majors with the most popular being psychology, economics/management and zoology and least popular being ancient studies, Black World studies and neuroscience. The school has a general core requirement. Cooperative education is not offered. All first-year students must maintain a 2.0 GPA or higher to avoid academic probation, and a minimum overall GPA of 2.0 is required to graduate. Other special academic programs that would appeal to a B student: self-designed majors · pass/fail grading option · independent study · double majors · dual degrees · honors program · Phi Beta Kappa · internships · certificate programs.

B Student Support and Success

Students who need additional attention or academic help at Ohio Wesleyan will find the assistance they need at the Academic Skills Center where the motto is "Improving the Student Inside You." The center offers individual counseling that helps students assess their strengths and weaknesses and gives support in areas like time management, note taking, reading from texts, test taking and overcoming procrastination and anxiety. Group presentations are available on the same topics and may be given in fraternity houses, residence halls and other spots across the campus.

A Lending Library gives students access to books on a variety of topics, including coping with learning disabilities and developing study skills. Computerized assessments help identify individual specific study skill deficits. In addition, the college offers a Quantitative Skills Center that helps students gain confidence in their ability to do math and related subjects like astronomy, chemistry and economics.

Ohio Wesleyan University provides a variety of support programs including dedicated guidance for: academic · career · personal · psychological · minority students · family planning · religious. The average freshman year GPA is 2.7, and 79 percent of freshmen students return for their sophomore year. What do students do after college? While many enter the work force, approximately 32 percent pursue a graduate degree immediately after graduation. Among students who enter the work force, approximately 80 percent enter a field related to their major within six months of graduation. Companies that most frequently hire graduates from Ohio Wesleyan University include: MBNA America · Fifth Third Bank · US Air Force · James Cancer Hospital · National Science Foundation · World Bank · Cardinal Health · Batelle Laboratories · Ross Laboratories · Ernst & Young · CSI International · Prudential Financial · Deloitte and Touche · Ohio State University Medical Center · Towne Square Animal Clinic · AC Nielson · Nexus Technology Group · Ohio Department of Health Laboratory · U.S. Forest Service · Ohio House of Representatives · Merrill Lynch · JP Morgan Chase · U.S. Peace Corps · Americorps · Columbus Public Schools · Citigroup Global Markets.

Support for Students with Learning Disabilities

Students with learning disabilities may take advantage of specific support programs offered by Ohio Wesleyan University. If necessary, the college will grant additional time to students with learning disabilities to complete their degree. Also, a lightened course load may be granted to LD students. Students with learning disabilities will find the following programs at Ohio Wesleyan University extremely

OHIO WESLEYAN UNIVERSITY

Highlights

Ohio Wesleyan University
Delaware, OH (Pop. 25,000)
Location: Large town
Website: http://web.owu.edu

Students
Total enrollment: 1,960
Undergrads: 917
Freshmen: 576
Part-time students: 1%
From out-of-state: 45%
Male/Female: 47%/53%
Live on-campus: 71%
In fraternities: 28%
In sororities: 26%
Off-campus employment rating: Excellent
Caucasian: 81%
African American: 5%
Hispanic: 1%
Asian or Pacific Islander: 2%
Native American: 1%
International: 9%

Academics
Student/faculty ratio: 12:1
Class size 9 or fewer: 25%
Class size 10-29: 62%
Class size 30-49: 13%
Class size 50-99: 1%
Class size 100 or more: 4%
Returning freshmen: 79%
Six-year graduation rate: 63%

Most Popular Fields of Study
Biological and Life Sciences
Business, Finance, Sales and Marketing
Area, Ethnic and Gender Studies
Visual and Performing Arts
Computer and Information Sciences
Communications, Journalism, Advertising
    and Comm. Technologies
Philosophy, Religion and Theology
Liberal Arts, Humanities and General
    Studies
English and Literature
Parks, Recreation and Fitness

335

OHIO WESLEYAN UNIVERSITY

Admissions
Applicants: 4,238
Accepted: 2,723
Acceptance rate: 64.3%
placed on wait list: 33
Average GPA: 3.4
ACT range: 23-30
SAT Math range: 520-650
SAT Reading range: 520-640
SAT Writing range: Not reported
Top 10% of class: 30%
Top 25% of class: 59%
Top 50% of class: 93%

Deadlines
Early Action: December 15
Early Decision: December 1
Regular Action: March 1 (priority)
Common Application: Accepted

Financial Aid
In-state tuition: $34,570
Out-of-state tuition: $34,570
Room: $4,490
Board: $4,734
Books: $2,402
Freshmen receiving need-based aid: 63%
Undergrads receiving need-based aid:
   59%
Avg. % of need met by financial aid: 78%
Avg. aid package (freshmen): $26,591
Avg. aid package (undergrads): $25,103
Freshmen receiving merit-based aid: 34%
Undergrads receiving merit-based aid:
   37%
Avg. student debt upon graduation:
   $26,704

Prominent Alumni
Byron Pitts, CBS national news correspondent; Branch Rickey, baseball executive who broke the Major League color
barrier in professional baseball.

School Spirit
Mascot: Battling Bishops

useful: remedial math · remedial English · special classes · tutors · learning center · extended time for tests · take-home exam · oral tests · note-taking services · tape recorders · waiver of math degree requirement. Individual or small group tutorials are also available in: time management · organizational skills · learning strategies · writing labs · math labs · study skills. An advisor/advocate from the Sagan Academic Resource Center is available to students.

How to Get Admitted

For admissions decisions, non-academic factors considered: interview · extracurricular activities · special talents, interests, abilities · char-acter/personal qualities · volunteer work · work experience · state of residency · geographical location · minority affiliation · alumni relationship. A high school diploma is required, although a GED is also accepted for admissions consideration. SAT or ACT test scores are required of all applicants. SAT Subject Test scores are considered, if submitted, but are not required. *According to the admissions office:* Minimum combined SAT score of 1000 (composite ACT score of 21) and minimum 2.5 GPA recommended. *Academic units recommended:* 4 Math, 4 Science, 4 Social Studies, 3 Foreign Language.

How to Pay for College

To apply for financial aid, students should submit the following: Free Application for Federal Student Aid (FAFSA) · institution's own financial aid forms. Ohio Wesleyan University participates in the Federal Work Study program. *Need-based aid programs include:* scholarships and grants · general need-based awards · Federal Pell grants · state scholarships and grants · college-based scholarships and grants · private scholarships and grants. *Non-Need-based aid programs include:* scholarships and grants · general need-based awards · state scholarships and grants · creative arts and performance awards · special achievements and activities awards · special characteristics awards.

OLD DOMINION UNIVERSITY

5115 Hampton Boulevard, Norfolk, VA 23529
Admissions: 800-348-7926 · Financial Aid: 757-683-3683
Email: admit@odu.edu · Website: http://www.odu.edu

From the College

"Old Dominion University is Virginia's forward-focused, public doctoral research university for high-performing students from around the world who want a rigorous academic experience in a fast-paced multicultural community. With an enrollment of more than 23,000 students, the university offers 70 bachelor's, 60 master's and 36 doctoral degree programs and two educational specialists degrees. A determined entrepreneurial approach to problem-solving drives cutting-edge research and strategic partnerships with government, business, industry, organizations and the arts."

Campus Setting

Founded in 1930 as a division of the College of William and Mary, Old Dominium became an independent state university in 1962. Programs are offered through the Colleges of Arts and Letters, Business and Public Administration, Education, Engineering and Technology, Health Sciences and Sciences. Its 188-acre campus in Norfolk reflects a Georgian architectural style. A four-year public institution, Old Dominion University has an enrollment of 23,086 students. In addition to a large, well-stocked library, the campus facilities include: art gallery · planetarium · sub-/super-sonic wind tunnels · marine science research vessel · random wave pool · laser optics and robotics labs. Old Dominion University provides on-campus housing with 1,566 units that can accommodate 4,062 students. Housing options: co-ed dorms · single-student apartments · special housing for disabled students · special housing for International students. Recreation and sports facilities include: basketball arena · fitness center · golf course · gymnasium · sand volleyball courts · soccer varsity and practice fields · tennis courts · baseball stadium · wrestling practice room · turf field stadium for field hockey and lacrosse · practice football fields · golf course · sailing center · water area.

Academics and Learning Environment

For the B student, the learning environment of a college is just as important as the quality of its academic program. Old Dominion University has 697 full-time and 449 part-time faculty members, offering a student-to-faculty ratio of 17:1. The most common course size is 10 to 19 students. Old Dominion University offers 141 majors with the most popular being interdisciplinary studies, psychology and criminal justice and least popular being African and African American Studies, music composition and acting. The school has a general core requirement. Cooperative education is available. All first-year students must maintain a 2.0 GPA or higher to avoid academic probation. Other special academic programs that would appeal to a B student: self-designed majors · pass/fail grading option · independent study · double majors · dual degrees ·

Old Dominion University
Norfolk, VA (Pop. 235,747)
Location: Medium city
Website: http://www.odu.edu

Students
Total enrollment: 23,086
Undergrads: 7,717
Freshmen: 3,959
Part-time students: 26%
From out-of-state: 7%
Male/Female: 45%/55%
Live on-campus: 71%
In fraternities: 28%
In sororities: 26%
Off-campus employment rating: Excellent
Caucasian: 61%
African American: 23%
Hispanic: 4%
Asian or Pacific Islander: 6%
Native American: 1%
International: 2%

Academics
Student/faculty ratio: 17:1
Class size 9 or fewer: 11%
Class size 10-29: 45%
Class size 30-49: 32%
Class size 50-99: 8%
Class size 100 or more: 5%
Returning freshmen: 80%
Six-year graduation rate: 47%

Most Popular Fields of Study
Business, Finance, Sales and Marketing
Biological and Life Sciences

Admissions
Applicants: 9,484
Accepted: 6,800
Acceptance rate: 71.7%
Average GPA: 3.3
ACT range: 18-23
SAT Math range: 490-590
SAT Reading range: 480-570
SAT Writing range: 460-560
Top 10% of class: 12%
Top 25% of class: 39%
Top 50% of class: 82%

OLD DOMINION UNIVERSITY

Deadlines
Early Action: December 1
Early Decision: No
Regular Action: Rolling admissions
Common Application: Accepted

Financial Aid
In-state tuition: $6,720
Out-of-state tuition: $18,390
Room: $4,234
Board: $568
Books: $1,000
Freshmen receiving need-based aid: 61%
Undergrads receiving need-based aid: 57%
Avg. % of need met by financial aid: 81%
Avg. aid package (freshmen): $7,571
Avg. aid package (undergrads): $7,597
Freshmen receiving merit-based aid: 4%
Undergrads receiving merit-based aid: 3%
Avg. student debt upon graduation: $17,250

Prominent Alumni
Michael J. Bloomfield, astronaut; Kenny Gattison, coach, New Jersey Nets basketball team; Mills Godwin, former governor, Virginia; William Lobeck, CEO, National Car Rental System; Nancy Lieberman-Cline, basketball coach and commentator.

School Spirit
Mascot: Monarchs
Colors: Silver and navy blue

accelerated study · honors program · internships · weekend college · distance learning.

B Student Support and Success

Old Dominion's Student Support Services provides academic support to increase the retention and graduation rates of eligible students. It includes tutorials, academic skills workshops, career exploration, advising services and cultural enrichment.

At the end of each semester, the Office of Continuance reviews the records of all students who do not maintain a 2.0 GPA. They are placed on academic warning and have one semester to bring their grades up or to be placed on suspension.

Old Dominion University provides a variety of support programs including dedicated guidance for: academic · career · personal · psychological · minority students · military · veterans · non-traditional students · family planning · religious. Additional counseling services include: alcohol/substance abuse, financial aid. The average freshman year GPA is 2.5, and 80 percent of freshmen students return for their sophomore year.

Support for Students with Learning Disabilities

Students with learning disabilities may take advantage of specific support programs offered by Old Dominion University. If necessary, the college will grant additional time to students with learning disabilities to complete their degree. Also, a lightened course load may be granted to LD students. According to the school, Disability Services strives to coordinate services using a developmental model that will enable students with disabilities to act as independently as possible in a supportive atmosphere that promotes self-reliance. Students with learning disabilities will find the following programs at Old Dominion University extremely useful: special classes · testing accommodations · extended time for tests · take-home exam · exam on tape or computer · readers · typist/scribe · note-taking services · tape recorders · texts on tape · early syllabus · priority registration · waiver of math degree requirement. Individual or small group tutorials are also available in: time management · organizational skills · learning strategies · specific subject areas · writing labs · study skills. An advisor/advocate from the Disability Services is available to students.

How to Get Admitted

For admissions decisions, non-academic factors considered: interview · extracurricular activities · special talents, interests, abilities · character/personal qualities · volunteer work · work experience · state of residency · alumni relationship. A high school diploma is required, although a GED is also accepted for admissions consideration. SAT or ACT test scores are required of all applicants. *According to the admissions office:* Admission based on eligibility index of standardized test scores and minimum 2.7 GPA. *Academic units recommended:* 4 English, 3 Math, 3 Science, 3 Social Studies, 3 Foreign Language.

How to Pay for College

To apply for financial aid, students should submit the following: Free Application for Federal Student Aid (FAFSA). Old Dominion University participates in the Federal Work Study program. *Need-based aid programs include:* scholarships and grants · general need-based awards · Federal Pell grants · state scholarships and grants · college-based scholarships and grants · private scholarships and grants · Federal Nursing scholarships · United Negro College Fund. *Non-Need-based aid programs include:* scholarships and grants · general need-based awards · state scholarships and grants · creative arts and performance awards · special achievements and activities awards · special characteristics awards · athletic scholarships · ROTC scholarships.

OREGON STATE UNIVERSITY

104 Kerr Administration Building, Corvallis, OR 97331
Admissions: 800-291-4192 · Financial Aid: 541-737-2241
Email: osuadmit@oregonstate.edu · Website: http://www.oregonstate.edu

From the College

"Oregon State University, a Carnegie Research University (very high research activity), is one of only two American universities to hold the Land-, Sea-, Sun- and Space-Grant designations. OSU is comprised of 11 academic colleges with strengths in natural resources, earth dynamics and sustainability, life sciences, entrepreneurship and the arts and sciences. More than 19,000 students attend the Corvallis and Cascades Campus locations. OSU has facilities and/or programs in every county in the state, including 13 regional experiment stations, 38 county extension offices, a major marine science center in Newport and a range of programs and facilities in the Portland region."

Campus Setting

Oregon State, founded in 1868, is a public, liberal arts university. Programs are offered through the Colleges of Agricultural Sciences, Business, Engineering, Forestry, Health and Human Performance, Home Economics and Education, Liberal Arts, Pharmacy and Science. Its 422-acre campus in Corvallis is 85 miles south of Portland. A four-year institution, Oregon State University has an enrollment of 20,320 students. In addition to a large, well-stocked library, the campus facilities include: art gallery · herbarium. Oregon State University provides on-campus housing with 2,430 units that can accommodate 4,204 students. Housing options: co-ed dorms · sorority housing · fraternity housing · single-student apartments · married-student apartments · special housing for disabled students · special housing for International students · cooperative housing. Recreation and sports facilities include: baseball · football and soccer stadiums · basketball · volleyball · gymnastics and wrestling coliseum · boathouse and docks · golf club · gymnastics and football centers · softball complex · swimming pool · weight room.

Student Life and Activities

Most students (77 percent) live off campus, which does impact the on-campus social scene. Nevertheless, like any college, students find time to create their own recreational outlets. There are some plays and concerts available to students, but to see anything good, a student has to go to Eugene or Portland, according to the editor of the student newspaper. Since all Greek parties are closed, "if you're not in a fraternity or a sorority, the party scene is dismal." Memorial Union Commons, the Beanery, American Dream Pizza and Top of the Peacock are favorite hangouts. Popular events include: Hawaii Night, Commencement, University Day, PowWow, Japan Night, China Night, India Night, Mom's Weekend, Dad's Weekend, Martin Luther King Jr. Breakfast, Homecoming and Civil War Football Weekend. Oregon State University has 300 official student organizations. Greeks have widespread influence on student social life. Oregon State University is a member of the Pacific-10 Conference (Division I, Football I-A).

Academics and Learning Environment

For the B student, the learning environment of a college is just as important as the quality of its academic program. Oregon State University has 880 full-time and 232 part-time faculty members, offering a student-to-faculty ratio of 19:1. The most common course size is 20 to 29 students. Oregon State University offers 249 majors with the most popular being business administration, human development and family science and liberal studies and least popular being agricultural and resource economics, rangeland resources and engineering physics. The school has a general core requirement. Cooperative education is available. All first-year students must maintain a 2.0 GPA or higher to avoid academic probation. Other special academic programs that would appeal to a B student: self-designed majors · pass/fail grading option · independent study · double majors · dual degrees · accelerated study · honors program · internships · distance learning certificate programs.

B Student Support and Success

OSU's College of Business Beta Alpha Psi is a co-ed professional accounting fraternity that sponsors an accounting library, provides resource materials and whose members tutor accounting students.

The Center for Writing and Learning gives instructions and advice to students and provides a study skills program. Basic writing skills such as organizing and revising are offered, and short grammar questions can be emailed for assistance.

A student chapter offers tutoring in chemical engineering, and the chemistry department has a tutor list for an hourly fee. A general chemistry tutorial room known as the Mole Hole is available during certain weeks of each term.

Free tutoring is available for undergrads in lower division core economics courses and for students of electrical engineering and computer science. Other departments offer assistance as well. The department of ethnic studies offers mentoring for students of color or anyone else interested in changing social patterns of race, gender, ethnic, class and other issues. Students taking French, German and Spanish can find tutorial support through the Department of Foreign Languages and Literatures. The College of Forestry offers tutoring to students in forestry or related classes. The Math Learning Center is available for drop-in tutoring from undergrads and volunteers and multiple resources, while the Microbiology Student Association tutors students in that subject, and physics grad students offer help to students in introductory physics courses. For students who have not yet declared a major, Exploratory Studies gives information, resources and other important materials to help.

Oregon State University provides a variety of support programs including dedicated guidance for: academic · career · personal · psychological · minority students · military · veterans · non-traditional students · family planning. Annually, 81 percent of freshmen students return for their sophomore year.

Support for Students with Learning Disabilities

Students with learning disabilities may take advantage of specific support programs offered by Oregon State University. If necessary, the college will grant additional time to students with learning disabilities to complete their degree. Also, a lightened course load may be granted to LD students. Students with learning disabilities will find the following programs at Oregon State University extremely useful: remedial math · remedial English · remedial reading · learning center · extended time for tests · oral tests · note-taking services · reading machines. Individual or small group tutorials are also available in: time management · organizational skills · learning

OREGON STATE UNIVERSITY

Highlights

Oregon State University
Corvallis, OR (Pop. 55,000)
Location: Large town
Website: http://www.oregonstate.edu

Students
Total enrollment: 20,320
Undergrads: 8,850
Freshmen: 4,376
Part-time students: 15%
From out-of-state: 15%
Male/Female: 53%/47%
Live on-campus: 23%
In fraternities: 9%
In sororities: 9%
Off-campus employment rating: Excellent
Caucasian: 72%
African American: 2%
Hispanic: 5%
Asian or Pacific Islander: 9%
Native American: 1%
International: 1%

Academics
Student/faculty ratio: 19:1
Class size 9 or fewer: 21%
Class size 10-29: 42%
Class size 30-49: 17%
Class size 50-99: 13%
Class size 100 or more: 6%
Returning freshmen: 81%
Six-year graduation rate: 62%

Most Popular Fields of Study
Business, Finance, Sales and Marketing
Biological and Life Sciences
Agriculture, Aquaculture and Animal Sciences

OREGON STATE UNIVERSITY

Highlights

Admissions
Applicants: 4,654
Accepted: 3,951
Acceptance rate: 84.9%
Average GPA: 3.5
ACT range: 20-26
SAT Math range: 480-610
SAT Reading range: 460-600
SAT Writing range: 440-560
Top 10% of class: 21%
Top 25% of class: 51%
Top 50% of class: 85%

Deadlines
Early Action: February 1
Early Decision: No
Regular Action: Rolling admissions
Common Application: Not accepted

Financial Aid
In-state tuition: $6,725
Out-of-state tuition: $19,417
Room: -
Board: -
Books: $1,527
Freshmen receiving need-based aid: 48%
Undergrads receiving need-based aid: 49%
Avg. % of need met by financial aid: 66%
Avg. aid package (freshmen): $8,812
Avg. aid package (undergrads): $9,528
Undergrads receiving merit-based aid: 0%
Avg. student debt upon graduation: $20,240

Prominent Alumni
Linus Pauling, Nobel Prize-winning chemist; Doug Englebart, inventor of the computer mouse; Mercedes Bates, vice president of Betty Crocker and first female officer at General Mills.

School Spirit
Mascot: Benny the Beaver
Colors: Orange and black
Song: *OSU Fight Song*

strategies · specific subject areas · writing labs · math labs · study skills. An advisor/advocate from the Office of Services for Students with Disabilities is available to students.

How to Get Admitted

For admissions decisions, non-academic factors considered: interview · extracurricular activities · special talents, interests, abilities · character/personal qualities · volunteer work · work experience · state of residency. A high school diploma is required, although a GED is also accepted for admissions consideration. SAT or ACT test scores are required of all applicants. SAT Subject Test scores are required for some applicants. *According to the admissions office:* Minimum cumulative grade point average of 3.0 and completion of 14 required subject area courses. Class rank taken in context with academic rigor and class size of high school attended. Performance on standardized tests will be considered when available. *Academic units recommended:* 4 English, 3 Math, 2 Science, 3 Social Studies, 2 Foreign Language.

How to Pay for College

To apply for financial aid, students should submit the following: Free Application for Federal Student Aid (FAFSA) · AFSA · USAF · SAAC · CSX. Oregon State University participates in the Federal Work Study program. *Need-based aid programs include:* scholarships and grants · general need-based awards · Federal Pell grants · state scholarships and grants · college-based scholarships and grants · private scholarships and grants. *Non-Need-based aid programs include:* scholarships and grants · general need-based awards · state scholarships and grants · athletic scholarships · ROTC scholarships.

PACE UNIVERSITY

1 Pace Plaza, New York, NY 10038
Admissions: 800-874-7223 · Financial Aid: 800-874-7223
Email: infoctr@pace.edu · Website: http://www.pace.edu

From the College

"Pace University offers a comprehensive education combining exceptional academics, professional experience and the New York edge. Diverse students take advantage of Pace's over 100 majors in the liberal arts and sciences, business, law, nursing, education and computer science. Located in lower Manhattan and Westchester County near centers of finance, accounting, media, healthcare, performing arts and technology, Pace enhances the student experience with one of the metropolitan area's largest cooperative education and internship program. Pace University draws strength from campuses in three locations, offering students choices of living and learning experiences, especially professional experiences that lead to careers and opportunities for students to improve their lives and the lives of others. Locations include our urban campus in New York City, blocks from Wall Street and South Street Seaport; our traditional suburban collegiate setting in the heart of Westchester County; and our White Plains campus with a 13-acre Law School campus and a Graduate Center directly across the street from the train station. Pace combines the benefits and resources of a large university with the warmth and personal attention usually associated with a small college, with class sizes averaging 28 students. Campus housing is available on each campus."

Campus Setting

Pace, founded in 1906, is a private, comprehensive university. A four-year private institution, Pace University has an enrollment of 12,704 students. In addition to a large, well-stocked library, the campus facilities include: actor's studio · theatre · environmental center · fitness center. Pace University provides on-campus housing that can accommodate 3,037 students. Housing options: co-ed dorms · single-student apartments. Recreation and sports facilities include: aerobics facility · weight rooms · arena · fitness and recreation centers.

Student Life and Activities

Most students (56 percent) live off campus, which does impact the on-campus social scene. Nevertheless, like any college, students find time to create their own recreational outlets. According to the student newspaper, on-campus activity is low on weekends, when most students go home. There are special dorm activities a couple of times each semester. Off-campus life all depends on whether students are involved in clubs, Greek life, etc. The campus student center and the gym/auditorium are popular gathering spots. New York City offers many attractions. Students in Westchester have options for activities in the Hudson Valley and also in New York City. Popular campus events include University Fest (combination of Homecoming, Alumni weekend, family weekend), Alternative Spring Break, Cariculture, Inside the Actor's Studio, Amateur Night, Spring Fest, Weekend in Montreal, Relay for Life, Townhouse Day, Ski Trips, Black Student Union Trip to Washington, DC, Community Service, RHA: Come out and Play. Pace University has 90 official student organizations. Greeks are influential on student life for parties, and sports teams to a lesser extent. For those interested in sports, there are intramural teams such as: basketball · dodgeball · flag football · soccer · volleyball. Pace University is a member of the Northeast-10 Conference (Division II).

PACE UNIVERSITY

Pace University
New York, NY (Pop. 8,250,000)
Location: Major city
Website: http://www.pace.edu

Students
Total enrollment: 12,704
Undergrads: 3,122
Freshmen: 2,891
Part-time students: 21%
From out-of-state: 42%
Male/Female: 40%/60%
Live on-campus: 44%
In fraternities: 5%
In sororities: 5%
Off-campus employment rating: Excellent
Caucasian: 45%
African American: 10%
Hispanic: 12%
Asian or Pacific Islander: 10%
Native American: 0%
International: 4%

Academics
Student/faculty ratio: 15:1
Class size 9 or fewer: 11%
Class size 10-29: 72%
Class size 30-49: 16%
Class size 50-99: 1%
Class size 100 or more: 1%
Returning freshmen: 74%
Six-year graduation rate: 56%

Most Popular Fields of Study
Business, Finance, Sales and Marketing
Protective Services, Criminal Justice and
    Public Administration
Psychology
Visual and Performing Arts
English and Literature
Computer and Information Sciences
Mathematics
Health Professions, Medicine and Re-
    lated Sciences
Liberal Arts, Humanities and General
    Studies

344

Academics and Learning Environment

For the B student, the learning environment of a college is just as important as the quality of its academic program. Pace University has 415 full-time and 640 part-time faculty members, offering a student-to-faculty ratio of 15:1. The most common course size is 10 to 19 students. Pace University offers 97 majors with the most popular being finance, nursing and accounting and least popular being mathematics, social services and history. The school has a general core requirement. Cooperative education is available. All first-year students must maintain a 2.0 GPA or higher to avoid academic probation, and a minimum overall GPA of 2.0 is required to graduate. Other special academic programs that would appeal to a B student: pass/fail grading option · independent study · dual degrees · accelerated study · honors program · internships · distance learning.

B Student Support and Success

Pace's Center for Academic Excellence is a comprehensive academic support network that helps students find their ideal path and make the transition from home to college life. It offers the following programs:

The Office of First Year Programs: This one-credit, Pass/Fail course helps all freshmen with the transition through academic advisement, and the UNV 101 program. It provides students with an in-depth look at the university's academic and cultural life, its support network and the services it provides for students. It meets for 13 weeks during fall semester and covers topics such as time management, study skills, critical thinking, health and wellness and campus diversity.

Academic Resources: The services of this program include meeting with an advisor, learning about different major and minors and choosing a course of study.

The Tutoring Center: Students can find assistance with classes that they find difficult by calling the Tutoring Center. It offers individualized and small group tutoring in upper and lower division courses.

Pace University provides a variety of support programs including dedicated guidance for: academic · career · psychological · minority students. Additional counseling services include: services for students with disabilities. The average freshman year GPA is 3.0, and 74 percent of freshmen students return for their sophomore year. What do students do after college? While many enter the work force, approximately 15 percent pursue a graduate degree immediately after graduation. Among students who enter the work force, approximately 84 percent enter a field related to their major within six months of graduation. Companies that most frequently hire graduates from Pace University include: Ernst & Young · Friedman · Protiviti · Rothstein Kass & Co. · IBM · Verizon · Lehman Brothers · KPMG · NY Presbyterian · New York City Department of Education · Westchester County School Districts · USB Financial Services Inc. · Merrill Lynch · AXA Advisors · PricewaterhouseCoopers · Deloitte & Touche · JPMorgan Chase & Co. · Goldman Sachs · Bank of New York · Morgan Stanley · RSM McGladrey & Pullen · Pace University · Pepsi Bottling Group · Citigroup · Westchester Medical Center.

Support for Students with Learning Disabilities

Students with learning disabilities may take advantage of specific support programs offered by Pace University. According to the school, students who are interested in receiving services for their disability must self-identify to the Office of Disability Services on their campus. High school math and foreign language waivers are granted on an individual basis. Student accommodations and services are also determined on an individual basis and not all services may be appropriate for all students. Students must contact the Coordinator of Disability Services on their campus in order to register with the office and arrange their services and, after the initial intake process, students can meet with their Disability Services Counselor as needed by appointment. Tutoring is available to all students and is not considered an accommodation. Students with learning disabilities will find the following programs at Pace University extremely useful: remedial math · remedial English · remedial reading · tutors · learning center · testing accommodations · untimed tests · extended time for tests · take-home exam · oral tests · exam on tape or computer · substitution of courses · readers · typist/scribe · note-taking services · proofreading services · reading machines · tape recorders · texts on tape · early syllabus · priority registration · priority seating · waiver of math degree requirement. Individual or small group tutorials are also available in: time management · organizational skills · writing labs · math labs · study skills. An advisor/advocate from the LD program is available to students.

How to Get Admitted

For admissions decisions, non-academic factors considered: extracurricular activities · special talents, interests, abilities · character/personal qualities · volunteer work · work experience · state of residency · alumni relationship. A high school diploma is required, although a GED is also accepted for admissions consideration. SAT or ACT test scores are required of all applicants. SAT Subject Test scores are required for some applicants. *According to the admissions office:* Minimum combined SAT Reasoning score of 1050 and minimum grade average of B required. *Academic units recommended:* 4 English, 4 Math, 2 Science, 2 Social Studies, 3 Foreign Language.

How to Pay for College

To apply for financial aid, students should submit the following: Free Application for Federal Student Aid (FAFSA) · state aid form. Pace University participates in the Federal Work Study program. *Need-based aid programs include:* scholarships and grants · general need-based awards · Federal Pell grants · state scholarships and grants · college-based scholarships and grants · private scholarships and grants · Federal Nursing scholarships · Endowed and Restricted Scholarships and Grants. *Non-Need-based aid programs include:* scholarships and grants · state scholarships and grants · athletic scholarships.

PACE UNIVERSITY

Highlights

Admissions
Applicants: 9,123
Accepted: 6,811
Acceptance rate: 74.7%
Average GPA: 3.2
ACT range: 20-26
SAT Math range: 490-590
SAT Reading range: 490-580
SAT Writing range: Not reported
Top 10% of class: 14%
Top 25% of class: 41%
Top 50% of class: 75%

Deadlines
Early Action: December 1
Early Decision: No
Regular Action: Rolling admissions
Common Application: Accepted

Financial Aid
In-state tuition: $30,632
Out-of-state tuition: $30,632
Room: -
Board: -
Books: $800
Freshmen receiving need-based aid: 76%
Undergrads receiving need-based aid: 71%
Avg. % of need met by financial aid: 70%
Avg. aid package (freshmen): $27,024
Avg. aid package (undergrads): $23,166
Freshmen receiving merit-based aid: 24%
Undergrads receiving merit-based aid: 21%
Avg. student debt upon graduation: $29,622

Prominent Alumni
Marie J. Toulantis, CEO of barnesandnoble.com; Ivan G. Seidenberg, chairman and CEO of Verizon Communications; Joseph R. Ficalora, chairman, president and CEO of New York Community Bancorp Inc.

School Spirit
Mascot: Setter
Colors: Navy and gold

Pacific Lutheran University

Tacoma, WA (Pop. 199,600)
Location: Medium city
Website: http://www.plu.edu

Students

Total enrollment: 3,586
Undergrads: 1,223
Freshmen: 827
Part-time students: 4%
From out-of-state: 25%
Male/Female: 37%/63%
Live on-campus: 51%
Off-campus employment rating: Excellent
Caucasian: 69%
African American: 2%
Hispanic: 2%
Asian or Pacific Islander: 6%
Native American: 1%
International: 5%

Academics

Student/faculty ratio: 15:1
Class size 9 or fewer: 15%
Class size 10-29: 53%
Class size 30-49: 30%
Class size 50-99: 2%
Class size 100 or more: 1%
Returning freshmen: 85%
Six-year graduation rate: 70%

Most Popular Fields of Study

Business, Finance, Sales and Marketing
Visual and Performing Arts
Social Sciences, History, Economics,
    Political Science
Protective Services, Criminal Justice and
    Public Administration
Biological and Life Sciences
Computer and Information Sciences
Communications, Journalism, Advertising
    and Comm. Technologies
Philosophy, Religion and Theology
English and Literature

America's
Best Colleges for
B Students

PACIFIC LUTHERAN UNIVERSITY

12180 Park Street S, Tacoma, WA 98447
Admissions: 800-274-6758 · Financial Aid: 800-678-3243
Email: admission@plu.edu · Website: http://www.plu.edu

From the College

"Pacific Lutheran University combines a rigorous academic program with a caring community ensuring challenge and support for every student. Students at PLU enjoy successful internship opportunities in world-class local businesses, a hands-on classroom experience with professors who are experts in their field of study, and a tradition of excellence and service to the world established by PLU alumni. The Tacoma/Seattle area also offers vast outdoor recreation, cultural events, art exhibits and museums, as well as music and theatre performances."

Campus Setting

Pacific Lutheran University, founded in 1890, is a church-affiliated university. Its 126-acre campus is located near Tacoma, Washington. A four-year private institution, Pacific Lutheran University has an enrollment of 3,586 students. The school is also affiliated with the Lutheran Church. In addition to a large, well-stocked library, the campus facilities include: art gallery · music center · Scandinavian cultural center · observatory · science center. Pacific Lutheran University provides on-campus housing with 947 units that can accommodate 1,725 students. Housing options: co-ed dorms · women's dorms · single-student apartments · married-student apartments · special housing for disabled students. Recreation and sports facilities include: field house · fitness center · gyms · swimming pool · tennis courts · track field.

Student Life and Activities

With 51 percent of students living on campus, there are plenty of social activities. The Cave and Marazano's restaurant are popular hang-outs. On the Road, Homecoming Dance, Miss Lute, EXPLORE! Retreat, PLU Idol, Campus Ministry Clothing Exchange, Spring Break Service Trips, Dance Ensemble, Relay for Life, Hawaii Luau, Spring Formal, Lute Loop 5k Run and Walk, Black and Gold Fridays, Outdoor Recreation Trips, University Congregation Mt. Rainier Hike, Sound Off, Songfest, Intramural Sports and Meant To Live Conference are popular events. Pacific Lutheran University has 72 official student organizations. The football team, Younglife and Rejoice are influential student groups. For those interested in sports, there are intramural teams such as: basketball · cycling club · flag football · softball · soccer · triathlon club · volleyball. Pacific Lutheran University is a member of the Northwest Conference (Division III).

Academics and Learning Environment

For the B student, the learning environment of a college is just as important as the quality of its academic program. Pacific Lutheran

University has 231 full-time and 33 part-time faculty members, offering a student-to-faculty ratio of 15:1. The most common course size is 20 to 29 students. Pacific Lutheran University offers 56 majors with the most popular being business administration, elementary education and secondary education and least popular being mathematics and philosophy. The school has a general core requirement as well as a religion requirement Cooperative education is available. All first-year students must maintain a 2.0 GPA or higher to avoid academic probation. Other special academic programs that would appeal to a B student: self-designed majors · pass/fail grading option · independent study · double majors · dual degrees · honors program · internships.

B Student Support and Success

PLU's Academic Assistance Center offers tutors, foreign language conversation groups, independent study strategies, group review sessions and even free flashcards—and a bonus: hand-outs on issues like critical reading, time management, note taking and test taking. There is a math lab, a computer science lab, a biology/chemistry lab and a geo-science lab. All services are free of charge.

Pacific Lutheran University provides a variety of support programs including dedicated guidance for: academic · career · personal · psychological · minority students · military · veterans · family planning · religious. Annually, 85 percent of freshmen students return for their sophomore year. Among students who enter the work force, approximately 86 percent enter a field related to their major within six months of graduation. Companies that most frequently hire graduates from Pacific Lutheran University include: Frank Russell · Enterprise · Boeing · Edward Jones · Thrivant Financial · Starbucks.

Support for Students with Learning Disabilities

Students with learning disabilities may take advantage of specific support programs offered by Pacific Lutheran University. If necessary, the college will grant additional time to students with learning disabilities to complete their degree. High school foreign language waivers are accepted. Students with learning disabilities will find the following programs at Pacific Lutheran University extremely useful: special classes · tutors · learning center · untimed tests · extended time for tests · take-home exam · oral tests · readers · typist/scribe · note-taking services · reading machines · tape recorders · videotaped classes · early syllabus · priority registration · priority seating · waiver of math degree requirement. Individual or small group tutorials are also available in: time management · organizational skills · learning strategies · specific subject areas · writing labs · math labs · study skills. An advisor/advocate from the Disability Support Services is available to students.

How to Get Admitted

For admissions decisions, non-academic factors considered: interview · extracurricular activities · special talents, interests, abilities · character/personal qualities · volunteer work · work experience · state of residency. A high school diploma is required, although a GED is also accepted for admissions consideration. SAT or ACT test scores

PACIFIC LUTHERN UNIVERSITY

Highlights

Admissions
Applicants: 2,555
Accepted: 1,914
Acceptance rate: 74.9%
Average GPA: 3.6
ACT range: 22-28
SAT Math range: 500-620
SAT Reading range: 490-630
SAT Writing range: 490-600
Top 10% of class: 32%
Top 25% of class: 66%
Top 50% of class: 92%

Deadlines
Early Action: No
Early Decision: No
Regular Action: Rolling admissions
Common Application: Accepted

Financial Aid
In-state tuition: $28,100
Out-of-state tuition: $28,100
Room: -
Board: -
Books: $972
Freshmen receiving need-based aid: 73%
Undergrads receiving need-based aid: 67%
Avg. % of need met by financial aid: 86%
Avg. aid package (freshmen): $25,805
Avg. aid package (undergrads): $26,063
Freshmen receiving merit-based aid: 24%
Undergrads receiving merit-based aid: 27%
Avg. student debt upon graduation: $22,484

Prominent Alumni
Elizabeth Pulliam, Pulitzer Prize-winning journalist; Joyce A. Barr, U.S. ambassador to Namibia.

School Spirit
Mascot: Lutes
Colors: Black and gold

347

PACIFIC LUTHERN UNIVERSITY

are required of all applicants. *Academic units recommended:* 4 English, 3 Math, 2 Science, 2 Social Studies, 2 Foreign Language.

How to Pay for College

To apply for financial aid, students should submit the following: Free Application for Federal Student Aid (FAFSA). Pacific Lutheran University participates in the Federal Work Study program. *Need-based aid programs include:* scholarships and grants · general need-based awards · Federal Pell grants · state scholarships and grants · college-based scholarships and grants · private scholarships and grants · Federal Nursing scholarships. *Non-Need-based aid programs include:* scholarships and grants · general need-based awards · state scholarships and grants · creative arts and performance awards · ROTC scholarships.

PAUL SMITH'S COLLEGE

Route 86 & 30, P.O. Box 265, Paul Smiths, NY 12970-0265
Admissions: 800-421-2605 · Financial Aid: 800-421-2605
Email: admissions@paulsmiths.edu
Website: http://www.paulsmiths.edu

Campus Setting

Paul Smith's College, founded in 1937, is a private, specialized institution located on a 14,200-acre wilderness campus. A four-year private institution, Paul Smith's College does not have on-campus housing for students.

Academics and Learning Environment

For the B student, the learning environment of a college is just as important as the quality of its academic program. Paul Smith's College offers 20 majors with the most popular being natural resources, hotel/resort/tourism management and culinary arts/service management. The school does not have a general core requirement. Cooperative education is not offered. All first-year students must maintain a 2.0 GPA or higher to avoid academic probation. Other special academic programs that would appeal to a B student: certificate programs.

B Student Support and Success

The theme at Paul Smith's Academic Center is "Helping Students Achieve their Goals for Academic Success." Here they offer peer tutoring, supplemental instruction, study groups and a Writing Center where experts strive to help students understand the assignment, build confidence, organize ideas, listen carefully, formulate comments and more.
The average freshman year GPA is 2.8, and 64 percent of freshmen students return for their sophomore year.

Support for Students with Learning Disabilities

Students with learning disabilities may take advantage of specific support programs offered by Paul Smith's College. Students with learning disabilities will find the following programs at Paul Smith's College extremely useful: tutors · waiver of math degree requirement.

How to Get Admitted

For admissions decisions, non-academic factors considered: state of residency. A high school diploma is required, although a GED is also accepted for admissions consideration. SAT or ACT test scores are required for some applicants. SAT Subject Test scores are recommended but not required. *According to the admissions office:* Minimum combined SAT Reasoning score of 800 (composite ACT score of 17) and rank in top half of secondary school class required.

How to Pay for College

To apply for financial aid, students should submit the following: Free Application for Federal Student Aid (FAFSA). Paul Smith's Col-

PAUL SMITH'S COLLEGE

Deadlines
Early Action: No
Early Decision: No
Regular Action: Rolling admissions
Common Application: Not accepted

Financial Aid
In-state tuition: $19,200
Out-of-state tuition: $19,200
Room: $4,720
Board: $4,220
Books: $1,000
Freshmen receiving need-based aid: 83%
Undergrads receiving need-based aid: 85%
Avg. % of need met by financial aid: 72%
Avg. aid package (freshmen): $15,254
Avg. aid package (undergrads): $15,953
Freshmen receiving merit-based aid: 14%
Undergrads receiving merit-based aid: 11%
Avg. student debt upon graduation: Not reported

lege participates in the Federal Work Study program. *Need-based aid programs include:* scholarships and grants · general need-based awards · Federal Pell grants · state scholarships and grants · college-based scholarships and grants · private scholarships and grants. *Non-Need-based aid programs include:* scholarships and grants · state scholarships and grants.

PINE MANOR COLLEGE

400 Heath Street, Chestnut Hill, MA 02467
Admissions: 800-762-1357 · Financial Aid: 800-762-1357
Email: admission@pmc.edu · Website: http://www.pmc.edu

From the College

"Pine Manor College prepares women for inclusive leadership and social responsibility in their workplaces, families and communities. We pursue this goal through: integration of an outcomes-based curriculum and co-curriculum demonstrated by portfolio presentations; active, collaborative, applied liberal arts learning; and college-wide mentoring teams and community partnerships-in an environment that celebrates diversity and respects the common good."

Campus Setting

Pine Manor, founded in 1911, is a private, liberal arts college for women. Its 65-acre campus is located in Chestnut Hill, five miles from downtown Boston. Pine Manor College has an enrollment of 501 students. In addition to a medium-sized library, the campus facilities include: art gallery · communication center · child study center. Pine Manor College provides on-campus housing that can accommodate 481 students. Housing options: women's dorms · special housing for disabled students. Recreation and sports facilities include: aerobics room · gymnasium · dance studio · soccer and lacrosse field · softball field · weight room.

Student Life and Activities

With 77 percent of students living on campus, there are plenty of social activities. Pine Manor College has 23 official student organizations. The most popular are: Anime club · Camerata Singers · dance ensemble · Campus Activites Board · The F-Group · psychology club. Bisexuals · Gays · Lesbians and Allies in Diversity. Pine Manor College is a member of the Great Northeast Athletic Conference (Division III).

Academics and Learning Environment

For the B student, the learning environment of a college is just as important as the quality of its academic program. Pine Manor College has 32 full-time and 44 part-time faculty members, offering a student-to-faculty ratio of 10:1. The most common course size is 10 to 19 students. Pine Manor College offers 16 majors with the most popular being business administration, psychology and biology and least popular being social/political systems. The school has a general core requirement. Cooperative education is not offered. All first-year students must maintain a 2.0 GPA or higher to avoid academic probation, and a minimum overall GPA of 2.0 is required to graduate. Other special academic programs that would appeal to a B student: self-designed majors · pass/fail grading option · independent study · double majors · internships.

B Student Support and Success

Freshmen at Pine Manor are required to take a First Year Experience Seminar that is led by faculty members, student life professionals and peer mentors. During their second year, they take a Portfolio Learning Seminar. Its purpose is to "encourage students to become reflective, self-directed learners, as well as to help them understand and fulfill degree requirements through development of a personalized learning portfolio." Presentation of this portfolio is one of the requirements for graduation.

Many students use the Brown Learning Resource Center, staffed by professional, full-time tutors. Assistance is offered in writing, math, reading, study skills and time management. According to the college, students who use the Resource Center are

PINE MANOR COLLEGE

Pine Manor College
Chestnut Hill, MA
Location: Major city
Website: http://www.pmc.edu

Students
Total enrollment: 501
Undergrads: 408
Freshmen: 172
Part-time students: 1%
From out-of-state: 34%
Male/Female: 0%/100%
Live on-campus: 77%
Off-campus employment rating: Excellent
Caucasian: 18%
African American: 47%
Hispanic: 14%
Asian or Pacific Islander: 5%
Native American: 1%
International: 6%

Academics
Student/faculty ratio: 10:1
Class size 9 or fewer: 31%
Class size 10-29: 69%
Class size 30-49: 12%
Class size 50-99: 5%
Class size 100 or more: -
Returning freshmen: 65%
Six-year graduation rate: 39%

Most Popular Fields of Study
Business, Finance, Sales and Marketing
Biological and Life Sciences
Psychology
English and Literature
Communications, Journalism, Advertising
    and Comm. Technologies
Education
Social Sciences, History, Economics,
    Political Science
Visual and Performing Arts

America's
Best Colleges for
B Students

"able to discover previously untapped strengths, adjust to new demands of the college environment, fill gaps in prior learning and most of all, learn how to take charge of their own learning."

Other advice from the college includes these statements: "Students can tell us about themselves and their accomplishments and their goals in their personal essay. Recommendation letters and personal interviews also give us great insights to the young women we counsel. There are many talented and deserving young women with B and C level grades that would grow and be successful at Pine Manor.

"Young women who attend PMC develop self confidence and leadership skills. You can really see these women transform themselves over the years."

Pine Manor College provides a variety of support programs including dedicated guidance for: academic · career · personal · psychological · minority students · family planning · religious. Recognizing that some students may need extra preparation, Pine Manor College offers remedial and refresher courses in: reading · writing · math · study skills. The average freshman year GPA is 2.7, and 65 percent of freshmen students return for their sophomore year. What do students do after college? While many enter the work force, approximately 5 percent pursue a graduate degree immediately after graduation, and another 20 percent enter graduate school within two years. Among students who enter the work force, approximately 20 percent enter a field related to their major within six months of graduation, while a further 40 percent enter a related career within two years of graduation. Companies that most frequently hire graduates from Pine Manor College include: Fidelity · Smith Barney · Bank of America · Sovereign Bank · Commonwealth of Massachusetts · Boston Financial · Jasmine Sola · Century Bank · the Second Step · Crayon College · Salem Hospital · Youth Build · Harbor Side Healthcare · Harvard Vanguard · Massachusetts Housing Partnership.

Support for Students with Learning Disabilities

Students with learning disabilities may take advantage of specific support programs. If necessary, the college will grant additional time to students with learning disabilities to complete their degree. Also, a lightened course load may be granted to LD students. Credit is given for remedial courses taken. According to the school, the Brown Learning Resource Center is open to all students and offers individual tutoring in writing, mathematics, reading, study skills and time management. Students with learning disabilities will find the following programs extremely useful: tutors · learning center · testing accommodations · untimed tests · extended time for tests · take-home exam · oral tests · readers · note-taking services · priority registration. Individual or small group tutorials are also available in: time management · organizational skills · learning strategies · writing labs · math labs · study skills. An advisor/advocate from the Brown Learning Resource Center/Mary Walsh is available. This member also sits on the admissions committee.

How to Get Admitted

For admissions decisions, non-academic factors considered: interview · extracurricular activities · special talents, interests, abilities · character/personal qualities · volunteer work · work experience · state of residency. A high school diploma is required, although a GED is also accepted for admissions consideration. SAT or ACT test scores are required of all applicants. SAT Subject Test scores are recommended but not required. *Academic units recommended:* 4 English, 3 Math, 3 Science, 2 Social Studies, 2 Foreign Language.

How to Pay for College

To apply for financial aid, students should submit the following: Free Application for Federal Student Aid (FAFSA). Pine Manor College participates in the Federal Work Study program. *Need-based aid programs include:* scholarships and grants · general need-based awards · Federal Pell grants · state scholarships and grants · college-based scholarships and grants · private scholarships and grants. *Non-Need-based aid programs include:* scholarships and grants · state scholarships and grants.

PINE MANOR COLLEGE

Highlights

Admissions
Applicants: 589
Accepted: 416
Acceptance rate: 70.6%
Average GPA: 2.5
ACT range: 16-18
SAT Math range: 350-460
SAT Reading range: 370-480
SAT Writing range: Not reported
Top 10% of class: 7%
Top 25% of class: 18%
Top 50% of class: 36%

Deadlines
Early Action: No
Early Decision: No
Regular Action: March 1 (priority)
Common Application: Accepted

Financial Aid
In-state tuition: $18,957
Out-of-state tuition: $18,957
Room: -
Board: -
Books: $800
Freshmen receiving need-based aid: 85%
Undergrads receiving need-based aid: 94%
Avg. % of need met by financial aid: 77%
Avg. aid package (freshmen): $17,425
Avg. aid package (undergrads): $15,768
Freshmen receiving merit-based aid: 2%
Undergrads receiving merit-based aid: 3%
Avg. student debt upon graduation: $18,000

School Spirit
Mascot: Gators
Colors: Green and white

PRESCOTT COLLEGE

220 Grove Avenue, Prescott, AZ 86301
Admissions: 800-628-6364 · Financial Aid: 877-350-2100, extension 1111
Email: admissions@prescott.edu · Website: http://www.prescott.edu

From the College

"Prescott College subscribes to the philosophy of experiential education or "learning by doing." We believe that doing is as important as reading and discussing. In cooperation with faculty, Prescott College students are able to work in such interdisciplinary fields as human development, ecopsychology, abstract art, environmental education and interpretation, teacher education, human ecology, agroecology, creative writing, outdoor adventure education, management, counseling and wilderness leadership. Our faculty recognize that some of the most important lessons are learned in situations that require action. Many courses have strong field components and some are conducted entirely in the field. Internships, apprenticeships, independent studies, community service and study abroad are encouraged so that students may study and live in cultural contexts outside their normal experience.

"Students are taught by full-time faculty members, not graduate assistants. Faculty members are role models and mentors and often become life-long friends and colleagues. Prescott College has a mission to educate students of diverse ages and backgrounds to understand, thrive in and enhance our world community and environment. Students are encouraged to think critically and act ethically with sensitivity to both the human community and the biosphere.

"Prescott College has a block and quarter academic calendar. Blocks are approximately four weeks in length and take place during September, January and May. A 10-week quarter follows each block. During the block, students enroll in only one course and learn through deep involvement in the subject. Many block courses are conducted partially or entirely in the field and can take students to the Grand Canyon, the Sea of Cortez, Eastern Europe, Latin America and throughout the Southwest and the world.

"We encourage students to tailor their curriculum to suit their needs and to include off-campus internships, work study, faculty-student research projects, group and independent study, community service, and study abroad. Prescott and the college are surrounded by 1,408,000 acres of National Forest, with more than 796 miles of trails. Prescott offers a diversity of outdoor activities, including rock climbing, hiking, mountain biking and nearby canoeing, rafting, kayaking and snow skiing. The old mining town of Jerome, the red rocks of Sedona, shopping in Phoenix and the Grand Canyon are all within a day's trip."

Campus Setting

Prescott College is a private college founded in 1966. The campus is located on four-acres in Prescott, approximately 100 miles north of Phoenix. Prescott College is an independent, liberal arts college offering bachelor's, master's and doctoral degrees, as well as teacher certification. A four-year institution, Prescott College has an enrollment of 1,065 students. In addition to a small library, the campus facilities include: performing arts center · visual arts building · farm · GIS laboratory. Prescott College provides on-campus housing with three units that can accommodate 27 students. Housing options: co-ed dorms.

Student Life and Activities

Most students (96 percent) live off campus, which does impact the on-campus social scene. Nevertheless, like any college, students find time to create their own recreational outlets. According to a school official, "College-sponsored activities, student groups and individuals throughout the college provide opportunities to meet and enjoy yourself outside of classes. Music and dance performances, photography exhibits, slide shows, poetry and fiction reading, yoga, lectures, panel discussions, plays and talent shows bring students together. Students frequently go hiking, camping, rock climbing, canoeing, mountain biking and, horseback riding." Popular on- and off-campus gathering spots include the Crossroads Cafe, Raven Cafe, Prescott Coffee Roasters, and Coyote Joe's Bar and Grill. Popular campus events include the Ripple Showcase, Vagina Monologues and the Drag Show. Prescott College has 17 official student organizations. Popular groups on campus include the Student Advisory Council, Aztlan Center, HUB (Helping Understand Bikes), WEB (Women's Empowerment Breakthrough), and Ripple Project.

Academics and Learning Environment

For the B student, the learning environment of a college is just as important as the quality of its academic program. Prescott College has 68 full-time and 43 part-time faculty members, offering a student-to-faculty ratio of 11:1. The most common course size is 10 to 19 students. Prescott College offers 21 majors with the most popular being education, counseling psychology and environmental studies and least popular being arts and letters, adventure education and cultural and regional studies. The school has a general core requirement. Cooperative education is available. Other special academic programs that would appeal to a B student: self-designed majors · pass/fail grading option · independent study · double majors · internships · certificate programs.

B Student Support and Success

According to the college, "Prescott is an ideal environment for both A and B students. Our programs are academically rigorous and experientially based. We are able to accommodate a variety of learning styles. Qualified applicants demonstrate solid, consistent academic performance, well-written college essays and a high level of personal motivation. We use holistic evaluation that looks at our applicant's overall prospects for success in the college."
Prescott College provides a variety of support programs including dedicated guidance for: academic · career · personal · psychological. Recognizing that some students may need extra preparation, Prescott College offers remedial and refresher courses in: reading · writing · math · study skills. Annually, 75 percent of freshmen students return for their sophomore year.

Support for Students with Learning Disabilities

Students with learning disabilities may take advantage of specific support programs offered by Prescott College. If necessary, the college will grant additional time to students with learning disabilities to complete their degree. Students with learning disabilities will find the following programs at Prescott College extremely useful: tutors · testing accommodations · untimed tests · extended time for tests · take-home exam · readers · note-taking services · tape recorders · texts on tape · early syllabus · priority registration · waiver of math degree requirement. Individual or small group tutorials are

PRESCOTT COLLEGE

Prescott College
Prescott, AZ (Pop. 43,217)
Location: Large town
Website: http://www.prescott.edu

Students
Total enrollment: 1,065
Undergrads: 286
Freshmen: 166
Part-time students: 11%
From out-of-state: 62%
Male/Female: 40%/60%
Live on-campus: 4%
Off-campus employment rating: Fair
Caucasian: 85%
African American: 2%
Hispanic: 7%
Asian or Pacific Islander: 1%
Native American: 1%
International: 1%

Academics
Student/faculty ratio: 11:1
Class size 9 or fewer: 37%
Class size 10-29: 63%
Class size 30-49: 23%
Class size 50-99: 3%
Class size 100 or more: -
Returning freshmen: 75%
Six-year graduation rate: 40%

Most Popular Fields of Study
Biological and Life Sciences
Protective Services, Criminal Justice and
    Public Administration
Psychology
Visual and Performing Arts
English and Literature
Philosophy, Religion and Theology
Physical Sciences, Chemistry, Physics
    and Astronomy
Parks, Recreation and Fitness
Interdisciplinary Studies
Health Professions, Medicine and Related Sciences

355

PRESCOTT COLLEGE

Admissions

Applicants: 365
Accepted: 280
Acceptance rate: 76.7%
Average GPA: Not reported
ACT range: 20-26
SAT Math range: 430-600
SAT Reading range: 460-660
SAT Writing range: 470-610

Deadlines

Early Action: No
Early Decision: December 1
Regular Action: Rolling admissions
Common Application: Accepted

Financial Aid

In-state tuition: $23,232
Out-of-state tuition: $23,232
Room: $3,630
Board: -
Books: $624
Freshmen receiving need-based aid: 58%
Undergrads receiving need-based aid:
   75%
Avg. % of need met by financial aid: 45%
Avg. aid package (freshmen): $12,786
Avg. aid package (undergrads): $10,721
Freshmen receiving merit-based aid: 39%
Undergrads receiving merit-based aid:
   21%
Avg. student debt upon graduation:
   $19,150

Prominent Alumni

Cody Lundin, author, survivalist, instructor, consultant; Craig Childs, author, adventurer, naturalist, desert ecologist.

also available in: time management · organizational skills · learning strategies · specific subject areas · writing labs · math labs · study skills. An advisor/advocate from the LD Program/Student Services is available to students.

How to Get Admitted

For admissions decisions, non-academic factors considered: interview · extracurricular activities · special talents, interests, abilities · character/personal qualities · volunteer work · work experience · state of residency. A high school diploma is required, although a GED is also accepted for admissions consideration. SAT or ACT test scores are required of all applicants. *Academic units recommended:* 4 English, 3 Math, 2 Science, 3 Social Studies, 1 Foreign Language.

Insight

"We welcome students from a variety of backgrounds," says Natalie Canfield, admissions counselor. "We look at each person as a whole, not just numbers and essays. We look at bad grades and try to see how we can fix them." At Prescott, the essay is particularly evaluative for both writing level and content. The school requires two kinds of essays: one that is autobiographical ("To get to know the student") and one that is an academic autobiography ("To learn the student's writing style"). "Interviews are optional," continues Canfield. "They are relaxed and we talk about past education and different situations. We also give students a chance to ask us questions to see if we are a fit."

Prescott College focuses on degrees having to do with the environment. According to Canfield, it has more 15-passenger vans for field trips than it does buildings on campus. "Many courses are field based and most courses involve weekend-long trips," she explains."

How to Pay for College

To apply for financial aid, students should submit the following: Free Application for Federal Student Aid (FAFSA). Prescott College participates in the Federal Work Study program. *Need-based aid programs include:* scholarships and grants · general need-based awards · Federal Pell grants · state scholarships and grants · college-based scholarships and grants · private scholarships and grants. *Non-Need-based aid programs include:* scholarships and grants · general need-based awards · state scholarships and grants.

PRINCIPIA COLLEGE

1 Maybeck Place, Elsah, IL 62028
Admissions: 800-277-4648, extension 2802
Financial Aid: 800-277-4648
Email: collegeadmissions@prin.edu
Website: http://www.prin.edu

From the College

"Principia College is a unique college in that it is the only college in the world whose educational mission is to educate students who are Christian Scientists. Its purpose is to "serve the Cause of Christian Science," as stated by its founder Mary Kimball Morgan. The mission of the college is to provide students who are Christian Scientists with a comprehensive, co-educational academic program of liberal arts and sciences, leading to a Bachelor of Arts or a Bachelor of Science degree. The college is also committed to academic excellence and development of the spiritual, intellectual, moral, social and physical development of each student. In this context, Principia offers its students an international perspective and challenges them to be ethically strong in service to the world community. The college campus contains and is surrounded by vast and diverse natural habitat, including forests, prairies and the Mississippi River. Situated on limestone bluffs 200 feet above the river, Principia has developed in its 75 years on the 2,600-acre site a harmonious blend of landscaped ground anchoring a variety of English Tudor buildings."

Campus Setting

Principia, founded in 1912, is a private, liberal arts college. Its campus is located in Elsah, 40 miles north of St. Louis. A four-year institution, Principia College has an enrollment of 509 students. The school is also affiliated with the Christian Science Church. In addition to a large, well-stocked library, the campus facilities include: Carillon Chapel · School of Nations Museum · science center · planetarium. Principia College provides on-campus housing with 14 units that can accommodate 560 students. Housing options: women's dorms · men's dorms · married-student apartments. Recreation and sports facilities include: baseball · football · soccer and softball field · basketball · tennis and volleyball courts · field house · golf course · swimming pools · outdoor track.

Student Life and Activities

Principia College has 28 official student organizations. The most popular are: Chorus · band · instrumental groups · drama group · concert and lecture series · amateur radio and camera clubs · fire crew · departmental · service and special-interest groups. For those interested in sports, there are intramural teams such as: basketball · soccer · softball · ultimate Frisbee · volleyball. Principia College is a member of the St. Louis Intercollegiate Athletic Conference (Division III) ; Upper Midwest Athletic Conference (NAIA).

PRINCIPIA COLLEGE

Financial Aid
In-state tuition: $22,650
Out-of-state tuition: $22,650
Room: $4,125
Board: $4,350
Books: $900
Avg. % of need met by financial aid: Not reported
Avg. aid package (freshmen): Not reported
Avg. aid package (undergrads): Not reported
Avg. student debt upon graduation: Not reported

School Spirit
Mascot: Panther
Colors: Navy blue and gold
Song: *The Gold and Blue*

Academics and Learning Environment

For the B student, the learning environment of a college is just as important as the quality of its academic program. Principia College has 55 full-time and 11 part-time faculty members. Principia College offers 25 majors with the most popular being business administration, studio art and education and least popular being art history, chemistry and engineering science. The school has a general core requirement as well as a religion requirement. Cooperative education is not offered. All first-year students must maintain a 2.0 GPA or higher to avoid academic probation, and a minimum overall GPA of 2.0 is required to graduate. Other special academic programs that would appeal to a B student: self-designed majors · independent study · double majors · internships.

B Student Support and Success

At Principia College's Academic and Career Advising Office, experts will help you explore majors, plan internships, research graduate schools, prepare resumes and investigate career opportunities. They also give new students guidance on subjects such as setting practical goals, managing your time and balancing your college demands. New students are assigned a faculty or staff advisor to help you make informed academic choices. The Writing Center sponsors a two week Writing Seminar that offers a wide range of reading and writing experiences, and tutors are available every evening for free assistance.

Principia College provides a variety of support programs including dedicated guidance for: academic · career · personal. Additional counseling services include: resident counselors reside in each dorm, available to counsel students at their request. The average freshman year GPA is 3.2. What do students do after college? While many enter the work force, approximately 5 percent pursue a graduate degree immediately after graduation, and another 18 percent enter graduate school within two years. Among students who enter the work force, approximately 33 percent enter a field related to their major within six months of graduation. Companies that most frequently hire graduates from Principia College include: Disney · A.G. Edwards · Edward D. Jones · Thompson Marketing (New York) · Windermere Farms (California).

How to Get Admitted

For admissions decisions, non-academic factors considered: interview · extracurricular activities · special talents, interests, abilities · character/personal qualities · volunteer work · work experience · state of residency · religious affiliation/commitment · minority affiliation · alumni relationship. A high school diploma is required, although a GED is also accepted for admissions consideration. SAT or ACT test scores are required of all applicants. SAT Subject Test scores are considered, if submitted, but are not required. *According to the admissions office:* Applicants must be Christian Scientists. Minimum combined SAT score of 920 (composite ACT score of 19) and minimum 2.0 GPA required. *Academic units recommended:* 4 English, 4 Math, 3 Science, 2 Social Studies, 3 Foreign Language.

How to Pay for College

To apply for financial aid, students should submit the following: · institution's own financial aid forms · CSS/Financial Aid PROFILE. Principia College does not participate in the Federal Work Study program. *Need-based aid programs include:* scholarships and grants · college-based scholarships and grants · private scholarships and grants. *Non-Need-based aid programs include:* scholarships and grants · state scholarships and grants.

PURDUE UNIVERSITY - WEST LAFAYETTE

475 Stadium Mall Drive, West Lafayette, IN 47907-2050
Admissions: 765-494-1776 · Financial Aid: 765-494-0998
Email: admissions@purdue.edu · Website: http://www.purdue.edu

From the College

"Founded in 1869, Purdue is Indiana's land-grant university. It has more than 200 areas of undergraduate study and renowned research initiatives. Purdue's programs in a wide variety of undergraduate and graduate disciplines consistently rank among the best in the country. Twenty-two of America's astronauts hold Purdue degrees. Students from all 50 states and more than 130 countries attend the main campus in West Lafayette. Although a large university, Purdue maintains an atmosphere that highly values individual needs and achievements."

Campus Setting

Purdue University - West Lafayette is a public, comprehensive institution. Founded in 1869, it adopted co-education in 1874. Its 2,468-acre campus is located in West Lafayette, 65 miles northwest of Indianapolis. A four-year institution, Purdue University - West Lafayette has an archives and special collections unit of the Purdue University Libraries. Purdue University - West Lafayette provides on-campus housing with 15 units that can accommodate 10,600 students. Housing options: co-ed dorms · women's dorms · men's dorms · sorority housing · fraternity housing · single-student apartments · married-student apartments · special housing for disabled students · cooperative housing.

Student Life and Activities

Most students (67 percent) live off campus, which does impact the on-campus social scene. Nevertheless, like any college, students find time to create their own recreational outlets. Popular events include: Activities Carnival, International Awareness Week, PMO Christmas Show, Senior Send-Off, Spring Fest/Bug Bowl, Step Shows, Athletic Events, Boiler Gold Rush, Concerts, Film Series, Grand Prix Race, Greek Week, Homecoming and Industrial Roundtable. Purdue University - West Lafayette has 815 official student organizations. The most popular are: Anime club · solar racing club · Student Orientation Committee · ballroom dance club · Beat Society · Camera club · College Mentors for Kids · Go Club · Old Masters · Queer Student Union · Reamer Club. For those interested in sports, there are intramural teams such as: badminton · basketball · football · golf · racquetball · soccer · softball · swimming and diving · tennis · track and field · ultimate Frisbee · volleyball. Purdue University - West Lafayette is a member of the Big Ten Conference (Division I, Football I-A).

Academics and Learning Environment

For the B student, the learning environment of a college is just as important as the quality of its academic program. Purdue University has 2,110 full-time and 317 part-time faculty members, offering a student-to-faculty ratio of 14:1. The most common course size is 20 to 29 students. Purdue University offers 348 majors with the most popular being general management, mechanical engineering and electrical/computer engineering. The school has a general core requirement. Cooperative education is not offered. All first-year students must maintain a 1.5 GPA or higher to avoid academic probation, and a minimum overall GPA of 2.0 is required to graduate. Other special academic programs that would appeal to a B student: pass/fail grading option · independent study · double majors · accelerated study · honors program · Phi Beta Kappa · internships · weekend college · distance learning.

B Student Support and Success

In order to "get the hang of college life quickly," Purdue offers a system called a "learning community". It consists of either a group of 20 to 30 first-year students who take two or three of the same courses together, a group of first-year students who share a common academic interest and live in the same residence hall or a group of first-year students who take part in both of these activities.

Purdue provides a variety of support programs including dedicated guidance for: academic · career · personal · psychological · minority students · military · veterans · non-traditional students · family planning. Recognizing that some students may need extra preparation, Purdue offers remedial and refresher courses in: reading · writing · math · study skills. The average freshman year GPA is 2.8, and 86 percent of freshmen students return for their sophomore year. What do students do after college? While many enter the work force, approximately 18 percent pursue a graduate degree immediately after graduation. Among students who enter the work force, approximately 74 percent enter a field related to their major within six months of graduation. Companies that most frequently hire graduates from Purdue include: Caterpillar · Eli Lilly · Boeing · Butler International · Cisco Systems · Cummins Engine · CVS Pharmacy · EDS · Exxon Mobil · Lockheed Martin · Procter and Gamble · Raytheon.

Support for Students with Learning Disabilities

Students with learning disabilities may take advantage of specific support programs offered by Purdue . Also, a lightened course load may be granted to LD students. According to the school, documentation must be provided before eligibility for classroom accommodations can be determined. Students with learning disabilities will find the following programs at Purdue extremely useful: remedial math · special classes · learning center · testing accommodations · extended time for tests · take-home exam · oral tests · exam on tape or computer · readers · typist/scribe · note-taking services · reading machines · tape recorders · texts on tape · early syllabus · diagnostic testing service · priority registration · waiver of math degree requirement. Individual or small group tutorials are also available in: time management · organizational skills · learning strategies · specific subject areas · writing labs · math labs · study skills. An advisor/advocate from the Adaptive Programs is available.

How to Get Admitted

For admissions decisions, non-academic factors considered: extracurricular activities · special talents, interests, abilities · character/personal qualities · volunteer work · work experience · geographical location · minority affiliation · alumni relationship. A high school diploma is required, although a GED is also accepted for admissions consideration. SAT or ACT test scores are required of all applicants. SAT Subject Test scores are not required. *Academic units recommended:* 4 English, 4 Math, 3 Science.

How to Pay for College

To apply for financial aid, students should submit the following: Free Application for Federal Student Aid (FAFSA). Purdue participates in

PURDUE UNIVERSITY – WEST LAFAYETTE

Highlights

Purdue University - West Lafayette
West Lafayette, IN (Pop. 28,778)
Location: Medium city
Website: http://www.purdue.edu

Students
Total enrollment: 40,090
Undergrads: 18,349
Freshmen: 7,063
Part-time students: 5%
From out-of-state: 31%
Male/Female: 58%/42%
Live on-campus: 33%
In fraternities: 9%
In sororities: 6%
Off-campus employment rating: Good
Caucasian: 80%
African American: 3%
Hispanic: 3%
Asian or Pacific Islander: 6%
Native American: 1%
International: 7%

Academics
Student/faculty ratio: 14:1
Class size 9 or fewer: 15%
Class size 10-29: 49%
Class size 30-49: 21%
Class size 50-99: 9%
Class size 100 or more: 6%
Returning freshmen: 86%
Six-year graduation rate: 72%

Most Popular Fields of Study
Business, Finance, Sales and Marketing
Agriculture, Aquaculture and Animal Sciences
Social Sciences, History, Economics, Political Science
Family and Consumer Sciences, Nutrition and Home Economics
Computer and Information Sciences
Communications, Journalism, Advertising and Comm. Technologies
Philosophy, Religion and Theology
English and Literature
Visual and Performing Arts
Health Professions, Medicine and Related Sciences

361

College Profiles

PURDUE UNIVERSITY – WEST LAFAYETTE

Admissions

Applicants: 29,952
Accepted: 21,423
Acceptance rate: 71.5%
Average GPA: 3.5
ACT range: 23-29
SAT Math range: 540-660
SAT Reading range: 490-610
SAT Writing range: 490-600
Top 10% of class: 30%
Top 25% of class: 65%
Top 50% of class: 93%

Deadlines

Early Action: No
Early Decision: No
Regular Action: March 1 (priority)
Common Application: Accepted

Financial Aid

In-state tuition: $8,060
Out-of-state tuition: $24,160
Room: -
Board: -
Books: $1,240
Freshmen receiving need-based aid: 48%
Undergrads receiving need-based aid: 43%
Avg. % of need met by financial aid: 94%
Avg. aid package (freshmen): $9,716
Avg. aid package (undergrads): $9,734
Freshmen receiving merit-based aid: 11%
Undergrads receiving merit-based aid: 7%
Avg. student debt upon graduation: $23,087

Prominent Alumni

Neil Armstrong, astronaut; Chesley "Sully" Sullenberger, heroic US Airways pilot; Robert "Bob" Griese, television commentator, retired professional football player

School Spirit

Mascot: Boilermaker Special
Colors: Old gold and black
Song: *Hail Purdue*

the Federal Work Study program. *Need-based aid programs include:* scholarships and grants · general need-based awards · Federal Pell grants · state scholarships and grants · college-based scholarships and grants · private scholarships and grants · Academic Competitiveness Grant (ACG) and National Smart Grant Program. *Non-Need-based aid programs include:* scholarships and grants · general need-based awards · state scholarships and grants · athletic scholarships · ROTC scholarships · leadership scholarships · music scholarships · drama scholarships.

QUINNIPIAC UNIVERSITY

275 Mount Carmel Avenue, Hamden, CT 06518
Admissions: 800-462-1944 · Financial Aid: 800-462-1944
Email: admissions@quinnipiac.edu · Website: http://www.quinnipiac.edu

From the College

"Quinnipiac University is committed to providing high-quality academic programs in a student-oriented environment, on a campus with a strong sense of community. The 600-acre campus (250-acre Mt. Carmel campus, plus nearby 250-acre York Hill campus plus 100-acre North Haven campus) is located minutes from New Haven, midway between New York City and Boston, and offers a variety of majors along with internship and clinical experiences in business, communications, health sciences, education, liberal arts and sciences and law to the 5,700 undergraduate and 2,000 graduate and part-time students.

"Facilities such as the fully digital high-definition production studio in the Ed McMahon Center for Communications, the sports biomechanics 'motion analysis' lab, the critical care lab for nursing and physician assistant students, and the Financial Technology Center (trading room), provide state-of-the-art training experiences.

"Quinnipiac is adjacent to the 1,700-acre Sleeping Giant State Park with trails for hiking and scenic views. Seventy-five percent of the entering class comes from out of state and 95 percent of the freshmen live on campus. Construction of new residence halls to add 2,000 beds (phased in opening beginning 2009) on the York Hill campus is underway. Housing is guaranteed to incoming freshmen for three years, housing for seniors is provided on a space available basis. Although resident freshmen may not bring a car to campus, the university maintains a campus shuttle system which brings students to nearby shopping, restaurants, museums and the New Haven train station with access to Metro North, and Amtrak."

Campus Setting

Quinnipiac, founded in 1929, is a private university offering 51 undergraduate and 17 graduate majors. Small classes, state-of-the-art facilities and opportunities for clinical experience, internships and study abroad highlight the academic life. Division I athletics, intramurals, recreation, clubs, organizations, leadership development, community involvement and student government provides a student focus and sense of community.

There is a large, well-stocked library. Quinnipiac University provides on-campus housing with 60 units that can accommodate 4,000 students. Housing options: co-ed dorms · single-student apartments. Recreation and sports facilities include: artificial turf field · baseball · field hockey · soccer and softball fields · basketball arena · tennis courts · ice hockey arena · indoor track · recreation center.

Student Life and Activities

With 75 percent of students living on campus, there are plenty of social activities. As reported by a school official, "Quinnipiac students have access to both on campus and near campus social and cultural activities throughout the year. A student life 'activity fair' starts the fall semester where each club and organization displays materials to attract new members. Student government supports the undergraduate clubs with budget assistance as well as supporting programming board's overall campus activity budget. Major weekend events are hosted several times during the year, as well as speakers, 'alternative spring break' trips and community service. Many groups fundraise for national and local charities through activities and awareness.' Popular on campus gathering spots include the recreation center and library. Popular off-campus

QUINNIPIAC UNIVERSITY

Highlights

Quinnipiac University
Hamden, CT (Pop. 59,000)
Location: Large town
Website: http://www.quinnipiac.edu

Students
Total enrollment: 7,413
Undergrads: 2,263
Freshmen: 1,484
Part-time students: 5%
From out-of-state: 79%
Male/Female: 39%/61%
Live on-campus: 75%
In fraternities: 3%
In sororities: 4%
Off-campus employment rating: Excellent
Caucasian: 80%
African American: 3%
Hispanic: 5%
Asian or Pacific Islander: 2%
Native American: 0%
International: 1%

Academics
Student/faculty ratio: 13:1
Class size 9 or fewer: 8%
Class size 10-29: 75%
Class size 30-49: 17%
Class size 50-99: 9%
Class size 100 or more: 6%
Returning freshmen: 90%
Six-year graduation rate: 75%

Most Popular Fields of Study
Business, Finance, Sales and Marketing
Psychology
English and Literature
Computer and Information Sciences
Mathematics
Law and Legal Studies
Health Professions, Medicine and Related Sciences
Liberal Arts, Humanities and General Studies
Communications, Journalism, Advertising and Comm. Technologies
Social Sciences, History, Economics, Political Science

364

gathering spots include Sleeping Giant State Park and various locations in Hamden and New Haven. Popular campus events include the December Holiday Party, Parents and Family Weekend, Little Siblings Weekend and Midnight Madness and spring concert weekend. Quinnipiac University has 72 official student organizations. Popular groups on campus include the Programming Board, Student Government, resident assistants and intramural athletics. For those interested in sports, there are intramural teams such as: basketball · beach volleyball · bowling · flag football · indoor soccer · kickball · softball · tennis · ultimate Frisbee · volleyball. Quinnipiac University is a member of the NCAA, Northeast Conference (Division I), ECAC Hockey.

Academics and Learning Environment

For the B student, the learning environment of a college is just as important as the quality of its academic program. Quinnipiac University has 304 full-time and 541 part-time faculty members, offering a student-to-faculty ratio of 13:1. The most common course size is 10 to 19 students. Quinnipiac University offers 57 majors with the most popular being management, psychology and mass communications and least popular being microbiology/biotechnology and mathematics. The school has a general core requirement. Cooperative education is not offered. All first-year students must maintain a 1.5 GPA or higher to avoid academic probation, and a minimum overall GPA of 2.0 is required to graduate. Other special academic programs that would appeal to a B student: self-designed majors · double majors · dual degrees · honors program · internships · distance learning.

B Student Support and Success

Quinnipiac students have three special courses open to them to help introduce them to major topics in university life: QU 101, 201 and 301.

The first course is QU 101, entitled "The Individual in the Community." It explores the relationship between individual and community identities, the rights and responsibilities of citizenship, ethics of community life and so on. In QU 201, "National Community," students explore the structure of the pluralistic American community, and in QU 301, "Global Community," students find out about the political, social, cultural, ecological and economic systems that shape global communities.

The college also offers a program called Writing across the Curriculum where students are engaged in hands-on learning experiences to become better writers, strong critical thinkers and innovative scholars.

Quinnipiac University provides a variety of support programs including dedicated guidance for: academic · career · personal · psychological · veterans · non-traditional students · religious. The average freshman year GPA is 2.9, and 90 percent of freshmen students return for their sophomore year. What do students do after college? While many enter the work force, approximately 32 percent pursue a graduate degree immediately after graduation, and another 6 percent enter graduate school within two years. Among students who enter the work force, approximately 82 percent enter a field related to their major within six months of graduation.

Companies that most frequently hire graduates from Quinnipiac University include: ABC stations and affiliates · Americorps · Bristol-Myers Squibb Medical Imaging · CBS · CNN · elementary and high schools in several states · ESPN · Deloitte and Touche · MTV · NBC · the Travelers.

Support for Students with Learning Disabilities

Students with learning disabilities may take advantage of specific support programs offered by Quinnipiac University. According to the school, students are encouraged to self-advocate for services needed and can self-disclose at any point following their admissions decision. Students with learning disabilities will find the following programs at Quinnipiac University extremely useful: tutors · learning center. Individual or small group tutorials are also available in: time management · organizational skills · learning strategies · specific subject areas · writing labs · math labs · study skills.

How to Get Admitted

For admissions decisions, non-academic factors considered: interview · extracurricular activities · character/personal qualities · volunteer work · work experience · state of residency · minority affiliation · alumni relationship. A high school diploma is required, although a GED is also accepted for admissions consideration. SAT or ACT test scores are required of all applicants. *According to the admissions office:* Minimum combined SAT Reasoning score of 1050, rank in top two-fifths of secondary school class, and minimum 3.0 GPA recommended. Minimum academic requirements may be higher for some majors. *Academic units recommended:* 4 English, 3 Math, 3 Science, 3 Social Studies, 2 Foreign Language.

How to Pay for College

To apply for financial aid, students should submit the following: Free Application for Federal Student Aid (FAFSA). Quinnipiac University participates in the Federal Work Study program. *Need-based aid programs include:* scholarships and grants · general need-based awards · Federal Pell grants · state scholarships and grants · college-based scholarships and grants · private scholarships and grants. *Non-Need-based aid programs include:* scholarships and grants · state scholarships and grants · athletic scholarships · ROTC scholarships.

QUINNIPIAC UNIVERSITY

Highlights

Admissions
Applicants: 14,994
Accepted: 6,721
Acceptance rate: 44.8%
placed on wait list: 1,787
Average GPA: 3.5
ACT range: 24-28
SAT Math range: 560-630
SAT Reading range: 540-610
SAT Writing range: Not reported
Top 10% of class: 25%
Top 25% of class: 66%
Top 50% of class: 100%

Deadlines
Early Action: No
Early Decision: No
Regular Action: Rolling admissions
Common Application: Accepted

Financial Aid
In-state tuition: $31,100
Out-of-state tuition: $31,100
Room: $10,380
Board: $2,000
Books: $800
Freshmen receiving need-based aid: 56%
Undergrads receiving need-based aid: 57%
Avg. % of need met by financial aid: 66%
Avg. aid package (freshmen): $18,592
Avg. aid package (undergrads): $18,306
Freshmen receiving merit-based aid: 16%
Undergrads receiving merit-based aid: 13%
Avg. student debt upon graduation: $37,849

Prominent Alumni
Murray Lender, Lender's Bagels; Bill Weldon, Johnson & Johnson.

School Spirit
Mascot: Bobcats
Colors: Navy and gold

365

RADFORD UNIVERSITY

P.O. Box 6890, Radford, VA 24142
Admissions: 800-890-4265 · Financial Aid: 540-831-5408
Email: admissions@radford.edu · Website: http://www.radford.edu

From the College

"Radford University is located in the heart of the New River Valley, Virginia, and features a student body of approximately 9,200, nationally recognized faculty-student collaborations, and a curriculum of more than 140 undergraduate and graduate programs. In the last year, RU has opened a state-of-the-art visual and performing arts center and welcomed three new graduate programs: doctoral degrees in nursing practice and physical therapy and a master's in occupational therapy. Outside the classroom, RU supports a diverse student population through co-curricular activities and events, NCAA Division I athletics and a commitment to environmental sustainability."

Campus Setting

Radford is a public, four-year, comprehensive university. Founded as a teachers college for women in 1910, it adopted co-education in 1972. Programs are offered through the Colleges of Business and Economics, Education and Human Development, Health and Human Services, Humanities and Behavioral Sciences, Science and Technology, Visual and Performing Arts and Graduate and Professional Studies. Its 177-acre campus is located in Radford, 45 miles west of Roanoke. In addition to a large, well-stocked library, the campus facilities include: gallery · museum · planetarium · nursing simulation lab · speech and hearing clinic · observatory · conservatory · athletic trainer lab · recital hall · forensics institute · advanced GIS and GPS capabilities · center for visual and performing arts. Radford University provides on-campus housing with 21 units that can accommodate 3,211 students. Housing options: co-ed dorms · single-student apartments · special housing for disabled students. Recreation and sports facilities include: arena · baseball park · field hockey · gymnasium · practice field · soccer and track stadiums · softball complex · swimming pool · tennis court · weight rooms.

Student Life and Activities

Most students (63 percent) live off campus, which does impact the on-campus social scene. Nevertheless, like any college, students find time to create their own recreational outlets. A popular on-campus gathering spot is the Bonnie Hurlburt Student Center. Popular campus events include Up All Night at the Bonnie, spring concert/major visiting performer(s), Bonnie Days of Spring, Homecoming, Family Weekend, Winter and Spring Commencement, movie series and Highlander Picnic. Radford University has 220 official student organizations. Popular groups on campus include the Student Government Association and fraternities and sororities. For those interested in sports, there are intramural teams such as: aerobics · basketball · bowling · climbing wall · disc golf · dodgeball · flag football · football · racquetball · soccer · softball · table tennis · tennis · volleyball · water polo. Radford University is a member of the Big South Conference (Division I), Northern Pacific Field Hockey Conference (Division I), Northeast Conference, Coastal Collegiate Swimming Association.

Academics and Learning Environment

For the B student, the learning environment of a college is just as important as the quality of its academic program. Radford University has 400 full-time and 232 part-time faculty members, offering a student-to-faculty ratio of 18:1. The most common course size is 20 to 29 students. Radford University offers 61 majors with the most popular being interdisciplinary studies, management and criminal justice and least popular being mathematics, philosophy and religious studies and geology. The school has a general core requirement. Cooperative education is not offered. All first-year students must maintain a 2.0 GPA or higher to avoid academic probation. Other special academic programs that would appeal to a B student: self-designed majors · pass/fail grading option · independent study · double majors · dual degrees · accelerated study · honors program · internships · distance learning certificate programs.

B Student Support and Success

Radford's Learning Assistance and Resource Center "strives to help all Radford University students achieve academic success in all disciplines." Through both individual and group tutoring sessions, students can get help from tutors who are certified by the College Reading and Learning Association. Writing tutors help with any writing assignments and math and science tutors helps with everything from grasping abstract concepts to reinforcing problem solving skills. Workshops and one-on-one consultations offer guidance in learning skills, reading comprehension and test taking strategies. Students with special needs, with language assistance, physical disabilities or learning challenges can get additional help.

Radford University provides a variety of support programs including dedicated guidance for: academic · career · personal · psychological · minority students · military · veterans · non-traditional students · family planning. Additional counseling services include: learning skills workshop. Recognizing that some students may need extra preparation, Radford University offers remedial and refresher courses in: reading · writing · math · study skills. Other remedial services include sciences and statistics, ESL. The average freshman year GPA is 2.7, and 78 percent of freshmen students return for their sophomore year. What do students do after college? While many enter the work force, approximately 10 percent pursue a graduate degree immediately after graduation, and another 27 percent enter graduate school within two years. Among students who enter the work force, approximately 55 percent enter a field related to their major within six months of graduation, while a further 25 percent enter a related career within two years of graduation. Companies that most frequently hire graduates from Radford University include: Blue Ridge Behavioral Health Care · Carilion Health Systems · Crate and Barrel · DMG Securities · Echo Star/Dish Network · Enterprise Rent-A-Car · State Farm Insurance Companies · Kroger · Medical Facilities of America · Pepsi Bottling Co. · SAIC · Sherwin Williams · Target Corp.· U.S. Army · U.S. Internal Revenue Service · Virginia Department of Transportation · Walgreens · Wells Fargo Financial.

Support for Students with Learning Disabilities

Students with learning disabilities may take advantage of specific support programs offered by Radford University. If necessary, the college will grant additional time to students with learning disabilities to complete their degree. Students with learning disabilities will find the following programs at Radford University extremely useful: tutors · learning center · testing accommodations · extended

RADFORD UNIVERSITY

Highlights

Radford University
Radford, VA (Pop. 15,859)
Location: Medium town
Website: http://www.radford.edu

Students
Total enrollment: 9,157
Undergrads: 3,503
Freshmen: 1,875
Part-time students: 5%
From out-of-state: 8%
Male/Female: 43%/57%
Live on-campus: 37%
In fraternities: 13%
In sororities: 14%
Off-campus employment rating: Good
Caucasian: 86%
African American: 6%
Hispanic: 3%
Asian or Pacific Islander: 2%
Native American: 0%
International: 1%

Academics
Student/faculty ratio: 18:1
Class size 9 or fewer: 9%
Class size 10-29: 59%
Class size 30-49: 27%
Class size 50-99: 3%
Class size 100 or more: 1%
Returning freshmen: 78%
Six-year graduation rate: 60%

Most Popular Fields of Study
Business, Finance, Sales and Marketing
Protective Services, Criminal Justice and
　　Public Administration
Visual and Performing Arts
Family and Consumer Sciences, Nutrition
　　and Home Economics
Computer and Information Sciences
Communications, Journalism, Advertising
　　and Comm. Technologies
Philosophy, Religion and Theology
English and Literature
Parks, Recreation and Fitness
Health Professions, Medicine and Related Sciences

RADFORD UNIVERSITY

Highlights

Admissions
Applicants: 7,819
Accepted: 5,768
Acceptance rate: 73.8%
placed on wait list: 199
Average GPA: 3.1
ACT range: 19-23
SAT Math range: 460-550
SAT Reading range: 460-550
SAT Writing range: Not reported
Top 10% of class: 6%
Top 25% of class: 25%
Top 50% of class: 71%

Deadlines
Early Action: December 15
Early Decision: No
Regular Action: February 1 (final)
Common Application: Accepted

Financial Aid
Room: -
Board: -
Books: $877
Freshmen receiving need-based aid: 33%
Undergrads receiving need-based aid: 37%
Avg. % of need met by financial aid: 79%
Avg. aid package (freshmen): $9,614
Avg. aid package (undergrads): $8,686
Freshmen receiving merit-based aid: 4%
Undergrads receiving merit-based aid: 4%
Avg. student debt upon graduation: $19,465

Prominent Alumni
Mr. R.J. Kirk, managing director and CEO, Third Securities; Charlene Curtis, ACC, coordinator of women's basketball officials; Jayma Mays, actress.

School Spirit
Mascot: Highlanders
Colors: Red, blue, green and white

time for tests · take-home exam · oral tests · readers · typist/scribe · note-taking services · reading machines · tape recorders · texts on tape · early syllabus · priority registration · waiver of math degree requirement. Individual or small group tutorials are also available in: time management · organizational skills · learning strategies · specific subject areas · writing labs · math labs · study skills. An advisor/advocate from the Disability Resource Office is available to students.

How to Get Admitted

For admissions decisions, non-academic factors considered: extracurricular activities · special talents, interests, abilities · character/personal qualities · volunteer work · work experience · geographical location · minority affiliation · alumni relationship. A high school diploma is required, although a GED is also accepted for admissions consideration. SAT or ACT test scores are required of all applicants. SAT Subject Test scores are not required. *Academic units recommended:* 4 English, 4 Math, 4 Science, 2 Social Studies, 3 Foreign Language.

How to Pay for College

To apply for financial aid, students should submit the following: Free Application for Federal Student Aid (FAFSA). Radford University participates in the Federal Work Study program. *Need-based aid programs include:* scholarships and grants · general need-based awards · Federal Pell grants · state scholarships and grants · college-based scholarships and grants · private scholarships and grants. *Non-Need-based aid programs include:* scholarships and grants · general need-based awards · state scholarships and grants · creative arts and performance awards · special achievements and activities awards · athletic scholarships · ROTC scholarships · alumni affiliation scholarships · leadership scholarships.

America's
Best Colleges for
B Students

RANDOLPH-MACON COLLEGE

P.O. Box 5005, Ashland, VA 23005-5505
Admissions: 800-888-1762 · Financial Aid: 804-752-7259
Email: admissions@rmc.edu · Website: http://www.rmc.edu

From the College

"Randolph-Macon College is located in Ashland just north of Richmond and is a co-educational, liberal arts and sciences college with a mission of developing the minds and character of its students. The college achieves this mission through a combination of personal interaction and academic rigor. Enrollment is kept near 1,200 to maintain an intimate atmosphere. Randolph-Macon College has a national reputation for its internships, study abroad and undergraduate research and offers a wealth of social and athletic programs. Founded in 1830, Randolph-Macon College is the oldest United Methodist Church- affiliated college in the nation, a Phi Beta Kappa college and ranked as a Baccalaureate I college by the Carnegie Foundation."

Campus Setting

Randolph-Macon, founded in 1830, has a 110-acre campus that includes three buildings on the National Register of Historic Buildings and one designated a National Historic Landmark. A four-year, private institution, Randolph-Macon College has an enrollment of 1,201 students. Randolph-Macon College has been co-ed since 1971. The school is also affiliated with the United Methodist Church. In addition to a large, well-stocked library, the campus facilities include: art gallery · observatory · greenhouse · historic buildings. Randolph-Macon College provides on-campus housing with 43 units that can accommodate 901 students. Housing options: co-ed dorms · women's dorms · men's dorms · sorority housing · fraternity housing · single-student apartments · special housing for disabled students · special housing for International students. Recreation and sports facilities include a recreational center.

Student Life and Activities

With 84 percent of students living on campus, there are plenty of social activities. Popular on-campus gathering spots include the Brown Campus Center and Brock Recreational Center. Popular campus events include the Dance Marathon, Springfest, Hampden-Sydney Week and Homecoming. Randolph-Macon College has 104 official student organizations. The most popular are: Chamber singers · concert choir · drama guild · jazz vocal · dance team · pep band · Anime Club · photography club (Vanishing Point) · Campus Activities Board · Student Education Association · Sociology and Anthropology Club · Amnesty International · Habitat for Humanity · Volunteers in Actions · philosophy club · Washington Literary Society · Society for Collegiate Journalists. For those interested in sports, there are intramural teams such as: basketball · flag football · racquetball · running · soccer · softball · ultimate Frisbee · volleyball. Randolph-Macon College is a member of the Old Dominion Athletic Conference (Division III).

Academics and Learning Environment

For the B student, the learning environment of a college is just as important as the quality of its academic program. Randolph-Macon College has 93 full-time and 52 part-time faculty members, offering a student-to-faculty ratio of 11:1. The most common course size is 10 to 19 students. Randolph-Macon College offers 29 majors with the most popular being economics/business, psychology and sociology and least popular being classical studies. The school has a general core requirement as well as a religion requirement. Cooperative education is not offered. All first-year students

RANDOLPH-MACON COLLEGE

Randolph-Macon College
Ashland, VA (Pop. 6,000)
Location: Small town
Website: http://www.rmc.edu

Students
Total enrollment: 1,201
Undergrads: 562
Freshmen: 362
Part-time students: 2%
From out-of-state: 37%
Male/Female: 47%/53%
Live on-campus: 84%
In fraternities: 34%
In sororities: 35%
Off-campus employment rating: Good
Caucasian: 81%
African American: 11%
Hispanic: 3%
Asian or Pacific Islander: 2%
Native American: 1%
International: 2%

Academics
Student/faculty ratio: 11:1
Class size 9 or fewer: 21%
Class size 10-29: 78%
Class size 30-49: 10%
Class size 50-99: -
Class size 100 or more: 1%
Returning freshmen: 77%
Six-year graduation rate: 65%

Most Popular Fields of Study
Business, Finance, Sales and Marketing
Biological and Life Sciences
Area, Ethnic and Gender Studies

must maintain a 2.0 GPA or higher to avoid academic probation, and a minimum overall GPA of 2.0 is required to graduate. Other special academic programs that would appeal to a B student: independent study · double majors · dual degrees · accelerated study · honors program · Phi Beta Kappa · internships.

B Student Support and Success

Randolph College offers a number of academic services to students. First-year students are assigned faculty advisors to help guide them in making course selections and career decisions. A Career Development Center focuses on helping students to "develop self knowledge related to their career choice and work performance by identifying, assessing, and understanding competencies, interests, values and personal characteristics."

The Ethyl Science and Mathematics Center provides tutoring to science and math students. The Learning Resources Center has interactive workshops, a Learning Strategies Program to help develop study strategies and clarify academic goals, tutors for every subject and printed and computerized materials.

Randolph-Macon College provides a variety of support programs including dedicated guidance for: academic · career · personal · psychological · minority students · religious. Recognizing that some students may need extra preparation, Randolph-Macon College offers remedial and refresher courses in: reading · writing · math · study skills. The average freshman year GPA is 2.5, and 77 percent of freshmen students return for their sophomore year. What do students do after college? While many enter the work force, approximately 26 percent pursue a graduate degree immediately after graduation. Among students who enter the work force, approximately 82 percent enter a field related to their major within six months of graduation. Companies that most frequently hire graduates from Randolph-Macon College include: Altria · BB&T · Hanover and Henrico County (VA) School System · Phillip Morris · U.S. Government · Virginia State Government.

Support for Students with Learning Disabilities

Students with learning disabilities may take advantage of specific support programs offered by Randolph-Macon College. If necessary, the college will grant additional time to students with learning disabilities to complete their degree. High school foreign language waivers are accepted. Students with learning disabilities will find the following programs at Randolph-Macon College extremely useful: tutors · learning center · testing accommodations · untimed tests · extended time for tests · take-home exam · exam on tape or computer · note-taking services · reading machines · tape recorders · early syllabus. Individual or small group tutorials are also available in: time management · organizational skills · learning strategies · specific subject areas · writing labs · math labs · study skills. An advisor/advocate from the LD program is available to students. This member also sits on the admissions committee.

How to Get Admitted

For admissions decisions, non-academic factors considered: interview · extracurricular activities · special talents, interests, abilities · character/personal qualities · volunteer work · work experience · state of residency · minority affiliation · alumni relationship. A high school diploma is required, although a GED is also accepted for admissions consideration. SAT or ACT test scores are required of all applicants. SAT Subject Test scores are considered, if submitted, but are not required. *Academic units recommended:* 4 English, 4 Math, 4 Science, 2 Social Studies, 4 Foreign Language.

How to Pay for College

To apply for financial aid, students should submit the following: Free Application for Federal Student Aid (FAFSA) · state aid form. Randolph-Macon College participates in the Federal Work Study program. *Need-based aid programs include:* scholarships and grants · general need-based awards · Federal Pell grants · state scholarships and grants · college-based scholarships and grants · private scholarships and grants · ACG · SMART grants. *Non-Need-based aid programs include:* scholarships and grants · general need-based awards · state scholarships and grants · ROTC scholarships.

RANDOLPH-MACON COLLEGE

Highlights

Admissions
Applicants: 3,502
Accepted: 2,034
Acceptance rate: 58.1%
placed on wait list: 322
Average GPA: 3.3
ACT range: Not reported
SAT Math range: 490-590
SAT Reading range: 500-590
SAT Writing range: 490-580
Top 10% of class: 20%
Top 25% of class: 49%
Top 50% of class: 82%

Deadlines
Early Action: November 15
Early Decision: No
Regular Action: February 1 (priority)
March 1 (final)
Common Application: Accepted

Financial Aid
In-state tuition: $28,397
Out-of-state tuition: $28,397
Room: $4,846
Board: $3,905
Books: $1,000
Freshmen receiving need-based aid: 66%
Undergrads receiving need-based aid: 61%
Avg. % of need met by financial aid: 79%
Avg. aid package (freshmen): $22,244
Avg. aid package (undergrads): $21,022
Freshmen receiving merit-based aid: 34%
Undergrads receiving merit-based aid: 39%
Avg. student debt upon graduation: $23,564

School Spirit
Mascot: Yellow Jackets
Colors: Yellow and black

RIDER UNIVERSITY

2083 Lawrenceville Road, Lawrenceville, NJ 08648-3099
Admissions: 800-257-9026 · Financial Aid: 800-257-9026
Email: admissions@rider.edu · Website: http://www.rider.edu

From the College

"Rider attracts and graduates talented and motivated students with diverse backgrounds from across the nation and around the world and puts them at the center of our learning and living community. As a learner-centered university dedicated to the education of the whole student, Rider provides students the intellectual resources and breadth of student life opportunities of a comprehensive university with the personal attention and close student-faculty interactions of a liberal arts college. Through a commitment to high quality teaching, scholarship and experiential opportunities, faculty on both campuses provide undergraduate and graduate students programs of study to expand their intellectual, cultural and personal horizons and develop their leadership skills. Our programs in the arts, social sciences, sciences, music, business and education challenge students to become active learners who can acquire, interpret, communicate and apply knowledge within and across disciplines to foster the integrative thinking required in a complex and rapidly changing world. Rider attracts faculty, staff and administrators with diverse backgrounds who create an environment which inspires intellectual and social engagement, stimulates innovation and service and encourages personal and professional development."

Campus Setting

With roots dating back to 1865, Rider is a private, co-educational university located on 280 acres on two campuses in New Jersey, one in Lawrenceville and one in Princeton, both within easy driving distance to New York City and Philadelphia. A four-year institution, Rider University has an enrollment of 6,011 students. Rider University has been co-ed since 1866. In addition to a large, well-stocked library, the campus facilities include: art gallery · Holocaust/genocide center · language and journalism labs · multimedia and finance/accounting rooms · multicultural center · flow cytometer · PCR machines · autoclaves · scintillation spectrometer · gamma counter · induction-coupled plasma emission spectro-photometer · nuclear magnetic resonance spectrometer · solomat (submersible instrument for environmental monitoring). Rider University provides on-campus housing with 1,329 units that can accommodate 2,375 students. Housing options: co-ed dorms · women's dorms · sorority housing · fraternity housing · single-student apartments · special housing for disabled students.

Student Life and Activities

With 54 percent of students living on campus, there are plenty of social activities. Rider University has 84 official student organizations. The most popular are: chorus · concert and jazz bands · dance group · debating · drama/theatre group · film society · inspirational choir · jazz ensemble · musical theatre · music ensembles · opera · symphony orchestra · departmental and special-interest groups. Rider University is a member of the Metro Atlantic Athletic Conference (Division I).

Academics and Learning Environment

For the B student, the learning environment of a college is just as important as the quality of its academic program. Rider University has 244 full-time and 347 part-time faculty members, offering a student-to-faculty ratio of 13:1. The most common course size is 10 to 19 students. Rider University offers 82 majors with the most popular being business/marketing, education and English and least popular being philosophy/religious studies, theology/religious vocations and foreign languages/literature. The school has a general core requirement. Cooperative education is not offered. All first-year students must maintain a 2.0 GPA or higher to avoid academic probation, and a minimum overall GPA of 2.0 is required to graduate. Other special academic programs that would appeal to a B student: pass/fail grading option · independent study · double majors · dual degrees · honors program · internships · weekend college · distance learning certificate programs.

B Student Support and Success

Tutoring services are available through the Rider Learning Center. Students struggling with academics can meet with peer tutors who have received excellent grades in their courses and are recommended by professors. Tutors work on both a drop-in and appointment basis. The center also offers a math skills lab. In addition to peer tutoring, Rider offers supplemental instruction for the most difficult classes. Students meet together to review notes, go over readings and learn test-taking strategies.

Rider has two core classes for first-year students who have not met the criteria for college-level reading. These are "Introduction to Academic Reading" and "College Reading." In the first class, which is required, reading and learning strategies are taught to help students increase their reading comprehension. This class earns two credits. In the second (elective) course, students may earn three credits by developing and improving reading comprehension skills and study strategies.

Rider University provides a variety of support programs including dedicated guidance for: academic · career · personal · psychological · minority students · veterans · non-traditional students · family planning · religious. Recognizing that some students may need extra preparation, Rider University offers remedial and refresher courses in: reading · writing · math · study skills. The average freshman year GPA is 3.0, and 80 percent of freshmen students return for their sophomore year.

Support for Students with Learning Disabilities

Students with learning disabilities may take advantage of specific support programs offered by Rider University. If necessary, the college will grant additional time to students with learning disabilities to complete their degree. Also, a lightened course load may be granted to LD students. According to the school, other services include screening and referral, supplementary assessment, advice to faculty and staff and instructional services. Students with learning disabilities will find the following programs at Rider University extremely useful: remedial math · remedial reading · special classes · tutors · learning center · testing accommodations · extended time for tests · take-home exam · oral tests · readers · typist/scribe · note-taking services · reading machines · tape recorders · texts on tape · diagnostic testing service · priority registration · waiver of math degree requirement. Individual or small group tutorials are also available in: time management · organizational skills · learning strategies · specific subject areas · writing labs · math labs · study skills. An advisor/advocate from the LD program is available to students.

RIDER UNIVERSITY

Highlights

Rider University
Lawrenceville, NJ (Pop. 4,000)
Location: Large town
Website: http://www.rider.edu

Students
Total enrollment: 6,011
Undergrads: 1,921
Freshmen: 12,994
Part-time students: 17%
From out-of-state: 25%
Male/Female: 40%/60%
Live on-campus: 54%
In fraternities: 7%
In sororities: 10%
Off-campus employment rating: Good
Caucasian: 71%
African American: 9%
Hispanic: 5%
Asian or Pacific Islander: 3%
Native American: 0%
International: 3%

Academics
Student/faculty ratio: 13:1
Class size 9 or fewer: 19%
Class size 10-29: 60%
Class size 30-49: 20%
Class size 50-99: 1%
Class size 100 or more: -
Returning freshmen: 80%
Six-year graduation rate: 58%

Most Popular Fields of Study
Business, Finance, Sales and Marketing
Biological and Life Sciences
Area, Ethnic and Gender Studies
Psychology
English and Literature
Philosophy, Religion and Theology
Computer and Information Sciences
Interdisciplinary Studies
Physical Sciences, Chemistry, Physics
    and Astronomy
Liberal Arts, Humanities and General
    Studies

373

RIDER UNIVERSITY

Admissions
Applicants: 6,829
Accepted: 5,053
Acceptance rate: 74.0%
placed on wait list: 56
Average GPA: 3.2
ACT range: 18-24
SAT Math range: 470-570
SAT Reading range: 470-560
SAT Writing range: 460-570
Top 10% of class: 14%
Top 25% of class: 37%
Top 50% of class: 75%

Deadlines
Early Action: November 15
Early Decision: November 15
Regular Action: Rolling admissions
Common Application: Accepted

Financial Aid
In-state tuition: $28,470
Out-of-state tuition: $28,470
Room: $6,420
Board: $4,300
Books: $1,500
Freshmen receiving need-based aid: 72%
Undergrads receiving need-based aid: 66%
Avg. % of need met by financial aid: 73%
Avg. aid package (freshmen): $20,878
Avg. aid package (undergrads): $20,013
Freshmen receiving merit-based aid: 19%
Undergrads receiving merit-based aid: 21%
Avg. student debt upon graduation: $33,156

Prominent Alumni
Jennifer Larmore-Powers, international mezzo-soprano opera singer; Thomas J. Lynch, CEO of Tyco Electronics Corp.; Richard 'Digger' Phelps, college basketball analyst for ESPN.

School Spirit
Mascot: Broncs
Colors: Cranberry, white and gray

How to Get Admitted

For admissions decisions, non-academic factors considered: interview · extracurricular activities · special talents, interests, abilities · character/personal qualities · volunteer work · work experience · geographical location · alumni relationship. A high school diploma is required, although a GED is also accepted for admissions consideration. SAT or ACT test scores are required of all applicants. SAT Subject Test scores are not required. *According to the admissions office:* Minimum combined SAT Reasoning score of 900, rank in top half of secondary school class, minimum grade average of 'B', essay, and two letters of recommendation recommended. *Academic units recommended:* 4 Math, 4 Science, 2 Social Studies, 2 Foreign Language.

How to Pay for College

To apply for financial aid, students should submit the following: Free Application for Federal Student Aid (FAFSA). Rider University participates in the Federal Work Study program. *Need-based aid programs include:* scholarships and grants · general need-based awards · Federal Pell grants · state scholarships and grants · college-based scholarships and grants · private scholarships and grants. *Non-Need-based aid programs include:* scholarships and grants · state scholarships and grants · creative arts and performance awards · athletic scholarships.

RIPON COLLEGE

300 Seward Street, Ripon, WI 54971-0248
Admissions: 800-94-RIPON · Financial Aid: 920-748-8101
Email: adminfo@ripon.edu · Website: http://www.ripon.edu

From the College

"Ripon College offers an intensely personal liberal arts education in a residential setting. Part of that education includes a one-on-one dynamic between the student and the faculty member. Communicating Plus emphasizes the development of written and oral communication, critical thinking and problem-solving skills. The curriculum focuses on exploring career choices, selecting opportunities to reach those goals and connecting with faculty and alumni through the classroom, internships and research. Student-faculty collaboration is paramount, which results in participation in state, regional and national conferences and published research articles in many disciplines. Among Ripon's distinctions are a nationally competitive forensics team which offers scholarships to members, three Rhodes Scholars (including a 2002 selection) and a chapter of Phi Beta Kappa."

Campus Setting

Ripon, founded in 1851, is a private, liberal arts college. Its 250-acre campus is located in Ripon, 80 miles northwest of Milwaukee. A four-year institution, Ripon College has an enrollment of 1,057 students. In addition to a large, well-stocked library, the campus facilities include: outdoor classroom and nature preserve · museum · planetarium. Ripon College provides on-campus housing with 496 units that can accommodate 944 students. Housing options: co-ed dorms · women's dorms · men's dorms · sorority housing · fraternity housing. Recreation and sports facilities include: gymnasium · racquetball · squash and tennis courts · swimming pool · weight rooms.

Student Life and Activities

With 88 percent of students living on campus, there are plenty of social activities. According to the editor of the school newspaper, "due to the interests of many professors and the more mature students, Ripon College has a rich cultural life. There are always great plays, concerts, art exhibits and comedians." Students gather at the library, cafeteria, pub, gym and the art building. Popular events include Homecoming, Murder Mystery, Late Night Breakfast, Joyce to the World (holiday celebration), Springfest, Iron Chef Cooking Competition, Couch Potato Play-offs, Martin Luther King Week, Diversity Week, International Night, Soul Food Dinners and Extrava-game-za. Ripon College has 45 official student organizations. Groups with a strong presence include Greek organizations and the Student Media and Activities Committee. For those interested in sports, there are intramural teams such as: basketball · bowling · flag football · floor hockey · indoor soccer · inner tube water polo · softball · tennis · volleyball. Ripon College is a member of the Midwest Conference (Division III).

Academics and Learning Environment

For the B student, the learning environment of a college is just as important as the quality of its academic program. Ripon College has 56 full-time and 37 part-time faculty members, offering a student-to-faculty ratio of 15:1. The most common course size is 10 to 19 students. Ripon College offers 31 majors with the most popular being history and English and least popular being environmental studies and computer science. The school has a general core requirement. Cooperative education is not offered. All first-year students must maintain a 1.8 GPA or higher to avoid academic

RIPON COLLEGE

probation. Other special academic programs that would appeal to a B student: self-designed majors · pass/fail grading option · independent study · double majors · accelerated study · Phi Beta Kappa · internships.

B Student Support and Success

Ripon offers new college students an extensive program called Communicating Plus that emphasizes the core basics of written and oral communication. The course focuses on communication, as well as critical thinking and problem solving skills. It involves student peer mentoring and outreach programming. Student Support Services offers a number of ways to help struggling students. Tutoring is available in a number of subject areas and serves as a supplement to faculty assistance. A group of peer contacts meet regularly with students to facilitate communication between participants and staff. The SSS also offers academic, life and career guidance. In addition, SSS offers cultural enrichment experiences on and off campus.

Ripon College provides a variety of support programs including dedicated guidance for: academic · career · personal · minority students · military · family planning. The average freshman year GPA is 3.0, and 85 percent of freshmen students return for their sophomore year. What do students do after college? While many enter the work force, approximately 21 percent pursue a graduate degree immediately after graduation. Among students who enter the work force, approximately 63 percent enter a field related to their major within six months of graduation. Companies that most frequently hire graduates from Ripon College include: Abbott Laboratories · U.S. Cellular · TEK Systems · US Bank · Environmental Protection Agency · Accenture · Americorps · Convance Labs · Hewitt Associates · M&I Bank · Peace Corps · Wells Fargo Financial · DNR.

Support for Students with Learning Disabilities

Students with learning disabilities may take advantage of specific support programs offered by Ripon College. High school foreign language waivers are accepted. Students with learning disabilities will find the following programs at Ripon College extremely useful: tutors · untimed tests · extended time for tests · take-home exam · oral tests · readers · note-taking services · tape recorders · early syllabus · waiver of math degree requirement. Individual or small group tutorials are also available in: time management · organizational skills · learning strategies · specific subject areas · writing labs · math labs · study skills. An advisor/advocate from the Student Support Services is available to students.

How to Get Admitted

For admissions decisions, non-academic factors considered: interview · extracurricular activities · special talents, interests, abilities · character/personal qualities · volunteer work · work experience · state of residency · minority affiliation · alumni relationship. A high school diploma is required, although a GED is also accepted for admissions consideration. SAT or ACT test scores are required of all applicants. *According to the admissions office:* Rank in top quarter of secondary school class recommended. *Academic units recommended:* 4 English, 4 Math, 4 Science, 4 Social Studies, 1 Foreign Language.

How to Pay for College

To apply for financial aid, students should submit the following: Free Application for Federal Student Aid (FAFSA). Ripon College participates in the Federal Work Study program. *Need-based aid programs include:* scholarships and grants · general need-based awards · Federal Pell grants · state scholarships and grants · college-based scholarships and grants · private scholarships and grants. *Non-Need-based aid programs include:* scholarships and grants · general need-based awards · state scholarships and grants · creative arts and performance awards · special achievements and activities awards · special characteristics awards · ROTC scholarships.

RIPON COLLEGE

Highlights

Admissions
Applicants: 1,081
Accepted: 853
Acceptance rate: 78.9%
Average GPA: 3.4
ACT range: 21-27
SAT Math range: 480-610
SAT Reading range: 490-620
SAT Writing range: Not reported
Top 10% of class: 26%
Top 25% of class: 50%
Top 50% of class: 83%

Deadlines
Early Action: No
Early Decision: No
Regular Action: Rolling admissions
Common Application: Accepted

Financial Aid
In-state tuition: $23,970
Out-of-state tuition: $23,970
Room: $3,490
Board: $3,280
Books: $0
Freshmen receiving need-based aid: 82%
Undergrads receiving need-based aid: 83%
Avg. % of need met by financial aid: 93%
Avg. aid package (freshmen): $20,890
Avg. aid package (undergrads): $20,438
Freshmen receiving merit-based aid: 17%
Undergrads receiving merit-based aid: 22%
Avg. student debt upon graduation: $19,929

Prominent Alumni
Spencer Tracy, actor; Harrison Ford, actor.

School Spirit
Mascot: Red Hawks
Colors: Crimson and white

ROANOKE COLLEGE

221 College Lane, Salem, VA 24153-3794
Admissions: 800-388-2276 · Financial Aid: 800-200-9221
Email: admissions@roanoke.edu · Website: http://roanoke.edu

From the College

"Roanoke College gives students depth and breadth in their education. The depth comes from intensive learning through strong majors and independent studies, special research opportunities, internships and other forms of experiential learning. The breadth comes from a series of core courses that span the four years of the undergraduate experience.

"At Roanoke College, students learn from professors who are experts in their fields. Ninety-five percent of the college's tenure-track faculty members have the highest degrees possible. Almost all professors practice what they teach or contribute to scholarly works in their academic areas—or do both. Because of this close-knit academic environment, students learn directly through the experiences of these experts. The type of mentoring relationship that many students have with their Roanoke professors leads them to excellent graduate school placement or directly into fulfilling careers. In fact, almost all seniors, about 95 percent, receive job offers within six months of graduation or go on to graduate school. With half of its students from Virginia and half from out of state, the college offers regional and national exposure. Alumni have attended graduate schools such as Johns Hopkins, Duke, Columbia, University of Pennsylvania and Yale. In addition, two recent Roanoke alumni were inducted into the national medical school honor society at the University of Virginia.

"Graduates also have gone on to careers ranging from scientific research, underwater archaeology and medicine to television production, humanitarianism and government as well as starting their own businesses."

Campus Setting

Roanoke, founded in 1842, is a church-affiliated, liberal arts college. The 68-acre campus, including several buildings registered as National Historic Landmarks, is located in Salem, five miles west of Roanoke. A four-year private institution, Roanoke College has an enrollment of 2,021 students. Roanoke College has been co-ed since 1930. The school is also affiliated with the Lutheran Church. The school has a library with 214,724 books. Roanoke College provides on-campus housing that can accommodate 1,400 students. Housing options: co-ed dorms · women's dorms · men's dorms · sorority housing · fraternity housing · single-student apartments. Recreation and sports facilities include: golf club · field · fitness center · stadium · YMCA located off-campus.

Student Life and Activities

With 64 percent of students living on campus, there are plenty of social activities. Popular gathering spots for students include the Colket student center, the back quad, and local restaurants such as Mac and Bob's and Macado's. Popular campus events include Fridays on the Quad, the President's Ball, Winterfest, Relay For Life and Alumni Weekend. Roanoke College has 85 official student organizations. The most popular are: Mainstreet (vocal) · Looking for an Echo (vocal) · Campus Activities Board · Outdoor Adventures · Earthbound · Habitat for Humanity. For those interested in sports, there are intramural teams such as: basketball · beach volleyball · canoeing · disc golf · dodgeball · flag football · hiking · kickball · mountain biking · soccer · softball. Roanoke College is a member of the Old Dominion Athletic Conference (Division III).

Academics and Learning Environment

For the B student, the learning environment of a college is just as important as the quality of its academic program. Roanoke College has 153 full-time and 37 part-time faculty members, offering a student-to-faculty ratio of 14:1. The most common course size is 10 to 19 students. Roanoke College offers 30 majors with the most popular being business administration, English and psychology and least popular being medical technology, physics and religion. The school has a general core requirement. Cooperative education is not offered. All first-year students must maintain a 1.7 GPA or higher to avoid academic probation, and a minimum overall GPA of 2.0 is required to graduate. Other special academic programs that would appeal to a B student: pass/fail grading option · independent study · double majors · dual degrees · accelerated study · honors program · Phi Beta Kappa · internships.

B Student Support and Success

Roanoke College's Center for Learning and Teaching offers a number of special services to help the B student. It is located in the Fintel Library, and all students are welcomed on a drop-in or appointment basis. A Writing Center provides students with assistance for creating papers for class, while peer mentoring is also available as is subject tutoring. A program called Success Skills Forum offers students access to workshops that deal with the transitional issues of college life. Workshop titles include these: "Getting Started, Getting Organized," "Time Management," "Reading Textbooks and Taking Notes," "Study Skills" and "Test Preparation."

Roanoke College provides a variety of support programs including dedicated guidance for: academic · career · personal · psychological · minority students · non-traditional students · religious. The average freshman year GPA is 2.7, and 76 percent of freshmen students return for their sophomore year. Among students who enter the work force, approximately 96 percent enter a field related to their major within six months of graduation.

Support for Students with Learning Disabilities

Students with learning disabilities may take advantage of specific support programs offered by Roanoke College. Students with learning disabilities will find the following programs at Roanoke College extremely useful: tutors · learning center · testing accommodations · untimed tests · extended time for tests · oral tests · note-taking services · tape recorders. Individual or small group tutorials are also available in: time management · organizational skills · learning strategies · specific subject areas · writing labs · study skills. An advisor/advocate from the LD program is available to students.

How to Get Admitted

For admissions decisions, non-academic factors considered: interview · extracurricular activities · special talents, interests, abilities · character/personal qualities · volunteer work · work experience · state of residency · minority affiliation · alumni relationship. A high school diploma is required, although a GED is also accepted for admissions consideration. SAT or ACT test scores are required of all applicants. SAT Subject Test scores are considered, if submitted, but are not required. *Academic units recommended:* 4 Foreign Language.

ROANOKE COLLEGE

Highlights

Roanoke College
Salem, VA (Pop. 25,000)
Location: Medium city
Website: http://roanoke.edu

Students
Total enrollment: 2,021
Undergrads: 905
Freshmen: 529
Part-time students: 5%
From out-of-state: 51%
Male/Female: 45%/55%
Live on-campus: 64%
In fraternities: 23%
In sororities: 23%
Off-campus employment rating: Excellent
Caucasian: 84%
African American: 3%
Hispanic: 3%
Asian or Pacific Islander: 1%
Native American: 0%
International: 1%

Academics
Student/faculty ratio: 14:1
Class size 9 or fewer: 22%
Class size 10-29: 72%
Class size 30-49: 6%
Class size 50-99: 2%
Class size 100 or more: -
Returning freshmen: 76%
Six-year graduation rate: 61%

Most Popular Fields of Study
Business, Finance, Sales and Marketing
Biological and Life Sciences

ROANOKE COLLEGE

Admissions
Applicants: 3,579
Accepted: 2,500
Acceptance rate: 69.9%
Average GPA: 3.3
ACT range: Not reported
SAT Math range: 510-600
SAT Reading range: 500-600
SAT Writing range: 470-570
Top 10% of class: 22%
Top 25% of class: 53%
Top 50% of class: 85%

Deadlines
Early Action: No
Early Decision:
Regular Action: March 15 (priority)
Common Application: Accepted

Financial Aid
In-state tuition: $28,734
Out-of-state tuition: $28,734
Room: $4,560
Board: $5,220
Books: $1,000
Freshmen receiving need-based aid: 63%
Undergrads receiving need-based aid: 61%
Avg. % of need met by financial aid: 83%
Avg. aid package (freshmen): $23,541
Avg. aid package (undergrads): $21,838
Freshmen receiving merit-based aid: 34%
Undergrads receiving merit-based aid: 36%
Avg. student debt upon graduation: $25,498

School Spirit
Mascot: Maroons

How to Pay for College

To apply for financial aid, students should submit the following: Free Application for Federal Student Aid (FAFSA) · state aid form. Roanoke College participates in the Federal Work Study program. *Need-based aid programs include:* scholarships and grants · general need-based awards · Federal Pell grants · state scholarships and grants · college-based scholarships and grants · private scholarships and grants. *Non-Need-based aid programs include:* scholarships and grants · general need-based awards · state scholarships and grants.

ROGER WILLIAMS UNIVERSITY

1 Old Ferry Road, Bristol, RI 02809
Admissions: 800-458-7144 · Financial Aid: 800-458-7144
Email: admit@rwu.edu · Website: http://www.rwu.edu

From the College

"Roger Williams University says that it is a regional leader in the liberal arts strengthened by professional schools. The 140-acre coastal campus lies in Bristol, Rhode Island, and is easily accessible from Boston and New York. Accredited by the New England Association of Schools and Colleges, the university draws over 5000 undergraduate, graduate and professional students. Nearly 40 undergraduate majors blend the traditional and innovative, cultivating multiple areas of expertise. The university also offers six graduate programs and the state's only law school. The campus includes modern facilities, recreation, athletics and social opportunities."

Campus Setting

Roger Williams University, founded in 1956, is a private, independent university located on a 140-acre campus on Mount Hope Bay in Bristol. A four-year institution, Roger Williams University has an enrollment of 5,166 students. In addition to a large, well-stocked library, the campus facilities include: performing arts center · center for marine and natural sciences. Roger Williams University provides on-campus housing with 1,368 units that can accommodate 2,949 students. Housing options: co-ed dorms · single-student apartments. Recreation and sports facilities include: aquatic center · athletic fields · fitness center · gymnasium · recreation center · tennis courts.

Student Life and Activities

With 79 percent of students living on campus, there are plenty of social activities. Roger Williams University has 92 official student organizations. The most popular are: animal rights/environmental club · art society · bagpipe and pep bands · chess club · chorus · Commuters in Action · creative writing club · dance club · Elizabethan society · faith choir · Habitat for Humanity · historic preservation club · lesbian/gay/bisexual/transgender alliance · political studies club · psychology club · stage company · Students Against Destructive Decisions · construction engineering society · aquaculture club · natural science club. For those interested in sports, there are intramural teams such as: basketball · indoor soccer · soccer · softball · water basketball. Roger Williams University is a member of the Commonwealth Coast Conference (Division III), New England College Wrestling Association (Division III).

Academics and Learning Environment

For the B student, the learning environment of a college is just as important as the quality of its academic program. Roger Williams University has 210 full-time and 374 part-time faculty members, offering a student-to-faculty ratio of 12:1. The most common course size is 10 to 19 students. Roger Williams University offers 42 majors with the most popular being criminal justice, business management and psychology and least popular being economics, American studies and environmental chemistry. The school has a general core requirement. Cooperative education is not offered. All first-year students must maintain a 1.4 GPA or higher to avoid academic probation, and a minimum overall GPA of 2.0 is required to graduate. Other special academic programs that would appeal to a B student: self-designed majors · pass/fail grading option · independent study · double majors · honors program · internships · distance learning.

ROGER WILLIAMS UNIVERSITY

Highlights

Roger Williams University
Bristol, RI (Pop. 22,469)
Location: Small town
Website: http://www.rwu.edu

Students
Total enrollment: 5,166
Undergrads: 2,202
Freshmen: 954
Part-time students: 14%
From out-of-state: 92%
Male/Female: 51%/49%
Live on-campus: 79%
Off-campus employment rating: Fair
Caucasian: 74%
African American: 2%
Hispanic: 2%
Asian or Pacific Islander: 1%
Native American: 0%
International: 2%

Academics
Student/faculty ratio: 12:1
Class size 9 or fewer: 14%
Class size 10-29: 77%
Class size 30-49: 9%
Class size 50-99: -
Class size 100 or more: -
Returning freshmen: 82%
Six-year graduation rate: 56%

Most Popular Fields of Study
Business, Finance, Sales and Marketing
Visual and Performing Arts
Social Sciences, History, Economics, Political Science
Protective Services, Criminal Justice and Public Administration
Communications, Journalism, Advertising and Comm. Technologies
Philosophy, Religion and Theology
English and Literature
Health Professions, Medicine and Related Sciences
Foreign Languages, Literature and Linguistics
Psychology

B Student Support and Success

Roger Williams University provides a number of helpful tools for the B student, including three university libraries on site. The school's Center for Academic Development offers workshops, seminars and individual tutorial sessions. Topics such as time management, organization, note taking, textbook strategies, test preparation, learning styles, classroom technology and academic success are all covered. A Writing Center helps with the development of papers from beginning to end, while a Math Center helps with homework in a number of math courses. Finally, a Core Tutoring Center provides peer tutors for the school's five-course interdisciplinary Core Curriculum.

Roger Williams University provides a variety of support programs including dedicated guidance for: academic · career · personal · psychological · minority students · military · veterans · non-traditional students · family planning. Recognizing that some students may need extra preparation, Roger Williams University offers remedial and refresher courses in: reading · writing · math · study skills. The average freshman year GPA is 3.0, and 82 percent of freshmen students return for their sophomore year. What do students do after college? While many enter the work force, approximately 13 percent pursue a graduate degree immediately after graduation, and another 13 percent enter graduate school within two years.

Support for Students with Learning Disabilities

Students with learning disabilities may take advantage of specific support programs offered by Roger Williams University. If necessary, the college will grant additional time to students with learning disabilities to complete their degree. Also, a lightened course load may be granted to LD students. Students with learning disabilities will find the following programs at Roger Williams University extremely useful: tutors · learning center · extended time for tests · readers · note-taking services. Individual or small group tutorials are also available in: time management · organizational skills · learning strategies · writing labs · math labs · study skills. An advisor/advocate from the LD program is available to students.

How to Get Admitted

For admissions decisions, non-academic factors considered: interview · extracurricular activities · special talents, interests, abilities · volunteer work · work experience · state of residency. A high school diploma is required, although a GED is also accepted for admissions consideration. SAT or ACT test scores are required of all applicants. SAT Subject Test scores are considered, if submitted, but are not required. *According to the admissions office:* Additional units of humanities, math, science, and social studies recommended. *Academic units recommended:* 4 English, 4 Math, 4 Science, 3 Social Studies, 2 Foreign Language.

How to Pay for College

To apply for financial aid, students should submit the following: Free Application for Federal Student Aid (FAFSA) · CSS/Financial Aid PROFILE · tax forms. Roger Williams University participates in the Federal Work Study program. *Need-based aid programs include:*

scholarships and grants · general need-based awards · Federal Pell grants · state scholarships and grants · college-based scholarships and grants · private scholarships and grants. *Non-Need-based aid programs include:* scholarships and grants · state scholarships and grants.

ROGER WILLIAMS UNIVERSITY

Highlights

Admissions
Applicants: 8,561
Accepted: 5,253
Acceptance rate: 61.4%
Average GPA: 3.2
ACT range: 21-25
SAT Math range: 520-600
SAT Reading range: 500-590
SAT Writing range: 500-590
Top 10% of class: 14%
Top 25% of class: 38%
Top 50% of class: 76%

Deadlines
Early Action: November 1
Early Decision: No
Regular Action: Rolling admissions
Common Application: Accepted

Financial Aid
In-state tuition: $26,880
Out-of-state tuition: $26,880
Room: $6,610
Board: $5,680
Books: $900
Freshmen receiving need-based aid: 57%
Undergrads receiving need-based aid: 57%
Avg. % of need met by financial aid: 86%
Avg. aid package (freshmen): $17,274
Avg. aid package (undergrads): $17,017
Freshmen receiving merit-based aid: 17%
Undergrads receiving merit-based aid: 10%
Avg. student debt upon graduation: $30,874

School Spirit
Mascot: Hawk
Colors: Blue and gold

RUST COLLEGE

150 Rust Avenue, Holly Springs, MS 38635
Admissions: 888-886-8492, extension 4059
Financial Aid: 888-886-8492, extension 4061
Email: admissions@rustcollege.edu
Website: http://www.rustcollege.edu

Rust College
Holly Springs, MS (Pop. 7,957)
Location: Rural
Website: http://www.rustcollege.edu

Students
Total enrollment: 979
Undergrads: 367
Freshmen: 348
Part-time students: 22%
From out-of-state: 40%
Male/Female: 37%/63%
Live on-campus: Not reported
Off-campus employment rating: Good

Academics
Student/faculty ratio: 16:1
Class size 9 or fewer: 14%
Class size 10-29: 77%
Class size 30-49: 9%
Class size 50-99: -
Class size 100 or more: -
Returning freshmen: 52%
Six-year graduation rate: 28%

Most Popular Fields of Study
Business, Finance, Sales and Marketing
Protective Services, Criminal Justice and
    Public Administration
Computer and Information Sciences
Parks, Recreation and Fitness
Communications, Journalism, Advertising
    and Comm. Technologies
Education
Social Sciences, History, Economics,
    Political Science
Physical Sciences, Chemistry, Physics
    and Astronomy
Visual and Performing Arts
Biological and Life Sciences

Campus Setting

Rust College, founded in 1866, is a private, church-affiliated college. Its 126-acre campus is located in Holly Springs, 45 miles southeast of Memphis. A four-year institution, Rust College is a historically black university with 979 students. The school is also affiliated with the Methodist Church. In addition to a large, well-stocked library, the campus has an African tribal art collection. Rust College provides on-campus housing that can accommodate 856 students. Housing options: women's dorms · men's dorms · married-student apartments. Recreation and sports facilities include: arena · multi-purpose athletic center · park.

Student Life and Activities

"The students interact well with each other, enjoying intelligent conversations and physical recreation," reports the student newspaper. "They are culturally aware and very proud of their African American heritage." Popular gathering spots include the student recreation center, gymnasium, library, laundry room, Doxey Fine Arts Building, McDonald's, KFC, Club Octagon, Pizza Hut, Pizza Inn and Victor's. Popular campus events include Founder's Weekend, Health Fair, SIAC Basketball Tournament, Religious Emphasis Week, Theatre Productions, dances, movies and commencement. Rust College has 38 official student organizations. Influential student groups include Omega Psi Phi, Zeta Phi Beta, the basketball team, the Baptist Student Union Choir and the Student Government Association. For those interested in sports, there are intramural teams such as: archery · basketball · billiards · dance · flag football · soccer · softball · swimming · table tennis · tennis · track · volleyball.

Academics and Learning Environment

For the B student, the learning environment of a college is just as important as the quality of its academic program. Rust College has 48 full-time and two part-time faculty members, offering a student-to-faculty ratio of 16:1. Rust College offers 21 majors with the most popular being biology, computer science and business administration and least popular being mathematics, English and chemistry. The school has a general core requirement as well as a religion requirement Cooperative education is not offered. All first-year students must maintain a 1.5 GPA or higher to avoid academic probation, and a minimum overall GPA of 2.0 is required to graduate. Other special academic programs that would appeal to a B student: independent study · double majors · honors program · internships.

B Student Support and Success

With its open admissions system, Rust College considers students whose "educational goals, career objectives and intellectual abilities match the institution's academic and non-academic programs." The Academic Counseling Program helps students plan their courses and careers based on needs and interests. Freshmen are assigned faculty advisors. After the first year, a major is declared, and each student is given an academic counselor from the faculty to help with any problems or questions that might follow.

Rust College provides a variety of support programs including dedicated guidance for: academic · career · minority students · religious. Recognizing that some students may need extra preparation, Rust College offers remedial and refresher courses in: reading · writing · math · study skills. Other remedial services include English. The average freshman year GPA is 2.6, and 52 percent of freshmen students return for their sophomore year. What do students do after college? While many enter the work force, approximately 10 percent pursue a graduate degree immediately after graduation. Among students who enter the work force, approximately 32 percent enter a field related to their major within six months of graduation, while 79 percent enter a related career within two years of graduation.

Support for Students with Learning Disabilities

Students with learning disabilities may take advantage of specific support programs offered by Rust College. Also, a lightened course load may be granted to LD students. Students with learning disabilities will find the following programs at Rust College extremely useful: remedial math · remedial English · tutors · diagnostic testing service.

How to Get Admitted

For admissions decisions, non-academic factors considered: interview · extracurricular activities · special talents, interests, abilities · character/personal qualities. A high school diploma is required, although a GED is also accepted for admissions consideration. SAT or ACT test scores *According to the admissions office:* Minimum 2.0 GPA required.

How to Pay for College

To apply for financial aid, students should submit the following: Free Application for Federal Student Aid (FAFSA) · institution's own financial aid forms · state aid form · Non-custodian (Divorced/Separated) Parent's Statement · Business/Farm Supplement. Rust College participates in the Federal Work Study program. *Need-based aid programs include:* scholarships and grants · general need-based awards · Federal Pell grants · state scholarships and grants · private scholarships and grants · United Negro College Fund. *Non-Need-based aid programs include:* scholarships and grants · general need-based awards · state scholarships and grants.

RUST COLLEGE

Highlights

Admissions
Applicants: 1,482
Accepted: 710
Acceptance rate: 47.9%
Average GPA: 2.6
ACT range: 14-17
SAT Math range: Not reported
SAT Reading range: Not reported
SAT Writing range: Not reported
Top 10% of class: 10%
Top 25% of class: 25%
Top 50% of class: 85%

Deadlines
Early Action: No
Early Decision: No
Regular Action: July 31 (priority)
Common Application: Not accepted

Financial Aid
In-state tuition: $7,000
Out-of-state tuition: $7,000
Room: -
Board: -
Books: -
Avg. % of need met by financial aid: Not reported
Avg. aid package (freshmen): Not reported
Avg. aid package (undergrads): Not reported
Avg. student debt upon graduation: Not reported

Prominent Alumni
Leslie McLemore, political science professor; F.C. Richardson, college president; Dimaggio Nichols, automobile dealership.

School Spirit
Mascot: Bearcats
Colors: Royal and white
Song: *Rust College Mine Mine Mine*

SALVE REGINA UNIVERSITY

100 Ochre Point Avenue, Newport, RI 02840-4192
Admissions: 888-GO-SALVE · Financial Aid: 888-GO-SALVE
Email: sruadmis@salve.edu · Website: http://www.salve.edu

From the College

"Salve Regina University is a small university with big opportunity. Salve Regina's oceanfront campus is a place where students feel at home. Students study and live in historic mansions, yet receive an education that prepares them for modern careers and a lifetime of serving their communities. Salve offers excellent professional and liberal arts programs (most popular are: business, education, administration of justice and biology). The classes are small and are all taught by professors (no grad assistants). Salve's small size also makes it easy for students to get involved on campus with clubs, activities, athletics or intramurals. At Salve, it is easy to become a leader, even in your first year. Newport offers the perfect location for students who love history, sailing and the outdoors. Students can surf, ocean kayak from First Beach or bike ride on Ocean Drive. Newport also hosts several festivals throughout the year. All students get a free statewide trolley/bus pass that takes them throughout Newport or to Providence 30 minutes away. Admission to Salve Regina is competitive. The Admissions Office looks at several factors in reviewing applications. Most important is your day-to-day academic work and the level of the courses you have taken. We also review recommendation letters and test scores. Leadership positions and community involvement are also considered in the review process."

Campus Setting

Salve Regina, founded in 1934, is a private, church-affiliated, liberal arts university. Its 65-acre campus is situated among turn-of-the-century summer estates listed with the National Register of Historic Places. A four-year institution, Salve Regina University has an enrollment of 2,691 students. Salve Regina University has been co-ed since 1973. The school is also affiliated with the Roman Catholic Church (Religious Sisters of Mercy). In addition to a large, well-stocked library, the campus has a public service center. Salve Regina University provides on-campus housing with 532 units that can accommodate 1,200 students. Housing options: co-ed dorms · women's dorms · men's dorms · single-student apartments · special housing for disabled students. Recreation and sports facilities include: fields · ice rink · fitness center · recreation center · tennis courts.

Student Life and Activities

With 58 percent of students living on campus, there are plenty of social activities. Students gather on campus at O'Hare Academic Center, Wakehurst Campus Center and Miley Hall. Off campus, students often head to the Brick Alley Pub and Restaurant. Popular campus events include Spring Weekend, Wakehurst Day and the all-campus BBQ and Salve Dance Company shows. Salve Regina University has 41 official student organizations. Influential campus groups include Sigma Phi Sigma honor society, the Student Life Senate, the Campus Activities Board and the Activities Office. For those interested in sports, there are intramural teams such as: several intramural/recreational sports. Salve Regina University is a member of the Commonwealth Coast Conference (Division III), ECAC Hockey League (Division III), New England Football Conference (Division III), New England Women's Lacrosse Alliance (Division III).

Academics and Learning Environment

For the B student, the learning environment of a college is just as important as the quality of its academic program. Salve Regina University has 120 full-time and 136 part-time faculty members, offering a student-to-faculty ratio of 14:1. The most common course size is 10 to 19 students. Salve Regina University offers 54 majors with the most popular being business administration, administration of justice and nursing and least popular being women's studies, secondary education/biology and anthropology. The school has a general core requirement as well as a religion requirement Cooperative education is not offered. All first-year students must maintain a 1.8 GPA or higher to avoid academic probation. Other special academic programs that would appeal to a B student: independent study · double majors · accelerated study · honors program · internships · distance learning.

B Student Support and Success

Salve Regina looks at a student's high school transcript, and one of the first things it does is recalculate the GPA. All extracurricular classes are eliminated and the average is obtained from the core academic classes only. Students who need academic assistance will find a Writing Center and Student Tutorial Center on campus. Faculty and staff make an extra effort to help first-year students with the transition from high school to college.

Salve Regina University provides a variety of support programs including dedicated guidance for: academic · career · personal · psychological · minority students · military · religious. The average freshman year GPA is 3.0, and 73 percent of freshmen students return for their sophomore year. What do students do after college? While many enter the work force, approximately 20 percent pursue a graduate degree immediately after graduation. Among students who enter the work force, approximately 63 percent enter a field related to their major within six months of graduation, while 76 percent enter a related career within two years of graduation. Companies that most frequently hire graduates from Salve Regina University include: Federal Bureau of Investigation · MTV · Pfizer · Ernst and Young · Mt. Sinai Hospital · Liberty Mutual Group · Boeing Co. · New York State Police · Child and Family Services · Sun Life Financial.

Support for Students with Learning Disabilities

Students with learning disabilities may take advantage of specific support programs offered by Salve Regina University. If necessary, the college will grant additional time to students with learning disabilities to complete their degree. Also, a lightened course load may be granted to LD students. Students with learning disabilities will find the following programs at Salve Regina University extremely useful: tutors · learning center · testing accommodations · untimed tests · extended time for tests · oral tests · readers · note-taking services · tape recorders · videotaped classes. Individual or small group tutorials are also available in: time management · organizational skills · learning strategies · specific subject areas · writing labs · math labs · study skills. An advisor/advocate from the Disability Services is available to students.

SALVE REGINA UNIVERSITY

Salve Regina University
Newport, RI (Pop. 27,000)
Location: Large town
Website: http://www.salve.edu

Students
Total enrollment: 2,691
Undergrads: 648
Freshmen: 556
Part-time students: 6%
From out-of-state: 89%
Male/Female: 30%/70%
Live on-campus: 58%
Off-campus employment rating: Good
Caucasian: 79%
African American: 1%
Hispanic: 3%
Asian or Pacific Islander: 1%
Native American: 0%
International: 1%

Academics
Student/faculty ratio: 14:1
Class size 9 or fewer: 17%
Class size 10-29: 64%
Class size 30-49: 19%
Class size 50-99: 1%
Class size 100 or more: -
Returning freshmen: 73%
Six-year graduation rate: 70%

Most Popular Fields of Study
Business, Finance, Sales and Marketing
Biological and Life Sciences
Protective Services, Criminal Justice and
    Public Administration
Visual and Performing Arts
Area, Ethnic and Gender Studies
Computer and Information Sciences
Communications, Journalism, Advertising
    and Comm. Technologies
Philosophy, Religion and Theology
Liberal Arts, Humanities and General
    Studies
English and Literature

SALVE REGINA UNIVERSITY

Admissions

Applicants: 5,937
Accepted: 3,484
Acceptance rate: 58.7%
placed on wait list: 614
Average GPA: 3.2
ACT range: 22-26
SAT Math range: 510-590
SAT Reading range: 510-580
SAT Writing range: Not reported
Top 10% of class: 20%
Top 25% of class: 56%
Top 50% of class: 90%

Deadlines

Early Action: November 1
Early Decision: No
Regular Action: Rolling admissions
Common Application: Accepted

Financial Aid

In-state tuition: $29,800
Out-of-state tuition: $29,800
Room: -
Board: -
Books: $900
Freshmen receiving need-based aid: 71%
Undergrads receiving need-based aid:
   68%
Avg. % of need met by financial aid: 67%
Avg. aid package (freshmen): $20,982
Avg. aid package (undergrads): $19,602
Freshmen receiving merit-based aid: 17%
Undergrads receiving merit-based aid:
   15%
Avg. student debt upon graduation:
   $30,138

Prominent Alumni

Janet Robinson, president and CEO
of *The New York Times*; General Carol
Mutter, U.S. Marine Corps (first female
three-star general); Kevin Favreau, special agent in charge/counter intelligence/
Washington, DC, FBI field office

School Spirit

Mascot: Seahawks
Colors: Blue, white and green

How to Get Admitted

For admissions decisions, non-academic factors considered: extracurricular activities · special talents, interests, abilities · character/personal qualities · volunteer work · work experience · state of residency · minority affiliation · alumni relationship. A high school diploma is required, although a GED is also accepted for admissions consideration. SAT or ACT test scores are required of all applicants. SAT Subject Test scores are considered, if submitted, but are not required.

Insight

"There is a college for everyone," says Amanda Warhurst Webster, senior associate director of admissions. "Here we look at the profile of the high school itself. Does it offer an honors curriculum? How many academic classes will the student choose to take, including their senior year? Do the students take state tests?" According to Warhurst Webster, emphasis is also put on recommendations. "We want to see the third party perspective," she says. "And we can tell when a letter is a general one or a truly personal one."

The essay is very important at Salve Regina. "It is the only part of the application process that is in the student's own voice," says Warhurst Webster. "The essays bring the kids to life. I always encourage students to think, 'How do I want to appear to the people in admissions?' " The essay topics are open-ended, and officers look at the concepts presented in the essay along with grammar, mechanics and usage issues. One common essay question is 'Tell us something more about yourself that you want us to know.' We certainly give leeway to students who do not have a support system," explains Warhurst Webster.

How to Pay for College

To apply for financial aid, students should submit the following: Free Application for Federal Student Aid (FAFSA) · CSS/Financial Aid PROFILE · Non-custodian (Divorced/Separated) Parent's Statement · Business/Farm Supplement. Salve Regina University participates in the Federal Work Study program. *Need-based aid programs include:* scholarships and grants · general need-based awards · Federal Pell grants · state scholarships and grants · college-based scholarships and grants · private scholarships and grants. *Non-Need-based aid programs include:* scholarships and grants · state scholarships and grants · ROTC scholarships · minority scholarships.

SARAH LAWRENCE COLLEGE

1 Mead Way, Bronxville, NY 10708-5999
Admissions: 800-888-2858 · Financial Aid: 914-395-2570
Email: slcadmit@sarahlawrence.edu
Website: http://www.sarahlawrence.edu

From the College

"Sarah Lawrence is a co-educational college of the liberal arts and sciences offering undergraduate and graduate degrees. The college is known for its rigorous academic standards, which are fostered by small seminars and individual student-faculty conferences, made possible by a low student-to -faculty ratio of 6-to-1. Students at SLC design their own course of study with the help of a faulty adviser or "don." Study abroad is a popular option for many juniors, and Sarah Lawrence has programs in Paris, Florence, Catania, Oxford, London and Havana. Students in all years frequently augment their classes and conferences with work in neighboring communities and New York City through service learning, volunteer opportunities and internships. Long respected in arts education, Sarah Lawrence recognizes the creative and performing arts as integral to a liberal arts education."

Campus Setting

Sarah Lawrence offers undergraduate as well as graduate degrees. A four-year, private institution, Sarah Lawrence College has an enrollment of 1,700 students. Although not originally a co-educational college, Sarah Lawrence College has been co-ed since 1968. In addition to a large, well-stocked library, the campus facilities include: art galleries · dance studios · music building · theatre · visual arts building · science center. Sarah Lawrence College provides on-campus housing with 716 units that can accommodate 1,000 students. Housing options: co-ed dorms · women's dorms · single-student apartments · cooperative housing. Recreation and sports facilities include: fitness center · gymnasium · softball field · swimming pool · tennis and squash courts.

Student Life and Activities

With 85 percent of students living on campus, there are plenty of social activities. Common Ground, the Pub and Westlands Lawn are favorite student hangouts. Popular campus events include Poetry Festival, Midnight Cabaret, Mayfair and Student Auction. Sarah Lawrence College has 61 official student organizations. The most popular are: Amnesty International · a cappella group · chamber music groups · chorus · dance group · drama group · environmental awareness group · feminist alliance · film society · jazz band · Model UN · orchestra · Positive Action · Queer Coalition · theatre outreach · outdoor club. For those interested in sports, there are intramural teams such as: badminton · basketball · bowling · fencing · martial arts · soccer · squash · tennis · ultimate Frisbee · volleyball. Sarah Lawrence College is a member of the Hudson Valley Men's Athletic Conference.

College Profiles

SARAH LAWRENCE COLLEGE

Highlights

Deadlines
Early Action: No
Early Decision: November 15
Regular Action: January 1 (priority)
January 1 (final)
Common Application: Accepted

Financial Aid
In-state tuition: $39,450
Out-of-state tuition: $39,450
Room: $8,756
Board: $4,348
Books: $600
Freshmen receiving need-based aid: 54%
Undergrads receiving need-based aid: 57%
Avg. % of need met by financial aid: 86%
Avg. aid package (freshmen): $26,288
Avg. aid package (undergrads): $27,454
Freshmen receiving merit-based aid: 11%
Undergrads receiving merit-based aid: 4%
Avg. student debt upon graduation: $15,581

Prominent Alumni
W. Ian Lipkin, '74, molecular neurobiologist who helped identify the West Nile Virus as the cause of the encephalitis outbreak in New York state in 1999; Vera Wang, '71, fashion designer.

School Spirit
Mascot: Gryphons
Colors: Hunter green and white

Academics and Learning Environment

For the B student, the learning environment of a college is just as important as the quality of its academic program. Sarah Lawrence College has 113 full-time and 221 part-time faculty members, offering a student-to-faculty ratio of 6:1. The most common course size is 10 to 19 students. Sarah Lawrence College offers 32 majors. The school does not have a general core requirement. Cooperative education is not offered. Other special academic programs that would appeal to a B student: self-designed majors · pass/fail grading option · independent study · dual degrees · internships.

B Student Support and Success

Sarah Lawrence College provides a variety of support programs including dedicated guidance for: academic · career · personal · psychological · minority students · non-traditional students · family planning. Annually, 80 percent of freshmen students return for their sophomore year. What do students do after college? While many enter the work force, approximately 10 percent pursue a graduate degree immediately after graduation, and another 10 percent enter graduate school within two years.

Support for Students with Learning Disabilities

Students with learning disabilities may take advantage of specific support programs offered by Sarah Lawrence College. If necessary, the college will grant additional time to students with learning disabilities to complete their degree. Students with learning disabilities will find the following programs at Sarah Lawrence College extremely useful: extended time for tests · take-home exam · readers · note-taking services · tape recorders · texts on tape · priority registration. Individual or small group tutorials are also available in: time management · organizational skills · learning strategies · study skills. An advisor/advocate from the LD program is available to students.

How to Get Admitted

For admissions decisions, non-academic factors considered: interview · extracurricular activities · special talents, interests, abilities · character/personal qualities · volunteer work · work experience · state of residency · geographical location · minority affiliation · alumni relationship. A high school diploma is required, although a GED is also accepted for admissions consideration. SAT or ACT test scores *Academic units recommended:* 4 Math, 4 Science, 4 Foreign Language.

How to Pay for College

To apply for financial aid, students should submit the following: Free Application for Federal Student Aid (FAFSA) · CSS/Financial Aid PROFILE · state aid form · Non-custodian (Divorced/Separated) Parent's Statement. Sarah Lawrence College participates in the Federal Work Study program. *Need-based aid programs include:* scholarships and grants · general need-based awards · Federal Pell grants · state scholarships and grants · college-based scholarships and grants · private scholarships and grants. *Non-Need-based aid programs include:*.

SCHREINER UNIVERSITY

2100 Memorial Boulevard, Kerrville, TX 78028
Admissions: 800-343-4919 · Financial Aid: 800-343-4919
Email: admissions@schreiner.edu · Website: http://www.schreiner.edu

From the College

"Mission: Schreiner University, a liberal arts institution affiliated by choice and covenant with the Presbyterian Church (USA), is committed to educating students holistically. Primarily undergraduate, the university offers a personalized, integrated education that prepares its students for meaningful work and purposeful lives. Vision: Schreiner University will always hold student success as its first priority, where students from a variety of backgrounds and experiences learn through educational programs equipping them to achieve, excel and lead. The university aspires to serve as a standard to others in programs and practices."

Campus Setting

Schreiner is a private, liberal arts university. Founded in 1923, it adopted co-education in 1971. Its 175-acre campus is located in Kerrville, 60 miles northwest of San Antonio. A four-year institution, Schreiner University has an enrollment of 974 students. The school is also affiliated with the Presbyterian Church. The school has a library with 89,000 books. Housing options: co-ed dorms · single-student apartments · married-student apartments · special housing for disabled students. Recreation and sports facilities include: baseball · soccer and softball fields · golf course · gymnasium · tennis courts.

Student Life and Activities

With 60 percent of students living on campus, there are plenty of social activities. Popular campus events include Late Night Breakfast, Monday Night Fiction, Mountaineer Leadership Conference, Chautauqua Lecture Series, Crate Lecture Series and Coffeehouse. Schreiner University has 38 official student organizations. The most popular are: AHG · Association of Texas Professional Educators · Rotaract · Asian Cultures Club · College Democrats · Non-Traditional and Commuter Student Association · Pre-Law Society · Unicycle Club · Schreiner Big · Schreiner Wellness Action Team · Trull Community Council · Delaney Community Council · Pecan Grove Community Council · The Oaks Community Council · Flato/LA Community Council · Spanish Club. For those interested in sports, there are intramural teams such as: basketball · cycling · dodgeball · flag football · kickball · soccer · tennis · ultimate Frisbee · volleyball · water polo. Schreiner University is a member of the Member of American Southwest Conference (Division III).

Academics and Learning Environment

For the B student, the learning environment of a college is just as important as the quality of its academic program. Schreiner University has 58 full-time and 43 part-time faculty members, offering a student-to-faculty ratio of 13:1. The most common course size is 10 to 19 students. Schreiner University offers 40 majors with the most popular being business administration, education and psychology and least popular being mathematics, humanities and philosophy. The school has a general core requirement. Cooperative education is not offered. All first-year students must maintain a 1.8 GPA or higher to avoid academic probation. Other special academic programs that would appeal to a B student: self-designed majors · independent study · double majors · accelerated study · honors program · Phi Beta Kappa · internships · certificate programs.

SCHREINER UNIVERSITY

Schreiner University
Kerrville, TX
Location: Small town
Website: http://www.schreiner.edu

Students
Total enrollment: 974
Undergrads: 405
Freshmen: 266
Part-time students: 5%
From out-of-state: 1%
Male/Female: 42%/58%
Live on-campus: 60%
In fraternities: 4%
In sororities: 8%
Off-campus employment rating: Fair
Caucasian: 73%
African American: 4%
Hispanic: 21%
Asian or Pacific Islander: 1%
Native American: 1%
International: 0%

Academics
Student/faculty ratio: 13:1
Class size 9 or fewer: 18%
Class size 10-29: 78%
Class size 30-49: 4%
Class size 50-99: 2%
Class size 100 or more: -
Returning freshmen: 63%
Six-year graduation rate: 42%

Most Popular Fields of Study
Business, Finance, Sales and Marketing
Biological and Life Sciences

B Student Support and Success

Because the student-to-faculty ratio at Schreiner is 13:1, students receive individual attention. In some instances, they can even help to design their own internships. There is also a strong honors program at Schreiner. Students with learning disabilities can find help through Schreiner's Learning Support Services Program. Tutoring for all classes is free.

Schreiner University provides a variety of support programs including dedicated guidance for: academic · career · personal · psychological · non-traditional students · family planning · religious. Annually, 63 percent of freshmen students return for their sophomore year.

Support for Students with Learning Disabilities

Students with learning disabilities may take advantage of specific support programs offered by Schreiner University. If necessary, the college will grant additional time to students with learning disabilities to complete their degree. Also, a lightened course load may be granted to LD students. High school foreign language waivers are accepted. High school math waivers are also accepted. According to the school, new freshmen in the program are enrolled in a special section of a required freshman studies class that focuses on issues of special concern to the success of LD college students. Staff is also available to work with students on course selection and registration. Students with learning disabilities will find the following programs at Schreiner University extremely useful: remedial math · remedial English · tutors · learning center · testing accommodations · untimed tests · extended time for tests · take-home exam · oral tests · exam on tape or computer · readers · note-taking services · reading machines · texts on tape · early syllabus · waiver of math degree requirement. Individual or small group tutorials are also available in: time management · organizational skills · learning strategies · specific subject areas · writing labs · study skills. An advisor/advocate from the Learning Support Services is available to students. This member also sits on the admissions committee.

How to Get Admitted

For admissions decisions, non-academic factors considered: interview · extracurricular activities · special talents, interests, abilities · character/personal qualities · volunteer work · work experience · state of residency. A high school diploma is required, although a GED is also accepted for admissions consideration. SAT or ACT test scores are required of all applicants. SAT Subject Test scores are not required. *According to the admissions office:* Minimum SAT scores of 410 verbal and 430 math (composite ACT score of 20), rank in top half of secondary school class, and minimum 2.0 GPA recommended. *Academic units recommended:* 4 English, 3 Math, 3 Science, 2 Social Studies, 2 Foreign Language.

Insight

Sandra Speed, dean of admission and financial aid, has important information for anyone thinking about coming to Schreiner. "If you want to fall through the cracks, do not come here," she warns. "If you don't come to class, you will be missed, and someone will try to help you resolve the problem before it becomes a bigger issue.

The faculty at Schreiner is very involved with each student's success. They have a real personal commitment to students and will even give you their home phone numbers. At Schreiner, counseling is consistent and ongoing." The school has a faith-based mission and a strong emphasis on extracurricular work within the community, school and church.

A student, Jay Govan III, took time to explain why he chose Schreiner University. "What led me to Schreiner was the ratio of students to professors," he explains. "I knew that would be a great benefit to me because if I were to struggle, the teachers always have their doors open to help students." He says the strong tutoring offered at Schreiner also led him to the school.

Govan's freshman and sophomore years of high school were at Trinity Christian Academy, a very small school, and he believes that is where he learned to be responsible in getting his work done on time. His junior and senior years were at Saint Anthony's Catholic High School, an all-boys school. He admits he was not looking forward to attending the school at first, but he says, "After a couple of weeks, things started going well. The good thing about an all-boys school is that you don't have to try to impress anyone but just worry about getting your studies done. While I was a senior there, my grades were good enough to allow me to also take a couple of college courses at the University of the Incarnate Word."

During his first year at Schreiner, Govan's GPA dropped from 3.0 to 2.5, an issue he is keenly aware of. "I have been working hard to continue to increase it to where it was in high school," he says. "The teachers are always persuading me to give it all I have and not hold anything back."

Govan has suggestions for students thinking about attending Schreiner. "This is a great school to come to. Be focused on your books and you won't get sidetracked like if you went to a college in a big city. I would also encourage students to get all the education you can get now because after school is over that's it, it's time to go out and look for a job, and no more thinking about skipping or being late."

He has learned some important things at college already. "You have to make goals for yourself and make studying and class your number one priority," he advises.

How to Pay for College

To apply for financial aid, students should submit the following: Free Application for Federal Student Aid (FAFSA) · TASFA. Schreiner University participates in the Federal Work Study program. *Need-based aid programs include:* scholarships and grants · general need-based awards · Federal Pell grants · state scholarships and grants · college-based scholarships and grants · private scholarships and grants. *Non-Need-based aid programs include:* scholarships and grants · state scholarships and grants · creative arts and performance awards · special achievements and activities awards · special characteristics awards.

SCHREINER UNIVERSITY

Highlights

Admissions
Applicants: 1,028
Accepted: 607
Acceptance rate: 59.0%
Average GPA: 3.5
ACT range: 18-24
SAT Math range: 440-550
SAT Reading range: 440-553
SAT Writing range: 430-540
Top 10% of class: 11%
Top 25% of class: 36%
Top 50% of class: 74%

Deadlines
Early Action: No
Early Decision: No
Regular Action: Rolling admissions
Common Application: Accepted

Financial Aid
In-state tuition: $18,131
Out-of-state tuition: $18,131
Room: -
Board: -
Books: -
Freshmen receiving need-based aid: 71%
Undergrads receiving need-based aid: 75%
Avg. % of need met by financial aid: 71%
Avg. aid package (freshmen): $12,376
Avg. aid package (undergrads): $12,944
Freshmen receiving merit-based aid: 24%
Undergrads receiving merit-based aid: 21%
Avg. student debt upon graduation: $7,562

Prominent Alumni
Dr. Richard Marrs, reproductive services; Sam Junkin, retired president of Schreiner University.

School Spirit
Mascot: Mountaineers
Colors: Maroon and white

SETON HILL UNIVERSITY

Seton Hill Drive, Greensburg, PA 15601
Admissions: 800-826-6234 · Financial Aid: 724-838-4293
Email: admit@setonhill.edu · Website: http://www.setonhill.edu

From the College

"Seton Hill University, chartered in 1918, is a liberal arts university in Greensburg, Pennsylvania, with more than 30 undergraduate programs and eight graduate programs, including an MBA. Seton Hill University brings the world to its students through lecturers and renowned centers, including the National Catholic Center for Holocaust Education and E-Magnify, the center for women entrepreneurs. Recognized three times by Entrepreneur magazine as one of the nation's Top 100 Entrepreneurial Universities, Seton Hill has also been named one of the Best in the Northeast by the Princeton Review and one of Pennsylvania's Top 100 Businesses by Pennsylvania Business Central."

Campus Setting

Located atop 200 acres of tree-lined hills, Seton Hill University offers an inspirational setting for a life-changing education. Founded by the Sisters of Charity and chartered in 1918, Seton Hill started out as a Catholic, liberal arts college for women. It has since grown into a co-educational university that embraces students of all faiths. Despite the years and despite the changes, we've continued to follow a sole mission - to educate students to think and act critically, creatively and ethically as productive members of society.. A four-year private institution, Seton Hill University has an enrollment of 2,093 students. Seton Hill University has been co-ed since 1997. The school is also affiliated with the Roman Catholic Church. In addition to a large, well-stocked library, the campus facilities include: art gallery · theatre. Seton Hill University provides on-campus housing with 8 units that can accommodate 750 students. Housing options: co-ed dorms · women's dorms · men's dorms. Recreation and sports facilities include: baseball · football · soccer and softball fields · equestrian facilities · gymnasium · field house · tennis courts · fitness center · weight room.

Student Life and Activities

With 67 percent of students living on campus, there are plenty of social activities. There is always something to do, reports the editor of the student newspaper. Hot spots for students include the Cove in Sullivan Hall, Griffin's Lounge, Rialto, Main Bowling, and Westmoreland Mall. Popular campus events include Midnight Breakfast, Step Afrika, Christmas on the Hill, Cosmic Bowling, Tron System Laser Tag, Comedian performances, Foam Dance and Halloween Dance. Seton Hill University has 40 official student organizations. Feminist collective, S.U.C.C.E.S.S., African-American students organization, International Student Organization, Respect Life Club, Student Education Association, Honors program and campus ministry have widespread influence on student life. For those interested in sports, there are intramural teams such as: basketball · flag football · volleyball. Seton Hill University is a member of the NCAA (Division II).

Academics and Learning Environment

For the B student, the learning environment of a college is just as important as the quality of its academic program. Seton Hill University has 75 full-time and 122 part-time faculty members, offering a student-to-faculty ratio of 16:1. The most common course size is 10 to 19 students. Seton Hill University offers 50 majors with the most popular being physician assistant and family/consumer science and least popular being philosophy, physics and religious studies/theology. The school has a general core requirement as well as a religion requirement. Cooperative education is not offered. All first-year students must maintain a 2.0 GPA or higher to avoid academic probation, and a minimum overall GPA of 2.0 is required to graduate. Other special academic programs that would appeal to a B student: self-designed majors · pass/fail grading option · independent study · double majors · dual degrees · accelerated study · honors program · internships · weekend college · distance learning.

B Student Support and Success

Seton Hill's Academic Support program provides assistance to students through a tutoring center, which offers individual and small group tutoring. There is a Writing Center, which helps with prewriting skills, organizing, drafting, revising and editing. The college also offers an Opportunity Program, which is a summer experience designed to help students get a head start by living on campus, participating in workshops and mastering the skills they will need for college work. The students who qualify for this program either have low SAT or ACT scores, a low high school GPA, non-academic courses in high school, or grades that simply don't truly reflect the student's potential. In addition to these services, Seton Hill also offers Academic Counseling on study skills such as taking notes, reading college textbooks, and taking tests. Common topics include time management, test anxiety, critical thinking and identifying personal learning styles.

Seton Hill University provides a variety of support programs including dedicated guidance for: academic · career · personal · psychological · minority students · veterans · non-traditional students · religious. The average freshman year GPA is 2.7, and 73 percent of freshmen students return for their sophomore year. What do students do after college? While many enter the work force, approximately 23 percent pursue a graduate degree immediately after graduation. Among students who enter the work force, approximately 57 percent enter a field related to their major within six months of graduation, while 67 percent enter a related career within two years of graduation. Companies that most frequently hire graduates from Seton Hill University include: Allegheny Energy Systems · Sony · University of Pittsburgh · Mine Safety Applications · Excela Westmoreland Health Care System · UPS · Citizen's Bank · YWCA · Family Behavioral Resources.

Support for Students with Learning Disabilities

Students with learning disabilities may take advantage of specific support programs offered by Seton Hill University. If necessary, the college will grant additional time to students with learning disabilities to complete their degree. Also, a lightened course load may be granted to LD students. Students with learning disabilities will find the following programs at Seton Hill University extremely useful: tutors · testing accommodations · untimed tests · extended time for tests · take-home exam · oral tests · readers · note-taking services · reading machines · tape recorders · texts on tape · videotaped classes · early syllabus · priority registration. Individual or small group tutorials are also available in: time management · organizational skills · learning strategies · specific subject areas ·

SETON HILL UNIVERSITY

Highlights

Seton Hill University
Greensburg PA (Pop. 16,000)
Location: Large town
Website: http://www.setonhill.edu

Students
Total enrollment: 2,093
Undergrads: 609
Freshmen: 454
Part-time students: 18%
From out-of-state: 25%
Male/Female: 37%/63%
Live on-campus: 67%
Off-campus employment rating: Good
Caucasian: 83%
African American: 8%
Hispanic: 1%
Asian or Pacific Islander: 1%
Native American: 0%
International: 2%

Academics
Student/faculty ratio: 16:1
Class size 9 or fewer: 20%
Class size 10-29: 66%
Class size 30-49: 12%
Class size 50-99: 2%
Class size 100 or more: -
Returning freshmen: 73%
Six-year graduation rate: 50%

Most Popular Fields of Study
Business, Finance, Sales and Marketing
Protective Services, Criminal Justice and
    Public Administration
Visual and Performing Arts
English and Literature
Philosophy, Religion and Theology
Computer and Information Sciences
Mathematics
Health Professions, Medicine and Related Sciences
Family and Consumer Sciences, Nutrition
    and Home Economics

SETON HILL UNIVERSITY

Admissions

Applicants: 1,701
Accepted: 1,079
Acceptance rate: 63.4%
Average GPA: 3.3
ACT range: Not reported
SAT Math range: 440-570
SAT Reading range: 440-560
SAT Writing range: Not reported
Top 10% of class: 24%
Top 25% of class: 51%
Top 50% of class: 75%

Deadlines

Early Action: No
Early Decision: No
Regular Action: May 1 (priority)
August 15 (final)
Common Application: Accepted

Financial Aid

In-state tuition: $25,802
Out-of-state tuition: $25,802
Room: -
Board: -
Books: $1,000
Freshmen receiving need-based aid: 83%
Undergrads receiving need-based aid:
    84%
Avg. % of need met by financial aid: 77%
Avg. aid package (freshmen): $22,854
Avg. aid package (undergrads): $21,103
Freshmen receiving merit-based aid: 16%
Undergrads receiving merit-based aid:
    13%
Avg. student debt upon graduation:
    $27,120

Prominent Alumni

Dr. Patricia Acquaviva-Grabow, CEO
and medical director at Denver General
Hospital; Rear Admiral Veronica Froman,
U.S. Navy.

School Spirit

Mascot: Griffins
Colors: Crimson and gold

writing labs · study skills. An advisor/advocate from the Office of Disability Services is available to students.

How to Get Admitted

For admissions decisions, non-academic factors considered: interview · extracurricular activities · special talents, interests, abilities · character/personal qualities · volunteer work · work experience · state of residency · alumni relationship. A high school diploma is required, although a GED is also accepted for admissions consideration. SAT or ACT test scores are recommended but not required. *Academic units recommended:* 2 Foreign Language.

How to Pay for College

To apply for financial aid, students should submit the following: Free Application for Federal Student Aid (FAFSA) · institution's own financial aid forms · state aid form. Seton Hill University participates in the Federal Work Study program. *Need-based aid programs include:* scholarships and grants · general need-based awards · Federal Pell grants · state scholarships and grants · college-based scholarships and grants · private scholarships and grants. *Non-Need-based aid programs include:* scholarships and grants · state scholarships and grants · creative arts and performance awards · athletic scholarships.

SHAW UNIVERSITY

118 East South Street, Raleigh, NC 27601
Admissions: 800-214-6683 · Financial Aid: 800-475-6190
Email: admissions@shawu.edu
Website: http://www.shawuniversity.edu

Campus Setting

Shaw, founded in 1865, is a private, church-affiliated, liberal arts university and is the oldest historically black college in the South. Its 30-acre campus is located in downtown Raleigh. A four-year institution, Shaw University has 2,702 students. The school is also affiliated with the Baptist Church. The school also has a library with 156,623 books. Shaw University provides on-campus housing with 1,220 units that can accommodate 2,440 students. Housing options: women's dorms · men's dorms.

Student Life and Activities

Most students (62 percent) live off campus, which does impact the on-campus social scene. Nevertheless, like any college, students find time to create their own recreational outlets. Shaw University has a number of official student organizations. The most popular are: Bands · choir · choral society · music ensembles · Shaw Players · Unique Horizon Dancers · debating · Order of Eastern Star · academic groups. Shaw University is a member of the Central Intercollegiate Athletic Association (Division II).

Academics and Learning Environment

For the B student, the learning environment of a college is just as important as the quality of its academic program. Shaw University has 114 full-time and 137 part-time faculty members, offering a student-to-faculty ratio of 15:1. The most common course size is 2 to 9 students. Shaw University offers 41 majors with the most popular being business management, criminal justice and sociology and least popular being environmental science and mathematics. The school has a general core requirement. Cooperative education is not offered. All first-year students must maintain a 1.5 GPA or higher to avoid academic probation. Other special academic programs that would appeal to a B student: self-designed majors · independent study · double majors · dual degrees · accelerated study · honors program · weekend college · distance learning.

B Student Support and Success

Shaw's Freshman Year Program is focused on providing the tools students need to reach their academic goals. It features a series of activities and events that help ease the transition as students become more familiar with college life. Every student must take this program as part of graduation requirements. It includes a number of classes, including a cultural and spiritual enrichment seminar.

Note that the college has a dress code, and community worship is mandatory, as is attendance to college events such as Homecoming, Senior Appreciation Day and University Awards Day.

A new, free program called Freshmen Academy earns credit

Highlights

Shaw University
Raleigh, NC
Location: Medium city
Website: http://www.shawuniversity.edu

Students
Total enrollment: 2,702
Undergrads: 890
Freshmen: 556
Part-time students: 10%
From out-of-state: 43%
Male/Female: 36%/64%
Live on-campus: Not reported
In fraternities: 4%
In sororities: 5%
Off-campus employment rating: Excellent
Caucasian: 2%
African American: 87%
Hispanic: 0%
Native American: 0%
International: 1%

Academics
Student/faculty ratio: 15:1
Class size 9 or fewer: 46%
Class size 10-29: 43%
Class size 30-49: 8%
Class size 50-99: 3%
Class size 100 or more: -
Returning freshmen: 58%
Six-year graduation rate: 28%

Most Popular Fields of Study
Business, Finance, Sales and Marketing
Protective Services, Criminal Justice and Public Administration
Psychology
English and Literature
Philosophy, Religion and Theology
Computer and Information Sciences
Parks, Recreation and Fitness
Health Professions, Medicine and Related Sciences
Liberal Arts, Humanities and General Studies
Communications, Journalism, Advertising and Comm. Technologies

SHAW UNIVERSITY

Highlights

Admissions
Applicants: 5,565
Accepted: 2,034
Acceptance rate: 36.5%
Average GPA: 2.5
ACT range: 13-17
SAT Math range: 320-420
SAT Reading range: 320-410
SAT Writing range: 320-410
Top 10% of class: 4%
Top 25% of class: 10%
Top 50% of class: 31%

Deadlines
Early Action: No
Early Decision: No
Regular Action: July 30 (final)
Common Application: Accepted

Financial Aid
In-state tuition: $9,336
Out-of-state tuition: $9,336
Room: $1,700
Board: $1,900
Books: -
Freshmen receiving need-based aid: 79%
Undergrads receiving need-based aid:
    88%
Avg. % of need met by financial aid: 58%
Avg. aid package (freshmen): $8,466
Avg. aid package (undergrads): $8,795
Freshmen receiving merit-based aid: 8%
Undergrads receiving merit-based aid:
    6%
Avg. student debt upon graduation:
    $22,308

School Spirit
Mascot: Bears
Colors: Maroon and white

hours. It is an intense summer academic program, and participants receive room, board, books and supplies. They attend workshops, seminars and presentations and go on field trips.

Shaw University provides a variety of support programs including dedicated guidance for: academic · career · personal · psychological · minority students · military · veterans · non-traditional students · family planning · religious. The average freshman year GPA is 2.4, and 58 percent of freshmen students return for their sophomore year.

Support for Students with Learning Disabilities

Students with learning disabilities may take advantage of specific support programs offered by Shaw University. If necessary, the college will grant additional time to students with learning disabilities to complete their degree. Also, a lightened course load may be granted to LD students. Students with learning disabilities will find the following programs at Shaw University extremely useful: tutors · untimed tests · extended time for tests · take-home exam · oral tests · note-taking services · tape recorders · diagnostic testing service · priority registration. Individual or small group tutorials are also available in: time management · organizational skills · learning strategies · specific subject areas · writing labs · math labs · study skills. An advisor/advocate from the LD program is available to students. This member also sits on the admissions committee.

How to Get Admitted

For admissions decisions, non-academic factors considered: extracurricular activities · character/personal qualities · geographical location · alumni relationship. A high school diploma is required, although a GED is also accepted for admissions consideration. SAT or ACT test scores are required of all applicants. *According to the admissions office:* Minimum 2.0 GPA required.

How to Pay for College

To apply for financial aid, students should submit the following: Free Application for Federal Student Aid (FAFSA) · institution's own financial aid forms · state aid form. Shaw University participates in the Federal Work Study program. *Need-based aid programs include:* scholarships and grants · general need-based awards · Federal Pell grants · state scholarships and grants · college-based scholarships and grants · private scholarships and grants · United Negro College Fund. *Non-Need-based aid programs include:* scholarships and grants · state scholarships and grants · creative arts and performance awards · athletic scholarships · ROTC scholarships.

SHENANDOAH UNIVERSITY

1460 University Drive, Winchester, VA 22601
Admissions: 800-432-2266 · Financial Aid: 800-432-2266
Email: admit@su.edu · Website: http://www.su.edu

From the College

"The main campus of the university is adjacent to Interstate 81 in Winchester, Virginia in the historic Shenandoah Valley of Virginia. The university's physical plant consists of 42 buildings, which includes residence halls, two leased facilities on the campus of the Winchester Medical Center and another leased facility on the Northern Virginia campus in Leesburg, Virginia, approximately 45 miles east of Winchester.

"Shenandoah University is comprised of six academic schools or colleges: (1) the School of Health Professions offering associate, baccalaureate and master's degrees, and post-master's certificates; (2) the Harry F. Byrd Jr., School of Business offering certificate programs and baccalaureate and master's degrees; (3) the College of Arts and Sciences offering baccalaureate degrees; (4) Shenandoah Conservatory offering certificate programs, baccalaureate, master's and doctoral degrees; (5) the Bernard J. Dunn School of Pharmacy offering doctoral degrees and (6) the newly established School of Education and Human Development offering certificates, master's and doctoral degrees. An impressive library system supports all academic programs."

Campus Setting

Shenandoah is a private, church-affiliated, comprehensive university. It was founded in 1875 and gained university status in 1991. Its 125-acre campus is located in Winchester, 72 miles from Washington, DC. A four-year institution, Shenandoah University has an enrollment of 3,511 students. The school is also affiliated with the United Methodist Church. The school has a library with 13,239 books. Shenandoah University provides on-campus housing with 451 units that can accommodate 805 students. Housing options: co-ed dorms · special housing for disabled students · special housing for International students. Recreation and sports facilities include: baseball · lacrosse · soccer and softball fields · golf and indoor tennis club · gymnasium · weight room.

Student Life and Activities

Most students (76 percent) live off campus, which does impact the on-campus social scene. Nevertheless, like any college, students find time to create their own recreational outlets. Students gather in the Shenandoah University Student Center. Popular campus events include the Sun Block Party, International Days, Home Coming, Family Weekend and Relay for Life. Shenandoah University has 50 official student organizations. Student theater/music groups and athletes are influential in student life. For those interested in sports, there are intramural teams such as: basketball · indoor soccer · indoor volleyball · sand volleyball · soccer · table tennis. Shenandoah University is a member of the USA South Athletic Conference (Division III), Pennsylvania Athletic Conference (Division III).

Academics and Learning Environment

For the B student, the learning environment of a college is just as important as the quality of its academic program. Shenandoah University has 200 full-time and 184 part-time faculty members, offering a student-to-faculty ratio of 8:1. The most common course size is 2 to 9 students. Shenandoah University offers 66 majors with the most popular being nursing, business administration and university studies and least popular being religion, composition and English. The school has a general

SHENANDOAH UNIVERSITY

Shenandoah University
Winchester, VA (Pop. 23,585)
Location: Large town
Website: http://www.su.edu

Students
Total enrollment: 3,511
Undergrads: 757
Freshmen: 697
Part-time students: 8%
From out-of-state: 43%
Male/Female: 44%/56%
Live on-campus: 24%
In fraternities: 9%
In sororities: 1%
Off-campus employment rating: Good
Caucasian: 47%
African American: 11%
Hispanic: 2%
Asian or Pacific Islander: 2%
Native American: 0%
International: 3%

Academics
Student/faculty ratio: 8:1
Class size 9 or fewer: 45%
Class size 10-29: 50%
Class size 30-49: 4%
Class size 50-99: -
Class size 100 or more: -
Returning freshmen: 70%
Six-year graduation rate: 49%

Most Popular Fields of Study
Biological and Life Sciences
Protective Services, Criminal Justice and
    Public Administration
Psychology
Visual and Performing Arts
Philosophy, Religion and Theology
Mathematics
Health Professions, Medicine and Re-
    lated Sciences
Liberal Arts, Humanities and General
    Studies
Foreign Languages, Literature and Lin-
    guistics

core requirement as well as a religion requirement Cooperative education is not offered. All first-year students must maintain a 1.0 GPA or higher to avoid academic probation, and a minimum overall GPA of 2.0 is required to graduate. Other special academic programs that would appeal to a B student: self-designed majors · independent study · double majors · dual degrees · accelerated study · honors program · internships · weekend college · distance learning certificate programs.

B Student Support and Success

Known as the "Yes, You Can" University, Shenandoah offers the Academic Enrichment Center whose mission is "to enhance student success, student learning and to help students become more effective and successful learners." It offers peer tutoring programs, study skills development course and workshops, services for students with disabilities and academic counseling. The staff works one on one with students and discusses topics such as the productive use of study time, goal setting for improved academic success, reading and note taking strategies, overcoming test taking challenges and any other academic skill students want to develop.

Shenandoah University provides a variety of support programs including dedicated guidance for: academic · career · personal · psychological · minority students · military · veterans · non-traditional students · family planning · religious. Recognizing that some students may need extra preparation, Shenandoah University offers remedial and refresher courses in: reading · writing · math · study skills. Annually, 70 percent of freshmen students return for their sophomore year. What do students do after college? While many enter the work force, approximately 20 percent pursue a graduate degree immediately after graduation. Among students who enter the work force, approximately 70 percent enter a field related to their major within six months of graduation. Companies that most frequently hire graduates from Shenandoah University include: Bank of America · BB&T Banks · Broadway shows · clinics · FedEx · hospitals · Metropolitan Opera · MSNBC · MTV · private medical practices · professional sports organizations · public and private schools · Shockey.

Support for Students with Learning Disabilities

Students with learning disabilities may take advantage of specific support programs offered by Shenandoah University. If necessary, the college will grant additional time to students with learning disabilities to complete their degree. Also, a lightened course load may be granted to LD students. Students with learning disabilities will find the following programs at Shenandoah University extremely useful: remedial math · tutors · learning center · testing accommodations · extended time for tests · take-home exam · oral tests · exam on tape or computer · readers · typist/scribe · note-taking services · reading machines · tape recorders · texts on tape · early syllabus · priority registration · waiver of math degree requirement. Individual or small group tutorials are also available in: time management · organizational skills · learning strategies · writing labs · study skills. An advisor/advocate from the Academic Success Services is available to students.

How to Get Admitted

For admissions decisions, non-academic factors considered: extracurricular activities · special talents, interests, abilities · volunteer work · work experience · state of residency. A high school diploma is required, although a GED is also accepted for admissions consideration. SAT or ACT test scores are required of all applicants. *According to the admissions office:* Minimum 2.5 GPA recommended. *Academic units recommended:* 4 Math, 4 Science, 4 Social Studies, 3 Foreign Language.

How to Pay for College

To apply for financial aid, students should submit the following: Free Application for Federal Student Aid (FAFSA) · state aid form · Virginia United Methodist Scholarship Application. Shenandoah University participates in the Federal Work Study program. *Need-based aid programs include:* scholarships and grants · general need-based awards · Federal Pell grants · state scholarships and grants · college-based scholarships and grants · private scholarships and grants · Federal Nursing scholarships. *Non-Need-based aid programs include:* scholarships and grants · general need-based awards · state scholarships and grants.

SHENANDOAH UNIVERSITY

Highlights

Admissions
Applicants: 1,279
Accepted: 1,109
Acceptance rate: 86.7%
Average GPA: 3.3
ACT range: 18-23
SAT Math range: 440-570
SAT Reading range: 440-570
SAT Writing range: 770-560
Top 10% of class: 14%
Top 25% of class: 40%
Top 50% of class: 73%

Deadlines
Early Action: No
Early Decision: No
Regular Action: March 1 (priority)
August 29 (final)
Common Application: Accepted

Financial Aid
In-state tuition: $23,850
Out-of-state tuition: $23,850
Room: -
Board: -
Books: $1,000
Freshmen receiving need-based aid: 85%
Undergrads receiving need-based aid: 67%
Avg. % of need met by financial aid: 92%
Avg. aid package (freshmen): $15,270
Avg. aid package (undergrads): $15,545
Freshmen receiving merit-based aid: 12%
Undergrads receiving merit-based aid: 8%
Avg. student debt upon graduation: $20,000

Prominent Alumni
Carl Tanner, world-renowned tenor; J. Robert Spencer, Broadway actor; Dr. Daniel Trzychodzyn, pharmacist; Thomson MicroMedex.

School Spirit
Mascot: Hornets
Colors: Navy, red and white
Song: *Shenandoah*

401

SHEPHERD UNIVERSITY

P.O. Box 5000, Shepherdstown, WV 25443-5000
Admissions: 800-344-5231 · Financial Aid: 800-344-5231, extension 5470
Email: admissions@shepherd.edu · Website: http://www.shepherd.edu

From the College

"Shepherd University is a public institution within the West Virginia system of higher education. Shepherd offers bachelor's and master's degrees in the liberal arts, business administration, teacher education, social and natural sciences and other career-oriented areas. Shepherd is dedicated to expanding its intellectual and cultural resources with the assistance of technological advances and its location 70 miles from the Baltimore/Washington metropolitan area. At the same time, the residential setting of the university creates an environment in which students are able to work closely with faculty, staff, administrators and industry."

Campus Setting

Shepherd University, founded in 1871, offers programs offered through the Schools of Arts and Humanities, Business and Social Sciences, Education and Professional Studies and Natural Science and Mathematics. Its 320-acre campus is located in Shepherdstown. A four-year institution, Shepherd University has an enrollment of 4,185 students. In addition to a large, well-stocked library, the campus also has a center for the study of the Civil War and legislature. Shepherd University provides on-campus housing with 14 units that can accommodate 1,308 students. Housing options: co-ed dorms · single-student apartments. Recreation and sports facilities include: athletic center · baseball · practice and softball fields · stadium · tennis courts.

Student Life and Activities

Most students (71 percent) live off campus, which does impact the on-campus social scene. Nevertheless, like any college, students find time to create their own recreational outlets. Popular campus events include ShepFest, Midnight Breakfast and Relay for Life. Shepherd University has 58 official student organizations. The most popular are: Allies · Interclass Council · Liberal Women's Association · Music Educators National Conference · Progressive Action Committee · Dance Team · Education Student Association · Environmental Association · Rude Mechanicals Players · Student Global Aids Council · Social Work Association · Sociology Club · Ram Marching Band · Student Life Council · Program Board · Debate and Forensics · 4-H. For those interested in sports, there are intramural teams such as: lacrosse. Shepherd University is a member of the West Virginia Intercollegiate Athletic Conference (Division II, NCAA).

Academics and Learning Environment

For the B student, the learning environment of a college is just as important as the quality of its academic program. Shepherd University has 119 full-time and 208 part-time faculty members, offering a student-to-faculty ratio of 18:1. The most common course size is 20 to 29 students. Shepherd University offers 29 majors with the most popular being Regents bachelor of arts, business administration and recreation and leisure studies and least popular being mathematics, music and Spanish. The school has a general core requirement. Cooperative education is available. All first-year students must maintain a 2.0 GPA or higher to avoid academic probation, and a minimum overall GPA of 2.0 is required to graduate. Other special academic programs that would appeal to a B student: pass/fail grading option · independent study · double majors · dual degrees · honors program · internships · distance learning.

B Student Support and Success

Shepherd has quite a bit to offer the B student. First, it has "stretch" model courses, i.e. courses that can be stretched to two semesters. The Academic Support Center offers tutoring and academic counseling and the Writing Center provides help for papers and writing assignments.

"We welcome students without straight A's. The mean incoming GPA for freshmen is 3.07. The mean freshman SAT composite is 1024, and the mean freshman ACT composite is 21.72. SU's admission requirements are 2.0 GPA and 920 SAT or 19 ACT for freshmen. Applicants with a B average are successful at Shepherd University if they are successful on the SAT or ACT.

Tutoring can aid students in their weaker skills. SU's philosophy toward B students and C students is that if they have completed a rigorous high school program, scored adequately on the ACT or SAT and have a good work ethic, the student will be successful here. We offer a good support system.

"Because of the size of the student body at Shepherd, students are known individually by faculty and staff. Shepherd is a very inclusive school allowing students to be accepted as themselves."
Shepherd University provides a variety of support programs including dedicated guidance for: academic · career · personal · psychological · minority students · military · veterans · non-traditional students · family planning. Recognizing that some students may need extra preparation, Shepherd University offers remedial and refresher courses in: reading · writing · math · study skills. Other remedial services include critical thinking. The average freshman year GPA is 2.5, and 65 percent of freshmen students return for their sophomore year. What do students do after college? While many enter the work force, approximately 16 percent pursue a graduate degree immediately after graduation. Among students who enter the work force, approximately 79 percent enter a field related to their major within six months of graduation. Companies that most frequently hire graduates from Shepherd University include: Businesses · federal agencies · hospitals · public schools.

Support for Students with Learning Disabilities

Students with learning disabilities may take advantage of specific support programs offered by Shepherd University. Also, a lightened course load may be granted to LD students. Students with learning disabilities will find the following programs at Shepherd University extremely useful: remedial math · remedial English · tutors · learning center · extended time for tests · take-home exam · readers · typist/scribe · note-taking services · tape recorders · texts on tape · videotaped classes · priority registration · waiver of math degree requirement · waiver of foreign language degree requirement. Individual or small group tutorials are also available in: time management · organizational skills · learning strategies · writing labs · math labs · study skills. An advisor/advocate from the Disability Support Services is available to students.

How to Get Admitted

For admissions decisions, non-academic factors considered: interview · extracurricular activities · special talents, interests, abilities · char-

SHEPHERD UNIVERSITY

Highlights

Shepherd University
Shepherdstown, WV (Pop. 1,287)
Location: Rural
Website: http://www.shepherd.edu

Students
Total enrollment: 4,185
Undergrads: 1,739
Freshmen: 910
Part-time students: 22%
From out-of-state: 42%
Male/Female: 43%/57%
Live on-campus: 29%
In fraternities: 3%
In sororities: 4%
Off-campus employment rating: Good
Caucasian: 86%
African American: 6%
Hispanic: 2%
Asian or Pacific Islander: 2%
Native American: 1%
International: 1%

Academics
Student/faculty ratio: 18:1
Class size 9 or fewer: 11%
Class size 10-29: 68%
Class size 30-49: 20%
Class size 50-99: 1%
Class size 100 or more: -
Returning freshmen: 65%
Six-year graduation rate: 34%

Most Popular Fields of Study
Business, Finance, Sales and Marketing
Protective Services, Criminal Justice and
    Public Administration
Visual and Performing Arts
Family and Consumer Sciences, Nutrition
    and Home Economics
Computer and Information Sciences
Communications, Journalism, Advertising
    and Comm. Technologies
Liberal Arts, Humanities and General
    Studies
English and Literature
Parks, Recreation and Fitness
Health Professions, Medicine and Re-
    lated Sciences

403

College Profiles

SHEPHERD UNIVERSITY

Highlights

Admissions
Applicants: 1,701
Accepted: 1,599
Acceptance rate: 94.0%
Average GPA: 3.1
ACT range: 19-24
SAT Math range: 450-550
SAT Reading range: 460-560
SAT Writing range: Not reported

Deadlines
Early Action: November 15
Early Decision: No
Regular Action: Common Application:
   Accepted

Financial Aid
In-state tuition: $4,898
Out-of-state tuition: $12,812
Room: $4,024
Board: $3,198
Books: $1,100
Freshmen receiving need-based aid: 50%
Undergrads receiving need-based aid:
   49%
Avg. % of need met by financial aid: 85%
Avg. aid package (freshmen): $9,828
Avg. aid package (undergrads): $10,628
Freshmen receiving merit-based aid: 25%
Undergrads receiving merit-based aid:
   22%
Avg. student debt upon graduation:
   $18,271

Prominent Alumni
Dr. Stanley Ikenberry, president emeritus,
University of Illinois; Linda Riegle, chief
judge, U.S. Bankruptcy Court, Nevada.

School Spirit
Mascot: Rams
Colors: Blue and gold

acter/personal qualities · volunteer work · work experience · state of residency. A high school diploma is required, although a GED is also accepted for admissions consideration. SAT or ACT test scores are required of all applicants. *According to the admissions office:* Minimum composite ACT score of 19 (combined SAT Reasoning score of 910) and minimum grade average of B required.

How to Pay for College

To apply for financial aid, students should submit the following: Free Application for Federal Student Aid (FAFSA) · state aid form. Shepherd University participates in the Federal Work Study program. *Need-based aid programs include:* scholarships and grants · general need-based awards · Federal Pell grants · state scholarships and grants · college-based scholarships and grants · private scholarships and grants. *Non-Need-based aid programs include:* scholarships and grants · general need-based awards · state scholarships and grants · creative arts and performance awards · special achievements and activities awards · athletic scholarships.

SIMMONS COLLEGE

300 The Fenway, Boston, MA 02115
Admissions: 800-345-8468 · Financial Aid: 617-521-2001
Email: ugadm@simmons.edu
Website: http://www.simmons.edu

From the College

"Simmons College was founded in 1899, and is a small university in the heart of Boston that upholds an educational "contract" with students and helps them achieve successful careers. Simmons honors this contract by delivering a strong education and professional preparation in a welcoming, collaborative environment. Students value the small classes, exceptional internship opportunities and individual attention from faculty who are experts and practitioners. Simmons offers more than 40 majors and programs for undergraduate women, the nation's only MBA designed for women and co-ed graduate programs in health studies, education, communications management, liberal arts, social work and library and information science."

Campus Setting

Simmons is a private undergraduate college for women. Its 12-acre campus includes nine Georgian-style dormitories. The graduate programs are open to men and women. Simmons College has an enrollment of 4,933 students. In addition to a large, well-stocked library, the campus facilities include: art gallery · technology resource center. Simmons College provides on-campus housing that can accommodate 1,139 students. Housing options: women's dorms · special housing for disabled students. Recreation and sports facilities include: basketball · racquetball · squash and volleyball courts · dance studio · fitness rooms · indoor running area · rowing · swimming pool · sauna.

Student Life and Activities

With 55 percent of students living on campus, there are plenty of social activities. Popular campus events include May Day Celebration, Honors Convocation, Culture Shock and Simmons Cup. Simmons College has 80 official student organizations. The most popular are: music · theatre · political · service and special-interest groups. Simmons College is a member of the Great Northeast Athletic Conference (Division III), North Atlantic Conference (Division III).

Academics and Learning Environment

For the B student, the learning environment of a college is just as important as the quality of its academic program. Simmons College has 250 full-time and 227 part-time faculty members, offering a student-to-faculty ratio of 13:1. The most common course size is 10 to 19 students. Simmons College offers 70 majors with the most popular being nursing, communications and psychology and least popular being East Asian studies, environmental science and retail management. The school has a general core requirement. Coopera-

Simmons College
Boston, MA (Pop. 600,000)
Location: Major city
Website: http://www.simmons.edu

Students
Total enrollment: 4,933
Undergrads: 2,060
Freshmen: 391
Part-time students: 10%
From out-of-state: 42%
Male/Female: 0%/100%
Live on-campus: 55%
Off-campus employment rating: Good

Academics
Student/faculty ratio: 13:1
Class size 9 or fewer: 15%
Class size 10-29: 73%
Class size 30-49: 8%
Class size 50-99: 5%
Class size 100 or more: -
Returning freshmen: 83%
Six-year graduation rate: 73%

Most Popular Fields of Study
Business, Finance, Sales and Marketing
Visual and Performing Arts
English and Literature
Philosophy, Religion and Theology
Computer and Information Sciences
Mathematics
Physical Sciences, Chemistry, Physics
 and Astronomy
Interdisciplinary Studies
Health Professions, Medicine and Related Sciences

Admissions
Applicants: 3,222
Accepted: 1,756
Acceptance rate: 54.5%
placed on wait list: 116
Average GPA: 3.2
ACT range: 22-26
SAT Math range: 500-590
SAT Reading range: 510-600
SAT Writing range: 520-620
Top 10% of class: 20%
Top 25% of class: 55%
Top 50% of class: 91%

405

College Profiles

SIMMONS COLLEGE

Highlights

Deadlines
Early Action: December 1
Early Decision: No
Regular Action: February 1 (priority)
February 1 (final)
Common Application: Accepted

Financial Aid
In-state tuition: $29,120
Out-of-state tuition: $29,120
Room: -
Board: -
Books: $1,120
Freshmen receiving need-based aid: 71%
Undergrads receiving need-based aid: 67%
Avg. % of need met by financial aid: 64%
Avg. aid package (freshmen): $18,344
Avg. aid package (undergrads): $19,758
Freshmen receiving merit-based aid: 22%
Undergrads receiving merit-based aid: 20%
Avg. student debt upon graduation: $42,174

Prominent Alumni
Gwen Ifill, journalist; Allyson Y. Schwartz, Congresswoman; Denise DiNovi, film producer.

School Spirit
Mascot: Sharks

tive education is not offered. All first-year students must maintain a 1.67 GPA or higher to avoid academic probation, and a minimum overall GPA of 1.7 is required to graduate. Other special academic programs that would appeal to a B student: self-designed majors · pass/fail grading option · independent study · double majors · dual degrees · accelerated study · honors program · internships.

B Student Support and Success

Simmons' Academic Support Center is focused on providing high-quality assistance to help students succeed academically. According to the college, its goal is to "help students become independent learners and to encourage them to take an active part in their educational and intellectual pursuits." The center achieves this through various methods. Academic Advising and Counseling assigns advisors to students who are having academic struggles. Placement examinations are given that provide results for math, language and chemistry levels. Services for Students with Disabilities is a program for those with a documented disability, while Tutorial Services matches students with course tutors in such subjects as biology, chemistry, foreign languages, math and physics. There are also study groups with weekly reviews of course material. Specialists offer one-on-one help by appointment and give instruction on study skills. Writing Assistance provides coaches to help students organize and structure their writing and learn how to self-edit.

Simmons College provides a variety of support programs including dedicated guidance for: academic · career · personal · psychological · minority students · non-traditional students · family planning · religious. Annually, 83 percent of freshmen students return for their sophomore year. What do students do after college? While many enter the work force, approximately 13 percent pursue a graduate degree immediately after graduation.

Support for Students with Learning Disabilities

Students with learning disabilities may take advantage of specific support programs offered by Simmons College. If necessary, the college will grant additional time to students with learning disabilities to complete their degree. Also, a lightened course load may be granted to LD students. Students with learning disabilities will find the following programs at Simmons College extremely useful: tutors · learning center · testing accommodations · extended time for tests · take-home exam · exam on tape or computer · readers · note-taking services · tape recorders · early syllabus · priority registration · priority seating. Individual or small group tutorials are also available in: time management · organizational skills · learning strategies · specific subject areas · writing labs · study skills. An advisor/advocate from the Disability Services is available to students.

How to Get Admitted

For admissions decisions, non-academic factors considered: interview · extracurricular activities · special talents, interests, abilities · character/personal qualities · volunteer work · work experience · state of residency. A high school diploma is not required for admissions consideration. SAT or ACT test scores are required of all applicants. SAT Subject Test scores are not required. *Academic*

units recommended: 4 English, 4 Math, 3 Science, 4 Social Studies, 4 Foreign Language.

How to Pay for College

To apply for financial aid, students should submit the following: Free Application for Federal Student Aid (FAFSA) · institution's own financial aid forms · federal tax returns. Simmons College participates in the Federal Work Study program. *Need-based aid programs include:* scholarships and grants · general need-based awards · Federal Pell grants · state scholarships and grants · college-based scholarships and grants · private scholarships and grants. *Non-Need-based aid programs include:* scholarships and grants · state scholarships and grants · special achievements and activities awards.

SONOMA STATE UNIVERSITY

1801 East Cotati Avenue, Rohnert Park, CA 94928
Admissions: 707-664-2778 · Financial Aid: 707-664-2389
Email: student.outreach@sonoma.edu · Website: http://www.sonoma.edu

From the College

"Sonoma State University is a relatively small (8,000 students), residential, public university committed to student retention, graduation and satisfaction. Its primary mission is to develop and maintain excellent programs of undergraduate instruction grounded in the liberal arts and sciences. Instructional programs are designed to challenge students not only to acquire knowledge but also to develop the skills of critical analysis, careful reasoning, creativity and self-expression.

"Within its 36 academic departments, SSU offers 41 bachelor's degree programs and 14 master's degree programs. In addition, the university offers a joint master's degree in mathematics with San Francisco State University and a joint doctorate in educational administration with California State University, Sacramento and the University of California - Davis. The University offers nine credential programs and eight undergraduate and graduate certificate programs. Basic teaching credential programs in education include multiple subject, multiple subject BCLAD, single subject, administrative services, reading/language arts (certificate or specialist), special education (mild/moderate or moderate/severe) and pupil personnel services (via the Counseling Department).

"The university is committed to creating a learning community in which people from diverse backgrounds and cultures are valued for the breadth of their perspectives and are encouraged in their intellectual pursuits. Sonoma's faculty maintain active scholarly lives and the university encourages faculty projects that involve students in research and other creative activities.

"Instead of dormitory-style housing, the SSU residential community offers a variety of accommodations from shared bedrooms in residential suites to private bedrooms and baths in apartments. A 58,000-square-foot student recreation center received the Outstanding Sports Facilities Award by the National Intramural Recreational Sports Association.

"The university was gifted the Fairfield Osborne Preserve, located within a mile of campus, which is dedicated to protecting and restoring natural communities and fostering ecological understanding through education and research. Additionally, the university accepted a 3,500-acre wilderness preserve in northern Sonoma County called the Galbreath Wildlands Preserve to promote environmental education and research, as well as to steward the diverse landscape of the preserve."

Campus Setting

Sonoma State, founded in 1960, is a public, comprehensive university. Its 269-acre campus is located in Rohnert Park, 45 miles north of San Francisco. A four-year institution, Sonoma State University has an enrollment of 8,921 students. In addition to a large, well-stocked library, the campus facilities include: performing art center · information/technology center · nature preserve · observatory · electron microscope · seismograph · environmental technology center · wildlands preserve. Sonoma State University provides on-campus housing with 588 units that can accommodate 3,163 students. Housing options: single-student apartments · special housing for disabled students. Recreation and sports facilities include: field · gymnasium · recreation center · track · tennis court.

Student Life and Activities

Most students (71 percent) live off campus, which does impact the on-campus social scene. Nevertheless, like any college, students find time to create their own recreational outlets. SSU has many on-campus activities. The SSU Seawolf Scene calendar posts daily events. Favorite student hangouts include the Pub, Northlight Books, Friar Tucks and Cotati Yacht Club. Popular events include Holocaust Lecture Series, Big Cats, Green Music Festival, Center for Performing Arts: Theater and Music, ASU Productions (multiple concerts and lectures), SF Comedy Night, Heritage Lecture Series and Gender Bender. Sonoma State University has 109 official student organizations. Groups with a strong presence in social life include: Greeks (fraternities and sororities), Associates Students (sponsors many events, concerts, dances, lectures, films) and Outdoor Pursuits (coordinates outdoor activities and trips). For those interested in sports, there are intramural teams such as: basketball · bowling · flag football · indoor soccer · soccer · softball · ultimate Frisbee · volleyball · group fitness · personal training · rock wall climbing. Sonoma State University is a member of the California Collegiate Athletic Conference (Division II), Western Water Polo Association (Division I).

Academics and Learning Environment

For the B student, the learning environment of a college is just as important as the quality of its academic program. Sonoma State University has 274 full-time and 353 part-time faculty members, offering a student-to-faculty ratio of 23:1. The most common course size is 20 to 29 students. Sonoma State University offers 57 majors with the most popular being business administration, psychology and liberal studies and least popular being women's/gender studies, chemistry and geology. The school has a general core requirement. Cooperative education is not offered. All first-year students must maintain a 2.0 GPA or higher to avoid academic probation. Other special academic programs that would appeal to a B student: self-designed majors · independent study · double majors · dual degrees · accelerated study · honors program · Phi Beta Kappa · internships · distance learning.

B Student Support and Success

Sonoma's Educational Mentoring Team helps students transition to college life with a Freshman Seminar and a strong advising department. They feel students should be connected to a faculty member, a student services professional and a peer mentor. The Freshman Seminar is an optional class, but all new students are encouraged to take it. The course focuses on the skills needed to succeed in college classes. Information is provided that teaches students how to be involved in their own education and individualized advising is available as well. Another part of the Freshman Seminar is the study of the university culture. SOAR, or Sonoma Orientation, Advising and Registration, is held each summer for entering freshmen and their parents and is geared to help with the transition to college life. Free tutoring is available for all undergraduate courses. Students are allowed four hours a week, with a maximum of two hours per subject.

SONOMA STATE UNIVERSITY

Admissions
Applicants: 12,240
Accepted: 9,270
Acceptance rate: 75.7%
Average GPA: 3.2
ACT range: 20-24
SAT Math range: 460-570
SAT Reading range: 450-550
SAT Writing range: Not reported

Deadlines
Early Action: No
Early Decision: No
Regular Action: Rolling admissions
Common Application: Not accepted

Financial Aid
Out-of-state tuition: $11,160
Room: -
Board: -
Books: $1,656
Freshmen receiving need-based aid: 23%
Undergrads receiving need-based aid: 37%
Avg. % of need met by financial aid: 65%
Avg. aid package (freshmen): $8,055
Avg. aid package (undergrads): $8,608
Freshmen receiving merit-based aid: 1%
Undergrads receiving merit-based aid: 1%
Avg. student debt upon graduation: $15,170

Prominent Alumni
Ed Sayres, president, American Society for the Prevention of Cruelty to Animals, New York City; Peter Rooney, deputy staff director of U.S. House of Representative Science Committee; Laurie MacDonald, co-head with Walter F. Parkes of Dream-Works Pictures, Motion Picture Division.

School Spirit
Mascot: Seawolves
Colors: Navy, columbia and white

Sonoma State University provides a variety of support programs including dedicated guidance for: academic · career · personal · psychological · minority students · military · veterans · non-traditional students · family planning. Recognizing that some students may need extra preparation, Sonoma State University offers remedial and refresher courses in: reading · writing · math · study skills. The average freshman year GPA is 2.8, and 74 percent of freshmen students return for their sophomore year.

Support for Students with Learning Disabilities

Students with learning disabilities may take advantage of specific support programs offered by Sonoma State University. Students with learning disabilities will find the following programs at Sonoma State University extremely useful: remedial math · remedial English · remedial reading · special classes · learning center · testing accommodations · extended time for tests · take-home exam · readers · typist/scribe · note-taking services · reading machines · tape recorders. Individual or small group tutorials are also available in: time management · organizational skills · learning strategies · specific subject areas · writing labs · math labs · study skills. An advisor/advocate from the Disabled Student Services is available to students.

How to Get Admitted

For admissions decisions, non-academic factors considered: geographical location. A high school diploma is required, although a GED is also accepted for admissions consideration. SAT or ACT test scores are required of all applicants. SAT Subject Test scores are not required. *According to the admissions office:* Electives should be taken from advanced math, agriculture, English, foreign language, history, lab science, social science, visual/performing arts. Minimum grade of C required in listed secondary school courses. Minimum eligibility index of 2800 for SAT Reasoning (694 for ACT) required of in-state applicants; minimum eligibility index of 3402 for SAT Reasoning (842 for ACT) required of out-of-state applicants.

How to Pay for College

To apply for financial aid, students should submit the following: Free Application for Federal Student Aid (FAFSA). Sonoma State University participates in the Federal Work Study program. *Need-based aid programs include:* scholarships and grants · general need-based awards · Federal Pell grants · state scholarships and grants · college-based scholarships and grants · private scholarships and grants · ACG and SMART grants. *Non-Need-based aid programs include:* scholarships and grants · state scholarships and grants · creative arts and performance awards · special achievements and activities awards · special characteristics awards · athletic scholarships.

SOUTHERN OREGON UNIVERSITY

1250 Siskiyou Boulevard, Ashland, OR 97520
Admissions: 800-482-7672 · Financial Aid: 800-482-7672
Email: admissions@sou.edu · Website: http://www.sou.edu

From the College

"Southern Oregon University is a contemporary, public, liberal arts and sciences university with a growing national reputation for excellence in teaching. It places student learning, inside and outside the classroom, at the heart of all programs and services. SOU is proud of its strengths in the sciences and humanities; its continuing tradition of preparing outstanding teachers, business leaders, and other professionals; and its designation as Oregon's Center of Excellence in the Fine and Performing Arts. SOU was recently selected by the New York Times as a 'hidden gem' in American higher education."

Campus Setting

Southern Oregon University, founded in 1869, has a 175-acre campus in southwestern Oregon. A four-year institution, Southern Oregon University has an enrollment of 4,675 students. In addition to a library, the campus facilities include: art museums · theatre complex · center of excellence for the performing arts · ecology center. Southern Oregon University provides on-campus housing that can accommodate 1,100 students. Housing options: co-ed dorms · single-student apartments · married-student apartments · special housing for disabled students · special housing for International students. Recreation and sports facilities include: fitness center · gymnasiums · swimming pool · tennis courts.

Student Life and Activities

Most students (77 percent) live off campus, which does impact the on-campus social scene. Nevertheless, like any college, students find time to create their own recreational outlets. Southern Oregon University has 70 official student organizations. The most popular are: Brass · concert and swing choirs · chamber ensemble · symphony · vocal and instrumental jazz groups · opera workshop · photography club · debating · public radio network. For those interested in sports, there are intramural teams such as: tennis · fitness · swimming · softball. Southern Oregon University is a member of the Cascade Collegiate Conference (NAIA).

Academics and Learning Environment

For the B student, the learning environment of a college is just as important as the quality of its academic program. Southern Oregon University has 193 full-time and 96 part-time faculty members. Southern Oregon University offers 45 majors with the most popular being business, psychology and communication and least popular being mathematics and interdisciplinary studies. The school has a general core requirement. Cooperative education is not offered. All first-year students must maintain a 2.0 GPA or higher to avoid

SOUTHERN OREGON UNIVERSITY

Admissions
Applicants: 1,871
Accepted: 1,744
Acceptance rate: 93.2%
Average GPA: 3.2
ACT range: Not reported
SAT Math range: Not reported
SAT Reading range: Not reported
SAT Writing range: Not reported

Deadlines
Early Action: No
Early Decision: No
Regular Action: July 1 (priority)
Common Application: Accepted

Financial Aid
In-state tuition: $4,168
Out-of-state tuition: $13,276
Room: -
Board: -
Books: -
Avg. % of need met by financial aid: Not reported
Avg. aid package (freshmen): Not reported
Avg. aid package (undergrads): Not reported
Avg. student debt upon graduation: Not reported

School Spirit
Mascot: Raider
Colors: Red and black

academic probation. Other special academic programs that would appeal to a B student: self-designed majors · pass/fail grading option · independent study · double majors · dual degrees · accelerated study · honors program · internships · distance learning.

B Student Support and Success

Southern Oregon University offers students help through its ACCESS Center, an acronym for Academic Advising, Counseling, Career Services and Educational Support Services. Their programs include a Writing Center and math tutoring. Academic advisors help students understand and organize the University Studies Requirements, i.e. General Studies.

Southern Oregon University provides a variety of support programs including dedicated guidance for: academic · career · personal · psychological · minority students · military · veterans · non-traditional students · family planning. The average freshman year GPA is 3.0, and

Support for Students with Learning Disabilities

Students with learning disabilities may take advantage of specific support programs offered by Southern Oregon University. If necessary, the college will grant additional time to students with learning disabilities to complete their degree. Also, a lightened course load may be granted to LD students. High school foreign language waivers are accepted. High school math waivers are also accepted. According to the school, Students with disabilities who do not meet university admission requirements are invited to participate in special admissions process, and to coordinate this with DSS. Support services available from both DSS and TRIO programs. Students with learning disabilities will find the following programs at Southern Oregon University extremely useful: remedial math · special classes · tutors · learning center · testing accommodations · extended time for tests · take-home exam · oral tests · readers · typist/scribe · note-taking services · reading machines · tape recorders. Individual or small group tutorials are also available in: time management · organizational skills · learning strategies · specific subject areas · writing labs · math labs · study skills. An advisor/advocate from the LD program is available to students.

How to Get Admitted

For admissions decisions, non-academic factors considered: extracurricular activities · special talents, interests, abilities · character/personal qualities · volunteer work · work experience · state of residency. A high school diploma is required, although a GED is also accepted for admissions consideration. SAT or ACT test scores are required of all applicants. SAT Subject Test scores are required for some applicants. *According to the admissions office:* Minimum combined SAT score of 1010 (composite ACT score of 21) or minimum 2.75 GPA required.

How to Pay for College

To apply for financial aid, students should submit the following: Free Application for Federal Student Aid (FAFSA). Southern Oregon University participates in the Federal Work Study program. *Need-based aid programs include:* scholarships and grants · general need-based awards · Federal Pell grants · state scholarships and grants · college-based scholarships and grants · private scholarships and grants. *Non-Need-based aid programs include:* scholarships and grants · general need-based awards · state scholarships and grants · creative arts and performance awards · special characteristics awards · athletic scholarships · Army GOLD scholarships.

SOUTHERN OREGON UNIVERSITY

Students
Total enrollment: 2,270
Undergrads: 2,270
Freshmen: 550
Part-time students: 5%
From out-of-state: 73%
Male/Female: 0%/100%
Live on-campus: 43%
Off-campus employment rating: Fair
Caucasian: 0%
African American: 96%
Asian or Pacific Islander: 0%
Native American: 0%
International: 3%

Academics
Student/faculty ratio: 12:1
Class size 9 or fewer: 22%
Class size 10-29: 69%
Class size 30-49: 8%
Class size 50-99: 1%
Class size 100 or more: 3%
Returning freshmen: 89%
Six-year graduation rate: 80%

Most Popular Fields of Study
Biological and Life Sciences

Admissions
Applicants: 6,033
Accepted: 2,122
Acceptance rate: 35.2%
Average GPA: 3.6
ACT range: 20-24
SAT Math range: 470-550
SAT Reading range: 490-570
SAT Writing range: Not reported
Top 10% of class: 29%
Top 25% of class: 69%
Top 50% of class: 94%

SPELMAN COLLEGE

From the College

"Spelman College promotes academic excellence in the liberal arts, and develops the intellectual, ethical and leadership potential of its students. A predominantly residential private college, Spelman seeks to empower the total person who appreciates the many cultures of the world and commits to positive social change. Spelman has been and expects to continue to be a major resource for cultivating leaders. A historically black college for women, Spelman reinforces a sense of pride and hope, develops character and inspires the love of learning imbued by a commitment to service. The programs of the college are created with the expectation that the community and society at large will benefit from a liberal arts educated student. Spelman College is a member of the Atlanta University Center consortium, and Spelman students enjoy access to the resources of the four participating institutions."

Campus Setting

Spelman's 32-acre campus is located one mile from downtown Atlanta and has 2,270 students. In addition to a large, well-stocked library, the campus facilities include: art museum · digital media lab. Spelman College provides on-campus housing with 11 units that can accommodate 1,174 students. Housing options: women's dorms · single-student apartments. Recreation and sports facilities include a gymnasium.

Student Life and Activities

Most students (57 percent) live off campus, which does impact the on-campus social scene. Nevertheless, like any college, students find time to create their own recreational outlets. "There is a lot to do," reports the editor of the student newspaper. "Although we are a small private college, we are part of a larger university system. We are within walking distance of three other colleges/universities. We are also five minutes from the downtown Atlanta area." Hot gathering spots include the Lower Manley Student Center Plaza and Friday Market. Popular campus events include: Founders Day, Spelman College Reunion, Family Weekend and Senior Soiree. Spelman College has 82 official student organizations. Student Government Association, sororities and AST (African Sisterhood) have widespread influence on student life. Spelman College is a member of the Great South Athletic Conference (Division III).

Academics and Learning Environment

For the B student, the learning environment of a college is just as important as the quality of its academic program. Spelman College has 174 full-time and 75 part-time faculty members, offering a student-to-faculty ratio of 12:1. The most common course size is

10 to 19 students. Spelman College offers 30 majors with the most popular being psychology, biology and English and least popular being sociology, human services and natural sciences. The school has a general core requirement. Cooperative education is not offered. All first-year students must maintain a 1.8 GPA or higher to avoid academic probation. Other special academic programs that would appeal to a B student: self-designed majors · independent study · double majors · dual degrees · honors program · Phi Beta Kappa · internships.

B Student Support and Success

Spelman's Learning Resources Center provides extra help to all students and offers services such as lab instruction, academic advisement, peer tutoring, workshops and instruction in study techniques and learning strategies. According to the college, the center's major objective is to "empower students who will become creative, independent learners and problem solvers capable of processing and handling volumes of information." Peer tutors are available on both a drop-in and appointment basis throughout the year. Students can get help in study techniques, reading, note taking, test-taking strategies, problem-solving and communication skills. Academic advising is also offered through the Learning Resources Center.

Spelman College provides a variety of support programs including dedicated guidance for: academic · career · personal · family planning. Annually, 89 percent of freshmen students return for their sophomore year. What do students do after college? While many enter the work force, approximately 38 percent pursue a graduate degree immediately after graduation. Among students who enter the work force, approximately 52 percent enter a field related to their major within six months of graduation. Companies that most frequently hire graduates from Spelman College include: Teach For America · Goldman Sachs · JP Morgan Chase · Deloitte Consulting · Freddie Mac.

Support for Students with Learning Disabilities

Students with learning disabilities may take advantage of specific support programs offered by Spelman College. Students with learning disabilities will find the following programs at Spelman College extremely useful: tutors · learning center · testing accommodations · extended time for tests · take-home exam · oral tests · readers · typist/scribe · note-taking services · tape recorders · priority registration · waiver of math degree requirement. Individual or small group tutorials are also available in: time management · organizational skills · writing labs · math labs. An advisor/advocate from the Office of Disability Services is available to students.

How to Get Admitted

For admissions decisions, non-academic factors considered: extracurricular activities · special talents, interests, abilities · character/personal qualities · volunteer work · work experience · state of residency · geographical location · alumni relationship. A high school diploma is required, although a GED is also accepted for admissions consideration. SAT or ACT test scores are required of all applicants. *Academic units recommended:* 4 English, 4 Math, 4 Science, 3 Social Studies, 4 Foreign Language.

SPELMAN COLLEGE

Highlights

Deadlines
Early Action: November 15
Early Decision: November 1
Regular Action: February 1 (final)
Common Application: Accepted

Financial Aid
In-state tuition: $17,266
Out-of-state tuition: $17,266
Room: -
Board: -
Books: -
Freshmen receiving need-based aid: 78%
Undergrads receiving need-based aid: 72%
Avg. % of need met by financial aid: Not reported
Avg. aid package (freshmen): $12,339
Avg. aid package (undergrads): $12,691
Freshmen receiving merit-based aid: 1%
Undergrads receiving merit-based aid: 2%
Avg. student debt upon graduation: $17,500

Prominent Alumni
Audrey Forbes Manley, academician, physician and public health professional; Marian Wright Edelman, founder and president of the Children's Defense Fund (CDF).

School Spirit
Mascot: Jaguar
Colors: Columbia blue
Song: *Spelman Hymn*

SPELMAN COLLEGE

How to Pay for College

To apply for financial aid, students should submit the following: Free Application for Federal Student Aid (FAFSA). Spelman College participates in the Federal Work Study program. *Need-based aid programs include:* scholarships and grants · general need-based awards · Federal Pell grants · state scholarships and grants · college-based scholarships and grants · private scholarships and grants · United Negro College Fund. *Non-Need-based aid programs include:* scholarships and grants · general need-based awards · state scholarships and grants · ROTC scholarships.

SPRINGFIELD COLLEGE

263 Alden Street, Springfield, MA 01109
Admissions: 800-343-1257 · Financial Aid: 413-748-3112
Email: admissions@spfldcol.edu · Website: http://www.springieldcollege.edu

From the College

"Springfield College's flexible and people-oriented approach reflects its commitment to the philosophy of humanics and to the development of the whole person in spirit, mind and body. Courses of study are designed to prepare young men and women for success in human-helping fields that enhance society and improve quality of life, especially for those in need. In the classroom, the humanics philosophy translates into a careful balance of theory and practice.

"Degrees are offered in 40 undergraduate and 14 graduate major areas of study, including doctoral degrees in physical education and physical therapy. Major areas of study are in health sciences, human and social services, sport management and movement studies and the arts and sciences. The academic experience encompasses coursework, research, laboratory experience and targeted fieldwork enhanced by co curricular and voluntary service activities on campus and in the community. The renovated Science Center is a state-of-the-art classroom and laboratory facility for science education, which over 85 percent of undergraduates take to complete their academic major or minor.

"Athletics and recreation facilities promote the athletic heritage and a campus-wide wellness initiative that reflects the balance of spirit, mind and body."

Campus Setting

Springfield, founded in 1885, is a private, multipurpose college. Its 167-acre campus is located in Springfield, 50 miles west of Worcester. A four-year institution, Springfield College has an enrollment of 4,946 students. Springfield College has been co-ed since 1949. The school also has a library with 159,081 books. Springfield College provides on-campus housing with 11 units that can accommodate 1,900 students. Housing options: co-ed dorms · men's dorms · single-student apartments · special housing for disabled students. Recreation and sports facilities include: arena · fields · gymnasium · tennis courts.

Student Life and Activities

With 88 percent of students living on campus, there are plenty of social activities. Popular events include: NCAA Division III Women's Basketball Championship, William Simpson Fine Arts Series, The Karpovich Lecture, The Britton C. and Lucile McCabe Lecture, Weckwerth Lecture, Greene Memorial Lecture in Physical Therapy, Girls and Women in Sports Day, Community Thanksgiving Dinner and Humanics in Action Day. Springfield College has 50 official student organizations. The most popular are: Best Buddies · Best of Broadway · Habitat for Humanity · history club · rehab club · Sti-Yu-Ka · Premedical Scholars · athletic training club · sports management cub · outing club · YMCA club. For those interested in sports, there are intramural teams such as: baseball · basketball · field hockey · flag football · floor hockey · inner-tube water polo · kickball · polo · punt-pass-kick · soccer · softball · triathlon · ultimate Frisbee · wiffle ball. Springfield College is a member of the ECAC (Division III, Football I-AA), Eastern Intercollegiate Volleyball Association (Division III), Empire Eight (Division III), New England College Wrestling Association (Division III), New England Women's and Men's Athletic Conference (Division III), Pilgrim League (Division III).

SPRINGFIELD COLLEGE

Springfield College

Springfield, MA
Location: Medium city
Website: http://www.springieldcollege.edu

Students

Total enrollment: 4,946
Undergrads: 1,444
Freshmen: 577
Part-time students: 12%
From out-of-state: 71%
Male/Female: 42%/58%
Live on-campus: 88%
Off-campus employment rating: Fair
Caucasian: 54%
African American: 22%
Hispanic: 8%
Asian or Pacific Islander: 1%
Native American: 0%
International: 0%

Academics

Student/faculty ratio: 13:1
Class size 9 or fewer: 16%
Class size 10-29: 71%
Class size 30-49: 12%
Class size 50-99: 1%
Class size 100 or more: 1%
Returning freshmen: 81%
Six-year graduation rate: 62%

Admissions

Applicants: 2,262
Accepted: 1,503
Acceptance rate: 66.4%
placed on wait list: 39
Average GPA: Not reported
ACT range: Not reported
SAT Math range: 470-570
SAT Reading range: 450-540
SAT Writing range: Not reported
Top 10% of class: 12%
Top 25% of class: 34%
Top 50% of class: 71%

Academics and Learning Environment

For the B student, the learning environment of a college is just as important as the quality of its academic program. Springfield College has 211 full-time and 415 part-time faculty members, offering a student-to-faculty ratio of 13:1. The most common course size is 20 to 29 students. Springfield College offers 60 majors with the most popular being physical education, rehabilitation services and physical therapy and least popular being computer graphics, medical informatics and history. The school has a general core requirement as well as a religion requirement Cooperative education is not offered. All first-year students must maintain a 1.7 GPA or higher to avoid academic probation. Other special academic programs that would appeal to a B student: pass/fail grading option · independent study · double majors · internships.

B Student Support and Success

Springfield's Academic Support Services includes access to one-on-one academic coaching. Qualified tutors help students in areas that include a variety of topics, including the following: taking and using class notes, preparing for exams, managing time, testing taking and alleviating test anxiety, actively reading and learning from your textbooks, concentrating during study sessions, organizing and outlining papers, avoiding procrastination and organizing study groups.

Springfield College provides a variety of support programs including dedicated guidance for: academic · career · personal · psychological · minority students · family planning · religious. The average freshman year GPA is 2.8, and 81 percent of freshmen students return for their sophomore year. What do students do after college? While many enter the work force, approximately 26 percent pursue a graduate degree immediately after graduation. Among students who enter the work force, approximately 55 percent enter a field related to their major within six months of graduation. Companies that most frequently hire graduates from Springfield College include: Baystate Health · New York Jets · Bank of America · Shriner's Hospital for Children · the May Institute · YMCAs Nationwide · Enterprise · Springfield Public Schools · ESPN Productions · MassMutual · Octogon · Jewish Family Services · Easter Seals.

Support for Students with Learning Disabilities

Students with learning disabilities may take advantage of specific support programs offered by Springfield College. If necessary, the college will grant additional time to students with learning disabilities to complete their degree. Also, a lightened course load may be granted to LD students. Students with learning disabilities will find the following programs at Springfield College extremely useful: remedial math · tutors · untimed tests · extended time for tests · readers · note-taking services · reading machines · tape recorders. Individual or small group tutorials are also available in: time management · organizational skills · learning strategies · study skills. An advisor/advocate from the Student Support Services is available to students.

How to Get Admitted

For admissions decisions, non-academic factors considered: interview · extracurricular activities · special talents, interests, abilities · character/personal qualities · volunteer work · work experience · state of residency · geographical location · minority affiliation · alumni relationship. A high school diploma is required, although a GED is also accepted for admissions consideration. SAT or ACT test scores are required of all applicants. SAT Subject Test scores are recommended but not required. *Academic units recommended:* 4 Math, 4 Science, 2 Social Studies, 3 Foreign Language.

How to Pay for College

To apply for financial aid, students should submit the following: Free Application for Federal Student Aid (FAFSA) · institution's own financial aid forms · state aid form. Springfield College participates in the Federal Work Study program. *Need-based aid programs include:* scholarships and grants · general need-based awards · Federal Pell grants · state scholarships and grants · college-based scholarships and grants · private scholarships and grants · Federal ACG · SMART Grants. *Non-Need-based aid programs include:* scholarships and grants · general need-based awards · state scholarships and grants · creative arts and performance awards · ROTC scholarships.

SPRINGFIELD COLLEGE

Highlights

Deadlines
Early Action: No
Early Decision: December 1
Regular Action: March 1 (priority)
April 1 (final)
Common Application: Accepted

Financial Aid
In-state tuition: $26,480
Out-of-state tuition: $26,480
Room: -
Board: -
Books: $900
Freshmen receiving need-based aid: 73%
Undergrads receiving need-based aid: 78%
Avg. % of need met by financial aid: 76%
Avg. aid package (freshmen): $16,730
Avg. aid package (undergrads): $16,231
Freshmen receiving merit-based aid: 15%
Undergrads receiving merit-based aid: 14%
Avg. student debt upon graduation: $29,226

School Spirit
Mascot: Pride
Colors: Maroon and white
Song: *Song For Springfield*

ST. JOHN'S UNIVERSITY

P.O. Box 7155, Collegeville, MN 56321
Admissions: 800-5441489 · Financial Aid: 800-544-1489
Email: admissions@csbsju.edu · Website: http://www.csbsju.edu

From the College

"The College of St. Benedict (CSB) and St. John's University (SJU) are liberal arts colleges whose partnership offers students the educational choices of a large university and the individual attention of a premier small college. Students attend classes and activities together and have access to the resources of both campuses. Ranked nationally among the top baccalaureate institutions for the number of students who study abroad, CSB/SJU are committed to preparing students for leadership and service in a global society. The colleges enroll students from around the world and integrate global citizenship into the curriculum. Nearly all students live on-campus or in the immediate neighborhood, providing them with opportunities for a highly engaged learning experience. The colleges are located on 3,300 acres of woods and lakes of Minnesota, an hour from Minneapolis/St. Paul and just west of Saint Cloud. A commitment to arts and culture creates an environment for creativity. The Hill Museum and Manuscript Library at SJU is home to the St. John's Bible and a collection of religious sculpture, paintings, prints and artifacts. The learning experience is enlivened by Catholic and Benedictine traditions of hospitality, stewardship, service and the lively engagement of faith and reason. The colleges' values have been shaped by a commitment to ecumenism and interfaith dialogue."

Campus Setting

St. John's is a church-affiliated, liberal arts university. Founded in 1857, it is a coordinate with College of St. Benedict for women. Its 2,500-acre campus is located in Collegeville, 75 miles north of Minneapolis. A four-year private men's college, St. John's University has an enrollment of 2,063 students. The school is also affiliated with the Roman Catholic Church (Benedictine). In addition to a large, well-stocked library, the campus facilities include: art gallery · arboretum · Sommers digital film studio on St John's campus. Benedicta Arts Center · St. Benedict's Monastery Heritage Museum on College of St. Benedict campus. St. John's University provides on-campus housing with 500 units that can accommodate 1,468 students. Housing options: men's dorms · single-student apartments · special housing for disabled students.

Student Life and Activities

With 79 percent of students living on campus, there are plenty of social activities. "Our college and the College of St. Benedict are close-knit schools; everyone tries to help everyone else," reports the student newspaper . On campus, students gather at Willy's Pub, Sexton Commons, the Loft, Mary Commons and Claire Lynch. Popular events include: Club Involvement Fair, Welcome Fest, Pinestock, Festival of Cultures, Battle of the Bands, Asian New Year, Little Sibs Weekend, Stella Maris Ball and Mother-Son Dance. St. John's University has 80 official student organizations. The most popular are: accounting club · international affairs club · Math Society · music club · nursing club · nutrition club · philosophy club · pre-dentistry club · Pre-Law Society · pre-med club · psychology club · art club · Pseudonym · social work club · Society for the Advancement of Management · American Sign Language · Amnesty International · Campus Groove Recordings · Campus Greens · College DFL/Democrats · College Republicans. For those interested in sports, there are intramural teams such as: aikido · ballroom dancing · basketball · bowling · climbing · cycling · disc golf · football · ice hockey · racquetball · sand volleyball · soccer · softball · table tennis ·

tae kwon do · tennis · volleyball · water polo. St. John's University is a member of the Minnesota Intercollegiate Athletic Conference (Division III).

Academics and Learning Environment

For the B student, the learning environment of a college is just as important as the quality of its academic program. St. John's University has 144 full-time and 32 part-time faculty members, offering a student-to-faculty ratio of 12:1. The most common course size is 20 to 29 students. St. John's University offers 82 majors with the most popular being business management, accounting and biology and least popular being classics, gender and women studies and social work. The school has a general core requirement as well as a religion requirement Cooperative education is not offered. All first-year students must maintain a 2.0 GPA or higher to avoid academic probation, and a minimum overall GPA of 2.5 is required to graduate. Other special academic programs that would appeal to a B student: self-designed majors · pass/fail grading option · independent study · double majors · honors program · internships · certificate programs.

B Student Support and Success

St. John's University offers help to its students through several programs and facilities. The Writing Center provides tutoring on both a drop-in and appointment basis. The Math Skills Center helps students with all 100-level math classes as well as preparation for the math proficiency exam. Tutors help students review algebra, geometry, trigonometry and pre-calculus as they work on assignments for math classes and prepare for the math portions of standardized tests. In addition, the college offers an Academic Skills Center Reading Lab.

St. John's University provides a variety of support programs including dedicated guidance for: academic · career · personal · psychological · minority students · religious. The average freshman year GPA is 3.1, and 90 percent of freshmen students return for their sophomore year.

Support for Students with Learning Disabilities

Students with learning disabilities may take advantage of specific support programs offered by St. John's University. According to the school, LD services are coordinated through the Academic Advising Office. While our disability services are limited, we are committed to providing academic accommodations on a case by case basis for enrolled students who provide adequate documentation of a disability. Students with learning disabilities will find the following programs at St. John's University extremely useful: tutors · testing accommodations · extended time for tests · typist/scribe · note-taking services · reading machines · texts on tape · waiver of math degree requirement. Individual or small group tutorials are also available in: writing labs · math labs · study skills. An advisor/advocate from the LD program is available to students.

How to Get Admitted

For admissions decisions, non-academic factors considered: interview · extracurricular activities · special talents, interests, abilities · char-

ST. JOHN'S UNIVERSITY

Highlights

St. John's University
Saint Cloud, MN (Pop. 67,000)
Location: Rural
Website: http://www.csbsju.edu

Students
Total enrollment: 2,063
Undergrads: 1,938
Freshmen: 503
Part-time students: 2%
From out-of-state: 16%
Male/Female: 100%/ 0%
Live on-campus: 79%
Off-campus employment rating: Fair
Caucasian: 88%
African American: 1%
Hispanic: 1%
Asian or Pacific Islander: 2%
Native American: 0%
International: 6%

Academics
Student/faculty ratio: 12:1
Class size 9 or fewer: 17%
Class size 10-29: 68%
Class size 30-49: 15%
Class size 50-99: -
Class size 100 or more: -
Returning freshmen: 90%
Six-year graduation rate: 83%

Most Popular Fields of Study
Business, Finance, Sales and Marketing
Biological and Life Sciences

ST. JOHN'S UNIVERSITY

Highlights

Admissions
Applicants: 1,557
Accepted: 1,152
Acceptance rate: 74.0%
placed on wait list: 7
Average GPA: 3.6
ACT range: 23-28
SAT Math range: 540-650
SAT Reading range: 480-650
SAT Writing range: Not reported
Top 10% of class: 24%
Top 25% of class: 58%
Top 50% of class: 91%

Deadlines
Early Action: November 15, December 15
Early Decision: No
Regular Action: November 15 (priority)
Common Application: Accepted

Financial Aid
In-state tuition: $29,388
Out-of-state tuition: $29,388
Room: $3,884
Board: $3,830
Books: $800
Freshmen receiving need-based aid: 60%
Undergrads receiving need-based aid: 56%
Avg. % of need met by financial aid: 88%
Avg. aid package (freshmen): $24,272
Avg. aid package (undergrads): $21,653
Freshmen receiving merit-based aid: 36%
Undergrads receiving merit-based aid: 38%
Avg. student debt upon graduation: Not reported

Prominent Alumni
Eugene McCarthy, former U.S. senator and presidential candidate; Jon Hassler, author; Dr. Tom Smith, microbiologist, researcher at the Mayo Clinic.

School Spirit
Mascot: Johnnies
Colors: Cardinal and blue
Song: *Johnnie Fight Song*

America's
Best Colleges for
B Students

acter/personal qualities · volunteer work · work experience · state of residency · geographical location · minority affiliation · alumni relationship. A high school diploma is required, although a GED is also accepted for admissions consideration. SAT or ACT test scores are required of all applicants. SAT Subject Test scores are not required. *According to the admissions office:* Minimum composite ACT score of 21 (combined SAT score of 1000), rank in top half of secondary school class, and minimum 3.0 GPA in college preparatory courses recommended. *Academic units recommended:* 2 Foreign Language.

How to Pay for College

To apply for financial aid, students should submit the following: Free Application for Federal Student Aid (FAFSA) · institution's own financial aid forms · tax forms. St. John's University participates in the Federal Work Study program. *Need-based aid programs include:* scholarships and grants · general need-based awards · Federal Pell grants · state scholarships and grants · college-based scholarships and grants. *Non-Need-based aid programs include:* scholarships and grants · state scholarships and grants · creative arts and performance awards · special achievements and activities awards · ROTC scholarships · leadership scholarships.

ST. LAWRENCE UNIVERSITY

23 Romoda Drive, Canton, NY 13617
Admissions: 800-285-1856 · Financial Aid: 800-355-0863
Email: admissions@stlawu.edu · Website: http://www.stlawu.edu

From the College

"St. Lawrence University, chartered in 1856, is a liberal arts learning community of inspiring faculty, serious students and accomplished alumni, guided by tradition and focused on the future. We provide a demanding undergraduate education to students selected for their seriousness of purpose and intellectual promise. St. Lawrence enrolls undergraduate students from 43 states and 49 nations, and about 120 graduate students in a non-residential Master of Education program. Located between the high peaks of the Adirondack Mountains and the national capital of Canada, the university provides access to international government, cultural and social opportunities and outdoor recreation. Among the features of St. Lawrence's curriculum are international programs in 15 nations and three domestic off-campus programs (including an Adirondack Semester), a model interdisciplinary program for first-year students; and 12 interdepartmental programs. St. Lawrence is in the midst of ambitious academic initiatives and major facilities improvements throughout campus but especially in the sciences and the arts.."

Campus Setting

St. Lawrence is a private university with a a 1,000-acre campus located in Canton, in northern New York. A four-year institution, St. Lawrence University has an enrollment of 2,325 students. In addition to a large, well-stocked library, the campus also has an art gallery. St. Lawrence University provides on-campus housing with 30 units that can accommodate 2,012 students. Housing options: co-ed dorms · sorority housing · fraternity housing · single-student apartments · special housing for disabled students · special housing for International students. Recreation and sports facilities include: arena · fitness center · football and practice fields · gymnasium · ice rink · stadium · swimming pool · tennis courts.

Student Life and Activities

With 99 percent of students living on campus, there are plenty of social activities. Campus events are plentiful and varied, and students are encouraged to develop programming. The Student Center, Newell Field House and ODY (library) are favorite student hangouts. Popular campus events include: Moving Up Day, 100th Night, Quad Experience, Winterfest, Peak Weekend and Festival of Science. St. Lawrence University has 125 official student organizations. Groups with an influence on campus social life include: athletes, student government and ACE, which provides a wide array of social and cultural activities from movies to plays to art openings. For those interested in sports, there are intramural teams such as: basketball · broomball · flag football · ice hockey · quadathalon · soccer · softball · volleyball. St. Lawrence University is a member of the Upstate Collegiate Athletic Association (Division III).

Academics and Learning Environment

For the B student, the learning environment of a college is just as important as the quality of its academic program. St. Lawrence University has 173 full-time and 21 part-time faculty members, offering a student-to-faculty ratio of 11:1. The most common course size is 10 to 19 students. St. Lawrence University offers 33 majors with the most popular being psychology, economics and English. The school has a general core requirement. Cooperative education is not offered. All first-year students

ST. LAWRENCE UNIVERSITY

St. Lawrence University
Canton, NY (Pop. 7,000)
Location: Rural
Website: http://www.stlawu.edu

Students

Total enrollment: 2,325
Undergrads: 999
Freshmen: 616
Part-time students: 1%
From out-of-state: 52%
Male/Female: 45%/55%
Live on-campus: 99%
In fraternities: 2%
In sororities: 20%
Off-campus employment rating: Poor
Caucasian: 68%
African American: 3%
Hispanic: 3%
Asian or Pacific Islander: 2%
Native American: 1%
International: 5%

Academics

Student/faculty ratio: 11:1
Class size 9 or fewer: 22%
Class size 10-29: 70%
Class size 30-49: 6%
Class size 50-99: 1%
Class size 100 or more: -
Returning freshmen: 88%
Six-year graduation rate: 76%

Most Popular Fields of Study

Biological and Life Sciences

must maintain a 2.0 GPA or higher to avoid academic probation. Other special academic programs that would appeal to a B student: self-designed majors · pass/fail grading option · independent study · double majors · Phi Beta Kappa · internships.

B Student Support and Success

According to St. Lawrence, it "is a student-centered institution which focuses on active learning. With a student to faculty ratio of 11:1, students are expected to be fully engaged in their academic coursework. Small seminar courses are common at St. Lawrence, allowing students to interact easily with faculty and other students. Professors are very accessible to students who need/want extra assistance. Our Academic Resources Department also offers students peer tutors as needed. We have writing and quantitative labs available to students who seek extra assistance with their communication and mathematical skills."

St. Lawrence University provides a variety of support programs including dedicated guidance for: academic · career · personal · psychological · family planning · religious. Annually, 88 percent of freshmen students return for their sophomore year. What do students do after college? While many enter the work force, approximately 20 percent pursue a graduate degree immediately after graduation. Among students who enter the work force, approximately 78 percent enter a field related to their major within six months of graduation. Companies that most frequently hire graduates from St. Lawrence University include: Goldman Sachs · Hartford Insurance · Amica Insurance · Morgan Stanley · Permal Asset Management.

Support for Students with Learning Disabilities

Students with learning disabilities may take advantage of specific support programs offered by St. Lawrence University. If necessary, the college will grant additional time to students with learning disabilities to complete their degree. Also, a lightened course load may be granted to LD students. High school foreign language waivers are accepted. High school math waivers are also accepted. According to the school, Reasonable accommodations are available for documented disabled students. All requests for accommodations must be supported by appropriate documentation provided. Students with learning disabilities will find the following programs at St. Lawrence University extremely useful: tutors · testing accommodations · untimed tests · extended time for tests · take-home exam · substitution of courses · readers · typist/scribe · note-taking services · reading machines · tape recorders · texts on tape · early syllabus · priority registration · waiver of math degree requirement. Individual or small group tutorials are also available in: time management · organizational skills · specific subject areas · writing labs · math labs · study skills. An advisor/advocate from the Office of Academic Services for Students with Special Needs is available to students.

How to Get Admitted

For admissions decisions, non-academic factors considered: interview · extracurricular activities · special talents, interests, abilities · character/personal qualities · volunteer work · work experience · state of residency · geographical location · minority affiliation · alumni relationship. A high school diploma is required, although a GED is also accepted for admissions consideration. SAT or ACT test scores are considered, if submitted, but are not required. SAT Subject Test scores are not required. *Academic units recommended:* 4 English, 4 Math, 4 Science, 2 Social Studies, 4 Foreign Language.

How to Pay for College

To apply for financial aid, students should submit the following: Free Application for Federal Student Aid (FAFSA) · institution's own financial aid forms · CSS/Financial Aid PROFILE · state aid form · Non-custodian (Divorced/Separated) Parent's Statement · W2 forms. St. Lawrence University participates in the Federal Work Study program. *Need-based aid programs include:* scholarships and grants · general need-based awards · Federal Pell grants · state scholarships and grants · college-based scholarships and grants. *Non-Need-based aid programs include:* scholarships and grants · general need-based awards · state scholarships and grants · special achievements and activities awards · athletic scholarships.

ST. LAWRENCE UNIVERSITY

Highlights

Admissions
Applicants: 5,419
Accepted: 1,829
Acceptance rate: 33.8%
placed on wait list: 658
Average GPA: 3.6
ACT range: 25-29
SAT Math range: 570-640
SAT Reading range: 570-640
SAT Writing range: 560-650
Top 10% of class: 44%
Top 25% of class: 74%
Top 50% of class: 96%

Deadlines
Early Action: No
Early Decision: November 15
Regular Action: February 1 (final)
Common Application: Accepted

Financial Aid
In-state tuition: $39,520
Out-of-state tuition: $39,520
Room: $5,460
Board: $4,700
Books: $650
Freshmen receiving need-based aid: 61%
Undergrads receiving need-based aid: 62%
Avg. % of need met by financial aid: 93%
Avg. aid package (freshmen): $36,230
Avg. aid package (undergrads): $35,622
Freshmen receiving merit-based aid: 19%
Undergrads receiving merit-based aid: 16%
Avg. student debt upon graduation: $16,941

Prominent Alumni
Susan Collins, Maine U.S. Senator; Jeff Boyd, CEO of priceline.com; Viggo Mortensen, actor.

School Spirit
Mascot: Saints
Colors: Scarlet and brown
Song: *Alma Mater*

425

St. Thomas University
Miami Gardens, FL
Location: Major city
Website: http://www.stu.edu

Students
Total enrollment: 2,454
Undergrads: 480
Freshmen: 213
Part-time students: 7%
From out-of-state: 10%
Male/Female: 43%/57%
Live on-campus: Not reported
Off-campus employment rating: Good
Caucasian: 10%
African American: 25%
Hispanic: 49%
Asian or Pacific Islander: 1%
Native American: 0%
International: 9%

Academics
Student/faculty ratio: 13:1
Class size 9 or fewer: 21%
Class size 10-29: 75%
Class size 30-49: 5%
Class size 50-99: 1%
Class size 100 or more: -
Returning freshmen: 69%
Six-year graduation rate: 37%

Most Popular Fields of Study
Business, Finance, Sales and Marketing
Protective Services, Criminal Justice and
    Public Administration
Psychology
English and Literature
Philosophy, Religion and Theology
Computer and Information Sciences
Health Professions, Medicine and Re-
    lated Sciences
Liberal Arts, Humanities and General
    Studies
Communications, Journalism, Advertising
    and Comm. Technologies
Education

ST. THOMAS UNIVERSITY

16401 N.W. 37th Avenue, Miami Gardens, FL 33054
Admissions: 800-367-9010 · Financial Aid: 800-367-9010
Email: signup@stu.edu · Website: http://www.stu.edu

From the College

"St. Thomas University is the only Catholic Archdiocesan-spon-
sored university in Florida and places an institutional emphasis on
social justice and ethical behavior. Our School of Law ranks first
among ABA- approved law schools in our proportion of Hispanic
students, and sixth among African American students. We are one of
the only law schools in the nation with a Human Rights Institute and
offer a joint M.B.A./J.D. in accounting, international business, mar-
riage and family counseling and sports administration in addition to
our 25 undergraduate and 12 graduate degrees. Approximately 90
percent of the faculty hold the highest degrees in their fields."

Campus Setting

St. Thomas is a private, church-affiliated, liberal arts university.
Founded in 1961, it adopted co-education in 1975. Its 140-acre
campus is located in Miami. A four-year institution, St. Thomas
University has an enrollment of 2,454 students. The school is also
affiliated with the Roman Catholic Church. In addition to a large,
well-stocked library, the campus has an archives and museum. St.
Thomas University provides on-campus housing with 3 units that
can accommodate 175 students. Housing options: women's dorms
· men's dorms. Recreation and sports facilities include: baseball ·
soccer and softball fields · gymnasium · tennis courts.

Student Life and Activities

St. Thomas University has 17 official student organizations. The
most popular are: Writers United · Lady Dimondettes · Men Achieving Leadership, Excellence and Success · Students Advocating and
Valuing Earth · Global Leadership Pax Romana Student Society
· political action club · psychology club · biology club. For those
interested in sports, there are intramural teams such as: basketball
· flag football · softball · volleyball. St. Thomas University is a
member of the NAIA, Florida Sun Conference.

Academics and Learning Environment

For the B student, the learning environment of a college is just as
important as the quality of its academic program. St. Thomas University has 100 full-time and part-time faculty members, offering
a student-to-faculty ratio of 13:1. The most common course size
is 10 to 19 students. St. Thomas University offers 48 majors with
the most popular being business/management and communication
arts and least popular being public administration. The school has a
general core requirement as well as a religion requirement Cooperative education is not offered. All first-year students must maintain
a 2.0 GPA or higher to avoid academic probation. Other special
academic programs that would appeal to a B student: independent

study · double majors · dual degrees · honors program · internships · distance learning certificate programs.

B Student Support and Success

The university's academic support program includes an ombudsman, or "a person who investigates and attempts to resolve complaints and problems between students and a university." At STU, the "ombud," as he/she is called, listens/evaluates/assists the student with academic concerns, clarifies any academic miscommunications and then helps with all aspect of solving the problem. In addition, the Writing Center offers help with all writing assignments in both one-on-one or group settings.

St. Thomas University provides a variety of support programs including dedicated guidance for: academic · career · personal · psychological · religious. Recognizing that some students may need extra preparation, St. Thomas University offers remedial and refresher courses in: reading · writing · math · study skills. The average freshman year GPA is 2.9, and 69 percent of freshmen students return for their sophomore year.

Support for Students with Learning Disabilities

Students with learning disabilities may take advantage of specific support programs offered by St. Thomas University. Students with learning disabilities will find the following programs at St. Thomas University extremely useful: remedial math · remedial English · remedial reading · tutors · learning center · untimed tests · extended time for tests · note-taking services. Individual or small group tutorials are also available in: writing labs · math labs · study skills. An advisor/advocate from the Academic Enhancement Center is available to students.

How to Get Admitted

For admissions decisions, non-academic factors considered: extracurricular activities · special talents, interests, abilities · character/personal qualities · volunteer work · work experience · state of residency · alumni relationship. A high school diploma is required, although a GED is also accepted for admissions consideration. SAT or ACT test scores are required of all applicants. SAT Subject Test scores are not required. *According to the admissions office:* Rank in top three-fifths of secondary school class and minimum 2.0 GPA required.

How to Pay for College

To apply for financial aid, students should submit the following: Free Application for Federal Student Aid (FAFSA) · state aid form. St. Thomas University participates in the Federal Work Study program. *Need-based aid programs include:* scholarships and grants · general need-based awards · Federal Pell grants · state scholarships and grants · college-based scholarships and grants · private scholarships and grants. *Non-Need-based aid programs include:* scholarships and grants · general need-based awards · state scholarships and grants · creative arts and performance awards · special achievements and activities awards · special characteristics awards · athletic scholarships · religious affiliation scholarships · alumni/ae affiliation scholarships.

ST. THOMAS UNIVERSITY

Highlights

Admissions
Applicants: 655
Accepted: 597
Acceptance rate: 91.1%
Average GPA: 3.0
ACT range: 16-21
SAT Math range: 380-490
SAT Reading range: 390-490
SAT Writing range: 400-490
Top 10% of class: 6%
Top 25% of class: 20%
Top 50% of class: 44%

Deadlines
Early Action: No
Early Decision: No
Regular Action: Common Application: Accepted

Financial Aid
In-state tuition: $27,930
Out-of-state tuition: $27,930
Room: -
Board: -
Books: $1,000
Freshmen receiving need-based aid: 83%
Undergrads receiving need-based aid: 71%
Avg. % of need met by financial aid: Not reported
Avg. aid package (freshmen): Not reported
Avg. aid package (undergrads): Not reported
Freshmen receiving merit-based aid: 17%
Undergrads receiving merit-based aid: 16%
Avg. student debt upon graduation: $18,300

School Spirit
Mascot: Bobcats
Colors: Columbia navy and white

STETSON UNIVERSITY

421 North Woodland Boulevard, Deland, FL 32723
Admissions: 800-688-0101 · Financial Aid: 800-688-7120
Email: admissions@stetson.edu · Website: http://www.stetson.edu

From the College

"Stetson University is a small, private, liberal arts university with a main campus in DeLand, between Orlando and Daytona, and a College of Law in Gulfport. From its founding in 1883, Stetson University has affirmed the importance of spiritual life and the quest for truth in its educational mission. The University motto, Pro Deo et Veritate ("For God and Truth"), is a symbol of this commitment and expresses our determination to integrate the pursuit of a liberal education with the search for meaning in our lives and communities.

"Stetson today offers undergraduate and pre-professional programs in its College of Arts and Sciences, School of Business Administration and School of Music. Graduate programs are offered in selected fields—business, teacher education, counselor education, and English—and the College of Law offers the JD and Master of Law degrees as well as a joint JD/MBA degree. Graduate programs are also offered in new academic centers in the planned community of Celebration (education and business) and in downtown Tampa (law). Through Stetson Undergraduate Research Experience (SURE) grants, students complete a summer research project in the field of their choice while receiving a stipend. All students in the College of Arts and Sciences are required to complete a research project prior to graduation. The research requirements in the College of Arts and Sciences have led to students receiving undergraduate awards such as the Truman scholarship and outstanding graduate school fellowships in the nation's leading research universities.

"Stetson's music program has produced many outstanding performers and music educators. The School of Music also offers students the opportunity to combine their degree in music with any other field offered by the university.

"The Roland George Investments Program offers a program of advanced education in investment management that equips students for positions in financial institutions such as banks, trust companies, brokerage firms and investment advisory firms. Stetson students in the program assume full responsibility for active management of a portfolio valued at approximately $3 million. Stetson's Family Business Center offers the nation's first major devoted to family enterprises.

"Stetson University offers a wide variety of international programs, including study abroad in France, Germany, Hong Kong, Mexico, Russia, Spain and Oxford in the United Kingdom. Stetson also offers two summer programs: intensive Spanish language study in Mexico and business in Austria. There are internship opportunities in Germany, England and Latin America. In addition, each year professors lead short Off-Campus Programs abroad during semester breaks."

Campus Setting

A four-year institution, Stetson University has a large, well-stocked library. The campus facilities include: art gallery · mineral museum · theatre. Stetson University provides on-campus housing with 922 units that can accommodate 1,847 students. Housing options: co-ed dorms · women's dorms · men's dorms · sorority housing · fraternity housing · single-student apartments.

Student Life and Activities

With 72 percent of students living on campus, there are plenty of social activities. As reported by a school representative, "an abundance of opportunities exist." Popular gathering spots include: the Commons on campus, around the fountain in the quad, the Abbey and beaches of the Atlantic Ocean. Popular campus events include: Greenfeather, School of Music concerts, Howard Thurman Lecture Series and Spring homecoming. Stetson University has 119 official student organizations. Greeks, the Student Government Association and a variety of student-run clubs influence campus life. For those interested in sports, there are intramural teams such as: baseball · basketball · billiards · bowling · cross-country/track · darts · dodgeball · flag football · floor ball/hockey · foosball · golf · inner-tube water polo · kickball · melonball · sand volleyball · soccer · softball · swimming · table tennis · tennis · ultimate Frisbee · volleyball · wiffle ball. Stetson University is a member of the Atlantic Sun Conference (Division I).

Academics and Learning Environment

For the B student, the learning environment of a college is just as important as the quality of its academic program. Stetson University has 231 full-time and 127 part-time faculty members, offering a student-to-faculty ratio of 11:1. The most common course size is 10 to 19 students. Stetson University offers 64 majors with the most popular being business administration, psychology and education and least popular being American studies, geography and Latin American studies. The school has a general core requirement as well as a religion requirement Cooperative education is available. All first-year students must maintain a 2.0 GPA or higher to avoid academic probation. Other special academic programs that would appeal to a B student: self-designed majors · pass/fail grading option · independent study · double majors · dual degrees · accelerated study · honors program · Phi Beta Kappa · internships · weekend college.

B Student Support and Success

Stetson offers a first-year program designed specifically to help the new student transition to college life. It features a center with a computer lab and study room, and F.O.C.U.S., or "Friends on Campus Uniting Students." This five-day orientation program teaches students about all about the resources available at Stetson. First-year seminars are offered in order to help students learn to read critically, analyze and interpret ideas, develop arguments, write persuasive text and produce different academic work.

Stetson University provides a variety of support programs including dedicated guidance for: academic · career · personal · psychological · minority students · family planning · religious. The average freshman year GPA is 2.7, and 77 percent of freshmen students return for their sophomore year.

Support for Students with Learning Disabilities

Students with learning disabilities may take advantage of specific support programs offered by Stetson University. If necessary, the college will grant additional time to students with learning disabilities to complete their degree. Also, a lightened course load may be granted to LD students. Students with learning disabilities will find the following programs at Stetson University extremely useful: tutors · learning center · extended time for tests · take-home exam · oral tests · exam on tape or computer · readers · note-taking

STETSON UNIVERSITY

429

College Profiles

STETSON UNIVERSITY

Highlights

Admissions
Applicants: 4,110
Accepted: 2,215
Acceptance rate: 53.9%
Average GPA: 3.7
ACT range: 21-26
SAT Math range: 500-600
SAT Reading range: 500-610
SAT Writing range: Not reported
Top 10% of class: 35%
Top 25% of class: 74%
Top 50% of class: 96%

Deadlines
Early Action: No
Early Decision: November 1
Regular Action: March 15 (priority)
Common Application: Accepted

Financial Aid
In-state tuition: $29,880
Out-of-state tuition: $29,880
Room: $5,014
Board: $3,920
Books: $1,000
Freshmen receiving need-based aid: 63%
Undergrads receiving need-based aid:
   59%
Avg. % of need met by financial aid: 83%
Avg. aid package (freshmen): $27,736
Avg. aid package (undergrads): $25,565
Freshmen receiving merit-based aid: 31%
Undergrads receiving merit-based aid:
   31%
Avg. student debt upon graduation:
   $28,775

School Spirit
Mascot: Hatters
Colors: Hunter green and white

services · tape recorders · texts on tape · early syllabus. Individual or small group tutorials are also available in: time management · organizational skills · learning strategies · specific subject areas · writing labs · math labs · study skills. An advisor/advocate from the Academic Resources Center is available to students.

How to Get Admitted

For admissions decisions, non-academic factors considered: interview · extracurricular activities · special talents, interests, abilities · character/personal qualities · volunteer work · work experience · geographical location · minority affiliation · alumni relationship. A high school diploma is required, although a GED is also accepted for admissions consideration. SAT or ACT test scores are required of all applicants. SAT Subject Test scores are recommended but not required.

How to Pay for College

To apply for financial aid, students should submit the following: Free Application for Federal Student Aid (FAFSA) · institution's own financial aid forms · state aid form. Stetson University participates in the Federal Work Study program. *Need-based aid programs include:* scholarships and grants · general need-based awards · Federal Pell grants · state scholarships and grants · college-based scholarships and grants · private scholarships and grants. *Non-Need-based aid programs include:* scholarships and grants · general need-based awards · state scholarships and grants · creative arts and performance awards · special achievements and activities awards · special characteristics awards · athletic scholarships · ROTC scholarships.

STEVENSON UNIVERSITY

1525 Greenspring Valley Road, Stevenson, MD 21153
Admissions: 877-468-6852 · Financial Aid: 877-468-6852
Email: admissions@stevenson.edu · Website: http://www.stevenson.edu

From the College

"Stevenson University (formerly Villa Julie College) is an independent, co-educational institution in Maryland. Students pursue undergraduate, master's and adult accelerated degrees at locations in Greenspring and Owings Mills. Stevenson has grown rapidly in recent years, setting new records for enrollment every year while maintaining quality academic programs and affordable tuition. Career Architecture allows students to undergo self-discovery exercises as soon as they arrive on campus in order to help them align their career goals with their personal interests and values.

"The Owings Mills campus opened in 2004 with seven apartment buildings and a community center for student events. The 100-acre campus now has four additional residence halls, a dining hall and student activities building, School of Business and Leadership, athletic fields and wellness center (formerly the home of the football Baltimore Ravens), and office and classroom space. Stevenson has added four-year programs in medical technology, public history and middle school education as well as the master's degree program in forensic studies. The forensic studies program, which includes tracks in law, accounting, information technology, investigations and interdisciplinary studies, is also available online.

"In addition to these new programs, Stevenson has expanded its offerings in the sciences and embraced distance-learning technology to bring its successful RN-to-BS nursing program to working nurses across the state. Since its founding in 1947 as a one-year school to train medical secretaries, Stevenson has focused on preparing its students to make positive contributions in the working world after graduation."

Campus Setting

Stevenson University's 62-acre campus in Stevenson is 10 miles from Baltimore. A four-year private institution, Stevenson University has an enrollment of 3,409 students. Although not originally a co-educational college, Stevenson University has been co-ed since 1972. In addition to a medium-sized library, the campus facilities include: art gallery · theatre · science center · labs · greenhouse. Stevenson University provides on-campus housing with 952 units that can accommodate 1,300 students. Housing options: single-student apartments. Recreation and sports facilities include: fitness centers · outdoor fields · training facilities · wellness center.

Student Life and Activities

Most students (59 percent) live off campus, which does impact the on-campus social scene. Nevertheless, like any college, students find time to create their own recreational outlets. As reported by a school representative, "Students meet friends on campus and organize off-campus activities. " Students gather on campus at the Student Center and the Exchange Cafe. Off campus, students frequent area night clubs and Baltimore Orioles baseball games at Camden Yard. Popular campus events include: Welcome Picnic, Villa Fest, Mr. and Ms. VJC, May Day and Founder's Day. Stevenson University has 45 official student organizations. Influential campus groups include: Greeks, student government, Black Student Union, Accounting Association, Student Nurses Association and political clubs. For those interested in sports, there are intramural teams such as: basketball · football · racquetball · soccer · tennis. Stevenson University is a member of the Capital Athletic Conference (Division III).

STEVENSON UNIVERSITY

America's
Best Colleges for
B Students

Academics and Learning Environment

For the B student, the learning environment of a college is just as important as the quality of its academic program. Stevenson University has 111 full-time and 171 part-time faculty members, offering a student-to-faculty ratio of 14:1. The most common course size is 10 to 19 students. Stevenson University offers 27 majors with the most popular being business systems, nursing and liberal arts/technology/computer/science/video. The school has a general core requirement. Cooperative education is available. All first-year students must maintain a 1.9 GPA or higher to avoid academic probation, and a minimum overall GPA of 2.0 is required to graduate. Other special academic programs that would appeal to a B student: self-designed majors · independent study · double majors · dual degrees · accelerated study · honors program · internships · weekend college · distance learning.

B Student Support and Success

Stevenson University provides a variety of support programs including dedicated guidance for: academic · career · personal · psychological · minority students · military · veterans · non-traditional students · family planning. Recognizing that some students may need extra preparation, Stevenson University offers remedial and refresher courses in: reading · writing · math · study skills. Other remedial services include Tutoring in all academic areas. Annually, 83 percent of freshmen students return for their sophomore year. Among students who enter the work force, approximately 96 percent enter a field related to their major within six months of graduation. Companies that most frequently hire graduates from Stevenson University include: Baltimore County School System · Blue Cross & Blue Shield · Carroll County School System · Greater Baltimore Medical Center · Harrford County School System · Johns Hopkins Hospital · Sinai Hospital · St. Joseph Medical Center · T. Rowe Price · various accounting firms.

Support for Students with Learning Disabilities

Students with learning disabilities may take advantage of specific support programs offered by Stevenson University. If necessary, the college will grant additional time to students with learning disabilities to complete their degree. Also, a lightened course load may be granted to LD students. High school foreign language waivers are accepted. High school math waivers are also accepted. Students with learning disabilities will find the following programs at Stevenson University extremely useful: remedial math · remedial English · remedial reading · tutors · learning center · testing accommodations · untimed tests · extended time for tests · oral tests · readers · note-taking services · reading machines · tape recorders · texts on tape · early syllabus · priority registration. Individual or small group tutorials are also available in: time management · organizational skills · learning strategies · specific subject areas · writing labs · math labs · study skills. An advisor/advocate from the Academic Support Services is available to students.

How to Get Admitted

For admissions decisions, non-academic factors considered: interview · extracurricular activities · special talents, interests, abilities · character/personal qualities · volunteer work · work experience · state of residency · geographical location · alumni relationship. A high school diploma is required, although a GED is also accepted for admissions consideration. SAT or ACT test scores are required of all applicants. *Academic units recommended:* 4 English, 3 Math, 3 Science, 2 Social Studies, 2 Foreign Language.

Insight

John Buettner, assistant vice president, says that Stevenson University is a former Catholic junior college (Villa Julie College before a name change in 2008) that has transitioned from a junior college for commuters to a four-year residential university over the last three decades, with the last 10 years being the university's time of greatest growth and acceleration.

How to Pay for College

To apply for financial aid, students should submit the following: Free Application for Federal Student Aid (FAFSA). Stevenson University participates in the Federal Work Study program. *Need-based aid programs include:* scholarships and grants · general need-based awards · Federal Pell grants · state scholarships and grants · college-based scholarships and grants · private scholarships and grants. *Non-Need-based aid programs include:* scholarships and grants · state scholarships and grants · creative arts and performance awards · special achievements and activities awards · special characteristics awards · ROTC scholarships.

STEVENSON UNIVERSITY

Highlights

Deadlines
Early Action: No
Early Decision: No
Regular Action: March 1 (priority)
Common Application: Accepted

Financial Aid
In-state tuition: $19,234
Out-of-state tuition: $19,234
Room: $6,750
Board: $1,596
Books: -
Freshmen receiving need-based aid: 67%
Undergrads receiving need-based aid: 61%
Avg. % of need met by financial aid: 71%
Avg. aid package (freshmen): $12,492
Avg. aid package (undergrads): $12,730
Freshmen receiving merit-based aid: 22%
Undergrads receiving merit-based aid: 25%
Avg. student debt upon graduation: $15,439

Prominent Alumni
Dr. P. Ann Cotten, director, Schaeffer Center for Public Policy, School of Public Affairs, University of Baltimore; Martha Kilma, former member of the Maryland House of Delegates.

School Spirit
Mascot: Mustangs
Colors: Green, black and white

STRATFORD UNIVERSITY

7777 Leesburg Pike, Suite 100, Falls Church, VA 22043
Admissions: 800-444-0804 · Financial Aid: 800-444-0804
Email: admissions@stratford.edu
Website: http://www.stratford.edu

Students
Total enrollment: 1,468
Undergrads: 474
Freshmen: Not reported
Live on-campus: 0%

Academics
Student/faculty ratio: 24:1
Class size 9 or fewer: 19%
Class size 10-29: 81%
Class size 30-49: 4%
Class size 50-99: 1%
Class size 100 or more: 1%
Returning freshmen: Not reported
Six-year graduation rate: Not reported

Admissions
Average GPA: Not reported
ACT range: Not reported
SAT Math range: Not reported
SAT Reading range: Not reported
SAT Writing range: Not reported

Deadlines
Early Action: No
Early Decision: No
Regular Action: Common Application: Not
  accepted

Financial Aid
In-state tuition: $14,000
Room: -
Board: -
Books: $1,560
Avg. % of need met by financial aid: Not
  reported
Avg. aid package (freshmen): Not re-
  ported
Avg. aid package (undergrads): Not
  reported

From the College

"The mission of Stratford University is to transition students into rewarding and challenging careers by providing quality, competency-based educational programs that meet the needs of employers in high demand industries."

Campus Setting

The campus in is Falls Church (population: 9,578), 10 miles from Washington, DC. A four-year, private (for-profit) institution, Stratford University has an enrollment of 1,468 students.

Student Life and Activities

All students live off campus.

Academics and Learning Environment

For the B student, the learning environment of a college is just as important as the quality of its academic program. Stratford University has a student-to-faculty ratio of 24:1 and offers 19 majors. Culinary arts and hospitality, health sciences, computer information systems and business administration are the most popular majors. The school does not have a general core requirement. Cooperative education is not offered. Other special academic programs that would appeal to a B student: academic/career counseling service · employment services for students · placement services for graduates.

B Student Support and Success

The Career and Student Services offers a variety of programs including an orientation program and a career development placement program that offers courses in effective resume writing techniques, effective interviewing techniques, interview opportunities and career planning and placement assistance.

Support for Students with Learning Disabilities

Students with learning disabilities may take advantage of specific support programs offered by Stratford University. Students with learning disabilities will find the following programs at Stratford University extremely useful: academic counseling service.

How to Get Admitted

The university has an open admissions policy. A high school diploma is required, although a GED is also accepted for admissions consideration.

How to Pay for College

To apply for financial aid, students should submit the following: Free Application for Federal Student Aid (FAFSA). Stratford University does participate in the Federal Work Study program. *Need-based aid programs include:* scholarships and grants · general need-based awards · Federal Pell grants · state scholarships and grants · college-based scholarships and grants · private scholarships and grants. *Non-Need-based aid programs include:* scholarships and grants · state scholarships and grants.

SUFFOLK UNIVERSITY

8 Ashburton Place, Boston, MA 02108
Admissions: 800-6-SUFFOL · Financial Aid: 617-573-8470
Email: admission@suffolk.edu · Website: http://www.suffolk.edu

From the College

"Suffolk University is a comprehensive university offering a wide range of undergraduate and graduate degrees in the College of Arts and Sciences, Sawyer Business School and Law School. The university's academic programs emphasize high-quality teaching, small class size and real-world career applications. Ninety-four percent of the faculty members hold Ph.D.'s, and many are practicing professionals in their fields. However, their first priority is teaching and mentoring. The undergraduate academic program offers more than 70 majors and 1,000 courses.

"Suffolk was selected to the first tier of "Best Universities Master's in the North" by U.S. News & World Report, as one of the "Best 361 Colleges" by the Princeton Review, to Barron's Best Buys in College Education and, most recently, as a College of Distinction by an independent committee of high school guidance counselors and college admissions professionals.

"Suffolk offers more than 75 student clubs and organizations, a nationally ranked debate team, three student-run publications, a strong performing arts program and numerous special events, dances, lectures and community service activities. Suffolk has three residence halls, a new state-of-the-art undergraduate library, and a new theater. Modern dormitory facilities provide Internet, cable and telephone access and beautiful views of the city.

"The university has campuses in Boston; Madrid, Spain; and Dakar, Senegal. Nearly 1,000 international students are enrolled at the Boston, Madrid and Dakar campuses. The University is committed to helping international students adjust to life in the United States. The Center for International Education assists students and advises them on immigration, administrative and cultural adjustment issues. Special social and cultural activities are offered to all international students. Courses in English as a second language, writing and tutoring are also offered."

Campus Setting

Suffolk University is located in the heart of Boston. Suffolk's campus is in Beacon Hill, a secure residential neighborhood of brick homes and the state capitol building. In addition to a large, well-stocked library, the campus facilities include: theatre · arts and design gallery · biology field station · law school gallery · audio · video and DVD equipment. Suffolk University provides on-campus housing with 550 units that can accommodate 1,048 students. Housing options: co-ed dorms · single-student apartments. Recreation and sports facilities include: fitness center · gymnasium · shared ice rink with Boston University · off-campus tennis courts and softball fields.

Student Life and Activities

Most students (76 percent) live off campus, which does impact the on-campus social scene. Nevertheless, like any college, students find time to create their own recreational outlets. Popular on-campus gathering spots include the Sawyer Library, local pubs, dance clubs and student lounges in the Sawyer and Donahue buildings. Popular campus events include: Commuter Fair, Spring Fling, Fall Fest, Various Performance Series, Winter Ball and Temple Street Fair. Suffolk University has 75 official student organizations. Popular groups on campus include: athletes, Student Government Association, Women in Business, Program Council and Council of Presidents, the Off-Campus Housing Office, Commuter Student Association, Suffolk University Hispanic Association (SUHA) and Black Student Union. For those interested in sports, there are intramural teams such as: basketball · volleyball. Suffolk University is a member of the NCAA, ECAC (Division III), GNAC Great Northeast Athletic Conference (Division III).

Academics and Learning Environment

For the B student, the learning environment of a college is just as important as the quality of its academic program. Suffolk University has 430 full-time and 607 part-time faculty members, offering a student-to-faculty ratio of 12:1. The most common course size is 20 to 29 students. Suffolk University offers 115 majors with the most popular being sociology, management and marketing and least popular being philosophy, computer science and mathematics. The school has a general core requirement. Cooperative education is available. All first-year students must maintain a 1.8 GPA or higher to avoid academic probation, and a minimum overall GPA of 2.0 is required to graduate. Other special academic programs that would appeal to a B student: pass/fail grading option · independent study · double majors · dual degrees · accelerated study · honors program · internships · weekend college · distance learning certificate programs.

B Student Support and Success

Suffolk has many different methods of helping students who are feeling a little lost or falling behind. At the Ballotti Learning Center, a Tutor Program matches students with peer tutors who can help students in two ways: 1) by providing extra support for students who are taking a course that is proving difficult for them or 2) through teaching general academic strategies like note taking, exam prep, time management, etc. The service is free, and tutors and students meet up to twice a week for one-hour sessions. In a survey done by the Learning Center, 97 percent of the students tutored reported that it helped them to become more independent learners. Study groups are also offered at the center. They focus on the traditionally high-risk courses and give students the time to review notes and prepare questions for class. Staff consultants at Ballotti are doctoral students in the field of psychology. Their job is to assist students with personal concerns and challenges. (Sessions are private and confidential.)

The AHANA (African Hispanic Asian Native American) International Program is an outreach program for students of color. Peer liaisons help with issues like second language, stereotypes and cultural differences that may occur.

Suffolk recognizes that some students may face academic challenges that could result in low grades. To help provide support for these struggling students, Suffolk has put two programs into place: High Profile and the Roster Project.

The school's High Profile Program is for students who are in "academic jeopardy." A team of counselors and technicians connect these students with services that can provide academic support.

The Roster Project identifies students who are heading for "academic risk" by mid-semester (at risk of failing because of missing class, poor study habits or communication skills, second language

SUFFOLK UNIVERSITY

Highlights

Suffolk University
Boston, MA (Pop. 599,531)
Location: Major city
Website: http://www.suffolk.edu

Students
Total enrollment: 9,435
Undergrads: 2,520
Freshmen: 1,570
Part-time students: 10%
From out-of-state: 39%
Male/Female: 43%/57%
Live on-campus: 24%
Off-campus employment rating: Good
Caucasian: 59%
African American: 3%
Hispanic: 6%
Asian or Pacific Islander: 6%
Native American: 0%
International: 10%

Academics
Student/faculty ratio: 12:1
Class size 9 or fewer: 14%
Class size 10-29: 72%
Class size 30-49: 13%
Class size 50-99: 1%
Class size 100 or more: -
Returning freshmen: 72%
Six-year graduation rate: 55%

Most Popular Fields of Study
Business, Finance, Sales and Marketing
Protective Services, Criminal Justice and
    Public Administration
English and Literature
Philosophy, Religion and Theology
Psychology
Engineering and Engineering Technologies
Law and Legal Studies
Foreign Languages, Literature and Linguistics
Communications, Journalism, Advertising
    and Comm. Technologies
Education

437

SUFFOLK UNIVERSITY

Admissions
Applicants: 9,171
Accepted: 7,513
Acceptance rate: 81.9%
placed on wait list: 308
Average GPA: 3.0
ACT range: 20-24
SAT Math range: 450-560
SAT Reading range: 450-550
SAT Writing range: 450-560
Top 10% of class: 11%
Top 25% of class: 32%
Top 50% of class: 70%

Deadlines
Early Action: November 20
Early Decision: No
Regular Action: Rolling admissions
Common Application: Accepted

Financial Aid
In-state tuition: $27,100
Out-of-state tuition: $27,100
Room: $1,204
Board: $2,340
Books: $1,000
Freshmen receiving need-based aid: 58%
Undergrads receiving need-based aid: 54%
Avg. % of need met by financial aid: 60%
Avg. aid package (freshmen): $15,063
Avg. aid package (undergrads): $15,232
Freshmen receiving merit-based aid: 6%
Undergrads receiving merit-based aid: 9%
Avg. student debt upon graduation: $17,006

Prominent Alumni
Robert L. Caret, president of Towson University; Jeanette G. Clough, president of Mt. Auburn Hospital; Dr. Karen De-Salvo, chief of general internal medicine at Tulane University.

School Spirit
Mascot: Rams
Colors: Blue and gold

America's
Best Colleges for
B Students

issues, etc.). Letters or calls are made as a warning and then students are encouraged to seek the help they need.

Educational consultants are on campus to address issues that affect a student's academic life. This often includes matching student with tutor and then monitoring the relationship to make sure it is successful and effective.

Suffolk University provides a variety of support programs including dedicated guidance for: academic · career · personal · psychological · minority students · veterans · non-traditional students · family planning · religious. Recognizing that some students may need extra preparation, Suffolk University offers remedial and refresher courses in: reading · writing · math · study skills. Other services are provided on an individual basis. The average freshman year GPA is 2.5, and 72 percent of freshmen students return for their sophomore year. What do students do after college? While many enter the work force, approximately 23 percent pursue a graduate degree immediately after graduation. Among students who enter the work force, approximately 70 percent enter a field related to their major within six months of graduation. Companies that most frequently hire graduates from Suffolk University include: Bank of America · Commonwealth of Massachusetts · Ernst & Young · Fidelity Investments · KPMG · Mass General Hospital · PricewaterhouseCoopers · State Street Corp.

Support for Students with Learning Disabilities

Students with learning disabilities may take advantage of specific support programs offered by Suffolk University. If necessary, the college will grant additional time to students with learning disabilities to complete their degree. Also, a lightened course load may be granted to LD students. According to the school, the LD program varies by student depending on needs. There are academic, psychological and student support groups and vocational counseling for all students, but the intensity and type of counseling is determined on an individual basis. LD students may meet with their advisor/advocate within the LD program as often or as little they and their advisor/advocate feel they need. Students with learning disabilities will find the following programs at Suffolk University extremely useful: remedial math · remedial English · remedial reading · tutors · learning center · testing accommodations · untimed tests · extended time for tests · take-home exam · oral tests · readers · typist/scribe · note-taking services · reading machines · tape recorders · texts on tape · early syllabus · priority registration · waiver of math degree requirement. Individual or small group tutorials are also available in: time management · organizational skills · learning strategies · specific subject areas · writing labs · math labs · study skills. An advisor/advocate from the Ballotti Learning Center is available to students.

How to Get Admitted

For admissions decisions, non-academic factors considered: interview · extracurricular activities · special talents, interests, abilities · character/personal qualities · volunteer work · work experience · state of residency · geographical location · alumni relationship. A high school diploma is required, although a GED is also accepted for admissions consideration. SAT or ACT test scores are required of all applicants. *According to the admissions office:* Minimum combined SAT Reasoning score of 950, rank in top half of secondary school class, and minimum 2.5 GPA is highly recommended. *Academic units recommended:* 4 English, 4 Math, 4 Science, 3 Foreign Language.

How to Pay for College

To apply for financial aid, students should submit the following: Free Application for Federal Student Aid (FAFSA) · institution's own financial aid forms. Suffolk University participates in the Federal Work Study program. *Need-based aid programs include:* scholarships and grants · general need-based awards · Federal Pell grants · state scholarships and grants · private scholarships and grants. *Non-Need-based aid programs include:* scholarships and grants · state scholarships and grants.

SUNY - PURCHASE COLLEGE

735 Anderson Hill Road, Purchase, NY 10577
Admissions: 914-251-6300 · Financial Aid: 914-251-6350
Email: admissn@purchase.edu
Website: http://www.purchase.edu

SUNY - Purchase College
Purchase, NY
Location: Large town
Website: http://www.purchase.edu

Students
Total enrollment: 4,251
Undergrads: 1,843
Freshmen: 1,099
Part-time students: 11%
From out-of-state: 27%
Male/Female: 45%/55%
Live on-campus: 68%
Off-campus employment rating: Fair
Caucasian: 56%
African American: 8%
Hispanic: 10%
Asian or Pacific Islander: 3%
Native American: 0%
International: 2%

Academics
Student/faculty ratio: 17:1
Class size 9 or fewer: 33%
Class size 10-29: 49%
Class size 30-49: 15%
Class size 50-99: 2%
Class size 100 or more: -
Returning freshmen: 79%
Six-year graduation rate: 50%

Most Popular Fields of Study
Psychology
English and Literature
Philosophy, Religion and Theology
Interdisciplinary Studies
Liberal Arts, Humanities and General
    Studies
Communications, Journalism, Advertising
    and Comm. Technologies
Social Sciences, History, Economics,
    Political Science
Visual and Performing Arts
Biological and Life Sciences

From the College

"SUNY - Purchase College combines conservatory programs in the arts with distinctive liberal arts programs. Its location in Westchester allows access to New York City 35 miles away but provides a safe self-contained 500-acre campus in a suburban location that contains facilities including a Performing Arts Center and the Neuberger Museum of Art. Its academic programs combine attention to general education with structured curricula; all programs culminate in a required senior project, and increasingly students enter learning communities that provide faculty and peer mentors, advisors and shared academic and co-curricular activities."

Campus Setting

SUNY - Purchase College, founded in 1967 as SUNY College at Purchase, is a public, multipurpose college and conservatory of liberal and fine arts. A four-year institution, SUNY - Purchase College has an enrollment of 4,251 students. In addition to a large, well-stocked library, the campus also has an art museum. SUNY - Purchase College provides on-campus housing that can accommodate 2,540 students. Housing options: co-ed dorms · single-student apartments · special housing for disabled students · special housing for International students. Recreation and sports facilities include: aerobics studio · baseball · softball and soccer fields · basketball and tennis courts · fitness center · gymnasium · weight room · Turf field with lights.

Student Life and Activities

With 68 percent of students living on campus, there are plenty of social activities. Popular campus events include Culture Shock and the Purchase Wide Open Festival. SUNY - Purchase College has 32 official student organizations. For those interested in sports, there are intramural teams such as: aerobics · basketball · bowling · dodgeball · flag football · floor hockey · golf · ice skating · Pilates · racquetball · rock climbing · soccer · softball · table tennis · tae kwon do · tennis · ultimate Frisbee · volleyball · weight lifting · yoga, ski trips. SUNY - Purchase College is a member of the NCAA, Skyline Conference (Division III), ECAC.

Academics and Learning Environment

For the B student, the learning environment of a college is just as important as the quality of its academic program. SUNY - Purchase College has 145 full-time and 233 part-time faculty members, offering a student-to-faculty ratio of 17:1. The most common course size is 10 to 19 students. SUNY - Purchase College offers 44 majors with the most popular being visual and performing arts, liberal arts/general studies and social sciences. The school has a general core requirement. Cooperative education is not offered. All first-year students must maintain a 2.0 GPA or higher to avoid academic probation. Other special academic programs that would appeal to a B student: self-designed majors · pass/fail grading option · independent study · double majors · internships · distance learning.

B Student Support and Success

Struggling students at SUNY can go to the Learning Center for free tutoring services in writing, math and foreign languages. Sessions with tutors in additional subjects can be arranged.

The center also offers students study skills help and printed materials in areas such as time management, making outlines, taking notes and studying. There are multimedia stations for computer assisted learning. Students interested in forming a study group can organize it through the Learning Center, and those with learning disabilities or other special needs can get help using a reading machine and other software.
SUNY - Purchase College provides a variety of support programs including dedicated guidance for: career · psychological. Recognizing that some students may need extra preparation, SUNY - Purchase College offers remedial and refresher courses in: reading · writing · math · study skills. Annually, 79 percent of freshmen students return for their sophomore year.

Support for Students with Learning Disabilities

Students with learning disabilities may take advantage of specific support programs offered by SUNY - Purchase College.

How to Get Admitted

For admissions decisions, non-academic factors considered: interview · extracurricular activities · special talents, interests, abilities · character/personal qualities · state of residency. A high school diploma is required, although a GED is also accepted for admissions consideration. SAT or ACT test scores are required of all applicants. SAT Subject Test scores are not required. *According to the admissions office:* Minimum combined SAT Reasoning score of 1100 or minimum grade average of 3.0 required. *Academic units recommended:* 4 English, 4 Math, 3 Science, 4 Social Studies, 3 Foreign Language.

How to Pay for College

To apply for financial aid, students should submit the following: Free Application for Federal Student Aid (FAFSA) · state aid form. SUNY - Purchase College participates in the Federal Work Study program. *Need-based aid programs include:* scholarships and grants · general need-based awards · Federal Pell grants · state scholarships and grants · college-based scholarships and grants · private scholarships and grants. *Non-Need-based aid programs include:* scholarships and grants · state scholarships and grants · creative arts and performance awards.

SUNY - PURCHASE COLLEGE

Highlights

Admissions
Applicants: 8,905
Accepted: 2,155
Acceptance rate: 24.2%
Average GPA: 3.2
ACT range: 22-26
SAT Math range: 490-590
SAT Reading range: 520-620
SAT Writing range: 510-610
Top 10% of class: 10%
Top 25% of class: 39%
Top 50% of class: 81%

Deadlines
Early Action: No
Early Decision: November 1
Regular Action: March 1 (priority)
July 15 (final)
Common Application: Not accepted

Financial Aid
In-state tuition: $4,350
Out-of-state tuition: $10,610
Room: -
Board: -
Books: $1,100
Freshmen receiving need-based aid: 53%
Undergrads receiving need-based aid: 51%
Avg. % of need met by financial aid: 61%
Avg. aid package (freshmen): $7,473
Avg. aid package (undergrads): $8,725
Freshmen receiving merit-based aid: 5%
Undergrads receiving merit-based aid: 8%
Avg. student debt upon graduation: $20,209

School Spirit
Mascot: panther
Colors: Royal blue and white

SWEET BRIAR COLLEGE

134 Chapel Road, Sweet Briar, VA 24595
Admissions: 800-381-6142 · Financial Aid: 800-381-6156
Email: admissions@sbc.edu · Website: http://www.sbc.edu

From the College

"Sweet Briar College grants bachelor's of arts, science and fine arts and master of arts in teaching and master of education degrees. The college offers more than 40 programs of study, including the new engineering science program, as well as self-designed and interdisciplinary majors. Students create and learn with faculty almost all of whom hold the doctorate or the appropriate terminal degree. Classes are small, and each student's educational program is customized."

Campus Setting

Sweet Briar, founded in 1901, is a private, liberal arts college for women. The campus has retained the Georgian architectural style of the original campus buildings. Its 3,300-acre campus is located in Sweet Briar, 12 miles from Lynchburg. Sweet Briar College has an enrollment of 828 students. In addition to a large, well-stocked library, the campus facilities include: museum · center for the creative arts. Sweet Briar College provides on-campus housing with 386 units that can accommodate 615 students. Housing options: women's dorms. Recreation and sports facilities include: field hockey · lacrosse · soccer and softball fields · fitness center · gymnasium · swimming pool · tennis court · trails · weight room.

Student Life and Activities

With 90 percent of students living on campus, there are plenty of social activities. Popular on-campus gathering spots include: Le Bistro and Vixen Den, Boat House, Bookstore Cafe, Prothro Dining Hall and Student Commons Courtyard. Popular campus events include: Spring Fling, Quadrocks and Student Involvement Fair and Parents' Weekend. Sweet Briar College has 61 official student organizations. The most popular are: Chamber orchestra · Sweet Tones · Paints and Patches · Amnesty International · Gay-Straight Alliance · Student Union-Campus Events Organization · Red Clay · College Republicans · Young Democrats · Model UN · Sociological Society. For those interested in sports, there are intramural teams such as: hiking · kayaking · mountain biking · riding · rock climbing · running · tennis · touch football. Sweet Briar College is a member of the Old Dominion Athletic Conference (Division III).

Academics and Learning Environment

For the B student, the learning environment of a college is just as important as the quality of its academic program. Sweet Briar College has 65 full-time and 36 part-time faculty members, offering a student-to-faculty ratio of 9:1. The most common course size is 10 to 19 students. Sweet Briar College offers 39 majors with the most popular being biology, business and psychology and least popular being engineering management, Italian studies and French. The school has a general core requirement. Cooperative education is not offered. All first-year students must maintain a 2.0 GPA or higher to avoid academic probation. Other special academic programs that would appeal to a B student: self-designed majors · independent study · double majors · dual degrees · accelerated study · honors program · internships.

B Student Support and Success

The Academic Resource Center (ARC) at Sweet Briar College provides many different opportunities for student support, including ways to help make college life and courses easier. The center is available to all students and is staffed by trained student assistants. ARC offers information on time management, writing, reading, study skills, stress management, peer tutoring and mentoring. ARC staff also offers assistance for students with learning differences, intent on "encouraging a higher standard of academic performance."

The writing tutoring service is ARC's main focus. The staff works with students on all stages of their papers' preparation, from forming a thesis to perfecting punctuation. Experienced student mentors help freshmen adjust to college academics.

ARC also offers online and printed resources on topics like weekly time management and course preparation. In addition, ARC assists with the social aspects of college life and the potential stress this can bring.

Sweet Briar College provides a variety of support programs including dedicated guidance for: academic · career · personal · psychological · religious. The average freshman year GPA is 2.8, and 71 percent of freshmen students return for their sophomore year. What do students do after college? While many enter the work force, approximately 29 percent pursue a graduate degree immediately after graduation. Among students who enter the work force, approximately 57 percent enter a field related to their major within six months of graduation. Companies that most frequently hire graduates from Sweet Briar College include: Ann Taylor · Books a Million · Center for Coastal Studies · Edelman Public Relations · Federal Bureau of Investigation · Freddie Mac · Genworth Financial · Merck Pharmaceuticals · National Association of Real Estate Executives · National Security Agency · Smith Barney · *Washington Post* · Yale University Cancer Center.

Support for Students with Learning Disabilities

Students with learning disabilities may take advantage of specific support programs offered by Sweet Briar College. If necessary, the college will grant additional time to students with learning disabilities to complete their degree. High school foreign language waivers are accepted. High school math waivers are also accepted. Students with learning disabilities will find the following programs at Sweet Briar College extremely useful: tutors · learning center · extended time for tests. Individual or small group tutorials are also available in: time management · organizational skills · learning strategies · specific subject areas · writing labs · study skills. An advisor/advocate from the Academic Advising is available to students. This member also sits on the admissions committee.

How to Get Admitted

For admissions decisions, non-academic factors considered: interview · extracurricular activities · special talents, interests, abilities · character/personal qualities · volunteer work · work experience · state of residency · minority affiliation · alumni relationship. A high school diploma is required, although a GED is also accepted for admissions consideration. SAT or ACT test scores are required of all applicants. SAT Subject Test scores are considered, if submitted, but are not required. *According to the admissions office:* Mathematics preparation must be at least through Algebra II. Foreign language must include two consecutive years of same language. *Academic*

SWEET BRIAR COLLEGE

Sweet Briar College
Sweet Briar, VA (Pop. 5,000)
Location: Rural
Website: http://www.sbc.edu

Students
Total enrollment: 828
Undergrads: 28
Freshmen: 212
Part-time students: 6%
From out-of-state: 56%
Male/Female: 3%/97%
Live on-campus: 90%
Off-campus employment rating: Poor
Caucasian: 87%
African American: 3%
Hispanic: 3%
Asian or Pacific Islander: 1%
Native American: 1%
International: 1%

Academics
Student/faculty ratio: 9:1
Class size 9 or fewer: 37%
Class size 10-29: 62%
Class size 30-49: 2%
Class size 50-99: 2%
Class size 100 or more: -
Returning freshmen: 71%
Six-year graduation rate: 72%

Most Popular Fields of Study
Biological and Life Sciences
Business, Finance, Sales and Marketing
Area, Ethnic and Gender Studies

SWEET BRIAR COLLEGE

Admissions
Applicants: 629
Accepted: 520
Acceptance rate: 82.7%
Average GPA: 3.5
ACT range: 23-28
SAT Math range: 470-600
SAT Reading range: 510-630
SAT Writing range: Not reported
Top 10% of class: 28%
Top 25% of class: 53%
Top 50% of class: 88%

Deadlines
Early Action: No
Early Decision: December 1
Regular Action: February 1 (priority)
February 1 (final)
Common Application: Accepted

Financial Aid
In-state tuition: $28,860
Out-of-state tuition: $28,860
Room: -
Board: -
Books: $900
Freshmen receiving need-based aid: 65%
Undergrads receiving need-based aid: 64%
Avg. % of need met by financial aid: 70%
Avg. aid package (freshmen): $15,051
Avg. aid package (undergrads): $13,633
Freshmen receiving merit-based aid: 33%
Undergrads receiving merit-based aid: 40%
Avg. student debt upon graduation: $25,373

Prominent Alumni
Sherri L. Manson, Equity Investors Ltd.; Elizabeth Harvey Fitzgerald, Alpha Laboratories.

School Spirit
Mascot: Vixen
Colors: Forest green and pink
Song: *Sweet Briar, Sweet Briar, Flower Fair*

units recommended: 4 English, 4 Math, 4 Science, 4 Social Studies, 4 Foreign Language.

How to Pay for College

To apply for financial aid, students should submit the following: Free Application for Federal Student Aid (FAFSA) · Non-custodian (Divorced/Separated) Parent's Statement. Sweet Briar College participates in the Federal Work Study program. *Need-based aid programs include:* scholarships and grants · general need-based awards · Federal Pell grants · state scholarships and grants · college-based scholarships and grants · private scholarships and grants. *Non-Need-based aid programs include:* scholarships and grants · general need-based awards · state scholarships and grants · creative arts and performance awards · special achievements and activities awards · special characteristics awards.

TEMPLE UNIVERSITY

1801 North Broad Street, Philadelphia, PA 19122-6096
Admissions: 888-340-2222 · Financial Aid: 215-204-8760
Email: tuadm@temple.edu · Website: http://www.temple.edu

From the College

"Temple University's faculty and its broad curriculum of over 300 academic programs provide educational opportunities for academically talented and highly motivated students, without regard to their status or station in life. Temple's richly diverse student population and the growth of its residential campus community enrich the educational and extracurricular life of all Temple's people. While the university especially serves students from Greater Philadelphia, it is enlivened by a rapidly increasing number of students from across Pennsylvania, throughout the nation and around the world. Temple maintains an international presence with campuses in Tokyo and Rome and programs in London, Beijing and six other locations worldwide. A long-time leader in professional education, Temple prepares the largest body of practitioners in Pennsylvania and is among the nation's largest educators in the combined fields of medicine, dentistry, pharmacy, podiatry and law. In addition, Temple offers more than four dozen doctoral and more than 100 master's degree programs that contribute to research and scholarship. Temple seeks to create new knowledge that improves the human condition and uplifts the human spirit. To achieve this goal, Temple maintains its commitment to recruiting, retaining and supporting outstanding faculty."

Campus Setting

Temple, founded in 1888, is a public, comprehensive, four-year university. Its 105-acre main campus is located in the center of Philadelphia. In addition to a large, well-stocked library, the campus facilities include: dentistry · pharmacy · podiatric museums. planetarium · observatory · art gallery · recording booths. Temple University provides on-campus housing with 1,806 units that can accommodate 4,891 students. Housing options: co-ed dorms · single-student apartments · special housing for disabled students. Recreation and sports facilities include: gymnastics · fencing and volleyball hall · baseball · football · soccer and softball fields · basketball center · recreation center · tennis pavilion.

Student Life and Activities

Most students (81 percent) live off campus, which does impact the on-campus social scene. Nevertheless, like any college, students find time to create their own recreational outlets. Temple has every type of person doing every type of thing. About 200 clubs and organizations are active on campus, with groups devoted to everything from fashion to the environment to community service. The sports enthusiast is well served at Temple, with 11 men's and 13 women's sports. Popular campus gathering spots include: the Tech Center, Howard Gittis Student Center, Liacouras Center, the Shops at Liacouras Walk and Bell Tower. Off campus, students gather at Liberty Bell, Penn's Landing, Philadelphia Art Museum, Olde City, South Street, Fairmount Park and Kelly's Drive, Kimmel Center for the Performing Arts, Liberty Place Shopping Mall and the Gallery Shopping Mall. Popular campus events include: Spring Fling, Homecoming, Ambler College Lecture Series, EarthFest, Free Friday, Welcome week, Memorable Moments, Welcome Back Week and Film Series at the Reel. The most popular student organizations are: Accounting Professional Society · American Medical Student Association · American Society of Civil Engineers · American Society of Mechanical Engineers · Association for Computing Machinery · Business Honors Student Association · Collegiate Music Educators Conference · Construc-

TEMPLE UNIVERSITY

Temple University
Philadelphia, PA (Pop. 1,500,000)
Location: Major city
Website: http://www.temple.edu

Students
Total enrollment: 35,490
Undergrads: 12,105
Freshmen: 4,186
Part-time students: 12%
From out-of-state: 26%
Male/Female: 46%/54%
Live on-campus: 19%
In fraternities: 1%
In sororities: 1%
Off-campus employment rating: Excellent
Caucasian: 58%
African American: 17%
Hispanic: 4%
Asian or Pacific Islander: 10%
Native American: 0%
International: 3%

Academics
Student/faculty ratio: 17:1
Class size 9 or fewer: 6%
Class size 10-29: 61%
Class size 30-49: 26%
Class size 50-99: 4%
Class size 100 or more: 3%
Returning freshmen: 87%
Six-year graduation rate: 65%

Most Popular Fields of Study
Business, Finance, Sales and Marketing
Visual and Performing Arts
Protective Services, Criminal Justice and
    Public Administration
Computer and Information Sciences
Communications, Journalism, Advertising
    and Comm. Technologies
Philosophy, Religion and Theology
Law and Legal Studies
English and Literature
Health Professions, Medicine and Re-
    lated Sciences

tion Management Student organization · Criminal Justice Society · Entrepreneurial Student Association. For those interested in sports, there are intramural teams such as: basketball · dodge ball · flag football · floor hockey · soccer · softball · volleyball. Temple University is a member of the Atlantic 10 Conference, Mid-American Conference (Division I, Football -A).

Academics and Learning Environment

For the B student, the learning environment of a college is just as important as the quality of its academic program. Temple University has 1,384 full-time and 1,506 part-time faculty members, offering a student-to-faculty ratio of 17:1. The most common course size is 20 to 29 students. Temple University offers 260 majors with the most popular being elementary education, psychology and marketing and least popular being environmental engineering technology, material sciences and mathematical economics. The school has a general core requirement. Cooperative education is available. All first-year students must maintain a 2.0 GPA or higher to avoid academic probation, and a minimum overall GPA of 2.0 is required to graduate. Other special academic programs that would appeal to a B student: self-designed majors · pass/fail grading option · independent study · double majors · dual degrees · honors program · Phi Beta Kappa · internships · distance learning certificate programs.

B Student Support and Success

Temple University offers plenty of support for its students, including computer labs, counseling and tutoring. The school provides students with the choice of more than 30 computer labs plus a Student Computer Center. Advisors are available to aid students with choosing majors and resolving academic and/or curriculum issues. Counselors are eager to provide "academic counseling for students to develop a meaningful education plan compatible with life goals." In addition, the advising center offers a new student orientation. The Student Support Services Program is part of the Russell Conwell Educational Service Center. It gives students intensive academic support through free year-round counseling and tutoring activities. In addition, the college offers a required six-week intensive Summer Bridge Program that includes skill building courses in math, computer technology, library usage, reading, writing and study skills as well as workshops on personal development, art appreciation and career choices.

Temple University provides a variety of support programs including dedicated guidance for: academic · career · personal · psychological · non-traditional students · family planning. Additional counseling services include: nutritionist/nutritional counseling, eating disorder counseling and support groups. Recognizing that some students may need extra preparation, Temple University offers remedial and refresher courses in: reading · writing · math · study skills. Annually, 87 percent of freshmen students return for their sophomore year.

Support for Students with Learning Disabilities

Students with learning disabilities may take advantage of specific support programs offered by Temple University. If necessary, the college will grant additional time to students with learning disabilities to complete their degree. Students with learning disabilities will find the following programs at Temple University extremely useful: testing accommodations · extended time for tests · take-home exam · exam on tape or computer · note-taking services · reading machines · tape recorders · texts on tape · videotaped classes · early syllabus · waiver of math degree requirement. Individual or small group tutorials are also available in: time management · specific subject areas · writing labs · math labs · study skills. An advisor/advocate from the Disability Resources and Services is available to students.

How to Get Admitted

For admissions decisions, non-academic factors considered: extracurricular activities · special talents, interests, abilities · character/personal qualities · volunteer work · work experience · state of residency · alumni relationship. A high school diploma is required, although a GED is also accepted for admissions consideration. SAT or ACT test scores are required of all applicants. *Academic units recommended:* 4 English, 4 Math, 3 Science, 2 Social Studies, 2 Foreign Language.

How to Pay for College

To apply for financial aid, students should submit the following: Free Application for Federal Student Aid (FAFSA). Temple University participates in the Federal Work Study program. *Need-based aid programs include:* scholarships and grants · general need-based awards · Federal Pell grants · state scholarships and grants · college-based scholarships and grants · private scholarships and grants · Federal Nursing scholarships. *Non-Need-based aid programs include:* scholarships and grants · state scholarships and grants · creative arts and performance awards · athletic scholarships · ROTC scholarships · music scholarships · drama scholarships.

TEMPLE UNIVERSITY

Highlights

Admissions
Applicants: 18,670
Accepted: 11,349
Acceptance rate: 60.8%
placed on wait list: 1,245
Average GPA: 3.4
ACT range: 21-26
SAT Math range: 510-610
SAT Reading range: 500-600
SAT Writing range: 490-590
Top 10% of class: 20%
Top 25% of class: 53%
Top 50% of class: 91%

Deadlines
Early Action: No
Early Decision: No
Regular Action: March 1 (final)
Common Application: Not accepted

Financial Aid
In-state tuition: $10,858
Out-of-state tuition: $19,878
Room: $5,866
Board: $3,018
Books: $1,000
Freshmen receiving need-based aid: 72%
Undergrads receiving need-based aid: 63%
Avg. % of need met by financial aid: 87%
Avg. aid package (freshmen): $14,579
Avg. aid package (undergrads): $13,958
Freshmen receiving merit-based aid: 17%
Undergrads receiving merit-based aid: 14%
Avg. student debt upon graduation: $26,064

Prominent Alumni
Dennis Alter, Advanta Co., chairman and CEO; Bill Cosby, TV personality and educator; John Dotson Jr., Pulitzer Prize-winning newspaper publisher.

School Spirit
Mascot: Owl
Colors: Cherry and white
Song: *T for Temple U University*

447

TEXAS TECH UNIVERSITY

Box 45005, Lubbock, TX 79409
Admissions: 806-742-1480 · Financial Aid: 806-742-3681
Email: admissions@ttu.edu · Website: http://www.ttu.edu

From the College

"Texas Tech University is a major comprehensive research university that retains the feel of a smaller liberal arts institution. Although enrollment is more than 28,000, our students have one-on-one interactions with faculty in a safe and traditional campus atmosphere. Our student body is diverse with students coming from nearly every state and more than 100 countries. Students choose from more than 150 undergraduate programs in 11 colleges, including an Honors College. Texas Tech is the only institution in the state with undergraduate and graduate schools, a law school and medical school all on the same campus, which facilitates your transition to professional studies. Texas Tech has a long history of involving undergraduates in research opportunities in areas such as alternative energy, food safety and other areas designed to solve real-world problems. We invest in the futures of talented and motivated students through the merit-based scholarship program. Any student with at least a 1250 SAT (reading and math only) or a 28 ACT (composite) and a top 10 percent high school class rank is eligible for a minimum of $10,000 in scholarships. Students who progress in the National Merit Scholarship Competition may receive scholarships totaling more than $60,000. Texas Tech is also committed to making college affordable for all students. The Red Raider Guarantee program offers four years of free tuition and fees to students whose families earn less than $40,000 per year. Lubbock, a city of more than 200,000, is large enough to offer great shopping, dining and entertainment options, but retains a friendly, college-focused atmosphere.."

Campus Setting

Texas Tech University, founded in 1923, has a 1,839-acre campus located in Lubbock. In addition to a large, well-stocked library, the campus facilities include: Southwest collection · Vietnam center and archives. Texas Tech University provides on-campus housing with 3,173 units that can accommodate 6,761 students. Housing options: co-ed dorms · women's dorms · men's dorms · single-student apartments · special housing for disabled students. Recreation and sports facilities include: aquatic center · arena · athletic training center · recreational fields · softball complex · tennis courts · track complex · leisure pool.

Student Life and Activities

Most students (74 percent) live off campus, which does impact the on-campus social scene. Nevertheless, like any college, students find time to create their own recreational outlets. Popular gathering spots on campus include: Tech Activities Board, Student Union and athletic venues. Popular gathering spots off campus include: Depot District, Greek Circle, Lone Star Pavilion and TTU Campus in Seville/Study Abroad. Popular campus events include: Homecoming Week Arbor Day, athletic and pre-athletic events (Raidergate), speakers and lectures, Hispanic Culture Week, Raider Welcome, Tech Activities Board activities, intramural sports, Relay for Life and community service. Texas Tech University has 421 student organizations. Popular groups on campus include: Greeks, community service organizations, multicultural and international student organizations, Student Government Association, Senate and Freshman Council and spirit groups. For those interested in sports, there are intramural teams such as: badminton · baseball · basketball · bowling disc golf · dodgeball · flag football · golf · inner-tube water polo · miniature golf · racquetball ·

sand volleyball · soccer · softball · swimming · table tennis · tennis · ultimate Frisbee · volleyball · water polo · weight lifting. Texas Tech University is a member of the Big 12 Conference (Division I, Football I-A).

Academics and Learning Environment

For the B student, the learning environment of a college is just as important as the quality of its academic program. Texas Tech University has 1,099 full-time and 81 part-time faculty members, offering a student-to-faculty ratio of 19:1. The most common course size is 10 to 19 students. Texas Tech University offers 281 majors with the most popular being human development and family studies, marketing and psychology and least popular being community/family/addiction services, German and theatre arts/design technology. The school has a general core requirement. Cooperative education is available. All first-year students must maintain a 2.0 GPA or higher to avoid academic probation. Other special academic programs that would appeal to a B student: self-designed majors · pass/fail grading option · independent study · double majors · dual degrees · accelerated study · honors program · Phi Beta Kappa · internships · distance learning certificate programs.

B Student Support and Success

The Discovery! Program's primary goal is to help students determine their major by examining their skills, values, interests and abilities. Texas Tech University provides other support programs including dedicated guidance for: academic · career · personal · psychological · minority students. Additional counseling services include: individual and group therapy for many psychological disorders. Recognizing that some students may need extra preparation, Texas Tech University offers remedial and refresher courses in: reading · writing · math · study skills. Other remedial services include advisement in course selection. Annually, 80 percent of freshmen students return for their sophomore year. What do students do after college? While many enter the work force, approximately 34 percent pursue a graduate degree immediately after graduation. Among students who enter the work force, approximately 84 percent enter a field related to their major within six months of graduation. Companies that most frequently hire graduates from Texas Tech University include: Weatherford International · General Dynamics, Cintas · Ernst & Young · ExxonMobil · IBM · Lockheed Martin · PriceWaterhouseCoopers · US Gypsum · Ferguson Enterprises · Chevron Phillips Chemical · Parkhill · Smith & Cooper · Raytheon · Texas Department of Transportation · Walgreens · Wells Fargo · 3M Co. · BWXT Pantex · Carter & Burgess · Halff Associates · Halliburton KBR · Freese & Nichols · Huitt-Zollars · Jacobs Engineering · KSA Engineers · Teague Nall & Perkings · Hurricane Text Lab · ConocoPhillips · BP.

Support for Students with Learning Disabilities

Students with learning disabilities may take advantage of specific support programs offered by Texas Tech University. Also, a lightened course load may be granted to LD students. Students with learning disabilities will find the following programs at Texas Tech University extremely useful: remedial math · remedial English ·

TEXAS TECH UNIVERSITY

Highlights

Texas Tech University
Lubbock, TX (Pop. 209,737)
Location: Medium city
Website: http://www.ttu.edu

Students
Total enrollment: 28,422
Undergrads: 12,917
Freshmen: 5,845
Part-time students: 8%
From out-of-state: 4%
Male/Female: 56%/44%
Live on-campus: 26%
In fraternities: 15%
In sororities: 20%
Off-campus employment rating: Excellent
Caucasian: 77%
African American: 4%
Hispanic: 14%
Asian or Pacific Islander: 3%
Native American: 1%
International: 1%

Academics
Student/faculty ratio: 19:1
Class size 9 or fewer: 4%
Class size 10-29: 42%
Class size 30-49: 33%
Class size 50-99: 13%
Class size 100 or more: 8%
Returning freshmen: 80%
Six-year graduation rate: 57%

Most Popular Fields of Study
Business, Finance, Sales and Marketing
Visual and Performing Arts
Social Sciences, History, Economics,
    Political Science
Family and Consumer Sciences, Nutrition
    and Home Economics
Computer and Information Sciences
Communications, Journalism, Advertising
    and Comm. Technologies
Philosophy, Religion and Theology
Liberal Arts, Humanities and General
    Studies
English and Literature

TEXAS TECH UNIVERSITY

Admissions

Applicants: 16,143
Accepted: 11,643
Acceptance rate: 72.1%
Average GPA: Not reported
ACT range: 22-26
SAT Math range: 520-620
SAT Reading range: 490-590
SAT Writing range: Not reported
Top 10% of class: 21%
Top 25% of class: 52%
Top 50% of class: 84%

Deadlines

Early Action: No
Early Decision: No
Regular Action: Rolling admissions
Common Application: Not accepted

Financial Aid

In-state tuition: $4,310
Out-of-state tuition: $12,650
Room: $3,980
Board: $3,330
Books: -
Freshmen receiving need-based aid: 41%
Undergrads receiving need-based aid: 39%
Avg. % of need met by financial aid: 60%
Avg. aid package (freshmen): $7,492
Avg. aid package (undergrads): $8,467
Freshmen receiving merit-based aid: 6%
Undergrads receiving merit-based aid: 3%
Avg. student debt upon graduation: $20,916

Prominent Alumni

Angela Braly, CEO, Wellpoint; Robert Condron, director of media relations, U.S. Olympic Committee; Pat Green, country music entertainer.

School Spirit

Mascot: Raider Red
Colors: Scarlet and black
Song: *Matador Song*

remedial reading · tutors · learning center · extended time for tests · take-home exam · readers · typist/scribe · note-taking services · tape recorders · priority registration. Individual or small group tutorials are also available in: time management · organizational skills · learning strategies · specific subject areas · writing labs · math labs · study skills. An advisor/advocate from the Student Disability Services is available to students.

How to Get Admitted

For admissions decisions, non-academic factors considered: extracurricular activities · special talents, interests, abilities · character/personal qualities · volunteer work · work experience · state of residency · minority affiliation · alumni relationship. A high school diploma is required, although a GED is also accepted for admissions consideration. SAT or ACT test scores are required of all applicants. *According to the admissions office:* Applicants with rank in top tenth of secondary school class may be admitted regardless of standardized test scores. Minimum combined SAT Reasoning score of 1140 (composite ACT score of 25) and rank in top quarter of secondary school class, minimum combined SAT Reasoning score of 1230 (composite ACT score of 28) and rank in second quarter of secondary school class, or combined SAT Reasoning score of 1270 (composite ACT score of 29) and rank in bottom half of secondary school class required.

How to Pay for College

To apply for financial aid, students should submit the following: Free Application for Federal Student Aid (FAFSA) · institution's own financial aid forms. Texas Tech University participates in the Federal Work Study program. *Need-based aid programs include:* scholarships and grants · general need-based awards · Federal Pell grants · state scholarships and grants · college-based scholarships and grants · private scholarships and grants. *Non-Need-based aid programs include:* scholarships and grants · state scholarships and grants · creative arts and performance awards · special achievements and activities awards · special characteristics awards · athletic scholarships · ROTC scholarships.

TUSKEGEE UNIVERSITY

P.O. Box 1239, Tuskegee, AL 36088
Admissions: 800-622-6531 · Financial Aid: 800-416-2831
Email: admissions@tuskegee.edu
Website: http://www.tuskegee.edu

From the College

"Imagine: Your assignment today involves more than reading a few pages from the textbook. Instead, you will measure forces at work inside a low turbulence wind tunnel, or you will be among the pioneer users of the most advanced surgical laser equipment. Perhaps you will work alongside professors studying nanocomposites - an emerging class of materials roughly 1,000 times smaller than a human hair. Welcome to Tuskegee University. Here, groundbreaking research and the quest for new knowledge are how we prepare our students. All of this doesn't just happen, of course. At Tuskegee, we have spent well over a century building this model in teaching and learning."

Campus Setting

Tuskegee, founded in 1881, is a private, state-related, comprehensive university. Programs are offered through the Colleges of Agriculture, Environmental, and Natural Sciences; Business and Information Science; Engineering, Architecture and Physical Sciences; Liberal Arts and Sciences; and Veterinary Medicine, Nursing, and Health Professions. Its 5,000-acre campus, located in Tuskegee, has been designated a National Historic Landmark. A four-year institution, Tuskegee University is a historically black university. In addition to a large, well-stocked library, the campus also has a George Washington Carver museum. Tuskegee University provides on-campus housing with 192 units that can accommodate 2,020 students. Housing options: women's dorms · men's dorms · single-student apartments · married-student apartments.

Student Life and Activities

With 55 percent of students living on campus, there are plenty of social activities. The most popular student organizations are: Chapel orchestra · choir · marching and concert bands · professional and special-interest groups. Tuskegee University is a member of the Southern Intercollegiate Athletic Conference (Division II).

Academics and Learning Environment

For the B student, the learning environment of a college is just as important as the quality of its academic program. Tuskegee University has 269 full-time and 53 part-time faculty members, offering a student-to-faculty ratio of 12:1. The most common course size is 10 to 19 students. Tuskegee University offers 51 majors with the most popular being electrical engineering, biology and business administration and least popular being medical technology. The school has a general core requirement. Cooperative education is not offered. All first-year students must maintain a 2.0 GPA or higher to avoid academic probation. Other special academic programs that would

Tuskegee University
Tuskegee, AL (Pop. 13,000)
Location: Rural
Website: http://www.tuskegee.edu

Students
Total enrollment: 2,842
Undergrads: 1,096
Freshmen: 697
Part-time students: 5%
From out-of-state: 64%
Male/Female: 45%/55%
Live on-campus: 55%
In fraternities: 6%
In sororities: 5%
Off-campus employment rating: Fair
Caucasian: 0%
African American: 78%
Hispanic: 0%
Asian or Pacific Islander: 0%
Native American: 0%
International: 1%

Academics
Student/faculty ratio: 12:1
Class size 9 or fewer: 4%
Class size 10-29: 71%
Class size 30-49: 18%
Class size 50-99: 10%
Class size 100 or more: -
Returning freshmen: 68%
Six-year graduation rate: 50%

Most Popular Fields of Study
Biological and Life Sciences
Agriculture, Aquaculture and Animal Sciences
Business, Finance, Sales and Marketing
Architecture

TUSKEGEE UNIVERSITY

appeal to a B student: pass/fail grading option · independent study · double majors · dual degrees · honors program · internships.

B Student Support and Success

Tuskegee offers a peer tutoring program for students who are taking first- or second-year courses in gross anatomy, microanatomy, neuroanatomy, physiology, microbiology, parasitology or clinical pathology, anatomic pathology and pharmacology. Peer tutors are available to help the needs of nursing, medical technology and occupational therapy students. These tutors give advice and guidance on information given in lectures; they also monitor more general study skills like questioning and answering and they help to establish study groups. An Academic Skills Guide discusses the importance of effective study skills. According to the college, the guide "addresses the how-to's of studying" and covers such elements as taking part in effective group study, developing thinking skills, taking tests and notes and managing time.

Tuskegee University provides a variety of support programs including dedicated guidance for: academic · career · personal · minority students · veterans · family planning · religious. Recognizing that some students may need extra preparation, Tuskegee University offers remedial and refresher courses in: reading · writing · math · study skills. The average freshman year GPA is 2.7, and 68 percent of freshmen students return for their sophomore year. What do students do after college? While many enter the work force, approximately 21 percent pursue a graduate degree immediately after graduation. Among students who enter the work force, approximately 21 percent enter a field related to their major within six months of graduation. Companies that most frequently hire graduates from Tuskegee University include: Amoco Oil · U.S. Department of Agriculture · General Electric · General Motors · IBM.

Support for Students with Learning Disabilities

Students with learning disabilities may take advantage of specific support programs offered by Tuskegee University. Students with learning disabilities will find the following programs at Tuskegee University extremely useful: remedial math · remedial English · remedial reading · learning center · diagnostic testing service.

How to Get Admitted

For admissions decisions, non-academic factors considered: extracurricular activities · special talents, interests, abilities · character/personal qualities · volunteer work · work experience · geographical location · minority affiliation · alumni relationship. A high school diploma is required, although a GED is also accepted for admissions consideration. SAT or ACT test scores are required of all applicants. *Academic units recommended:* 4 English, 3 Math, 2 Science, 3 Social Studies.

How to Pay for College

To apply for financial aid, students should submit the following: Free Application for Federal Student Aid (FAFSA) · institution's own financial aid forms. Tuskegee University participates in the Federal Work Study program. *Need-based aid programs include:* scholarships and grants · general need-based awards · Federal Pell grants · state scholarships and grants · college-based scholarships and grants · private scholarships and grants · Federal Nursing scholarships · United Negro College Fund. *Non-Need-based aid programs include:* scholarships and grants · state scholarships and grants · athletic scholarships · ROTC scholarships.

UNIVERSITY OF ALABAMA

Box 870100, Tuscaloosa, AL 35487-0100
Admissions: 800-933-BAMA · Financial Aid: 205-348-6756
Email: admissions@ua.edu · Website: http://www.ua.edu

From the College

"The University of Alabama is a major, comprehensive, student-centered research university founded in 1831 as Alabama's first public college. We provide a creative, nurturing campus environment where our students can become the best individuals possible, learn from the best and brightest faculty, and make a positive difference in the community, the state and the world. On a typical day on our campus, an undergraduate student works side by side with a top molecular biologist researching Parkinson's disease, students openly debate controversial topics at the Center for Ethics and Social Responsibility, and volunteers tutor in local schools through the Community Service Center. Fall weekends are alive with the excitement of Alabama football—and "Roll Tide, Roll" echoes across the campus.

"UA's graduates and students include numerous Rhodes, Goldwater, Truman and Hollings Scholars. Participation in original research and creative activities is becoming a hallmark of the undergraduate experience at UA, with students working closely with faculty on a wide variety of projects. In addition to equipping our students to succeed academically, the University of Alabama's programs set the bar high for character, service and citizenship. Students are encouraged to participate campus organizations. Campus ministries are thriving."

Campus Setting

The University of Alabama is a public, four-year, comprehensive doctoral and research institution. Its 1,000-acre campus is located in west central Alabama, approximately 50 miles southwest of Birmingham. University of Alabama has been co-ed since 1893. In addition to a large, well-stocked library, the campus facilities include: art gallery · natural history museum · concert hall · archaeologic site and museum · arboretum · observatory · simulated coal mine · robotics lab · wind tunnel · artificial intelligence lab · jet propulsion engine mini-lab · special collections building. The University of Alabama provides on-campus housing with 4,009 units that can accommodate 8,225 students. Housing options: co-ed dorms · women's dorms · men's dorms · sorority housing · fraternity housing · single-student apartments · married-student apartments · special housing for disabled students. Recreation and sports facilities include: aquatic center · park · fields complex · golf course · lake · intramural fields · ice arena · regional rock climbing facilities · outdoor swimming pool · recreation center · tennis courts.

Student Life and Activities

Most students (70 percent) live off campus, which does impact the on-campus social scene. Nevertheless, like any college, students find time to create their own recreational outlets. As reported by a school representative, "With more than 300 student organizations on campus, UA offers activities of interest to just about everyone. Students plan and take advantage of concerts and lectures, participate in and enjoy musical, dance and theatre performances, play on intramural sports teams and take part in student government. Many students are involved in community service and religious organizations. Fall football weekends are a major event on campus, and students also support UA's many other Division I athletic teams. Whatever your interests, you'll find opportunities to get involved at UA." Popular on-campus gathering spots include: Ferguson Student Center, Recreation Center and the Quad. Popular campus events include:

Homecoming, A-Day Game, African-American Heritage Month, Bama Bound Orientation, Beat Auburn Beat Hunger, Capstone Creed Week, Flava Fest, Hispanic Heritage Month, Iron Bowl, Kick-Off on the Quad, Navigating the Tide, Get on Board Day, Realizing the Dream Concert, Student Government Association Elections, University Day, Urban Comedy Tour, Sakura Festival, Earth Day, Honors Week, Bama Blast, Welcome Back Concert and Family Weekend. Popular campus groups include: Greek organizations, campus ministries and intramural sports. For those interested in sports, there are intramural teams such as: badminton · basketball · bowling · dodgeball · flag football · golf · horseshoes · inner-tube water polo · kickball · punt-pass-kick competition · racquetball · rock climbing · soccer · softball · squash · swimming · table tennis · tennis · track and field · turkey trot · ultimate Frisbee · volleyball · wallyball · wiffleball. The University of Alabama is a member of the Southeastern Conference (Division I, Football I-A).

Academics and Learning Environment

For the B student, the learning environment of a college is just as important as the quality of its academic program. The University of Alabama has 1,028 full-time and 339 part-time faculty members, offering a student-to-faculty ratio of 20:1. The most common course size is 10 to 19 students. The University of Alabama offers 186 majors with the most popular being finance, marketing and accounting. The school has a general core requirement. Cooperative education is available. All first-year students must maintain a 2.0 GPA or higher to avoid academic probation, and a minimum overall GPA of 2.0 is required to graduate. Other special academic programs that would appeal to a B student: self-designed majors · pass/fail grading option · independent study · double majors · dual degrees · accelerated study · honors program · Phi Beta Kappa · internships · weekend college · distance learning certificate programs.

B Student Support and Success

The University of Alabama has several programs in place to help the new college student who might be struggling. WOW, the Week of Welcome, helps students get familiar with all aspects of campus life before classes begin. The Tide Early Alert program allows faculty, staff, parents and students the chance to help any student who is having a tough time maintaining grades. The system identifies any students who have received a D or F on an assignment, test or paper. It also pinpoints students who have had excessive absences or has exhibited behavior that indicates a problem. This alert is transmitted to the staff and they, in turn, link the student to the most helpful campus resources. UA also offers Peer Mentoring from upper class students.

The University of Alabama provides a variety of support programs including dedicated guidance for: academic · career · personal · psychological · minority students · military · veterans · non-traditional students · family planning · religious. Recognizing that some students may need extra preparation, The University of Alabama offers remedial and refresher courses in: reading · writing · math · study skills. Other remedial services include supplemental instruction, course review, help sessions, professional entrance exam

UNIVERSITY OF ALABAMA

University of Alabama
Tuscaloosa, AL (Pop. 78,000)
Location: Medium city
Website: http://www.ua.edu

Students
Total enrollment: 27,014
Undergrads: 10,568
Freshmen: 7,198
Part-time students: 8%
From out-of-state: 37%
Male/Female: 47%/53%
Live on-campus: 30%
In fraternities: 22%
In sororities: 29%
Off-campus employment rating: Fair
Caucasian: 84%
African American: 11%
Hispanic: 2%
Asian or Pacific Islander: 1%
Native American: 1%
International: 1%

Academics
Student/faculty ratio: 20:1
Class size 9 or fewer: 16%
Class size 10-29: 52%
Class size 30-49: 18%
Class size 50-99: 9%
Class size 100 or more: 6%
Returning freshmen: 84%
Six-year graduation rate: 65%

Most Popular Fields of Study
Business, Finance, Sales and Marketing
Protective Services, Criminal Justice and
    Public Administration
Visual and Performing Arts
Family and Consumer Sciences, Nutrition
    and Home Economics
Philosophy, Religion and Theology
Communications, Journalism, Advertising
    and Comm. Technologies
Library Science
English and Literature
Parks, Recreation and Fitness
Military Science and Technologies

455

UNIVERSITY OF ALABAMA

Admissions
Applicants: 18,500
Accepted: 11,172
Acceptance rate: 60.4%
Average GPA: 3.4
ACT range: 21-27
SAT Math range: 500-610
SAT Reading range: 490-600
SAT Writing range: Not reported
Top 10% of class: 42%
Top 25% of class: 55%
Top 50% of class: 80%

Deadlines
Early Action: No
Early Decision: No
Regular Action: Rolling admissions
Common Application: Not accepted

Financial Aid
In-state tuition: $6,400
Out-of-state tuition: $18,000
Room: $4,100
Board: $2,330
Books: $1,000
Freshmen receiving need-based aid: 33%
Undergrads receiving need-based aid:
    35%
Avg. % of need met by financial aid: 71%
Avg. aid package (freshmen): $11,921
Avg. aid package (undergrads): $11,705
Freshmen receiving merit-based aid: 36%
Undergrads receiving merit-based aid:
    29%
Avg. student debt upon graduation:
    $24,412

Prominent Alumni
Harper Lee, author, *To Kill a Mockingbird*;
John McKinley, former CEO, Texaco;
Hugo Black, former Supreme Court
justice.

School Spirit
Mascot: Big Al
Colors: Crimson and white
Song: *Yea Alabama*

preparation. The average freshman year GPA is 3.1, and 84 percent of freshmen students return for their sophomore year.

Support for Students with Learning Disabilities

Students with learning disabilities may take advantage of specific support programs offered by the University of Alabama. If necessary, the college will grant additional time to students with learning disabilities to complete their degree. Also, a lightened course load may be granted to LD students. According to the school, accommodations for students with learning disabilities are coordinated through the Office of Disability Services (ODS), which is the designated unit at the university serving all students with disabilities who have self-identified and requested disability-related assistance. Services such as tutoring and writing assistance are offered through the same channels as for students who do not have disabilities. ODS is not specific to students with learning disabilities. Students with learning disabilities will find the following programs at the University of Alabama extremely useful: remedial math · tutors · learning center · testing accommodations · extended time for tests · take-home exam · oral tests · exam on tape or computer · typist/scribe · note-taking services · reading machines · texts on tape · early syllabus · priority registration · waiver of math degree requirement. Individual or small group tutorials are also available in: time management · organizational skills · learning strategies · specific subject areas · writing labs · math labs · study skills. An advisor/advocate from the Office of Disability Services is available to students.

How to Get Admitted

For admissions decisions, non-academic factors considered: interview · extracurricular activities · special talents, interests, abilities · character/personal qualities · volunteer work · work experience · state of residency · alumni relationship. A high school diploma is required, although a GED is also accepted for admissions consideration. SAT or ACT test scores are required of all applicants. SAT Subject Test scores are not required. *According to the admissions office:* Minimum composite ACT score of 21 (combined SAT score of 990) and minimum 3.0 GPA highly considered if submitted. *Academic units recommended:* 4 English, 3 Math, 3 Science, 4 Social Studies, 1 Foreign Language.

How to Pay for College

To apply for financial aid, students should submit the following: Free Application for Federal Student Aid (FAFSA). The University of Alabama participates in the Federal Work Study program. *Need-based aid programs include:* scholarships and grants · general need-based awards · Federal Pell grants · state scholarships and grants · college-based scholarships and grants · private scholarships and grants · Federal Nursing scholarships. *Non-Need-based aid programs include:* scholarships and grants · general need-based awards · state scholarships and grants · creative arts and performance awards · special achievements and activities awards · special characteristics awards · athletic scholarships · ROTC scholarships · alumni/ae affiliation scholarships.

UNIVERSITY OF ARIZONA

P.O. Box 210066, Tucson, AZ 85721-0066
Admissions: 520-621-3237 · Financial Aid: 520-621-5200
Email: appinfo@arizona.edu · Website: http://www.arizona.edu

From the College

"Located in the heart of Tucson, the University of Arizona is one of the top-ranked research universities in the nation. Surrounded by mountains and the high Sonoran desert, the campus offers a distinctive Southwestern look and enjoys more than 300 days of sunshine each year. Approximately 38,000 students are enrolled at the University of Arizona, coming from all 50 states and more than 100 countries. The UA offers more than 100 academic and professional degree tracks and a vibrant campus atmosphere at a cost well below most other colleges and universities in the U.S."

Campus Setting

The University of Arizona, founded in 1885, offers programs through the Colleges of Agriculture, Architecture, Business and Public Administration, Education, Engineering and Mines, Fine Arts, Humanities, Nursing, Pharmacy, Science and Social and Behavioral Sciences; the Schools of Family and Consumer Resources and Health-Related Professions; and the University College and Arizona International College. A four-year public institution, the University of Arizona has a 353-acre campus. In addition to a large, well-stocked library, the campus facilities include: art, minerals and pharmacy museums · herbarium · science center · planetarium. The University of Arizona provides on-campus housing with 44 units that can accommodate 6,300 students. Housing options: co-ed dorms · women's dorms · sorority housing · fraternity housing · single-student apartments · special housing for disabled students · special housing for International students.

Student Life and Activities

Most students (80 percent) live off campus, which does impact the on-campus social scene. Nevertheless, like any college, students find time to create their own recreational outlets. Students gather at University Blvd. and Fourth Ave. The University of Arizona has 450 official student organizations. The most popular are: marching and pep bands · chess · baton twirling · team managers. The University of Arizona is a member of the Mountain Pacific Sports Federation (Division I), Pacific-10 Conference (Division I, Football I-A).

Academics and Learning Environment

For the B student, the learning environment of a college is just as important as the quality of its academic program. The University of Arizona has 1,280 full-time and 783 part-time faculty members, offering a student-to-faculty ratio of 19:1. The most common course size is 20 to 29 students. The University of Arizona offers 425 majors with the most popular being psychology, management information systems and finance. The school has a general core requirement. Cooperative education is not offered. All first-year students must maintain a 2.0 GPA or higher to avoid academic probation. Other special academic programs that would appeal to a B student: pass/fail grading option · independent study · double majors · dual degrees · accelerated study · honors program · Phi Beta Kappa · internships · weekend college · distance learning.

B Student Support and Success

The University of Arizona offers an extensive Student Support Services designed to help students manage the demands of college life. Their programs include: Aca-

UNIVERSITY OF ARIZONA

University of Arizona
Tucson, AZ (Pop. 600,000)
Location: Major city
Website: http://www.arizona.edu

Students
Total enrollment: 38,057
Undergrads: 14,163
Freshmen: 6,331
Part-time students: 13%
From out-of-state: 38%
Male/Female: 48%/52%
Live on-campus: 20%
In fraternities: 10%
In sororities: 11%
Off-campus employment rating: Excellent
Caucasian: 65%
African American: 3%
Hispanic: 17%
Asian or Pacific Islander: 7%
Native American: 2%
International: 3%

Academics
Student/faculty ratio: 19:1
Class size 9 or fewer: 19%
Class size 10-29: 55%
Class size 30-49: 15%
Class size 50-99: 6%
Class size 100 or more: 5%
Returning freshmen: 79%
Six-year graduation rate: 57%

Most Popular Fields of Study
Business, Finance, Sales and Marketing
Biological and Life Sciences
Visual and Performing Arts
Social Sciences, History, Economics,
    Political Science
Protective Services, Criminal Justice and
    Public Administration
Family and Consumer Sciences, Nutrition
    and Home Economics
Computer and Information Sciences
Communications, Journalism, Advertising
    and Comm. Technologies
Philosophy, Religion and Theology
English and Literature

demic Career Advising, Peer Advising, a three-credit Connections Course that "explores and critically discusses a variety of topics to help students successfully transition into the UA," and the SSS Colloquia called "Leadership in Student Support Services." The course promotes career and academic related leadership skills, critical thinking and civic engagement projects.

The University of Arizona provides a variety of support programs including dedicated guidance for: academic · career · personal · psychological · minority students · military · veterans · family planning. The average freshman year GPA is 2.6, and 79 percent of freshmen students return for their sophomore year.

Support for Students with Learning Disabilities

Students with learning disabilities may take advantage of specific support programs offered by the University of Arizona. If necessary, the college will grant additional time to students with learning disabilities to complete their degree. Also, a lightened course load may be granted to LD students. According to the school, the SALT Center is an enhanced service program for LD students, and charges fees for some services. Students with learning disabilities will find the following programs at the University of Arizona extremely useful: remedial math · remedial English · tutors · learning center · testing accommodations · extended time for tests · take-home exam · readers · note-taking services · reading machines · tape recorders · texts on tape · early syllabus. Individual or small group tutorials are also available in: time management · organizational skills · learning strategies · specific subject areas · writing labs · math labs · study skills. An advisor/advocate from the Disability Resources is available to students. This member also sits on the admissions committee.

How to Get Admitted

For admissions decisions, non-academic factors considered: interview · extracurricular activities · special talents, interests, abilities · character/personal qualities · volunteer work · work experience · geographical location · minority affiliation. A high school diploma is required, although a GED is also accepted for admissions consideration. SAT or ACT test scores are recommended but not required. SAT Subject Test scores are considered, if submitted, but are not required. *According to the admissions office:* Minimum combined SAT Reasoning score of 1040 (composite ACT score of 22), rank in top half of secondary school class, or minimum 2.5 GPA required of in-state applicants; minimum combined SAT Reasoning score of 1110 (composite ACT score of 24), rank in top quarter of secondary school class, or minimum 3.0 GPA required of out-of-state applicants. *Academic units recommended:* 4 English, 3 Math, 3 Science, 2 Social Studies, 2 Foreign Language.

How to Pay for College

To apply for financial aid, students should submit the following: Free Application for Federal Student Aid (FAFSA). The University of Arizona participates in the Federal Work Study program. *Need-based aid programs include:* scholarships and grants · general need-based awards · Federal Pell grants · state scholarships and grants · college-based scholarships and grants · private scholarships and grants · Federal Nursing scholarships. *Non-Need-based aid programs include:*

scholarships and grants · state scholarships and grants · creative arts and performance awards · ROTC scholarships.

UNIVERSITY OF ARIZONA

Admissions
Applicants: 22,544
Accepted: 18,158
Acceptance rate: 80.5%
Average GPA: 3.3
ACT range: 21-26
SAT Math range: 500-620
SAT Reading range: 480-600
SAT Writing range: Not reported
Top 10% of class: 32%
Top 25% of class: 61%
Top 50% of class: 88%

Deadlines
Early Action: No
Early Decision: No
Regular Action: Rolling admissions
Common Application: Not accepted

Financial Aid
In-state tuition: $7,248
Out-of-state tuition: $20,976
Room: $5,044
Board: $2,768
Books: $1,000
Freshmen receiving need-based aid: 36%
Undergrads receiving need-based aid: 38%
Avg. % of need met by financial aid: 63%
Avg. aid package (freshmen): $8,138
Avg. aid package (undergrads): $8,529
Freshmen receiving merit-based aid: 35%
Undergrads receiving merit-based aid: 23%
Avg. student debt upon graduation: $18,025

Prominent Alumni
Richard Russo, Pulitzer Prize winner; Richard Carmona, U.S. surgeon general.

School Spirit
Mascot: Wildcats

UNIVERSITY OF CALIFORNIA - DAVIS

1 Shields Avenue, Davis, CA 95616
Admissions: 530-752-2971 · Financial Aid: 530-752-2390
Email: undergraduateadmissions@ucdavis.edu
Website: http://www.ucdavis.edu

From the College

"Fueled by learning and energized by discovery, the UC-Davis tradition of engagement with the local community, the nation and the world guides all that it does. The commitment to providing an attentive and research-enriched education creates a supportive learning environment for both students and faculty. UC Davis is a pioneer in interdisciplinary problem-solving, and its four colleges, five professional schools, more than 100 academic majors and 86 graduate programs make it the most comprehensive of all the University of California campuses."

Campus Setting

UC-Davis, founded in 1905, is a public, four-year, comprehensive university. Programs are offered through the Colleges of Agricultural and Environmental Science, Engineering, and Letters and Science and the Graduate School of Management. Its 5,200-acre campus is located in Davis, 15 miles from Sacramento. In addition to a large, well-stocked library, the campus facilities include: art galleries · arboretum · herbarium · entomology and design museums. University of California - Davis provides on-campus housing with 5,534 units. Housing options: co-ed dorms · women's dorms · single-student apartments · married-student apartments · special housing for disabled students · special housing for International students · cooperative housing. Recreation and sports facilities include: aquatic center · athletic and recreational fields · gymnasium · recreation center · stadium · swimming pool.

Student Life and Activities

Most students (80 percent) live off campus, which does impact the on-campus social scene. Nevertheless, like any college, students find time to create their own recreational outlets. University of California - Davis has 452 official student organizations. The most popular are: AIDS education project · American Field Service · anime club · ballroom dance group · Block and Bridle · Coalition Against Genocide · comedy troupe · gospel choir · law society · marching and pep bands · Model UN · Parents Under Pressure · square dance group · modern dance group · wildlife society · visually-impaired persons group · International Association of Business Communicators · Vet Student Association · astronomy club · team managers. For those interested in sports, there are intramural teams such as: basketball · flag football · floor hockey · golf · grass volleyball · indoor soccer · racquetball · roller hockey · soccer · softball · table tennis · tennis · ultimate Frisbee · volleyball. University of California - Davis is a member of the Big West Conference, Mountain Pacific Sports Federation, Pacific-10 Conference, Great West Football Conference, Western Water Polo Association, Western Intercollegiate Rowing Association, NorPac Conference.

Academics and Learning Environment

For the B student, the learning environment of a college is just as important as the quality of its academic program. University of California - Davis has 1,568 full-time and 311 part-time faculty members, offering a student-to-faculty ratio of 19:1. The most common course size is 20 to 29 students. University of California - Davis offers 235 majors with the most popular being psychology, economics and biological sciences and least popular being agricultural science and management, food biochemistry and

Afro American studies. The school has a general core requirement. Cooperative education is not offered. All first-year students must maintain a 2.0 GPA or higher to avoid academic probation. Other special academic programs that would appeal to a B student: self-designed majors · pass/fail grading option · independent study · double majors · dual degrees · accelerated study · honors program · Phi Beta Kappa · internships.

B Student Support and Success

The Learning Skills Center offers courses in a number of helpful topics including General Study Skills, Time Scheduling, Top Ten Survival Tips, Developing a Growth Mind Set for Academic Success, Critical Reading, Lecture Note Taking Strategies, Annotating, Multiple Choice Exam Prep and Test Taking Skills and Essay Exam Strategies. In addition to these general courses, there are specific subject courses for writing skills (pre-writing techniques, term paper assistance, grammar, etc.), ESL, science and math. All workshops are free.

University of California - Davis provides a variety of support programs including dedicated guidance for: academic · career · personal · psychological · minority students · military · veterans · non-traditional students · family planning. Recognizing that some students may need extra preparation, University of California - Davis offers remedial and refresher courses in: reading · writing · math · study skills. Annually, 90 percent of freshmen students return for their sophomore year. Among students who enter the work force, approximately 39 percent enter a field related to their major within six months of graduation, while a further 43 percent enter a related career within two years of graduation. Companies that most frequently hire graduates from University of California - Davis include: Calgene · California school districts · Genentech · Hewlett-Packard · government agencies · Intel · Kaiser Permanente · Oracle · Washington Mutual · Wells Fargo.

Support for Students with Learning Disabilities

Students with learning disabilities may take advantage of specific support programs offered by University of California - Davis. According to the school, UC-Davis is committed to ensuring equal access to educational opportunities for students with disabilities. An integral component in the implementation of that commitment is the coordination of academic accommodations and support services through the Student Disability Center (SDC). Students requesting accommodations must first establish eligibility by providing documentation of an impairment that limits a major life activity. The university reserves the right to request supplemental information to verify a student's current functional limitations. Documentation must meet the following criteria: 1) Appropriate standardized testing measures that are adult-normed and reflect current abilities and achievement; 2) Comprehensive written report discussing student's medical, educational and learning history, including current presenting concerns; 3) Clear statement of the existence of an impairment, and a summary indicating the current functional limitations and their extent, and; 4) Report must be signed by a qualified diagnosing professional (e.g., licensed educational or clinical psychologist). Requests for accommodations are considered on an individual basis

UNIVERSITY OF CALIFORNIA - DAVIS

Highlights

University of California - Davis
Davis, CA (Pop. 64,401)
Location: Medium city
Website: http://www.ucdavis.edu

Students
Total enrollment: 30,568
Undergrads: 10,588
Freshmen: 4,972
Part-time students: 1%
From out-of-state: 3%
Male/Female: 44%/56%
Live on-campus: 20%
Off-campus employment rating: Good
Caucasian: 35%
African American: 3%
Hispanic: 13%
Asian or Pacific Islander: 40%
Native American: 1%
International: 2%

Academics
Student/faculty ratio: 19:1
Class size 9 or fewer: 13%
Class size 10-29: 48%
Class size 30-49: 11%
Class size 50-99: 15%
Class size 100 or more: 14%
Returning freshmen: 90%
Six-year graduation rate: 81%

Most Popular Fields of Study
Biological and Life Sciences
Agriculture, Aquaculture and Animal Sciences
Visual and Performing Arts
Family and Consumer Sciences, Nutrition and Home Economics
Computer and Information Sciences
Communications, Journalism, Advertising and Comm. Technologies
Philosophy, Religion and Theology
English and Literature
Psychology
Engineering and Engineering Technologies

UNIVERSITY OF CALIFORNIA - DAVIS

Admissions
Applicants: 40,605
Accepted: 21,357
Acceptance rate: 52.6%
Average GPA: 3.8
ACT range: 22-28
SAT Math range: 550-670
SAT Reading range: 500-630
SAT Writing range: 510-640
Top 10% of class: 96%
Top 25% of class: 100%
Top 50% of class: 100%

Deadlines
Early Action: No
Early Decision: No
Regular Action: November 30 (final)
Common Application: Not accepted

Financial Aid
In-state tuition: $10,404
Out-of-state tuition: $33,073
Room: -
Board: -
Books: $1,590
Freshmen receiving need-based aid: 55%
Undergrads receiving need-based aid: 54%
Avg. % of need met by financial aid: 79%
Avg. aid package (freshmen): $15,811
Avg. aid package (undergrads): $14,275
Freshmen receiving merit-based aid: 4%
Undergrads receiving merit-based aid: 4%
Avg. student debt upon graduation: $15,155

Prominent Alumni
Steve Robinson, astronaut; Ann Veneman, executive director of UNICEF and former U.S. secretary of agriculture; Timothy Mondavi, president and CEO Continuum Wines.

School Spirit
Mascot: Mustang
Colors: Yale blue and gold
Song: *Aggie Fight*

by taking into account institutional obligations to provide equal access to educational opportunities, documented current functional limitation, and the student's course requirements. It is the student's responsibility to submit all requests for disability-based accommodations to the SDC each academic quarter. Students with learning disabilities will find the following programs at University of California - Davis extremely useful: waiver of math degree requirement. An advisor/advocate from the Advising Services - Student Disability Center is available to students.

How to Get Admitted

For admissions decisions, non-academic factors considered: extracurricular activities · special talents, interests, abilities · character/personal qualities · volunteer work · work experience. A high school diploma is required, although a GED is also accepted for admissions consideration. SAT or ACT test scores are required of all applicants. SAT Subject Test scores are required from all applicants. *According to the admissions office:* Minimum 3.3 GPA required of in-state applicants; minimum 3.4 GPA required of out-of-state applicants. Specific SAT Reasoning or ACT scores required of applicants with 2.82-3.29 GPA. Applicants meeting specific requirements on SAT Reasoning or ACT and SAT Subject may be admitted on the basis of test scores alone. *Academic units recommended:* 4 English, 4 Math, 3 Science, 2 Social Studies, 3 Foreign Language.

How to Pay for College

To apply for financial aid, students should submit the following: Free Application for Federal Student Aid (FAFSA). University of California - Davis participates in the Federal Work Study program. *Need-based aid programs include:* scholarships and grants · general need-based awards · Federal Pell grants · state scholarships and grants · college-based scholarships and grants · private scholarships and grants · Academic Competitiveness Grant · National SMART grant. *Non-Need-based aid programs include:* scholarships and grants · ROTC scholarships.

UNIVERSITY OF CALIFORNIA - RIVERSIDE

900 University Avenue, Riverside, CA 92521
Admissions: 951-827-4531 · Financial Aid: 951-827-3878
Email: discover@ucr.edu · Website: http://www.ucr.edu

From the College

"The University of California - Riverside lays claim to graduate Richard Schrock sharing the Nobel Prize in Chemistry; the opening of a new downtown art gallery; the women's basketball team making it to the NCAA Division I tournament; and 100 years of agricultural research discoveries. UC-Riverside puts a quality education within every student's reach through strong core programs, new and emerging disciplines, and faculty recognized for their dedication, high standards and accessibility to students."

Campus Setting

UC Riverside, founded as an agricultural research center in 1907, is a public, comprehensive university. Programs are offered through the Colleges of Natural and Agricultural Sciences, Humanities, Arts and Social Sciences and Engineering. Its 1,200-acre campus is located 60 miles east of Los Angeles. In addition to a large, well-stocked library, the campus facilities include: art gallery · museum · research centers · agricultural research institute · gardens · salinity laboratory. University of California - Riverside provides on-campus housing with 2,915 units that can accommodate 5,095 students. Housing options: co-ed dorms · single-student apartments · married-student apartments. Recreation and sports facilities include: baseball stadium · recreation center · softball and soccer fields · track and tennis courts.

Student Life and Activities

Most students (70 percent) live off campus, which does impact the on-campus social scene. Nevertheless, like any college, students find time to create their own recreational outlets. According to a school official, "Life at Riverside can be "very calm, and the school's atmosphere in general is very quiet." One contributor to this sense of calm is the fact that many students commute to school. "We are not a huge party school," students admit, but "there is always a party to go to if that's what you're into." Although the city of Riverside has "very little to offer in the way of entertainment," students compensate by joining various clubs and student organizations, including sororities and fraternities, which have a noticeable presence on campus. The school also offers "countless events, including free movie screenings, concerts, academic discussion forums, plays, and trips." Popular campus hangouts include "a great rec center," "the student commons" and "a campus movie theater, where some of our classes are held." Students seem to agree, however, that "intercollegiate sports need more student support." Those with cars leave campus relatively frequently on the weekends, finding plenty to do outside of town; one student explains, "Within an hour's drive you can ski in the mountains, go sunbathing at the beach, visit a major theme park or even hang out in Hollywood for a day. Popular campus events include: Block Party, Welcome Week, Homecoming, Spring Splash and Heat. University of California - Riverside has 203 official student organizations. The most popular are: bagpipe and pep bands · jazz ensemble · drill team · performing arts program · film society · folk dance club · chess · team managers · service groups · human corps program · academic · environmental and recreational clubs. For those interested in sports, there are intramural teams such as: badminton · basketball · bowling · flag football · hockey · in-line skating · racquetball · soccer · softball · table tennis · tennis

UNIVERSITY OF CALIFORNIA - RIVERSIDE

University of California - Riverside
Riverside, CA (Pop. 260,000)
Location: Medium city
Website: http://www.ucr.edu

Students
Total enrollment: 18,079
Undergrads: 7,545
Freshmen: Not reported
Part-time students: 2%
From out-of-state: Not reported
Male/Female: 48%/52%
Live on-campus: 30%
In fraternities: 6%
In sororities: 6%
Off-campus employment rating: Excellent
Caucasian: 17%
African American: 8%
Hispanic: 28%
Asian or Pacific Islander: 40%
Native American: 0%
International: 2%

Academics
Student/faculty ratio: 18:1
Class size 9 or fewer: 13%
Class size 10-29: 59%
Class size 30-49: 9%
Class size 50-99: 10%
Class size 100 or more: 10%
Returning freshmen: 84%
Six-year graduation rate: 64%

Most Popular Fields of Study
Business, Finance, Sales and Marketing
Biological and Life Sciences
Area, Ethnic and Gender Studies

· volleyball. University of California - Riverside is a member of the Big West Conference (Division I).

Academics and Learning Environment

For the B student, the learning environment of a college is just as important as the quality of its academic program. University of California - Riverside has 765 full-time and 154 part-time faculty members, offering a student-to-faculty ratio of 18:1. The most common course size is 20 to 29 students. University of California - Riverside offers 155 majors with the most popular being business, management, marketing, and related support services, social sciences and biological and biomedical sciences. The school has a general core requirement. Cooperative education is not offered. All first-year students must maintain a 2.0 GPA or higher to avoid academic probation. Other special academic programs that would appeal to a B student: self-designed majors · pass/fail grading option · independent study · double majors · dual degrees · accelerated study · honors program · Phi Beta Kappa · internships.

B Student Support and Success

Educators, counselors and advanced students help with academic performance through services at the school's Learning Center. Any student who is not satisfied with the grade he/she is getting in a class is welcome, including freshmen and students on academic probation. Virtually all services are free.

University of California - Riverside provides a variety of support programs including dedicated guidance for: academic · career · personal · psychological · minority students · military · veterans · non-traditional students · family planning · religious. Recognizing that some students may need extra preparation, University of California - Riverside offers remedial and refresher courses in: reading · writing · math · study skills. The average freshman year GPA is 2.7, and 84 percent of freshmen students return for their sophomore year. What do students do after college? While many enter the work force, approximately 30 percent pursue a graduate degree immediately after graduation. Among students who enter the work force, approximately 70 percent enter a field related to their major within six months of graduation. Companies that most frequently hire graduates from University of California - Riverside include: Abbott Vascular · Anheuser Busch Sales Co. · BDO Seidman · CIA · Cintas Corp. · Countrywide Financial · Deloitte & Touche · Eli Lilly and Co. · Enterprise Rent-a-Car · Ernst and Young · ESRI · FedEX Ground · GlaxoSmithKline · Grant Thornton · IRS · Jacobs Engineering · Kaiser Permanente · KPMG · Maxim Healthcare Services · Merck · Northrup Grumman · Novartis Pharmaceuticals · Pacific Life · Pepsi Bottling Group · Schlumberger Technology · Sherwin-Williams Co. · Southern California Gas Co. · Target Corp. · Walt Disney · Washington Mutual · Wells Fargo · Wolseley North America-Fergusun · Verizon.

Support for Students with Learning Disabilities

Students with learning disabilities may take advantage of specific support programs offered by University of California - Riverside. According to the school, accommodations are individually tailored to meet each student's disability-related needs and are based on the student's current functional limitations and the requirements of the specific class in which the student is enrolled.

How to Get Admitted

For admissions decisions, non-academic factors considered: special talents, interests, abilities. A high school diploma is required, although a GED is also accepted for admissions consideration. SAT or ACT test scores are required of all applicants. SAT Subject Test scores are required from all applicants. *According to the admissions office:* Minimum grade of C in listed secondary school units required of in-state applicants; minimum 3.4 GPA required of out-of-state applicants. In-state applicants with minimum 3.3 GPA are eligible regardless of test scores. Applicants meeting specific requirements on SAT Reasoning or ACT and SAT Subject may be admitted on the basis of test scores alone. *Academic units recommended:* 4 English, 4 Math, 3 Science, 3 Foreign Language.

How to Pay for College

To apply for financial aid, students should submit the following: Free Application for Federal Student Aid (FAFSA) · state aid form. University of California - Riverside participates in the Federal Work Study program. *Need-based aid programs include:* scholarships and grants · general need-based awards · Federal Pell grants · state scholarships and grants · college-based scholarships and grants · private scholarships and grants. *Non-Need-based aid programs include:* scholarships and grants · state scholarships and grants · creative arts and performance awards · athletic scholarships · ROTC scholarships.

UNIVERSITY OF CALIFORNIA - RIVERSIDE

Highlights

Admissions
Applicants: 21,453
Accepted: 16,817
Acceptance rate: 78.4%
Average GPA: 3.4
ACT range: Not reported
SAT Math range: Not reported
SAT Reading range: Not reported
SAT Writing range: Not reported
Top 10% of class: 94%
Top 25% of class: 100%
Top 50% of class: 100%

Deadlines
Early Action: No
Early Decision: No
Regular Action: Rolling admissions
Common Application: Not accepted

Financial Aid
In-state tuition: $7,845
Out-of-state tuition: $28,453
Room: -
Board: -
Books: $4,800
Freshmen receiving need-based aid: 65%
Undergrads receiving need-based aid: 64%
Avg. % of need met by financial aid: 83%
Avg. aid package (freshmen): $16,754
Avg. aid package (undergrads): $15,342
Freshmen receiving merit-based aid: 2%
Undergrads receiving merit-based aid: 1%
Avg. student debt upon graduation: $15,414

Prominent Alumni
Stephen Breen, Pulitzer Prize-Editorial cartoonist; Billy Collins, poet laureate; Richard Schrock, Nobel Prize recipient, chemistry.

School Spirit
Mascot: Highlanders
Colors: Blue and gold
Song: *Brave Scots/Sons of California*

University of Cincinnati
Cincinnati, OH (Pop. 332,000)
Location: Major city
Website: http://www.uc.edu

Students
Total enrollment: 29,617
Undergrads: 10,309
Freshmen: 3,166
Part-time students: 17%
From out-of-state: 8%
Male/Female: 49%/51%
Live on-campus: 21%
Off-campus employment rating: Excellent
Caucasian: 78%
African American: 11%
Hispanic: 2%
Asian or Pacific Islander: 3%
Native American: 0%
International: 1%

Academics
Student/faculty ratio: :1
Class size 9 or fewer: 16%
Class size 10-29: 61%
Class size 30-49: 15%
Class size 50-99: 5%
Class size 100 or more: 3%
Returning freshmen: 83%
Six-year graduation rate: 55%

Most Popular Fields of Study
Business, Finance, Sales and Marketing
Architecture
Protective Services, Criminal Justice and
    Public Administration
Visual and Performing Arts
Computer and Information Sciences
Communications, Journalism, Advertising
    and Comm. Technologies
Law and Legal Studies
Liberal Arts, Humanities and General
    Studies
Biological and Life Sciences
English and Literature

America's
Best Colleges for
B Students

UNIVERSITY OF CINCINNATI

2600 Clifton Avenue, Cincinnati, OH 45221-0063
Admissions: 800-827-8728 · Financial Aid: 513-556-1000
Email: admissions@uc.edu · Website: http://www.uc.edu

From the College

"Students looking for real-world experience on a dynamic campus flourish at the University of Cincinnati. Located in a region with 11 Fortune 500 companies, UC links education to the workplace and the community. Beyond co-op, UC connects through partnerships, service learning and research. UC offers more than 250 undergraduate degree programs providing many pathways to success for motivated students."

Campus Setting

The University of Cincinnati, founded in 1819, is a public, four-year, urban research university dedicated to undergraduate, graduate and professional education, experience-based learning and research. Its 137-acre campus is located two miles from downtown Cincinnati. The school also has a library. Housing options: co-ed dorms · women's dorms · men's dorms · sorority housing · fraternity housing · single-student apartments · married-student apartments · special housing for international students. Recreation and sports facilities include: baseball · football · soccer and track stadium · basketball and volleyball arena · tennis courts.

Student Life and Activities

Most students (79 percent) live off campus, which does impact the on-campus social scene. Nevertheless, like any college, students find time to create their own recreational outlets. University of Cincinnati has many official student organizations. The most popular are: choral groups · concert · jazz · marching and pep bands · music ensembles · opera · symphony orchestra · musical theatre · drama · dance · film society · baton twirling · drill team · team managers · student community involvement · Showboat Majestic · special-interest groups. For those interested in sports, there are intramural teams such as: basketball · flag football · soccer · softball · volleyball · wallyball. University of Cincinnati is a member of the Big East Conference (Division I, Football I-A).

Academics and Learning Environment

For the B student, the learning environment of a college is just as important as the quality of its academic program. University of Cincinnati has 1,208 full-time and 41 part-time faculty members, offering a student-to-faculty ratio of 14:1. The most common course size is 20 to 29 students. University of Cincinnati offers 389 majors with the most popular being marketing, clinical laboratory science and nursing. The school does not have a general core requirement. Cooperative education is not offered. A minimum overall GPA of 2.0 is required to graduate. Other special academic programs that would appeal to a B student: pass/fail grading option · independent study · double majors · dual degrees · accelerated study · honors program · Phi Beta Kappa · internships · weekend college · distance learning certificate programs.

B Student Support and Success

At the University of Cincinnati, helping new students with lower GPAs get up to speed is usually achieved through the Center for Access and Transition. CAT is geared to help students have the knowledge, skills and resources to earn their degree. This is accomplished through one-on-one advising and individually tailored academic plans. (For an example of this kind of plan, go to the website.) Services include free tutoring and academic skill-enhancing workshops designed to increase GPAs, to improve study skills and time management strategies and to increase classroom attendance. Each student who is assisted by CAT has an advisor to create the personalized learning agreement. This will show the student how to meet each requirement for his/her major and may include required homework, workshop attendance or use of various campus resources. The plan clearly outlines the student's responsibilities, which commonly include meeting with his/her academic advisor and regular progress reports from instructors. Tutoring at no charge is available to all UC students and the campus has a Writing Lab and a Math Resource Center for students as well.

University of Cincinnati provides a variety of support programs including dedicated guidance for: career · psychological · non-traditional students. Recognizing that some students may need extra preparation, University of Cincinnati offers remedial and refresher courses in: reading · writing · math · study skills. The average freshman year GPA is 3.0, and 83 percent of freshmen students return for their sophomore year.

How to Get Admitted

For admissions decisions, non-academic factors considered: extracurricular activities · state of residency. A high school diploma is required, although a GED is also accepted for admissions consideration. SAT or ACT test scores are required of all applicants. SAT Subject Test scores are not required. *Academic units recommended:* 4 Math, 3 Science.

How to Pay for College

To apply for financial aid, students should submit the following: Free Application for Federal Student Aid (FAFSA). University of Cincinnati participates in the Federal Work Study program. *Need-based aid programs include:* scholarships and grants · general need-based awards · Federal Pell grants · state scholarships and grants · college-based scholarships and grants · private scholarships and grants · Federal Nursing scholarships · United Negro College Fund · ACG · SMART · TEACH. *Non-Need-based aid programs include:* scholarships and grants · general need-based awards · state scholarships and grants · creative arts and performance awards · special achievements and activities awards · special characteristics awards · athletic scholarships · ROTC scholarships.

UNIVERSITY OF CINCINNATI

Highlights

Admissions
Applicants: 14,333
Accepted: 8,798
Acceptance rate: 61.4%
Average GPA: 3.4
ACT range: 22-27
SAT Math range: 520-640
SAT Reading range: 500-610
SAT Writing range: 490-600
Top 10% of class: 22%
Top 25% of class: 49%
Top 50% of class: 81%

Deadlines
Early Action: No
Early Decision: No
Regular Action: February 1 (priority)
September 1 (final)
Common Application: Not accepted

Financial Aid
In-state tuition: $7,896
Out-of-state tuition: $22,419
Room: $5,523
Board: $3,717
Books: $1,275
Avg. % of need met by financial aid: Not reported
Avg. aid package (freshmen): Not reported
Avg. aid package (undergrads): Not reported

School Spirit
Mascot: Bearcat
Colors: Red and black
Song: *Fight Cincinnati*

UNIVERSITY OF HARTFORD

200 Bloomfield Avenue, West Hartford, CT 06117-1599
Admissions: 800-947-4303 · Financial Aid: 800-947-4303
Email: admission@hartford.edu · Website: http://www.hartford.edu

From the College

"The University of Hartford provides a learning environment in which students may transform themselves intellectually, personally and socially. We provide students with educational experiences that blend the feel of a small residential college with an array of academic programs and opportunities characteristic of a large university. Through relationships with faculty and staff dedicated to teaching, scholarship, research, the arts and civic engagement, every student may prepare for a lifetime of learning and for personal and professional success."

Campus Setting

The University of Hartford, founded in 1877, is a private, four-year, comprehensive institution. Its 200-acre campus is located in West Hartford, two miles from downtown Hartford. In addition to a large, well-stocked library, the campus facilities include: gallery · hall of fame. The University of Hartford provides on-campus housing with 17 units that can accommodate 3,784 students. Housing options: co-ed dorms · women's dorms · men's dorms · single-student apartments · special housing for disabled students. Recreation and sports facilities include a sports arena.

Student Life and Activities

With 60 percent of students living on campus, there are plenty of social activities. Popular on-campus gathering spots include the Hawks Nest and the Gengras Student Union. Popular campus events include: Parents Weekend and Spring Fling. The University of Hartford has 46 official student organizations. The most popular are: chorus · jazz ensemble · orchestra · university players · film series · art magazine · amateur radio club · residence hall association · student union board of governors · program council · commuter/transfer association · team managers. For those interested in sports, there are intramural teams such as: basketball · football · handball · racquetball · soccer · softball · tennis · volleyball. The University of Hartford is a member of the American East Conference (Division I).

Academics and Learning Environment

For the B student, the learning environment of a college is just as important as the quality of its academic program. The University of Hartford has 337 full-time and 539 part-time faculty members, offering a student-to-faculty ratio of 14:1. The most common course size is 10 to 19 students. The University of Hartford offers 118 majors with the most popular being visual and performing arts, business/marketing and engineering/engineering technologies and least popular being biological/life studies, mathematics and physical sciences. The school has a general core requirement. Cooperative education is available. All first-year students must maintain a 1.8 GPA or higher to avoid academic probation. Other special academic programs that would appeal to a B student: self-designed majors · pass/fail grading option · independent study · double majors · dual degrees · honors program · internships · weekend college · distance learning.

B Student Support and Success

The Center for Reading and Writing (CRW) at Hartford provides writing tutors that work one on one with students in all phases of writing, from start to finish. Hartford also has a math and physics tutoring lab, chemistry tutors, computer science tutoring labs and an on-campus tutoring service that matches new students with trained and experienced student tutors.

The All University Curriculum covers 11 categories of learning, from arts and culture to responsibility for civic life and values identification. These classes are taught through a variety of methods including simulations, debates, field trips, interviews, surveys, discussions, oral reports and skits or dramatic scenes. Students are required to take at least four of these courses over a four-year period.

The University of Hartford provides a variety of support programs including dedicated guidance for: academic · career · personal · psychological · minority students · veterans · family planning · religious. Additional counseling services include: high school advanced enrollment program. Recognizing that some students may need extra preparation, the University of Hartford offers remedial and refresher courses in: reading · writing · math · study skills. The average freshman year GPA is 2.9, and 75 percent of freshmen students return for their sophomore year. What do students do after college? While many enter the work force, approximately 17 percent pursue a graduate degree immediately after graduation. Among students who enter the work force, approximately 73 percent enter a field related to their major within six months of graduation. Companies that most frequently hire graduates from the University of Hartford include: Bank of America · Cigna · ESPN · Prudential Financial · St. Francis Hospital · United Technologies · University of Hartford · Yale University.

Support for Students with Learning Disabilities

Students with learning disabilities may take advantage of specific support programs offered by the University of Hartford. If necessary, the college will grant additional time to students with learning disabilities to complete their degree. Also, a lightened course load may be granted to LD students. Students with learning disabilities will find the following programs at the University of Hartford extremely useful: learning center · extended time for tests · take-home exam · readers · typist/scribe · note-taking services · reading machines · tape recorders · texts on tape · waiver of math degree requirement. Individual or small group tutorials are also available in: time management · organizational skills · learning strategies · writing labs · study skills. An advisor/advocate from the Learning Plus is available to students.

How to Get Admitted

For admissions decisions, non-academic factors considered: interview · extracurricular activities · special talents, interests, abilities · character/personal qualities · state of residency. A high school diploma is required, although a GED is also accepted for admissions consideration. SAT or ACT test scores are required of all applicants. SAT Subject Test scores are not required. *Academic units recommended:* 3 Math, 3 Science, 3 Social Studies, 2 Foreign Language.

How to Pay for College

To apply for financial aid, students should submit the following: Free Application for Federal Student Aid (FAFSA) · institution's own

UNIVERSITY OF HARTFORD

Highlights

University of Hartford
West Hartford, CT (Pop. 64,000)
Location: Large town
Website: http://www.hartford.edu

Students
Total enrollment: 7,366
Undergrads: 2,720
Freshmen: 1,469
Part-time students: 15%
From out-of-state: 74%
Male/Female: 48%/52%
Live on-campus: 60%
Off-campus employment rating: Good
Caucasian: 64%
African American: 12%
Hispanic: 6%
Asian or Pacific Islander: 3%
Native American: 0%
International: 3%

Academics
Student/faculty ratio: 14:1
Class size 9 or fewer: 19%
Class size 10-29: 74%
Class size 30-49: 6%
Class size 50-99: 1%
Class size 100 or more: -
Returning freshmen: 75%
Six-year graduation rate: 58%

Most Popular Fields of Study
Business, Finance, Sales and Marketing
Protective Services, Criminal Justice and
　　Public Administration
Psychology
English and Literature
Computer and Information Sciences
Engineering and Engineering Technolo-
　　gies
Law and Legal Studies
Interdisciplinary Studies
Health Professions, Medicine and Re-
　　lated Sciences

College Profiles

UNIVERSITY OF HARTFORD

Admissions
Applicants: 11,627
Accepted: 6,574
Acceptance rate: 56.5%
Average GPA: Not reported
ACT range: 20-25
SAT Math range: 480-590
SAT Reading range: 470-570
SAT Writing range: Not reported

Deadlines
Early Action:
Early Decision: No
Regular Action: Rolling admissions
Common Application: Accepted

Financial Aid
In-state tuition: $27,750
Out-of-state tuition: $27,750
Room: $6,908
Board: $4,330
Books: $1,000
Freshmen receiving need-based aid: 74%
Undergrads receiving need-based aid:
    67%
Avg. % of need met by financial aid: 80%
Avg. aid package (freshmen): $17,117
Avg. aid package (undergrads): $17,441
Freshmen receiving merit-based aid: 26%
Undergrads receiving merit-based aid:
    26%
Avg. student debt upon graduation:
    $38,852

Prominent Alumni
John C. Shaw, investment banker and
buyout specialist; Jerome P. Kelly, professional golfer.

School Spirit
Mascot: Hawks
Colors: Red and white

America's
Best Colleges for
B Students

financial aid forms. The University of Hartford participates in the Federal Work Study program. *Need-based aid programs include:* scholarships and grants · general need-based awards · Federal Pell grants · state scholarships and grants · college-based scholarships and grants · private scholarships and grants. *Non-Need-based aid programs include:* scholarships and grants · state scholarships and grants · creative arts and performance awards · athletic scholarships.

UNIVERSITY OF HAWAI`I - MANOA

2500 Campus Road, Honolulu, HI 96822
Admissions: 800-823-9771 · Financial Aid: 808-956-7251
Email: ar-info@hawaii.edu · Website: http://www.manoa.hawaii.edu

From the College

"The University of Hawai`i - Manoa's special distinction is found in its Hawaiian, Asian and Pacific orientation and its unique location in the middle of the Pacific Ocean. Its setting and the diversity of its students and faculty foster advantages in the study of Asian and Pacific cultures, foreign languages, tropical agriculture, tropical medicine, ocean and marine sciences, astronomy, volcanology and international business. Our geographical, cultural and historical heritage suggests that Manoa values and the responsibilities inherent in embracing those values include the following: A focus on developing an awareness of and sensitivity to diversity and commonality. A focus on global awareness and local responsibility. A focus on sustainability and renewability. Cultivating, practicing and communicating these values are our university's gifts and obligation to the rest of the world."

Campus Setting

The University of Hawai`i - Manoa, founded in 1907, is a public institution. Programs are offered through the Colleges of Arts and Sciences, Business Administration, Education, Engineering, and Tropical Agriculture and the Schools of Accountancy, Architecture, Hawaiian, Asian, and Pacific Studies, Law, Medicine, Nursing, Ocean and Earth Science Technology, Public Health, Social Work and Travel Industry Management. Its 300-acre campus is located in Manoa Valley, a residential area near the center of metropolitan Honolulu. A four-year institution, the University of Hawai`i - Manoa has an enrollment of 20,169 students. In addition to a large, well-stocked library, the campus facilities include: art museum · center for Hawaiian studies · Korean studies center · arboretum · aquarium · institute for astronomy · cancer research center · undersea research lab · institution of geophysics and planetology · institute of marine biology. The University of Hawai`i - Manoa provides on-campus housing with 1,298 units that can accommodate 3,605 students. Housing options: co-ed dorms · single-student apartments · married-student apartments · special housing for disabled students. Recreation and sports facilities include: aquatic complex · gymnasium · marine training facility · tennis courts · track · weight room.

Student Life and Activities

Most students (83 percent) live off campus, which does impact the on-campus social scene. Nevertheless, like any college, students find time to create their own recreational outlets. Students gather at the Campus Center, Manoa Gardens, Manoa Marketplace and Puck's Alley. Football games, orientation week and Friday concerts are popular events. The University of Hawai`i - Manoa has 150 official student organizations. The most popular are: music · theatre · political · service and special-interest groups. For those interested in sports, there are intramural teams such as: badminton · basketball · bench press · free-throw contest · golf · indoor soccer · table tennis · tennis · turkey trot · volleyball. The University of Hawai`i - Manoa is a member of the Mountain Pacific Sports Federation (Division I), Western Athletic Conference (Division I, Football I-A).

Academics and Learning Environment

For the B student, the learning environment of a college is just as important as the quality of its academic program. The University of Hawai`i - Manoa has 1,222 full-

471

College Profiles

UNIVERSITY OF HAWAI'I - MANOA

University of Hawai'i - Manoa
Honolulu, HI (Pop. 359,694)
Location: Major city
Website: http://www.manoa.hawaii.edu

Students
Total enrollment: 20,169
Undergrads: 6,309
Freshmen: 1,812
Part-time students: 19%
From out-of-state: 30%
Male/Female: 46%/54%
Live on-campus: 17%
In fraternities: 1%
In sororities: 1%
Off-campus employment rating: Excellent
Caucasian: 24%
African American: 1%
Hispanic: 3%
Asian or Pacific Islander: 65%
Native American: 0%
International: 5%

Academics
Student/faculty ratio: 15:1
Class size 9 or fewer: 14%
Class size 10-29: 63%
Class size 30-49: 14%
Class size 50-99: 5%
Class size 100 or more: 3%
Returning freshmen: 78%
Six-year graduation rate: 55%

Most Popular Fields of Study
Business, Finance, Sales and Marketing
Visual and Performing Arts
Social Sciences, History, Economics,
    Political Science
Protective Services, Criminal Justice and
    Public Administration
Biological and Life Sciences
Family and Consumer Sciences, Nutrition
    and Home Economics
Computer and Information Sciences
Communications, Journalism, Advertising
    and Comm. Technologies
Philosophy, Religion and Theology
Liberal Arts, Humanities and General
    Studies

America's
Best Colleges for
B Students

time and 84 part-time faculty members, offering a student-to-faculty ratio of 15:1. The most common course size is 10 to 19 students. The University of Hawai'i - Manoa offers 216 majors with the most popular being information/computer science, psychology and biology and least popular being German, Korean and real estate. The school has a general core requirement. Cooperative education is available. All first-year students must maintain a 2.0 GPA or higher to avoid academic probation. Other special academic programs that would appeal to a B student: self-designed majors · pass/fail grading option · independent study · double majors · dual degrees · honors program · Phi Beta Kappa · internships · distance learning certificate programs.

B Student Support and Success

The Learning Center at UH has a variety of services including testing, tutoring, study skills information and computer services. Practical skills are taught in areas like speed reading, test taking and time management. Tutoring in math, English, foreign language and other subjects is available by appointment or walk-in. The university also has two computer labs that provide extra assistance to students.

The University of Hawai'i - Manoa provides a variety of support programs including dedicated guidance for: academic · career · personal · psychological · military · family planning. The average freshman year GPA is 2.8, and 78 percent of freshmen students return for their sophomore year. Among students who enter the work force, approximately 86 percent enter a field related to their major within six months of graduation, while a further 6 percent enter a related career within two years of graduation. Companies that most frequently hire graduates from the University of Hawai'i - Manoa include: Bank of Hawaii · Marriott International Hotels and Resorts · Kaiser Permanente · Hawaiian Airlines · Grant Thornton LLP; Japanese English Teaching (JET) Program; KMH LLP; KPMG LLP; Pearl Harbor Naval Shipyard and Immediate Maintenance Facility; PriceWaterhouseCoopers LLP; U.S. Undersea Naval Warfare Center Detachment · Hawaiian Electric Industries · Verizon Hawaii · Hilton Hawaii · Kamehameha Schools.

Support for Students with Learning Disabilities

Students with learning disabilities may take advantage of specific support programs offered by the University of Hawai'i - Manoa. If necessary, the college will grant additional time to students with learning disabilities to complete their degree. Also, a lightened course load may be granted to LD students. Students with learning disabilities will find the following programs at the University of Hawai'i - Manoa extremely useful: tutors · extended time for tests · take-home exam · readers · typist/scribe · note-taking services · reading machines · tape recorders · texts on tape · early syllabus. An advisor/advocate from the KOKUA Program is available to students.

How to Get Admitted

For admissions decisions, non-academic factors considered: interview · extracurricular activities · special talents, interests, abilities · geographical location. A high school diploma is required, although a

GED is also accepted for admissions consideration. SAT or ACT test scores are required of all applicants. SAT Subject Test scores are not required. *According to the admissions office:* Minimum SAT Reasoning score of 510 in both verbal and math (composite ACT score of 22), rank in top two-fifths of secondary school class, and minimum 2.8 GPA required.

How to Pay for College

To apply for financial aid, students should submit the following: Free Application for Federal Student Aid (FAFSA). The University of Hawai`i - Manoa participates in the Federal Work Study program. *Need-based aid programs include:* scholarships and grants · general need-based awards · Federal Pell grants · state scholarships and grants · college-based scholarships and grants · private scholarships and grants · Federal Nursing scholarships. *Non-Need-based aid programs include:* scholarships and grants · general need-based awards · state scholarships and grants · creative arts and performance awards · athletic scholarships · ROTC scholarships.

UNIVERSITY OF HAWAI`I - MANOA

Highlights

Admissions
Applicants: 7,029
Accepted: 4,688
Acceptance rate: 66.7%
Average GPA: 3.4
ACT range: 21-25
SAT Math range: 500-610
SAT Reading range: 480-570
SAT Writing range: 470-560
Top 10% of class: 25%
Top 25% of class: 58%
Top 50% of class: 91%

Deadlines
Early Action: No
Early Decision: No
Regular Action: Rolling admissions
Common Application: Not accepted

Financial Aid
In-state tuition: $6,768
Out-of-state tuition: $18,816
Room: $3,672
Board: $2,382
Books: $1,226
Freshmen receiving need-based aid: 32%
Undergrads receiving need-based aid: 32%
Avg. % of need met by financial aid: 60%
Avg. aid package (freshmen): $6,926
Avg. aid package (undergrads): $7,687
Freshmen receiving merit-based aid: 21%
Undergrads receiving merit-based aid: 18%
Avg. student debt upon graduation: $14,818

Prominent Alumni
U.S. Senator Daniel Akaka; U.S. Senator Daniel K. Inouye ; Jay H. Shidler, philanthropist.

School Spirit
Mascot: Warriors, Rainbow Warriors, Rainbow Wahine, Rainbows
Colors: Green, white, black and silver

473

UNIVERSITY OF HOUSTON

212 Ezekiel Cullen Building, Houston, TX 77204
Admissions: 713-743-1010 · Financial Aid: 713-743-1010
Email: admissions@uh.edu · Website: http://www.uh.edu

From the College

"The University of Houston is a metropolitan research and teaching institution that is recognized throughout the world as a leader in energy research, law, business and environmental education. Located in America's fourth -argest city, the University of Houston ranks as one of the two most ethnically diverse major research universities in the nation—a student population of more than 34,000 students from 133 countries. In addition to preparing its students to succeed in today's global economy, the University of Houston is also a catalyst within its own community—changing lives through health, education and outreach projects that help build a future for children in Houston, in Texas and in the world. Other merits of the University of Houston include a strong student experience, a Division I athletics program and a faculty including eight National Academy members, a Nobel laureate and winners of the National Medal of Science, Pulitzer and Tony awards."

Campus Setting

University of Houston, founded in 1927, is a public institution. Programs are offered through the Colleges of Architecture, Business Administration, Education, Humanities and Fine Arts, Natural Science and Mathematics, Optometry, Pharmacy, Social Sciences, and Technology; the Graduate School of Social Work; the Cullen College of Engineering; the Hilton College of Hotel and Restaurant Management; and the Bates College of Law. Its 550-acre campus is located in a residential area, three miles from downtown Houston. A four-year institution, the University of Houston has an enrollment of 36,104 students. In addition to a large, well-stocked library, the campus also has a gallery. The University of Houston provides on-campus housing with 2,786 units that can accommodate 4,385 students. Housing options: co-ed dorms · sorority housing · fraternity housing · single-student apartments · married-student apartments · special housing for disabled students. Recreation and sports facilities include: field · pavilion · recreation center · stadium · softball complex · track · tennis courts.

Student Life and Activities

Most students (92 percent) live off campus, which does impact the on-campus social scene. Nevertheless, like any college, students find time to create their own recreational outlets. Frontier Fiesta and Homecoming are popular events. The University of Houston has 350 official student organizations. The most popular are: Frontier Fiesta Association · Residence Hall Association · Metropolitan Volunteer Program. The University of Houston is a member of the Member of Conference USA (Division I, Football I-A).

Academics and Learning Environment

For the B student, the learning environment of a college is just as important as the quality of its academic program. The University of Houston has 1,229 full-time and 544 part-time faculty members, offering a student-to-faculty ratio of 22:1. The most common course size is 20 to 29 students. The University of Houston offers 274 majors with the most popular being psychology, accounting and finance and least popular being merchandise and industrial distribution, German area studies and Chinese studies. The school has a general core requirement. Cooperative education is available. All first-year students must maintain a 2.0 GPA or higher to avoid academic probation, and a minimum overall GPA of 2.0 is required to graduate. Other special academic programs that would appeal to a B student: pass/fail grading option · independent study · double majors · dual degrees · accelerated study · honors program · internships · weekend college · distance learning certificate programs.

B Student Support and Success

Learning and Assessment Services at UH offers workshops covering topics such as improving memory power, overcoming procrastination, reducing test anxiety, preparing for exams and time management. Tutoring is available for no cost on both a walk-in and appointment basis. Multimedia Resources can help students who learn best on the computer, and math, science and business majors can find supplemental instruction study groups that meet on a regular basis. The Texas Success Initiative Program provides non-course, non-credit developmental instruction in reading, writing, math and test preparation.

The University of Houston provides a variety of support programs including dedicated guidance for: academic · career · personal · psychological · minority students · military · veterans · non-traditional students · family planning · religious. Recognizing that some students may need extra preparation, the University of Houston offers remedial and refresher courses in: reading · writing · math · study skills. Annually, 79 percent of freshmen students return for their sophomore year.

Support for Students with Learning Disabilities

Students with learning disabilities may take advantage of specific support programs offered. If necessary, the college will grant additional time to students with learning disabilities to complete their degree. Also, a lightened course load may be granted to LD students. According to the school, the Center for Students with Disabilities (CSD) provides numerous academic support services to individuals with any type of learning disability, health impairment, physical limitation or psychiatric disorder. Our goal is to help ensure that qualified students with disabilities at the University of Houston are able to successfully compete with non-disabled students. CSD services are confidential. CSD student information is shared only with the student's written permission to do so. Students with learning disabilities will find the following programs extremely useful: remedial math · remedial English · remedial reading · tutors · learning center · testing accommodations · extended time for tests · take-home exam · oral tests · readers · typist/scribe · note-taking services · reading machines · tape recorders · texts on tape · videotaped classes · early syllabus · diagnostic testing service · priority registration · priority seating · waiver of math degree requirement · waiver of foreign language degree requirement. Individual or small group tutorials are also available in: time management · organizational skills · learning strategies · specific subject areas · writing labs · math labs · study skills. An advisor/advocate from the Center for Students with Disabilities is available to students.

How to Get Admitted

For admissions decisions, non-academic factors considered: extracurricular activities · special talents, interests, abilities · character/personal

UNIVERSITY OF HOUSTON

University of Houston
Houston, TX (Pop. 1,953,631)
Location: Major city
Website: http://www.uh.edu

Students
Total enrollment: 36,104
Undergrads: 14,133
Freshmen: 6,867
Part-time students: 28%
From out-of-state: 2%
Male/Female: 49%/51%
Live on-campus: 8%
In fraternities: 4%
In sororities: 3%
Off-campus employment rating: Good
Caucasian: 33%
African American: 15%
Hispanic: 23%
Asian or Pacific Islander: 22%
Native American: 0%
International: 4%

Academics
Student/faculty ratio: 22:1
Class size 9 or fewer: 10%
Class size 10-29: 46%
Class size 30-49: 20%
Class size 50-99: 15%
Class size 100 or more: 9%
Returning freshmen: 79%
Six-year graduation rate: 42%

Most Popular Fields of Study
Business, Finance, Sales and Marketing
Social Sciences, History, Economics, Political Science
Visual and Performing Arts
Family and Consumer Sciences, Nutrition and Home Economics
Computer and Information Sciences
Communications, Journalism, Advertising and Comm. Technologies
Biological and Life Sciences
English and Literature
Health Professions, Medicine and Related Sciences

UNIVERSITY OF HOUSTON

Admissions
Applicants: 11,542
Accepted: 9,093
Acceptance rate: 78.8%
Average GPA: 3.3
ACT range: 19-24
SAT Math range: 490-600
SAT Reading range: 460-570
SAT Writing range: Not reported
Top 10% of class: 21%
Top 25% of class: 51%
Top 50% of class: 81%

Deadlines
Early Action: No
Early Decision: No
Regular Action: Rolling admissions
Common Application: Not accepted

Financial Aid
In-state tuition: $8,532
Out-of-state tuition: $14,108
Room: -
Board: -
Books: $1,100
Freshmen receiving need-based aid: 58%
Undergrads receiving need-based aid:
    53%
Avg. % of need met by financial aid: 73%
Avg. aid package (freshmen): $11,469
Avg. aid package (undergrads): $11,660
Freshmen receiving merit-based aid: 5%
Undergrads receiving merit-based aid:
    2%

School Spirit
Mascot: Cougars
Colors: Red and white
Song: *University*

476

qualities · volunteer work · work experience · state of residency. A high school diploma is required, although a GED is also accepted for admissions consideration. SAT or ACT test scores are required of all applicants. SAT Subject Test scores are recommended but not required. *According to the admissions office:* Minimum SAT critical reading and math scores of 440 (combined ACT score of 19) required. *Academic units recommended:* 4 English, 3 Math, 2 Science, 3 Social Studies, 2 Foreign Language.

How to Pay for College

To apply for financial aid, students should submit the following: Free Application for Federal Student Aid (FAFSA). The University of Houston participates in the Federal Work Study program. *Need-based aid programs include:* scholarships and grants · general need-based awards · Federal Pell grants · state scholarships and grants · college-based scholarships and grants · private scholarships and grants. *Non-Need-based aid programs include:* scholarships and grants · general need-based awards · state scholarships and grants · creative arts and performance awards · athletic scholarships · ROTC scholarships.

UNIVERSITY OF IDAHO

P.O. Box 442282, Moscow, ID 83844-2282
Admissions: 888-884-3246 · Financial Aid: 888-884-3246
Email: admissions@uidaho.edu · Website: http://www.uidaho.edu

From the College

"The University of Idaho offers a complete living and learning experience. It's a residential campus located in a small, friendly community. There are fresh air outdoor activities and surprising cultural gems, including the Lionel Hampton International Jazz Festival and Moscow's active art scene. Many students take advantage of an emphasis on undergraduate research opportunities in computer security, transportation innovations, environmental science, evolutionary biology and biomedical research. Our facilities include: the stunning Student Recreation Center, Kibbie Dome, Idaho Commons, Student Union and Pritchard Art Gallery. The University of Idaho is nationally ranked as a best buy for the quality and value and ranked as one of the most unwired college campuses in the United States."

Campus Setting

The University of Idaho, founded in 1889, is a public, comprehensive, land-grant institution. Its 1,450-acre campus and university farm are located in Moscow, 90 miles southeast of Spokane, Wash. A four-year public institution, the University of Idaho has an enrollment of 11,791 students. In addition to a large, well-stocked library, the campus also has art galleries. The University of Idaho provides on-campus housing that can accommodate 2,226 students. Housing options: co-ed dorms · women's dorms · men's dorms · sorority housing · fraternity housing · single-student apartments · married-student apartments · special housing for disabled students · special housing for International students. Recreation and sports facilities include: fields · gymnasium · golf course · recreation center · track and field complex · weight rooms · swim center · activity center.

Student Life and Activities

Many students (45 percent) live off campus, which does impact the on-campus social scene. Nevertheless, like any college, students find time to create their own recreational outlets. Students gather at Idaho Commons, Student Union, Kibbie Dome, Arboretum, Latah Trail, Kenworthy Performing Arts Center, Moscow downtown restaurants and Palouse mall. Popular events include: Lional Hampton International Jazz Festival, Cruise the World, Martini Forum, Dancers, Drummers and Dreamers, Tuxinmepu PowWow, Borah Symposium, student musical and theatre productions, student recitals and Kibbie Dome athletic events. The University of Idaho has 234 official student organizations. Greeks, Associated Students University of Idaho and international groups are influential in campus life. For those interested in sports, there are intramural teams such as: badminton · basketball · billiards · disc golf · dodgeball · flag football · floor hockey · foosball · horseshoes · kickball · power lifting · racquetball · roller hockey · soccer · softball · swimming · tennis · ultimate Frisbee · volleyball · wiffleball · wrestling. The University of Idaho is a member of the Western Athletic Conference (Division I, Football Bowl 1-A).

Academics and Learning Environment

For the B student, the learning environment of a college is just as important as the quality of its academic program. The University of Idaho has 582 full-time and 126 part-time faculty members, offering a student-to-faculty ratio of 16:1. The most common course size is 2 to 9 students. The University of Idaho offers 236 majors

UNIVERSITY OF IDAHO

Highlights

University of Idaho
Moscow, ID (Pop. 24,955)
Location: Small town
Website: http://www.uidaho.edu

Students
Total enrollment: 11,791
Undergrads: 4,994
Freshmen: 1,665
Part-time students: 12%
From out-of-state: 35%
Male/Female: 54%/46%
Live on-campus: 21%
In fraternities: 28%
In sororities: 28%
Off-campus employment rating: Excellent
Caucasian: 83%
African American: 1%
Hispanic: 5%
Asian or Pacific Islander: 2%
Native American: 1%
International: 2%

Academics
Student/faculty ratio: 16:1
Class size 9 or fewer: 27%
Class size 10-29: 48%
Class size 30-49: 17%
Class size 50-99: 6%
Class size 100 or more: 1%
Returning freshmen: 77%
Six-year graduation rate: 57%

Most Popular Fields of Study
Business, Finance, Sales and Marketing
Visual and Performing Arts
Social Sciences, History, Economics,
    Political Science
Protective Services, Criminal Justice and
    Public Administration
Family and Consumer Sciences, Nutrition
    and Home Economics
Computer and Information Sciences
Communications, Journalism, Advertising
    and Comm. Technologies
Philosophy, Religion and Theology
Liberal Arts, Humanities and General
    Studies

America's
Best Colleges for
B Students

with the most popular being psychology, elementary education and mechanical engineering. The school has a general core requirement. Cooperative education is available. All first-year students must maintain a 2.0 GPA or higher to avoid academic probation, and a minimum overall GPA of 2.0 is required to graduate. Other special academic programs that would appeal to a B student: self-designed majors · pass/fail grading option · independent study · double majors · dual degrees · accelerated study · honors program · Phi Beta Kappa · internships · distance learning certificate programs.

B Student Support and Success

The University of Idaho offers three academic assistance programs, each with its own focus. Tutoring and Learning Services provides one-on-one tutoring as well as a series of workshops called the College Success Series. These workshops cover such areas as note taking, active learning, college textbook reading and time management. Freshmen are also offered a one-credit study skills course, and there is an online learning center as well. Students in accounting, computer science and chemistry have their own learning labs and study groups, and there is a separate Math Lab. The English Writing Center helps with all facets of written communication. Student Support Services is designed to provide academic support and assistance to students who meet the TRIO eligibility standards: 1) neither parent has a college degree, 2) they come from a low-income family or 3) they are physically/learning disabled. The Disability Support Services is geared to assist students who are physically challenged as defined by the American Disabilities Act.

The University of Idaho provides a variety of support programs including dedicated guidance for: academic · career · personal · psychological · minority students · military · veterans · non-traditional students · family planning. Recognizing that some students may need extra preparation, the University of Idaho offers remedial and refresher courses in: reading · writing · math · study skills. The average freshman year GPA is 3.0, and 77 percent of freshmen students return for their sophomore year. Among students who enter the work force, approximately 87 percent enter a field related to their major within six months of graduation.

Support for Students with Learning Disabilities

Students with learning disabilities may take advantage of specific support programs. Also, a lightened course load may be granted to LD students. According to the school, Diagnostic Testing Service offered through the Counseling and Testing Center. Students with learning disabilities will find the following programs at the University of Idaho extremely useful: tutors · learning center · extended time for tests · oral tests · readers · note-taking services · reading machines · tape recorders · videotaped classes · waiver of math degree requirement. Individual or small group tutorials are also available in: time management · organizational skills · learning strategies · specific subject areas · writing labs · math labs · study skills. An advisor/advocate from the LD program is available.

How to Get Admitted

For admissions decisions, non-academic factors considered: state of residency. A high school diploma is required, although a GED is also accepted for admissions consideration. SAT or ACT test scores are required of all applicants. SAT Subject Test scores are not required. *According to the admissions office:* One unit of fine arts, foreign language, history, literature or philosophy required. Applicants evaluated on a sliding scale based on secondary school GPA and ACT or SAT Reasoning scores.

How to Pay for College

To apply for financial aid, students should submit the following: Free Application for Federal Student Aid (FAFSA). The University of Idaho participates in the Federal Work Study program. *Need-based aid programs include:* scholarships and grants · general need-based awards · Federal Pell grants · state scholarships and grants · college-based scholarships and grants · private scholarships and grants. *Non-Need-based aid programs include:* scholarships and grants · general need-based awards · state scholarships and grants · creative arts and performance awards · special achievements and activities awards · special characteristics awards · athletic scholarships · ROTC scholarships.

UNIVERSITY OF IDAHO

Highlights

Admissions
Applicants: 4,935
Accepted: 3,844
Acceptance rate: 77.9%
Average GPA: 3.4
ACT range: 20-26
SAT Math range: 490-610
SAT Reading range: 480-600
SAT Writing range: Not reported
Top 10% of class: 18%
Top 25% of class: 44%
Top 50% of class: 76%

Deadlines
Early Action: No
Early Decision: No
Regular Action: Rolling admissions
Common Application: Accepted

Financial Aid
In-state tuition: $4,932
Out-of-state tuition: $15,012
Room: -
Board: -
Books: $1,474
Freshmen receiving need-based aid: 56%
Undergrads receiving need-based aid: 58%
Avg. % of need met by financial aid: 74%
Avg. aid package (freshmen): $10,472
Avg. aid package (undergrads): $10,609
Freshmen receiving merit-based aid: 30%
Undergrads receiving merit-based aid: 22%
Avg. student debt upon graduation: $21,702

Prominent Alumni
Jeffrey Ashby, astronaut; Dirk Kempthorne, secretary of the interior, former governor of Idaho, former U.S. Senator; Jack Lemley, construction manager for Europe's Channel Tunnel.

School Spirit
Mascot: Vandal
Colors: Silver and gold
Song: *Here We Have Idaho (alma mater)*

479

UNIVERSITY OF KENTUCKY

101 Main Building, Lexington, KY 40506
Admissions: 859-257-2000 · Financial Aid: 859-257-3172
Email: admissions@uky.edu · Website: http://www.uky.edu

From the College

"The University of Kentucky is a public land grant institution that prepares students for an increasingly diverse and technological world. The university offers a broad array of undergraduate, graduate and professional degree programs. The university strives to nurture a true learning community—one that inspires academic growth and learning among faculty, staff and students. Research, scholarship and creative activities support human and economic development through the expansion of knowledge and its applications in the sciences, social sciences, education, arts, humanities, business and the professions."

Campus Setting

University of Kentucky, founded in 1865, is a public, comprehensive university. Programs are offered through the Colleges of Agriculture, Allied Health Professions, Architecture, Arts and Sciences, Business and Economics, Communications and Information Studies, Education, Engineering, Fine Arts, Human Environmental Sciences, Law, Nursing, Pharmacy and Social Work. Its 685-acre campus is located in Lexington, 75 miles from Cincinnati. A four-year institution, the University of Kentucky has an enrollment of 26,054 students. In addition to a large, well-stocked library, the campus facilities include: art galleries · center for American music · art and anthropology museums. The University of Kentucky provides on-campus housing with 2,918 units that can accommodate 6,349 students. Housing options: co-ed dorms · women's dorms · men's dorms · sorority housing · fraternity housing · single-student apartments · married-student apartments · special housing for disabled students · special housing for International students. Recreation and sports facilities include: aquatics and tennis recreation center · basketball and volleyball courts · gymnasium · track.

Student Life and Activities

Most students (71 percent) live off campus, which does impact the on-campus social scene. Nevertheless, like any college, students find time to create their own recreational outlets. The University of Kentucky has 348 official student organizations. The most popular are: chorus · glee club · marching and pep bands · symphonic band and orchestra · opera workshop · drill team · modern dance club · theatre · debate club · team managers · other academic and special-interest groups. For those interested in sports, there are intramural teams such as: basketball · flag football · golf · inner-tube water polo · racquetball · soccer · softball · swimming · table tennis · tennis · team handball · track · tug-of-war · turkey trot · ultimate Frisbee · volleyball. The University of Kentucky is a member of the Southeastern Conference (Division I, Football I-A).

Academics and Learning Environment

For the B student, the learning environment of a college is just as important as the quality of its academic program. The University of Kentucky has 1,047 full-time and 614 part-time faculty members, offering a student-to-faculty ratio of 18:1. The most common course size is 20 to 29 students. The University of Kentucky offers 186 majors with the most popular being accounting, biology and marketing and least popular being Latin American studies and Russian/East European studies. The school has a general core requirement. Cooperative education is available. All first-year students must maintain a 2.0 GPA or higher to avoid academic probation, and a minimum overall GPA of 2.0 is required to graduate. Other special academic programs that would appeal to a B student: pass/fail grading option · independent study · double majors · dual degrees · accelerated study · honors program · Phi Beta Kappa · internships · weekend college · distance learning certificate programs.

B Student Support and Success

The University of Kentucky has an Academic Enhancement Program which is typically referred to as "the Study." It is geared to help students reach their academic goals through study groups, tutoring or learning skills workshops. The Writing Center offers free individual or group consultations and helps with class assignments, creative writing, dissertations, reports, articles and more. The Math Resource Center (Mathskeller) has tutors for 100-level math courses, and the Counseling and Testing Center offers personal sessions as well as interactive workshops.

The University of Kentucky provides a variety of support programs including dedicated guidance for: academic · career · psychological · minority students · military. Annually, 81 percent of freshmen students return for their sophomore year.

Support for Students with Learning Disabilities

Students with learning disabilities may take advantage of specific support programs. If necessary, the college will grant additional time to students with learning disabilities to complete their degree. According to the school, each student with Learning Disabilities receives accommodations that are specific to his/her needs and that are supported by documentation. All students with Learning Disabilities are not eligible for all accommodations. Students with learning disabilities will find the following programs extremely useful: remedial math · testing accommodations · extended time for tests · take-home exam · oral tests · readers · typist/scribe · reading machines · tape recorders · early syllabus · diagnostic testing service. Individual or small group tutorials are also available in: time management · organizational skills · learning strategies · specific subject areas · writing labs · math labs · study skills. An advisor/advocate from the Disability Resource Center is available to students.

How to Get Admitted

For admissions decisions, non-academic factors considered: interview · extracurricular activities · special talents, interests, abilities · character/personal qualities · volunteer work · state of residency · geographical location · minority affiliation · alumni relationship. A high school diploma is required, although a GED is also accepted for admissions consideration. SAT or ACT test scores are required of all applicants. *According to the admissions office:* Minimum 2.0 GPA required. *Academic units recommended:* 4 English, 4 Math, 4 Science, 3 Social Studies, 2 Foreign Language.

How to Pay for College

To apply for financial aid, students should submit the following: Free Application for Federal Student Aid (FAFSA). The University of

UNIVERSITY OF KENTUCKY

Highlights

University of Kentucky
Lexington, KY (Pop. 261,000)
Location: Medium city
Website: http://www.uky.edu

Students
Total enrollment: 26,054
Undergrads: 9,369
Freshmen: 4,110
Part-time students: 9%
From out-of-state: 24%
Male/Female: 49%/51%
Live on-campus: Not reported
In fraternities: 9%
In sororities: 12%
Off-campus employment rating: Excellent
Caucasian: 87%
African American: 7%
Hispanic: 1%
Asian or Pacific Islander: 2%
Native American: 0%
International: 1%

Academics
Student/faculty ratio: 18:1
Class size 9 or fewer: 9%
Class size 10-29: 53%
Class size 30-49: 22%
Class size 50-99: 10%
Class size 100 or more: 6%
Returning freshmen: 81%
Six-year graduation rate: 58%

Most Popular Fields of Study
Business, Finance, Sales and Marketing
Visual and Performing Arts
Protective Services, Criminal Justice and
    Public Administration
Family and Consumer Sciences, Nutrition
    and Home Economics
Computer and Information Sciences
Communications, Journalism, Advertising
    and Comm. Technologies
Philosophy, Religion and Theology
English and Literature
Health Professions, Medicine and Re-
    lated Sciences
Psychology

481

College Profiles

UNIVERSITY OF KENTUCKY

Admissions
Applicants: 11,120
Accepted: 8,757
Acceptance rate: 78.8%
Average GPA: 3.4
ACT range: 22-27
SAT Math range: 500-630
SAT Reading range: 490-610
SAT Writing range: 480-600
Top 10% of class: 26%
Top 25% of class: 54%
Top 50% of class: 82%

Deadlines
Early Action: No
Early Decision: No
Regular Action: February 15 (priority)
February 15 (final)
Common Application: Not accepted

Financial Aid
In-state tuition: $7,214
Out-of-state tuition: $7,214
Room: $3,975
Board: $5,150
Books: $800
Freshmen receiving need-based aid: 46%
Undergrads receiving need-based aid: 40%
Avg. % of need met by financial aid: 82%
Avg. aid package (freshmen): $8,978
Avg. aid package (undergrads): $8,794
Freshmen receiving merit-based aid: 22%
Undergrads receiving merit-based aid: 19%
Avg. student debt upon graduation: $15,891

School Spirit
Mascot: Wildcats
Colors: Blue and white
Song: *On, On U of K*

Kentucky participates in the Federal Work Study program. *Need-based aid programs include:* scholarships and grants · general need-based awards · Federal Pell grants · state scholarships and grants · college-based scholarships and grants · private scholarships and grants. *Non-Need-based aid programs include:* scholarships and grants · general need-based awards · state scholarships and grants · creative arts and performance awards · special achievements and activities awards · athletic scholarships · ROTC scholarships · alumni affiliation scholarships · leadership scholarships · minority scholarships · music and drama scholarships.

UNIVERSITY OF LOUISIANA - LAFAYETTE

P.O. Drawer 41008, Lafayette, LA 70504-1008
Admissions: 337-482-6553 · Financial Aid: 337-482-6506
Email: enroll@louisiana.edu · Website: http://www.louisiana.edu

From the College

"The university takes as its primary purpose the examination, transmission, preservation and extension of mankind's intellectual traditions. The university provides intellectual leadership for the educational, cultural and economic development of the region and state through its instructional, research, and service activities. The university extends its resources to diverse constituency groups it serves through research centers, continuing education, public outreach programs cultural activities and access to campus facilities."

Campus Setting

Southwestern Louisiana, founded in 1898, is a public, comprehensive university. Programs are offered through the Colleges of Applied Life Sciences, the Arts, Business Administration, Education, Engineering, General Studies, Liberal Arts, Nursing and Sciences, and through the Graduate School. Its 1,375-acre campus is located in Lafayette, 50 miles from Baton Rouge. A four-year institution, the University of Louisiana - Lafayette has an enrollment of 16,302 students. In addition to a large, well-stocked library, the campus also has art museums. The University of Louisiana - Lafayette provides on-campus housing with 20 units that can accommodate 2,154 students. Housing options: women's dorms · men's dorms · fraternity housing · single-student apartments · married-student apartments.

Student Life and Activities

Most students (88 percent) live off campus, which does impact the on-campus social scene. Nevertheless, like any college, students find time to create their own recreational outlets. The University of Louisiana - Lafayette has 134 official student organizations. The most popular are: Accounting Society · Club for Academic Competition · College Democrats · College Republicans · Ducks Unlimited · Gospel Choir · Greek Council · Computer Society · Interfraternity Council · American Institute of Architecture Students · Law Club · MBA Association · National Panhellenic Conference · Outdoor Club · Pre-Vet Society · Pride Society · Residence Hall Association · American Institute of Chemical Engineers Student Chapter · American Society of Civil Engineers · Anime Club · ACM · Beacon Club · Best Buddies · Bowling Club. For those interested in sports, there are intramural teams such as: basketball · flag football · racquetball · soccer · softball · tennis · triathlon · volleyball · water polo. The University of Louisiana - Lafayette is a member of the Sun Belt Conference (Division I, Football I-A).

Academics and Learning Environment

For the B student, the learning environment of a college is just as important as the quality of its academic program. The University of Louisiana - Lafayette has 530 full-time and 165 part-time faculty members, offering a student-to-faculty ratio of 25:1. The most common course size is 20 to 29 students. The University of Louisiana - Lafayette offers 119 majors with the most popular being elementary education, finance and nursing. The school has a general core requirement. Cooperative education is not offered. All first-year students must maintain a 2.0 GPA or higher to avoid academic probation. Other special academic programs that would appeal to a B student: self-designed majors · independent study · double majors · dual degrees ·

UNIVERSITY OF LOUISIANA - LAFAYETTE

University of Louisiana - Lafayette
Lafayette, LA (Pop. 195,000)
Location: Medium city
Website: http://www.louisiana.edu

Students
Total enrollment: 16,302
Undergrads: 6,308
Freshmen: 2,914
Part-time students: 15%
From out-of-state: 5%
Male/Female: 42%/58%
Live on-campus: 12%
In fraternities: 3%
In sororities: 5%
Off-campus employment rating: Fair
Caucasian: 72%
African American: 19%
Hispanic: 2%
Asian or Pacific Islander: 2%
Native American: 0%
International: 1%

Academics
Student/faculty ratio: 25:1
Class size 9 or fewer: 7%
Class size 10-29: 54%
Class size 30-49: 30%
Class size 50-99: 6%
Class size 100 or more: 3%
Returning freshmen: 73%
Six-year graduation rate: 40%

Most Popular Fields of Study
Business, Finance, Sales and Marketing
Protective Services, Criminal Justice and
    Public Administration
Visual and Performing Arts
Family and Consumer Sciences, Nutrition
    and Home Economics
Computer and Information Sciences
Communications, Journalism, Advertising
    and Comm. Technologies
Liberal Arts, Humanities and General
    Studies
Biological and Life Sciences
English and Literature

484

America's
Best Colleges for
B Students

accelerated study · honors program · internships · distance learning certificate programs.

B Student Support and Success

Students may be admitted through the University of Louisiana's Guaranteed Admission requirements, which are these:

Completion of the Louisiana Board of Regents' high school core curriculum and a mathematics ACT score of at least 18 (430 math SAT) or an English ACT score of at least 18 (450 critical reading SAT) and one of the following:

High school GPA of 2.5 or higher using an unweighted 4.0 scale ACT composite score of at least 23 (SAT 1060) with at least a 2.0 GPA or rank in the top 25 percent of the high school graduating class and at least a 2.0 GPA.

Students who don't meet the Guaranteed Admission requirements may apply for Admission by Committee by submitting a completed application.

Once students are accepted and enrolled at the University of Louisiana, they can find help for succeeding in their studies. The Learning Center offers walk-in tutoring, although appointments are sometimes recommended. The Writing Center helps students with all stages of the writing process. Free online tutoring is offered through Smart Thinking. With it, students can access live tutorials in writing, math, accounting, statistics and economics. They can also consult writing manuals, sample problems, research tools and study skills manuals.

Study groups are available on campus so that several students can get help on a weekly basis. They are student led, and sessions cover problems and questions from weekly class material.

Study skills and time management helps are found on the college website, including information on reading, note taking, studying, test anxiety, test taking and general study skills.

The college also offers a Career Counseling Center that can provide help to a student in deciding a major. A career counselor is there to guide students to resources and informational material. Along with this, a half-semester, one-credit course on career decision-making assists students who want an in-depth career analysis.

The University of Louisiana - Lafayette provides a variety of support programs including dedicated guidance for: academic · career · personal. Recognizing that some students may need extra preparation, the University of Louisiana - Lafayette offers remedial and refresher courses in: reading · writing · math · study skills. Annually, 73 percent of freshmen students return for their sophomore year.

Support for Students with Learning Disabilities

Students with learning disabilities may take advantage of specific support programs offered by the University of Louisiana - Lafayette. If necessary, the college will grant additional time to students with learning disabilities to complete their degree. Also available are math study groups, special five-days a week math classes, videos in remedial math and college algebra classes and online tutoring. Smart Thinking is available through the university, and a writing lab is available in the English Department. There are workshops in study skills, time management and individual counseling. Students with learning disabilities will find the following programs at the University of Louisiana - Lafayette extremely useful: remedial math · remedial English · remedial reading · special classes · tutors · learning center · untimed tests · extended time for tests · oral tests · readers · typist/scribe · note-taking services · reading machines · tape recorders · diagnostic testing service · priority registration · waiver of foreign language degree requirement. An advisor/advocate from the LD program is available to students.

How to Get Admitted

For admissions decisions, non-academic factors considered: A high school diploma is required, although a GED is also accepted for admissions consideration. SAT or ACT test scores are required of all applicants. SAT Subject Test scores are recommended but not required. *According to the admissions office:* Minimum 2.0 GPA required. Minimum composite ACT score of 17 required of out-of-state applicants.

How to Pay for College

To apply for financial aid, students should submit the following: Free Application for Federal Student Aid (FAFSA). The University of Louisiana - Lafayette participates in the Federal Work Study program. *Need-based aid programs include:* scholarships and grants · general need-based awards · Federal Pell grants · state scholarships and grants · college-based scholarships and grants · private scholarships and grants · Federal Nursing scholarships · United Negro College Fund. *Non-Need-based aid programs include:* scholarships and grants · state scholarships and grants · creative arts and performance awards · athletic scholarships.

UNIVERSITY OF LOUISIANA - LAFAYETTE

Highlights

Admissions
Applicants: 7,140
Accepted: 5,219
Acceptance rate: 73.1%
Average GPA: 3.2
ACT range: 19-25
SAT Math range: Not reported
SAT Reading range: Not reported
SAT Writing range: Not reported
Top 10% of class: 14%
Top 25% of class: 38%
Top 50% of class: 72%

Deadlines
Early Action: No
Early Decision: No
Regular Action: July 20 (priority)
Common Application: Not accepted

Financial Aid
In-state tuition: $3,401
Out-of-state tuition: $9,581
Room: -
Board: -
Books: $1,000
Freshmen receiving need-based aid: 47%
Undergrads receiving need-based aid: 48%
Avg. % of need met by financial aid: 48%
Avg. aid package (freshmen): $5,137
Avg. aid package (undergrads): $5,490
Freshmen receiving merit-based aid: 11%
Undergrads receiving merit-based aid: 6%
Avg. student debt upon graduation: Not reported

Prominent Alumni
Jake Delhomme, professional football player; Kathleen Blanco, governor of Louisiana.

School Spirit
Mascot: Ragin' Cajuns
Colors: Vermillion and White
Song: *UL Fight Song*

485

UNIVERSITY OF MAINE

168 College Avenue, Orono, ME 04469
Admissions: 877-486-2364 · Financial Aid: 207-581-1324
Email: um-admit@maine.edu · Website: http://www.umaine.edu

From the College

"While the University of Maine embraces its tradition of providing high-quality education, research and service all relevant and important to Maine, it also recognizes that its work affects people far beyond the state's borders. Its nationally and internationally programs in areas like climate change provide outstanding learning opportunities for its students, while advancing knowledge in critical disciplines. UMaine is also a leader in developing teaching and research partnerships with other institutions—both educational and research—to maximize resources and share expertise, with the ultimate goal of producing high-quality results."

Campus Setting

The University of Maine, founded in 1865, is a public, land-grant institution. Programs are offered through the Colleges of Business, Public Policy, and Health, Education and Human Development, Engineering, Liberal Arts and Sciences, Natural Resources, Forestry and Agriculture. Its 3,300-acre main campus is located in Orono, eight miles north of Bangor. A four-year institution, the University of Maine has an enrollment of 11,912 students. The University of Maine has been co-ed since 1872. In addition to a large, well-stocked library, the campus facilities include: arts · Canadian-American and Franco-American center · art museum · digital media lab · hall for performing arts · anthropology museum · aquatic production facility · farm museum · botanical gardens · environmental research facility · marine lab · woodland preserve · observatory · planetarium · woods composites building · advanced manufacturing center · lab for advanced surface science and technology · climbing wall. The University of Maine provides on-campus housing that can accommodate 3,875 students. Housing options: co-ed dorms · sorority housing · fraternity housing · single-student apartments · married-student apartments · special housing for disabled students · special housing for International students.

Student Life and Activities

Most students (58 percent) live off campus, which does impact the on-campus social scene. Nevertheless, like any college, students find time to create their own recreational outlets. The University of Maine has 234 official student organizations. The most popular are: concert · jazz · marching and symphonic bands · varsity and pep bands · orchestra · music ensembles · university singers · women's glee club · Oratorio Society · opera workshop · Maine Masque Theatre · musical theatre · dance club · debating · language clubs · Sophomore Eagles · Blade Society · Maine Bound · drill team. The University of Maine is a member of the American East Conference (Division I), Atlantic 10 Conference (Division I, Football I-AA), Hockey East Association (Division I).

Academics and Learning Environment

For the B student, the learning environment of a college is just as important as the quality of its academic program. The University of Maine has 608 full-time and 221 part-time faculty members, offering a student-to-faculty ratio of 15:1. The most common course size is 10 to 19 students. The University of Maine offers 173 majors with the most popular being business administration, nursing and psychology and least popular being German, Earth sciences and Latin. The school has a general core requirement. Cooperative education is not offered. All first-year students must maintain a 1.6 GPA or higher to avoid academic probation. Other special academic programs that would appeal to a B student: pass/fail grading option · independent study · double majors · accelerated study · honors program · Phi Beta Kappa · internships · distance learning certificate programs.

B Student Support and Success

The Tutor Program at the University of Maine is designed to meet with students in small group settings who need help in their 100- and 200-level, non-web-based courses. Peer tutors meet with students two or three times a week throughout the semester. One student is quoted on the website as saying, "I was not grasping the problems in lecture, and I was often confused on which technique to apply. Having students explain ideas and concepts to each other has been very helpful. I have had to be prepared for each session, which keeps me on task." This no-cost service is open to any student who has registered for at least six credit hours as well as students who need help in math classes.

For those needing help with writing, the college's Writing Center staff is there to give advice as well.

The University of Maine provides a variety of support programs including dedicated guidance for: academic · career · personal · psychological · minority students · military · veterans · non-traditional students · family planning · religious. The average freshman year GPA is 2.9, and 76 percent of freshmen students return for their sophomore year.

Support for Students with Learning Disabilities

Students with learning disabilities may take advantage of specific support programs offered by the University of Maine. If necessary, the college will grant additional time to students with learning disabilities to complete their degree. Also, a lightened course load may be granted to LD students. Students with learning disabilities will find the following programs at the University of Maine extremely useful: remedial math · remedial English · remedial reading · tutors · testing accommodations · extended time for tests · take-home exam · oral tests · readers · note-taking services · tape recorders · early syllabus. Individual or small group tutorials are also available in: learning strategies · study skills. An advisor/advocate from the College Success Programs is available to students.

How to Get Admitted

For admissions decisions, non-academic factors considered: interview · extracurricular activities · special talents, interests, abilities · character/personal qualities · volunteer work · work experience · geographical location. A high school diploma is required, although a GED is also accepted for admissions consideration. SAT or ACT test scores are required of all applicants. SAT Subject Test scores are recommended but not required. *According to the admissions office:* Rank in top half of secondary school class and minimum 2.5 GPA recommended. *Academic units recommended:* 4 English, 4 Math, 4 Science, 3 Social Studies, 2 Foreign Language.

UNIVERSITY OF MAINE

Highlights

University of Maine
Orono, ME (Pop. 9,000)
Location: Rural
Website: http://www.umaine.edu

Students
Total enrollment: 11,912
Undergrads: 4,750
Freshmen: 1,972
Part-time students: 18%
From out-of-state: 22%
Male/Female: 49%/51%
Live on-campus: 42%
Off-campus employment rating: Fair
Caucasian: 79%
African American: 1%
Hispanic: 1%
Asian or Pacific Islander: 1%
Native American: 1%
International: 1%

Academics
Student/faculty ratio: 15:1
Class size 9 or fewer: 16%
Class size 10-29: 54%
Class size 30-49: 17%
Class size 50-99: 10%
Class size 100 or more: 3%
Returning freshmen: 76%
Six-year graduation rate: 59%

Most Popular Fields of Study
Business, Finance, Sales and Marketing
Visual and Performing Arts
Social Sciences, History, Economics,
    Political Science
Family and Consumer Sciences, Nutrition
    and Home Economics
Computer and Information Sciences
Communications, Journalism, Advertising
    and Comm. Technologies
Philosophy, Religion and Theology
Liberal Arts, Humanities and General
    Studies
English and Literature

UNIVERSITY OF MAINE

Admissions
Applicants: 7,407
Accepted: 5,721
Acceptance rate: 77.2%
Average GPA: 3.2
ACT range: 20-25
SAT Math range: 480-600
SAT Reading range: 480-580
SAT Writing range: 470-570
Top 10% of class: 21%
Top 25% of class: 52%
Top 50% of class: 86%

Deadlines
Early Action: December 15
Early Decision: No
Regular Action: Rolling admissions
Common Application: Accepted

Financial Aid
In-state tuition: $9,100
Out-of-state tuition: $22,510
Room: -
Board: -
Books: -
Freshmen receiving need-based aid: 67%
Undergrads receiving need-based aid: 67%
Avg. % of need met by financial aid: 78%
Avg. aid package (freshmen): $11,855
Avg. aid package (undergrads): $11,369
Freshmen receiving merit-based aid: 18%
Undergrads receiving merit-based aid: 19%
Avg. student debt upon graduation: $24,330

School Spirit
Mascot: Black Bears
Colors: Maine blue, navy blue, and white
Song: *Stein Song*

How to Pay for College
To apply for financial aid, students should submit the following: Free Application for Federal Student Aid (FAFSA). The University of Maine participates in the Federal Work Study program. *Need-based aid programs include:* scholarships and grants · general need-based awards · Federal Pell grants · state scholarships and grants · college-based scholarships and grants · private scholarships and grants. *Non-Need-based aid programs include:* scholarships and grants · general need-based awards · state scholarships and grants · creative arts and performance awards · athletic scholarships · ROTC scholarships.

America's
Best Colleges for
B Students

UNIVERSITY OF MARYLAND – EASTERN SHORE

J.T. Williams Hall, Room 2106, Princess Anne, MD 21853
Admissions: 410-651-6410 · Financial Aid: 410-651-6172
Email: umesadmissions@umes.edu
Website: http://www.umes.edu

Campus Setting

U Maryland - Eastern Shore is a public, multipurpose institution. It was founded in 1886, became a state college in 1948 and gained university status in 1970. Its 620-acre campus is located in Princess Anne, 15 miles from Salisbury. A four-year institution, the University of Maryland - Eastern Shore is a historically black university with 4,130 students. The school also has a library with 217,429 books. The University of Maryland - Eastern Shore provides on-campus housing that can accommodate 2,100 students. Housing options: co-ed dorms · women's dorms · men's dorms. Recreation and sports facilities include: bowling alley · center · field · gymnasium · stadium.

Student Life and Activities

Popular events include: Homecoming, Mr. and Miss UMES and National Women's History Month. The University of Maryland - Eastern Shore has 75 official student organizations. The most popular is Biology Society. For those interested in sports, there are intramural teams such as: basketball · billiards · bowling · flag football · soccer · table tennis · volleyball. The University of Maryland - Eastern Shore is a member of the Mid-Eastern Athletic Conference (Division I).

Academics and Learning Environment

For the B student, the learning environment of a college is just as important as the quality of its academic program. The University of Maryland - Eastern Shore has 174 full-time and 104 part-time faculty members, offering a student-to-faculty ratio of 18:1. The most common course size is 20 to 29 students. The University of Maryland - Eastern Shore offers 55 majors with the most popular being criminal justice and rehabilitation services and least popular being physical education, fine arts and mathematics. The school has a general core requirement. Cooperative education is not offered. All first-year students must maintain a 1.66 GPA or higher to avoid academic probation, and a minimum overall GPA of 2.0 is required to graduate. Other special academic programs that would appeal to a B student: pass/fail grading option · independent study · dual degrees · honors program · internships · distance learning.

B Student Support and Success

UMES has an extensive Academic Support Center, which includes a tutorial program that helps students in all lower-level courses. Both individual and small group tutoring are available and all services are free.

Highlights

University of Maryland - Eastern Shore
Princess Anne, MD (Pop. 10,343)
Location: Rural
Website: http://www.umes.edu

Students
Total enrollment: 4,130
Undergrads: 1,435
Freshmen: 1,181
Part-time students: 8%
From out-of-state: 30%
Male/Female: 39%/61%
Live on-campus: Not reported
Off-campus employment rating: Poor
Caucasian: 6%
African American: 84%
Hispanic: 1%
Asian or Pacific Islander: 1%
Native American: 0%
International: 3%

Academics
Student/faculty ratio: 18:1
Class size 9 or fewer: 25%
Class size 10-29: 56%
Class size 30-49: 15%
Class size 50-99: 4%
Class size 100 or more: -
Returning freshmen: 65%
Six-year graduation rate: 34%

Most Popular Fields of Study
Business, Finance, Sales and Marketing
Biological and Life Sciences
Agriculture, Aquaculture and Animal Sciences

489

UNIVERSITY OF MARYLAND - EASTERN SHORE

Admissions
Applicants: 3,595
Accepted: 2,833
Acceptance rate: 78.8%
Average GPA: 2.7
ACT range: 15-18
SAT Math range: 350-460
SAT Reading range: 360-460
SAT Writing range: Not reported

Deadlines
Early Action:
Early Decision: No
Regular Action: March 1 (priority)
July 15 (final)
Common Application: Accepted

Financial Aid
In-state tuition: $4,112
Out-of-state tuition: $10,900
Room: $3,460
Board: $3,000
Books: $1,600
Freshmen receiving need-based aid: 73%
Undergrads receiving need-based aid: 75%
Avg. % of need met by financial aid: 84%
Avg. aid package (freshmen): $14,372
Avg. aid package (undergrads): $12,250
Freshmen receiving merit-based aid: 7%
Undergrads receiving merit-based aid: 10%
Avg. student debt upon graduation: Not reported

School Spirit
Mascot: Fighting Hawks/Lady Hawks
Colors: Maroon and grey

Through the school's Computer Assisted Instruction Program, students can use a system known as Accuplacer to obtain a comprehensive analysis of where they stand in reading, math and English. Developmental skills classes are offered by professional staff specialists. Students who need a stronger background in liberal arts may find help through the General Studies Program.

Additionally, students who are 1) from families with low income, 2) first generation college enrollees or 3) disabled (learning or physical) can take part in the federally funded Student Support Services Program.

The University of Maryland - Eastern Shore provides a variety of support programs including dedicated guidance for: academic · career · personal · psychological · minority students · veterans · religious. Recognizing that some students may need extra preparation, the University of Maryland - Eastern Shore offers remedial and refresher courses in: reading · writing · math · study skills. Other remedial services include Pre-admission summer program. The average freshman year GPA is 2.7, and 65 percent of freshmen students return for their sophomore year.

Support for Students with Learning Disabilities

Students with learning disabilities may take advantage of specific support programs offered by the University of Maryland - Eastern Shore. If necessary, the college will grant additional time to students with learning disabilities to complete their degree. Students with learning disabilities will find the following programs at the University of Maryland - Eastern Shore extremely useful: remedial math · remedial English · remedial reading · tutors · untimed tests · extended time for tests · note-taking services · tape recorders · waiver of math degree requirement. An advisor/advocate from the Office of Services for Students with Disabilities is available to students.

How to Get Admitted

For admissions decisions, non-academic factors considered: interview · extracurricular activities · special talents, interests, abilities · character/personal qualities. A high school diploma is required, although a GED is also accepted for admissions consideration. SAT or ACT test scores are required of all applicants. SAT Subject Test scores are not required. *According to the admissions office:* Minimum combined SAT score of 860 and minimum 2.5 GPA recommended. In-state applicants with secondary school diploma and minimum 2.5 GPA may be admitted on basis of predictive index weighting SAT scores and GPA.

How to Pay for College

To apply for financial aid, students should submit the following: Free Application for Federal Student Aid (FAFSA). The University of Maryland - Eastern Shore participates in the Federal Work Study program. *Need-based aid programs include:* scholarships and grants · general need-based awards · Federal Pell grants · state scholarships and grants · college-based scholarships and grants · private scholarships and grants. *Non-Need-based aid programs include:* scholarships and grants · state scholarships and grants · creative arts and performance awards · athletic scholarships.

UNIVERSITY OF MASSACHUSETTS - AMHERST

37 Mather Drive, Amherst, MA 01003-9313
Admissions: 413-545-0222 · Financial Aid: 413-545-0801
Email: mail@admissions.umass.edu · Website: http://www.umass.edu

From the College

"The University of Massachusetts - Amherst combines the academic resources of a research university with the support and individualized attention usually reserved for a small college. Students come from every state and over 100 countries, making this New England campus a national and international center for intellectual and cultural activity. With over 85 majors, UMass Amherst offers its students a wide array of academic disciplines and nationally known programs of study, including the Bachelor's Degree with Individual Concentration (BDIC), which allows students to create their own major. (If you are a legal resident of Connecticut, Maine, New Hampshire, Rhode Island or Vermont, and the major you want at UMass Amherst is not available at your public college, you may qualify for reduced tuition through the New England Regional Student Program.)

"Students complement their classroom work with internships, co-ops and research, working side-by-side their faculty. Students take what they learn in the classroom and apply it in the studio, the lab, the concert hall and the field. With this intersection of learning and doing, students find their intellectual voice and independence. Commonwealth College, the honors program, welcomes students who seek additional academic challenge and meet the requirements for acceptance. The extensive library system is the largest at any public institution in the Northeast and offers students a state-of-the-art learning environment through the Learning Commons, a place that fosters academic collaboration and social interaction. Through the Five College Interchange, students enroll in classes at nearby Amherst, Hampshire, Mount Holyoke, and Smith Colleges at no extra charge. A free bus system connects these five campuses, allowing students to participate in a wide array of social and cultural events.

"UMass Amherst first-year students participate in the Residential First Year Experience, choosing a living option based on themes and shared interests. Living and learning together, students take field trips, organize events and interact with faculty and staff. Other opportunities for personal development are found through the Center for Student Development, which brings together more than 220 clubs and organizations.

"Appearing on "the top ten" lists for college towns, Amherst has a combination of New England charm and international sophistication. Boston is less than two hours away, and New York City just three hours south. For outdoor enthusiasts, the mountains of Vermont are less than an hour away and offer skiing and hiking."

Campus Setting

The University of Massachusetts Amherst is a public research university located in the New England town of Amherst. Undergraduates choose from almost 90 areas of academic study, and UMass Amherst provides almost unlimited possibilities for personal growth and professional development. A four-year institution, the University of Massachusetts - Amherst has an enrollment of 25,873 students. The school also has a library with 3,233,990 books. The University of Massachusetts - Amherst provides on-campus housing with 44 units that can accommodate 11,970 students. Housing options: co-ed dorms · women's dorms · men's dorms · sorority housing · fraternity housing · single-student apartments · married-student apartments · special housing for disabled students · special housing for international students. Recreation

UNIVERSITY OF MASSACHUSETTS - AMHERST

University of Massachusetts - Amherst
Amherst, MA (Pop. 34,874)
Location: Large town
Website: http://www.umass.edu

Students
Total enrollment: 25,873
Undergrads: 10,090
Freshmen: 4,144
Part-time students: 7%
From out-of-state: 23%
Male/Female: 50%/50%
Live on-campus: 60%
In fraternities: 4%
In sororities: 4%
Off-campus employment rating: Excellent
Caucasian: 74%
African American: 5%
Hispanic: 4%
Asian or Pacific Islander: 8%
Native American: 0%
International: 1%

Academics
Student/faculty ratio: 17:1
Class size 9 or fewer: 15%
Class size 10-29: 49%
Class size 30-49: 19%
Class size 50-99: 8%
Class size 100 or more: 9%
Returning freshmen: 84%
Six-year graduation rate: 67%

Most Popular Fields of Study
Business, Finance, Sales and Marketing
Visual and Performing Arts
Social Sciences, History, Economics, Political Science
Computer and Information Sciences
Communications, Journalism, Advertising and Comm. Technologies
Philosophy, Religion and Theology
Liberal Arts, Humanities and General Studies
English and Literature
Health Professions, Medicine and Related Sciences
Physical Sciences, Chemistry, Physics and Astronomy

492

and sports facilities include: arena · artificial turf · dance studio · recreational fitness center · gymnasium · handball · racquetball and squash courts · ice rinks · indoor track · playing fields · soccer and softball fields · stadium · swimming pools · weight training room · wrestling room.

Student Life and Activities

With 60 percent of students living on campus, there are plenty of social activities. Time has not tarnished the city's small town connectedness, and the downtown itself is still centered on a traditional New England town common, with shops, cafés and restaurants lining the streets around it. While UMass's 10,000-seat Mullins Center is a venue for sports events and pop concerts, the Fine Arts Center hosts performing arts groups and houses a visual arts gallery. Popular gathering spots include: the Learning Commons, Campus Center/Student Union, downtown Amherst and nearby Northampton. Popular campus events include: Something Every Friday, First Week, Festival of the Arts, Multicultural Film Festival, Haitian/Dominican/CASA Cultural Night, Jazz in July and Magic Triangle Jazz series. The University of Massachusetts - Amherst has 227 official student organizations. The most popular are: music · theatre · political · service and special-interest groups. For those interested in sports, there are intramural teams such as: basketball · field hockey · flag football · ice hockey · soccer · softball · tennis · ultimate Frisbee · volleyball · wallyball · wrestling. The University of Massachusetts - Amherst is a member of the Atlantic 10 Conference (Division I, Football I-AA), ECAC (Division I, Football I-AA), Hockey East Association (Division I).

Academics and Learning Environment

For the B student, the learning environment of a college is just as important as the quality of its academic program. The University of Massachusetts - Amherst has 1,175 full-time and 186 part-time faculty members, offering a student-to-faculty ratio of 17:1. The most common course size is 10 to 19 students. The University of Massachusetts - Amherst offers 214 majors with the most popular being psychology, management and biology. The school has a general core requirement. Cooperative education is available. All first-year students must maintain a 2.0 GPA or higher to avoid academic probation. Other special academic programs that would appeal to a B student: self-designed majors · pass/fail grading option · independent study · double majors · dual degrees · accelerated study · honors program · Phi Beta Kappa · internships · distance learning certificate programs.

B Student Support and Success

UMass's General Studies program offers students the chance to develop skills like critical thinking, communication and learning skills. It consists of 14 required courses and assistance is possible through the Learning Commons and an academic advisor. A Learning Resource Center offers free help through tutoring, and supplemental instruction.

The University of Massachusetts - Amherst provides a variety of support programs including dedicated guidance for: academic · career · personal · psychological · minority students · veterans ·

family planning. The average freshman year GPA is 3.1, and 84 percent of freshmen students return for their sophomore year. What do students do after college? While many enter the work force, approximately 17 percent pursue a graduate degree immediately after graduation.

Support for Students with Learning Disabilities

Students with learning disabilities may take advantage of specific support programs offered by the University of Massachusetts - Amherst. If necessary, the college will grant additional time to students with learning disabilities to complete their degree. Also, a lightened course load may be granted to LD students. Credit is given for remedial courses taken. High school foreign language waivers are accepted. High school math waivers are also accepted. Students with learning disabilities will find the following programs at the University of Massachusetts - Amherst extremely useful: special classes · testing accommodations · untimed tests · extended time for tests · take-home exam · oral tests · exam on tape or computer · readers · typist/scribe · note-taking services · proofreading services · reading machines · tape recorders · early syllabus · priority registration · priority seating · waiver of math degree requirement · waiver of foreign language degree requirement. Individual or small group tutorials are also available in: time management · organizational skills · learning strategies · specific subject areas · study skills. An advisor/advocate from the Disability Services is available to students.

How to Get Admitted

For admissions decisions, non-academic factors considered: extracurricular activities · special talents, interests, abilities · character/personal qualities · volunteer work · work experience · geographical location · minority affiliation. A high school diploma is required, although a GED is also accepted for admissions consideration. SAT or ACT test scores are required of all applicants.

How to Pay for College

To apply for financial aid, students should submit the following: Free Application for Federal Student Aid (FAFSA). The University of Massachusetts - Amherst participates in the Federal Work Study program. *Need-based aid programs include:* scholarships and grants · general need-based awards · Federal Pell grants · state scholarships and grants · college-based scholarships and grants · private scholarships and grants. *Non-Need-based aid programs include:* scholarships and grants · general need-based awards · state scholarships and grants · creative arts and performance awards · special achievements and activities awards · special characteristics awards · athletic scholarships · ROTC scholarships.

UNIVERSITY OF MASSACHUSETTS - AMHERST

Highlights

Admissions
Applicants: 27,138
Accepted: 17,815
Acceptance rate: 65.6%
placed on wait list: 2,881
Average GPA: 3.5
ACT range: Not reported
SAT Math range: 520-630
SAT Reading range: 510-610
SAT Writing range: Not reported
Top 10% of class: 22%
Top 25% of class: 58%
Top 50% of class: 94%

Deadlines
Early Action: November 1
Early Decision: No
Regular Action: January 15 (final)
Common Application: Accepted

Financial Aid
In-state tuition: $1,714
Out-of-state tuition: $9,937
Room: $4,524
Board: $3,590
Books: $1,000
Freshmen receiving need-based aid: 52%
Undergrads receiving need-based aid: 51%
Avg. % of need met by financial aid: 86%
Avg. aid package (freshmen): $12,018
Avg. aid package (undergrads): $12,551
Freshmen receiving merit-based aid: 10%
Undergrads receiving merit-based aid: 6%
Avg. student debt upon graduation: $21,614

Prominent Alumni
Catherine "Cady" Coleman, astronaut; Bill Pullman, actor; Jeff Corwin, the Jeff Corwin Experience of *Animal Planet.*

School Spirit
Mascot: Minutemen, Minutewomen
Colors: Maroon and white
Song: *Fight UMass*

493

College Profiles

UNIVERSITY OF MEMPHIS

101 Wilder Tower, Memphis, TN 38152
Admissions: 800-669-2678 · Financial Aid: 901-678-4825
Email: recruitment@memphis.edu · Website: http://www.memphis.edu

From the College

"The University of Memphis was founded in 1912 by the Tennessee legislature and is one of only two doctoral research-extensive public universities in the state and is designated as "community engaged" by the Carnegie Foundation for the Advancement of Teaching. Home to students from all 50 states and 100 foreign countries, the University of Memphis strives to provide a close community for its students through its Learning Communities, Emerging Leaders Program, Honors Program, residence life and 180 student organizations. Our students are National Merit finalists, Goldwater Scholars, Emerging Leaders, Honors students and Merck Research scholars. They have won national competitions in robotics/artificial intelligence, music, journalism, investment challenges, moot court, architecture and mathematics. Men's basketball has a 20-year tradition of excellence, including repeated trips to the NCAA tournament and appearances in the famed Final Four.

"The UofM is comprised of five undergraduate colleges: arts and sciences, business, education, communication and fine arts, and engineering, the University College, as well as a graduate school, law school, nursing school and a School of Audiology and Speech-Language Pathology. The University offers 15 bachelor's degrees in more than 50 majors and 70 concentrations, master's degrees in more than 45 subjects, and doctoral degrees in 21 disciplines, in addition to the juris doctor (law) and specialist in education degrees. Our academic programs enable our students to compete at the highest level offering programs in education, psychology, philosophy, audiology and speech-language pathology, earthquake science, biomedical engineering, discrete mathematics, among others. The Loewenberg School of Nursing has a longstanding 100 percent first-time passage rate for state licensure, and the Cecil C. Humphreys School of Law graduates have the overall highest first-time bar exam passage of any law school in Tennessee. Our faculty in the College of Communication and Fine Arts has received Grammy Awards, Peabody Awards, and CINE Eagle Awards. Within that college, the Rudi E. Scheidt School of Music is the only one in the Southeast region to offer a doctorate in music.

"The university is closely connected to the community via internships and research conducted in conjunction with area businesses and industries. The university is dedicated to lifelong learning and to making higher education accessible to as many people as possible. Toward that end, it makes significant use of online courses and offers classes at 34 off-site community locations and four satellite campuses in West Tennessee."

Campus Setting

University of Memphis is a comprehensive, public university. It changed its name from Memphis State University in 1994. Its 1,178-acre campus is located in Memphis. A four-year institution, the University of Memphis has an enrollment of 20,214 students. In addition to a large, well-stocked library, the campus facilities include: art gallery · biological center · art and archaeological museums · Egyptian art and archaeology and technology institutes. The University of Memphis provides on-campus housing with 1,294 units that can accommodate 2,541 students. Housing options: co-ed dorms · women's dorms · men's dorms · sorority housing · fraternity housing · single-student apartments · married-student apartments · special housing for disabled students.

Student Life and Activities

Most students (86 percent) live off campus, which does impact the on-campus social scene. Nevertheless, like any college, students find time to create their own recreational outlets. Popular campus events include: Up 'til Dawn, Cultural Arts Series, Wednesday Night Live Series, major concerts and comedy, Domestic Violence Awareness Week, Why Do You Hate Me Week, debates, Homosexuality and Morality, Black History Month, Women's History Month and Black Scholars Breakfast. The University of Memphis has 181 official student organizations. The most popular are: music · theatre · political · service and special-interest groups. The University of Memphis is a member of the Conference USA (Division I, Football I-AA).

Academics and Learning Environment

For the B student, the learning environment of a college is just as important as the quality of its academic program. The University of Memphis has 851 full-time and 533 part-time faculty members, offering a student-to-faculty ratio of 15:1. The most common course size is 20 to 29 students. The University of Memphis offers 123 majors with the most popular being business/marketing, interdisciplinary studies and education and least popular being family and consumer sciences, history and computer and information sciences. The school has a general core requirement. Cooperative education is available. All first-year students must maintain a 1.4 GPA or higher to avoid academic probation, and a minimum overall GPA of 2.0 is required to graduate. Other special academic programs that would appeal to a B student: self-designed majors · pass/fail grading option · independent study · double majors · dual degrees · accelerated study · honors program · internships · distance learning certificate programs.

B Student Support and Success

The University of Memphis offers its students help through its Advanced Learning Center. A Learning Lab provides consultations, open forum learning, special topics training and educational seminars.

The University of Memphis provides a variety of support programs including dedicated guidance for: academic · career · personal · psychological · minority students · military · veterans · non-traditional students · family planning · religious. Recognizing that some students may need extra preparation, the University of Memphis offers remedial and refresher courses in: reading · writing · math · study skills. The average freshman year GPA is 2.7, and 75 percent of freshmen students return for their sophomore year. What do students do after college? While many enter the work force, approximately 26 percent pursue a graduate degree immediately after graduation. Among students who enter the work force, approximately 61 percent enter a field related to their major within six months of graduation. Companies that most frequently hire graduates from the University of Memphis include: Pricewaterhouse Cooper · Nike · Thompson Dunavant · Phillip Morris · Cummins · Schering-Plough Corp.· Smith and Nephew · Williams Sonoma · Hilton Hotels Corp.· Reynolds · Bone and Griesbeck · First Tennessee Bank · Pfizer · Dell · Regions Financial Corp.·

UNIVERSITY OF MEMPHIS

Highlights

University of Memphis
Memphis, MN (Pop. 680,800)
Location: Major city
Website: http://www.memphis.edu

Students
Total enrollment: 20,214
Undergrads: 6,074
Freshmen: Not reported
Part-time students: 25%
From out-of-state: 9%
Male/Female: 38%/62%
Live on-campus: 14%
In fraternities: 7%
In sororities: 5%
Off-campus employment rating: Excellent
Caucasian: 53%
African American: 39%
Hispanic: 2%
Asian or Pacific Islander: 2%
Native American: 0%
International: 2%

Academics
Student/faculty ratio: 15:1
Class size 9 or fewer: 14%
Class size 10-29: 55%
Class size 30-49: 20%
Class size 50-99: 7%
Class size 100 or more: 2%
Returning freshmen: 75%
Six-year graduation rate: 35%

Most Popular Fields of Study
Business, Finance, Sales and Marketing
Visual and Performing Arts
Social Sciences, History, Economics, Political Science
Family and Consumer Sciences, Nutrition and Home Economics
Computer and Information Sciences
Communications, Journalism, Advertising and Comm. Technologies
Philosophy, Religion and Theology
Liberal Arts, Humanities and General Studies
English and Literature
Health Professions, Medicine and Related Sciences

College Profiles

UNIVERSITY OF MEMPHIS

Morgan Keegan · Wells Fargo · International Paper · FedEx · Merrill Lynch · Medtronic.

Support for Students with Learning Disabilities

Students with learning disabilities may take advantage of specific support programs offered by the University of Memphis. If necessary, the college will grant additional time to students with learning disabilities to complete their degree. Also, a lightened course load may be granted to LD students. According to the school, The LD/ADHD Program at University of Memphis promotes development and independence of students with LD and ADHD (attention deficit hyperactivity disorder) through early intervention and education about disability-related functional limitations. Through counseling and coaching, students learn appropriate techniques and accommodation to compensate for functional limitations and move toward academic success. Students with learning disabilities will find the following programs at the University of Memphis extremely useful: remedial math · remedial English · remedial reading · tutors · learning center · testing accommodations · extended time for tests · take-home exam · exam on tape or computer · readers · typist/scribe · note-taking services · reading machines · tape recorders · texts on tape · early syllabus · diagnostic testing service · priority registration · waiver of math degree requirement · waiver of foreign language degree requirement. Individual or small group tutorials are also available in: time management · organizational skills · learning strategies · specific subject areas · writing labs · math labs · study skills. An advisor/advocate from the Student Disability Services is available to students.

How to Get Admitted

For admissions decisions, non-academic factors considered: special talents, interests, abilities · character/personal qualities · work experience · state of residency. A high school diploma is required, although a GED is also accepted for admissions consideration. SAT or ACT test scores are required of all applicants. *Academic units recommended:* 4 Math.

How to Pay for College

To apply for financial aid, students should submit the following: Free Application for Federal Student Aid (FAFSA). The University of Memphis participates in the Federal Work Study program. *Need-based aid programs include:* scholarships and grants · general need-based awards · Federal Pell grants · state scholarships and grants · college-based scholarships and grants · private scholarships and grants. *Non-Need-based aid programs include:* scholarships and grants · general need-based awards · state scholarships and grants · creative arts and performance awards · athletic scholarships · ROTC scholarships.

UNIVERSITY OF MISSISSIPPI

P.O. Box 1848, University, MS 38677-1848
Admissions: 800-OLEMISS (in-state)
Financial Aid: 800-OLEMISS (in-state)
Email: admissions@olemiss.edu · Website: http://www.olemiss.edu

From the College

"The University of Mississippi, one of the oldest but also most progressive public institutions of higher learning in the South, is a classical liberal arts institution that offers a selection of professional programs. Known affectionately as Ole Miss, the main campus is located in the picturesque city of Oxford, which combines the charm and safety of a small town with the sophistication of a larger city. With 100 academic programs to choose from, University of Mississippi students are exposed to a diversity of academic disciplines that emphasize cultural breadth, intellectual depth and independence of mind. They also participate in a full range of extracurricular and entertainment programs in a residential environment. The university emphasizes strong classroom teaching supported by excellent library, laboratory and technical facilities.

"The campus in Oxford, home of the late Nobel Prize-winning author William Faulkner, is an incubator for writers and literary scholars and houses the College of Liberal Arts; the schools of Accountancy, Applied Sciences, Business Administration, Education, Engineering, Pharmacy and Law; and the graduate school, as well as 35 research centers and institutes. The Center for the Study of Southern Culture and William Winter Institute for Racial Reconciliation are located here, as are the nation's most extensive Blues Archive and Faulkner's papers. The complete library of the accountancy profession is housed in the J.D. Williams Library. More than $100 million in research is conducted annually, including studies in atmospheric physics, cardiovascular disease, pharmaceutical sciences, physical acoustics, remote sensing, space law and tropical diseases.

"Ole Miss was the first public university in Mississippi to shelter a chapter of Phi Beta Kappa, the nation's oldest and most prestigious undergraduate honor society. The Croft Institute for International Studies provides students with intensive training that can lead to careers in law, international business, journalism or public service, and the Lott Leadership Institute offers the state's only undergraduate degree program in public policy studies and strengthens the university's tradition of producing national leaders. The accountancy school's graduate and undergraduate programs are ranked in the nation's top 25. The National Science Foundation ranks UM 20th nationally for total R&D expenditures in physics, and the School of Pharmacy ranks fifth among America's 92 pharmacy schools for total extramural funding for research. The university has produced 25 Rhodes Scholars. Since 1998, the university also has produced eight Goldwater scholars, six Truman scholars, six Fulbright scholars and a Marshall scholar. UM's 18 sports teams compete at the NCAA's highest level."

Campus Setting

The University of Mississippi, founded in 1844, is a comprehensive, public institution. Its 2,500-acre campus is located in Oxford, 70 miles southeast of Memphis. A four-year institution, the University of Mississippi has an enrollment of 15,389 students. The University of Mississippi has been co-ed since 1882. In addition to a library, the campus facilities include: art galleries · museums. Housing options: women's dorms · men's dorms · sorority housing · fraternity housing · married-student apartments.

UNIVERSITY OF MISSISSIPPI

Highlights

University of Mississippi
Oxford, MS (Pop. 19,000)
Location: Small town
Website: http://www.olemiss.edu

Students
Total enrollment: 15,389
Undergrads: 6,114
Freshmen: 3,488
Part-time students: 9%
From out-of-state: Not reported
Male/Female: 48%/52%
Live on-campus: Not reported
In fraternities: 32%
In sororities: 34%
Caucasian: 80%
African American: 13%
Hispanic: 1%
Asian or Pacific Islander: 1%
Native American: 0%
International: 1%

Academics
Student/faculty ratio: 18:1
Class size 9 or fewer: 18%
Class size 10-29: 53%
Class size 30-49: 14%
Class size 50-99: 11%
Class size 100 or more: 3%
Returning freshmen: 78%
Six-year graduation rate: 56%

Most Popular Fields of Study
Business, Finance, Sales and Marketing
Visual and Performing Arts
Social Sciences, History, Economics,
   Political Science
Protective Services, Criminal Justice and
   Public Administration
Biological and Life Sciences
Family and Consumer Sciences, Nutrition
   and Home Economics
Computer and Information Sciences
Communications, Journalism, Advertising
   and Comm. Technologies
Liberal Arts, Humanities and General
   Studies

Student Life and Activities
Popular campus events include: Welcome Week, Homecoming, Rumble in the Grove, Miss University Scholarship Pageant, Red and Blue Week, Greek Week and Spring Fest. The University of Mississippi has 200 official student organizations. The most popular are: music · theatre · political · service and special-interest groups. The University of Mississippi is a member of the Southeastern Conference (Division I, Football I-A).

Academics and Learning Environment
For the B student, the learning environment of a college is just as important as the quality of its academic program. The University of Mississippi has 725 full-time and 142 part-time faculty members, offering a student-to-faculty ratio of 18:1. The most common course size is 10 to 19 students. The University of Mississippi offers 126 majors with the most popular being business/marketing, family consumer science and elementary education and least popular being German, philosophy and classics. The school has a general core requirement. Cooperative education is not offered. All first-year students must maintain a 1.6 GPA or higher to avoid academic probation, and a minimum overall GPA of 2.0 is required to graduate. Other special academic programs that would appeal to a B student: pass/fail grading option · independent study · double majors · accelerated study · honors program · internships · distance learning.

B Student Support and Success
The Academic Support Center at the University of Mississippi aids struggling students and those who have not yet declared a major. It helps with scheduling classes, exploring possible majors and fulfilling core requirements for a bachelor's degree. In addition, the center assists with questions or problems with student schedules, explanations of university policies and procedures as well as providing referrals to other offices as needed.

The University of Mississippi provides a variety of support programs including dedicated guidance for: academic · personal · psychological. Additional counseling services include: science. Annually, 78 percent of freshmen students return for their sophomore year.

Support for Students with Learning Disabilities
Students with learning disabilities may take advantage of specific support programs offered by the University of Mississippi. According to the school, reasonable accommodations to verified students with disabilities are provided; accommodations are approved on an individual basis.

How to Get Admitted
For admissions decisions, non-academic factors considered: special talents, interests, abilities · alumni relationship. A high school diploma is required, although a GED is also accepted for admissions consideration. SAT or ACT test scores are required for some applicants. SAT Subject Test scores are not required. *According to the admissions office: Academic units recommended:* 4 Math, 4 Science, 2 Social Studies, 2 Foreign Language.

How to Pay for College

To apply for financial aid, students should submit the following: • institution's own financial aid forms. The University of Mississippi participates in the Federal Work Study program. *Need-based aid programs include:* scholarships and grants. *Non-Need-based aid programs include:* scholarships and grants • special achievements and activities awards • ROTC scholarships.

UNIVERSITY OF MISSISSIPPI

Highlights

Admissions
Applicants: 7,946
Accepted: 6,630
Acceptance rate: 83.4%
Average GPA: Not reported
ACT range: 20-26
SAT Math range: 460-580
SAT Reading range: 450-580
SAT Writing range: Not reported

Deadlines
Early Action: No
Early Decision: No
Regular Action: Rolling admissions
Common Application: Not accepted

Financial Aid
In-state tuition: $5,272
Out-of-state tuition: $13,216
Room: -
Board: -
Books: $1,200
Freshmen receiving need-based aid: 38%
Undergrads receiving need-based aid: 41%
Avg. % of need met by financial aid: 76%
Avg. aid package (freshmen): $8,111
Avg. aid package (undergrads): $6,890
Freshmen receiving merit-based aid: 23%
Undergrads receiving merit-based aid: 18%
Avg. student debt upon graduation: $20,047

Prominent Alumni
Shepard Smith, anchor, Fox News; John Grisham, author; Larry Speakes, White House press secretary for President Ronald Reagan.

School Spirit
Mascot: Ole Miss Rebels
Colors: Cardinal red and navy

499

UNIVERSITY OF NEVADA - LAS VEGAS

4505 Maryland Parkway, Las Vegas, NV 89154
Admissions: 702-774-8658 · Financial Aid: 702-895-3424
Email: admissions@unlv.edu · Website: http://www.unlv.edu

From the College

"UNLV is an doctoral degree-granting institution of approximately 28,000 students and 3,300 faculty and staff. Founded in 1957, the university offers more than 220 undergraduate, master's and doctoral degree programs. UNLV is located on a 350-acre campus in southern Nevada and is classified in the category of research universities (high research activity) by the Carnegie Foundation for the Advancement of Teaching. UNLV's programs include the William F. Harrah College of Hotel Administration, William S. Boyd School of Law, an accomplished English department featuring a creative writing program and an international literary center, as well as Honors, environmental studies, architecture, health sciences, social work, business, physical therapy, liberal and fine arts, engineering and science programs. There are numerous research centers and interdisciplinary programs. UNLV is also home to the International Institute of Modern Letters. UNLV's main campus, located minutes away from the Las Vegas Strip, features a 300,000 square-foot library as its centerpiece. Among the university's newest facilities are a Science and Engineering Building, featuring more than 200,000 square feet of flexible laboratory and teaching space, offices, high-tech conference rooms and integrated research areas; Greenspun Hall, the home of the Greenspun College of Urban Affairs and broadcast studios for UNLV's radio and television stations; and the UNLV Student Recreation and Wellness Center, a technologically advanced recreation, fitness and wellness facility. Additionally, the university is actively engaged in the development of "Midtown UNLV," a long-term, public-private endeavor to create a culturally diverse university district. UNLV's regional Shadow Lane campus stands on 18 acres in the heart of the downtown Las Vegas medical district. This campus is home to the UNLV School of Dental Medicine. UNLV's first international campus, UNLV Singapore, celebrated its third anniversary in 2009."

Campus Setting

A four-year public institution, the University of Nevada - Las Vegas has an enrollment of 28,617 students. In addition to a large, well-stocked library, the campus facilities include: art galleries · recording studio and MIDI lab · recital hall · dental education complex · science and engineering complex · moot court facility · natural history museum · desert research institute · center for environmental studies · exercise physiology and cognitive interference lab. The University of Nevada - Las Vegas provides on-campus housing with 11 units that can accommodate 1,735 students. Housing options: co-ed dorms · special housing for disabled students · special housing for International students. Recreation and sports facilities include: basketball and volleyball courts · physical education complex · football field and stadium · student recreation and wellness center.

Student Life and Activities

Most students (97 percent) live off campus, which does impact the on-campus social scene. Nevertheless, like any college, students find time to create their own recreational outlets. Students gather at the Student Recreation and Wellness Center, Student Union, Thomas & Mack Center and Cox Pavilion. Popular events include: Charles Vanda Master Series, Barrick Lecture Series, University Forum Lecture Series, Moskow Distinguished Speaker Series, William S. Boyd School of Law Saltman

Center for Conflict Resolution Lectures, UNLV Jazz Ensemble concerts and Las Vegas Philharmonic Concerts. The University of Nevada - Las Vegas has 180 official student organizations. The most popular are: academic and sports clubs · International Civic Engagement & Advocacy. For those interested in sports, there are intramural teams such as: basketball · bowling · football · racquetball · soccer · softball · swimming and diving · tennis · volleyball. The University of Nevada - Las Vegas is a member of the Mountain West Conference (Division I, Football I-A).

Academics and Learning Environment

For the B student, the learning environment of a college is just as important as the quality of its academic program. The University of Nevada - Las Vegas has 902 full-time and 526 part-time faculty members, offering a student-to-faculty ratio of 20:1. The most common course size is 20 to 29 students. The University of Nevada - Las Vegas offers 190 majors with the most popular being hospitality and hotel administration, education and psychology and least popular being physics, health physics and romance languages. The school has a general core requirement. Cooperative education is available. All first-year students must maintain a 2.0 GPA or higher to avoid academic probation. Other special academic programs that would appeal to a B student: self-designed majors · pass/fail grading option · independent study · double majors · dual degrees · accelerated study · honors program · Phi Beta Kappa · internships · distance learning certificate programs.

B Student Support and Success

Student Support Services at UNLV helps students "overcome personal concerns, academic deficiencies and financial difficulties that could impair their chances of succeeding in college." It focuses on the development of good study habits and decision-making skills through tutoring and workshops on subjects such as study skills, time management, note taking, listening skills, reading and outlining textbooks, test-taking strategies, motivation, concentration and stress reduction. These services are free.

An academic enrichment program for high school students called Upward Bound offers academic counseling, career exploration, tutoring, college admission testing workshops, motivation, personal development and concentration in computer literacy, English, foreign language, history, government, math and science. Upward Bound students are often involved in weekend or after-school instruction. During the summer, they can participate in daily classes emphasizing academic skills, study techniques and test preparation.

The University of Nevada - Las Vegas provides a variety of support programs including dedicated guidance for: academic · career · personal · psychological · minority students · veterans · non-traditional students · family planning · religious. Recognizing that some students may need extra preparation, the University of Nevada - Las Vegas offers remedial and refresher courses in: reading · writing · math · study skills. The average freshman year GPA is 3.3, and 76 percent of freshmen students return for their sophomore year. What do students do after college? While many enter the work force, approximately 21 percent pursue a graduate degree im-

UNIVERSITY OF NEVADA - LAS VEGAS

Highlights

University of Nevada - Las Vegas
Las Vegas, NV (Pop. 2,000,000)
Location: Major city
Website: http://www.unlv.edu

Students
Total enrollment: 28,617
Undergrads: 9,915
Freshmen: Not reported
Part-time students: 28%
From out-of-state: 18%
Male/Female: 45%/55%
Live on-campus: 6%
In fraternities: 5%
In sororities: 3%
Off-campus employment rating: Excellent
Caucasian: 46%
African American: 9%
Hispanic: 14%
Asian or Pacific Islander: 18%
Native American: 1%
International: 4%

Academics
Student/faculty ratio: 20:1
Class size 9 or fewer: 6%
Class size 10-29: 50%
Class size 30-49: 28%
Class size 50-99: 12%
Class size 100 or more: 4%
Returning freshmen: 76%
Six-year graduation rate: 41%

Most Popular Fields of Study
Business, Finance, Sales and Marketing
Visual and Performing Arts
Personal Services, Culinary and Cosmetology
Social Sciences, History, Economics, Political Science
Protective Services, Criminal Justice and Public Administration
Computer and Information Sciences
Communications, Journalism, Advertising and Comm. Technologies
Liberal Arts, Humanities and General Studies
English and Literature
Health Professions, Medicine and Related Sciences

501

College Profiles

UNIVERSITY OF NEVADA - LAS VEGAS

Admissions

Applicants: 8,679
Accepted: 6,317
Acceptance rate: 72.8%
Average GPA: 3.3
ACT range: 19-24
SAT Math range: 450-580
SAT Reading range: 440-560
SAT Writing range: Not reported
Top 10% of class: 20%
Top 25% of class: 52%
Top 50% of class: 85%

Deadlines

Early Action: No
Early Decision: No
Regular Action: Rolling admissions
Common Application: Not accepted

Financial Aid

In-state tuition: $4,200
Out-of-state tuition: $16,540
Room: $6,546
Board: $3,910
Books: $100
Freshmen receiving need-based aid: 43%
Undergrads receiving need-based aid: 39%
Avg. % of need met by financial aid: 62%
Avg. aid package (freshmen): $8,308
Avg. aid package (undergrads): $7,910
Freshmen receiving merit-based aid: 2%
Undergrads receiving merit-based aid: 3%
Avg. student debt upon graduation: $19,700

Prominent Alumni

Anthony Zuiker, television writer (*CSI*); Eric Whitacre, composer of choral, wind band and electronic music; Guy Fieri, author, co-owner of five restaurants and Food Network host.

School Spirit

Mascot: Rebel
Colors: Scarlet and gray

502

mediately after graduation. Among students who enter the work force, approximately 69 percent enter a field related to their major within six months of graduation. Companies that most frequently hire graduates from the University of Nevada - Las Vegas include: Clark County School District · Marriott International · Nevada Gaming Control Board · Walt Disney World · Fairmont Hotel & Resorts · Hilton Hotels · PricewaterhouseCoopers · Ernst & Young · Deloitte · Four Seasons Hotels & Resorts.

Support for Students with Learning Disabilities

Students with learning disabilities may take advantage of specific support programs offered by the University of Nevada - Las Vegas. If necessary, the college will grant additional time to students with learning disabilities to complete their degree. Also, a lightened course load may be granted to LD students. Students with learning disabilities will find the following programs at the University of Nevada - Las Vegas extremely useful: tutors · learning center · testing accommodations · extended time for tests · take-home exam · oral tests · exam on tape or computer · readers · typist/scribe · note-taking services · reading machines · tape recorders · texts on tape · early syllabus · diagnostic testing service · priority registration · waiver of math degree requirement. Individual or small group tutorials are also available in: time management · organizational skills · learning strategies · specific subject areas · writing labs · math labs · study skills. An advisor/advocate from the Disability Resource Center is available to students.

How to Get Admitted

For admissions decisions, non-academic factors considered: state of residency. A high school diploma is required, although a GED is also accepted for admissions consideration. SAT or ACT test scores are recommended but not required. SAT Subject Test scores are not required. *According to the admissions office:* Minimum weighted 3.0 GPA in the 13 required high school academic units or any one of the following required: a combined score from the SAT Critical Reading and Math sections of at least 1040, an ACT composite score of at least 22, a Nevada Advanced High School Diploma.

How to Pay for College

To apply for financial aid, students should submit the following: Free Application for Federal Student Aid (FAFSA) · institution's own financial aid forms. The University of Nevada - Las Vegas participates in the Federal Work Study program. *Need-based aid programs include:* scholarships and grants · general need-based awards · Federal Pell grants · state scholarships and grants · college-based scholarships and grants · private scholarships and grants. *Non-Need-based aid programs include:* scholarships and grants · general need-based awards · state scholarships and grants · creative arts and performance awards · athletic scholarships.

UNIVERSITY OF NEW HAVEN

300 Boston Post Road, West Haven, CT 06516
Admissions: 800-DIAL-UNH · Financial Aid: 800-DIAL-UNH
Email: adminfo@newhaven.edu · Website: http://www.newhaven.edu

From the College

"The University of New Haven is for students seeking quality education in liberal arts and in professionally oriented careers. We combine hands-on learning and a focused curriculum with a solid foundation in liberal arts and sciences. UNH brings practice into the classroom and the classroom into the workplace. We are committed to small classes and to tailoring coursework to everyday life in the selected field of study. Internships, special events and an experiential learning series enhance the UNH experience. Our most popular programs are: forensic science, criminal justice, music and sound recording, music industry, management of sports industries, engineering, fire science, dental Hygiene, and the biological sciences."

Campus Setting

The University of New Haven, founded in 1920, is a private university. Programs are offered through the Schools of Arts and Sciences; Business Administration; Engineering; Hotel, Restaurant and Tourism Administration; and Public Safety and Professional Studies. Its 78-acre campus is located in West Haven, two miles from New Haven. A four-year institution, the University of New Haven has an enrollment of 5,233 students. In addition to a large, well-stocked library, the campus also has an art gallery The University of New Haven provides on-campus housing that can accommodate 2,300 students. Housing options: co-ed dorms · single-student apartments. Recreation and sports facilities include: baseball · practice and softball fields · basketball · racquetball · handball and tennis courts · exercise and weight rooms · gymnasium · indoor track · stadium.

Student Life and Activities

With 59 percent of students living on campus, there are plenty of social activities. According to a school official, UNH has a family-like atmosphere with numerous community events and activities. This past year UNH had three major bands for concerts on campus. The variety of activities keeps students on campus during the weekends. In addition, because New Haven is a college town, there are many meeting places available off-campus. Where people go off-campus? Popular gathering spots include: the Student Center, Sports Spot, Beckman Recreation Center, Eddie's Bar and Century Diver. Popular campus events include: Homecoming Weekend, Parents Weekend, Spring Fling Weekend, Black History Month, Latino Awareness Week, Bean House open mike nights, International Festival and International Coffee Hours. The University of New Haven has 84 official student organizations. Influential groups on campus are student government, Student Committee on Programs and Events (SCOPE), Black Student Union, Latin American Student Association and Fire Science Club. For those interested in sports, there are intramural teams such as: badminton · basketball · cheerleading/dance team · dodge ball · lightweight football · racquetball · soccer · softball · team handball · table tennis · tennis · volleyball. The University of New Haven is a member of the Northeast-10 Conference.

Academics and Learning Environment

For the B student, the learning environment of a college is just as important as the quality of its academic program. The University of New Haven has 183 full-time and 320 part-time faculty members, offering a student-to-faculty ratio of 15:1. The

UNIVERSITY OF NEW HAVEN

University of New Haven
West Haven, CT (Pop. 52,000)
Location: Large town
Website: http://www.newhaven.edu

Students
Total enrollment: 5,233
Undergrads: 1,770
Freshmen: 1,516
Part-time students: 13%
From out-of-state: 59%
Male/Female: 50%/50%
Live on-campus: 59%
In fraternities: 3%
In sororities: 3%
Off-campus employment rating: Excellent
Caucasian: 67%
African American: 9%
Hispanic: 9%
Asian or Pacific Islander: 3%
Native American: 0%
International: 2%

Academics
Student/faculty ratio: 15:1
Class size 9 or fewer: 36%
Class size 10-29: 56%
Class size 30-49: 7%
Class size 50-99: 1%
Class size 100 or more: 4%
Returning freshmen: 76%
Six-year graduation rate: 45%

Most Popular Fields of Study
Business, Finance, Sales and Marketing
Biological and Life Sciences
Architecture

America's
Best Colleges for
B Students

most common course size is 10 to 19 students. The University of New Haven offers 79 majors with the most popular being forensic science, fire science and criminal justice and least popular being occupational safety/health technology, public administration and mathematics. The school has a general core requirement. Cooperative education is available. All first-year students must maintain a 1.75 GPA or higher to avoid academic probation, and a minimum overall GPA of 2.0 is required to graduate. Other special academic programs that would appeal to a B student: independent study · double majors · dual degrees · accelerated study · honors program · internships · distance learning certificate programs.

B Student Support and Success

The Center for Learning Resources at UNH offers students support for writing assignments, plus sophomore-level core courses. It is made up of three labs: 1) Mathematics, Science and Business, 2) Writing and 3) Computer.

In addition, the Office of Academic Services has many different programs. The Freshman Year Program is a one-credit seminar required for graduation. It helps to make the transition from high school to college. Academic Skills Counseling is offered individually and in small groups. The focus is on study and time management skills. Developmental mentoring assists students with developing the skills needed for college-level math and/or English.

The University of New Haven provides a variety of support programs including dedicated guidance for: academic · career · personal · psychological · minority students · religious. Recognizing that some students may need extra preparation, the University of New Haven offers remedial and refresher courses in: reading · writing · math · study skills. The average freshman year GPA is 2.8, and 76 percent of freshmen students return for their sophomore year.

Support for Students with Learning Disabilities

Students with learning disabilities may take advantage of specific support programs. If necessary, the college will grant additional time to students with learning disabilities to complete their degree. Also, a lightened course load may be granted to LD students. According to the school, assisted technology is available, such as writing, talking word processors, graphic organizers and more. Students with learning disabilities will find the following programs at the University of New Haven extremely useful: remedial math · remedial English · remedial reading · tutors · learning center · testing accommodations · untimed tests · extended time for tests · take-home exam · exam on tape or computer · readers · note-taking services · reading machines · tape recorders · texts on tape · early syllabus · diagnostic testing service · priority registration · waiver of math degree requirement · waiver of foreign language degree requirement. Individual or small group tutorials are also available in: time management · organizational skills · learning strategies · specific subject areas · writing labs · math labs · study skills. An advisor/advocate from the Office of Disability Services and Resources is available to students.

How to Get Admitted

For admissions decisions, non-academic factors considered: interview · extracurricular activities · character/personal qualities · volunteer work · work experience · state of residency. A high school diploma is required, although a GED is also accepted for admissions consideration. SAT or ACT test scores are required of all applicants. SAT Subject Test scores are recommended but not required. *According to the admissions office:* Minimum combined SAT Reasoning score of 750 and minimum 2.75 GPA recommended.

How to Pay for College

To apply for financial aid, students should submit the following: Free Application for Federal Student Aid (FAFSA) · institution's own financial aid forms. The University of New Haven participates in the Federal Work Study program. *Need-based aid programs include:* scholarships and grants · general need-based awards · Federal Pell grants · state scholarships and grants · college-based scholarships and grants. *Non-Need-based aid programs include:* scholarships and grants · state scholarships and grants · special achievements and activities awards · athletic scholarships.

UNIVERSITY OF NEW HAVEN

Highlights

Admissions
Applicants: 5,623
Accepted: 3,824
Acceptance rate: 68.0%
Average GPA: 3.0
ACT range: 19-24
SAT Math range: 450-570
SAT Reading range: 450-550
SAT Writing range: 440-550
Top 10% of class: 7%
Top 25% of class: 20%
Top 50% of class: 83%

Deadlines
Early Action: No
Early Decision: No
Regular Action: Rolling admissions
Common Application: Accepted

Financial Aid
In-state tuition: $28,250
Out-of-state tuition: $28,250
Room: $7,600
Board: $4,604
Books: $1,000
Freshmen receiving need-based aid: 83%
Undergrads receiving need-based aid: 78%
Avg. % of need met by financial aid: 65%
Avg. aid package (freshmen): $18,781
Avg. aid package (undergrads): $17,762
Freshmen receiving merit-based aid: 15%
Undergrads receiving merit-based aid: 10%
Avg. student debt upon graduation: Not reported

School Spirit
Mascot: Charger
Colors: Gold and blue
Song: *UNH Fight Song*

UNIVERSITY OF NEW MEXICO

1 University of New Mexico, Albuquerque, NM 87131-0001
Admissions: 505-277-2446 · Financial Aid: 505-277-3012
Email: apply@unm.edu · Website: http://www.unm.edu

From the College

"The University of New Mexico seeks to serve as a significant knowledge resource for New Mexico, the nation and the world, by offering a high-quality educational, research and service programs. UNM is situated near an international border and resides in a state noted for its rich demographic and cultural diversity. Its proximity to the internationally prominent scientific communities of the Los Alamos and Sandia National Laboratories provides many opportunities for collaboration in scientific and engineering education and research. UNM is located in the midst of a world-class arts center, enabling it to provide educational opportunities in the arts and humanities."

Campus Setting

The University of New Mexico, founded in 1889, is a public, comprehensive institution. Programs are offered through the Colleges of Architecture, Arts and Sciences, Dental Programs, Education, Engineering, Fine Arts, Nursing and Pharmacy and the Schools of Management and Medicine. Its 769-acre campus is located in Albuquerque. A four-year institution, the University of New Mexico has an enrollment of 25,754 students. In addition to a large, well-stocked library, the campus facilities include: art · anthropology · meteorite · geology · biology museums. The University of New Mexico provides on-campus housing with 1,975 units that can accommodate 2,365 students. Housing options: co-ed dorms · sorority housing · fraternity housing · single-student apartments · married-student apartments · special housing for disabled students · special housing for International students. Recreation and sports facilities include: center · fields.

Student Life and Activities

Freshman Family Day, Welcome Back Days, Red Rally, Homecoming, Nihzoni Days, Hanging of the Greens, Black History Month, Lobo Day, Spring Storm and Cherry and Silver Game are popular events. The University of New Mexico has 375 official student organizations. The most popular are: academic and departmental organizations · graduate organizations · military organizations · political organizations · service organizations · special-interest organizations · sport and recreation organizations · honorary organizations. For those interested in sports, there are intramural teams such as: archery · badminton · basketball · bowling · cross-country · flag football · golf · miniature golf · racquetball · soccer · swimming · volleyball · weightlifting. The University of New Mexico is a member of the Mountain West Conference (Division I, Football I-A).

Academics and Learning Environment

For the B student, the learning environment of a college is just as important as the quality of its academic program. The University of New Mexico has 934 full-time and 507 part-time faculty members, offering a student-to-faculty ratio of 20:1. The most common course size is 20 to 29 students. The University of New Mexico offers 201 majors with the most popular being business, nursing and psychology. The school has a general core requirement. Cooperative education is available. All first-year students must maintain a 2.0 GPA or higher to avoid academic probation. Other special academic programs that would appeal to a B student: self-designed majors · pass/fail grading option · independent study · double majors · dual degrees · accelerated study · honors program · Phi Beta Kappa · internships · weekend college · distance learning certificate programs.

B Student Support and Success

UNM's Center for Academic Program Support offers free educational assistance through individualized peer tutoring (done by upper division undergraduates and graduate students) for courses numbered 100-499 as well as library and study strategies (by appointment only). Drop-in tutoring labs are available for biology, chemistry, physics, astronomy, writing, pre-calculus, statistics, calculus and engineering. In a new program called CAPS Across Campus, tutoring will be offered in the theater, library and student resident center commons room.

The University of New Mexico provides a variety of support programs including dedicated guidance for: academic · career · personal · psychological · minority students · veterans. Recognizing that some students may need extra preparation, the University of New Mexico offers remedial and refresher courses in: reading · writing · math · study skills. Annually, 77 percent of freshmen students return for their sophomore year.

Support for Students with Learning Disabilities

Students with learning disabilities may take advantage of specific support programs offered by the University of New Mexico. Also, a lightened course load may be granted to LD students. Students with learning disabilities will find the following programs at the University of New Mexico extremely useful: remedial math · remedial English · remedial reading · tutors · learning center · testing accommodations · untimed tests · extended time for tests · take-home exam · readers · note-taking services · tape recorders · videotaped classes · early syllabus · priority registration · waiver of math degree requirement. Individual or small group tutorials are also available in: time management · organizational skills · learning strategies · specific subject areas · writing labs · math labs · study skills. An advisor/advocate from the Accessibility Resource Center is available to students.

How to Get Admitted

For admissions decisions, non-academic factors considered: extracurricular activities · special talents, interests, abilities · character/personal qualities · volunteer work · work experience · state of residency. A high school diploma is required, although a GED is also accepted for admissions consideration. SAT or ACT test scores are required of all applicants. SAT Subject Test scores are required for some applicants. *According to the admissions office:* Minimum 2.25 GPA required.

How to Pay for College

To apply for financial aid, students should submit the following: Free Application for Federal Student Aid (FAFSA). The University of New Mexico participates in the Federal Work Study program. *Need-based aid programs include:* scholarships and grants · general need-based awards · Federal Pell grants · state scholarships and grants · college-based scholarships and grants · private scholarships

UNIVERSITY OF NEW MEXICO

University of New Mexico
Albuquerque, NM (Pop. 500,000)
Location: Major city
Website: http://www.unm.edu

Students
Total enrollment: 25,754
Undergrads: 8,722
Freshmen: Not reported
Part-time students: 25%
From out-of-state: Not reported
Male/Female: 44%/56%
Live on-campus: Not reported
Off-campus employment rating: Good
Caucasian: 45%
African American: 3%
Hispanic: 36%
Asian or Pacific Islander: 4%
Native American: 7%
International: 1%

Academics
Student/faculty ratio: 20:1
Class size 9 or fewer: 17%
Class size 10-29: 57%
Class size 30-49: 13%
Class size 50-99: 9%
Class size 100 or more: 4%
Returning freshmen: 77%
Six-year graduation rate: 44%

Most Popular Fields of Study
Business, Finance, Sales and Marketing
Biological and Life Sciences
Visual and Performing Arts
Social Sciences, History, Economics, Political Science
Protective Services, Criminal Justice and Public Administration
Family and Consumer Sciences, Nutrition and Home Economics
Computer and Information Sciences
Communications, Journalism, Advertising and Comm. Technologies
Philosophy, Religion and Theology
Liberal Arts, Humanities and General Studies

507

College Profiles

UNIVERSITY OF NEW MEXICO

Admissions
Applicants: 8,788
Accepted: 5,964
Acceptance rate: 67.9%
Average GPA: 3.3
ACT range: 19-25
SAT Math range: 460-600
SAT Reading range: 470-610
SAT Writing range: Not reported
Top 10% of class: 20%
Top 25% of class: 45%
Top 50% of class: 77%

Deadlines
Early Action: No
Early Decision: No
Regular Action: Rolling admissions
Common Application: Not accepted

Financial Aid
In-state tuition: $5,101
Out-of-state tuition: $17,254
Room: -
Board: -
Books: $920
Avg. % of need met by financial aid: Not reported
Avg. aid package (freshmen): Not reported
Avg. aid package (undergrads): Not reported
Avg. student debt upon graduation: Not reported

Prominent Alumni
Pete Domenici, former U.S. senator; Brian Urlacher, professional football Chicago Bears; N. Scott Momaday, author, Pulitzer Prize winner; Leslie Marmon Silko, author, recipient of the McArthur "Genius" Grant.

School Spirit
Mascot: Lobos
Colors: Cherry and silver
Song: *Hail to Thee New Mexico*

and grants · Federal Nursing scholarships · United Negro College Fund. *Non-Need-based aid programs include:* scholarships and grants · general need-based awards · state scholarships and grants · creative arts and performance awards · special achievements and activities awards · special characteristics awards · athletic scholarships · ROTC scholarships.

UNIVERSITY OF NEW ORLEANS

2000 Lakeshore Drive, New Orleans, LA 70148
Admissions: 800-256-5-UNO · Financial Aid: 504-280-6603
Email: admissions@uno.edu · Website: http://www.uno.edu

From the College

"The University of New Orleans a major urban university and provides essential support for the further development of the educational, economic, cultural and social well being of the New Orleans metropolitan area. Located in an international city, the university serves as an important link between Louisiana, the nation and the world. Its partnership approach strategically serves the needs of the region and builds on its success through mutually beneficial engagements with public and private bodies whose missions and goals are consistent with and supportive of the university's teaching, scholarly and community service missions. Focused local partnerships with public schools, government, foundations, business and civic groups enrich opportunities for learning and creative discovery as well as help enhance the opportunities for career and community growth. Graduate study and research are integral to the university's purpose. Doctoral programs will continue to focus on fields of study in which UNO has the ability to achieve national competitiveness and/or to respond to specific state / regional needs. UNO is categorized as an SREB Four-Year 2 institution, as a Carnegie Doctoral Intensive and as a COC/SACS Level VI institution. UNO will offer no associate degree programs. At a minimum, the university will implement Selective II admissions criteria. UNO is located in Region I."

Campus Setting

University of New Orleans, founded in 1958, is a public institution. Programs are offered through the Colleges of Business Administration, Education, Engineering, Liberal Arts, Sciences and Urban and Public Affairs and the Metropolitan College. Its 195-acre campus is located in a residential section of New Orleans. A four-year institution, the University of New Orleans has an enrollment of 11,428 students. The school also has a library with 896,000 books. The University of New Orleans provides on-campus housing that can accommodate 1,426 students. Housing options: co-ed dorms · single-student apartments · married-student apartments · special housing for disabled students.

Student Life and Activities

Most students (95 percent) live off campus, which does impact the on-campus social scene. Nevertheless, like any college, students find time to create their own recreational outlets. International Night is a popular event on campus. The University of New Orleans has 73 official student organizations. The most popular are: Louisiana Restaurant Association · Chess Club · UNO Filmmakers · Society for Earth and Environmental Science · Circle K · Rainbow Alliance. The University of New Orleans is a member of the Sun Belt Conference (Division I, Football I-A).

Academics and Learning Environment

For the B student, the learning environment of a college is just as important as the quality of its academic program. The University of New Orleans has 449 full-time and 155 part-time faculty members, offering a student-to-faculty ratio of 18:1. The most common course size is 10 to 19 students. The University of New Orleans offers 87 majors with the most popular being general studies, business administration and elementary education and least popular being Spanish, art history and music. The school has a general core requirement. Cooperative education is available. All first-

UNIVERSITY OF NEW ORLEANS

University of New Orleans
New Orleans, LA (Pop. 225,000)
Location: Major city
Website: http://www.uno.edu

Students
Total enrollment: 11,428
Undergrads: 4,177
Freshmen: 1,267
Part-time students: 24%
From out-of-state: 7%
Male/Female: 48%/52%
Live on-campus: 5%
In fraternities: 1%
In sororities: 1%
Off-campus employment rating: Excellent
Caucasian: 59%
African American: 18%
Hispanic: 7%
Asian or Pacific Islander: 6%
Native American: 1%
International: 4%

Academics
Student/faculty ratio: 18:1
Class size 9 or fewer: 13%
Class size 10-29: 54%
Class size 30-49: 23%
Class size 50-99: 7%
Class size 100 or more: 3%
Returning freshmen: 69%
Six-year graduation rate: 24%

Most Popular Fields of Study
Business, Finance, Sales and Marketing
Psychology
English and Literature
Philosophy, Religion and Theology
Computer and Information Sciences
Mathematics
Engineering and Engineering Technologies
Parks, Recreation and Fitness
Interdisciplinary Studies
Liberal Arts, Humanities and General Studies

year students must maintain a 2.0 GPA or higher to avoid academic probation. Other special academic programs that would appeal to a B student: self-designed majors · independent study · double majors · dual degrees · honors program · internships · weekend college · distance learning.

B Student Support and Success

UNO's Learning Resource Center offers free writing and math tutoring on both an individual and group basis. The computer lab has 24 workstations, and tutors are available for biology, business, chemistry, foreign language, psychology and physics. Much of the tutoring is performed by upperclassmen. Classes on time management, test taking, note taking and communication are offered, as are short workshops on test taking and note taking. A media library supplies videotapes and CD ROMs in math, science and liberal arts.

The college's Writing Center guides students through their papers, while the Math Tutor Center and Study Hall assists students in math requirements to "maximize their math potential."
The University of New Orleans provides a variety of support programs including dedicated guidance for: academic · career · personal · psychological · minority students · military · veterans · family planning. The average freshman year GPA is 2.5, and 69 percent of freshmen students return for their sophomore year.

Support for Students with Learning Disabilities

Students with learning disabilities may take advantage of specific support programs offered by the University of New Orleans. According to the school, we have no specific LD program. ODS offers academic accommodations to students with documented disabilities. Tutoring and other content specific programming is open to all students through the Learning Resource Center or Counseling Services. Students with learning disabilities will find the following programs at the University of New Orleans extremely useful: learning center · testing accommodations · extended time for tests · take-home exam · exam on tape or computer · note-taking services · reading machines · tape recorders · texts on tape · early syllabus · priority registration. Individual or small group tutorials are also available in: time management · organizational skills · learning strategies · specific subject areas · writing labs · math labs · study skills. An advisor/advocate from the Office of Disability Services is available to students.

How to Get Admitted

For admissions decisions, non-academic factors considered: geographical location. A high school diploma is required, although a GED is also accepted for admissions consideration. SAT or ACT test scores are required of all applicants. *According to the admissions office:* Minimum composite ACT score of 20 (combined SAT Reasoning score of 950) or minimum 2.0 GPA required.

How to Pay for College

To apply for financial aid, students should submit the following: Free Application for Federal Student Aid (FAFSA). The University of New Orleans participates in the Federal Work Study program. *Need-based aid programs include:* scholarships and grants · general need-based awards · Federal Pell grants · state scholarships and grants · college-based scholarships and grants · private scholarships and grants. *Non-Need-based aid programs include:* scholarships and grants · state scholarships and grants · athletic scholarships.

UNIVERSITY OF NEW ORLEANS

Highlights

Admissions
Applicants: 3,615
Accepted: 1,998
Acceptance rate: 55.3%
Average GPA: 3.1
ACT range: 20-25
SAT Math range: 490-650
SAT Reading range: 470-600
SAT Writing range: 460-580
Top 10% of class: 16%
Top 25% of class: 35%
Top 50% of class: 67%

Deadlines
Early Action: No
Early Decision: No
Regular Action: July 1 (priority)
August 20 (final)
Common Application: Accepted

Financial Aid
In-state tuition: $3,488
Out-of-state tuition: $10,884
Room: -
Board: -
Books: $1,200
Freshmen receiving need-based aid: 55%
Undergrads receiving need-based aid: 98%
Avg. % of need met by financial aid: 70%
Avg. aid package (freshmen): $9,196
Avg. aid package (undergrads): $9,312
Freshmen receiving merit-based aid: 28%
Undergrads receiving merit-based aid: 12%
Avg. student debt upon graduation: $14,911

School Spirit
Mascot: Privateers

UNIVERSITY OF NORTH CAROLINA - GREENSBORO

P.O. Box 26170, Greensboro, NC 27402
Admissions: 336-334-5243 · Financial Aid: 336-334-5702
Email: admissions@uncg.edu · Website: http://www.uncg.edu

From the College

"The University of North Carolina - Greensboro is a student-centered research university, linking the Triad and North Carolina to the world through learning, discovery and service. As a doctoral-granting university, it is committed to teaching based in scholarship and advancing knowledge through research. The College of Arts and Sciences and six professional schools offer graduate and undergraduate programs in which students are mentored by teachers including nationally and internationally recognized researchers and artists. Affirming the liberal arts as the foundation for life-long learning, the university provides learning environments on campus and through distance education so that students can acquire knowledge, develop intellectual skills and become more thoughtful and responsible members of a global society. Co-curricular, residential and other programs contribute to students' social, aesthetic and ethical development. The University of North Carolina - Greensboro is a community in which people of any racial or ethnic identity, age or background can achieve an informed appreciation of their own and different cultures. It is a community of actively engaged students, faculty, staff and alumni founded on open dialogue, shared responsibility and respect for the distinct contributions of each member."

Campus Setting

The University of North Carolina - Greensboro is a public, liberal arts university founded in 1891. It became co-educational in 1963. Its 210-acre campus is located one mile from the center of Greensboro, NC. A four-year institution, the University of North Carolina - Greensboro has an enrollment of 17,407 students. In addition to a large, well-stocked library, the campus also has an art museum. The University of North Carolina - Greensboro provides on-campus housing that can accommodate 4,500 students. Housing options: co-ed dorms · women's dorms · single-student apartments · special housing for International students. Recreation and sports facilities include: gymnasium · weight and exercise rooms · fitness course · athletic training facility · indoor swimming pool · dance studios · golf holes · tennis courts · soccer · softball and other field sports practice fields.

Student Life and Activities

Most students (69 percent) live off campus, which does impact the on-campus social scene. Nevertheless, like any college, students find time to create their own recreational outlets. UNC-Greensboro has a large commuter population, reports the school news paper. And of the on-campus residents, over 75 percent of them leave for the weekend. Popular off-campus gathering spots include: Spring Garden Bar & Grill and New York Pizza. Popular campus events include: UNCG Open House, athletic events, Students Taking Active Responsibility (STAR), Family Weekend, Spring Fling, intramural sports, Commuter Student Deli, Leadership Education and Development Seminars (LEAD Seminars), Career Days, Fitness Testing, Fall Kickoff, UNCG Theatre, Martin Luther King, Jr. Celebration, Office of Student Life Movie Series, International Festival, Outdoor Adventures, University Concert/Lecture Series, and African American History Events. The University of North Carolina - Greensboro has 170 official student organizations. Student media organizations have widespread influence in student social life. For those interested in sports, there are intramural teams such as: basketball · flag football · indoor soccer · outdoor soccer · softball · volleyball. The University of North Carolina - Greensboro is a member of the Southern Conference (Division I, Football I-AA).

Academics and Learning Environment

For the B student, the learning environment of a college is just as important as the quality of its academic program. The University of North Carolina - Greensboro has 816 full-time and 389 part-time faculty members, offering a student-to-faculty ratio of 16:1. The most common course size is 20 to 29 students. The University of North Carolina - Greensboro offers 126 majors with the most popular being biology, psychology and exercise and sport science and least popular being social studies, nutrition and food service systems, finance, insurance and real estate. The school has a general core requirement. Cooperative education is not offered. All first-year students must maintain a 1.5 GPA or higher to avoid academic probation, and a minimum overall GPA of 2.0 is required to graduate. Other special academic programs that would appeal to a B student: independent study · double majors · dual degrees · accelerated study · honors program · Phi Beta Kappa · internships · distance learning certificate programs.

B Student Support and Success

The Student Success Center at Greensboro's University of North Carolina has three divisions to help students succeed academically: the Learning Assistance Center, Resource Lab and Special Support Services.

The Learning Assistance Center provides tutoring, academic skills assessment and counseling, academic workshops and a resource lab with computers, academic software and handouts. Tutoring is done on an individual basis for at least one hour a week or through small groups of no more than three students in sessions that last one and one-half to two hours a week. Walk-in tutoring is available also.

The Resource Lab gives students a peaceful place to study and to receive tutoring. Students have access to computers, a text book library, academic-skills assessment, as well as computer tutorials in math and foreign languages and handouts on academic skills like time management, note taking, textbook reading and test taking. In addition to this, the LAC works to help students increase their understanding of course content, enhance self-confidence and encourage positive attitudes toward learning.

Special Support Services provides aid to students who are 1) first-generation college enrollees, 2) from low-income families or 3) have a documented disability. This program offers counseling, tutoring and a learning lab.

A program known as Supplemental Instruction provides a series of weekly discussion/review sessions for students taking notoriously difficult courses. Each class is led by students who have successfully completed the course. According to the college, students who attend these supplemental classes attain grades that are one-third to one whole grade higher than the grades of those who do not participate.

UNIVERSITY OF NORTH CAROLINA - GREENSBORO

Highlights

University of North Carolina - Greensboro
Greensboro, NC (Pop. 258,671)
Location: Medium city
Website: http://www.uncg.edu

Students
Total enrollment: 17,407
Undergrads: 4,480
Freshmen: 2,492
Part-time students: 13%
From out-of-state: 8%
Male/Female: 33%/67%
Live on-campus: 31%
Off-campus employment rating: Excellent
Caucasian: 65%
African American: 22%
Hispanic: 3%
Asian or Pacific Islander: 4%
Native American: 0%
International: 1%

Academics
Student/faculty ratio: 16:1
Class size 9 or fewer: 19%
Class size 10-29: 56%
Class size 30-49: 15%
Class size 50-99: 10%
Class size 100 or more: 3%
Returning freshmen: 76%
Six-year graduation rate: 53%

Most Popular Fields of Study
Business, Finance, Sales and Marketing
Biological and Life Sciences
Visual and Performing Arts
Protective Services, Criminal Justice and Public Administration
Family and Consumer Sciences, Nutrition and Home Economics
Computer and Information Sciences
Communications, Journalism, Advertising and Comm. Technologies
Philosophy, Religion and Theology
Liberal Arts, Humanities and General Studies
English and Literature

513

College Profiles

UNIVERSITY OF NORTH CAROLINA - GREENSBORO

Admissions
Applicants: 9,187
Accepted: 6,634
Acceptance rate: 72.2%
Average GPA: 3.6
ACT range: Not reported
SAT Math range: 470-570
SAT Reading range: 460-560
SAT Writing range: 7-8
Top 10% of class: 13%
Top 25% of class: 45%
Top 50% of class: 85%

Deadlines
Early Action:
Early Decision: No
Regular Action: March 1 (priority)
August 1 (final)
Common Application: Accepted

Financial Aid
In-state tuition: $2,632
Out-of-state tuition: $14,351
Room: $3,392
Board: $2,440
Books: $1,282
Freshmen receiving need-based aid: 74%
Undergrads receiving need-based aid: 71%
Avg. % of need met by financial aid: 59%
Avg. aid package (freshmen): $9,364
Avg. aid package (undergrads): $9,920
Freshmen receiving merit-based aid: 6%
Undergrads receiving merit-based aid: 5%
Avg. student debt upon graduation: $16,326

School Spirit
Mascot: Spartans

The University of North Carolina - Greensboro provides a variety of support programs including dedicated guidance for: academic · career · personal · psychological · minority students · family planning. Recognizing that some students may need extra preparation, the University of North Carolina - Greensboro offers remedial and refresher courses in: reading · writing · math · study skills. The average freshman year GPA is 2.8, and 76 percent of freshmen students return for their sophomore year.

Support for Students with Learning Disabilities

Students with learning disabilities may take advantage of specific support programs offered by the University of North Carolina - Greensboro. Students with learning disabilities will find the following programs at the University of North Carolina - Greensboro extremely useful: remedial English · remedial reading · tutors · learning center · testing accommodations · extended time for tests · oral tests · readers · note-taking services · reading machines · tape recorders · diagnostic testing service. Individual or small group tutorials are also available in: time management · organizational skills · learning strategies · specific subject areas · writing labs · math labs · study skills. An advisor/advocate from the Office of Disability Services is available to students.

How to Get Admitted

For admissions decisions, non-academic factors considered: state of residency. A high school diploma is required and a GED is not accepted for admissions consideration. SAT or ACT test scores are required of all applicants. SAT Subject Test scores are not required. *Academic units recommended:* 4 English, 4 Math, 3 Science, 2 Social Studies, 2 Foreign Language.

How to Pay for College

To apply for financial aid, students should submit the following: Free Application for Federal Student Aid (FAFSA). The University of North Carolina - Greensboro participates in the Federal Work Study program. *Need-based aid programs include:* scholarships and grants · general need-based awards · Federal Pell grants · state scholarships and grants · college-based scholarships and grants · private scholarships and grants. *Non-Need-based aid programs include:* scholarships and grants · general need-based awards · state scholarships and grants · creative arts and performance awards · special achievements and activities awards · special characteristics awards · athletic scholarships · ROTC scholarships.

UNIVERSITY OF OREGON

1226 University of Oregon, Eugene, OR 97403-1226
Admissions: 800-232-3825 · Financial Aid: 800-760-6953
Email: uoadmit@uoregon.edu · Website: http://www.uoregon.edu

Campus Setting

The University of Oregon, founded in 1876, is a public, comprehensive, liberal arts institution. Programs are offered through the College of Arts and Sciences, Charles H. Lundquist College of Business, College of Education, and Schools of Journalism, Music and Dance and Architecture and Allied Arts. Its 295-acre campus is located in Eugene, south of Portland. A four-year institution, the University of Oregon has an enrollment of 21,452 students. In addition to a large, well-stocked library, the campus facilities include: art and natural and cultural history museums · sports marketing center · center for entrepreneurship · instrumentation center · music center · green chemistry laboratory. The University of Oregon provides on-campus housing with 2,358 units that can accommodate 3,875 students. Housing options: co-ed dorms · sorority housing · fraternity housing · single-student apartments · married-student apartments · cooperative housing. Recreation and sports facilities include: student recreation center with gyms and training facilities with exercise and weight training equipment · swimming pool · indoor track · climbing wall · stadium · arena · track and field complex · softball complex · grass fields.

Student Life and Activities

Most students (79 percent) live off campus, which does impact the on-campus social scene. Nevertheless, like any college, students find time to create their own recreational outlets. Erb Memorial Union, the EMU amphitheater and the quad are favorite hangouts. Cinco de Mayo Celebration, Hawaii Club Luau, Native American Pow Wow, Willamette Valley Folk Festival (three days of free folk music, food and crafts), Martin Luther King Events (a week or more of events surrounding the Martin Luther King holiday), InterMingle, Athletic Events, Miller Theatre Complex, Oregon Bach Festival, Concerts in Beall Hall, Jordan Schnitzer Museum of Art, Oregon Museum of Natural and Cultural History, and Convocation (a festive tradition in which the university welcomes new faculty and students) are popular events. The University of Oregon has 250 official student organizations. The most popular are: music · theatre · political · service and special-interest groups. For those interested in sports, there are intramural teams such as: badminton · basketball · cross-country · dodgeball · flag football · floor hockey · golf · racquetball · soccer · softball · swimming · tennis · track and field · volleyball · ultimate Frisbee. The University of Oregon is a member of the Member of Mountain Pacific Sports Federation (Division I), Pacific-10 Conference (Division I, Football I-A).

Academics and Learning Environment

For the B student, the learning environment of a college is just as important as the quality of its academic program. The University of Oregon has 844 full-time and 365 part-time faculty members, offering a student-to-faculty ratio of 19:1. The most common course size is 20 to 29 students. The University of Oregon offers 207 majors with the most popular being business administration, journalism and political science and least popular being fine arts, independent study and Greek. The school has a general core requirement. Cooperative education is not offered. All first-year students must maintain a 2.0 GPA or higher to avoid academic probation. Other special academic programs that would appeal to a B student: self-designed majors ·

UNIVERSITY OF OREGON

pass/fail grading option · independent study · double majors · dual degrees · honors program · Phi Beta Kappa · internships · distance learning certificate programs.

B Student Support and Success

UO's Academic Learning Services offers a number of one-credit and multiple-credit courses each quarter to help with test taking, time management, communication skills and group dynamics. In the fall, the college offers "Get Savvy: Focus on Academic Success," a get-together geared to help students improve their study approaches, meet new people and even win prizes! Other workshops include "Active Learning," "Grammar Hour" and "Statistics." Math and Writing Labs are available, as is tutoring in small group or private settings. Workshops to help prepare for standardized test preparation (GRE, GMAT, SAT, MCAT, etc.) are also offered.

The University of Oregon provides a variety of support programs including dedicated guidance for: academic · career · personal · psychological · minority students · military · veterans · non-traditional students · family planning. Recognizing that some students may need extra preparation, the University of Oregon offers remedial and refresher courses in: reading · writing · math · study skills. The average freshman year GPA is 3.0, and 84 percent of freshmen students return for their sophomore year.

Support for Students with Learning Disabilities

Students with learning disabilities may take advantage of specific support programs offered by the University of Oregon. If necessary, the college will grant additional time to students with learning disabilities to complete their degree. Also, a lightened course load may be granted to LD students. High school foreign language waivers are accepted. High school math waivers are also accepted. According to the school, most services are provided as requested by the student. Paid tutoring groups offered in Academic Learning Services are available to any student. Average paid tutoring group size is 6. Students with learning disabilities will find the following programs at the University of Oregon extremely useful: tutors · learning center · testing accommodations · untimed tests · extended time for tests · take-home exam · oral tests · exam on tape or computer · substitution of courses · readers · note-taking services · reading machines · tape recorders · texts on tape · priority registration · waiver of math degree requirement. Individual or small group tutorials are also available in: time management · organizational skills · learning strategies · writing labs · math labs · study skills. An advisor/advocate from the Disability Services is available to students. This member also sits on the admissions committee.

How to Get Admitted

For admissions decisions, non-academic factors considered: extracurricular activities · special talents, interests, abilities · volunteer work · work experience · geographical location · minority affiliation. A high school diploma is required, although a GED is also accepted for admissions consideration. SAT or ACT test scores are required of all applicants. SAT Subject Test scores are required for some applicants. *According to the admissions office:* Minimum 3.25 GPA, 16 credits of college prep work, and SAT/ACT score submission required for guaranteed admission. *Academic units recommended:* 4 English, 3 Math, 2 Science, 3 Social Studies, 2 Foreign Language.

How to Pay for College

To apply for financial aid, students should submit the following: Free Application for Federal Student Aid (FAFSA). The University of Oregon participates in the Federal Work Study program. *Need-based aid programs include:* scholarships and grants · general need-based awards · Federal Pell grants · state scholarships and grants · college-based scholarships and grants · private scholarships and grants. *Non-Need-based aid programs include:* scholarships and grants · general need-based awards · state scholarships and grants · athletic scholarships · ROTC scholarships.

UNIVERSITY OF OREGON

Highlights

Admissions
Applicants: 15,013
Accepted: 12,801
Acceptance rate: 85.3%
Average GPA: 3.5
ACT range: Not reported
SAT Math range: 499-612
SAT Reading range: 489-607
SAT Writing range: Not reported
Top 10% of class: 26%
Top 25% of class: 58%
Top 50% of class: 90%

Deadlines
Early Action: November 1
Early Decision: No
Regular Action: Rolling admissions
Common Application: Not accepted

Financial Aid
In-state tuition: $7,428
Out-of-state tuition: $23,718
Room: -
Board: -
Books: $1,050
Freshmen receiving need-based aid: 34%
Undergrads receiving need-based aid: 37%
Avg. % of need met by financial aid: 72%
Avg. aid package (freshmen): $8,112
Avg. aid package (undergrads): $8,735
Freshmen receiving merit-based aid: 12%
Undergrads receiving merit-based aid: 6%
Avg. student debt upon graduation: $18,805

Prominent Alumni
Ken Kesey, author; Ann Bancroft, first woman explorer to cross the North and South Poles; Phil Knight, founder and CEO of Nike.

School Spirit
Mascot: Ducks
Colors: Green and yellow
Song: *Mighty Oregon*

517

College Profiles

UNIVERSITY OF PORTLAND

5000 North Willamette Boulevard, Portland, OR 97203
Admissions: 888-627-5601 · Financial Aid: 503-943-7311
Email: admissio@up.edu · Website: http://www.up.edu

From the College

"The University of Portland, Oregon's Catholic university, has received several national faculty awards from the Carnegie Foundation in recent years, among them the U.S. Professor of the Year and three Oregon Professor of the Year honors. Its faculty and students have earned many Fulbright, Marshall, Mitchell and Goldwater fellowships, and have received both the Oregon's Governor's Award for more than 10,000 hours of volunteer service annually and Washington Monthly magazine's national top ranking for service to the nation. The university is renowned for its extensive study-abroad programs (in Asia, Australia, Latin America and Europe), its cross-disciplinary entrepreneurship program, education, biology, and theater programs, state-of-the-art nursing and science laboratories, and its global business and environmental ethics majors—the latter the only one of its kind in the U.S. The university also sponsors a creative center for freshman support, savors its NCAA national champion women's soccer team (twice in four years), and has been dedicated for more than a century to creating a campus community where 'teachable moments' in and out of the classroom are not only prized but the true epiphanies sparking lifelong learning."

Campus Setting

The University of Portland, founded in 1901, is a private institution with programs offered through the College of Arts and Sciences; and the Schools of Business Administration, Education, Engineering and Nursing. Its 125-acre is located four miles from downtown Portland. A private institution, the University of Portland has an enrollment of 3,661 students. The University of Portland has been co-ed since 1951. The school is also affiliated with the Roman Catholic Church. In addition to a large, well-stocked library, the campus has a museum. The University of Portland provides on-campus housing that can accommodate 1,400 students. Housing options: co-ed dorms · women's dorms · men's dorms. Recreation and sports facilities include: aerobics · cardio and weight rooms · grass and artificial fields · gymnasium · swimming pool.

Student Life and Activities

Most students (51 percent) live off campus, which does impact the on-campus social scene. Nevertheless, like any college, students find time to create their own recreational outlets. Espresso UP, Coffeehouse, Junior Parents Weekend, Service Plunge, International Night, Relay for Life, Dance of the Decades, Three Wise Monkeys Art Festival, Homecoming Dance and Guam Night are popular events. The University of Portland has 60 official student organizations. The most popular are: Accounting Club · ActUP · American Chemical Society · American Society of Civil Engineers · Association for Computing Machinery · Institute of Electrical and Electronics Engineers · Investment Association (formerly known as the Finance Club) · Mechanical Engineers Club · Operations Management Association · Philosophy · Pre-Dental Student Association · Social Sciences · Social Work Club · Society of Women Engineers. For those interested in sports, there are intramural teams such as: basketball · dodgeball · flag football · kickball · soccer · softball · ultimate Frisbee · volleyball. The University of Portland is a member of the West Coast Conference (Division I).

Academics and Learning Environment

For the B student, the learning environment of a college is just as important as the quality of its academic program. The University of Portland has 205 full-time and 102 part-time faculty members, offering a student-to-faculty ratio of 12:1. The most common course size is 20 to 29 students. The University of Portland offers 47 majors with the most popular being nursing and management/marketing and least popular being engineering management and theatre management. The school has a general core requirement as well as a religion requirement Cooperative education is not offered. All first-year students must maintain a 2.0 GPA or higher to avoid academic probation. Other special academic programs that would appeal to a B student: independent study · double majors · dual degrees · honors program · internships.

B Student Support and Success

The University of Portland's Academic Resources offers services that are extensive. An Integrated Writing Center, Speech Resource Center and Math Resource Center give information and advice for academic skills. The Shepard Freshman Resource Center is a one-stop place for first year students who want to know more about the campus and college life. The Learning Assistance program is geared to teach students' various learning strategies and skills. Counselors help guide students to improving learning skills like time management and prioritizing assignments, plus how to deal with overdue assignments, text anxiety, study overload and difficulty with reading and note taking.

The University of Portland provides a variety of support programs including dedicated guidance for: academic · career · personal · psychological · religious. The average freshman year GPA is 3.1, and 86 percent of freshmen students return for their sophomore year. What do students do after college? While many enter the work force, approximately 25 percent pursue a graduate degree immediately after graduation.

Support for Students with Learning Disabilities

Students with learning disabilities may take advantage of specific support programs offered by the University of Portland. If necessary, the college will grant additional time to students with learning disabilities to complete their degree. Also, a lightened course load may be granted to LD students. Students with learning disabilities will find the following programs at the University of Portland extremely useful: extended time for tests · readers · note-taking services · reading machines · waiver of math degree requirement. Individual or small group tutorials are also available in: time management · organizational skills · learning strategies · writing labs · math labs · study skills. An advisor/advocate from the LD program is available to students.

How to Get Admitted

For admissions decisions, non-academic factors considered: interview · extracurricular activities · special talents, interests, abilities · character/personal qualities · volunteer work · work experience · state of residency · geographical location · religious affiliation/commitment · minority affiliation · alumni relationship. A high school diploma is required, although a GED is also accepted for admissions consideration. SAT or ACT test scores are required of all applicants.

UNIVERSITY OF PORTLAND

Highlights

University of Portland
Portland, OR (Pop. 500,000)
Location: Medium city
Website: http://www.up.edu

Students
Total enrollment: 3,661
Undergrads: 1,125
Freshmen: 794
Part-time students: 3%
From out-of-state: 60%
Male/Female: 37%/63%
Live on-campus: 49%
Off-campus employment rating: Fair
Caucasian: 71%
African American: 1%
Hispanic: 5%
Asian or Pacific Islander: 10%
Native American: 1%
International: 2%

Academics
Student/faculty ratio: 12:1
Class size 9 or fewer: 13%
Class size 10-29: 61%
Class size 30-49: 23%
Class size 50-99: 3%
Class size 100 or more: -
Returning freshmen: 86%
Six-year graduation rate: 72%

Most Popular Fields of Study
Business, Finance, Sales and Marketing
Biological and Life Sciences
Visual and Performing Arts
English and Literature
Philosophy, Religion and Theology
Computer and Information Sciences
Psychology
Engineering and Engineering Technologies
Health Professions, Medicine and Related Sciences
Liberal Arts, Humanities and General Studies

519

College Profiles

UNIVERSITY OF PORTLAND

Admissions
Applicants: 8,271
Accepted: 4,867
Acceptance rate: 58.8%
placed on wait list: 1,181
Average GPA: 3.7
ACT range: Not reported
SAT Math range: 540-650
SAT Reading range: 540-660
SAT Writing range: Not reported
Top 10% of class: 44%
Top 25% of class: 74%
Top 50% of class: 95%

Deadlines
Early Action: No
Early Decision: No
Regular Action: Rolling admissions
Common Application: Accepted

Financial Aid
In-state tuition: $30,800
Out-of-state tuition: $30,800
Room: $4,245
Board: $5,120
Books: $1,000
Freshmen receiving need-based aid: 61%
Undergrads receiving need-based aid:
     38%
Avg. % of need met by financial aid: 90%
Avg. aid package (freshmen): $25,192
Avg. aid package (undergrads): $26,970
Freshmen receiving merit-based aid: 32%
Undergrads receiving merit-based aid:
     37%
Avg. student debt upon graduation:
     $22,787

Prominent Alumni
Fedele Bauccio, founder of *Bon Appetit*;
Jean Auel, author.

School Spirit
Colors: Purple

SAT Subject Test scores are considered, if submitted, but are not required. *According to the admissions office:* Minimum combined SAT score of 950 and minimum 2.8 GPA required. *Academic units recommended:* 4 English, 3 Math, 2 Science, 2 Social Studies.

How to Pay for College

To apply for financial aid, students should submit the following: Free Application for Federal Student Aid (FAFSA). The University of Portland participates in the Federal Work Study program. *Need-based aid programs include:* scholarships and grants · general need-based awards · Federal Pell grants · state scholarships and grants · college-based scholarships and grants · private scholarships and grants. *Non-Need-based aid programs include:* scholarships and grants · state scholarships and grants · athletic scholarships · ROTC scholarships.

UNIVERSITY OF REDLANDS

P.O. Box 3080, Redlands, CA 92373
Admissions: 800-455-5064 · Financial Aid: 888-867-5544
Email: admissions@redlands.edu · Website: http://www.redlands.edu

From the College

"The University of Redlands is a private, independent university committed to providing a personalized education that frees students to make enlightened choices. Redlands emphasizes academic rigor, curricular diversity and innovative teaching. Redlands fosters a community of scholars and encourages a pluralistic notion of values by challenging assumptions and stereotypes in both classes and activities. A Redlands education goes beyond training to embrace a reflective understanding of our world; it proceeds from information to insight, from knowledge to meaning. Welcoming intellectually curious students of diverse religious, ethnic, national and socio-economic backgrounds, the university seeks to develop responsible citizenship as part of a complete education. Redlands encourages a community atmosphere with exception opportunity for student leadership and interaction. For working adults, the University offers programs at convenient locations and times. Redlands blends liberal arts and professional programs, applied and theoretical study, traditional majors and self-designed contracts for graduation. Small classes enable each student to participate in class discussion, to work closely with professors and to receive extensive individual attention. Redlands remains sensitive to contemporary trends in society and challenges students to commit themselves to a lifetime of learning."

Campus Setting

Redlands, founded in 1907, is a liberal arts university. Its 140-acre campus is located in Redlands, 65 miles east of Los Angeles. A four-year institution, the University of Redlands has an enrollment of 2,427 students. In addition to a large, well-stocked library, the campus facilities include: art gallery · center for communicative disorders · language lab · anthropology lab · physics laser photonics lab · geographic information system lab. The University of Redlands provides on-campus housing with 30 units that can accommodate 1,634 students. Housing options: co-ed dorms · women's dorms · men's dorms · sorority housing · fraternity housing · single-student apartments · special housing for disabled students. Recreation and sports facilities include: aquatic center · baseball · soccer and softball fields · fitness center · football stadium · golf country club · gymnasium · tennis court · track.

Student Life and Activities

With 67 percent of students living on campus, there are plenty of social activities. Popular campus events include Feast of Lights and Multicultural Festival. The University of Redlands has 102 official student organizations. The most popular are: Accounting Club · Philosophy Club · Pre-Med Club (AMSA) · Student Athletic Advisory Committee · Wilderness Connections · Art Club · Dance Company · Astronomy Club · Glenn Wallichs Theatre Association · Improv Company · Mixed Blend · Music Educators National Conference (MENC) · Musical Theatre · Peer Theatre · Those Guys · Women's Ensemble · Amnesty International · Coalition for Non-Violent Activism · Biology Club. For those interested in sports, there are intramural teams such as: basketball · beach volleyball · dodgeball · flag football · kickball · life vest water polo · racquetball · soccer · softball · tennis · ultimate Frisbee. The University of Redlands is a member of the Southern California Intercollegiate Athletic Conference (Division III), Western Water Polo Association (Division III).

UNIVERSITY OF REDLANDS

University of Redlands
Redlands, CA (Pop. 63,591)
Location: Large town
Website: http://www.redlands.edu

Students
Total enrollment: 2,427
Undergrads: 1,000
Freshmen: 605
Part-time students: 0%
From out-of-state: 39%
Male/Female: 42%/58%
Live on-campus: 67%
In fraternities: 5%
In sororities: 7%
Caucasian: 56%
African American: 4%
Hispanic: 14%
Asian or Pacific Islander: 5%
Native American: 0%
International: 2%

Academics
Student/faculty ratio: 11:1
Class size 9 or fewer: 28%
Class size 10-29: 67%
Class size 30-49: 4%
Class size 50-99: 1%
Class size 100 or more: 1%
Returning freshmen: 86%
Six-year graduation rate: 66%

Most Popular Fields of Study
Business, Finance, Sales and Marketing
Biological and Life Sciences

America's
Best Colleges for
B Students

Academics and Learning Environment

For the B student, the learning environment of a college is just as important as the quality of its academic program. The University of Redlands has 214 full-time and 267 part-time faculty members, offering a student-to-faculty ratio of 11:1. The most common course size is 10 to 19 students. The University of Redlands offers 42 majors with the most popular being business administration, liberal studies and psychology and least popular being French and philosophy. The school has a general core requirement. Cooperative education is not offered. All first-year students must maintain a 2.0 GPA or higher to avoid academic probation, and a minimum overall GPA of 2.0 is required to graduate. Other special academic programs that would appeal to a B student: self-designed majors · pass/fail grading option · independent study · double majors · honors program · Phi Beta Kappa · internships · certificate programs.

B Student Support and Success

The University of Redlands' Academic Support Services helps students develop and strengthen the skills they will need most for academic success, accomplishing this through academic counseling, subject tutoring, writing tutoring and a learning skills course. With academic counseling, students are encouraged to talk to their advisors when choosing a major, planning for possible study abroad and learning time management and study skills. The tutoring center provides time management calendars, study skills handouts and other materials. A learning skills course is offered each semester and covers time management, improving memory, understanding learning styles and developing positive attitudes and motivation. Time is spent discussing goal setting, career planning, test taking and note taking. Redlands also offers up to two hours a week of free peer tutoring. Students with documented learning disabilities may receive more. Writing tutors can be accessed on a drop-in basis. Students are able to receive help at all stages of their writing assignments from outlining to footnoting.

The University of Redlands provides a variety of support programs including dedicated guidance for: academic · career · personal · psychological · religious. The average freshman year GPA is 3.0, and 86 percent of freshmen students return for their sophomore year. What do students do after college? While many enter the work force, approximately 44 percent pursue a graduate degree immediately after graduation, and another 10 percent enter graduate school within two years.

Support for Students with Learning Disabilities

Students with learning disabilities may take advantage of specific support programs offered by the University of Redlands. If necessary, the college will grant additional time to students with learning disabilities to complete their degree. Also, a lightened course load may be granted to LD students. High school foreign language waivers are accepted. High school math waivers are also accepted. Students with learning disabilities will find the following programs at the University of Redlands extremely useful: tutors · testing accommodations · untimed tests · extended time for tests · take-home exam · oral tests · exam on tape or computer · readers · note-taking services · reading machines · tape recorders · early syllabus. Individual or small group tutorials are also available in: time management · organizational skills · learning strategies · specific subject areas · writing labs · math labs · study skills. An advisor/advocate from the Disability Services is available to students.

How to Get Admitted

For admissions decisions, non-academic factors considered: interview · extracurricular activities · special talents, interests, abilities · character/personal qualities · volunteer work · work experience · state of residency · geographical location · minority affiliation · alumni relationship. A high school diploma is required, although a GED is also accepted for admissions consideration. SAT or ACT test scores are required of all applicants. SAT Subject Test scores are not required. *Academic units recommended:* 4 English, 3 Math, 3 Science, 3 Social Studies, 3 Foreign Language.

How to Pay for College

To apply for financial aid, students should submit the following: Free Application for Federal Student Aid (FAFSA) · state aid form · in-state GPA verification form. The University of Redlands participates in the Federal Work Study program. *Need-based aid programs include:* scholarships and grants · general need-based awards · Federal Pell grants · state scholarships and grants · college-based scholarships and grants · private scholarships and grants. *Non-Need-based aid programs include:* scholarships and grants · state scholarships and grants · creative arts and performance awards · special achievements and activities awards · special characteristics awards.

UNIVERSITY OF REDLANDS

Highlights

Admissions
Applicants: 3,607
Accepted: 2,270
Acceptance rate: 62.9%
Average GPA: 3.6
ACT range: 22-26
SAT Math range: 540-630
SAT Reading range: 520-620
SAT Writing range: Not reported
Top 10% of class: 31%
Top 25% of class: 70%
Top 50% of class: 93%

Deadlines
Early Action: No
Early Decision: No
Regular Action: Rolling admissions
Common Application: Accepted

Financial Aid
In-state tuition: $33,594
Out-of-state tuition: $33,594
Room: $5,814
Board: $4,658
Books: $1,638
Freshmen receiving need-based aid: 63%
Undergrads receiving need-based aid: 68%
Avg. % of need met by financial aid: 83%
Avg. aid package (freshmen): $29,046
Avg. aid package (undergrads): $29,203
Freshmen receiving merit-based aid: 15%
Undergrads receiving merit-based aid: 11%
Avg. student debt upon graduation: $15,125

Prominent Alumni
Cynthia J. Hoffman, chair, Department of Voice, the Julliard School; Gaddi H. Vasquez, U.S. Representative, United Nations Food and Agricultural Organization.

School Spirit
Mascot: Bulldogs
Colors: Maroon and gray
Song: *Och Tamale*

523

UNIVERSITY OF RHODE ISLAND

Undergraduate Admissions Office, 14 Upper College Road,
Kingston, RI 02881-0806
Admissions: 401-874-7100 · Financial Aid: 401-874-9500
Email: admission@uri.edu · Website: http://www.uri.edu

From the College

"We are the largest university in the nation's smallest state, but with 13,000 under-graduates and 2,600 graduate students, URI is small enough to be friendly, intimate, safe and student-centered. Our students come from most states in the U.S. and dozens of countries all over the world. More than 100 undergraduate and 80 graduate degree programs, plus more than 100 student clubs and activities spark creativity and inspire our students' pioneering spirit. Six miles from Rhodes Island's coastal beaches and easy driving distances from Providence, Boston and New York, our rural setting is close enough to big-city culture to make anyone feel at home."

Campus Setting

URI, founded in 1892, is a public, comprehensive university. Programs are offered through the Colleges of Arts and Science, Business Administration, Engineering, Environmental and Life Sciences, Human Science and Services, Nursing and Pharmacy. Its 1,200-acre campus is located in Kingston, 30 miles south of Providence. A four-year institution, the University of Rhode Island has an enrollment of 15,904 students. The school also has a library with 1,385,958 books. The University of Rhode Island provides on-campus housing with 2,601 units that can accommodate 5,041 students. Housing options: co-ed dorms · sorority housing · fraternity housing · single-student apartments · married-student apartments · special housing for disabled students. Recreation and sports facilities include: basketball · tennis · volleyball courts · fields · gymnasium · ice arena · swimming pool.

Student Life and Activities

Most students (55 percent) live off campus, which does impact the on-campus social scene. Nevertheless, like any college, students find time to create their own recreational outlets. The Union, Fraternity houses, dance clubs, bars and pool halls are hot spots for students. Popular campus events include: First Night, Welcome Week, Winterfest, Springfest, Block Party, Oozeball, Greek Week, Rainville Awards Banquet, Ram Tours and Relay for Life. The University of Rhode Island has 80 official student organizations. Greeks are influential in student life. For those interested in sports, there are intramural teams such as: badminton · basketball · beach volleyball · billiards · bowling · flag football · floor hockey · golf · ice hockey · indoor soccer · soccer · softball · tennis · volleyball. The University of Rhode Island is a member of the Atlantic 10 Conference (Division I, Football I-AA), ECAC (Division I, Football I-AA).

Academics and Learning Environment

For the B student, the learning environment of a college is just as important as the quality of its academic program. The University of Rhode Island has 683 full-time and 16 part-time faculty members, offering a student-to-faculty ratio of 17:1. The most common course size is 20 to 29 students. The University of Rhode Island offers 260 majors with the most popular being communication studies, psychology (general) and human development/family studies and least popular being Italian, classical studies and comparative literature. The school has a general core requirement. Cooperative education is not offered. All first-year students must maintain a GPA or higher to avoid academic probation, and a minimum overall GPA of 2.0 is required to graduate. Other special academic programs that would appeal to a B student: pass/fail grading option · independent study · double majors · dual degrees · honors program · Phi Beta Kappa · internships · distance learning.

B Student Support and Success

URI's Academic Enhancement Center's motto is "Teaching Is Learning." This phrase reflects its belief that "learning happens best when the learner is engaged in teaching subject matter to others." Thus, students are helped through peer tutoring and study groups that focus both on general study skills topics as well as specific courses. The college advocates study groups that get together once a week and share responsibility for the material they are all learning. Students are encouraged to discuss class materials, work together to solve problems, compare notes and help each other to succeed.

The URI Writing Center is free to all students who need help with all levels of writing. Additionally, the online assistance center has excellent materials to be read and/or downloaded.

The University of Rhode Island provides a variety of support programs including dedicated guidance for: academic · career · personal · psychological · minority students · military · veterans · non-traditional students · family planning · religious. Additional counseling services include: Graduate student counseling. Recognizing that some students may need extra preparation, the University of Rhode Island offers remedial and refresher courses in: reading · writing · math · study skills. Other remedial services include Time Management. Annually, 80 percent of freshmen students return for their sophomore year.

Support for Students with Learning Disabilities

Students with learning disabilities may take advantage of specific support programs offered by the University of Rhode Island. If necessary, the college will grant additional time to students with learning disabilities to complete their degree. Also, a lightened course load may be granted to LD students. High school foreign language waivers are accepted. According to the school, Disability Services for Students coordinates accommodations and support for all students with disabilities. All accommodation requests are considered on a case-by-case basis and rely on complete documentation to substantiate the request. Students with learning disabilities will find the following programs at the University of Rhode Island extremely useful: learning center · testing accommodations · extended time for tests · take-home exam · readers · typist/scribe · note-taking services · reading machines · tape recorders · special bookstore section · priority registration · waiver of math degree requirement. Individual or small group tutorials are also available in: time management · organizational skills · learning strategies · specific subject areas · writing labs · math labs · study skills. An advisor/advocate from the Disability Services for Students is available to students. This member also sits on the admissions committee.

How to Get Admitted

For admissions decisions, non-academic factors considered: extracurricular activities · special talents, interests, abilities · character/personal

UNIVERSITY OF RHODE ISLAND

University of Rhode Island
South Kingstown, RI (Pop. 28,000)
Location: Rural
Website: http://www.uri.edu

Students
Total enrollment: 15,904
Undergrads: 5,626
Freshmen: 3,247
Part-time students: 12%
From out-of-state: 50%
Male/Female: 44%/56%
Live on-campus: 45%
In fraternities: 11%
In sororities: 11%
Off-campus employment rating: Good
Caucasian: 73%
African American: 5%
Hispanic: 5%
Asian or Pacific Islander: 3%
Native American: 0%
International: 0%

Academics
Student/faculty ratio: 17:1
Class size 9 or fewer: 8%
Class size 10-29: 58%
Class size 30-49: 25%
Class size 50-99: 5%
Class size 100 or more: 4%
Returning freshmen: 80%
Six-year graduation rate: 58%

Most Popular Fields of Study
Business, Finance, Sales and Marketing
Personal Services, Culinary and Cosmetology
Social Sciences, History, Economics, Political Science
Visual and Performing Arts
Computer and Information Sciences
Communications, Journalism, Advertising and Comm. Technologies
English and Literature
Health Professions, Medicine and Related Sciences
Psychology

525

College Profiles

UNIVERSITY OF RHODE ISLAND

Admissions
Applicants: 15,887
Accepted: 12,724
Acceptance rate: 80.1%
Average GPA: 3.1
ACT range: Not reported
SAT Math range: 500-590
SAT Reading range: 480-570
SAT Writing range: Not reported
Top 10% of class: 16%

Deadlines
Early Action: December 1
Early Decision: No
Regular Action: Rolling admissions
Common Application: Not accepted

Financial Aid
In-state tuition: $7,454
Out-of-state tuition: $23,552
Room: $5,316
Board: $3,510
Books: $1,000
Freshmen receiving need-based aid: 53%
Undergrads receiving need-based aid:
   55%
Avg. % of need met by financial aid: 57%
Avg. aid package (freshmen): $12,194
Avg. aid package (undergrads): $12,654
Freshmen receiving merit-based aid: 5%
Undergrads receiving merit-based aid:
   4%
Avg. student debt upon graduation:
   $22,500

School Spirit
Mascot: Rams
Colors: Light blue and white
Song: *Rhode Island Bowm*

qualities · volunteer work · work experience · geographical location · minority affiliation · alumni relationship. A high school diploma is required, although a GED is also accepted for admissions consideration. SAT or ACT test scores are required of all applicants.

How to Pay for College

To apply for financial aid, students should submit the following: Free Application for Federal Student Aid (FAFSA). The University of Rhode Island participates in the Federal Work Study program. *Need-based aid programs include:* scholarships and grants · general need-based awards · Federal Pell grants · state scholarships and grants · college-based scholarships and grants · private scholarships and grants. *Non-Need-based aid programs include:* scholarships and grants · state scholarships and grants · creative arts and performance awards · special achievements and activities awards · athletic scholarships · ROTC scholarships.

UNIVERSITY OF SAN FRANCISCO

2130 Fulton Street, San Francisco, CA 94117-1080
Admissions: 800-CALL-USF · Financial Aid: 415-422-2620
Email: admission@usfca.edu
Website: http://www.usfca.edu

From the College

"The core mission of the university is to promote learning in the Jesuit Catholic tradition. The university offers undergraduate, graduate and professional students the knowledge and skills needed to succeed as persons and professionals, and the values and the sensitivity necessary to be men and women for others. The university will distinguish itself as a diverse, socially responsible learning community of high quality scholarship and academic rigor sustained by a faith that does justice."

Campus Setting

University of San Francisco, founded in 1855, is a private, Jesuit Catholic University. Programs are offered through the Colleges of Arts and Sciences and Professional Studies, the McLaren College of Business and the Schools of Education, Law and Nursing. The 55-acre campus is located in San Francisco, three miles from downtown. A four-year institution, the University of San Francisco has an enrollment of 8,750 students. The University of San Francisco has been co-ed since 1964. The school is also affiliated with the Roman Catholic Church. In addition to a large, well-stocked library, the campus also has an Institute for Chinese-Western cultural history. The University of San Francisco provides on-campus housing with 8 units that can accommodate 2,200 students. Housing options: co-ed dorms · women's dorms · single-student apartments. Recreation and sports facilities include a health and recreation center.

Student Life and Activities

Most students (54 percent) live off campus, which does impact the on-campus social scene. Nevertheless, like any college, students find time to create their own recreational outlets. Homecoming is a popular event. The University of San Francisco has 90 official student organizations. For those interested in sports, there are intramural teams such as: basketball · flag football · volleyball. The University of San Francisco is a member of the West Coast Conference (Division I).

Academics and Learning Environment

For the B student, the learning environment of a college is just as important as the quality of its academic program. The University of San Francisco has 380 full-time and 510 part-time faculty members, offering a student-to-faculty ratio of 15:1. The most common course size is 10 to 19 students. The University of San Francisco offers 46 majors with the most popular being business, nursing and psychology. The school has a general core requirement as well as a religion requirement Cooperative education is not offered. All first-year students must maintain a 2.0 GPA or higher to avoid academic pro-

UNIVERSITY OF SAN FRANCISCO

Admissions

Applicants: 8,485
Accepted: 5,399
Acceptance rate: 63.6%
placed on wait list: 325
Average GPA: 3.5
ACT range: 22-27
SAT Math range: 530-630
SAT Reading range: 510-620
SAT Writing range: 510-620
Top 10% of class: 26%
Top 25% of class: 67%
Top 50% of class: 91%

Deadlines

Early Action: November 15
Early Decision: No
Regular Action: February 1 (final)
Common Application: Accepted

Financial Aid

In-state tuition: $34,430
Out-of-state tuition: $34,430
Room: $7,730
Board: $3,810
Books: $1,000
Freshmen receiving need-based aid: 62%
Undergrads receiving need-based aid: 56%
Avg. % of need met by financial aid: 69%
Avg. aid package (freshmen): $25,158
Avg. aid package (undergrads): $23,076
Freshmen receiving merit-based aid: 4%
Undergrads receiving merit-based aid: 3%
Avg. student debt upon graduation: $26,523

Prominent Alumni

Paul Otellini, president, Intel Corp.; Gordon Getty, business leader and philanthropist.

School Spirit

Mascot: Dons
Colors: Green, gold, and white

bation, and a minimum overall GPA of 2.0 is required to graduate. Other special academic programs that would appeal to a B student: self-designed majors · pass/fail grading option · independent study · double majors · dual degrees · accelerated study · honors program · internships · distance learning certificate programs.

B Student Support and Success

The Learning Center at USF provides assistance to students through tutors in a variety of academic disciplines. The tutors are undergrads and graduate students that have excelled in certain academic areas and who have had special tutorial training. These students offer help on such topics as math, science, business, languages, computers, arts and general education. Study skills videos, textbooks and reference books are available, and the center also provides students a place to study that is peaceful and supportive.

The Writing Center features tutors that tailor programs of instruction to meet each student's needs. The center's primary goal is to "guide students in developing their writing skills in rhetoric, style and correctness, through one-on-one interactive conferences with rhetoric and composition faculty who have been chosen to work as consultants."

The University of San Francisco provides a variety of support programs including dedicated guidance for: academic · career · personal · psychological · minority students · non-traditional students · religious. Additional counseling services include: Learning Disabilities services. The average freshman year GPA is 3.0, and 83 percent of freshmen students return for their sophomore year.

Support for Students with Learning Disabilities

Students with learning disabilities may take advantage of specific support programs offered by the University of San Francisco. If necessary, the college will grant additional time to students with learning disabilities to complete their degree. Also, a lightened course load may be granted to LD students. Students with learning disabilities will find the following programs at the University of San Francisco extremely useful: tutors · learning center · testing accommodations · untimed tests · extended time for tests · take-home exam · oral tests · readers · note-taking services · reading machines · tape recorders · videotaped classes · diagnostic testing service · waiver of math degree requirement. Individual or small group tutorials are also available in: time management · organizational skills · learning strategies · specific subject areas · writing labs · math labs · study skills. An advisor/advocate from the Student Disability Services is available to students.

How to Get Admitted

For admissions decisions, non-academic factors considered: extracurricular activities · special talents, interests, abilities · character/personal qualities · volunteer work · state of residency · alumni relationship. A high school diploma is required, although a GED is also accepted for admissions consideration. SAT or ACT test scores are required of all applicants. SAT Subject Test scores are required for some applicants. *According to the admissions office:* Minimum 2.8 GPA required; rank in top quarter of secondary school class and minimum 3.0 GPA recommended.

How to Pay for College

To apply for financial aid, students should submit the following: Free Application for Federal Student Aid (FAFSA). The University of San Francisco participates in the Federal Work Study program. *Need-based aid programs include:* scholarships and grants · general need-based awards · Federal Pell grants · state scholarships and grants · college-based scholarships and grants · private scholarships and grants · Federal Nursing scholarships. *Non-Need-based aid programs include:* scholarships and grants · state scholarships and grants · special achievements and activities awards · athletic scholarships · ROTC scholarships · University Scholars Program.

UNIVERSITY OF SAN FRANCISCO

UNIVERSITY OF SOUTH CAROLINA - COLUMBIA

Columbia, SC 29208
Admissions: 800-868-5872 · Financial Aid: 803-777-8134
Email: admissions-ugrad@sc.edu · Website: http://www.sc.edu

From the College

"Chartered in 1801 as South Carolina College, the University of South Carolina – Columbia blends historic charm with a 21st century attitude. The original campus, popularly known as the Horseshoe, is listed on the National Register of Historic Places. Today's students have access to world-class facilities, including the Strom Thurmond Wellness and Fitness Center and the world's largest "green" dorm. USC Columbia offers more than 350 undergraduate and graduate courses of study. Programs range from liberal arts and sciences to business, law, medicine and other professional studies. The international business program is very popular. Study abroad, undergraduate research and interdisciplinary programs of study are encouraged. The Honors College is strong."

Campus Setting

The University of South Carolina – Columbia is a public, comprehensive university. Programs are offered through the Colleges of Business, Criminal Justice, Education, Engineering, Hospitality, Retail, and Sport Management, Journalism and Mass Communications, Library and Information Science, Liberal Arts, Nursing, Pharmacy, Science and Mathematics and Social Work; through the Schools of the Environment, Law, Medicine, Music and Public Health; and through the South Carolina Honors College. Its 351-acre campus, including a pre-Civil War area, is located in Columbia, in central South Carolina. A four-year institution, the University of South Carolina - Columbia has an enrollment of 27,488 students. The University of South Carolina - Columbia has been co-ed since 1893. In addition to a large, well-stocked library, the campus facilities include: museum · observatory · arboretum · green dorm with learning center focusing on sustainability · filtration research engineering demonstration unit. The University of South Carolina - Columbia provides on-campus housing with 4,325 units that can accommodate 7,015 students. Housing options: co-ed dorms · women's dorms · men's dorms · sorority housing · fraternity housing · single-student apartments · married-student apartments · special housing for disabled students · special housing for International students. Recreation and sports facilities include: baseball and softball fields · basketball center · football · soccer and tennis stadium · golf club · natatorium · track and field · volleyball.

Student Life and Activities

Most students (64 percent) live off campus, which does impact the on-campus social scene. Nevertheless, like any college, students find time to create their own recreational outlets. Popular campus events include: Caught in the Creative Act: Writers Talk about their Writing, Garnet Jacket Classic Golf Tournament, Parents Weekend, Dance Marathon, Black History Month, Carolina Spirit Week and Tiger Burn, Homecoming Week, Carolina - Clemson Food Fight, First-Year Reading Experience and Carolina Cuisine at the McCutcheon House. The University of South Carolina - Columbia has 300 official student organizations. The most popular are: music · theatre · political · service and special-interest groups. For those interested in sports, there are intramural teams such as: badminton · basketball · bench press · bowling · flag football · floor hockey · football · golf · indoor soccer · racquetball · sand volleyball · soccer · softball · swimming · tennis · track · tug-of-war · ultimate

Frisbee · volleyball · wallyball. The University of South Carolina - Columbia is a member of the Southeastern Conference (Division I, Football I-A).

Academics and Learning Environment

For the B student, the learning environment of a college is just as important as the quality of its academic program. The University of South Carolina - Columbia has 1,201 full-time and 508 part-time faculty members, offering a student-to-faculty ratio of 18:1. The most common course size is 10 to 19 students. The University of South Carolina - Columbia offers 246 majors with the most popular being biological sciences, experimental psychology and sport management/exercise science and least popular being contemporary European studies, Latin American studies and Italian. The school has a general core requirement. Cooperative education is not offered. All first-year students must maintain a 2.0 GPA or higher to avoid academic probation. Other special academic programs that would appeal to a B student: self-designed majors · pass/fail grading option · independent study · double majors · dual degrees · accelerated study · honors program · Phi Beta Kappa · internships · weekend college · distance learning.

B Student Support and Success

At the University of South Carolina, where students are known as "Gamecocks," the Academic Center for Excellence provides free writing consultations, math tutoring and other services. Guidance from ACE coaches is offered in areas of time management, procrastination, reading comprehension, note taking, goal setting, test taking, motivation, anxiety management, concentration and information processing. In addition, USC has a site called "My Game Plan" that helps each student design a personal approach for achieving academic success in college. It includes a personal assessment, study strategies and much more.

The University of South Carolina - Columbia provides a variety of support programs including dedicated guidance for: academic · career · personal · psychological · minority students · military · veterans · non-traditional students · family planning. Recognizing that some students may need extra preparation, the University of South Carolina - Columbia offers remedial and refresher courses in: reading · writing · math · study skills. The average freshman year GPA is 3.3, and 87 percent of freshmen students return for their sophomore year.

Support for Students with Learning Disabilities

Students with learning disabilities may take advantage of specific support programs offered by the University of South Carolina - Columbia. If necessary, the college will grant additional time to students with learning disabilities to complete their degree. Also, a lightened course load may be granted to LD students. Credit is given for remedial courses taken. High school foreign language waivers are accepted. Students with learning disabilities will find the following programs at the University of South Carolina - Columbia extremely useful: untimed tests · extended time for tests · readers · note-taking services · reading machines · tape recorders. Individual or small group tutorials are also available in: time man-

UNIVERSITY OF SOUTH CAROLINA - COLUMBIA

University of South Carolina - Columbia
Columbia, SC (Pop. 250,000)
Location: Medium city
Website: http://www.sc.edu

Students
Total enrollment: 27,488
Undergrads: 8,990
Freshmen: 5,493
Part-time students: 7%
From out-of-state: 38%
Male/Female: 45%/55%
Live on-campus: 36%
In fraternities: 14%
In sororities: 15%
Off-campus employment rating: Excellent
Caucasian: 73%
African American: 12%
Hispanic: 2%
Asian or Pacific Islander: 3%
Native American: 0%
International: 1%

Academics
Student/faculty ratio: 18:1
Class size 9 or fewer: 18%
Class size 10-29: 53%
Class size 30-49: 18%
Class size 50-99: 8%
Class size 100 or more: 3%
Returning freshmen: 87%
Six-year graduation rate: 67%

Most Popular Fields of Study
Business, Finance, Sales and Marketing
Social Sciences, History, Economics, Political Science
Protective Services, Criminal Justice and Public Administration
Visual and Performing Arts
Computer and Information Sciences
Communications, Journalism, Advertising and Comm. Technologies
Philosophy, Religion and Theology
Liberal Arts, Humanities and General Studies
English and Literature
Parks, Recreation and Fitness

531

College Profiles

UNIVERSITY OF SOUTH CAROLINA - COLUMBIA

Admissions
Applicants: 17,018
Accepted: 9,954
Acceptance rate: 58.5%
Average GPA: 3.9
ACT range: 24-28
SAT Math range: 550-650
SAT Reading range: 540-630
SAT Writing range: Not reported
Top 10% of class: 30%
Top 25% of class: 69%
Top 50% of class: 91%

Deadlines
Early Action: October 1
Early Decision: No
Regular Action: December 1 (priority)
December 1 (final)
Common Application: Not accepted

Financial Aid
In-state tuition: $8,438
Out-of-state tuition: $22,508
Room: $3,620
Board: -
Books: $936
Freshmen receiving need-based aid: 42%
Undergrads receiving need-based aid: 46%
Avg. % of need met by financial aid: 71%
Avg. aid package (freshmen): $10,994
Avg. aid package (undergrads): $11,283
Freshmen receiving merit-based aid: 47%
Undergrads receiving merit-based aid: 36%
Avg. student debt upon graduation: $21,315

Prominent Alumni
Gary Parsons, founder, XM Satellite Radio; Tonique Williams-Darling, Olympic gold medalist, 400-meter champion; Dean Felber, Mark Bryan, Jim Sonefeld and Darius Rucker, Grammy Award-winning musicians, Hootie and the Blowfish.

School Spirit
Mascot: Cocky
Colors: Garnet and black
Song: *We Hail Thee Carolina*

532

agement · organizational skills · learning strategies · study skills. An advisor/advocate from the Student Disability Services is available to students.

How to Get Admitted

For admissions decisions, non-academic factors considered: extracurricular activities · special talents, interests, abilities · character/personal qualities · volunteer work · work experience · minority affiliation · alumni relationship. A high school diploma is required, although a GED is also accepted for admissions consideration. SAT or ACT test scores are required of all applicants. SAT Subject Test scores are not required.

How to Pay for College

To apply for financial aid, students should submit the following: Free Application for Federal Student Aid (FAFSA). The University of South Carolina - Columbia participates in the Federal Work Study program. *Need-based aid programs include:* scholarships and grants · general need-based awards · Federal Pell grants · state scholarships and grants · college-based scholarships and grants · private scholarships and grants · Federal Nursing scholarships · United Negro College Fund · USC Opportunity Grant. *Non-Need-based aid programs include:* scholarships and grants · general need-based awards · state scholarships and grants · creative arts and performance awards · special achievements and activities awards · athletic scholarships · ROTC scholarships.

UNIVERSITY OF TENNESSEE

320 Student Services Building, Knoxville, TN 37996
Admissions: 865-974-2184 · Financial Aid: 865-974-3131
Email: admissions@utk.edu · Website: http://www.utk.edu

From the College

"The University of Tennessee, Knoxville, intends to be the preeminent public research and teaching university linking the people of Tennessee to the nation and the world. The core of UT's mission is to educate students and prepare them for the world. To do so, UT offers a broad array of majors and programs, internships, and hands-on research opportunities to internationalize your education, options for leadership and campus involvement. UT also focuses on making a college education accessible to all qualified students. From special first-year programs to intercultural initiatives, UT strives to ensure that students are prepared in Tennessee and for service around the world. The university offers several programs and opportunities to help students succeed at the university level. The Tennessee Pledge and Tennessee Promise scholarships target students from high schools that have not traditionally sent many of their graduates to UT-Knoxville. They also allow students to graduate debt-free by paying for mandatory college costs not covered by other federal and state aid.

"The Chancellor's Honors Program enrolls students who have excelled in rigorous high school curricula and demonstrated exceptional leadership. In addition, UT recently established the Haslam Scholars program, an honors program for 15 of the nation's top students.

"The College of Arts and Sciences offers courses of study in several interdisciplinary programs, including African Studies, Cinema Studies and Medieval Studies. Another specialized opportunity is the College Scholars program for highly motivated and academically talented students with clear goals for their undergraduate education that require them to work outside the colleges' traditional academic requirements.

"UT also has many programs that focus on enhancing diversity. Ready for the World is a long-range plan to transform the Knoxville campus into a culture of diversity that best prepares students for working and competing in the 21st century. As many as 100 general educational courses have been reworked to integrate cultural awareness as part of Ready for the World. UT LEAD Summer Institute is a center that groups many services and resources, like tutoring and advising, into one location as part of a comprehensive hub of academic services. The program allows incoming freshmen to get acquainted with campus and preview what courses and homework assignments will be like before classes begin. The UT College of Engineering is home to the Engage Engineering Fundamentals Program. All qualified first-year engineering students have the option to live in the Engage Community, making it easier to share notes and form study groups."

Campus Setting

The University of Tennessee is a public, comprehensive university. Founded as a private college in 1794, it became the first campus of the University of Tennessee in 1879. Programs are offered through the Colleges of Agricultural Sciences and Natural Resources, Architecture and Design, Arts and Sciences, Business Administration, Communication and Information, Education Health and Human Sciences, Engineering, Law, Nursing, Social Work and Veterinary Medicine. Its 550-acre campus is located in Knoxville. A four-year institution, the University of Tennessee has an enrollment of 30,410 students. The University of Tennessee has been co-ed since 1892. In addition to a large, well-stocked library, the campus facilities include: gallery · museum · gardens · international house · music hall · public policy and black

UNIVERSITY OF TENNESSEE

University of Tennessee
Knoxville, TN (Pop. 200,500)
Location: Medium city
Website: http://www.utk.edu

Students
Total enrollment: 30,410
Undergrads: 10,871
Freshmen: 5,918
Part-time students: 6%
From out-of-state: 13%
Male/Female: 50%/50%
Live on-campus: 26%
In fraternities: 22%
In sororities: 14%
Off-campus employment rating: Good
Caucasian: 85%
African American: 8%
Hispanic: 2%
Asian or Pacific Islander: 3%
Native American: 0%
International: 1%

Academics
Student/faculty ratio: 16:1
Class size 9 or fewer: 11%
Class size 10-29: 59%
Class size 30-49: 23%
Class size 50-99: 5%
Class size 100 or more: 3%
Returning freshmen: 84%
Six-year graduation rate: 59%

Most Popular Fields of Study
Business, Finance, Sales and Marketing
Visual and Performing Arts
Social Sciences, History, Economics,
    Political Science
Protective Services, Criminal Justice and
    Public Administration
Family and Consumer Sciences, Nutrition
    and Home Economics
Computer and Information Sciences
Communications, Journalism, Advertising
    and Comm. Technologies
Philosophy, Religion and Theology
English and Literature
Health Professions, Medicine and Re-
    lated Sciences

534

cultural centers. The University of Tennessee provides on-campus housing that can accommodate 8,053 students. Housing options: co-ed dorms · women's dorms · men's dorms · fraternity housing · single-student apartments · married-student apartments · special housing for disabled students · special housing for international students. Recreation and sports facilities include: aquatic center · arena · athletic center · baseball stadium · basketball courts · intramural fields · paddleball and handball courts · recreational center · recreational sports field · sand volleyball court · soccer complex · softball stadium · tennis courts · track.

Student Life and Activities

Most students (73 percent) live off campus, which does impact the on-campus social scene. Nevertheless, like any college, students find time to create their own recreational outlets. Students have a large number of social and special interest groups to join. Every effort is made to expose students to music, theater, and artistic venues that will foster personal growth and enhance the university experience. Popular on-campus gathering spots include: University Center, T-Rec and other sports/fitness facilities and the Strip. Popular campus events include: Homecoming activities, Smokey's Howl, Cheerleading Competition, Box Car Races, Parade with Float and Miss Homecoming Queen Competition, All Sing Musical Competition, Carnicus (parodies and satire performance), Vol Night Long, Volapalooza, Volunteer Challenge, football and basketball games and other sports. The University of Tennessee has 260 official student organizations. Popular groups on campus include: Student Government, Greeks, athletics, religious groups and sports clubs. For those interested in sports, there are intramural teams such as: basketball · billiards · bowling · cycling · fencing · field hockey · flag football · football · ice hockey · lacrosse · martial arts · rugby · sailing · sand volleyball · scuba diving · skiing · soccer · softball · swimming · tennis · volleyball · water polo · water skiing · weightlifting. The University of Tennessee is a member of the Southeastern Conference (Division I, Football I-A).

Academics and Learning Environment

For the B student, the learning environment of a college is just as important as the quality of its academic program. The University of Tennessee has 1,550 full-time and 116 part-time faculty members, offering a student-to-faculty ratio of 16:1. The most common course size is 20 to 29 students. The University of Tennessee offers 207 majors with the most popular being business/marketing, psychology and communications/journalism and least popular being philosophy, computer science and education. The school has a general core requirement. Cooperative education is available. All first-year students must maintain a 2.0 GPA or higher to avoid academic probation. Other special academic programs that would appeal to a B student: self-designed majors · independent study · double majors · dual degrees · honors program · internships · distance learning.

B Student Support and Success

According to its website, UT offers "First Year Studies 101: a one credit course to introduce students to the university and resources, a Student Success Center: one stop shopping for academic referrals and resources, a Math Tutorial Center and Writing Center and a College academic advising center." Students are encouraged to "take a challenging curriculum of academic courses." UT offers this advice to those wishing to apply for acceptance: "Complete the personal statement with your application—it will be read! Letters of recommendation are not required but if you wish to include them, be sure that they are from teachers of academic subjects. Tell us about your academic challenges and successes. Tell about your special talents and abilities. UT welcomes B students with strong and diverse academic backgrounds."

The University of Tennessee provides a variety of support programs including dedicated guidance for: academic · career · personal · psychological · minority students · military · veterans · non-traditional students · family planning. The average freshman year GPA is 3.0, and 84 percent of freshmen students return for their sophomore year. What do students do after college? While many enter the work force, approximately 10 percent pursue a graduate degree immediately after graduation. Among students who enter the work force, approximately 85 percent enter a field related to their major within six months of graduation. Companies that most frequently hire graduates from the University of Tennessee include: 21st Mortgage · Pricewaterhouse Coopers · Ernst & Young · Dell · KPMG · Kimberly-Clark · Marriott Business Services · Nissan · Pepsi Bottling Group · University of Tennessee · Wolseley North America · Deloitte & Touche · Eaton Electrical · Enterprise Rent-a-Car · Gresham · Smith & Partners · International Paper · Pugh & Co. · Square D/Schneider Electric · Tennessee Valley Authority · Whirlpool · ADTRAN · ALSTROM Power · Baker Hughes · Dixon Hughes · Dow Chemical Co. · ExxonMobil · Honeywell · Joseph Decosimo & Co. · Manhattan Associates · Michael Brady · APL Logistics · Brunswick Corporation/BBG/Sea Ray Boats · CHEP USA · CIGNA Healthcare · Clayton Homes · Crowe Chizek and Co. · Fed-Ex · Frito Lay · Johnson & Johnson · Knight Transportation · Knoxville Utilities Board · Kroger · Newell Rubbermaid · Pershing Yoakley · Regions Bank · Shaw Industries Group · Siemens · SPX Corp. · Target Stores · Turner Broadcasting · Wal-Mart.

Support for Students with Learning Disabilities

Students with learning disabilities may take advantage of specific support programs offered by the University of Tennessee. If necessary, the college will grant additional time to students with learning disabilities to complete their degree. Also, a lightened course load may be granted to LD students. High school foreign language waivers are accepted. High school math waivers are also accepted. According to the school, No separate admissions process for students with disabilities. Eligibility for accommodations/services are established by the disability documentation provided by the student in accordance with institutional standards. Accommodations/services are coordinated through the Disability Services Office and are based on needs specified in the student's documentation. Other offices on campus may also provide services, some of which are not mandated by laws and/or regulations. Students with learning disabilities will find the following programs at the University of Tennessee extremely useful: tutors · learning center · testing accommodations · extended time for tests · take-home exam · oral tests

UNIVERSITY OF TENNESSEE

Highlights

Admissions
Applicants: 13,894
Accepted: 8,999
Acceptance rate: 64.8%
Average GPA: 3.7
ACT range: 24-29
SAT Math range: 540-640
SAT Reading range: 530-630
SAT Writing range: Not reported
Top 10% of class: 41%
Top 25% of class: 71%
Top 50% of class: 94%

Deadlines
Early Action: No
Early Decision: No
Regular Action: December 1 (final)
Common Application: Not accepted

Financial Aid
In-state tuition: $5,428
Out-of-state tuition: $18,086
Room: $3,728
Board: $3,160
Books: $1,326
Freshmen receiving need-based aid: 47%
Undergrads receiving need-based aid: 45%
Avg. % of need met by financial aid: 72%
Avg. aid package (freshmen): $9,731
Avg. aid package (undergrads): $9,611
Freshmen receiving merit-based aid: 19%
Undergrads receiving merit-based aid: 12%
Avg. student debt upon graduation: $24,690

UNIVERSITY OF TENNESSEE

Prominent Alumni

Howard H. Baker Jr., former U.S. senator and ambassador to Japan, Presidential Medal of Freedom, White House chief of staff (Ronald Reagan); Pat Summitt, NCAA college basketball coach; Cormac McCarthy, author, National Book Award winner, Pulitzer Prize winner; Peyton Manning, Indianapolis Colts football player; Candace Parker, professional basketball player.

School Spirit

Mascot: Blue-Tic Coon Hound
Colors: Orange and white
Song: *Rocky Top*

· exam on tape or computer · readers · typist/scribe · note-taking services · reading machines · tape recorders · texts on tape · early syllabus · diagnostic testing service · priority registration. Individual or small group tutorials are also available in: time management · organizational skills · specific subject areas · writing labs · math labs · study skills. An advisor/advocate from the LD program is available to students.

How to Get Admitted

For admissions decisions, non-academic factors considered: extracurricular activities · special talents, interests, abilities · character/personal qualities · volunteer work · work experience · geographical location · minority affiliation · alumni relationship. A high school diploma is required, although a GED is also accepted for admissions consideration. SAT or ACT test scores are required of all applicants. *According to the admissions office:* Minimum 2.0 GPA required; holistic review of all parts of the application.

How to Pay for College

To apply for financial aid, students should submit the following: Free Application for Federal Student Aid (FAFSA) · institution's own financial aid forms. The University of Tennessee participates in the Federal Work Study program. *Need-based aid programs include:* scholarships and grants · general need-based awards · Federal Pell grants · state scholarships and grants · college-based scholarships and grants · private scholarships and grants · Federal Nursing scholarships. *Non-Need-based aid programs include:* scholarships and grants · general need-based awards · state scholarships and grants · creative arts and performance awards · special achievements and activities awards · special characteristics awards · athletic scholarships · ROTC scholarships.

UNIVERSITY OF THE PACIFIC

3601 Pacific Avenue, Stockton, CA 95211
Admissions: 800-959-2867 · Financial Aid: 209-946-2421
Email: admissions@pacific.edu · Website: http://www.pacific.edu

From the College

"The University of the Pacific is a study in contrasts. The community has the attitude of a California university and the pioneering spirit of the American West. But the campus looks like a school set in the countryside of New England, complete with old brick buildings, ivy and a lot of green spaces. In each of our 91 majors, students share the common experiences of mentoring faculty, small classes and guarantees of internships and graduation within four years."

Campus Setting

University of the Pacific, founded in 1851, is a private, comprehensive university. Programs are offered through College of the Pacific, Schools of Engineering, International Studies and Pharmacy, Benerd School of Education, Eberhardt School of Business and the Conservatory of Music. Its 175-acre campus is located in Stockton, 85 miles east of San Francisco. A four-year institution, the University of the Pacific has an enrollment of 6,251 students. The school also has a library with 364,030 books. The University of the Pacific provides on-campus housing with 1,445 units that can accommodate 2,208 students. Housing options: co-ed dorms · sorority housing · fraternity housing · single-student apartments · married-student apartments · special housing for disabled students. Recreation and sports facilities include: fitness center · gymnasium.

Student Life and Activities

With 57 percent of students living on campus, there are plenty of social activities. Popular campus events include: Diversity Week, Alumni Weekend, Homecoming, Festival of Lights and Founder's Day. The University of the Pacific has 100 official student organizations. The most popular are: Students for Environmental Action · Pacific Forensics Society · Celebrate Diversity · Music and Entertainers Industry Student Association · Pacific American Marketing Association · Association for Computing Machinery · Association of Engineering Students · American Society of Civil Engineers · American Society of Mechanical Engineers · American Society for Engineering Management · Snow bound · Biomedical Engineering Society. The University of the Pacific is a member of the Member of Big West Conference (Division I, Football I-A), Mountain Pacific Sports Federation (Division I), Northern Pacific Field Hockey Conference (Division I).

Academics and Learning Environment

For the B student, the learning environment of a college is just as important as the quality of its academic program. The University of the Pacific has 426 full-time and 298 part-time faculty members, offering a student-to-faculty ratio of 13:1. The most common course size is 2 to 9 students. The University of the Pacific offers 80 majors with the most popular being. The school has a general core requirement. Cooperative education is available. All first-year students must maintain a 2.0 GPA or higher to avoid academic probation, and a minimum overall GPA of 2.0 is required to graduate. Other special academic programs that would appeal to a B student: self-designed majors · pass/fail grading option · independent study · double majors · accelerated study · honors program · internships.

UNIVERSITY OF THE PACIFIC

University of the Pacific
Stockton, CA (Pop. 279,513)
Location: Medium city
Website: http://www.pacific.edu

Students
Total enrollment: 6,251
Undergrads: 1,515
Freshmen: 882
Part-time students: 3%
From out-of-state: 18%
Male/Female: 44%/56%
Live on-campus: 57%
In fraternities: 16%
In sororities: 18%
Caucasian: 35%
African American: 4%
Hispanic: 11%
Asian or Pacific Islander: 34%
Native American: 1%
International: 3%

Academics
Student/faculty ratio: 13:1
Class size 9 or fewer: 35%
Class size 10-29: 48%
Class size 30-49: 12%
Class size 50-99: 5%
Class size 100 or more: -
Returning freshmen: 82%
Six-year graduation rate: 68%

Most Popular Fields of Study
Biological and Life Sciences
Business, Finance, Sales and Marketing
Social Sciences, History, Economics, Political Science
Visual and Performing Arts
Computer and Information Sciences
Communications, Journalism, Advertising and Comm. Technologies
Liberal Arts, Humanities and General Studies
English and Literature
Parks, Recreation and Fitness
Health Professions, Medicine and Related Sciences

B Student Support and Success

University of the Pacific's Retention Services offers tutoring, study skills sessions, peer mentoring, career counseling and academic counseling. Their student-to-student advising program has 40 undergrads that are there to help with time management, preparing for tests, choosing a major, meeting general education requirements and even dealing with homesickness.

University of the Pacific provides a variety of support programs including dedicated guidance for: academic · career · personal · psychological · veterans. Annually, 82 percent of freshmen students return for their sophomore year. What do students do after college? While many enter the work force, approximately 17 percent pursue a graduate degree immediately after graduation. Among students who enter the work force, approximately 30 percent enter a field related to their major within six months of graduation, while a further 40 percent enter a related career within two years of graduation. Companies that most frequently hire graduates from University of the Pacific include: Accenture · Alcatel USA · American Express · AT&T Wireless · Biosource · California Human Development Corp.· Celebrity Cruise Lines · Cingular Wireless · Cisco Systems · Citgo Fund Services · Dresdner RCM Global Investors · Edward Jones · Enterprise · E-Trade · First Financial · Frito Lay · Gallo Wineries · Gap · General Mills · General Motors · George Simons International · Herzog Transit · Houston Astros · IRS · JET · Kaiser Permanente · Lawrence Livermore National Laboratory · Mervyns · Northwestern Mutual Financial · NY Life · Pacida International Maersk · PricewaterhouseCoopers · Quad Knopf · Rite Aid · Sandia National Laboratory · State of California · various school districts and non-profit organizations · Walgreens · Xerox.

Support for Students with Learning Disabilities

Students with learning disabilities may take advantage of specific support programs offered by the University of the Pacific. If necessary, the college will grant additional time to students with learning disabilities to complete their degree. Also, a lightened course load may be granted to LD students. Students with learning disabilities will find the following programs at University of the Pacific extremely useful: remedial math · remedial English · remedial reading · tutors · learning center · extended time for tests · reading machines · waiver of math degree requirement. Individual or small group tutorials are also available in: writing labs · math labs. An advisor/advocate from the Services for Students with Disabilities is available to students.

How to Get Admitted

For admissions decisions, non-academic factors considered: extracurricular activities · special talents, interests, abilities · character/personal qualities · volunteer work · work experience · state of residency · geographical location · minority affiliation · alumni relationship. A high school diploma is required, although a GED is also accepted for admissions consideration. SAT or ACT test scores are required of all applicants. SAT Subject Test scores are recommended but not required. *According to the admissions office:* Minimum grade average of 'B' in college-preparatory courses required. *Academic*

units recommended: 4 English, 3 Math, 2 Science, 3 Social Studies, 2 Foreign Language.

How to Pay for College

To apply for financial aid, students should submit the following: Free Application for Federal Student Aid (FAFSA). The University of the Pacific participates in the Federal Work Study program. *Need-based aid programs include:* scholarships and grants · general need-based awards · Federal Pell grants · state scholarships and grants · college-based scholarships and grants · private scholarships and grants. *Non-Need-based aid programs include:* scholarships and grants · state scholarships and grants · special achievements and activities awards · special characteristics awards · athletic scholarships.

UNIVERSITY OF THE PACIFIC

Highlights

Admissions
Applicants: 5,450
Accepted: 3,783
Acceptance rate: 69.4%
placed on wait list: 50
Average GPA: 3.5
ACT range: 22-28
SAT Math range: 543-670
SAT Reading range: 510-630
SAT Writing range: 510-630
Top 10% of class: 39%
Top 25% of class: 75%
Top 50% of class: 93%

Deadlines
Early Action:
Early Decision: No
Regular Action: Rolling admissions
Common Application: Accepted

Financial Aid
In-state tuition: $31,730
Out-of-state tuition: $31,730
Room: -
Board: -
Books: -
Freshmen receiving need-based aid: 69%
Undergrads receiving need-based aid: 67%
Avg. % of need met by financial aid: Not reported
Avg. aid package (freshmen): $27,556
Avg. aid package (undergrads): $27,263
Freshmen receiving merit-based aid: 18%
Undergrads receiving merit-based aid: 13%
Avg. student debt upon graduation: Not reported

Prominent Alumni
Alex Spanos, developer; Michael Olowokandi, professional basketball player; Janet Leigh, actress.

School Spirit
Mascot: Tigers
Colors: Orange and black
Song: *Tiger Fight Song*

UNIVERSITY OF UTAH

201 Presidents Circle, Salt Lake City, UT 84112
Admissions: 801-581-7281 · Financial Aid: 801-581-6211
Email: admissions@sa.utah.edu · Website: http://www.utah.edu

From the College

"The mission of the University of Utah is to educate the individual and to discover, refine and disseminate knowledge. As a teaching and research university, the flagship institution of the Utah state system of higher education, the University of Utah strives to create an academic environment where the highest standards of scholarship and professional practice are observed and where responsibilities to students are conscientiously met. It recognizes the mutual relevance and interdependence of teaching and research as essential components of academic excellence. It welcomes students who are committed to learning and who conform to high academic standards. The right of free inquiry is zealously preserved; diversity is encouraged and respected; critical examination and creativity are promoted; and intellectual integrity and social responsibility are fostered. Add in the spectacular mountain setting—a one-of-a-kind environment."

Campus Setting

The University of Utah, founded in 1850, is a public institution. Its main campus is located in Salt Lake City. A four-year institution, the University of Utah has an enrollment of 28,211 students. In addition to a large, well-stocked library, the campus facilities include: theatre · dance center · fine arts and natural history museum · arboretum · cancer research center · research park · hospital · neuropsychiatric institute. University of Utah provides on-campus housing with 3,347 units that can accommodate 4,262 students. Housing options: co-ed dorms · fraternity housing · single-student apartments · married-student apartments · special housing for disabled students. Recreation and sports facilities include: courts · fields · gymnasium · recreation centers.

Student Life and Activities

Most students (92 percent) live off campus, which does impact the on-campus social scene. Nevertheless, like any college, students find time to create their own recreational outlets. According to the school, there exists a diverse student body and thus there are many different cultural and ethnic events on campus for students. These include: independent film series, cultural awareness week, dance concerts and plays. Popular gathering places are Port-O-Call Social Club, Bar-X, Lumpy's Social Club, the Bayou, The Park Cafe and The Pie. Popular events include: tailgate party at the homecoming game, Crimson Nights, Oktoberfest, Family Day, Friday Night Live, Union Film Festival, Union Art Gallery and Union Bowling League Tournament. The University of Utah has 160 official student organizations. Greeks, the football team, and the bar scene are heavy influences on student social life. For those interested in sports, there are intramural teams such as: basketball · billiards · bowling · dodgeball · flag football · golf · racquetball · sand volleyball · soccer · softball · table tennis · target shooting · tennis · ultimate Frisbee. The University of Utah is a member of the Mountain West Conference (FBS Division I, Football).

Academics and Learning Environment

For the B student, the learning environment of a college is just as important as the quality of its academic program. The University of Utah has 1,276 full-time and 656 part-time faculty members, offering a student-to-faculty ratio of 13:1. The most common course size is 10 to 19 students. University of Utah offers 277 majors with the most popular being business, exercise and sport science and biology and least popular being women studies, consumer studies and family economics and Middle East studies. The school has a general core requirement. Cooperative education is available. All first-year students must maintain a 2.0 GPA or higher to avoid academic probation. Other special academic programs that would appeal to a B student: self-designed majors · pass/fail grading option · independent study · double majors · dual degrees · accelerated study · honors program · Phi Beta Kappa · internships · distance learning certificate programs.

B Student Support and Success

Students at the University of Utah can turn to PASS, or Programs for Academic Support, for help in subject areas. Through PASS, students receive free peer tutoring in physics, chemistry, science, some foreign languages and math. Sessions can be either one on one or in a group. Online tutoring has recently been expanded as well. A Self-Help Learning Lab features audio and videotapes, books and computer software for development of study skills. Assistance is available in reading, algebra, calculus, trigonometry, statistics, differential equations, chemistry, foreign language and more. Academic advising covers topics such as study skills and time management, effective listening and note taking, improving reading comprehension, test taking, test anxiety and learning style. Supplemental instruction is provided for the historically difficult entry-level classes.

University of Utah provides a variety of support programs including dedicated guidance for: academic · career · personal · psychological · minority students · military · veterans · non-traditional students · family planning. The average freshman year GPA is 2.9, and 83 percent of freshmen students return for their sophomore year.

Support for Students with Learning Disabilities

Students with learning disabilities may take advantage of specific support programs offered by the University of Utah. If necessary, the college will grant additional time to students with learning disabilities to complete their degree. Also, a lightened course load may be granted to LD students. High school foreign language waivers are accepted. Students with learning disabilities will find the following programs at the University of Utah extremely useful: tutors · testing accommodations · extended time for tests · take-home exam · oral tests · exam on tape or computer · readers · typist/scribe · note-taking services · reading machines · tape recorders · early syllabus · priority registration · waiver of math degree requirement. Individual or small group tutorials are also available in: time management · organizational skills · learning strategies · specific subject areas · writing labs · math labs · study skills. An advisor/advocate from the Center for Disability Services is available to students. This member also sits on the admissions committee.

How to Get Admitted

For admissions decisions, non-academic factors considered: interview · extracurricular activities · special talents, interests, abilities · state of

UNIVERSITY OF UTAH

University of Utah
Salt Lake City, UT (Pop. 948,172)
Location: Major city
Website: http://www.utah.edu

Students
Total enrollment: 28,211
Undergrads: 11,895
Freshmen: 3,724
Part-time students: 33%
From out-of-state: 19%
Male/Female: 55%/45%
Live on-campus: 8%
In fraternities: 2%
In sororities: 2%
Off-campus employment rating: Excellent
Caucasian: 79%
African American: 1%
Hispanic: 5%
Asian or Pacific Islander: 6%
Native American: 1%
International: 3%

Academics
Student/faculty ratio: 13:1
Class size 9 or fewer: 20%
Class size 10-29: 48%
Class size 30-49: 17%
Class size 50-99: 11%
Class size 100 or more: 4%
Returning freshmen: 83%
Six-year graduation rate: 51%

Most Popular Fields of Study
Business, Finance, Sales and Marketing
Visual and Performing Arts
Social Sciences, History, Economics, Political Science
Protective Services, Criminal Justice and Public Administration
Family and Consumer Sciences, Nutrition and Home Economics
Computer and Information Sciences
Communications, Journalism, Advertising and Comm. Technologies
Philosophy, Religion and Theology
English and Literature

541

UNIVERSITY OF UTAH

Admissions
Applicants: 7,234
Accepted: 5,868
Acceptance rate: 81.1%
Average GPA: 3.5
ACT range: 21-27
SAT Math range: 500-635
SAT Reading range: 490-610
SAT Writing range: 470-610
Top 10% of class: 29%
Top 25% of class: 49%
Top 50% of class: 76%

Deadlines
Early Action: No
Early Decision: No
Regular Action: Rolling admissions
Common Application: Not accepted

Financial Aid
In-state tuition: $4,956
Out-of-state tuition: $17,346
Room: $3,096
Board: $1,270
Books: $1,080
Freshmen receiving need-based aid: 30%
Undergrads receiving need-based aid:
    36%
Avg. % of need met by financial aid: 57%
Avg. aid package (freshmen): $9,295
Avg. aid package (undergrads): $9,146
Freshmen receiving merit-based aid: 9%
Undergrads receiving merit-based aid:
    5%
Avg. student debt upon graduation:
    $11,749

Prominent Alumni
Willard Marriott, CEO of Marriott International Inc.; Stephen Covey, founder of Covey Leadership Center and author of "The 7 Habits of Highly Effective People."

School Spirit
Mascot: Swoop (red tailed hawk)
Colors: Crimson and white
Song: *Utah Man*

residency · minority affiliation. A high school diploma is required, although a GED is also accepted for admissions consideration. SAT or ACT test scores are required of all applicants. SAT Subject Test scores are considered, if submitted, but are not required. *According to the admissions office:* The university uses an admission index based on ACT score (or SAT scores) and high school GPA. *Academic units recommended:* 4 English, 2 Math, 3 Science, 2 Foreign Language.

How to Pay for College

To apply for financial aid, students should submit the following: Free Application for Federal Student Aid (FAFSA) · institution's own financial aid forms. The University of Utah participates in the Federal Work Study program. *Need-based aid programs include:* scholarships and grants · general need-based awards · Federal Pell grants · state scholarships and grants · college-based scholarships and grants · private scholarships and grants. *Non-Need-based aid programs include:* scholarships and grants · general need-based awards · state scholarships and grants · creative arts and performance awards · athletic scholarships · ROTC scholarships.

UNIVERSITY OF VERMONT

South Prospect Street, Burlington, VT 05405-0160
Admissions: 802-656-3370 · Financial Aid: 802-656-5700
Email: admissions@uvm.edu · Website: http://www.uvm.edu

From the College

"Students at the University of Vermont benefit from a setting that combines the resources of a major research university with the intimate feeling of a liberal arts college. Renowned Professors, rather than graduate assistants, are students' teachers and advisors, and many students assist their professors with their research projects. The nation's premier environmental university, UVM is located in Burlington, a small city regularly hailed as a top college town, surrounded by the mountains and lakes of the Vermont countryside. The university is noted for its academic programs and faculty, newly established Honors College, hands-on teaching, engaged student body and its quality of life."

Campus Setting

The University of Vermont, founded in 1791, is a public, comprehensive institution. Undergraduate programs are offered through the Colleges of Agriculture and Life Sciences, Arts and Sciences, Education and Social Services, Engineering and Mathematical Sciences and Nursing and Health Sciences, the School of Business Administration and the Rubenstein School of Environment and Natural Resources. Outstanding undergraduates are invited to concurrent enrollment in the Honors College. The university also offers master's and doctoral programs through the Graduate College and the doctor of medicine through the College of Medicine. A four-year institution, University of Vermont has an enrollment of 12,800 students. University of Vermont has been co-ed since 1871. In addition to a large, well-stocked library, the campus facilities include: art galleries · museums · center for cultural pluralism · research vessel · agricultural and environmental testing laboratory · agricultural experiment station · biomedical research complex · dairy farm and herd · entomology research laboratory · greenhouses · institute for ecological economics · horse-riding arena · horticultural research center. The University of Vermont provides on-campus housing with 3,049 units that can accommodate 5,717 students. Housing options: co-ed dorms · sorority housing · fraternity housing · single-student apartments · married-student apartments. Recreation and sports facilities include: fields · gymnasium · ice arena · natatorium.

Student Life and Activities

With 53 percent of students living on campus, there are plenty of social activities. UVM students are active - nearly 80 percent are involved in one or more academic, arts, athletic, environmental, media, cultural, political or service organizations. All first- and second-year students live on campus, with many choosing special interest housing ranging from careers in medicine to live music to language and culture houses. While individuals tend to be passionate about their particular interests, the campus as a whole is noted for being exceptionally open and friendly. Many students arrive and nearly all leave with heightened appreciation and active concern for the natural environment. Popular gathering spots on campus include: Davis Center (atrium, fireplace lounges, game room, green roof and food court), Bailey Beach'(main library steps), the University Green, central campus amphitheatre, Gucciardi fitness center and the Williams Hall fire escape for sunset views. Popular gathering spots off campus include: Church Street Marketplace, Higher Ground (live music venue), local ski areas, North Beach and Waterfront Park. Popular campus events include:

UNIVERSITY OF VERMONT

Highlights

University of Vermont
Burlington, VT (Pop. 40,000)
Location: Medium city
Website: http://www.uvm.edu

Students
Total enrollment: 12,800
Undergrads: 4,841
Freshmen: 2,778
Part-time students: 11%
From out-of-state: 74%
Male/Female: 44%/56%
Live on-campus: 53%
In fraternities: 6%
In sororities: 5%
Off-campus employment rating: Good
Caucasian: 92%
African American: 1%
Hispanic: 2%
Asian or Pacific Islander: 2%
Native American: 0%
International: 1%

Academics
Student/faculty ratio: 16:1
Class size 9 or fewer: 16%
Class size 10-29: 55%
Class size 30-49: 18%
Class size 50-99: 7%
Class size 100 or more: 5%
Returning freshmen: 86%
Six-year graduation rate: 71%

Most Popular Fields of Study
Business, Finance, Sales and Marketing
Biological and Life Sciences
Agriculture, Aquaculture and Animal Sciences
Visual and Performing Arts
Social Sciences, History, Economics, Political Science
Protective Services, Criminal Justice and Public Administration
Family and Consumer Sciences, Nutrition and Home Economics
Area, Ethnic and Gender Studies
Computer and Information Sciences
Communications, Journalism, Advertising and Comm. Technologies

544

Fall Activities Fest, Homecoming and Family Weekend, the Hunger Banquet, Week of Welcome, Martin Luther King Celebration, Random Acts of Kindness Day (aka free hot dog day), Springfest, Community Works, hockey and basketball games, speakers and concerts. University of Vermont has 132 official student organizations. Groups that have a strong presence on campus include: the Outing Club, Volunteers In Action (VIA), Vermont Student Environmental Program (VSTEP), Ski and Snowboard Club, fraternities and sororities, intramural leagues and club sports, Alternative Breaks (service trips), the Vermont Cynic (student newspaper), Free2Be and Feel Good (world hunger relief). For those interested in sports, there are intramural teams such as: basketball · bowling · broomball · flag football · homerun derby · horseshoes · ice hockey · inner-tube water polo · racquetball · soccer · softball · tennis · volleyball · wiffle ball. The University of Vermont is a member of the American East Conference (Division I), Hockey East Association (Division I).

Academics and Learning Environment

For the B student, the learning environment of a college is just as important as the quality of its academic program. University of Vermont has 609 full-time and 156 part-time faculty members, offering a student-to-faculty ratio of 16:1. The most common course size is 10 to 19 students. University of Vermont offers 178 majors with the most popular being business administration, psychology and English. The school does not have a general core requirement. Cooperative education is available. A minimum overall GPA of 2.0 is required to graduate. Other special academic programs that would appeal to a B student: self-designed majors · pass/fail grading option · independent study · double majors · honors program · Phi Beta Kappa · internships · distance learning certificate programs.

B Student Support and Success

UVM has the Learning Cooperative, a place "where students help students learn." It offers individual tutoring, group study sessions and writing and learning skills conferences. The Learning Skills program is there to help students develop learning skills and study habits that lead to a successful college career. They do this through free tutoring and workshops. Along with individualized tutoring, the cooperative offers a number of group study sessions for the college's most traditionally difficult courses. A Writing Center helps with any class papers.

The University of Vermont provides a variety of support programs including dedicated guidance for: academic · career · personal · psychological · minority students · military · veterans · non-traditional students · family planning · religious. Recognizing that some students may need extra preparation, University of Vermont offers remedial and refresher courses in: reading · writing · math · study skills. The average freshman year GPA is 3.0, and 86 percent of freshmen students return for their sophomore year.

Support for Students with Learning Disabilities

Students with learning disabilities may take advantage of specific support programs offered by the University of Vermont. If necessary, the college will grant additional time to students with learning disabilities to complete their degree. Also, a lightened course load may be granted to LD students. High school foreign language waivers are accepted. Students with learning disabilities will find the following programs at University of Vermont extremely useful: special classes · tutors · learning center · testing accommodations · extended time for tests · take-home exam · oral tests · substitution of courses · readers · note-taking services · reading machines · tape recorders · texts on tape · early syllabus · priority registration · priority seating · waiver of math degree requirement. Individual or small group tutorials are also available in: time management · organizational skills · learning strategies · specific subject areas · writing labs · math labs · study skills. An advisor/advocate from the ACCESS Academic Support Services is available to students.

How to Get Admitted

For admissions decisions, non-academic factors considered: interview · extracurricular activities · special talents, interests, abilities · character/personal qualities · volunteer work · work experience · geographical location · minority affiliation · alumni relationship. A high school diploma is required, although a GED is also accepted for admissions consideration. SAT or ACT test scores are required of all applicants. SAT Subject Test scores are considered, if submitted, but are not required.

How to Pay for College

To apply for financial aid, students should submit the following: Free Application for Federal Student Aid (FAFSA). The University of Vermont participates in the Federal Work Study program. *Need-based aid programs include:* scholarships and grants · general need-based awards · Federal Pell grants · state scholarships and grants · college-based scholarships and grants · private scholarships and grants · Federal Nursing scholarships. *Non-Need-based aid programs include:* scholarships and grants · state scholarships and grants · creative arts and performance awards · special achievements and activities awards · special characteristics awards · athletic scholarships · ROTC scholarships.

UNIVERSITY OF VERMONT

Highlights

Admissions
Applicants: 21,062
Accepted: 13,651
Acceptance rate: 64.8%
placed on wait list: 3,074
Average GPA: Not reported
ACT range: 23-28
SAT Math range: 550-650
SAT Reading range: 540-640
SAT Writing range: 540-640
Top 10% of class: 29%
Top 25% of class: 72%
Top 50% of class: 98%

Deadlines
Early Action:
Early Decision: No
Regular Action: January 15 (final)
Common Application: Accepted

Financial Aid
In-state tuition: $11,048
Out-of-state tuition: $27,886
Room: $5,752
Board: $2,782
Books: $990
Freshmen receiving need-based aid: 57%
Undergrads receiving need-based aid: 55%
Avg. % of need met by financial aid: 76%
Avg. aid package (freshmen): $21,537
Avg. aid package (undergrads): $19,519
Freshmen receiving merit-based aid: 32%
Undergrads receiving merit-based aid: 21%
Avg. student debt upon graduation: $25,599

Prominent Alumni
Jody Williams, 1997 Nobel Peace laureate for heading the international campaign to ban land mines; Dr. John McCall, section leader for Doctors Without Borders when the organization was awarded the Nobel Peace Prize in 1999; Jon Kilik, film producer, *Malcolm X*, *Do the Right Thing* and *Dead Man Walking*.

School Spirit
Mascot: Catamount
Colors: Green and gold
Song: *Champlain*

545

UNIVERSITY OF WYOMING

1000 East University Avenue, Laramie, WY 82071
Admissions: 800-342-5996 · Financial Aid: 307-766-2116
Email: why-wyo@uwyo.edu · Website: http://www.uwyo.edu

From the College

"The University of Wyoming is the state's only provider of baccalaureate and graduate education, research and outreach services. UW combines major-university benefits and small-school advantages, with more than 175 programs of study set against the idyllic backdrop of southeastern Wyoming's rugged mountains and high plains. The main campus is located in Laramie, approximately two hours north of Denver. The university also maintains the UW/Casper College Center, nine outreach education centers across Wyoming and Cooperative Extension Service centers in each of the state's 23 counties and on the Wind River Indian Reservation."

Campus Setting

University of Wyoming, founded in 1886, is a public, multipurpose institution. Programs are offered through the Colleges of Agriculture, Arts and Sciences, Education, Engineering, Law, Health Sciences, and Business. Its 780-acre campus is located in Laramie, in southeastern Wyoming, 50 miles west of Cheyenne, and 155 miles north of Denver. A four-year institution, University of Wyoming has an enrollment of 12,067 students. In addition to a large, well-stocked library, the campus facilities include: art · geological · anthropology and insect museums · on site elementary school · Rocky Mountain and Solheim Herbarium · Spatial Data and Visualization Center · Williams Botany Conservatory · Learning Resource Center · National Park research center · Planetarium · State Veterinary Laboratory · Materials Characterization Lab · Cooperative Research Unit · Infrared Telescope · Star · Red Bullet and Elk Mountain Observatories · Survey Analysis Center · Institute of Environment and Natural Resources · Fishery and Wildlife Research Unit · American Heritage Center · Microscopy Facility. The University of Wyoming provides on-campus housing that can accommodate 3,400 students. Housing options: co-ed dorms · sorority housing · fraternity housing · single-student apartments · married-student apartments · special housing for disabled students. Recreation and sports facilities include: athletic center · fieldhouse training room.

Student Life and Activities

Wyoming Union, Library Book and Bean, Coal Creek Coffee, Turtle Rock Cafe, Classroom Lounge and Prexys Pasture are popular gathering spots. The Student Activities Council schedules many concerts, convocations and quality programming that promotes student development. Popular events include: Friday Night Fever, UW theatre and dance performances, cultural programs, sports events and activities and art exhibitions. The University of Wyoming has 223 official student organizations. The most popular are: departmental · musical · recreational · political · professional and special-interest groups. For those interested in sports, there are intramural teams such as: slam dunk contest · hot shot competition · table tennis · basketball · tube water polo · wallyball · racquetball · billiards · bowling · flag football · Fantasy Football League · Outdoor Soccer · Golf Tournament · Paintball · Ultimate Frisbee · Punt-Pass and Kick · Miniature Golf · Home Run Contest · Disc Golf · Floor Hockey · 5K Fun Run · 3 on 3 Basketball · Bench Press Competition · Free Throw Contest · Bowling · Sports Trivia · Volleyball. University of Wyoming is a member of the Mountain West Conference (Division I, Football I-A).

Academics and Learning Environment

For the B student, the learning environment of a college is just as important as the quality of its academic program. The University of Wyoming has 715 full-time and 52 part-time faculty members, offering a student-to-faculty ratio of 14:1. The most common course size is 20 to 29 students. University of Wyoming offers 175 majors with the most popular being elementary education, nursing and psychology and least popular being astronomy and astrophysics, botany and self-designed major. The school has a general core requirement. Cooperative education is available. All first-year students must maintain a 2.0 GPA or higher to avoid academic probation. Other special academic programs that would appeal to a B student: self-designed majors · pass/fail grading option · independent study · double majors · dual degrees · accelerated study · honors program · Phi Beta Kappa · internships · distance learning certificate programs.

B Student Support and Success

Academic Services provides support for undergraduates through tutoring and study skills development. It includes a series of study skills workshops and individual advising.

Student Success Services is a program designed for students who meet one of these three criteria: 1) first-generation college student, 2) low-income family or 3) documented disability, learning or physical. This support system offers individual and group tutoring, study skills workshops, individualized math assistance, career exploration and more to eligible students.

The University of Wyoming provides a variety of support programs including dedicated guidance for: academic · career · personal · psychological · minority students · military · veterans · non-traditional students · family planning. The average freshman year GPA is 3.5, and 73 percent of freshmen students return for their sophomore year.

Support for Students with Learning Disabilities

Students with learning disabilities may take advantage of specific support programs offered by University of Wyoming. If necessary, the college will grant additional time to students with learning disabilities to complete their degree. Also, a lightened course load may be granted to LD students. Students with learning disabilities will find the following programs at University of Wyoming extremely useful: tutors · learning center · testing accommodations · extended time for tests · take-home exam · oral tests · exam on tape or computer · readers · typist/scribe · note-taking services · reading machines · tape recorders · texts on tape · early syllabus. Individual or small group tutorials are also available in: time management · organizational skills · learning strategies · specific subject areas · writing labs · math labs · study skills. An advisor/advocate from the University Disability Support Services is available to students.

How to Get Admitted

For admissions decisions, non-academic factors considered: interview · extracurricular activities · special talents, interests, abilities · character/personal qualities. A high school diploma is required, although a GED is also accepted for admissions consideration. SAT or ACT

University of Wyoming
Laramie, WY (Pop. 27,204)
Location: Large town
Website: http://www.uwyo.edu

Students
Total enrollment: 12,067
Undergrads: 4,524
Freshmen: 2,390
Part-time students: 17%
From out-of-state: 54%
Male/Female: 47%/53%
Live on-campus: Not reported
In fraternities: 5%
In sororities: 6%
Off-campus employment rating: Excellent
Caucasian: 82%
African American: 1%
Hispanic: 4%
Asian or Pacific Islander: 1%
Native American: 1%
International: 3%

Academics
Student/faculty ratio: 14:1
Class size 9 or fewer: 14%
Class size 10-29: 57%
Class size 30-49: 20%
Class size 50-99: 4%
Class size 100 or more: 4%
Returning freshmen: 73%
Six-year graduation rate: 57%

Most Popular Fields of Study
Business, Finance, Sales and Marketing
Agriculture, Aquaculture and Animal Sciences
Biological and Life Sciences
Visual and Performing Arts
Social Sciences, History, Economics, Political Science
Protective Services, Criminal Justice and Public Administration
Family and Consumer Sciences, Nutrition and Home Economics
Computer and Information Sciences
Communications, Journalism, Advertising and Comm. Technologies

547

College Profiles

UNIVERSITY OF WYOMING

Admissions
Applicants: 3,589
Accepted: 3,444
Acceptance rate: 96.0%
Average GPA: 3.5
ACT range: 21-27
SAT Math range: 500-640
SAT Reading range: 470-610
SAT Writing range: Not reported
Top 10% of class: 23%
Top 25% of class: 51%
Top 50% of class: 81%

Deadlines
Early Action: No
Early Decision: No
Regular Action: Rolling admissions
Common Application: Not accepted

Financial Aid
In-state tuition: $2,820
Out-of-state tuition: $10,740
Room: $3,364
Board: $2,175
Books: $1,200
Freshmen receiving need-based aid: 42%
Undergrads receiving need-based aid:
   46%
Avg. % of need met by financial aid: 43%
Avg. aid package (freshmen): $7,612
Avg. aid package (undergrads): $8,050
Freshmen receiving merit-based aid: 10%
Undergrads receiving merit-based aid:
   16%
Avg. student debt upon graduation:
   $16,307

Prominent Alumni
Dick Cheney, former vice president; Alan
K. Simpson, former U.S. senator; Ardis
J. Meier, chief pharmacy consultant to
USAF surgeon.

School Spirit
Mascot: Cowboy Joe
Colors: Brown and gold
Song: *Ragtime Cowboy Joe*

test scores are required of all applicants. SAT Subject Test scores are not required. *According to the admissions office:* 13 units is required pre-college curriculum. Minimum 2.75 GPA required of in-state applicants, minimum 3.0 GPA or minimum 2.75 GPA with minimum composite ACT score of 20 (combined SAT Reasoning score of 960) required of out-of-state applicants. *Academic units recommended:* 4 English, 4 Math, 4 Science, 2 Foreign Language.

How to Pay for College

To apply for financial aid, students should submit the following: Free Application for Federal Student Aid (FAFSA). The University of Wyoming participates in the Federal Work Study program. *Need-based aid programs include:* scholarships and grants · general need-based awards · Federal Pell grants · state scholarships and grants · college-based scholarships and grants · private scholarships and grants. *Non-Need-based aid programs include:* scholarships and grants · general need-based awards · state scholarships and grants · creative arts and performance awards · special achievements and activities awards · special characteristics awards · athletic scholarships · ROTC scholarships.

VALPARAISO UNIVERSITY

Kretzmann Hall, 1700 Chapel Drive, Valparaiso, IN 46383
Admissions: 888-GO-VALPO · Financial Aid: 888-GO-VALPO
Email: undergrad.admissions@valpo.edu · Website: http://www.valpo.edu

From the College

"All American colleges and universities bear a family resemblance to one another as they come from a common set of ancestors in Europe and colonial America. Within that larger family, Valparaiso University is neither a large research university nor a small liberal arts college. At the same time that it promotes a basic liberal arts curriculum, it features strong undergraduate colleges of other areas. Broad enough in curriculum and in variety of programs to be a university, still Valparaiso University emphasizes undergraduate teaching in the manner of the traditional small college, with many small classes and strong individual guidance. While the university focuses on undergraduate education, it maintains a modest graduate program as well as a law school. Valparaiso University is also a founding member of the Associated New American Colleges, a national consortium of small to mid-sized colleges and universities that are committed to the ideal of integrating liberal and professional studies. Valparaiso University's status as an independent Lutheran University supplies the rationale for this special combination of liberal and professional studies. No church body has control or authority over the university, which is owned and operated by the Lutheran University Association. Valparaiso is therefore both free and responsible to realize an educational ideal informed by the best traditions of Lutheran Christianity and of liberal and professional studies."

Campus Setting

An independent university of 4,000 students, Valparaiso University belongs to a small group of institutions of higher education that is characterized by the integration of liberal arts and professional studies. Students pursue majors in more than 70 fields of study in five colleges—Arts and Sciences, Business Administration, Engineering, Nursing, and Christ College. Also part of the university are a Division of Graduate Studies and Continuing Education and the School of Law. Founded in 1859, Valparaiso University is located on 320 acres in northwest Indiana near the city of Chicago and the Indiana Dunes National Lakeshore on Lake Michigan. A four-year private institution, Valparaiso University has an enrollment of 3,975 students. The school is also affiliated with the Lutheran Church. In addition to a large, well-stocked library, the campus facilities include: art museum · center for the arts · chapel · audiovisual and language labs · virtual nursing learning center · Doppler radar facility · weather center · planetarium · observatory · scientific visualization lab · athletics recreation center. Valparaiso University provides on-campus housing with 983 units that can accommodate 1,972 students. Housing options: co-ed dorms · women's dorms · fraternity housing · single-student apartments. Recreation and sports facilities include: basketball · racquetball · handball and tennis courts · playing fields · track · swimming pool · weight room · fitness center · golf course · bowling alley.

Student Life and Activities

With 68 percent of students living on campus, there are plenty of social activities. Popular gathering spots include: Harre Student Union, Grinders Cyber Cafe, Athletics and Recreation Center and Maria Elena's Restaurant. Popular campus events include: Martin Luther King Jr. Day, Christ College Freshman Production, Homecoming Weekend, Siblings Weekend, JazzFest, Songfest, Battle of the Bands, International Dinners, Christ College Debates and Advent Vespers. Valparaiso University has 105

VALPARAISO UNIVERSITY

Valparaiso University
Valparaiso, IN (Pop. 30,000)
Location: Large town
Website: http://www.valpo.edu

Students
Total enrollment: 3,975
Undergrads: 1,372
Freshmen: 695
Part-time students: 5%
From out-of-state: 64%
Male/Female: 48%/52%
Live on-campus: 68%
In fraternities: 23%
In sororities: 19%
Off-campus employment rating: Good
Caucasian: 82%
African American: 5%
Hispanic: 4%
Asian or Pacific Islander: 2%
Native American: 0%
International: 3%

Academics
Student/faculty ratio: 12:1
Class size 9 or fewer: 14%
Class size 10-29: 66%
Class size 30-49: 16%
Class size 50-99: 4%
Class size 100 or more: -
Returning freshmen: 85%
Six-year graduation rate: 75%

Most Popular Fields of Study
Business, Finance, Sales and Marketing
Visual and Performing Arts
Social Sciences, History, Economics,
    Political Science
Computer and Information Sciences
Communications, Journalism, Advertising
    and Comm. Technologies
Philosophy, Religion and Theology
Liberal Arts, Humanities and General
    Studies
English and Literature
Parks, Recreation and Fitness

official student organizations. The most popular are: Acabellas · Biology Club · Chemistry Club · College Democrats · Crusader Pep Band · VU Ballroom · Earthtones · Engineers without Borders · GAMMA - BACCHUS · Air Force - ROTC · Geography Club · German Club · Green Peas · Habitat for Humanity · Honor Council · Interfraternity Council · French Club · Alliance · Music Enterprise Student Association · Northwest Indiana National Weather Association · Panhellenic Council. For those interested in sports, there are intramural teams such as: badminton · basketball, billiards · bowling · cheerleading · dodgeball · flag football · floor hockey · foosball · golf · kickball · racquetball · soccer · softball · swimming · table tennis · tennis · ultimate Frisbee · volleyball · water basketball · wiffle ball. Valparaiso University is a member of the Horizon League (Division I); Pioneer Football League (Division I, Football I-AA).

Academics and Learning Environment

For the B student, the learning environment of a college is just as important as the quality of its academic program. Valparaiso University has 257 full-time and 119 part-time faculty members, offering a student-to-faculty ratio of 12:1. The most common course size is 10 to 19 students. Valparaiso University offers 94 majors with the most popular being nursing, psychology and political science and least popular being American studies, middle level education and environmental science. The school has a general core requirement as well as a religion requirement Cooperative education is available. All first-year students must maintain a 2.0 GPA or higher to avoid academic probation. Other special academic programs that would appeal to a B student: self-designed majors · pass/fail grading option · independent study · double majors · dual degrees · accelerated study · honors program · Phi Beta Kappa · internships · distance learning certificate programs.

B Student Support and Success

Valpo's Academic Success Center has a wide selection of helpful programs including tutoring, help sessions, study group sessions, academic advisement, learning assistance, learning enrichment workshops, career planning, student support groups and disability support services. The Peer Tutoring Program helps students one on one. The tutors have completed the courses for which they provide tutoring and receive recommendations from their professors.

Valparaiso University provides a variety of support programs including dedicated guidance for: academic · career · personal · psychological · minority students · military · non-traditional students · religious. The average freshman year GPA is 3.0, and 85 percent of freshmen students return for their sophomore year.

Support for Students with Learning Disabilities

Students with learning disabilities may take advantage of specific support programs offered by Valparaiso University. According to the school, Students should submit documentation to the DSS office following admission into the university. Students with learning disabilities will find the following programs at Valparaiso University extremely useful: tutors · testing accommodations · extended time for tests · oral tests · readers · typist/scribe · note-taking services · tape recorders · priority registration · waiver of math degree requirement. Individual or small group tutorials are also available in: time management · organizational skills · writing labs · study skills. An advisor/advocate from the Valparaiso University Disability Support Services is available to students.

How to Get Admitted

For admissions decisions, non-academic factors considered: interview · extracurricular activities · special talents, interests, abilities · character/personal qualities · volunteer work · state of residency · religious affiliation/commitment · minority affiliation · alumni relationship. A high school diploma is required, although a GED is also accepted for admissions consideration. SAT or ACT test scores are required of all applicants. SAT Subject Test scores are not required. *Academic units recommended:* 4 English, 4 Math, 3 Science, 1 Social Studies, 2 Foreign Language.

How to Pay for College

To apply for financial aid, students should submit the following: Free Application for Federal Student Aid (FAFSA). Valparaiso University participates in the Federal Work Study program. *Need-based aid programs include:* scholarships and grants · general need-based awards · Federal Pell grants · state scholarships and grants · college-based scholarships and grants · private scholarships and grants. *Non-Need-based aid programs include:* scholarships and grants · state scholarships and grants · creative arts and performance awards · special achievements and activities awards · special characteristics awards · athletic scholarships · ROTC scholarships.

VALPARAISO UNIVERSITY

Highlights

Admissions
Applicants: 3,022
Accepted: 2,773
Acceptance rate: 91.8%
Average GPA: 3.3
ACT range: 22-28
SAT Math range: 500-630
SAT Reading range: 490-600
SAT Writing range: 480-590
Top 10% of class: 31%
Top 25% of class: 61%
Top 50% of class: 87%

Deadlines
Early Action: November 1
Early Decision: No
Regular Action: Rolling admissions
Common Application: Accepted

Financial Aid
In-state tuition: $27,360
Out-of-state tuition: $27,360
Room: $4,910
Board: $2,640
Books: $1,200
Freshmen receiving need-based aid: 76%
Undergrads receiving need-based aid: 71%
Avg. % of need met by financial aid: 82%
Avg. aid package (freshmen): $20,616
Avg. aid package (undergrads): $24,061
Freshmen receiving merit-based aid: 19%
Undergrads receiving merit-based aid: 23%
Avg. student debt upon graduation: $28,784

Prominent Alumni
Rebecca Pallmeyer, district judge, U.S. District Court, Chicago; Paul Sieving, director, National Eye Institute; Jay W. Christopher, chairman, Thatcher Corp.

School Spirit
Mascot: Crusaders
Colors: Brown and gold

VIRGINIA COMMONWEALTH UNIVERSITY

P.O. Box 842527, Richmond, VA 23284
Admissions: 800-841-3638 · Financial Aid: 804-828-6669
Email: ugrad@vcu.edu · Website: http://www.vcu.edu

From the College

"Virginia Commonwealth University is a research university located in Richmond, the state capital. VCU was founded in 1838 as the medical department of Hampden-Sydney College, becoming the Medical College of Virginia in 1854. In 1968, the General Assembly merged MCV with the Richmond Professional Institute, founded in 1917, to create Virginia Commonwealth University. Students pursue 208 degree and certificate programs through VCU's 15 schools and one college. The VCU Health System supports the university's health care education, research and patient care mission. With more than $220 million a year in sponsored research funding, VCU is designated as a research university with high research activity by the Carnegie Foundation. Eighteen university-approved centers and institutes of excellence involving faculty from multiple disciplines in public policy, biotechnology and health care discoveries support the university's research mission. Twenty-one graduate and first-professional programs are ranked by *US News & World Report* as among the best in the country."

Campus Setting

Virginia Commonwealth is a public, multipurpose university. Programs are offered through the Centers for Environmental Sciences and Public Policy; the College of Humanities and Sciences; and the Schools of Allied Health Professions, the Arts, Business, Dentistry, Education, Engineering, Mass Communications, Medicine, Nursing, Pharmacy and Social Work. Two campuses of 141 acres are both located in downtown Richmond. A four-year institution, Virginia Commonwealth University has an enrollment of 32,284 students. In addition to a large, well-stocked library, the campus facilities include: gallery · life sciences building. Virginia Commonwealth University provides on-campus housing with 8 units that can accommodate 4,976 students. Housing options: co-ed dorms · women's dorms · men's dorms · single-student apartments · special housing for disabled students · special housing for International students. Recreation and sports facilities include a sports medicine building.

Student Life and Activities

Students gather at Student Commons, Shafer Court Area and the library. Popular campus events include: Homecoming, Spring Fest, Welcome Week, Annual Fall Step Show, VCU Block Party, Intercultural Festival, Family Day, Greek Week, Black History Month, Spring Fest and Career Fair. Virginia Commonwealth University has 330 official student organizations. The most popular include: Americans for Informed Democracy · College Panhellenic Council · Interfraternity Council · MCV Campus Class of 2011 · Multicultural Greek Council · National Pan-Hellenic Council · College Republicans · International Students for Social Equality · Network of Spiritual Progressive · Young Democrats · AD Club. For those interested in sports, there are intramural teams such as: badminton · basketball · light weight football · martial arts · racquetball · soccer · softball · tennis · volleyball. Virginia Commonwealth University is a member of the Colonial Athletic Association (Division I).

Academics and Learning Environment

For the B student, the learning environment of a college is just as important as the quality of its academic program. Virginia Commonwealth University has 1,927 full-time and 1,161 part-time faculty members, offering a student-to-faculty ratio of 18:1. The most common course size is 20 to 29 students. Virginia Commonwealth University offers 146 majors with the most popular being visual and performing arts, business, management, marketing, and related support services and health professions and related clinical sciences. The school has a general core requirement. Cooperative education is available. All first-year students must maintain a 2.0 GPA or higher to avoid academic probation. Other special academic programs that would appeal to a B student: self-designed majors · independent study · double majors · accelerated study · honors program · internships · distance learning.

B Student Support and Success

VCU has a College Success Program that works to "provide assistance to students that will help them attain their academic potential." Along with academic counseling and tutoring, students who need additional development in some academic areas are involved in a mandatory year-long program during their freshman year. The school also offers UNIV 101, An Introduction to the University, which is a one-credit class that guides students to resources and services, plus promotes the development of intellectual, personal and social skills. It examines learning styles and study skills as well.

Virginia Commonwealth University provides a variety of support programs including dedicated guidance for: academic · career · personal · psychological · minority students · military · veterans · non-traditional students · family planning · religious. Additional counseling services include: non-traditional student. The average freshman year GPA is 2.6, and 85 percent of freshmen students return for their sophomore year.

Support for Students with Learning Disabilities

Students with learning disabilities may take advantage of specific support programs offered by Virginia Commonwealth University. If necessary, the college will grant additional time to students with learning disabilities to complete their degree. Students with learning disabilities will find the following programs at Virginia Commonwealth University extremely useful: tutors · testing accommodations · extended time for tests · take-home exam · oral tests · exam on tape or computer · readers · typist/scribe · note-taking services · reading machines · tape recorders · texts on tape · early syllabus · priority registration. Individual or small group tutorials are also available in: time management · organizational skills · learning strategies · specific subject areas · writing labs · math labs · study skills. An advisor/advocate from the Disability Support Services is available to students.

How to Get Admitted

For admissions decisions, non-academic factors considered: extracurricular activities · special talents, interests, abilities · volunteer work · work experience · state of residency. A high school diploma is required, although a GED is also accepted for admissions consideration. SAT or ACT test scores SAT Subject Test scores are not required. *Academic units recommended:* 4 English, 4 Math, 4 Science, 1 Social Studies, 3 Foreign Language.

VIRGINIA COMMONWEALTH UNIVERSITY

Highlights

Virginia Commonwealth University
Richmond, VA (Pop. 200,123)
Location: Medium city
Website: http://www.vcu.edu

Students
Total enrollment: 32,284
Undergrads: 9,608
Freshmen: 5,048
Part-time students: 19%
From out-of-state: 9%
Male/Female: 42%/58%
Live on-campus: Not reported
In fraternities: 5%
In sororities: 4%
Off-campus employment rating: Fair
Caucasian: 53%
African American: 20%
Hispanic: 4%
Asian or Pacific Islander: 11%
Native American: 1%
International: 3%

Academics
Student/faculty ratio: 18:1
Class size 9 or fewer: 11%
Class size 10-29: 60%
Class size 30-49: 16%
Class size 50-99: 6%
Class size 100 or more: 6%
Returning freshmen: 85%
Six-year graduation rate: 49%

Most Popular Fields of Study
Business, Finance, Sales and Marketing
Visual and Performing Arts
Social Sciences, History, Economics, Political Science
Protective Services, Criminal Justice and Public Administration
Computer and Information Sciences
Communications, Journalism, Advertising and Comm. Technologies
Philosophy, Religion and Theology
English and Literature
Parks, Recreation and Fitness
Health Professions, Medicine and Related Sciences

553

College Profiles

VIRGINIA COMMONWEALTH UNIVERSITY

Admissions
Applicants: 17,489
Accepted: 10,193
Acceptance rate: 58.3%
placed on wait list: 650
Average GPA: 3.4
ACT range: 19-25
SAT Math range: 480-590
SAT Reading range: 490-600
SAT Writing range: Not reported
Top 10% of class: 17%
Top 25% of class: 46%
Top 50% of class: 86%

Deadlines
Early Action: No
Early Decision: No
Regular Action: February 1st (priority)
Common Application: Accepted

Financial Aid
In-state tuition: $7,063
Out-of-state tuition: $20,695
Room: -
Board: -
Books: -
Freshmen receiving need-based aid: 44%
Undergrads receiving need-based aid:
   44%
Avg. % of need met by financial aid: 57%
Avg. aid package (freshmen): $7,872
Avg. aid package (undergrads): $8,133
Freshmen receiving merit-based aid: 4%
Undergrads receiving merit-based aid:
   2%

School Spirit
Mascot: Rams
Colors: Black and gold

How to Pay for College
To apply for financial aid, students should submit the following: Free Application for Federal Student Aid (FAFSA). Virginia Commonwealth University participates in the Federal Work Study program. *Need-based aid programs include:* scholarships and grants · general need-based awards · Federal Pell grants · state scholarships and grants · college-based scholarships and grants · private scholarships and grants · Federal Nursing scholarships. *Non-Need-based aid programs include:* scholarships and grants · state scholarships and grants · creative arts and performance awards · special achievements and activities awards · athletic scholarships.

VIRGINIA WESLEYAN COLLEGE

1584 Wesleyan Drive, Norfolk, VA 23502-5599
Admissions: 800-737-8684 · Financial Aid: 800-737-8684
Email: admissions@vwc.edu · Website: http://ww2.vwc.edu

From the College

"Virginia Wesleyan College is a small, private, liberal arts college located on the border of Norfolk and Virginia Beach. It focuses on creatively mixing core academic courses, extracurricular activities and opportunities to gain real-world experience through internships, fieldwork, study abroad and community service. Through the college's partnerships with businesses, government agencies and non-profit organizations, VWC's students explore various career paths, "shadow" professionals as they go about their work and take a hands-on approach to helping solve local community problems. VWC is affiliated with the United Methodist Church."

Campus Setting

Virginia Wesleyan, founded in 1961, is a private, liberal arts college. Its 300-acre campus is located in Norfolk/Virginia Beach, 10 miles from downtown areas and 15 miles from the ocean. A four-year institution, Virginia Wesleyan College has an enrollment of 1,381 students. The school is also affiliated with the Methodist Church. In addition to a large, well-stocked library, the campus has centers for the study of religious freedom and sacred music. Virginia Wesleyan College provides on-campus housing with 335 units that can accommodate 800 students. Housing options: co-ed dorms · women's dorms · sorority housing · fraternity housing · single-student apartments · special housing for disabled students · special housing for international students. Recreation and sports facilities include: baseball or softball complex · field hockey · lacrosse and soccer field.

Student Life and Activities

With 57 percent of students living on campus, there are plenty of social activities. Popular campus events include: Seafood Party in the Dell, Mud Games, Greek Week, village cookouts, poetry slams, Arts Alive, academic fair, Potato Drop, Celebration of Women's Voices, Native American fair, Marlin Spirit Pregame, Lake Taylor Music Festival, Lively in the Ivy Concert, Spring Fling, Homecoming, Airband, Intercultural Fashion Show, Comedy Club and Relay for Life. Virginia Wesleyan College has 65 official student organizations. The most popular are: French, German and Spanish clubs · drama club · anime club · Wesleyan Ambassadors · Wesleyan Traditional Music Society · Record Label DJs · Step Team · Electronic Music Society · Campus Kaleidoscope · Commuter Club · Fairy Godmothers · Gay Straight Alliance · Circle K · Habitat for Humanity · Youth Matters · Order of Infinity · IMAGINE · the Link · Honors and Scholars · Residence Hall Association · Wesleyan Activities Council · Greek Presidents · Relay for Life · Panhellenic Council · Interfraternal Council · SEAL · Beekeepers Association · College Republicans · Democracy Matters · Model UN · Young Democrats · Political Science Association · Society for the Advancement of Management · Recreation Majors Club · Psychology Club · Science Club. For those interested in sports, there are intramural teams such as: basketball · canoeing · flag football · mud games · running · soccer · swimming · volleyball. Virginia Wesleyan College is a member of the Old Dominion Athletic Conference (Division III).

Academics and Learning Environment

For the B student, the learning environment of a college is just as important as the quality of its academic program. Virginia Wesleyan College has 85 full-time and 64

VIRGINIA WESLEYAN COLLEGE

Virginia Wesleyan College
Norfolk, VA (Pop. 231,954)
Location: Major city
Website: http://www.vwc.edu

Students
Total enrollment: 1,381
Undergrads: 521
Freshmen: 329
Part-time students: 16%
From out-of-state: 28%
Male/Female: 38%/62%
Live on-campus: 57%
In fraternities: 10%
In sororities: 5%
Off-campus employment rating: Good
Caucasian: 71%
African American: 19%
Hispanic: 4%
Asian or Pacific Islander: 2%
Native American: 0%
International: 1%

Academics
Student/faculty ratio: 12:1
Class size 9 or fewer: 27%
Class size 10-29: 72%
Class size 30-49: 6%
Class size 50-99: 6%
Class size 100 or more: 6%
Returning freshmen: 65%
Six-year graduation rate: 44%

Most Popular Fields of Study
Business, Finance, Sales and Marketing
Biological and Life Sciences

part-time faculty members, offering a student-to-faculty ratio of 12:1. The most common course size is 10 to 19 students. Virginia Wesleyan College offers 39 majors with the most popular being liberal arts management/business, criminal justice and social sciences and least popular being computer science and mathematics. The school has a general core requirement. Cooperative education is not offered. All first-year students must maintain a 2.0 GPA or higher to avoid academic probation, and a minimum overall GPA of 2.5 is required to graduate. Other special academic programs that would appeal to a B student: self-designed majors · pass/fail grading option · independent study · double majors · dual degrees · accelerated study · honors program · internships · distance learning.

B Student Support and Success

The Learning Center at VWC offers tutoring and resource materials as well as study skills workshops. With a 13:1 student/teacher ratio, teachers are often willing to take the time to help students with one-on-one counseling and guidance. Career Services assists students with choosing a major and scheduling courses.

Virginia Wesleyan College provides a variety of support programs including dedicated guidance for: academic · career · personal · psychological · minority students · military · veterans · non-traditional students · family planning · religious. Recognizing that some students may need extra preparation, Virginia Wesleyan College offers remedial and refresher courses in: reading · writing · math · study skills. The average freshman year GPA is 2.6, and 65 percent of freshmen students return for their sophomore year. What do students do after college? While many enter the work force, approximately 19 percent pursue a graduate degree immediately after graduation. Among students who enter the work force, approximately 84 percent enter a field related to their major within six months of graduation. Companies that most frequently hire graduates from Virginia Wesleyan College include: American Funds Group · Chesapeake Public Schools · City of Virginia Beach · Landmark Communications · Norfolk Public Schools · Tidewater Community College · USAA · Virginia Beach Police · Virginia Beach Public Schools · Virginia Wesleyan College.

Support for Students with Learning Disabilities

Students with learning disabilities may take advantage of specific support programs offered by Virginia Wesleyan College. If necessary, the college will grant additional time to students with learning disabilities to complete their degree. Also, a lightened course load may be granted to LD students. According to the school, students file the same application and apply to the Learning Center program separately. The Learning Center Coordinator serves as a consultant to the Admissions Committee. Students with learning disabilities will find the following programs at Virginia Wesleyan College extremely useful: remedial math · remedial English · remedial reading · special classes · tutors · learning center · testing accommodations · untimed tests · extended time for tests · oral tests · readers · typist/scribe · note-taking services · tape recorders · priority registration · waiver of foreign language degree requirement. Individual or small group tutorials are also available in: time management · organizational skills · learning strategies · specific subject areas ·

writing labs · math labs · study skills. An advisor/advocate from the Learning Center is available to students.

How to Get Admitted

For admissions decisions, non-academic factors considered: interview · extracurricular activities · special talents, interests, abilities · character/personal qualities · volunteer work · work experience · state of residency · alumni relationship. A high school diploma is required, although a GED is also accepted for admissions consideration. SAT or ACT test scores are required of all applicants. SAT Subject Test scores are considered, if submitted, but are not required. *According to the admissions office:* Minimum combined SAT Reasoning score of 900 required with rank in top half of secondary school class, and minimum 2.5 GPA recommended; students submitting combined SAT Reasoning scores that are lower than 900 may be admitted provisionally. *Academic units recommended:* 4 English, 3 Math, 2 Science, 2 Foreign Language.

How to Pay for College

To apply for financial aid, students should submit the following: Free Application for Federal Student Aid (FAFSA) · state aid form. Virginia Wesleyan College participates in the Federal Work Study program. *Need-based aid programs include:* scholarships and grants · general need-based awards · Federal Pell grants · state scholarships and grants · college-based scholarships and grants · private scholarships and grants. *Non-Need-based aid programs include:* scholarships and grants · general need-based awards · state scholarships and grants · creative arts and performance awards · special characteristics awards · ROTC scholarships · religious affiliation scholarship · army ROTC scholarships · affiliation with Old Dominion U. scholarships.

VIRGINIA WESLEYAN COLLEGE

Highlights

Admissions
Applicants: 1,447
Accepted: 1,114
Acceptance rate: 77.0%
Average GPA: 3.1
ACT range: 18-26
SAT Math range: 450-550
SAT Reading range: 450-550
SAT Writing range: 445-540
Top 10% of class: 14%
Top 25% of class: 36%
Top 50% of class: 70%

Deadlines
Early Action: No
Early Decision: No
Regular Action: March 1 (priority)
Common Application: Accepted

Financial Aid
In-state tuition: $26,976
Out-of-state tuition: $26,976
Room: -
Board: -
Books: $1,000
Freshmen receiving need-based aid: 79%
Undergrads receiving need-based aid: 75%
Avg. % of need met by financial aid: 71%
Avg. aid package (freshmen): $18,953
Avg. aid package (undergrads): $16,935
Freshmen receiving merit-based aid: 20%
Undergrads receiving merit-based aid: 24%
Avg. student debt upon graduation: $18,365

School Spirit
Mascot: Marlin
Colors: Navy blue, silver, and white

WASHINGTON & JEFFERSON COLLEGE

60 South Lincoln Street, Washington, PA 15301
Admissions: 888-926-3529 · Financial Aid: 724-223-6019
Email: admission@washjeff.edu · Website: http://www.washjeff.edu

From the College

"Washington & Jefferson College has been ranked first in the country per capita for producing attorneys and third in the country for producing physicians and medical researchers. Routinely, 90 percent of our applicants to medical and law schools are admitted. More than 85 percent of seniors seeking employment find work in their fields or admission to graduate school before graduation. W&J offers students a personalized learning experience, with over 70 percent of classes having fewer than 20 students.

"Alumni around the world offer students networking opportunities in nearly every discipline. The result is student achievement of the highest caliber. Our students land research internships at the Pasteur Institute, Mayo Clinic, and Los Alamos Labs, to name a few. W&J challenges our students by sending them to national meetings where their research is presented alongside that of professional researchers, graduate students and faculty from other institutions.

"More than half of our students take advantage of 40+ study abroad programs in countries such as Australia, China, France, Germany, Spain, and South Africa. The Intersession term, a feature of our 4-1-4 academic calendar, allows students to take one course, intensively, during January. They may travel to London to study theatre, camp out in Africa to watch animals migrate or stay on campus to design robots or study with a prize-winning journalist.

"W&J was honored with the President's Honor Roll for Community Service with Distinction; students volunteer more than 15,000 hours a year in service to our community.

"W&J also has a strong tradition of producing student-athletes. The college fields 24 intercollegiate sports. W&J has graduated leaders in almost every field, from architecture to zoology."

Campus Setting

Washington & Jefferson is a private, liberal arts college. Tracing its origin to three schools established between 1781 and 1787, it had become a college for men by 1869 and became co-educational in 1970. Its 52-acre campus is located in Washington, 30 miles southwest of Pittsburgh. A four-year institution, Washington & Jefferson College has an enrollment of 1,519 students. In addition to a large, well-stocked library, campus facilities include: microplate reader · cell culture labs · isolator lab · X-ray diffraction unit · neuropsychology lab · atomic absorption unit · nuclear magnetic resonance (NMR) lab · refrigerated centrifuge · global learning unit · language lab · spectrometers · laser scanning confocal microscope facility · field station. Washington & Jefferson College provides on-campus housing with 893 units that can accommodate 1,437 students. Housing options: co-ed dorms · women's dorms · men's dorms · sorority housing · fraternity housing · single-student apartments · special housing for disabled students. Recreation and sports facilities include: natatorium · parks · stadiums · tennis courts · wellness center.

Student Life and Activities

With 95 percent of students living on campus, there are plenty of social activities. Popular gathering sports include: the Hub (Student Center), Swanson Wellness Center, Monticellos Coffee House, Burnett, Technology Center, ski lodge/Barista in the Commons, cultural areas of Pittsburgh, professional sports, local nightclubs and dining, Washington Park and Trinity Point. Popular events include: Spring Concert, Homecoming Weekend, International Week, Street Fair, Family Weekend, Greek Week, V Day Monologues and Holiday Light-up Night. Washington & Jefferson College has 70 official student organizations. Greek organizations, athletic teams, Student Activities Board, G.I.V.E., Asian Cultural Association and club sports are influential groups on campus. For those interested in sports, there are intramural teams such as: basketball · billiards · bowling · cross-country · dodge ball · flag football · foul shooting · kickball · pilates · racquetball · slow pitch softball · soccer · street hockey · table tennis · tennis · triathlon · ultimate Frisbee · volleyball · wallyball · water aerobics · yoga. Washington & Jefferson College is a member of the Presidents' Athletic Conference (Division III).

Academics and Learning Environment

For the B student, the learning environment of a college is just as important as the quality of its academic program. Washington & Jefferson College has 112 full-time and 37 part-time faculty members, offering a student-to-faculty ratio of 12:1. The most common course size is 10 to 19 students. Washington & Jefferson College offers 30 majors with the most popular being business administration, psychology and English and least popular being religion, theatre and biophysics. The school has a general core requirement. Cooperative education is not offered. All first-year students must maintain a 2.0 GPA or higher to avoid academic probation. Other special academic programs that would appeal to a B student: self-designed majors · pass/fail grading option · independent study · double majors · dual degrees · accelerated study · honors program · Phi Beta Kappa · internships.

B Student Support and Success

The Center for Learning and Teaching supports Washington and Jefferson students by providing peer-assisted learning in which study skills are taught by fellow students. In addition, assistance is also provided for areas such as memory and concentration, class participation, how to talk to your instructor, stress management and more. The Associate Director of the Center helps students assess their current academic skills by identifying strengths and weaknesses. Specific feedback is then given so that students know what areas to concentrate on within the Center.

Washington & Jefferson College provides a variety of support programs including dedicated guidance for: academic · career · personal · psychological · minority students · family planning · religious. The average freshman year GPA is 3.0, and 87 percent of freshmen students return for their sophomore year. What do students do after college? While many enter the work force, approximately 35 percent pursue a graduate degree immediately after graduation. Among students who enter the work force, approximately 62 percent enter a field related to their major within six months of graduation. Companies that most frequently hire graduates from Washington & Jefferson College include: AmeriCorps · CVS Pharmacy · Dick's Sporting Goods Corporate Headquarters · Enterprise Rent-A-Car · ESPN · MetLife · Washington & Jefferson College · Wesley

WASHINGTON & JEFFERSON COLLEGE

Highlights

Washington & Jefferson College
Washington, PA (Pop. 17,198)
Location: Large town
Website: http://www.washjeff.edu

Students
Total enrollment: 1,519
Undergrads: 823
Freshmen: 399
Part-time students: 1%
From out-of-state: 28%
Male/Female: 54%/46%
Live on-campus: 95%
In fraternities: 40%
In sororities: 44%
Off-campus employment rating: Good
Caucasian: 86%
African American: 3%
Hispanic: 1%
Asian or Pacific Islander: 1%
Native American: 0%
International: 0%

Academics
Student/faculty ratio: 12:1
Class size 9 or fewer: 24%
Class size 10-29: 73%
Class size 30-49: 3%
Class size 50-99: 6%
Class size 100 or more: 6%
Returning freshmen: 87%
Six-year graduation rate: 73%

Most Popular Fields of Study
Business, Finance, Sales and Marketing
Biological and Life Sciences

WASHINGTON & JEFFERSON COLLEGE

Admissions
Applicants: 6,826
Accepted: 2,611
Acceptance rate: 38.3%
placed on wait list: 139
Average GPA: 3.4
ACT range: 22-26
SAT Math range: 530-630
SAT Reading range: 510-610
SAT Writing range: Not reported
Top 10% of class: 39%
Top 25% of class: 74%
Top 50% of class: 97%

Deadlines
Early Action: January 15
Early Decision: December 1
Regular Action: Rolling admissions
Common Application: Accepted

Financial Aid
In-state tuition: $32,495
Out-of-state tuition: $32,495
Room: $5,256
Board: $3,669
Books: $800
Freshmen receiving need-based aid: 75%
Undergrads receiving need-based aid:
    73%
Avg. % of need met by financial aid: 77%
Avg. aid package (freshmen): $23,554
Avg. aid package (undergrads): $22,221
Freshmen receiving merit-based aid: 24%
Undergrads receiving merit-based aid:
    22%
Avg. student debt upon graduation:
    $20,000

Prominent Alumni
Roger Goodell, professional football
NFL commissioner; Luke Ravenstahl,
mayor, PIttsburgh; John Reed, former
CEO, Citibank, president, New York Stock
Exchange.

School Spirit
Mascot: Presidents
Colors: Red and black

Spectrum Services · West Shore School District · Westlake School District · Wyeth Pharmaceuticals.

Support for Students with Learning Disabilities

Students with learning disabilities may take advantage of specific support programs offered by Washington & Jefferson College. If necessary, the college will grant additional time to students with learning disabilities to complete their degree. High school foreign language waivers are accepted. Students with learning disabilities will find the following programs at Washington & Jefferson College extremely useful: tutors · learning center · testing accommodations · extended time for tests · take-home exam · oral tests · early syllabus · priority registration · priority seating. Individual or small group tutorials are also available in: time management · organizational skills · learning strategies · specific subject areas · writing labs · math labs · study skills. An advisor/advocate from the LD program is available to students.

How to Get Admitted

For admissions decisions, non-academic factors considered: interview · extracurricular activities · special talents, interests, abilities · character/personal qualities · volunteer work · geographical location · minority affiliation · alumni relationship. A high school diploma is required, although a GED is also accepted for admissions consideration. SAT or ACT test scores are considered, if submitted, but are not required. SAT Subject Test scores are considered, if submitted, but are not required. *Academic units recommended:* 6 English, 6 Math, 6 Foreign Language.

How to Pay for College

To apply for financial aid, students should submit the following: Free Application for Federal Student Aid (FAFSA). Washington & Jefferson College participates in the Federal Work Study program. *Need-based aid programs include:* scholarships and grants · general need-based awards · Federal Pell grants · state scholarships and grants · college-based scholarships and grants · private scholarships and grants · ACG · SMART Grants. *Non-Need-based aid programs include:* scholarships and grants · state scholarships and grants · special achievements and activities awards · special characteristics awards · Pittsburgh Promise.

WASHINGTON STATE UNIVERSITY

French Administration Building, Pullman, WA 99164
Admissions: 888-468-6978 · Financial Aid: 509-335-9711
Email: admiss2@wsu.edu · Website: http://www.wsu.edu

From the College

"Washington State conducts research that empowers students and improves people's lives. Motivated, high-achieving students work side by side with faculty, gaining insights and research experience. Across the university's 11 colleges, many academic programs rank among the nation's finest. Faculty researchers have earned international recognition in many fields, including the biological and physical sciences, engineering, mathematics, social sciences, humanities and the arts. Fortune 500 and other employers recruit the university's graduates."

Campus Setting

Washington State, founded in 1890, is a public, co-educational university. Its 620-acre campus is located in Pullman, 80 miles from Spokane. A four-year institution, Washington State University has an enrollment of 25,352 students. In addition to a large, well-stocked library, the campus facilities include: art · anthropology and natural history museums · special collections · theatres · concert halls · creamery · observatory · planetarium. Washington State University provides on-campus housing with 3,998 units that can accommodate 7,604 students. Housing options: co-ed dorms · women's dorms · men's dorms · sorority housing · fraternity housing · single-student apartments · married-student apartments · special housing for disabled students · special housing for international students. Recreation and sports facilities include: aquatic center · city playfields · golf course · gymnasium · mini golf course · recreation center · stadium · walking and hiking trails.

Student Life and Activities

Most students (64 percent) live off campus, which does impact the on-campus social scene. Nevertheless, like any college, students find time to create their own recreational outlets. Popular on-campus gathering spots include the Compton Union Building (CUB), Student Recreation Center, Ferdinand's Ice Cream Shoppe, Palouse Ridge Golf Club and WSU Art Museum. Popular off-campus locations include: Steptoe Butte State Park, Daily Grind Espresso, Palouse Discovery Science Center, Bill Chipman Palouse Trail, Little Fairways at Airway Hills, Moscow Farmer's Market and the Palouse Ice Rink in Moscow, Idaho.. Popular campus events include: Springfest, Cougfest and multiple Up All Night events throughout the year. Washington State University has 260 official student organizations. The most popular are: Cable 8 Productions · 2nd Amendment Gun Club · Turf Club · American Civil Liberties Union · American Medical Student Association · Arnold Air Society · Anime Club · Belly Dance Club · Block & Bridle · Art Sudent Union · College of Vet Med Canine Club · College of Vet Med Wellness Club · Badminton Club · CAHNRS Ambassadors · Draft Horse Club · Electronic Music Association · Capoeira. For those interested in sports, there are intramural teams such as: badminton · basketball · bowling · flag football · golf · lawn games · racquetball · soccer · softball · table tennis · tennis · volleyball · water polo · wiffle ball · Wii tournaments. Washington State University is a member of the Pacific-10 Conference (Division I, Football I-A).

Academics and Learning Environment

For the B student, the learning environment of a college is just as important as the quality of its academic program. Washington State University has 1,204 full-time and

WASHINGTON STATE UNIVERSITY

Washington State University
Pullman, WA (Pop. 27,000)
Location: Large town
Website: http://www.wsu.edu

Students
Total enrollment: 25,352
Undergrads: 10,152
Freshmen: 5,123
Part-time students: 15%
From out-of-state: 11%
Male/Female: 48%/52%
Live on-campus: 36%
In fraternities: 15%
In sororities: 20%
Off-campus employment rating: Good
Caucasian: 75%
African American: 2%
Hispanic: 5%
Asian or Pacific Islander: 6%
Native American: 1%
International: 3%

Academics
Student/faculty ratio: 14:1
Class size 9 or fewer: 17%
Class size 10-29: 47%
Class size 30-49: 18%
Class size 50-99: 12%
Class size 100 or more: 6%
Returning freshmen: 82%
Six-year graduation rate: 67%

Most Popular Fields of Study
Business, Finance, Sales and Marketing
Visual and Performing Arts
Social Sciences, History, Economics,
    Political Science
Protective Services, Criminal Justice and
    Public Administration
Family and Consumer Sciences, Nutrition
    and Home Economics
Computer and Information Sciences
Communications, Journalism, Advertising
    and Comm. Technologies
Liberal Arts, Humanities and General
    Studies
English and Literature
Health Professions, Medicine and Re-
    lated Sciences

562

458 part-time faculty members, offering a student-to-faculty ratio of 14:1. The most common course size is 10 to 19 students. Washington State University offers 224 majors with the most popular being business administration, nursing and social sciences and least popular being American studies, recreation administration/leisure studies and agribusiness economics and management. The school has a general core requirement. Cooperative education is not offered. All first-year students must maintain a 2.0 GPA or higher to avoid academic probation. Other special academic programs that would appeal to a B student: self-designed majors · independent study · double majors · dual degrees · accelerated study · honors program · Phi Beta Kappa · internships · distance learning certificate programs.

B Student Support and Success

WSU students go to the SALC, or Student Advising and Learning Center, for academic assistance. The staff at SALC provides advising, tutoring and other help. Academic Assistance offers services such as learning-strategies workshops, handouts, videos and a peer-tutorial program for one-on-one assistance in a wide range of subjects for an hourly fee. A two-credit elective class called the Freshman Seminar is designed to "help first-year students enhance critical thinking, research, writing and presentation skills as well as deal with transition issues faced when entering into the university." Students enrolled in this class develop a research project about the lessons learned in the course.

Washington State University provides a variety of support programs including dedicated guidance for: academic · career · personal · psychological · minority students · military · veterans · non-traditional students · family planning. The average freshman year GPA is 2.8, and 82 percent of freshmen students return for their sophomore year.

Support for Students with Learning Disabilities

Students with learning disabilities may take advantage of specific support programs offered by Washington State University. If necessary, the college will grant additional time to students with learning disabilities to complete their degree. Also, a lightened course load may be granted to LD students. Students with learning disabilities will find the following programs at Washington State University extremely useful: waiver of math degree requirement. Individual or small group tutorials are also available in: time management · organizational skills · learning strategies · specific subject areas · writing labs · math labs · study skills. An advisor/advocate from the Disability Resource Center is available to students.

How to Get Admitted

For admissions decisions, non-academic factors considered: extracurricular activities · special talents, interests, abilities · character/personal qualities · volunteer work · work experience · state of residency. A high school diploma is required, although a GED is also accepted for admissions consideration. SAT or ACT test scores are required of all applicants. *According to the admissions office:* Admission based on a combination of test scores, secondary school GPA, personal statement, core coursework and other factors. *Academic units recom-*

mended: 4 English, 4 Math, 2 Science, 3 Social Studies, 2 Foreign Language.

How to Pay for College

To apply for financial aid, students should submit the following: Free Application for Federal Student Aid (FAFSA). Washington State University participates in the Federal Work Study program. *Need-based aid programs include:* scholarships and grants · general need-based awards · Federal Pell grants · state scholarships and grants · college-based scholarships and grants · private scholarships and grants · Federal Nursing scholarships · United Negro College Fund. *Non-Need-based aid programs include:* scholarships and grants · general need-based awards · state scholarships and grants · creative arts and performance awards · special achievements and activities awards · special characteristics awards · athletic scholarships · ROTC scholarships.

WASHINGTON STATE UNIVERSITY

Highlights

Admissions
Applicants: 11,983
Accepted: 8,677
Acceptance rate: 72.4%
placed on wait list: 1,073
Average GPA: 3.5
ACT range: 21-26
SAT Math range: 510-610
SAT Reading range: 490-600
SAT Writing range: Not reported
Top 10% of class: 44%
Top 25% of class: 61%
Top 50% of class: 84%

Deadlines
Early Action: No
Early Decision: No
Regular Action: Rolling admissions
Common Application: Accepted

Financial Aid
In-state tuition: $7,600
Out-of-state tuition: $18,676
Room: $5,616
Board: $3,714
Books: $936
Freshmen receiving need-based aid: 42%
Undergrads receiving need-based aid: 47%
Avg. % of need met by financial aid: 87%
Avg. aid package (freshmen): $9,254
Avg. aid package (undergrads): $10,366
Freshmen receiving merit-based aid: 19%
Undergrads receiving merit-based aid: 7%
Avg. student debt upon graduation: $18,815

Prominent Alumni
Sherman Alexie, award-winning poet, author, screenwriter, director; Paul Allen, Microsoft cofounder; Neva Martin Abelson, research physician, pediatrician, co-developer of Rh blood test.

School Spirit
Mascot: Cougar
Colors: Crimson and gray
Song: *Cougar Fight Song*

563

WELLS COLLEGE

170 Main Street, Aurora, NY 13026
Admissions: 800-952-9355 · Financial Aid: 315-364-3289
Email: admissions@wells.edu · Website: http://www.wells.edu

From the College

"Wells College is a co-educational, private, liberal arts college located on a 365-acre lakeside campus situated in the heart of the Finger Lakes Region of New York State in the historical village of Aurora. The college prides itself on offering on a collaborative learning environment. The Wells experience is deeply personal and intensely focused on superior academic achievement. Wells offers 16 majors and more than 35 minors. With one professor for every eight students, professors get to know everyone. The average class size has 13 students and is taught seminar-style, with discussions taking precedence over lectures.

"Since 1868 we've been encouraging our students to step outside the classroom. Why? Because the best education combines traditional studies with real-world experiences. Last year, the Wells Office of Career Services coordinated internships in twenty states, the District of Columbia, France and Senegal. By graduation, 97 percent of seniors had completed at least one internship. Your education won't stop at the edge of campus. Recent internships include: the White House, ABC Television, Aquarium of the Pacific, Rock and Roll Hall of Fame and Museum, Smithsonian Institution and many more. Wells also offers a study abroad program with affiliated programs in 13 different countries. Our staff will help you pursue your academic interests wherever they lead you.

"We also work with affiliated institutions to make sure your learning opportunities are as rich and varied as possible. For example, if you find the perfect course at Cornell University or the London School of Economics, we'll do our best to get you there. There are many opportunities for you to develop your leadership skills through more than 40 different organizations. Wells students are intellectually curious, open-minded and creative."

Campus Setting

Wells, founded in 1868, is 40 miles southwest of Syracuse. A four-year institution, Wells College has an enrollment of 579 students. Wells College has been co-ed since 2005. In addition to a large, well-stocked library, the campus facilities include: photography · social science and arts labs · art gallery · book arts center. Wells College provides on-campus housing with 8 units that can accommodate 487 students. Housing options: co-ed dorms · women's dorms. Recreation and sports facilities include: cardio room · field hockey · fitness center · gymnasium · indoor and outdoor tennis courts · lacrosse · soccer and softball fields · swimming pool.

Student Life and Activities

With 88 percent of students living on campus, there are plenty of social activities. Popular gathering spots include the Sommer Center and the Fargo. Popular campus events include: Spring Weekend, Odd/Even Weekend and Convocation. Wells College has 48 official student organizations. The most popular are: American Red Cross Club · Amnesty International · Appointed · Bell Ringer · Campus Greens · Cardinal · Chamber Singers · Concert Choir · Chronicle · College Democrats · College Republicans · Dance Collective · Early Music Ensemble · history society · Japanese club · literary society · Model UN · orchestra · Programming Board · Queers and Allies · Student Diversity Committee · Symposium club · Whirligigs · Women in Lifelong Learning · outdoor club · Student-Athlete Advisory Committee. For those interested in sports, there are intramural teams such as: basketball · canoeing · cross-country skiing · fitness training · flag football · floor hockey · golf · indoor soccer · running · sailing · ultimate Frisbee · volleyball. Wells College is a member of the North Eastern Athletic Conference (Division III).

Academics and Learning Environment

For the B student, the learning environment of a college is just as important as the quality of its academic program. Wells College has 44 full-time and 44 part-time faculty members, offering a student-to-faculty ratio of 9:1. The most common course size is 10 to 19 students. Wells College offers 23 majors with the most popular being psychology, sociology/anthropology and English and least popular being religious studies, computer science and foreign languages. The school has a general core requirement. Cooperative education is not offered. All first-year students must maintain a 1.75 GPA or higher to avoid academic probation. Other special academic programs that would appeal to a B student: self-designed majors · pass/fail grading option · independent study · double majors · accelerated study · Phi Beta Kappa · internships.

B Student Support and Success

The First Year Experience (WLLS 101) is required for freshman enrolled at Wells. The course is designed to acquaint students with the four divisions of social sciences, humanities, sciences and fine arts and their connection to liberal arts. The class helps students to think, read and write critically, discuss complex issues, communicate effectively, use college resources precisely and learn as a group. It is taught in a combination of discussion and workshop.

Wells College provides a variety of support programs including dedicated guidance for: academic · career · personal · psychological · minority students · non-traditional students · family planning · religious. Annually, 72 percent of freshmen students return for their sophomore year. What do students do after college? While many enter the work force, approximately 25 percent pursue a graduate degree immediately after graduation.

Support for Students with Learning Disabilities

Students with learning disabilities may take advantage of specific support programs offered by Wells College. If necessary, the college will grant additional time to students with learning disabilities to complete their degree. Also, a lightened course load may be granted to LD students. Students with learning disabilities will find the following programs at Wells College extremely useful: tutors · extended time for tests · oral tests · note-taking services · tape recorders · waiver of math degree requirement. Individual or small group tutorials are also available in: writing labs · math labs. An advisor/advocate from the LD program is available to students.

How to Get Admitted

For admissions decisions, non-academic factors considered: interview · extracurricular activities · special talents, interests, abilities · character/personal qualities · volunteer work · work experience · state of residency · alumni relationship. A high school diploma is required, although a GED is also accepted for admissions consideration. SAT

WELLS COLLEGE

Highlights

Wells College
Aurora, NY (Pop. 736)
Location: Rural
Website: http://www.wells.edu

Students
Total enrollment: 579
Undergrads: 176
Freshmen: 155
Part-time students: 2%
From out-of-state: 36%
Male/Female: 30%/70%
Live on-campus: 88%
Off-campus employment rating: Fair
Caucasian: 69%
African American: 7%
Hispanic: 5%
Asian or Pacific Islander: 2%
Native American: 1%
International: 1%

Academics
Student/faculty ratio: 9:1
Class size 9 or fewer: 41%
Class size 10-29: 57%
Class size 30-49: 2%
Class size 50-99: 12%
Class size 100 or more: 6%
Returning freshmen: 72%
Six-year graduation rate: 52%

Most Popular Fields of Study
Biological and Life Sciences
Area, Ethnic and Gender Studies
Business, Finance, Sales and Marketing

WELLS COLLEGE

Admissions

Applicants: 1,117
Accepted: 713
Acceptance rate: 63.8%
Average GPA: 3.5
ACT range: 21-27
SAT Math range: 490-600
SAT Reading range: 500-620
SAT Writing range: 470-600
Top 10% of class: 35%
Top 25% of class: 67%
Top 50% of class: 89%

Deadlines

Early Action: December 15
Early Decision: December 15
Regular Action: December 15 (priority)
March 1 (final)
Common Application: Accepted

Financial Aid

In-state tuition: $28,180
Out-of-state tuition: $28,180
Room: $4,500
Board: $4,500
Books: $800
Freshmen receiving need-based aid: 73%
Undergrads receiving need-based aid:
   77%
Avg. % of need met by financial aid: 86%
Avg. aid package (freshmen): $18,810
Avg. aid package (undergrads): $19,260
Freshmen receiving merit-based aid: 21%
Undergrads receiving merit-based aid:
   15%
Avg. student debt upon graduation:
   $18,277

Prominent Alumni

Dr. Margaret Pericak-Vance, medical
geneticist; Lisa Marsh Ryerson, first
alumna president of Wells College; Pleasant Thiele Rowland, founder of Pleasant
Co./American Girl Doll

School Spirit

Mascot: Express
Colors: Red and white

or ACT test scores are required of all applicants. SAT Subject Test scores are considered, if submitted, but are not required. *According to the admissions office:* Standardized tests are considered on sliding scale depending on GPA and rigor of secondary school curriculum and preparation. *Academic units recommended:* 4 English, 4 Math, 3 Science, 2 Social Studies, 2 Foreign Language.

How to Pay for College

To apply for financial aid, students should submit the following: Free Application for Federal Student Aid (FAFSA). Wells College participates in the Federal Work Study program. *Need-based aid programs include:* scholarships and grants · general need-based awards · Federal Pell grants · state scholarships and grants · college-based scholarships and grants · private scholarships and grants. *Non-Need-based aid programs include:* scholarships and grants · state scholarships and grants.

WESLEYAN COLLEGE

4760 Forsyth Road, Macon, GA 31210-4462
Admissions: 800-447-6610 · Financial Aid: 888-665-5723
Email: admissions@wesleyancollege.edu
Website: http://www.wesleyancollege.edu

From the College

"Founded in 1836 as the first college in the world for women, Wesleyan College offers an education that leads to lifelong intellectual, personal and professional growth. Our academic community attracts those with a passion for learning and making a difference. The Wesleyan experience has four cornerstones: Academics, Women, Faith and Community. We believe that real education is a lifelong endeavor, fueled by curiosity, challenge and discovery. Wesleyan is committed to the goals of educating women to understand and appreciate the liberal and fine arts and preparing them for careers through high-quality professional programs."

Campus Setting

Wesleyan's 200-acre campus is located in Macon, 90 miles south of Atlanta. A four-year, private, liberal arts college, Wesleyan College has an enrollment of 739 students. The school is also affiliated with the United Methodist Church. In addition to a large, well-stocked library, the campus facilities include: art and history museums · equestrian center · specialized labs. Wesleyan College provides on-campus housing with 361 units that can accommodate 622 students. Housing options: women's dorms · single-student apartments. Recreation and sports facilities include: athletic complex · gymnasium.

Student Life and Activities

With 76 percent of students living on campus, there are plenty of social activities. As reported by a school representative, "One of Wesleyan's strongest traditions is our class system. No, it's definitely nothing like the one Marx critiqued. It's based on a strong class-year system going back to the early 1900s. Each class is identified by a color and a mascot. They even have their own songs and cheers. Another one of our most popular traditions would have to be the annual class theatrics of STUNT. Performed each year since 1897, classes write, direct, act, and produce their own skits to raise money for scholarships." Popular off-campus gathering spots include: Ingleside Village Pizza, Starbuck's, the Stack, Joshua Cup, and El Sombero. Homecoming, spring formal and STUNT are popular campus events. Wesleyan College has 44 official student organizations. Popular groups on campus include: Student Government Association, Campus Activities Board and Student Recreation Council. For those interested in sports, there are intramural teams such as: basketball · dodgeball · fencing · fitness challenge · floor hockey · soccer. Wesleyan College is a member of the Great South Athletic Conference (Division III).

Academics and Learning Environment

For the B student, the learning environment of a college is just as important as the quality of its academic program. Wesleyan College has 50 full-time and one part-time faculty members, offering a student-to-faculty ratio of 9:1. The most common course size is 2 to 9 students. Wesleyan College offers 38 majors with the most popular being business administration, psychology and biology and least popular being dual degree engineering, French and physics. The school has a general core requirement. Cooperative education is not offered. All first-year students must maintain a 2.0 GPA or higher to avoid academic probation, and a minimum overall GPA of 2.0 is required

WESLEYAN COLLEGE

Wesleyan College
Macon, GA (Pop. 154,709)
Location: Large town
Website: http://www.wesleyancollege.edu

Students
Total enrollment: 739
Undergrads: 14
Freshmen: 83
Part-time students: 38%
From out-of-state: 26%
Male/Female: 2%/98%
Live on-campus: 76%
Off-campus employment rating: Fair
Caucasian: 46%
African American: 33%
Hispanic: 2%
Asian or Pacific Islander: 3%
Native American: 0%
International: 14%

Academics
Student/faculty ratio: 9:1
Class size 9 or fewer: 49%
Class size 10-29: 50%
Class size 30-49: 2%
Class size 50-99: 12%
Class size 100 or more: 6%
Returning freshmen: 77%
Six-year graduation rate: 62%

Most Popular Fields of Study
Business, Finance, Sales and Marketing
Visual and Performing Arts
English and Literature
Philosophy, Religion and Theology
Mathematics
Interdisciplinary Studies
Foreign Languages, Literature and Linguistics
Communications, Journalism, Advertising and Comm. Technologies
Social Sciences, History, Economics, Political Science

to graduate. Other special academic programs that would appeal to a B student: self-designed majors · pass/fail grading option · independent study · double majors · dual degrees · accelerated study · honors program · internships · weekend college.

B Student Support and Success

Student-to-faculty ratio is 11:1, and class sizes are 19 and under. The school offers an Academic Center that provides free tutoring and counseling for students who may be struggling in their classes. Group and individual sessions are available year round, either by appointment or as on a drop-in basis. In addition, Wesleyan has a Writing Center for students who need assistance with any kind of writing project. The Computer Science Lab and Help Desk is also available and is staffed by peer tutors. It offers a quiet place to study, work on projects or conduct study groups. The director of the Academic Center also offers confidential counseling for academic issues with individual students.

Wesleyan College provides a variety of support programs including dedicated guidance for: academic · career · personal · psychological · family planning · religious. Recognizing that some students may need extra preparation, Wesleyan College offers remedial and refresher courses in: reading · writing · math · study skills. The average freshman year GPA is 3.2, and 77 percent of freshmen students return for their sophomore year. What do students do after college? While many enter the work force, approximately 32 percent pursue a graduate degree immediately after graduation. Among students who enter the work force, approximately 28 percent enter a field related to their major within six months of graduation.

Support for Students with Learning Disabilities

Students with learning disabilities may take advantage of specific support programs offered by Wesleyan College. If necessary, the college will grant additional time to students with learning disabilities to complete their degree. Also, a lightened course load may be granted to LD students. Students with learning disabilities will find the following programs at Wesleyan College extremely useful: tutors · learning center · testing accommodations · extended time for tests · oral tests · readers · note-taking services · priority registration · waiver of foreign language degree requirement. Individual or small group tutorials are also available in: time management · organizational skills · learning strategies · specific subject areas · writing labs · math labs · study skills. An advisor/advocate from the Academic Center is available to students.

How to Get Admitted

For admissions decisions, non-academic factors considered: extracurricular activities · special talents, interests, abilities · character/personal qualities · volunteer work · work experience · state of residency · alumni relationship. A high school diploma is required, although a GED is also accepted for admissions consideration. SAT or ACT test scores are required of all applicants. SAT Subject Test scores are considered, if submitted, but are not required. *Academic units recommended:* 4 English, 4 Math, 4 Science, 4 Social Studies, 4 Foreign Language.

How to Pay for College

To apply for financial aid, students should submit the following: Free Application for Federal Student Aid (FAFSA) · institution's own financial aid forms · state aid form · Non-custodian (Divorced/Separated) Parent's Statement. Wesleyan College participates in the Federal Work Study program. *Need-based aid programs include:* scholarships and grants · general need-based awards · Federal Pell grants · state scholarships and grants · college-based scholarships and grants · private scholarships and grants · HOPE Scholarship · Georgia Tuition Equalization Grant Georgia LEAP Grant. *Non-Need-based aid programs include:* scholarships and grants · general need-based awards · state scholarships and grants · creative arts and performance awards · special achievements and activities awards · special characteristics awards · United Methodist Church-related scholarships.

WESLEYAN COLLEGE

Highlights

Admissions
Applicants: 536
Accepted: 286
Acceptance rate: 53.4%
Average GPA: 3.5
ACT range: 28-21
SAT Math range: 460-600
SAT Reading range: 500-610
SAT Writing range: Not reported
Top 10% of class: 32%
Top 25% of class: 55%
Top 50% of class: 87%

Deadlines
Early Action: No
Early Decision: November 15
Regular Action: May 1 (priority)
August 1 (final)
Common Application: Accepted

Financial Aid
In-state tuition: $17,500
Out-of-state tuition: $17,500
Room: -
Board: -
Books: $1,000
Freshmen receiving need-based aid: 65%
Undergrads receiving need-based aid: 58%
Avg. % of need met by financial aid: 83%
Avg. aid package (freshmen): $14,559
Avg. aid package (undergrads): $15,038
Freshmen receiving merit-based aid: 29%
Undergrads receiving merit-based aid: 34%
Avg. student debt upon graduation: $20,896

School Spirit
Mascot: Pioneers
Colors: Purple and white
Song: *Hail Wesleyan*

569

WEST VIRGINIA UNIVERSITY

P.O. Box 6201, Morgantown, WV 26506-6201
Admissions: 800-344-9881 · Financial Aid: 800-344-WVU1
Email: go2wvu@mail.wvu.edu · Website: http://www.wvu.edu

From the College

"West Virginia University has produced 25 Rhodes Scholars, 32 Goldwater Scholars, 20 Truman Scholars and five members of USA Today's All-USA College Academic First team. Whether your goal is to be an aerospace engineer, reporter, physicist, athletic trainer, forensic investigator, pharmacist or CEO, WVU's 185 degree choices can make it happen. Student-centered initiatives extend learning beyond the classroom. Resident faculty leaders live next to the residence halls to mentor students, and WVUp All Night provides free food and activities on weekends. The Mountaineer Parents Club connects 18,500 WVU families, and a helpline leads to a parent advocate. The Student Recreation Center includes athletic courts, pools, weight/fitness equipment and a 50-foot indoor climbing wall. Students come from every 50 states and Washington, DC, and 99 countries. As a major research institution, WVU attracts more than $125 million in annual grant funding. The campus is one of the safest in the nation, and the area's natural beauty provides chances to ski, bike and hike."

Campus Setting

West Virginia University, founded in 1867, is a public, comprehensive institution. Programs are offered through the Colleges of Agriculture, Forestry, and Consumer Sciences, Arts and Sciences, Business and Economics, Creative Arts, Engineering and Mineral Resources, Law and Human Resources and Education and the Schools of Dentistry, Journalism, Medicine, Nursing, Pharmacy and Physical Education. The two campuses, totaling 1,456 acres, are located in Morgantown and Evansdale, 75 miles south of Pittsburgh. A four-year institution, West Virginia University has an enrollment of 28,840 students. West Virginia University has been co-ed since 1889. In addition to a large, well-stocked library, the campus facilities include: museums · arboretum · herbarium · planetarium · experimental farms · natatorium · coliseum · stadium · software development · fluidization · black culture and research · cancer research · recreation and creative arts centers. West Virginia University provides on-campus housing with 17 units that can accommodate 5,351 students. Housing options: co-ed dorms · women's dorms · men's dorms · sorority housing · fraternity housing · single-student apartments · married-student apartments · special housing for disabled students · special housing for international students. Recreation and sports facilities include: coliseum · football stadium · halls · intramural fields · natatorium · recreational center · swimming pool · track.

Student Life and Activities

Most students (74 percent) live off campus, which does impact the on-campus social scene. Nevertheless, like any college, students find time to create their own recreational outlets. "Morgantown is a small city with cosmopolitan appeal," reports the student newspaper. "Major musical acts from the Ramones to Alan Jackson have played here recently, while artists and actors are showcased in WVU's Creative Arts Center. Even with easy access to Washington, DC, and Pittsburgh, Morgantown is minutes away from recreational lakes, parks, and wilderness." Popular student gathering spots include: Side Pocket Pub, Maximillian's, the Blue Moose Coffee Shop, Student Union and Mario's Back Door. Popular campus events include: Festival of Ideas, basketball games, FallFest, outdoor recreation trips, concerts by touring musical artists, football, Mountaineer Week and performing arts events at Creative Arts Center. West Virginia

University has 360 official student organizations. Popular groups on campus include: the student newspaper and campus radio station. West Virginia University is a member of the Big East Conference (Division I, Football I-A), Eastern Wrestling League (Division I).

Academics and Learning Environment

For the B student, the learning environment of a college is just as important as the quality of its academic program. West Virginia University has 876 full-time and 312 part-time faculty members, offering a student-to-faculty ratio of 23:1. The most common course size is 2 to 9 students. West Virginia University offers 253 majors with the most popular being nursing, exercise physiology and psychology. The school has a general core requirement. Cooperative education is available. All first-year students must maintain a 2.0 GPA or higher to avoid academic probation, and a minimum overall GPA of 2.0 is required to graduate. Other special academic programs that would appeal to a B student: self-designed majors · pass/fail grading option · independent study · double majors · accelerated study · honors program · Phi Beta Kappa · internships · weekend college · distance learning certificate programs.

B Student Support and Success

With almost 4,000 freshmen entering WVU each year, the school has designed a large program that provides students academic support. University 101 is a class geared to help freshmen adjust to university life and its demands. A passing grade in this course is required for graduation. In the fall semester, students also may take the SSS Orientation Course, which is designed to introduce them to academic requirements and acquaint them with how student support services can help. In assigning residence halls, the college places freshmen with similar majors and/or passions in the same dorm, enabling them to form peer study groups and meet others with the same interests. Other support systems include a math lab at the Learning Center and the availability of writing assistance through sessions geared to help with everything from letters to research papers. Free tutoring is available for most general classes in either one-on-one or study group sessions. Students who are still not sure about their major can get assistance through the Student Support Services professional staff of advisors.

West Virginia University provides a variety of support programs including dedicated guidance for: academic · career · personal · psychological · minority students · military · veterans · non-traditional students · family planning · religious. Recognizing that some students may need extra preparation, West Virginia University offers remedial and refresher courses in: reading · writing · math · study skills. The average freshman year GPA is 2.5, and 81 percent of freshmen students return for their sophomore year. Among students who enter the work force, approximately 55 percent enter a field related to their major within six months of graduation. Companies that most frequently hire graduates from West Virginia University include: Alpern · Rosenthal · Dixon Hughes · Arnett & Foster · American Income Life · Bank of New York · Beers and Cutler · Deloitte & Touche · Deloitte Consulting · Department of the Treasury · Dow Chemical · Ernst & Young · FedEx Ground · Geico · Grant Thornton · Halliburton · Insight Global · KPMG ·

WEST VIRGINIA UNIVERSITY

Highlights

West Virginia University
Morgantown, WV (Pop. 60,000)
Location: Large town
Website: http://www.wvu.edu

Students
Total enrollment: 28,840
Undergrads: 12,064
Freshmen: 6,479
Part-time students: 6%
From out-of-state: 53%
Male/Female: 55%/45%
Live on-campus: 26%
In fraternities: 12%
In sororities: 13%
Off-campus employment rating: Fair
Caucasian: 89%
African American: 3%
Hispanic: 2%
Asian or Pacific Islander: 2%
Native American: 0%
International: 2%

Academics
Student/faculty ratio: 23:1
Class size 9 or fewer: 27%
Class size 10-29: 42%
Class size 30-49: 15%
Class size 50-99: 10%
Class size 100 or more: 6%
Returning freshmen: 81%
Six-year graduation rate: 56%

Most Popular Fields of Study
Business, Finance, Sales and Marketing
Visual and Performing Arts
Social Sciences, History, Economics, Political Science
Protective Services, Criminal Justice and Public Administration
Family and Consumer Sciences, Nutrition and Home Economics
Computer and Information Sciences
Communications, Journalism, Advertising and Comm. Technologies
Liberal Arts, Humanities and General Studies

571

WEST VIRGINIA UNIVERSITY

Admissions

Applicants: 15,094
Accepted: 13,232
Acceptance rate: 87.7%
Average GPA: 3.3
ACT range: 20-26
SAT Math range: 480-580
SAT Reading range: 470-560
SAT Writing range: Not reported
Top 10% of class: 19%
Top 25% of class: 44%
Top 50% of class: 63%

Deadlines

Early Action: No
Early Decision: No
Regular Action: Rolling admissions
Common Application: Accepted

Financial Aid

In-state tuition: $5,100
Out-of-state tuition: $15,770
Room: -
Board: -
Books: $1,160
Freshmen receiving need-based aid: 41%
Undergrads receiving need-based aid: 43%
Avg. % of need met by financial aid: 75%
Avg. aid package (freshmen): $6,466
Avg. aid package (undergrads): $6,938
Freshmen receiving merit-based aid: 24%
Undergrads receiving merit-based aid: 15%

Prominent Alumni

Charles M. Vest, former president, MIT; Jerry West, president of basketball operation, Memphis Grizzlies; Don Knotts, actor.

School Spirit

Mascot: Mountaineer
Colors: Old gold and blue
Song: *Hail West Virginia*

Lockheed Martin · Microsoft · Milliken & Co. · NAVAIR · NASA · Northrop Grumman · Northwestern Mutual Financial Network · Pepsi Bottling Group · PPG · PricewaterhouseCoopers · Raytheon Co. · Schlumberger · Siemens Energy · Sherwin Williams · Target · United Bank · Westinghouse · Yount · Hyde & Barbour..

Support for Students with Learning Disabilities

Students with learning disabilities may take advantage of specific support programs offered by West Virginia University. If necessary, the college will grant additional time to students with learning disabilities to complete their degree. Also, a lightened course load may be granted to LD students. According to the school, the Mountaineer Academic Program (MAP) is an academic enhancement program that provides student-centered supplemental academic support services for students with disabilities. MAP coaches provide consistency through regular contact and individualized support, accountability through weekly meetings, guidance to improve study skills, time management, and organizational skills, and referrals and regular contact with various academic and personal support services. MAP tutors provide individual content tutoring and support. Students with learning disabilities will find the following programs at West Virginia University extremely useful: remedial math · tutors · learning center · testing accommodations · untimed tests · extended time for tests · take-home exam · oral tests · exam on tape or computer · readers · typist/scribe · note-taking services · reading machines · tape recorders · texts on tape · early syllabus · diagnostic testing service · priority registration · priority seating. Individual or small group tutorials are also available in: time management · organizational skills · learning strategies · specific subject areas · writing labs · math labs · study skills. An advisor/advocate from the Mountaineer Academic Program is available to students.

How to Get Admitted

For admissions decisions, non-academic factors considered: extracurricular activities · special talents, interests, abilities · volunteer work. A high school diploma is required, although a GED is also accepted for admissions consideration. SAT or ACT test scores are required of all applicants. SAT Subject Test scores are required from all applicants. *According to the admissions office:* English units should include composition, grammar and literature. Math units should include algebra I, algebra II and geometry. Electives in computer science, fine arts and humanities recommended. Minimum combined SAT Reasoning score of 910 (composite ACT score of 19) and minimum 2.0 GPA required of in-state applicants. Minimum combined SAT Reasoning score of 990 (composite ACT score of 21) and minimum 2.25 GPA required of out-of-state applicants. Higher requirements for some programs.

How to Pay for College

To apply for financial aid, students should submit the following: Free Application for Federal Student Aid (FAFSA) · state aid form. West Virginia University participates in the Federal Work Study program. *Need-based aid programs include:* scholarships and grants · general need-based awards · Federal Pell grants · state scholarships and grants · college-based scholarships and grants · private scholarships and grants. *Non-Need-based aid programs include:* scholarships and grants • general need-based awards • state scholarships and grants • creative arts and performance awards • special achievements and activities awards • special characteristics awards • athletic scholarships • ROTC scholarships.

WESTERN CONNECTICUT STATE UNIVERSITY

181 White Street, Danbury, CT 06810
Admissions: 877-837-9278 · Financial Aid: 203-837-8580
Email: admissions@wcsu.edu · Website: http://www.wcsu.edu

From the College

"According to New England Association of Schools and Colleges Inc., Commission on Institutions of Higher Education, Western Connecticut State University is effectively accomplishing its mission as an urban, public, comprehensive university and seems well positioned to meet future challenges."

Campus Setting

Western Connecticut State University, founded in 1903, has two campuses: the original, 34-acre campus located in downtown Danbury and a newer 364-acre campus west of the city's center. A four-year institution, Western Connecticut State University has an enrollment of 6,462 students. Western Connecticut State University has been co-ed since 1933. The school also has a library with 215,096 books. Western Connecticut State University provides on-campus housing with 845 units that can accommodate 1,679 students. Housing options: co-ed dorms · single-student apartments. Recreation and sports facilities include: athletic complex · baseball and softball fields · gymnasium · tennis courts.

Student Life and Activities

Most students (72 percent) live off campus, which does impact the on-campus social scene. Nevertheless, like any college, students find time to create their own recreational outlets. Popular campus events include: the President's Lecture Series, Bauhaus Art Club spoken word events, English Society readings, Black Student Alliance summits and formals, German Studies Center talks, percussion ensemble performances, Concert Choir and Chamber Singers performances, Continuing Research Seminar series, art department bus trips to New York City museums and Department of Social Science's the Social Hour. Western Connecticut State University has 89 official student organizations. Popular groups on campus include: fraternities and sororities, Catholic Campus Ministry, Jewish Student Association, Newman Club and WestConn Christian Ministry. For those interested in sports, there are intramural teams such as: basketball · football · soccer · softball. Western Connecticut State University is a member of the Freedom Football Conference (Division III), Little East Conference (Division III), New England Women's Lacrosse Alliance (Division III), New Jersey Athletic Conference (Division III).

Academics and Learning Environment

For the B student, the learning environment of a college is just as important as the quality of its academic program. Western Connecticut State University has 221 full-time and 316 part-time faculty members, offering a student-to-faculty ratio of 16:1. The most common course size is 20 to 29 students. Western Connecticut State University offers 52 majors with the most popular being justice/law administration, management and psychology and least popular being American studies/history, business administration/management and medical technology. The school has a general core requirement. Cooperative education is available. All first-year students must maintain a 2.0 GPA or higher to avoid academic probation. Other special academic programs that would appeal to a B student: self-designed majors · pass/fail grading option · independent study · double majors · dual degrees · honors program · internships · distance learning.

B Student Support and Success

Western Connecticut offers a Study Skills/Reading Lab to help students with skills such as reading, outlining, note taking, studying, time management, test taking, researching and word processing. The Math Clinic helps with everything from math skills to math anxiety. Tutors help student study for tests and solve homework problems. The Writing Lab provides assistance on writing, grammar, development, style, organization and mechanics.

Western Connecticut State University provides a variety of support programs including dedicated guidance for: academic · career · personal · psychological · minority students · veterans · non-traditional students · family planning · religious. Additional counseling services include: Myers-Briggs Type Indicator (MBTI), Strong Interest Inventory. Recognizing that some students may need extra preparation, Western Connecticut State University offers remedial and refresher courses in: reading · writing · math · study skills. Other remedial services include Educational Achievement and Access Program. The average freshman year GPA is 2.5, and 74 percent of freshmen students return for their sophomore year. What do students do after college? While many enter the work force, approximately 2 percent pursue a graduate degree immediately after graduation.

Support for Students with Learning Disabilities

Students with learning disabilities may take advantage of specific support programs offered by Western Connecticut State University. If necessary, the college will grant additional time to students with learning disabilities to complete their degree. Also, a lightened course load may be granted to LD students. Students with learning disabilities will find the following programs at Western Connecticut State University extremely useful: remedial math · remedial English · tutors · learning center · testing accommodations · untimed tests · extended time for tests · take-home exam · oral tests · exam on tape or computer · typist/scribe · note-taking services · reading machines · tape recorders · early syllabus · priority registration. Individual or small group tutorials are also available in: time management · organizational skills · learning strategies · specific subject areas · writing labs · math labs · study skills. An advisor/advocate from the Disability Services is available to students.

How to Get Admitted

For admissions decisions, non-academic factors considered: interview · extracurricular activities · special talents, interests, abilities · character/personal qualities · volunteer work · work experience · minority affiliation · alumni relationship. A high school diploma is required, although a GED is also accepted for admissions consideration. SAT or ACT test scores are required of all applicants. SAT Subject Test scores are recommended but not required. *According to the admissions office:* Minimum combined SAT Reasoning score of 1000, rank in top half of secondary school class, and minimum 2.67 GPA recommended. *Academic units recommended:* 3 Foreign Language.

WESTERN CONNECTICUT STATE UNIVERSITY

Highlights

Western Connecticut State University
Danbury, CT (Pop. 78,765)
Location: Medium city
Website: http://www.wcsu.edu

Students
Total enrollment: 6,462
Undergrads: 2,658
Freshmen: 1,894
Part-time students: 20%
From out-of-state: 10%
Male/Female: 46%/54%
Live on-campus: 28%
In fraternities: 3%
In sororities: 2%
Off-campus employment rating: Excellent
Caucasian: 76%
African American: 7%
Hispanic: 8%
Asian or Pacific Islander: 3%
Native American: 0%
International: 0%

Academics
Student/faculty ratio: 16:1
Class size 9 or fewer: 7%
Class size 10-29: 62%
Class size 30-49: 30%
Class size 50-99: -
Class size 100 or more: -
Returning freshmen: 74%
Six-year graduation rate: 40%

Most Popular Fields of Study
Business, Finance, Sales and Marketing
Protective Services, Criminal Justice and Public Administration
Visual and Performing Arts
English and Literature
Computer and Information Sciences
Mathematics
Physical Sciences, Chemistry, Physics and Astronomy
Health Professions, Medicine and Related Sciences
Liberal Arts, Humanities and General Studies
Foreign Languages, Literature and Linguistics

575

WESTERN CONNECTICUT STATE UNIVERSITY

Admissions
Applicants: 4,221
Accepted: 2,315
Acceptance rate: 54.8%
Average GPA: 2.8
ACT range: Not reported
SAT Math range: 440-550
SAT Reading range: 440-540
SAT Writing range: 440-530
Top 10% of class: 6%
Top 25% of class: 19%
Top 50% of class: 57%

Deadlines
Early Action: No
Early Decision: No
Regular Action: Rolling admissions
Common Application: Accepted

Financial Aid
In-state tuition: $3,514
Out-of-state tuition: $11,373
Room: $5,384
Board: $3,774
Books: $1,200
Freshmen receiving need-based aid: 54%
Undergrads receiving need-based aid: 49%
Avg. % of need met by financial aid: 76%
Avg. aid package (freshmen): $10,628
Avg. aid package (undergrads): $10,946
Freshmen receiving merit-based aid: 2%
Undergrads receiving merit-based aid: 1%
Avg. student debt upon graduation: $23,970

School Spirit
Mascot: Colonials
Colors: Dark blue, metallic copper and white

How to Pay for College

To apply for financial aid, students should submit the following: Free Application for Federal Student Aid (FAFSA) · institution's own financial aid forms. Western Connecticut State University participates in the Federal Work Study program. *Need-based aid programs include:* scholarships and grants · general need-based awards · Federal Pell grants · state scholarships and grants · college-based scholarships and grants · private scholarships and grants. *Non-Need-based aid programs include:* scholarships and grants · state scholarships and grants · private scholarships.

WESTERN NEW ENGLAND COLLEGE

1215 Wilbraham Road, Springfield, MA 01119-2684
Admissions: 800-325-1122, extension 1321
Financial Aid: 800-325-1122, extension 2080
Email: ugradmis@wnec.edu · Website: http://www.wnec.edu

From the College

"Western New England College is committed to being a leader regionally and recognized nationally in providing integrated professional and liberal learning. The college is characterized by a synergy that results internally from the collaboration of its programs in arts and sciences, business, engineering, pre-pharmacy and law and externally from the strategic partnerships and alliances forged with the local and regional business, educational, and civic community."

Campus Setting

Western New England, founded in 1919, is a private, comprehensive, co-educational institution. Its 215-acre campus is located in a residential section of Springfield, 90 miles west of Boston. A four-year institution, Western New England College has an enrollment of 3,722 students. The school also has a library with 131,500 books. Western New England College provides on-campus housing that can accommodate 2,110 students. Housing options: co-ed dorms · single-student apartments · special housing for disabled students. Recreation and sports facilities include: athletic center · field · park · stadium.

Student Life and Activities

With 79 percent of students living on campus, there are plenty of social activities. Some of the most popular social events are: Parent's Weekend, First Week and Senior Week. Western New England College has 60 official student organizations. The Student Senate and the Council of Peer Advisors are two of the influential groups on campus. For those interested in sports, there are intramural teams such as: badminton · basketball · bocce · flag football · floor hockey · horseshoes · indoor soccer · inner-tube water polo · kickball · rock climbing · softball · table tennis · ultimate Frisbee · volleyball. Western New England College is a member of the ECAC Hockey (Division III), New England College Wrestling Association (Division III), New England Football Conference (Division III), Commonwealth Coast Conference (Division III).

Academics and Learning Environment

For the B student, the learning environment of a college is just as important as the quality of its academic program. Western New England College has 180 full-time and 125 part-time faculty members, offering a student-to-faculty ratio of 15:1. The most common course size is 20 to 29 students. Western New England College offers 61 majors with the most popular being engineering, psychology and business/marketing. The school has a general core requirement. Cooperative education is not offered. All first-year students must maintain a 1.9 GPA or higher to avoid academic probation. Other special academic programs that would appeal to a B student: self-designed majors · independent study · double majors · accelerated study · honors program · internships · distance learning certificate programs.

B Student Support and Success

Information from Western New England College explains aspects of the school that are of interest to the B student: "Math and science tutoring centers, academic advisors, peer advisors, small classes (average 21-22); all professors are required to

WESTERN NEW ENGLAND COLLEGE

Western New England College
Springfield, MA (Pop. 152,082)
Location: Medium city
Website: http://www.wnec.edu

Students
Total enrollment: 3,722
Undergrads: 1,692
Freshmen: 736
Part-time students: 11%
From out-of-state: 62%
Male/Female: 61%/39%
Live on-campus: 79%
Off-campus employment rating: Fair
Caucasian: 87%
African American: 3%
Hispanic: 3%
Asian or Pacific Islander: 2%
Native American: 0%
International: 0%

Academics
Student/faculty ratio: 15:1
Class size 9 or fewer: 14%
Class size 10-29: 76%
Class size 30-49: 9%
Class size 50-99: -
Class size 100 or more: -
Returning freshmen: 75%
Six-year graduation rate: 57%

Most Popular Fields of Study
Business, Finance, Sales and Marketing
Protective Services, Criminal Justice and
    Public Administration
Psychology
English and Literature
Philosophy, Religion and Theology
Computer and Information Sciences
Mathematics
Engineering and Engineering Technolo-
    gies
Law and Legal Studies
Liberal Arts, Humanities and General
    Studies

hold office hours. First year seminar course for freshmen students." Advice for prospective students includes these remarks: "Students should challenge themselves academically, show consistency in their grades and get involved in their school and community. When the Admission Office reviews a student's application, we calculate their transcript to obtain an overall GPA. We calculate all college prep courses (full credit) from freshmen to senior year. We look for a consistent performance over four years and we like to see students challenging themselves academically. Western New England College facilitates student learning."

Western New England College provides a variety of support programs including dedicated guidance for: academic · career · personal · psychological · minority students · military · veterans · non-traditional students · family planning · religious. Annually, 75 percent of freshmen students return for their sophomore year.

Support for Students with Learning Disabilities

Students with learning disabilities may take advantage of specific support programs offered by Western New England College. If necessary, the college will grant additional time to students with learning disabilities to complete their degree. Also, a lightened course load may be granted to LD students. High school foreign language waivers are accepted. According to the school, Student Disability Services assists students with challenges in developing strategies to participate fully in the college experience. Students with learning disabilities will find the following programs at Western New England College extremely useful: remedial English · remedial reading · tutors · learning center · extended time for tests · take-home exam · readers · typist/scribe · note-taking services · reading machines · tape recorders · texts on tape · early syllabus · priority registration · waiver of math degree requirement. Individual or small group tutorials are also available in: time management · organizational skills · learning strategies · specific subject areas · writing labs · math labs · study skills. An advisor/advocate from the WNEC Student Disability Services is available to students.

How to Get Admitted

For admissions decisions, non-academic factors considered: interview · extracurricular activities · special talents, interests, abilities · character/personal qualities · volunteer work · work experience · state of residency · minority affiliation · alumni relationship. A high school diploma is required, although a GED is also accepted for admissions consideration. SAT or ACT test scores are required of all applicants. SAT Subject Test scores are not required. *Academic units recommended:* 4 English, 4 Math, 2 Science, 2 Social Studies, 2 Foreign Language.

How to Pay for College

To apply for financial aid, students should submit the following: Free Application for Federal Student Aid (FAFSA) · federal income tax forms and W2(s). Western New England College participates in the Federal Work Study program. *Need-based aid programs include:* scholarships and grants · general need-based awards · Federal Pell grants · state scholarships and grants · college-based scholarships and grants · private scholarships and grants. *Non-Need-based aid pro-*

grams include: scholarships and grants · state scholarships and grants · creative arts and performance awards · ROTC scholarships.

WESTERN NEW ENGLAND COLLEGE

Admissions
Applicants: 4,809
Accepted: 3,526
Acceptance rate: 73.3%
Average GPA: 3.1
ACT range: 20-24
SAT Math range: 490-600
SAT Reading range: 470-550
SAT Writing range: Not reported
Top 10% of class: 14%
Top 25% of class: 36%
Top 50% of class: 77%

Deadlines
Early Action: No
Early Decision: No
Regular Action: Rolling admissions
Common Application: Accepted

Financial Aid
In-state tuition: $26,822
Out-of-state tuition: $26,822
Room: -
Board: -
Books: $1,050
Freshmen receiving need-based aid: 76%
Undergrads receiving need-based aid: 72%
Avg. % of need met by financial aid: 70%
Avg. aid package (freshmen): $19,273
Avg. aid package (undergrads): $17,604
Freshmen receiving merit-based aid: 13%
Undergrads receiving merit-based aid: 11%

School Spirit
Mascot: Golden Bear
Colors: Blue and gold
Song: *The Time Has Come*

WESTMINSTER COLLEGE

Students
Total enrollment: 1,569
Undergrads: 562
Freshmen: 626
Part-time students: 5%
From out-of-state: 20%
Male/Female: 39%/61%
Live on-campus: 85%
In fraternities: 35%
In sororities: 36%
Off-campus employment rating: Excellent
Caucasian: 75%
African American: 2%
Hispanic: 0%
Asian or Pacific Islander: 0%
Native American: 0%

Academics
Student/faculty ratio: 12:1
Class size 9 or fewer: 27%
Class size 10-29: 68%
Class size 30-49: 4%
Class size 50-99: -
Class size 100 or more: -
Returning freshmen: 85%
Six-year graduation rate: 78%

Admissions
Applicants: 1,149
Accepted: 899
Acceptance rate: 78.2%
Average GPA: 3.4
ACT range: 20-25
SAT Math range: 480-590
SAT Reading range: 470-580
SAT Writing range: Not reported
Top 10% of class: 23%
Top 25% of class: 59%
Top 50% of class: 89%

South Market Street, New Wilmington, PA 16172
Admissions: 800-942-8033 · Financial Aid: 724-946-7102
Email: admis@westminster.edu
Website: http://www.westminster.edu

From the College

"It is the mission of Westminster College to bring to our students a world-class education that integrates the liberal arts with a major. Extra- and co-curricular activities are integrated into the learning experience. The college promotes active and collaborative learning experiences. More than 76 percent of our first-year students graduate on time."

Campus Setting

Westminster, founded in 1852, is a church-affiliated, liberal arts college. Its 300-acre campus is located in New Wilmington, 65 miles north of Pittsburgh. A four-year private institution, the school is affiliated with the Presbyterian Church (USA). The school also has a library with 283,070 books. Westminster College provides on-campus housing with 700 units that can accommodate 1,100 students. Housing options: women's dorms · men's dorms · fraternity housing. Recreation and sports facilities include: baseball, football, soccer and softball fields · fitness center · gymnasium · natatorium · indoor and outdoor track and field.

Student Life and Activities

With 85 percent of students living on campus, there are plenty of social activities. "Socially, fraternities provide the greatest amount of activity; culturally, there's not much happening, but Pittsburgh is close for concerts and museums," reports the Holcad. Popular on-campus gathering spots include: fraternity houses, Student Union and campus pub; students gather off-campus at Seafood Express and Quaker Steak & Lube. Popular events include: Homecoming, Christmas Vespers, Greek Week and Volley Rock. Westminster College has 69 official student organizations. According to the editor of the school newspaper, the most influential groups on campus are Christian organizations and the Greeks. For those interested in sports, there are intramural teams such as: aerobics · basketball · bowling · canoe racing · flag football · golf · indoor soccer · inner-tube water polo · kickball · racquetball · softball · table tennis · volleyball. Westminster College is a member of the Presidents' Athletic Conference (Division III).

Academics and Learning Environment

For the B student, the learning environment of a college is just as important as the quality of its academic program. Westminster College has 101 full-time and 53 part-time faculty members, offering a student-to-faculty ratio of 12:1. The most common course size is 10 to 19 students. Westminster College offers 35 majors with the most popular being business administration, elementary education and biology and least popular being theatre, Spanish and philosophy. The school has a general core requirement. Cooperative education is not offered. All first-year students must maintain a 1.8 GPA or higher to avoid academic probation. Other special academic programs that would appeal to a B student: self-designed majors · pass/fail grading option · independent study · double majors · accelerated study · honors program · internships.

B Student Support and Success

The Westminster Plan provides a complete core curriculum in science, humanities, math, computer science and religion. All students graduate with two majors. Student-to-faculty ratio is 13:1, and most classes are no more than 19 students. The school emphasizes that it takes education seriously and that this is not a "party school." Westminster offers a First Year Program as well as the Next Chapter, a summer reading program for all incoming first-year students. The Learning Center is open for students who need assistance to "improve their academic performance."

Westminster College provides a variety of support programs including dedicated guidance for: academic · career · personal · psychological · minority students · non-traditional students · religious. Annually, 85 percent of freshmen students return for their sophomore year.

Support for Students with Learning Disabilities

Students with learning disabilities may take advantage of specific support programs. If necessary, the college will grant additional time to students with learning disabilities to complete their degree. Students with learning disabilities will find the following programs at Westminster College extremely useful: remedial reading · tutors · learning center · untimed tests · extended time for tests · oral tests · readers · note-taking services · reading machines · tape recorders · videotaped classes · priority registration · waiver of math degree requirement. Individual or small group tutorials are also available in: time management · organizational skills · learning strategies · specific subject areas · study skills. An advisor/advocate from the Office of Disability Support Services is available to students.

How to Get Admitted

For admissions decisions, non-academic factors considered: interview · extracurricular activities · special talents, interests, abilities · character/personal qualities · volunteer work · work experience · state of residency · religious affiliation/commitment · minority affiliation · alumni relationship. A high school diploma is required, although a GED is also accepted for admissions consideration. SAT or ACT test scores are required of all applicants.

How to Pay for College

To apply for financial aid, students should submit the following: Free Application for Federal Student Aid (FAFSA) · institution's own financial aid forms. Westminster College participates in the Federal Work Study program. *Need-based aid programs include:* scholarships and grants · general need-based awards · Federal Pell grants · college-based scholarships and grants · private scholarships and grants. *Non-Need-based aid programs include:* scholarships and grants · state scholarships and grants.

WESTMINSTER COLLEGE

Highlights

Deadlines
Early Action:
Early Decision: No
Regular Action: Rolling admissions
Common Application: Accepted

Financial Aid
In-state tuition: $26,225
Out-of-state tuition: $26,225
Room: -
Board: -
Books: $1,000
Freshmen receiving need-based aid: 81%
Undergrads receiving need-based aid: 79%
Avg. % of need met by financial aid: 88%
Avg. aid package (freshmen): $21,108
Avg. aid package (undergrads): $20,157
Freshmen receiving merit-based aid: 18%
Undergrads receiving merit-based aid: 20%
Avg. student debt upon graduation: $23,592

School Spirit
Mascot: Titans/Lady Titans
Colors: Blue and white
Song: *Victory*

WHEELOCK COLLEGE

200 The Riverway, Boston, MA 02215
Admissions: 800-734-5212 · Financial Aid: 800-734-5212
Email: undergrad@wheelock.edu · Website: http://www.wheelock.edu

From the College

"Making the world a better place by educating people to improve the lives of children and families is the cornerstone of a Wheelock education. Wheelock's academic environment values excellence and equity, delivering an education that expands intellectual capabilities and provides students with the knowledge and skills needed to succeed in personal and professional life. What makes a Wheelock education distinctive is what is common across programs. No matter what is studied here at Wheelock, a student leaves a caring, creative and competent person with professional knowledge and skills and the confidence to apply learning to make a difference."

Campus Setting

A four-year private institution, Wheelock College has an enrollment of 1,081 students. Wheelock College has been co-ed since 1972. The school also has a library with 83,267 books. Wheelock College provides on-campus housing with 5 units that can accommodate 545 students. Housing options: co-ed dorms · women's dorms · special housing for disabled students · cooperative housing.

Student Life and Activities

With 70 percent of students living on campus, there are plenty of social activities. On campus, students like to gather at the college center and the cafeteria. Popular events include: Spring Concert, Spring Formal, Oktoberfest, Explore Your Major Day, Black History Month, Red Sox games, Vagina Monologues, Fall Family Weekend. Wheelock College has 26 official student organizations. The most popular are: Best Buddies · Boston Association for the Education of Young Children · Campus Activities Board · Campus Association of Social Workers · Child Life Organization · dance team · Divine Harmony · drama club · Queer Co-Op · sign choir · Students Against Destructive Decisions · Math Mania. Wheelock College is a member of the Great Northeast Athletic Conference (Division III), North Atlantic Conference (Division III).

Academics and Learning Environment

For the B student, the learning environment of a college is just as important as the quality of its academic program. Wheelock College has 62 full-time and 117 part-time faculty members, offering a student-to-faculty ratio of 9:1. The most common course size is 10 to 19 students. Wheelock College offers 17 majors with the most popular being human development and social work. The school has a general core requirement. Cooperative education is not offered. All first-year students must maintain a 1.5 GPA or higher to avoid academic probation. Other special academic programs that would appeal to a B student: pass/fail grading option · independent study · double majors · dual degrees · internships.

B Student Support and Success

According to Mike Akillian, assistant to the president of Wheelock, the college "has been providing a transformational education to students who aim to improve society by improving the lives of children and families." Akillian says that many of Wheelock's students focus on making contributions to society, electing to work in professions like education, social work, child life (in medical settings), juvenile justice and youth advocacy. "We believe it is our close collaboration with faculty, a blend of arts and sciences programs coupled with professional programs (most students graduate with double majors), a focus on mission and the integration of theory and scholarship with real-world practice that serves as a catalyzing force for change," says Akillian.

Wheelock College provides a variety of support programs including dedicated guidance for: academic · career · personal · psychological · non-traditional students. The average freshman year GPA is 3.1, and 69 percent of freshmen students return for their sophomore year. What do students do after college? While many enter the work force, approximately 60 percent pursue a graduate degree immediately after graduation. Among students who enter the work force, approximately 95 percent enter a field related to their major within six months of graduation. Companies that most frequently hire graduates from Wheelock College include: Boston Public Schools · Brookline Public Schools · Cambridge Public Schools · Framingham Public Schools · LEAP School · Kingsley Montessori · May Institute · South Bay · Children's Hospital · Mass. General Hospital · UMass Medical · New York Public Schools · Criterion Child Enrichment · Associated early Care and Eduction · Lawrence Public Schools · Lowell Public Schools · right Horizons · Quincy Public Schools · Stoughton Public Schools · Taunton Public Schools · Social Work PRN · Belmont Day School.

Support for Students with Learning Disabilities

Students with learning disabilities may take advantage of specific support programs offered by Wheelock College. If necessary, the college will grant additional time to students with learning disabilities to complete their degree. Also, a lightened course load may be granted to LD students. High school foreign language waivers are accepted. Students with learning disabilities will find the following programs at Wheelock College extremely useful: tutors · learning center · testing accommodations · untimed tests · extended time for tests · readers · typist/scribe · note-taking services · reading machines · tape recorders · texts on tape · early syllabus · priority registration. Individual or small group tutorials are also available in: time management · organizational skills · learning strategies · specific subject areas · writing labs · math labs · study skills. An advisor/advocate from the Office of Academic Advising and Assistance is available to students.

How to Get Admitted

For admissions decisions, non-academic factors considered: interview · extracurricular activities · special talents, interests, abilities · character/personal qualities · volunteer work · work experience · state of residency · alumni relationship. A high school diploma is required, although a GED is also accepted for admissions consideration. SAT or ACT test scores are required of all applicants. SAT Subject Test scores are not required. *According to the admissions office:* Experience in child care recommended. *Academic units recommended:* 4 English, 3 Math, 3 Science, 2 Social Studies, 2 Foreign Language.

How to Pay for College

To apply for financial aid, students should submit the following: Free Application for Federal Student Aid (FAFSA). Wheelock College

WHEELOCK COLLEGE

Highlights

Wheelock College
Boston, MA (Pop. 600,000)
Location: Major city
Website: http://www.wheelock.edu

Students
Total enrollment: 1,081
Undergrads: 52
Freshmen: 225
Part-time students: 7%
From out-of-state: 40%
Male/Female: 7%/93%
Live on-campus: 70%
Off-campus employment rating: Fair
Caucasian: 74%
African American: 9%
Hispanic: 5%
Asian or Pacific Islander: 2%
Native American: 0%
International: 1%

Academics
Student/faculty ratio: 9:1
Class size 9 or fewer: 19%
Class size 10-29: 79%
Class size 30-49: 3%
Class size 50-99: -
Class size 100 or more: -
Returning freshmen: 69%
Six-year graduation rate: 63%

Admissions
Applicants: 1,144
Accepted: 719
Acceptance rate: 62.8%
Average GPA: 3.0
ACT range: 16-19
SAT Math range: 410-550
SAT Reading range: 430-550
SAT Writing range: Not reported
Top 10% of class: 7%
Top 25% of class: 30%
Top 50% of class: 70%

583

WHEELOCK COLLEGE

Deadlines
Early Action: December 1
Early Decision: No
Regular Action: Rolling admissions
Common Application: Accepted

Financial Aid
In-state tuition: $27,150
Out-of-state tuition: $27,150
Room: -
Board: -
Books: $800
Freshmen receiving need-based aid: 82%
Undergrads receiving need-based aid: 87%
Avg. % of need met by financial aid: 58%
Avg. aid package (freshmen): $15,101
Avg. aid package (undergrads): $16,823
Freshmen receiving merit-based aid: 9%
Undergrads receiving merit-based aid: 6%
Avg. student debt upon graduation: $18,231

School Spirit
Mascot: Wildcats

participates in the Federal Work Study program. *Need-based aid programs include:* scholarships and grants · general need-based awards · Federal Pell grants · state scholarships and grants · college-based scholarships and grants · private scholarships and grants. *Non-Need-based aid programs include:* scholarships and grants · state scholarships and grants · special achievements and activities awards.

WHITTIER COLLEGE

13406 East Philadelphia Street, P.O. Box 634, Whittier, CA 90608
Admissions: 562-907-4238 · Financial Aid: 562-907-4285
Email: admission@whittier.edu · Website: http://www.whittier.edu

From the College

"Whittier College is a residential, four-year, liberal arts institution where intellectual inquiry and experiential learning are fostered in a community that promotes respect for diversity of thought and culture. With 43 percent of its students from traditionally under-represented groups, and its federal designation as a Hispanic-Serving Institution, Whittier College remains one of the most diverse liberal arts schools in the nation. The college's location at the crossroads of Los Angeles and Orange Counties—Southern California's centers of urban and cultural life—provides opportunities to explore a full range of thought, cultures and talents.

"Recognized for its Whittier Scholars Program, interdisciplinary curriculum and emphasis on linking theory and practice, Whittier College's academic program is progressive; students gain a wide breadth of knowledge and the confidence to apply that knowledge. Working closely with professors and with the advantage of small class size, students have extensive undergraduate research opportunities, which atypically extend beyond the natural and physical sciences to include social sciences, humanities and the arts. Multitudes of students have become published authors through joint research endeavors and have actively participated in national professional conferences. Whittier faculty also embrace the educational advantages provided through experiential learning; a high percentage of students engage in off-campus study both locally and abroad, academically supported through research trips, fieldwork, service projects and professional internships.

"Popular with students is the January Interim session, an abbreviated but rigorous term that offers intense focus on subject matter, typically followed by a field trip to apply learning. Recent courses included travel to Mexico to study multinational management practices; Chile to analyze the politics of race, religion and gender in action; Paris to examine historical social construct through city planning; and Rome to explore origins of art and architecture. Whittier's 50-year association with the DIS-Copenhagen program remains the most popular semester abroad option, though recent choice destinations have included India, China, Egypt, Africa, and South America.

"In particular, strong faculty-student relationships are forged here—through collaborative projects, mentoring and social interaction - that extend well beyond the college years and most often result in professional networking, graduate study references and career assistance later in life. Whittier graduates serve across a variety of sectors, including public service, education and social work, science and health, entrepreneurial business and the arts."

Campus Setting

Whittier College, founded in 1887, has a 75-acre campus located in Whittier, 18 miles east of Los Angeles. A four-year private institution, Whittier College has an enrollment of 1,948 students. In addition to a large, well-stocked library, the campus facilities include: center for the performing arts · language resource center · image processing lab · analytical instrumentation and mass spectrometry lab · nuclear magnetic resonance spectrometry research lab. Whittier College provides on-campus housing with 8 units that can accommodate 800 students. Housing options: co-ed dorms. Recreation and sports facilities include: aquatics center · fitness center · lacrosse and soccer fields · stadium · tennis courts.

WHITTIER COLLEGE

Whittier College
Whittier, CA (Pop. 85,000)
Location: Large town
Website: http://www.whittier.edu

Students
Total enrollment: 1,948
Undergrads: 591
Freshmen: 312
Part-time students: 1%
From out-of-state: 40%
Male/Female: 46%/54%
Live on-campus: 59%
In fraternities: 8%
In sororities: 18%
Off-campus employment rating: Fair
Caucasian: 43%
African American: 4%
Hispanic: 30%
Asian or Pacific Islander: 8%
Native American: 1%
International: 2%

Academics
Student/faculty ratio: 13:1
Class size 9 or fewer: 17%
Class size 10-29: 74%
Class size 30-49: 9%
Class size 50-99: -
Class size 100 or more: -
Returning freshmen: 78%
Six-year graduation rate: 58%

Admissions
Applicants: 2,186
Accepted: 1,581
Acceptance rate: 72.3%
Average GPA: 3.1
ACT range: 22-24
SAT Math range: 460-580
SAT Reading range: 470-580
SAT Writing range: 460-580
Top 10% of class: 21%
Top 25% of class: 35%
Top 50% of class: 87%

586

America's
Best Colleges for
B Students

Student Life and Activities

With 59 percent of students living on campus, there are plenty of social activities. Popular events include: Sportsfest, Late Night Breakfast, Random Acts of Kindness Week, Diverse Identities Week, Asian Heritage Month, Black History Month, Hispanic Heritage Month, Spring Sing, Mona Kai, Luminarias, Helping Hands Day, Asian Night, Soul Food Night, Tardeada, Martin Luther King, Jr. Oratorical Contest and the Hawaiian Islanders Club Lu'au. Whittier College has 68 official student organizations. The most popular are: Anthropology Club · International Relations Club · Les Copians (French Club) · Poet Democrats Club · Photography Club · Psychology Club · Reaching Equiality and Diversity (READ) · Richard M. Nixon Republican Club · Society of Physics Students · Students for Community Medicine · Anime Ikkimasu · Whittier College Choir · Spanish Club · Breakdancing Club · Whittier College Dance Team · Wickets and Balls (Cricket Club) · Intramurals · Artorian Order of the Knights of Pendragon (AOKP) · Art Club · Biology Club · Circle K · Coalition of Activist Leders (COAL) · Consulting club · Economics Club. Whittier College is a member of the Southern California Intercollegiate Athletic Conference (Division III), Western Water Polo Association (Division III).

Academics and Learning Environment

For the B student, the learning environment of a college is just as important as the quality of its academic program. Whittier College has 90 full-time and 34 part-time faculty members, offering a student-to-faculty ratio of 13:1. The most common course size is 10 to 19 students. Whittier College offers 31 majors with the most popular being business administration, political science and English and least popular being French, music and religious studies. The school has a general core requirement. Cooperative education is not offered. All first-year students must maintain a 2.0 GPA or higher to avoid academic probation. Other special academic programs that would appeal to a B student: self-designed majors · pass/fail grading option · independent study · double majors · internships.

B Student Support and Success

At Whittier's Center for Academic Success (CAS), tutoring is free and classes that have been identified as historically challenging for most students are supported through supplemental instruction. Students in group sessions review notes, practice quizzes and work to reinforce the knowledge and skills they need for the class.

CAS also offers a class called Succeeding in College that helps students find out how to do well in school, both academically and personally. The class features individual exercises, cooperative learning, reading and lectures and is available each spring. Students that need assistance in the writing process can find all the help they need through the Writing Program.

Whittier College provides a variety of support programs including dedicated guidance for: academic · career · personal · psychological · minority students · family planning. The average freshman year GPA is 2.7, and 78 percent of freshmen students return for their sophomore year. What do students do after college? While many enter the work force, approximately 20 percent pursue a graduate degree immediately after graduation. Among students who enter the work force, approximately 66 percent enter a field related to their major within six months of graduation. Companies that most frequently hire graduates from Whittier College include: Beckman Coulter · Sony Pictures · Warner Brothers Entertainment · Wells Fargo · U.S. Congress · U.S. Department of State · University of Southern California Medical Center · Deloitte and Touche · Expeditors International · I Have a Dream Foundation · IBM.· KMG Consultants · Smith Barney · Northrup Grumman Corp. · Peace Corps.

Support for Students with Learning Disabilities

Students with learning disabilities may take advantage of specific support programs offered by Whittier College. High school foreign language waivers are accepted. LD students complete the same requirements for admission as other students, and self- identify when they enter as freshmen or transfer students. Students with learning disabilities will find the following programs at Whittier College extremely useful: special classes · tutors · learning center · testing accommodations · extended time for tests · take-home exam · oral tests · readers · note-taking services · reading machines · tape recorders · texts on tape · early syllabus · priority seating. Individual or small group tutorials are also available in: time management · organizational skills · learning strategies · specific subject areas · writing labs · math labs · study skills. An advisor/advocate from the Whittier College Disability Services is available to students.

How to Get Admitted

For admissions decisions, non-academic factors considered: interview · extracurricular activities · special talents, interests, abilities · character/personal qualities · volunteer work · work experience · geographical location · minority affiliation · alumni relationship. A high school diploma is required, although a GED is also accepted for admissions consideration. SAT or ACT test scores are required of all applicants. SAT Subject Test scores are considered, if submitted, but are not required. *Academic units recommended:* 4 English, 3 Math, 2 Science, 2 Social Studies, 3 Foreign Language.

How to Pay for College

To apply for financial aid, students should submit the following: Free Application for Federal Student Aid (FAFSA) · institution's own financial aid forms · CSS/Financial Aid PROFILE · state aid form. Whittier College participates in the Federal Work Study program. *Need-based aid programs include:* scholarships and grants · general need-based awards · Federal Pell grants · state scholarships and grants · college-based scholarships and grants · private scholarships and grants. *Non-Need-based aid programs include:* scholarships and grants · state scholarships and grants · creative arts and performance awards · ROTC scholarships.

WHITTIER COLLEGE

Highlights

Deadlines
Early Action: December 1
Early Decision: No
Regular Action: February 1 (priority)
Common Application: Accepted

Financial Aid
In-state tuition: $33,868
Out-of-state tuition: $33,868
Room: -
Board: -
Books: $1,638
Freshmen receiving need-based aid: 68%
Undergrads receiving need-based aid: 67%
Avg. % of need met by financial aid: 91%
Avg. aid package (freshmen): $31,833
Avg. aid package (undergrads): $31,869
Freshmen receiving merit-based aid: 27%
Undergrads receiving merit-based aid: 25%
Avg. student debt upon graduation: $40,862

Prominent Alumni
Edward Petersen, co-founder Intelius; George Stults and Geoff Stults, actors.

School Spirit
Mascot: Poets
Colors: Purple and gold

WILKES UNIVERSITY

84 West South Street, Wilkes-Barre, PA 18766
Admissions: 800-WILKES-U · Financial Aid: 800-WILKES-U
Email: admissions@wilkes.edu · Website: http://www.wilkes.edu

From the College

"At Wilkes, we change lives. We recognize that giving our students the extra personal attention they need is the difference - the key to our students' success. It's why a student who may not have succeeded elsewhere thrives at Wilkes. It's why we can count so many Wilkes alumni as leaders in their careers and communities. We're not just about diplomas and degrees. We're about more than teaching. We're about mentoring."

Campus Setting

Wilkes is a private university. Founded as a junior college in 1933, it achieved college status in 1947 and university status in 1989. Its 25-acre campus is located in Wilkes-Barre, 20 miles from Scranton. A four-year institution, Wilkes University has an enrollment of 5,901 students. In addition to a library, the campus facilities include: art gallery · performing arts and sports centers · electron microscope · pharmacy information center. Wilkes University provides on-campus housing that can accommodate 973 students. Housing options: co-ed dorms · women's dorms · men's dorms · single-student apartments. Recreation and sports facilities include: athletic center · basketball and tennis courts · football and soccer fields · field house · recreation and weight room.

Student Life and Activities

Most students (57 percent) live off campus, which does impact the on-campus social scene. Nevertheless, like any college, students find time to create their own recreational outlets. Wilkes University has 60 official student organizations. The most popular are: Choral club · Circle K · commuter council · Cue and Curtain · debating · film society · madrigal singers · men's and women's choruses · music ensembles · pep band · academic and community service clubs · special-interest groups. For those interested in sports, there are intramural teams such as: basketball · golf · racquetball · soccer · softball · tennis. Wilkes University is a member of the Freedom Conference (Division III), Middle Atlantic States Collegiate Athletic Conference (Division III).

Academics and Learning Environment

For the B student, the learning environment of a college is just as important as the quality of its academic program. Wilkes University has 146 full-time and 283 part-time faculty members, offering a student-to-faculty ratio of 15:1. The most common course size is 10 to 19 students. Wilkes University offers 41 majors with the most popular being business administration, health professions and psychology and least popular being philosophy, mathematics and interdisciplinary studies. The school has a general core requirement. Cooperative education is not offered. All first-year students must maintain a 1.75 GPA or higher to avoid academic probation. Other special academic programs that would appeal to a B student: self-designed majors · pass/fail grading option · independent study · double majors · dual degrees · honors program · internships · weekend college · distance learning.

B Student Support and Success

Wilkes has a deep interest in helping the B student achieve excellence through a dedicated faculty and personal tutoring. Admissions are based on secondary-school record, class rank and results of the SAT or ACT. Interviews are not required but highly recommended. Essays and letters of recommendation are not required but will be accepted and considered if submitted.

Wilkes University provides a variety of support programs including dedicated guidance for: academic · career · personal · psychological · minority students · military · veterans · non-traditional students. Recognizing that some students may need extra preparation, Wilkes University offers remedial and refresher courses in: reading · writing · math · study skills. The average freshman year GPA is 2.9, and 78 percent of freshmen students return for their sophomore year.

Support for Students with Learning Disabilities

Students with learning disabilities may take advantage of specific support programs offered by Wilkes University. If necessary, the college will grant additional time to students with learning disabilities to complete their degree. Also, a lightened course load may be granted to LD students. Credit is given for remedial courses taken. High school foreign language waivers are accepted. High school math waivers are also accepted. Students with learning disabilities will find the following programs at Wilkes University extremely useful: remedial math · remedial English · remedial reading · tutors · learning center · testing accommodations · extended time for tests · take-home exam · oral tests · readers · typist/scribe · note-taking services · reading machines · tape recorders · texts on tape · diagnostic testing service · priority registration. Individual or small group tutorials are also available in: time management · organizational skills · learning strategies · specific subject areas · writing labs · math labs · study skills. An advisor/advocate from the University College is available to students.

How to Get Admitted

For admissions decisions, non-academic factors considered: interview · extracurricular activities · special talents, interests, abilities · character/personal qualities · volunteer work · work experience · state of residency · alumni relationship. A high school diploma is required, although a GED is also accepted for admissions consideration. SAT or ACT test scores are required of all applicants. SAT Subject Test scores are considered, if submitted, but are not required. *According to the admissions office:* Minimum combined SAT Reasoning score of 920 and rank in top three-fifths of secondary school class required. Minimum 2.5 GPA recommended. *Academic units recommended:* 4 English, 3 Math, 2 Science, 3 Social Studies.

Insight

Wilkes was founded to educate first-generation students. "What sets us apart from other colleges can't be measured by numbers on a page. Students succeed here because of the unique atmosphere and philosophy. At Wilkes you will find someone who believes in you," explains Mike Frantz, vice president of enrollment and marketing. "Our professors do everything they can to help students reach their goals. They even help them figure out what those goals are."

According to Frantz, Wilkes is actively looking for reasons to include B students. "We look for signs of potential," he says. "Our faculty and staff truly take a deep interest in students' dreams and

WILKES UNIVERSITY

Wilkes University
Wilkes-Barre, PA (Pop. 50,000)
Location: Medium city
Website: http://www.wilkes.edu

Students
Total enrollment: 5,901
Undergrads: 1,150
Freshmen: 770
Part-time students: 10%
From out-of-state: 25%
Male/Female: 50%/50%
Live on-campus: 43%
Off-campus employment rating: Good
Caucasian: 84%
African American: 4%
Hispanic: 2%
Asian or Pacific Islander: 2%
Native American: 0%
International: 3%

Academics
Student/faculty ratio: 15:1
Class size 9 or fewer: 16%
Class size 10-29: 61%
Class size 30-49: 19%
Class size 50-99: 4%
Class size 100 or more: -
Returning freshmen: 78%
Six-year graduation rate: 58%

Most Popular Fields of Study
Business, Finance, Sales and Marketing
Protective Services, Criminal Justice and Public Administration
English and Literature
Computer and Information Sciences
Psychology
Engineering and Engineering Technologies
Health Professions, Medicine and Related Sciences
Liberal Arts, Humanities and General Studies
Foreign Languages, Literature and Linguistics
Communications, Journalism, Advertising and Comm. Technologies

589

College Profiles

WILKES UNIVERSITY

Admissions

Applicants: 2,778
Accepted: 2,091
Acceptance rate: 75.3%
Average GPA: Not reported
ACT range: Not reported
SAT Math range: 460-600
SAT Reading range: 460-570
SAT Writing range: 450-560
Top 10% of class: 22%
Top 25% of class: 52%
Top 50% of class: 83%

Deadlines

Early Action: No
Early Decision: No
Regular Action: May 1 (priority)
Common Application: Accepted

Financial Aid

In-state tuition: $24,690
Out-of-state tuition: $24,690
Room: $6,680
Board: $4,420
Books: $1,100
Freshmen receiving need-based aid: 84%
Undergrads receiving need-based aid:
    79%
Avg. % of need met by financial aid: 75%
Avg. aid package (freshmen): $20,731
Avg. aid package (undergrads): $19,642
Freshmen receiving merit-based aid: 11%
Undergrads receiving merit-based aid:
    14%
Avg. student debt upon graduation:
    $31,935

School Spirit

Mascot: Colonels
Colors: Blue and gold

aspirations." For those students struggling with any particular skills, Wilkes offers individual tutoring as well as a staff that assists in career strategies and study skills. "We can take any students if they honestly express the desire to improve," explains Frantz. "This campus is full of passionate faculty who treat students as equals and challenge them to strive towards greater accomplishments."

How to Pay for College

To apply for financial aid, students should submit the following: Free Application for Federal Student Aid (FAFSA). Wilkes University participates in the Federal Work Study program. *Need-based aid programs include:* scholarships and grants · general need-based awards · Federal Pell grants · state scholarships and grants · college-based scholarships and grants · private scholarships and grants. *Non-Need-based aid programs include:* scholarships and grants · state scholarships and grants · ROTC scholarships.

WITTENBERG UNIVERSITY

P.O. Box 720, Springfield, OH 45501
Admissions: 800-677-7558, extension 6314
Financial Aid: 800-677-7558
Email: admission@wittenberg.edu
Website: http://www.wittenberg.edu

From the College

"Wittenberg University provides a liberal arts education dedicated to intellectual inquiry and wholeness of person within a diverse residential community. Reflecting its Lutheran heritage, Wittenberg challenges students to become responsible global citizens, to discover their callings, and to lead personal, professional and civic lives of creativity, service, compassion and integrity. Home to more than 50 majors and special programs, including interdisciplinary ones in East Asian Studies, and Russian and Central Eurasian studies, Wittenberg requires community service to graduate. Every year, hundreds of students spend time in service locally and around the world, and many more go on to build homes with Habitat for Humanity, work in inner-city schools with Teach for America or enter the Peace Corps post-graduation. Wittenberg also supports a study-abroad program that annually sends students around the world. At the same time, Wittenberg graduates regularly land coveted positions in all fields as well as entry to prestigious graduate schools."

Campus Setting

Wittenberg, founded in 1845, is a church-affiliated university. Its 71-acre campus is located in Springfield, 25 miles northeast of Dayton. A four-year private institution, Wittenberg University has an enrollment of 2,536 students. Wittenberg University has been co-ed since 1874. The school is also affiliated with the Lutheran Church. In addition to a large, well-stocked library, the campus has a gallery. Wittenberg University provides on-campus housing with 742 units that can accommodate 1,646 students. Housing options: co-ed dorms • women's dorms • sorority housing • fraternity housing • single-student apartments • special housing for International students. Recreation and sports facilities include: athletic arena • field house • fitness center • football • field hockey • lacrosse • soccer and softball field • recreation center • tennis complex • track • stadium.

Student Life and Activities

With 88 percent of students living on campus, there are plenty of social activities. Since we are a small school, it's easy to make friends and find social events, reports the editor of the school newspaper. There are many alternatives to parties, like Union Board cultural activities and sports. The Pub, fraternity houses, area bars and off-campus houses are the most frequented student gathering spots. Popular events include: Witt Fest and Lil' Sibs Weekend. Wittenberg University has 129 official student organizations. Greeks, Student Senate, athletes, the Union Board and Concerned Black Students have widespread influence on student social life at Wit-

WITTENBERG UNIVERSITY

Admissions
Applicants: 3,344
Accepted: 2,299
Acceptance rate: 68.8%
Average GPA: 3.4
ACT range: 23-29
SAT Math range: 540-640
SAT Reading range: 520-640
SAT Writing range: Not reported
Top 10% of class: 33%
Top 25% of class: 61%
Top 50% of class: 89%

Deadlines
Early Action: December 1
Early Decision: November 15
Regular Action: Rolling admissions
Common Application: Accepted

Financial Aid
In-state tuition: $33,890
Out-of-state tuition: $33,890
Room: $4,554
Board: $4,218
Books: $1,000
Freshmen receiving need-based aid: 69%
Undergrads receiving need-based aid: 71%
Avg. % of need met by financial aid: 88%
Avg. aid package (freshmen): $27,461
Avg. aid package (undergrads): $26,618
Freshmen receiving merit-based aid: 31%
Undergrads receiving merit-based aid: 28%

Prominent Alumni
Wesley C. Bates, chairman and CEO Stanley Steamer; John McLaughlin, former deputy director CIA; John F. Meier, chairman and CEO Libby Inc.

School Spirit
Mascot: Tiger
Colors: Red and white

tenberg. For those interested in sports, there are intramural teams such as: basketball · cheerleading · Chinese dance · crew · dance · dodgeball · flag football · hockey · indoor soccer · martial arts · outdoor caving · rugby · sand volleyball · softball · swing club · volleyball · wiffle ball. Wittenberg University is a member of the North Coast Athletic Conference (Division III).

Academics and Learning Environment

For the B student, the learning environment of a college is just as important as the quality of its academic program. Wittenberg University has 142 full-time and 53 part-time faculty members, offering a student-to-faculty ratio of 12:1. The most common course size is 10 to 19 students. Wittenberg University offers 34 majors with the most popular being biology, business administration and social sciences and least popular being computer science, philosophy and religious studies and mathematics. The school has a general core requirement. Cooperative education is not offered. All first-year students must maintain a 1.8 GPA or higher to avoid academic probation, and a minimum overall GPA of 2.5 is required to graduate. Other special academic programs that would appeal to a B student: self-designed majors · pass/fail grading option · independent study · double majors · dual degrees · honors program · Phi Beta Kappa · internships.

B Student Support and Success

Wittenberg offers a First Year Experience program with Wittenberg Seminars or WittSems. These small courses introduce students to the core matters of "academic inquiry" through the skills of close reading, problem solving and critical thinking. They offer a Foreign Language Learning Center, Math Workshop, and Writing Center to help students who are struggling with basic courses.

Wittenberg University provides a variety of support programs including dedicated guidance for: academic · career · personal · psychological · minority students · family planning · religious. The average freshman year GPA is 2.7, and 73 percent of freshmen students return for their sophomore year.

Support for Students with Learning Disabilities

Students with learning disabilities may take advantage of specific support programs offered by Wittenberg University. Students with learning disabilities will find the following programs at Wittenberg University extremely useful: tutors · extended time for tests · take-home exam · exam on tape or computer. Individual or small group tutorials are also available in: writing labs · math labs. An advisor/advocate from the LD program is available to students.

How to Get Admitted

For admissions decisions, non-academic factors considered: interview · extracurricular activities · special talents, interests, abilities · character/personal qualities · volunteer work · work experience · state of residency · alumni relationship. A high school diploma is required, although a GED is also accepted for admissions consideration. SAT or ACT test scores are considered, if submitted, but are not required. *Academic units recommended:* 4 English, 4 Math, 5 Science, 3 Foreign Language.

How to Pay for College

To apply for financial aid, students should submit the following: Free Application for Federal Student Aid (FAFSA) · state aid form · Non-custodian (Divorced/Separated) Parent's Statement · verification form. Wittenberg University participates in the Federal Work Study program. *Need-based aid programs include:* scholarships and grants · general need-based awards · Federal Pell grants · state scholarships and grants · college-based scholarships and grants · private scholarships and grants. *Non-Need-based aid programs include:* scholarships and grants · general need-based awards · state scholarships and grants · creative arts and performance awards · special achievements and activities awards · ROTC scholarships.

Woodbury University

Burbank, CA (Pop. 100,316)
Location: Major city
Website: http://www.woodbury.edu

Students

Total enrollment: 1,547
Undergrads: 575
Freshmen: 166
Part-time students: 18%
From out-of-state: 7%
Male/Female: 46%/54%
Live on-campus: 15%
In fraternities: 1%
In sororities: 1%
Off-campus employment rating: Fair
Caucasian: 43%
African American: 4%
Hispanic: 33%
Asian or Pacific Islander: 11%
Native American: 0%
International: 8%

Academics

Student/faculty ratio: 9:1
Class size 9 or fewer: 30%
Class size 10-29: 69%
Class size 30-49: 2%
Class size 50-99: -
Class size 100 or more: -
Returning freshmen: 74%
Six-year graduation rate: 51%

Most Popular Fields of Study

Architecture
Business, Finance, Sales and Marketing
Computer and Information Sciences
Visual and Performing Arts
Psychology
Communications, Journalism, Advertising
   and Comm. Technologies
Interdisciplinary Studies

WOODBURY UNIVERSITY

7500 Glenoaks Boulevard, Burbank, CA 91510
Admissions: 800-784-9663 · Financial Aid: 818-252 5273
Email: admissions@woodbury.edu
Website: http://www.woodbury.edu

From the College

"At Woodbury University, the integrated nature of our educational environment cultivates successful students with a strong and enduring sense of personal and social responsibility. Woodbury fosters academic excellence and individual development in an environment that honors the following values: integrity and ethical behavior, diversity, empowering students to determine and manage their own decisions, academic rigor, liberal arts-based professional education that effectively prepares students for careers, and student focus in all aspects of the university's operations."

Campus Setting

Woodbury, founded in 1884, is a private university of business administration and professional design. Its 22-acre campus is located in Burbank, in the Los Angeles metropolitan area. A four-year institution, Woodbury University has an enrollment of 1,547 students. The school also has a library with 66,648 books. Woodbury University provides on-campus housing with 146 units that can accommodate 226 students. Housing options: co-ed dorms · single-student apartments.

Student Life and Activities

Most students (85 percent) live off campus, which does impact the on-campus social scene. Nevertheless, like any college, students find time to create their own recreational outlets. Woody's Cafe is a popular gathering spot. University Gala, Winter Formal, Springfest and Commencement are popular events. Woodbury University has 24 official student organizations. The most popular are: American Institute of Graphic Arts (AIGA) · American Society of Interior Designers (ASID) · Architecture Student Forum · Collegiate Entrepreneurs' Organization · Organization Name Common Threads · Communication Club · MBA Association · Social Animals · Society of Accounting and Business · Society of Interior Architecture Students · Business & Professional Women of Woodbury · Winter Formal · Woodstock · Founders' Week · Midnight Breakfast.

Academics and Learning Environment

For the B student, the learning environment of a college is just as important as the quality of its academic program. Woodbury University has 51 full-time and 214 part-time faculty members, offering a student-to-faculty ratio of 9:1. The most common course size is 10 to 19 students. Woodbury University offers 18 majors with the most popular being business/management, architecture and fashion design. The school has a general core requirement. Cooperative education is not offered. All first-year students must maintain a 2.0 GPA or higher to avoid academic probation. Other special academic programs that would appeal to a B student: double majors · accelerated study · internships · weekend college.

B Student Support and Success

Woodbury offers a variety of services to help B students through OASIS (Office of Academic Success and Instructional Services). Services include academic peer mentors, faculty advising, individual and small-group tutoring. The school also provides supplemental instruction for historically challenging courses in weekly study sessions. In addition, each freshman student is assigned a Student Orientation, Advising and Registration (SOAR) peer advisor who helps students with all aspects of college life.

Woodbury University provides a variety of support programs including dedicated guidance for: academic · career · psychological. Annually, 74 percent of freshmen students return for their sophomore year. Among students who enter the work force, approximately 62 percent enter a field related to their major within six months of graduation, while a further 7 percent enter a related career within two years of graduation. Companies that most frequently hire graduates from Woodbury University include: Warner Bros · Universal Studios · Bloomingdales · Office Pavilion · City of Los Angeles · DWP · NBC · Good Swartz Brown & Brown LLP · First Commerce Bank · Countrywide Mortgage · JC Penney · Americorps · Paramount · Washington Mutual · Bank of America · Citibank · Disney · Guess · Los Angeles Sheriff's Department · Los Angeles Superior Court · Nestle · Boeing · IKEA · Los Angeles County Office of Public Safety · State of California · Gensler · Escada · Port of Los Angeles · Shell Oil · Williams-Sanoma · ABC · Dreamworks · Technicolor · Nickelodeon.

Support for Students with Learning Disabilities

Students with learning disabilities may take advantage of specific support programs offered by Woodbury University. High school foreign language waivers are accepted. Students with learning disabilities will find the following programs at Woodbury University extremely useful: tutors · learning center · testing accommodations · untimed tests · extended time for tests · oral tests · note-taking services · tape recorders. Individual or small group tutorials are also available in: time management · organizational skills · writing labs. An advisor/advocate is available to students.

How to Get Admitted

For admissions decisions, non-academic factors considered: interview · extracurricular activities · volunteer work · work experience · state of residency · alumni relationship. A high school diploma is required, although a GED is also accepted for admissions consideration. SAT or ACT test scores are required of all applicants. SAT Subject Test scores are not required. *According to the admissions office:* Minimum 2.5 GPA recommended. *Academic units recommended:* 4 English, 3 Math, 2 Science, 1 Social Studies, 2 Foreign Language.

How to Pay for College

To apply for financial aid, students should submit the following: Free Application for Federal Student Aid (FAFSA) · institution's own financial aid forms. Woodbury University participates in the Federal

WOODBURY UNIVERSITY

Highlights

Admissions
Applicants: 494
Accepted: 361
Acceptance rate: 73.1%
Average GPA: 3.3
ACT range: 15-21
SAT Math range: 420-550
SAT Reading range: 370-510
SAT Writing range: Not reported

Deadlines
Early Action: No
Early Decision: No
Regular Action: Rolling admissions
Common Application: Accepted

Financial Aid
In-state tuition: $27,928
Out-of-state tuition: $27,928
Room: $5,651
Board: $3,555
Books: $1,638
Freshmen receiving need-based aid: 73%
Undergrads receiving need-based aid: 78%
Avg. % of need met by financial aid: 55%
Avg. aid package (freshmen): $19,273
Avg. aid package (undergrads): $18,917
Freshmen receiving merit-based aid: 16%
Undergrads receiving merit-based aid: 12%
Avg. student debt upon graduation: $43,854

Prominent Alumni
Helen Gurley Brown, editor in chief, Cosmopolitan Magazine.

Work Study program. *Need-based aid programs include:* scholarships and grants · general need-based awards · Federal Pell grants · state scholarships and grants · college-based scholarships and grants · private scholarships and grants. *Non-Need-based aid programs include:* scholarships and grants · state scholarships and grants.

XAVIER UNIVERSITY OF LOUISIANA

1 Drexel Drive, New Orleans, LA 70125
Admissions: 877-XAVIERU · Financial Aid: 877-XAVIERU
Email: apply@xula.edu · Website: http://www.xula.edu

From the College

"Xavier University of Louisiana is Catholic and historically black. The ultimate purpose of the university is the promotion of a more just and humane society. To this end, Xavier prepares its students to assume roles of leadership and service in society. This preparation takes place in a pluralistic teaching and learning environment that incorporates all relevant educational means, including research and community service. So that they will be able to assume roles of leadership and service, Xavier graduates will be: prepared for continual spiritual, moral and intellectual development; liberally educated in the knowledge and skills required for leadership and service; and educated in a major field so that they are prepared to complete graduate or professional school and to succeed in a career and in life."

Campus Setting

Xavier, founded in 1925, is a liberal arts university. Its 29-acre campus is located in New Orleans. A four-year, private institution, Xavier University of Louisiana has 3,236 students. The school is also affiliated with the Roman Catholic Church. The school has a library with 261,000 books. Xavier University of Louisiana provides on-campus housing with 824 units that can accommodate 1,692 students. Housing options: co-ed dorms · women's dorms · men's dorms · special housing for disabled students. Recreation and sports facilities include: fitness center · gymnasium.

Student Life and Activities

Most students (57 percent) live off campus, which does impact the on-campus social scene. Nevertheless, like any college, students find time to create their own recreational outlets. The Student Union is a popular on-campus gathering spot. Popular campus events include: Spring Fest, October Fest, Festival of Scholars and Greek shows. Xavier University of Louisiana has a number of official student organizations. The most popular are: music · theatre · political · service · special-interest groups. Xavier University of Louisiana is a member of the NAIA, Gulf Coast Athletic Conference.

Academics and Learning Environment

For the B student, the learning environment of a college is just as important as the quality of its academic program. Xavier University of Louisiana has 212 full-time and 28 part-time faculty members, offering a student-to-faculty ratio of 13:1. The most common course size is 20 to 29 students. Xavier University of Louisiana offers 53 majors with the most popular being biology, psychology and chemistry and least popular being art education, economics and theology. The school has a general core requirement as well as a

XAVIER UNIVERSITY OF LOUISIANA

Admissions
Applicants: 3,516
Accepted: 2,307
Acceptance rate: 65.6%
Average GPA: 3.1
ACT range: 18-23
SAT Math range: 400-520
SAT Reading range: 410-530
SAT Writing range: 410-520
Top 10% of class: 18%
Top 25% of class: 36%
Top 50% of class: 52%

Deadlines
Early Action: January 15
Early Decision: No
Regular Action: March 1 (priority)
July 1 (final)
Common Application: Accepted

Financial Aid
In-state tuition: $14,500
Out-of-state tuition: $14,500
Room: -
Board: -
Books: $1,200
Freshmen receiving need-based aid: 87%
Undergrads receiving need-based aid: 80%
Avg. % of need met by financial aid: 24%
Avg. aid package (freshmen): $17,348
Avg. aid package (undergrads): $17,684
Freshmen receiving merit-based aid: 4%
Undergrads receiving merit-based aid: 3%
Avg. student debt upon graduation: $25,227

School Spirit
Mascot: Gold Rush
Colors: Gold and white

religion requirement Cooperative education is available. All first-year students must maintain a 2.0 GPA or higher to avoid academic probation. Other special academic programs that would appeal to a B student: independent study · double majors · dual degrees · accelerated study · honors program · internships.

B Student Support and Success

The Office of Academic Support Programs at Xavier provides academic assistance to students who need extra help. Services include one-on-one tutoring, academic counseling, study techniques, test-taking strategies, enrichment and development, time management skills and referrals to the math, reading and writing labs. Tutoring services are free.

The Math Lab helps student develop their mathematical abilities in an informal manner. The college states that the overall goal of the lab is to "increase each student's understanding of her or his course material. This takes time and active participation on the student's part."

Students may also use the Reading Lab to read and study more effectively. Software can be utilized that helps improve vocabulary and comprehension skills. A Speech Lab is also available, as is a Writing Center website for online tutoring in the different stages of the writing process.

Xavier University of Louisiana provides a variety of support programs including dedicated guidance for: academic · career · personal · psychological · religious. Recognizing that some students may need extra preparation, Xavier University of Louisiana offers remedial and refresher courses in: reading · writing · math · study skills. Annually, 73 percent of freshmen students return for their sophomore year. What do students do after college? While many enter the work force, approximately 39 percent pursue a graduate degree immediately after graduation.

Support for Students with Learning Disabilities

Students with learning disabilities may take advantage of specific support programs offered by Xavier University of Louisiana. If necessary, the college will grant additional time to students with learning disabilities to complete their degree. Students with learning disabilities will find the following programs at Xavier University of Louisiana extremely useful: tutors · testing accommodations · untimed tests · extended time for tests · take-home exam · oral tests · typist/scribe · tape recorders · early syllabus · priority registration · waiver of math degree requirement. Individual or small group tutorials are also available in: time management · learning strategies · writing labs · math labs · study skills. An advisor/advocate from the LD program is available to students.

How to Get Admitted

For admissions decisions, non-academic factors considered: interview · extracurricular activities · special talents, interests, abilities · character/personal qualities · volunteer work · work experience · state of residency · alumni relationship. A high school diploma is required, although a GED is also accepted for admissions consideration. SAT or ACT test scores are required of all applicants. *Academic units recommended:* 4 Math, 3 Science, 1 Foreign Language.

How to Pay for College

To apply for financial aid, students should submit the following: Free Application for Federal Student Aid (FAFSA). Xavier University of Louisiana participates in the Federal Work Study program. *Need-based aid programs include:* scholarships and grants · general need-based awards · Federal Pell grants · state scholarships and grants · college-based scholarships and grants · private scholarships and grants · United Negro College Fund. *Non-Need-based aid programs include:* scholarships and grants · state scholarships and grants · creative arts and performance awards · athletic scholarships · religious affiliation scholarships.

XAVIER UNIVERSITY OF LOUISIANA

INDEX OF AMERICA'S BEST COLLEGES FOR B STUDENTS

America's Best Colleges
for B Students

America's Best Colleges
for B Students

INDEX OF COLLEGES BY LOCATION

NEW HAMPSHIRE
Granite State College, 227

NEW JERSEY
Caldwell College, 123
Drew University, 174
Rider University, 372

NEW MEXICO
College of Santa Fe, 151
University of New Mexico, 506

NEW YORK
Adelphi University, 65
Alfred University, 80
Elmira College, 189
Hartwick College, 245
Hilbert College, 251
Manhattanville College, 290
Marymount Manhattan College, 296
Pace University, 343
Paul Smith's College, 349
Sarah Lawrence College, 389
St. Lawrence University, 423
SUNY - Purchase College, 440
Wells College, 564

NORTH CAROLINA
Campbell University, 126
Chowan University, 135
Guilford College, 232
High Point University
Shaw University, 397
University of North Carolina - Greensboro, 512

OHIO
Bowling Green State University, 111
Hiram College, 254
Marietta College, 293
Muskingum College, 323
Ohio Northern University, 328
Ohio University, 331
Ohio Wesleyan University, 334
University of Cincinnati, 466
Wittenberg University, 591

OREGON
Oregon State University, 340
Southern Oregon University, 411
University of Oregon, 515
University of Portland, 518

PENNSYLVANIA
Albright College, 75
Drexel University, 177
Duquesne University, 180
Harrisburg University of Science and Technology, 244
Indiana University of Pennsylvania, 272
Lycoming College, 284
Seton Hill University, 394
Temple University, 445
Washington & Jefferson College, 558
Westminster College, 580
Wilkes University, 588

RHODE ISLAND
Bryant University, 120
Roger Williams University, 381
Salve Regina University, 386
University of Rhode Island, 524

SOUTH CAROLINA
Coastal Carolina University, 140
University of South Carolina - Columbia, 530

TENNESSEE
Fisk University, 201
University of Memphis, 494
University of Tennessee, 533

TEXAS
Angelo State University, 89
Schreiner University, 391
Texas Tech University, 448
University of Houston, 474

UTAH
University of Utah, 540

VERMONT
Champlain College, 132
Green Mountain College, 229
Norwich University, 326
University of Vermont, 543

VIRGINIA
Christopher Newport University, 137
George Mason University, 219
Hampden-Sydney College, 238
Hampton University, 241
Hollins University, 257
Longwood University, 278
Old Dominion University, 337
Radford University, 366
Randolph-Macon College, 369
Roanoke College, 378
Shenandoah University, 399
Stratford University, 434
Sweet Briar College, 442
Virginia Commonwealth University, 552
Virginia Wesleyan College, 555

WASHINGTON
Evergreen State College, 195
Pacific Lutheran University, 346
Washington State University, 561

WEST VIRGINIA
Fairmont State University, 198
Shepherd University, 399
West Virginia University, 570

WISCONSIN
Alverno College, 86
Ripon College, 375

WYOMING
University of Wyoming, 546

CONTRIBUTORS

Shirley Bloomquist, MA, Ed M, NCC
College and Educational Counselor
sbloomqu@aol.com

Marilyn Emerson
Independent Educational Consultant
www.collplan.com
111 E. 85th Street
New York, NY 10028
212-671-1972 or
84 Old Farm Road North
Chappaqua, NY 10514
914-747-1760

Todd Fothergill
President of Strategies for College
www.strategiesforcollege.com

Marjorie Ann Goode
Educational Consultant/School Counselor
Start Early: College and Career Planning Services
agoode2003@yahoo.com

Laura Jeanne Hammond
Editor in Chief
Next Step Magazine
800-771-3117
www.nextstepmagazine.com
AIM screenname: nsmanswergirl

Todd Johnson
College Admissions Partners
2600 15th Street SW
Willmar, MN 56201
320-262-9955
todd@collegeadmissionspartners.com

Judith Mackenzie
Mackenzie College Consulting
4705 16th Avenue NE
Seattle, WA 98105
206-527-2287

Lynda McGee
College Counselor
Downtown Magnets High School
lmcgee00@aol.com

Maureen McQuaid
College Focus LLC
Independent Counselor
www.collegefocus.com
niep1@aol.com
650-343-3940

David Miller
Director of College Counseling
Stevenson School
www.rlstevenson.org

Laurie Nimmo
Career Center and College Admissions Coordinator/
Independent College Advising
Healdsburg, CA 95448
lnimmo@sonic.net

Terry O'Banion
Former President of the League for Innovation in the
Community College
www.league.org

Patrick O'Brien
Former Admission Officer and Consultant-
Ambassador for the ACT

Judi Robinovitz
Judi Robinovitz Associates and Educational
Consulting
www.scoreatthetop.com

Jennifer Tabbush, MBA, CEP
Headed for College
17328 Ventura Boulevard, Suite 216
Encino, CA 91316
818-996-9540
jtabbush@headedforcollege.com
www.headedforcollege.com

Sarah Wilburn
Campus Bound
617-769-0400
swilburn@campusbound.com
Campus Bound helps families across the country find
the right colleges, fill out all the applications and
apply for financial aid.

ABOUT THE AUTHOR

Tamra B. Orr is a full-time educational writer and author originally from Indiana and now living in the Pacific Northwest (where she takes a long look at the mountains every single day!). She is the author of more than 250 nonfiction titles for kids, teens and families. Her book, *Violence in Our Schools: Halls of Hope, Halls of Fear* (Scholastic), won the Best Nonfiction Book of the Year for Teens from the New York Public Library. She is also the author of *Ace the SAT Writing Even If You Hate to Write: Shortcuts and Strategies to Score Higher Regardless of Your Skill Level* (SuperCollege), *The Purple Cow Guide to Extraordinary Essays* (Scholastic) and *The Encyclopedia of Notable Hispanic-Americans* (Publications International).

Orr is involved in education in almost every imaginable way. She writes dozens of nonfiction books each year on a huge variety of topics (from face lifts to fire ants!) and she writes hundreds of stories and items for standardized tests for more than a dozen educational companies. She has a degree in Secondary Education and English from Ball State University in Muncie, Indiana. Orr has been married for more than half of her life to Joseph and together, they have four children ranging in age from 21 to 9. The three that are still living at home are all homeschooled (in between her writing and his messing around with old Volkswagens). Orr has appeared on numerous radio and television shows and has done countless book signings/appearances to promote her books and talk about a variety of issues within education. Since she was once so shy she almost flunked speech class in high school, this is still an amazing fact to her (and her parents!).

And to think she did all this . . . and was a mere B student!